# Mastering Civil Procedure

## Carolina Academic Press Mastering Series
### Russell Weaver, Series Editor

**Mastering Administrative Law**
William R. Andersen

**Mastering Adoption Law and Policy**
Cynthia Hawkins DeBose

**Mastering Alternative Dispute Resolution**
Kelly M. Feeley, James A. Sheehan

**Mastering American Indian Law**
Angelique Wambdi EagleWoman, Stacy L. Leeds

**Mastering Appellate Advocacy and Process, Revised Printing**
Donna C. Looper, George W. Kuney

**Mastering Art Law**
Herbert Lazerow

**Mastering Bankruptcy**
George W. Kuney

**Mastering Civil Procedure, Third Edition**
David Charles Hricik

**Mastering Constitutional Law, Second Edition**
John C. Knechtle, Christopher J. Roederer

**Mastering Contract Law**
Irma S. Russell, Barbara K. Bucholtz

**Mastering Corporate Tax**
Reginald Mombrun, Gail Levin Richmond, Felicia Branch

**Mastering Corporations and Other Business Entities, Second Edition**
Lee Harris

**Mastering Criminal Law, Second Edition**
Ellen S. Podgor, Peter J. Henning, Neil P. Cohen

**Mastering Criminal Procedure, Volume 1:**
**The Investigative Stage, Second Edition**
Peter J. Henning, Andrew Taslitz, Margaret L. Paris, Cynthia E. Jones, Ellen S. Podgor

**Mastering Criminal Procedure, Volume 2:**
**The Adjudicatory Stage, Second Edition**
Peter J. Henning, Andrew Taslitz, Margaret L. Paris, Cynthia E. Jones, Ellen S. Podgor

**Mastering Elder Law, Second Edition**
Ralph C. Brashier

**Mastering Employment Discrimination Law**
Paul M. Secunda, Jeffrey M. Hirsch

# Mastering Civil Procedure

## THIRD EDITION

### David Charles Hricik
MERCER UNIVERSITY
WALTER F. GEORGE SCHOOL OF LAW

CAROLINA ACADEMIC PRESS
Durham, North Carolina

Library of Congress Cataloging-in-Publication Data

Names: Hricik, David, author.
Title: Mastering civil procedure / David Charles Hricik.
Description: Third edition. | Durham, North Carolina : Carolina Academic
  Press, 2017. | Series: Carolina Academic Press Mastering Series | Includes
  bibliographical references and index.
Identifiers: LCCN 2017009731 | ISBN 9781611637342 (alk. paper)
Subjects: LCSH: Civil procedure--United States.
Classification: LCC KF8841 .H75 2017 | DDC 347.73/5--dc23
LC record available at https://lccn.loc.gov/2017009731

eISBN 978-1-53100-714-0


Carolina Academic Press, LLC
700 Kent Street
Durham, North Carolina 27701
Telephone (919) 489-7486
Fax (919) 493-5668
www.cap-press.com


Printed in the United States of America

*For Abby, Alex, Houston, and Julian*

# Contents

## Part A
### To Anchor the Action in a Federal Court, a Plaintiff Must Plead One Claim Where (1) Subject Matter Jurisdiction, (2) Personal Jurisdiction, and (3) Venue Are Proper.

## PART C

### SPECIAL PROCEDURES FOR RESOLVING SIMILAR
### CLAIMS AMONG MANY PARTIES

# Table of Cases

# Series Editor's Foreword

The Carolina Academic Press Mastering Series is designed to provide you with a tool that will enable you to easily and efficiently "master" the substance and content of law school courses. Throughout the series, the focus is on quality writing that makes legal concepts understandable. As a result, the series is designed to be easy to read and is not unduly cluttered with footnotes or cites to secondary sources.

In order to facilitate student mastery of topics, the Mastering Series includes a number of pedagogical features designed to improve learning and retention. At the beginning of each chapter, you will find a "Roadmap" that tells you about the chapter and provides you with a sense of the material that you will cover. A "Checkpoint" at the end of each chapter encourages you to stop and review the key concepts, reiterating what you have learned. Throughout the book, key terms are explained and emphasized. Finally, a "Master Checklist" at the end of each book reinforces what you have learned and helps you identify any areas that need review or further study.

We hope that you will enjoy studying with, and learning from, the Mastering Series.

Russell L. Weaver
Professor of Law & Distinguished University Scholar
University of Louisville, Louis D. Brandeis School of Law

# Introduction and Acknowledgments

This book is the product of 15 years of teaching civil procedure on top of almost 30 doing federal civil litigation. It is designed to bring the practical aspects of civil procedure in focus while addressing the policy issue often focused on in law school. Profound thanks to Cindy Schiesel at Palo Verde High School and Ruth Gardner at the University of Arizona for helping me learn to write more clearly.

# Mastering Civil Procedure

# Chapter 1

# Courts Decide Claims

---

### Claims Roadmap

This chapter explains the basic building block of civil procedure: that federal courts resolve claims between parties. The "claim" is the fundamental unit of federal civil procedure.

---

This book is about civil procedure, and more particularly the rules and law that govern adjudication of civil lawsuits filed in federal court in the United States. Many states have rules that govern civil lawsuits filed in state court that are quite similar to the law we will discuss here, so much of what you learn in this book likely applies in state courts. On the other hand, however, many states have differently worded rules, or rules that, despite being identical to the Federal Rules of Civil Procedure (the "Rules"), have been interpreted differently. So, our focus will be solely on the Rules, but some of what we study will apply in state court practice.

What is a civil lawsuit? It is when somebody sues someone. Civil lawsuits are typically filed by a private party with the goal of having the government— through a court—resolve a dispute by issuing some sort of decision that binds both parties. More specifically, a civil lawsuit is usually filed to have a court (jury or judge) determine whether the party who believes it has been harmed— the plaintiff—has proven facts that entitles it to obtain relief against the party it has sued—the defendant. In the simplest case, a court decides whether the plaintiff can recover for a claim against the defendant, and, if so, what relief (*e.g.*, money for damages the defendant caused to the plaintiff) the plaintiff is entitled to receive.

## A. Lawsuits Begin with Clients

With that brief background, let us start at the beginning. A lawsuit starts when a client walks into a lawyer's office and says, "I think I've been wronged" (or more colorful language). Lawyers know that it is not enough to justify filing a suit. It may be that a client feels they have been wronged, or even that the lawyer concludes that something unfair or immoral has happened to the client. But that does not mean the law provides a remedy.

Instead, lawyers know that, before a lawsuit can be filed, the lawyer must investigate and determine whether the lawyer can likely prove a "claim" that entitles the client to relief in court. *Substantive* law "creates" claims. At the most basic level of civil lawsuits, a court decides whether one party, called the plaintiff, proved the elements of a "claim" against the other party, called the defendant. Substantive law defines the "elements" of a claim.

For example, a plaintiff injured by a defendant in a car wreck can prove a claim of negligence; if the plaintiff does so, a "judgment" will be entered that can result in the defendant having to pay the plaintiff money. Another example of a claim is one called "battery." If a client tells a lawyer that someone punched her, the lawyer will examine the substantive law to determine whether this action constitutes a claim upon which relief can be granted — if believed by a jury, the court will enter a judgment that makes the defendant pay the plaintiff money (if the defendant has any). In your torts class, you will learn that punching someone gives rise to a claim for battery, or negligence, or both. If, under the *substantive* law, these facts, if true, show the plaintiff is entitled to relief, then the lawyer may file a lawsuit. *Substantive law* is what you will study in most classes.

If the lawyer believes that the law and facts show his client has claim against a defendant, the lawyer can file a lawsuit. At its core, the essential purpose of civil litigation is to decide which party is entitled to prevail on one or more "claims" by a plaintiff against a defendant.

Procedural law regulates *how* the plaintiff's lawyer begins the process of litigating a claim, and then *how* the parties and the court proceed to determine whether the plaintiff will recover money. Procedure is about how to resolve a claim, not defining the circumstances in which the plaintiff should get money, or not, for what the defendant has done. Procedural law governs what the lawyer must do to file a lawsuit (she files a "complaint," we'll see.) Procedural law also controls the various steps that the parties will then go through. The end result, at least in the trial court, may be a jury trial. If the plaintiff persuades a jury that the facts needed to establish a claim are true, then after the jury verdict, the court will enter an order, called a "judgment," awarding the plaintiff damages. The plaintiff can use a judgment to force the defendant to pay money up to the amount of those damages.

In most of your classes, you will study substantive, not procedural, law. Although substance and procedure are distinct, they are both important. A lawyer who knows substantive law, but not procedure, will not do a good job for their client. Likewise, a lawyer who understands procedural law, but not the underlying substantive law, will fail.

Since what constitutes a "claim" turns on substantive law—the stuff learned in your other courses—those other courses, in some ways, provide the foundation for civil procedure. Without knowing what a "claim" is, or what elements of law make up a claim, you will be unable to understand civil procedure. This chapter, therefore, provides some forest-from-the-trees views of what a "claim" is.

# B. What Is a "Claim"?

The key point to take away is that courts follow rules of procedure to decide each claim (and, as we will see, defenses to claims), not "lawsuits" or "disputes." A "claim" is a set of allegations that, if true, would mean that the party asserting the claim is entitled to relief (usually money) from the party against whom the claim is asserted. The substantive law dictates what facts are needed to support a claim and how much money (or other remedies) a party can get. If you start with a focus on what "claim" or "claims" are involved, a lot of the Rules and law we will cover will make sense.

Oddly, however, despite the repeated mention of a "claim" in the Rules and pertinent federal statutes, these sources of law do not define it. For example, Rule 8(a) provides that a "pleading that states a claim for relief" must contain a "short and plain statement of the claim showing that the pleader is entitled to relief." Similarly, Rule 12(b)(6) allows a party against whom a claim is asserted (typically the defendant) to move to dismiss the claim for "failure to state a claim upon which relief can be granted." In summation, the Rules state a court may dismiss a pleading if the pleading does not set forth a "statement of the claim showing that the pleader is entitled to relief," yet the Rules fail to explain precisely what a "claim" is.

Rather than the Rules describing the definition of a claim, state common law and state and federal statutes—the focus of your other courses—tell what a "claim" is. Particularly, within the realms of those sources of law, claims define the boundaries of when someone can sue for breach of contract, for battery, or for negligence. So let us look at a few claims you have probably explored or are about to learn in your other classes.

In torts, for example, the laws of most states do not create a general "duty to rescue." If I am walking along the beach and you are drowning, I can just stand there, and no one can sue me for not rescuing you. Instead, to state a claim upon which relief can be granted, a plaintiff must allege more than simply stating that "he was walking by and did nothing." In many states, the substantive law necessitates that stating a claim requires (1) a special relationship between the plaintiff and defendant—one that causes defendant to owe a duty to plaintiff; (2) which was breached by the defendant; (3) which caused (in fact and proximately) (4) damages to the plaintiff. Typically, are the four elements of a negligence claim.

In continuing with the above example, a claim for failing to rescue someone is *only* stated when the plaintiff's complaint *alleges* facts to support each element. Thus, a complaint that failed to allege the plaintiff was harmed would fail to state a claim upon which relief could be granted because the complaint would lack establishing "damages to the plaintiff." Likewise, a complaint that failed to allege facts to support the existence of a duty—for example, the complaint did not allege that the defendant had a "special relationship" with the plaintiff—does not state a claim upon which relief can be granted. If the party against whom the claim is asserted can say "so what"—even if the facts are true, they do not support imposing liability on me to you—then the complaint fails to state a claim upon which relief can be granted.

Solely the pleadings may notify the opposing party of the claims a party asserts against it and the allegations that, if true, support each element of every asserted claim. To state a claim in this example, the Rules require a plaintiff to give notice of facts that support each element of the negligence claim based upon the duty to rescue, and they must give that notice through the pleadings.

However, to construct the pleadings, the plaintiff's lawyer must analyze and research not procedure, but substantive law (state common law in this example) to identify the elements of the claim. A lawyer researching the substantive law will find, in most states at least, that I may have been morally corrupt for not rescuing you, but that I cannot be legally liable. As a result, you cannot state a claim for relief against me because there are no facts you can allege (making them up is not an option, as we will see) showing a special relationship exists between us. Thus, there is no duty, and duty is an element of this tort. There is, as a result, no basis to award you, as the plaintiff, money.

To reiterate, substantive law—that is, state common law in a duty to rescue claim—defines the elements of a claim. The law of procedure tells how the plaintiff must notify the defendant of the claims and, after that, how to resolve the dispute between the parties concerning whether the plaintiff is entitled to have the government order the defendant to pay the plaintiff money for what happened.

The same concepts about "claims" lurk, perhaps less obviously, in contracts classes. In general, only a party to an agreement can sue for a breach of the contract. To use contract lingo, the plaintiff and defendant must commonly be in "privity" for the plaintiff to state a claim for breach of contract. Thus, a complaint that falls short of alleging privity between plaintiff and defendant fails to state a claim upon which relief can be granted for breach of contract.

(A central exception to the requirement of privity is that an intended third-party beneficiary can sue for breach of a contract; if you are thinking of that, you are correct and thinking of substantive contract law. What do you suppose you would need to plead if your client was not a party to a contract, but was a third-party beneficiary to it? That is right: you would have to plead allegations that show, if true, that your client was a third-party beneficiary.)

Since privity frequently is an element of the claim for breach of contract, let us try an example. If I were to sue you because you failed to pay for a car you agreed to buy from Bob, and as a result, Bob could not pay a debt he owed to me, your response would be that I have failed to state a claim for breach of contract because you and I were not in privity; only you and Bob were.

How do you, as a lawyer, make that response if your client was sued despite lack of privity? How does a lawyer respond if you (or your estate) sue me for failing to rescue you? Those are the questions procedure addresses; it does not tell us *what* someone must allege, like a special relationship or privity. Rather, procedure tells us *how* to allege something and, subsequently, gives the rules to resolve the dispute.

One final point that may not be intuitive: the same set of facts often gives rise to multiple claims. For example, a party can bring a negligence claim *and* an intentional tort claim arising from the same basic facts. For example, the plaintiff who had been punched might claim both battery and negligence, essentially alleging that if the defendant's act was not intentional, then it was negligent. Or, as is common, a medical malpractice plaintiff might assert both a battery claim—intentional nonconsensual contact—and negligence. Both claims arise out of the same botched operation. For various reasons concerning remedies, insurance coverage, and other factors, lawyers may choose not to assert every claim the facts present. However, one set of facts will almost always give rise to more than one claim.

# C. Affirmative Defenses Compared to Claims

It is also important to distinguish between an affirmative defense and a claim. A claim is what the plaintiff has the burden to plead and prove, and if the plaintiff fails to do either, then the plaintiff loses. Even if the plaintiff proves all elements of a claim, however, they can still lose if the defendant pleads and proves an affirmative defense to the claim.

Suppose the plaintiff sues for breach of contract. It alleges all of the elements of breach of contract and, later, prove them. The defendant can still prevail on this proven breach of contract claim — the plaintiff takes nothing even though the defendant breached the contract — if the defendant proves an affirmative defense. Consider, for example, that the statute of limitations bars the claim; meaning it was filed "too long" after the breach occurred. (For a list of common affirmative defenses, see Rule 8(c).) This statute of limitations serves as an affirmative defense to the plaintiff's breach of contract claim, no matter how severe the claim may be, and the plaintiff cannot prevail.

Keeping the roles of claims and affirmative defenses distinct will help throughout the study of civil procedure, as well as your other courses. Why is this distinction important? Generally, the party asserting a claim possesses the burden to plead allegations to support it and to produce evidence to prove it later. Analogously, the party asserting an affirmative defense has those same obligations. If someone with the burden of pleading or production of evidence fails to meet that burden on even one element of the claim or defense, they lose that claim or defense. But, it is important to note that the plaintiff does not have to plead or prove it filed their suit on time, just as the defendant does not have to plead or prove that it was not negligent. Each party has its own burdens.

## D. Destroying a Myth and an Important Note About Studying Procedure

This final short section is more important than its length might suggest. Its first goal is to destroy a myth; if you believe this myth, it makes learning procedure unnecessarily difficult.

The myth is that some judge sits in their courtroom eagerly waiting to independently examine the allegations to hear in court; for example, whether a complaint states a claim. *Judges are passive in the litigation process.* Parties control lawsuits. The adversary process resolves lawsuits; meaning, a lawyer representing a client who has been sued must read the complaint and respond appropriately. If the complaint does not state a claim, the judge will do nothing. Instead, defense counsel must file a motion to ask the court to dismiss that claim. In our simple hypotheticals, defense counsel would move to dismiss for failure to state a claim upon which relief could be granted. *See* FRCP 12(b)(6). If the lawyer does not do that, the judge is not going to do it for them. We will see that theme arise over and over again. It is not the judge's responsibility to point out defects or raise objections because, with few exceptions, the rules put that responsibility on the lawyers.

This duty on lawyers leads to an important point about the word "require." If a Rule or statute "requires" something, that obligation only means that the opposing party can raise the problem with the court for the other party's failure to establish a requirement. So, for example, if a party fails to abide by a deadline "required" by a Rule, *nothing will happen* unless either the opposing party does something to raise the violation with the court or it is one of the *rare* instances when a court will raise the issue on its own.

When reading that something is "required" by a Rule or statute, or that something "must" be done, keep it clear that a party's failure to abide by a Rule or statute usually means that an opposing party has the power to raise the issue with the court. We will see that a party can almost always waive the other party's violation of the Rules or statute by not promptly and correctly raising the violation with the court.

The second point of this section is this: In civil procedure, the first place to look for an answer is the Rules or a few federal statutes. That may not be the case in your other courses, which are probably not as regulated by statutes and rules to the same degree as civil procedure. In many instances, a Rule or federal statute specifically addresses a common issue, or a dispute arising between the parties. Thus, always start with the text of the Rule or statute and read it carefully. Other classes may regularly reference and turn on what a *court* said, and while court decisions play a role in civil procedure, the first step differs. Rather than looking to an opinion first, look to the particular rule or statute; a skill that you may not be developing in your other classes. Develop it here because statutes and rules are everywhere, not just in civil procedure.

---

## Checkpoints

- Can you describe what a "claim" is?
- Can you distinguish a claim from an affirmative defense?
- Can you explain who has the burden to plead and prove both a claim and an affirmative defense to a claim?
- Do you understand why substantive law, not procedural law, provides the meaning of what a "claim" is?

## Part A

## To Anchor the Action in a Federal Court, a Plaintiff Must Plead One Claim Where (1) Subject Matter Jurisdiction, (2) Personal Jurisdiction, and (3) Venue Are Proper.

# Chapter 2

# A Preview of Part A of This Book

## A. The Three Requirements to Adjudicate an Anchor Claim: Subject Matter Jurisdiction, Personal Jurisdiction, and Venue

In many law schools, professors teach civil procedure in two semesters, with the first semester focusing on subject matter jurisdiction, personal jurisdiction, and venue, and the second semester focusing on the "rules" aspect of civil procedure. While these two portions are keenly interrelated, this book organizationally mirrors how professors commonly teach the course. Additionally, the first part of the book points to where, in the second part of the book, the rules explain what to do if, for example, the court lacks subject matter jurisdiction, personal jurisdiction, or venue over a claim. Remember, as a general rule, the court does not act on its own, so parties must *move* the court to take action.

Accordingly, the first part of this book, Part A, addresses and summarizes the three requirements for a federal district court to have the power to resolve a plaintiff's claim against a defendant. In a complaint, a plaintiff must assert at least one claim over which the court has "subject matter jurisdiction" over the action, "personal jurisdiction" over the defendant, and proper "venue."

Starting with the hardest one to grasp of the three requirements, "subject matter jurisdiction" is an awkward phrase that essentially means the federal courts possess Constitutional and statutory authority to adjudicate a claim. In the U.S. Constitution, the States gave power to Congress to create federal courts that resolve certain types of claims, including the two claims this book (and most civil procedure courses) focus on: (1) claims created by federal law (called "federal question" jurisdiction), and (2) claims between citizens of different states (called "diversity" jurisdiction).

A federal court lacks the *power*—in civil procedure lingo, a federal court lacks *subject matter jurisdiction*—to decide a claim unless two things have occurred: (1) the Constitution authorized Congress to create federal courts to adjudicate that type of claim, and (2) pursuant to that authority, Congress enacted a statute that gave federal courts the power to do so. Without Constitutional and statutory power, federal courts cannot resolve the claim—even despite of what the parties may want. Neither the parties nor the court may expand the scope of subject matter jurisdiction conferred by Congress as limited by the Constitution. The court must have the power to resolve the action, or it must dismiss the claim.

"Personal jurisdiction," perhaps, is a bit more intuitive than subject matter jurisdiction. No court—state or federal—can force a party to defend itself against a claim in that state unless the facts leading to the claim have enough connection to the state to make litigation a fair trial. For example, if a person has never been to Ohio, that person likely cannot be forced to defend themselves in Ohio for a claim arising out of a car wreck that happened in Iowa. In large measure, determining whether personal jurisdiction exists over a claim depends on the defendant's "minimum contacts" with the state in which the plaintiff filed suit. However, despite the required "connection" to the state, personal jurisdiction is not a question of convenience. Rather, the concept of personal jurisdiction springs from the Constitution's requirement that a person cannot be deprived of property without Due Process of law—without a fair hearing.

However, unlike subject matter jurisdiction, a lack of personal jurisdiction is something that a party can "waive"—and in various ways. Sometimes, parties agree that if a dispute arises between them, a claim must be filed in a certain state. Absent unusual circumstances, that kind of contractual clause will be upheld and waive any objection that personal jurisdiction is lacking. Furthermore, if the lawyer representing that Iowa driver, from the earlier example, fails to follow the proper procedure by neglecting to object to a lack of personal jurisdiction in Ohio for the Iowa car wreck (remember, the judge won't do it for her), then any future objection of theirs would be waived.

"Venue" is a concept that primarily seeks to litigate claims in the particular district (almost every state is, by federal statute, divided into more than one district and has more than one federal district court) in which most of the witnesses and other information are likely to be. While personal jurisdiction generally turns on whether a person has sufficient contacts with a *state* to expose that person to suit in that state, venue mainly examines *which district in that state* will likely be the most convenient for the court, parties, and witnesses to try the lawsuit.

Venue, like personal jurisdiction, can be waived. Similar to personal jurisdiction, parties sometimes agree that venue will lie in a particular state or district before there is even a dispute. Absent unusual circumstances, that contract will waive any objection to that chosen venue. Likewise, the judge does not raise an objection to venue on their own. If the defendant's lawyer fails to object to improper venue, a claim can be tried in a district that is totally unconnected to the dispute.

Accordingly, lawyers for both plaintiffs and defendants must know how to determine whether subject matter jurisdiction, personal jurisdiction, and venue are proper. Plaintiffs' counsel needs to know these things to determine in which district suit can be filed. Defense counsel equally needs to discern whether these three requirements are proper so they can see if any of them are missing and, if so, how to object. Again, the first part of this book, Part A, focuses on the substance of the three requirements, and the second part, Part B, analyzes (among other things) what to do if a party believes one is missing.

The flowchart below ties the two steps together. Notice that you need to analyze all three requirements: it may be possible that subject matter jurisdiction and personal jurisdiction are lacking and that venue is proper, or other various combinations. Also, remember that this analysis generally is done on a claim-by-claim basis, with the exceptions discussed below.

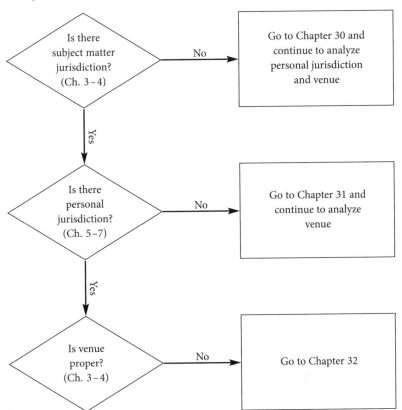

# Chapter 3

# The Foundations of Subject Matter Jurisdiction

---

### Subject Matter Jurisdiction Roadmap

The next several chapters, including this one, explain that there must be at least one claim — the "anchor claim" — to allow a particular federal court to decide that claim and, perhaps, others.

These chapters show that the three principal requirements for a federal court to have the power to adjudicate an "anchor" claim are: subject matter jurisdiction, personal jurisdiction, and venue. To anchor a claim — and a *case with other claims* — in federal court, the plaintiff must plead *one* claim over which the court has all three, or the defendant can move to dismiss the claim (and case) for lack of whichever is missing. (Once a plaintiff has *one* anchor claim, it can *join* other claims and parties to the suit as part of that *case*, which we will explore later in this book. But without one claim anchored, there is nothing to join other claims or parties to.)

This chapter focuses on the consequences of our divided government — divided between state and federal power — on federal judicial power. It explains why the Constitution both *grants* and *limits* federal judicial power to decide claims — what we call subject matter jurisdiction — and explains that Congress has not authorized federal courts to have that power to the fullest extent possible under the Constitution.

Although this book presents subject matter jurisdiction first, a court may analyze whether it has personal jurisdiction first, without determining whether it has subject matter jurisdiction. Civil procedure course books discuss these three principal requirements in different orders, but the courses tend to address subject matter jurisdiction first. While this book tracks that approach, the chapters can be tackled in the order your professor takes.

---

# A. A Divided System of Government: States and the Federal Government

In the United States, there are two broad divisions of government: state and federal. (Obviously, there are other divisions within each of those two broader categories, such as the legislative, executive, and judicial sectors; moreover, state governments often have various entities, such as counties, cities, and so on. However, the two expansive divisions implicated by subject matter jurisdiction are state and federal.)

This divided form of government creates many complexities for litigators.

One is that substantive law and procedural law can be created by both state and federal courts. Substantive law can be created by states and by the federal government. For example, state legislatures can enact statutes, as can Congress. State courts create "common law," and so too (to a very limited extent) can federal courts. That creates issues: Which law, state or federal, governs a particular claim? If a state law claim is filed in federal court, does the federal court apply federal law even if state law creates the claim? If the federal court applies state law, what if the state law conflicts with federal law?

Second, there are both state and federal court systems. Do both state and federal courts have the power to decide any given claim, or does only one have that power? If both do, who gets to pick? More simply, do state courts only decide claims created by state law, while federal courts only decide claims arising under federal law, or can the two courts overlap?

Third, what if a claim created by state law is in federal court? Does a federal court apply state law, or does federal law apply? What about procedure?

We will see that these questions must be asked separately. Sometimes, state law applies to a claim, and it must be filed in state court, while at other times, state law creates a claim and it *can* but need not be filed in federal court. Some federal claims can be filed in state court, while a few *must* be filed in federal court. Usually, the plaintiff gets to pick which system to file in but—sometimes—if the plaintiff picks state court the defendant can "remove" the case from state to federal court. A party could have two claims that arise out of the same set of facts—one arising under state law, the other under federal law—and a federal court would apply state federal substantive law to one claim and state substantive law to the other. Despite all of these variables, usually, in federal court, federal *procedural* rules control even if state *substantive* law applies to the claim.

The federal judicial branch has power to adjudicate a claim only when the Constitution authorizes it to do so and, further, Congress has enacted a statute that extends the subject matter jurisdiction of federal courts to decide that claim. This chapter focuses on that principle.

In light of the dual system of government, it is important to remember that the federal judiciary must have the power to adjudicate a claim, that such power is limited by the Constitution and Congress, and that the limited power has immediate consequences for someone who wants to file a civil lawsuit. Mainly, they must determine if the suit *may* or *must* be filed in federal court, or if they can choose where to file the action. (If there is a choice, practical issues may influence which forum—state or federal—is better for the suit, a point this book will discuss later.) If the Constitution does not authorize Congress to allow federal courts to decide the claim, or if the Constitution does but Congress has not enacted a statute authorizing federal courts to hear a claim, then federal courts lack power to decide the claim, no matter what the parties might want.

Let's be clear. Lawyers and judges typically do not explicitly discuss whether the Constitution gives federal courts power to decide a claim. For example, they don't ask, "Does the Constitution give a federal court the power to decide this claim, and did Congress enact a statute that 'turned on' that power?" Instead, they implicitly address the issue by analyzing whether a federal court has "subject matter jurisdiction" over a claim. However, the two questions ask exactly the same thing. Be sure to understand that when saying a federal court "lacks subject matter jurisdiction," that phrase indicates that particular federal court lacks the power to adjudicate the claim, either because the claim is beyond the reach of the Constitution or because it is beyond the reach of a statute that Congress adopted pursuant to its Constitutional power. Almost always, the issue is the latter: is the claim within the scope of a statute giving the federal courts power?

## B. Power to Resolve a Claim: Subject Matter Jurisdiction

Although, as Chapter 4 shows, federal *law* is the supreme law of the land and can "preempt" conflicting state law, the federal *government*'s power is limited. Specifically, the States in the Constitution delegated only limited powers to the federal government, and any power not expressly given to the federal government is reserved for the States. *See* U.S. Const. Am. 10 ("The powers not delegated to the United States by the Constitution, nor prohibited by it to the States, are reserved to the States respectively, or to the people.") Consequently, unless States delegated a specific power to the federal government in the Constitution, the federal government does not have that particular power; the States do.

Pertinent here, through Article III of the Constitution, the States authorized Congress to create "inferior" federal courts (that is, courts with lesser power than the Supreme Court) to adjudicate certain claims. Notably, the States gave Congress power to create what are now the federal district courts in Section 1 of Article 2. This Article confers judicial power to "one Supreme Court, and in such inferior Courts as the Congress may from time to time ordain and establish." Thus, the Constitution itself creates only the Supreme Court, and the

States permitted, but did not require, Congress to create these other "inferior" federal courts.

While States gave power to Congress to create lower federal courts, Article II also limits that authority. Section 2 of Article III provides:

> The judicial Power shall extend to all Cases, in Law and Equity, aris-
> ing under this Constitution, the Laws of the United States, and Trea-
> ties made, or which shall be made, under their Authority; to all Cases
> affecting Ambassadors, other public Ministers and Consuls; to all Cases
> of admiralty and maritime Jurisdiction; to Controversies to which the
> United States shall be a Party; to Controversies between two or more
> States; between a State and Citizens of another State; between Citizens
> of different States; between Citizens of the same State claiming Lands
> under Grants of different States, and between a State, or the Citizens
> thereof, and foreign States, Citizens or Subjects.

Though this language clearly delegates power from the States to the federal government, it is also limited by its own terms. The States did not authorize federal courts to decide *all* disputes—only those enumerated in Section 2 of Article III. Put another way, Section 2 of Article III and the Tenth Amendment both create *and* limit the power of federal courts. *See Moe v. Avions Marcel Dassault-Breguet Aviation,* 727 F.2d 917, 932–33 (10th Cir. 1984) ("The enumerated powers set forth for the . . . Judiciary in Article III are by implication limited powers, and the notion of limited federal authority is reinforced by the Tenth Amendment.").

There's one counter-intuitive point that is important to confront: you must keep separate the power to adjudicate the claim from what law applies to it. The Constitution does not make federal judicial power turn on which law governs a claim. One possibility mentioned above ties to the notion that the States in the Constitution could have agreed that claims arising under federal law could be tried only in federal court, while claims arising under state law had to be decided in state court. However, the States did not do so. Instead, the States limited federal judicial power to two types of cases, and the law that creates the claim is only part of the limitation for one of type.

One type of claim over which federal courts have subject matter jurisdiction, *federal question jurisdiction,* turns solely on which law created the claim. If federal law created the claim (meaning, almost always, a federal *statute* created the claim), then the Constitution permits Congress to allow federal courts to decide it. But the other type of subject matter jurisdiction, *diversity jurisdiction,* requires not just that state law created the claim, but also on whether the parties are *citizens of different states.* While there are many subsections in Section 2 of Article III, this book (as well as most civil procedure courses) focus on those two main bases for federal subject matter jurisdiction, which are (1) to adjudicate cases "arising under this Constitution" or "arising under . . . the Laws of the United States" and (2) to adjudicate cases "between Citizens of different States." Again, the first of these grounds for subject matter jurisdiction is "federal question" jurisdiction, and the second is "diversity" jurisdiction.

It is important you recognize that this discussion is about constitutional power and limitations. Remember, the Constitution demonstrates only that the States gave Congress the power to create federal courts with "jurisdiction" over certain claims. Congress could have chosen not to exercise that power; and, it could have only used *some* of that power. We'll see that when it enacted statutes pursuant to the power in the Constitution, Congress did not go as far as it could have. Although Section 1 of Article III authorizes Congress to enact statutes to create lower federal courts and Section 2 of Article III allows Congress to delegate certain powers to those federal courts, federal courts only have power to the extent that Congress actually enacted a statute.

Accordingly, "federal courts may assume only that portion of the Article III judicial power which Congress, by statute, entrusts to them." *Senate Select Comm. v. Nixon,* 366 F. Supp. 51, 55 (D.D.C. 1973). Said differently, the Constitution simply authorizes Congress to act while simultaneously setting the outer limit of such power; however, it does not itself create or require jurisdiction. Since Congress has power to not create lower courts *at all,* Congress can establish them while concurrently limiting their authority to hear claims, provided that, the creation is still within the bounds of Article III. *Kline v. Burke Constr. Co.,* 260 U.S. 226, 234 (1922).

As discussed, for a federal district court to have subject matter jurisdiction, Congress must have enacted a statute. As a result, subject matter jurisdiction turns on whether a federal statute gives federal courts certain power to hear a particular type of claim. Accordingly, so long as any statute Congress creates does not exceed jurisdictional boundaries set by Article III, the scope of subject matter jurisdiction turns on the scope of the statute, not the Constitution. To put it visually:

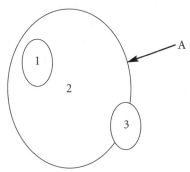

In this diagram, Circle A represents one of the clauses of Article III, Section 2. For example, the clause "between Citizens of different States" authorizes Congress to create what we've come to call "diversity subject matter jurisdiction." Congress *could* enact a statute that gives federal courts *less* power than the Constitution lets it—a statute could not go to the full extent authorized by the Constitution (represented here by Circle 1, which illustrates what Congress *has actually done*). On the other hand, Congress could enact a statute that goes to the maximum extent allowed in the Constitution, which is represented by the same circle; however, call it Circle 2 to distinguish the statute (Circle 2) from the Constitution (Circle 1). (A statute that exceeds the scope of authority permitted by the Constitution is represented here by Circle 3. It would be *un*constitutional since it exceeds the delegated authority in Article III, and thus that power remains with the States under the 10th Amendment.)

Most likely, your professor will emphasize that Congress did not give to the federal courts all of the constitutionally-permitted power to adjudicate claims that it could have. The statutes that implement each principal form of subject matter jurisdiction—diversity and federal question—do not extend to the limits of Article III. Thus, Circle 1 exemplifies the statutes that Congress has enacted, which do not extend to the limits of Article III. That point becomes important because neither the federal question nor diversity statutes extend to the limits of Article III. They're like Circle 1, not Circle 2.

## C. Which Law Applies Can be Distinct from Subject Matter Jurisdiction

I emphasize to my students is that they have to keep the issues in this course separated. Analyze each one separately. Keep 'em separated, to coin a phrase.

It would be simpler if only state courts could decide claims created by state law, and only federal courts could decide claims created by federal law, but our Founders did not choose that dividing line. Instead, federal courts have "subject matter jurisdiction"—power to decide a claim—over a claim created by state law, if there is diversity (or, for claims beyond the anchor claim, also if there is "supplemental jurisdiction"). Likewise, state courts have power to decide federal claims; very few federal claims must be filed in federal court.

The focus of subject matter jurisdiction is *may* the claim be in federal court? (And, in rare instances, *must* it be in federal court?)

## Checkpoints

- Do you understand the difference between power to adjudicate a claim (what is called subject matter jurisdiction) and what substantive law applies to the claim?

- Do you understand why the Constitution both grants and limits Congressional power to enact statutes that give federal courts subject matter jurisdiction?

- Can you identify the language in the Constitution that creates diversity jurisdiction? What about the language for federal question jurisdiction?

- Do you understand why, even though the Constitution gave Congress power to adopt jurisdictional statutes, the terms of any statute controls whether a court has subject matter jurisdiction, unless the statute exceeds the scope of Congressional authority under the Constitution?

Chapter 4

# Federal Question and Diversity Subject Matter Jurisdiction

---

## Federal Question and Diversity Subject Matter Jurisdiction Roadmap

This chapter describes federal question subject matter jurisdiction and distinguishes it from diversity subject matter jurisdiction, and identifies the Constitutional and statutory sources for both types of jurisdiction.

This chapter shows that the Supreme Court has held that, although the Constitution gives Congress broader power to authorize federal question jurisdiction in the lower courts, Section 1331 does not go to the full breadth of the Constitution. Instead, a claim "arises under" federal law, and so can be heard in a lower federal court, in only three circumstances: (a) when a federal statute creates the claim; (b) when federal law preempts state law; or (c) when the claim, though created by state law, turns on a substantial question of federal law. This chapter explains how to identify each type of federal claim, and emphasizes the narrow nature of the latter two types.

This chapter shows that the Supreme Court has held that, although the Constitution gives Congress broader power to authorize diversity jurisdiction, it, again, did not enact a statute that gives the lower federal courts power that goes to the limits of the Constitution. Instead, Section 1332 gives lower federal courts subject matter jurisdiction to hear state law claims only if every plaintiff is a "citizen" of a different state from every defendant, *and* the "amount in controversy" exceeds $75,000. This chapter explains how to determine which state(s) a party is a citizen of, and how to determine the amount in controversy.

Finally, the chapter ends by emphasizing that this discussion is only the first part of the subject matter jurisdiction story: there must be one claim in a lawsuit over which a lower federal court has subject matter jurisdiction under either Section 1331 or Section 1332 (or, rarely, some other federal claim-specific statute), but if there is one such claim then additional related claims might be able to "tag along" under Section 1367, the supplemental subject matter jurisdiction statute.

---

As we saw above, the States in Article III delegated power to Congress to enact statutes to authorize lower federal courts to decide claims (a) "arising under" the Constitution or laws of the United States or (b) between citizens of different states. We also saw that, while Article III allows Congress to create federal courts to decide those claims, Article III is not itself a self-executing grant of power to the judicial branch. Instead, "the district courts only have only that jurisdiction that Congress grants through statute." *Int'l Science & Technology Institute, Inc. v. Inacom Comms., Inc.,* 106 F.3d 1146, 1153 (4th Cir. 1997). Thus, a federal district court does not have federal question jurisdiction — or any subject matter jurisdiction, for that matter — simply because the Constitution authorizes Congress to enact statutes to permit the courts to have the power to decide certain claims. Instead, a federal statute must authorize federal subject matter jurisdiction over a claim. While any statute must be within Article III of the Constitution, the routine inquiry is whether a claim is within the scope of a statute: does the claim "arise under" federal law, or does it satisfy the requirements for "diversity"?

Many federal statutes that create federal claims also explicitly give federal courts subject matter jurisdiction over those claims. A federal court has power to adjudicate a federal claim if the statute that creates the claim and also creates subject matter jurisdiction over the claim.

Not all statutes that create claims have specific statutes like that, however. Congress also enacted two general statutes on which civil procedure courses focus: (1) one gives federal courts power to adjudicate over claims "arising under" the U.S. Constitution or federal statutes, and (2) the other gives them power to adjudicate claims between citizens of different states if the amount in controversy exceeds $75,000. Thus, while a federal court will have subject matter jurisdiction over every claim "arising under" federal law, if a claim arises under state law, a federal court will not have jurisdiction it unless the parties to the claim are "diverse" and more than $75,000 is "in controversy."

It is important to note that the statutes are mutually exclusive: a claim can meet the requirements of the federal question statute, or be a state law claim that meets the requirements of the diversity statute, but not both. There is no such thing as a "diverse federal claim." Put the other way, if a claim arises under federal law, then it doesn't matter either whether the amount in controversy exceeds $75,000 or whether the parties are "diverse."

# A. Do Federal Courts Have Power to Adjudicate the Claim?

## 1. Federal Question Subject Matter Jurisdiction under Section 1331

The Constitution gave Congress broad power to confer federal question jurisdiction on the federal courts. The scope of the federal question prong of Article III was examined in *Osborn v. Bank of the U.S.*, 22 U.S. 738, 822–23 (1824), where Chief Justice Marshall held that a claim "arises under" federal law in terms of Article III if

> the title or right set up by the party, may be defeated by one construction of the Constitution or law of the United States, and sustained by the opposite construction. We think, then, that when a question to which the judicial power of the Union is extended by the Constitution, forms an ingredient of the original [claim], it is in the power of Congress to give [federal district courts] jurisdiction of that [claim], although other questions of fact or law may be involved in it.

Thus, the phrase "arising under" in Article III reaches claims where federal law is merely an "ingredient" in it: a claim is within the "federal question" prong Article III if the claim is sustained by one construction of federal law, but defeated by another. *See Bell v. Hood*, 327 U.S. 678, 681 (1946).

Again, simply because the Constitution gives federal courts this broad authority over federal claims, the key issue is the scope of the statutes that Congress has enacted that actually create the power in federal courts. Although there are many claim-specific grants of federal subject matter jurisdiction in federal statutes, most civil procedure courses focus on what is called the "general federal question" statute. That statute gives federal district courts subject matter jurisdiction over "all civil actions arising under the Constitution, laws, or treaties of the United States." 28 U.S.C. § 1331.

Somewhat surprisingly, even though Section 1331 uses exactly the same phrase as the Constitution—"arising under" federal law—the Supreme Court long ago interpreted Section 1331 to not reach as far as Article III permits. Put the other way, Congress gave federal courts less power to adjudicate claims than it could have. *Louisville & Nashville R.R. v. Mottley*, 211 U.S. 149 (1908) is the case you will study for this point and a related one.

The first important point from *Mottley* is the scope of Section 1331. In *Mottley*, the L&N railroad had agreed to provide the plaintiffs with lifetime free passes for transportation. Plaintiffs sued for breach of contract, a state law claim, seeking an order for specific performance of the contract. In their complaint, the plaintiffs pled that the railroad had defended its decision to stop honoring the passes because Congress had, later, passed a federal statute that prohibited railroads from giving free transportation. In their complaint, the plaintiffs also alleged that the federal statute did not apply to their contract for free passes and, if it did, the statute was unconstitutional. Even though clearly federal law was an ingredient of this state law claim, the Court held there was no federal question subject matter jurisdiction under what is now Section 1331:

> It is the settled interpretation of . . . [Section 1331] that a suit arises under the Constitution and laws of the United States only when the plaintiff's statement of his own cause of action shows that it is based upon those laws or that Constitution. It is not enough that the plaintiff alleges some anticipated defense to his cause of action, and asserts that the defense is invalidated by some provision of the Constitution of the United States. Although such allegations show that very likely, in the course of the litigation, a question under the Constitution would arise, they do not show that the suit, that is, the plaintiff's original cause of action, arises under the Constitution.

*Id.* at 152. Note that the Court reached this conclusion even though the outcome turned on federal law: if the federal statute was interpreted one way, plaintiffs won, but if it were interpreted the other way, they lost. Clearly, the claim "arose under" federal law if Section 1331 reached to the extent permitted by the Constitution as construed by *Osborn*.

*Mottley* established the proposition that Section 1331 did not reach that far. Although the phrase "arising under" in Article III allowed Congress to enact a statute that would have given federal courts subject matter jurisdiction over their claim, the Court held that Congress had not done so — even though it uses the same words. (Again, referring to the diagram in the prior chapter, Section 1331 is like Circle 1, not Circle 2.) "Although the constitutional meaning of 'arising under' may extend to all cases in which a federal question is 'an ingredient' of the action . . . the statutory grants of federal-question jurisdiction . . . confers a more limited power." *Merrell Dow Pharm., Inc. v. Thompson*, 478 U.S. 804, 807 (1986).

*Mottley* established a second fundamental principle of subject matter jurisdiction: whether a claim "arises under" federal law turns on application of the "well-pleaded complaint" rule. A "complaint" is the pleading the plaintiff files with a federal court to commence a lawsuit. Among other things, a complaint must state at least one claim that anchors the case in federal court. *See*

Chapter 13. Under the well-pleaded complaint rule, two principles are important: first, the focus is on claims actually pled, second, on a some-what imaginary "well-pleaded" complaint.

First, the focus is solely on the complaint. Whether federal question subject matter jurisdiction exists is determined by looking solely at the complaint and examining each claim in it. This means that a federal court determines from the complaint itself whether or not the claim "arises under" federal law. The focus solely on the complaint excludes things pled in the defendant's answer (which is the pleading a defendant files in response to being served with a complaint, *see* Chapter 37):

> Affirmative defenses that are based on federal law raised in a defendant's answer cannot show a federal question exists, *Bracken v. Matgouranis*, 296 F. 3d 160 (3rd Cir. 2002) (state law defamation claim did not raise federal question where complaint anticipated defendant's First Amendment defense), *unless the defense is that federal law completely preempts the state law claim. McCullough v. Ligon*, 430 F. Supp. 2d 846, 849–50 (E.D. Ark. 2006). (Complete preemption is discussed below.)

Thus, for example, a defendant's counterclaim cannot be used to show a federal question exists. *Price v. Alfa Mut. Ins. Co.*, 877 F. Supp. 597, 600 n. 7 (M.D. Ala. 1995) ("a defendant's counterclaim constitutes a subsequent pleading by the defendant, and a federal claim raised (by a defendant) in a counterclaim does not provide an independent basis for jurisdiction").

Second, not only does the well-pleaded complaint rule focus only on the plaintiff's complaint and not the defendant's answer, the well-pleaded complaint rule even filters out some things that may be in the plaintiff's complaint. The rule limits federal question subject matter jurisdiction to a claim in a well-pleaded complaint that either:

(A) is created by federal law either (i) expressly or (ii) impliedly through complete preemption or

(B) "the plaintiff's right to relief necessarily depends on resolution of a substantial question of federal law."

*Franchise Tax Bd. of Cal. v. Constr. Laborers Vacation Trust*, 463 U.S. 1, 27–28 (1983). The next section explores these two categories: *the claim* must either be created by federal law *or* depend on resolution of a substantial question of federal law. We'll explore these next, but it is not enough if the plaintiff, like the Mottley's, predicts in its complaint the obvious federal defense to their claim, and proactively pleads why that federal defense fails. The *claim* is what matters, and a complaint that pleads to avoid a defense is not "well pleaded" since *avoiding the federal defense is not an element of a claim.*

This is sometimes a difficult concept. One way to think about it is ask yourself: what must the plaintiff plead to win, without considering reasons why it might lose. So, for example, in a car wreck case a plaintiff must plead duty, breach, causation, and damages. In a breach of contract, it must plead a contract, breach, and damage. A plaintiff does not have to plead that it sued on time, or that it was not at fault. This will take practice!

### a.  Federal Question Subject Matter Jurisdiction

### i.  The Typical "Arising Under" Federal Claim: A Federal Statute Creates the Claim

The first step to determine if federal question jurisdiction exists is to determine what law creates the claim. Remember to apply the well-pleaded complaint rule, which means focusing on the elements of plaintiff's claim, not what a court will have to decide to resolve the claim. Simply because a federal statute bars enforcement of a contract does not mean the claim for breach of contract arises under federal law.

Notice that the well-pleaded complaint rule often gives a plaintiff control over whether a federal claim will be stated in the complaint. As you should be recognizing, the same set of facts often give rise to different claims. *See* Chapter 1. The same set of facts sometimes gives rise even to a claim under state law and another that arises under federal law. But plaintiff does not have to plead every claim it has, and so it can choose to assert only the state law claims to avoid federal question jurisdiction. *Caterpillar, Inc. v. Williams,* 482 U.S. 386, 392 (1987). A defendant cannot argue that federal question jurisdiction can be based upon a claim that the plaintiff has not alleged. *Merrell Dow,* 478 U.S. at 809 n. 6; *E.g., Merrill Lynch, Pierce, Fenner & Smith, Inc. v. Manning,* 136 S. Ct. 1562 (2016) (no jurisdiction under Section 1331 where plaintiff pled only state law security fraud claims, even though a federal statute created federal claims and that statute gave federal courts exclusive jurisdiction over claims created by that statute).

If you apply the well-pleaded complaint rule, and the claim is *not* created by federal law, then (absent the very narrow circumstances required for preemption or present in *Grable,* discussed below), there will not be federal question jurisdiction.

And it is usually easy to spot a federal claim. The vast majority of federal claims arise because a federal *statute* creates the claim. And federal statutes are identified by the letters "U.S.C." (for United States Code). So, if you see

"Plaintiff asserts a claim under 35 U.S.C. § 271," you've got a federal claim and—almost without doubt—federal subject matter jurisdiction.

Where a party asserts a claim created by a federal statute, questions about federal question jurisdiction are rarely raised. These are the easy ones, and for two reasons.

First, if a federal statute creates the claim, often that same statute will give federal courts jurisdiction to decide the claim. More likely than not, your professor will not test you on this, but in the real world, a federal statute that creates a claim often has a provision that makes it clear federal courts have power to decide that claim.

The second source for subject matter jurisdiction over a claim created by federal law is Section 1331. If a federal statute creates the claim, then it "arises under" federal law and is within Section 1331. There are only very narrow exceptions, but some casebooks cover them. *See, e.g., Shoshone Mining Co. v. Rutter,* 177 U.S. 505 (1900) (holding there was no federal question jurisdiction over claims authorized by federal statute to determine who owns certain interests in mines). These, however, are rare. Ordinarily, if federal law creates a claim, either there will be a statute specific to that claim giving federal courts power to decide it, or it will be covered by Section 1331.

There are two instances, however, when federal courts have power to hear a claim created by state law, and they can do so even when the requirements for diversity are lacking.

### ii. Plaintiff's State Law Claim Necessarily Turns on a Substantial Question of Federal Law

The second category of federal question subject matter jurisdiction is conceptually difficult, but very narrow. Be sure to keep *Mottley* in mind!

Suppose state law creates the claim, but to adjudicate it, a court must decide a *very* significant issue of federal law? As an element of the state law claim, the plaintiff must prove something that turns on the meaning of important federal law. Federal law is not a defense; it's part of plaintiff's claim.

Remember, first, that the Constitution permits Congress to enact a statute that gives federal courts jurisdiction over these claims, because federal law is at least an "ingredient" of the state law claim. Despite its narrow interpretation of Section 1331, the Supreme Court has held that Section 1331 includes *state* law claims but only the claim *necessarily depends* on resolution of a *substantial question of federal law.* That rule is very narrow and has several components.

First, only the plaintiff's *claim* counts: the question is not whether the court must, to decide whether the plaintiff "wins" a lawsuit, resolve a substantial question of federal law. Instead, the question is whether prevailing on plaintiff's state law claim requires resolution of a substantial question of federal law. So, for example, there is no federal question if a plaintiff pleads a state law contract claim and includes in its complaint facts that, if true, would overcome a federal law defense that the defendant might raise in its answer. (As was the case in *Mottley*.) As noted above, the existence of a federal defense to a state law claim is normally irrelevant (absent complete preemption) to determining federal question jurisdiction. *Aetna Health, Inc. v. Davila*, 542 U.S. 200, 207 (2004). To enforce that principle, it is irrelevant to federal question jurisdiction that a plaintiff pleads "around" a federal defense in the complaint. *Metropolitan Life Ins. Co. v. Taylor*, 481 U.S. 58, 63 (1987). Put another way, it does not matter if the defendant might have a federal defense to a claim; the resolution of the state law claim itself must necessarily depend on a substantial question of federal law.

Second, the federal issue implicated by the state law claim must be "substantial" or "significant." *Grable & Sons Metal Prods., Inc. v. Daure Engineering & Mfg.*, 545 U.S. 308 (2005) states that the "mere presence of a federal issue in a state cause of action does not automatically confer federal-question jurisdiction." *Merrell Dow*, 478 U.S. at 807. Instead, a federal question exists only where a substantial, disputed question of federal law is an element of the plaintiff's state law claim. *Id.* at 813.

The meaning of "substantial" is not subject to a precise, single test. *Grable*, 545 U.S. at 313. The Court has characterized "substantial" as meaning that the state claim must "really and substantially involve a dispute or controversy respecting the validity, construction or effect of federal law." *Id.* at 313. Similarly, the Court has stated that "substantial" in this context "demands not only a contested federal issue, but a substantial one, indicating a serious federal interest in claiming the advantages thought to be inherent in a federal forum." *Id.*

In addition, and even if there is a disputed substantial federal issue, "the federal issue will ultimately qualify for a federal forum only if federal jurisdiction is consistent with congressional judgment about the sound division of labor between state and federal courts governing application of § 1331." *Id.* Amplifying on this point, the Court stated that "the question is, does a state-law claim necessarily raise a stated federal issue, actually disputed and substantial, which a federal forum may entertain without disturbing any congressionally approved balance of federal and state judicial responsibilities." *Grable*, 545 U.S. at 314. Thus, at the outer reaches of Section 1331, "determinations about federal jurisdiction require sensitive judgments about congressional intent, judicial power, and the federal system." *Merrell Dow*, 478 U.S. at 810.

This requirement of a "substantial issue" of federal law is more difficult to establish than it sounds. Suppose, for example, that a plaintiff files a state tort law claim, alleging that a product was negligently designed, and in so alleging the plaintiff relies on the fact that the product failed to satisfy certain federal safety regulations. If "substantial" is read broadly, the plaintiff's claim necessarily turns on federal law since to figure out if the product was negligently designed the court will have to apply federal regulations to it. The following cases show both that it is not read that broadly, but that its boundaries are far from clear, with Justices often disagreeing on whether federal question jurisdiction existed. In cases with remarkably similar facts, the Court has reached different results.

On the one hand, in a few cases the Court concluded that a substantial federal question was necessary to the state law claim, and so federal question subject matter jurisdiction existed. Foremost, in *Smith v. Kansas City Title & Trust Co.*, 255 U.S. 180 (1921), the plaintiff pled a state law breach of fiduciary duty claim against a bank. However, whether the bank had breached its duty, or not, turned on—necessarily depended on—whether the bank had bought bonds that were unconstitutionally issued by the government. Because the question of whether the bonds were unconstitutionally issued turned on a question of federal law, the Court held that the plaintiff's state law claim necessarily depended on resolution of a substantial question of federal law, and so federal question subject matter jurisdiction was present.

More recently, in *Grable & Sons Metal Prods., Inc. v. Darue Eng'g & Mfg'g*, 545 U.S. 308 (2005), to satisfy a tax lien the IRS seized property owned by Grable, and then sold the property to Darue. Five years later, Grable sued Darue in state court to "quiet title" to that property (*i.e.*, for a judicial determination of who owned the property). Grable asserted that Darue's title was invalid because the IRS had not properly notified Grable of the sale, as required by a federal statute. Darue removed the case to federal court, and ultimately the Court held that the claim presented a federal question: whether Grable received adequate notice of the sale was "an essential element of [Grable's] quite title claim" and "appear[ed] to be the only . . . issue contested in the case." *Id.* at 315. Thus, it was a substantial question, and one that the claim necessarily depended on. Finally, the Court noted that the meaning of the federal tax notice provision was "an important issue of federal law that sensibly belongs in a federal court." *Id.* Thus, the resolution of the federal question was dispositive, and the resolution of that issue would involve litigation of the propriety of an act by the federal government.

The Court reached the opposite conclusion in three other cases. In the oldest, *Gully v. First Nat'l Bank*, 299 U.S. 109 (1936), Bank A had agreed to pay Bank B's debts and taxes. Both banks were national banks. The state filed suit against Bank A to collect the taxes Bank B owed. Court held the state law claim did not create any substantial federal question even though a federal law permitted states to tax banks, and the state had enacted its tax pursuant to that federal statute. Although the Court did not use the term, clearly Bank A's argument that the taxes were not validly assessed did not arise out of the state's well-pleaded complaint, but was at best a defense to enforcement of the state-law contract for debt.

In only a few cases, the Court has found question subject matter jurisdiction lacking even though federal law played an important role in adjudicating the state law claim. For example, in *Merrell Dow*, the plaintiff filed suit in state court alleging a state claim based on the allegation that a drug had been defectively made, in part relying on an allegation that the drug had been "misbranded" in terms of the federal Food Drug and Cosmetic Act ("FDCA"). The Court held there was no substantial federal question, heavily relying on the fact that Congress had not created a federal claim for violating the FDCA, and on the fact that, because breach of a federal regulation is often used to establish negligence in products liability cases, allowing federal question jurisdiction would seriously alter the federal-state balance, since those claims historically had been decided in state court.

Similarly, in *Empire Healthchoice Assurance, Inc. v. McVeigh*, 547 U.S. 677 (2006), after an accident an insured federal employee recovered money from a defendant who settled a tort claim. The employee's insurance company then sued the employee in federal district court seeking reimbursement, since it had paid the employee's medical bills, a portion of which the insured employee had obtained from the settling defendant. The insurer and insured disputed how much the insurer was entitled to, a matter which in part turned on application of federal regulations and statutes. The district court found no federal question and so dismissed the claim. In a 5–4 decision, the Court held that there was no substantial federal question, even though the insured had been a federal employee and the insurer subject to federal regulation.

The *Empire* Court identified several distinctions with *Grable* that justified a different result: First, the reimbursement claim "was triggered, not by the action of any federal department, agency, or service, but by the settlement of a personal-injury action launched in state court." Second, the claim did not involve a dispositive "pure issue of law" as in *Grable* but instead "the bottom line practical issue is the share of that settlement properly payable to" the insurer. *Id.* Finally, the majority noted that the federal interests in attracting able workers "do not warrant turning into a discrete and costly 'federal case' an insurer's contract-driven claim to be reimbursed from the proceeds of a federal worker's state-court-initiated tort litigation." *Id.*

More recently, the Court found no substantial federal question in *Gunn v. Minton*, 133 S.Ct. 1059 (2013). Gunn had represented Minton in a patent lawsuit that had been filed in federal court. Patent suits are required to be, and Minton's was, in federal court. During that lawsuit, the defendant asserted that Minton's patent was invalid. The court agreed and dismissed Minton's suit. Minton's lawyers then, in a motion to reconsider dismissal, argued for the first time that an exception applied and, as a result, the patent was not invalid. Specifically, although patent laws provide that an inventor must file for a patent within one-year of putting his invention in public use, an exception allowed an inventor to engage in "experimental use." An invention was not in "public use" if its use was experimental. The district court held that this argument was made too late, and waived.

Minton sued Gunn for legal malpractice, a claim created by state law. He filed the case in Texas state court. Minton argued that Gunn should have raised the experimental use exception earlier, and, had Gunn done so, the patent would not have been found invalid. The trial court ruled for Gunn, granting summary judgment. On appeal in the Texas Supreme Court, Minton argued that the state courts lacked subject matter jurisdiction since it was an exclusively federal issue (patent law is one of those rare exclusively federal issues). The Texas Supreme Court agreed, undoing Minton's loss and giving Minton the opportunity to file in federal court. The Supreme Court, however, granted certiorari and held that—even though central issues in the case turned on patent law—there was no federal subject matter jurisdiction. The Court emphasized that the relief Minton sought would not affect a patent (his was invalid) and any interpretation by a state court of federal patent law would not bind federal courts.

The fact that the line between these cases is not bright is confirmed by the fact that there were dissenting opinions in these decisions (except *Gunn*), and the lower appellate courts, too, have struggled with the boundary. *See, e.g., Verizon Md., Inc. v. Global Naps, Inc.*, 377 F.3d 355 (4th Cir. 2004) (appellate court split on whether a claim arising out of the breach of a contract that was required by federal statute presented a federal question).

Finally, a recent case addressed the scope of *Grable* in passing and in *dicta*. In *Merrill Lynch, Pierce, Fenner & Smith, Inc. v. Manning*, 136 S. Ct. 1562 (2016), the plaintiff's state court complaint contained only claims created by state law, alleging that the defendant had committed securities fraud. The Court stated that if the state statute had created a state claim for "any violation of the" federal statute, there would be *Grable* type jurisdiction because an element of the plaintiff's claim would have been a determination that very important federal laws—the securities laws—had been violated.

### iii. Federal Question Jurisdiction if Federal Law Completely Preempts a State Law Claim

Some casebooks address this very narrow form of federal question jurisdiction, but your professor may not.

As noted above, under the well-pleaded complaint rule, only the elements of claims that "needed" to be pled in the complaint "count." Thus, anything in the defendant's answer, including affirmative defenses, do not. However, there is one exception: the defense of complete preemption by federal law. Congress sometimes completely precludes (or "preempts") state law from applying to certain subjects. Where Congress intends to preclude states from making law in a field—whether through common law or state legislation—Congress is said to have "completely preempted" that subject.

The fact that Congress has enacted a federal statute does not usually lead to a finding of complete preemption. Instead, there are various kinds, or degrees, of preemption. Federal preemption often arises as a defense to a plaintiff's state-law claim, and without more does not change federal court jurisdiction: the well-pleaded complaint rule would ignore the defense. However, where federal law *completely* preempts state law, a claim is available, if at all, only under federal law. "A federal statute carrying the power of complete preemption wholly displaces a claim couched in state law, and such a claim is considered to be one arising under federal law." *Aetna Health, Inc. v. Davila*, 542 U.S. 200, 207–08 (2004).

This is a narrow exception to the well-pleaded complaint rule, but be sure you recognize it is just that—narrow. It is narrow for two reasons.

First, a federal statute that *completely* preempts a plaintiff's state law claim provides a basis for federal question subject matter jurisdiction even though preemption will be raised in the defendant's answer, not the plaintiff's complaint. *Aetna Health, Inc. v. Davila*, 542 U.S. 200, 207 (1984). This doctrine, which conceptually permits federal question jurisdiction over a something not raised in the complaint "recognizes that some federal laws evince such a strong federal interest that, when they apply to the facts underpinning the plaintiff's state-law claim, they convert that claim into one arising under federal law." *In re Blackwater Security Consulting, LLC*, 460 F.3d 576, 583 (4th Cir. 2006). Congress has completely preempted state law in only a few areas: § 301 of the Labor Management Relations Act, *Avco Corp. v. Aero Lodge No. 735, Int'l Ass'n of Machinists*, 390 U.S. 557, 560 (1968), § 502(a)(1)(B) of ERISA, *Metro. Life Ins. Co. v. Taylor*, 481 U.S. 58, 63–66 (1987), and §§ 85 and 86 of the National Bank Act, *Beneficial Nat'l Bank v. Andersen*, 539 U.S. 1, 10–11 (2003).

Second, complete preemption usually only matters when a defendant "removes" a state law case from state to federal court. *See* Chapter 10. Complete preemption gets used almost exclusively when a plaintiff files a state law claim in *state* court, but the defendant wants to "remove" the case to *federal* court. Without diversity jurisdiction, the claim is proper in federal court only if there is complete federal preemption of state law. A defendant can rely on federal question subject matter jurisdiction to remove a state law claim that is completely preempted by federal law. *See EFCO Corp. v. Iowa Ass'n of Bus. & Indus.,* 447 F. Supp. 2d 985 (N.D. Iowa 2006). So, the second way that this doctrine is narrow is that it applies almost only in determining whether a defendant properly removed a case from state to federal court based upon the complete preemption of a state law claim.

One counter-intuitive point about complete preemption is that it may be that federal law will provide the plaintiff with a claim, or federal law may preclude the plaintiff's claim entirely: whether the plaintiff has a federal claim, or not, is irrelevant to whether state law is completely preempted!

## 2. Diversity Subject Matter Jurisdiction

As shown above, in the vast majority of cases, if federal law (almost without exception, a federal statute) creates a claim, then federal question jurisdiction exists because that claim arises under federal. If state law creates the claim, federal question jurisdiction will not exist, unless resolution of the state law claim necessarily depends on resolution of a substantial federal question, or there is complete preemption.

The other source of original jurisdiction (remember, we'll cover supplemental jurisdiction later) is diversity. We turn there next.

The States in Article III of the Constitution granted Congress the power to enact statutes to allow federal courts to decide claims created by state law, but only if the dispute is "between Citizens of different States."

Before turning to what this means, consider why this exists. After all, it makes sense for federal courts to have the power to decide federal claims. As we'll see in Chapter 46, when deciding a state claim because of diversity jurisdiction, a federal court will apply state, not federal, law. Thus, a federal court with diversity jurisdiction over a claim will apply the same law as would the state court. So why did the States authorize Congress to create federal courts that could decide disputes between citizens of different states? The answer, back then at least, was bias: each State was concerned that if its citizens were sued in another State, that the jury would disfavor its citizen. At the time of the Constitution, the States concluded that a federal forum might be closer to neutral, and so they authorized Congress to let federal courts decide matters of state law when the dispute was between citizens of different States.

The Court has held that the Constitution permits Congress to enact statutes that permit federal courts to hear claims where there is merely "minimal diversity." Minimal diversity exists so long as at least one plaintiff is a citizen of a different state of at least one defendant. If so, there is a claim "between Citizens of different States" in terms of Article III. *State Farm Fire & Cas. Co. v Tashire,* 386 U.S. 523 (1967). Much like the Constitution merely required that any federal question jurisdiction statute require at least that federal law be an "ingredient" of a claim, the Constitution only limits Congress to giving courts power to hear claims with "minimal diversity."

Rather than going to the limits allowed by Article III, however, Section 1332(a) requires "complete diversity," meaning that no plaintiff may be a citizen of the same state as any defendant. *Strawbridge v. Curtiss,* 7 U.S. (3 Cranch) 267 (1806). Just like federal question jurisdiction, diversity jurisdiction is not co-extensive with Article III. It is symbolized by Circle 2, not Circle 1, in the illustration that appears in Chapter 2. So, to illustrate the difference, if two plaintiffs, one from Texas and another from California, sue a defendant in California, there is minimal diversity, but there is not complete diversity. Further, Congress included in Section 1332(a) an "amount in controversy" requirement. Neither it nor complete diversity are required by the Constitution. But, again, what matters is whether a claim is not within Section 1332, not whether Congress could have enacted a statute giving jurisdiction over the claim.

### a. Section 1332 Requires Complete Diversity and More Than $75,000 Exclusive of Costs and Interests be in Controversy

Using the power delegated to it in Article III, Congress enacted 28 U.S.C. § 1332. In full, Section 1332 provides:

(a) The district courts shall have original jurisdiction of all civil actions where the matter in controversy exceeds the sum or value of $75,000, exclusive of interest and costs, and is between—
   (1) citizens of different States;
   (2) citizens of a State and citizens or subjects of a foreign state;
   (3) citizens of different States and in which citizens or subjects of a foreign state are additional parties; and
   (4) a foreign state, defined in section 1603 (a) of this title, as plaintiff and citizens of a State or of different States.

For the purposes of this section, section 1335, and section 1441, an alien admitted to the United States for permanent residence shall be deemed a citizen of the State in which such alien is domiciled.

(b) Except when express provision therefor is otherwise made in a statute of the United States, where the plaintiff who files the case originally in the Federal courts is finally adjudged to be entitled to recover less than the sum or value of $75,000, computed without regard to any setoff or counterclaim to which the defendant may be adjudged to be entitled, and exclusive of interest and costs, the district court may deny costs to the plaintiff and, in addition, may impose costs on the plaintiff.

(c) For the purposes of this section and section 1441 of this title —

  (1) a corporation shall be deemed to be a citizen of any State by which it has been incorporated and of the State where it has its principal place of business, except that in any direct action against the insurer of a policy or contract of liability insurance, whether incorporated or unincorporated, to which action the insured is not joined as a party-defendant, such insurer shall be deemed a citizen of the State of which the insured is a citizen, as well as of any State by which the insurer has been incorporated and of the State where it has its principal place of business; and

  (2) the legal representative of the estate of a decedent shall be deemed to be a citizen only of the same State as the decedent, and the legal representative of an infant or incompetent shall be deemed to be a citizen only of the same State as the infant or incompetent.

(d) The word "States", as used in this section, includes the Territories, the District of Columbia, and the Commonwealth of Puerto Rico.

Again, like Section 1331, Section 1332(a) does not extend to the limits of Article III. It is narrower in two ways: it requires complete, not minimal, diversity *and* it imposes a minimum "amount in controversy." To analyze whether there is diversity subject matter jurisdiction over a claim, you'll need to know what complete diversity means, what "citizenship" means, and how to determine whether the amount in controversy exceeds $75,000.

## i. Section 1332(a) Requires Complete Diversity

Because subject matter jurisdiction turns on meeting the requirements of the statute, there is no diversity jurisdiction because the statute requires complete diversity. Even though complete diversity is not mandated by Article III or the statutory language, the Court has "adhered to the complete diversity rule in light of the purpose of" diversity jurisdiction, "which is to provide a federal forum for important disputes where state courts might favor, or be perceived as favoring, home-state litigants. The presence of parties from the same State on both sides of a case dispels this concern. . . ." *ExxonMobil Corp. v. Allapattah Serv., Inc.,* 545 U.S. 546 (2005).

This is an important point: if a plaintiff is a citizen of the same state as a defendant, then there can be no "anchor claim" under Section 1332. "Contamination" occurs, according to *ExxonMobil.*

We'll now explore how to determine "citizenship" and the "amount in controversy."

## *(a)  Determining Citizenship of a Party*
### (1)  When Is Citizenship Determined?

Citizenship is measured at the time of filing the pleading that contains the ostensibly diverse claim. Because jurisdiction is measured as of the time of filing suit, or the claim at issue if that comes later (we will see that parties may amend pleadings to add claims after the suit has been initiated) the focus generally is on the time the claim is filed and events after that point are irrelevant. If there is diversity at the time of filing the complaint (or of amending a complaint to add the new claim) then there is diversity subject matter jurisdiction even if after the claim is filed the parties become citizens of the same state. (In the next section, you'll also see the same principle applies to the amount in controversy requirement: it is measured as of the time of filing the claim, and subsequent events cannot divest a court of jurisdiction.) So, if an Alabama plaintiff files a $100,000 state law claim against a Texas defendant, there is diversity jurisdiction. Even if the plaintiff later moves to Texas, there is still diversity jurisdiction and even if the plaintiff amends his complaint to add another state law claim based upon diversity.

Conversely, if the parties are citizens of the same state when the claim is filed, the lack of diversity cannot be "cured" if afterwards the parties move and become citizens of different states. If a plaintiff was a citizen of the same state as a defendant at the time the claim was filed, but then becomes a citizen of a different state from the defendant, there still was no diversity at the time of filing, and so there is no diversity jurisdiction. *Grupo Dataflux v. Atlas Global Group, L.P.,* 541 U.S. 567 (2004).

So, we will see that citizenship of a corporation turns in part on its principal place of business. That determination is also made at the time the claim is filed, *Stock West Corp. v. Taylor,* 964 F.2d 912, 917 (9th Cir.1992), or the case with the pertinent claim is removed from federal to state court, *Miller v. Grgurich,* 763 F.2d 372, 373 (9th Cir.1985), or the amendment with a new claim is filed. Because subject matter jurisdiction turns on the facts at the time the claim is filed, changes in a corporation's activities or state of incorporation subsequent to that time are irrelevant.

Citizenship at the time the claim is filed is what counts. Note, that in addition to meaning that post-filing changes to a particular plaintiff's citizenship are irrelevant, this bright line also means that a party's citizenship at the time of the events that led to the lawsuit is irrelevant, too. Finally, don't overstate what this section says: if a party is added to a lawsuit later, its citizenship is determined at that time, not when the lawsuit was initially filed. *Century Commodity Corp. v. Data-Trend Commodities Inc.*, 1986 WL 9557 (N.D. Ill. Aug. 22, 1986) (citizenship of party subsequently joined to a suit is measured at time of joinder, not time suit was originally filed).

## (2) How Is Citizenship Determined?

### aa. *A Natural Person Is a Citizen of His State of Domicile*

"For purposes of diversity jurisdiction, citizenship [of a natural person] usually is equated with domicile." *Valentinn v. Hosp. Bella Vista*, 254 F.3d 358, 366 (1st Cir. 2001). Thus, the domicile of a human being named as a party determines his or her place of citizenship for purposes of determining whether a federal court has diversity subject matter jurisdiction. "A person's domicile is the place where he has his true, fixed home and principal establishment, and to which, whenever he is absent, he has the intention of returning. Domicile requires both physical presence in a place and the intent to make that place one's home." *Id. See Mas v. Perry*, 489 F.2d 1396 (5th Cir. 1974). Note that a person has *only one domicile*, even though she can have *more than one residence*. A residence is not the same as a domicile.

*Mas v. Perry*, 489 F.2d 1396 (5th Cir. 1974), illustrates these two requirements. There, Mrs. Mas had married her husband, a French citizen, at her parent's home in Mississippi during a time when both were teaching graduate school in Louisiana. Shortly after their marriage, they returned to Baton Rouge to resume teaching duties. They rented an apartment and after several months discovered that their landlord had installed a "two way mirror" enabling him to look into the bedroom of their Baton Rouge apartment. After suit was filed, they moved to Illinois to continue teaching, but always intending to return to Baton Rouge so Mr. Mas could complete his degree in Louisiana, but they testified that they intended once he completed his studies to move elsewhere, but did not know precisely where. Louisiana was simply a place for them to study and work.

They filed suit against the landlord in Louisiana, basing jurisdiction on diversity, alleging that Mrs. Mas was a Mississippi citizen, Mr. Mas a French Citizen, and the landlord a citizen of Louisiana. The district court denied the landlord's motion to dismiss for lack of subject matter jurisdiction, and the Fifth Circuit affirmed. The court held that the fact that Mrs. Mas had lived for a year in Louisiana did not change her domicile even though she testified that she had no intention of returning to the Mississippi home of her parents, that she was a Mississippi domicile because she was in Louisiana only as a student and lacked the requisite intent to remain there. "Until she acquires a new domicile, she remains a domiciliary, and thus a citizen, of Mississippi." *Id.* at 1400.

In the typical case, determining a person's state of domicile is straightforward: most people own one home and, though they may travel or have a vacation spot, they intend to return to that home. However, if a party's domicile is unclear (imagine they spend half the year in New Hampshire, and the other half in Georgia), then the courts look to the totality of the circumstances to determine domicile. In making that determination, there are no bright line rules. Some of the factors that courts often consider include:

(1) the person's place of voting;
(2) the location of the person's real and personal property;
(3) the state issuing the person's driver's license;
(4) the state where the person's bank accounts are maintained;
(5) club, church, or membership in other organizations;
(6) the person's place of employment;
(7) the state or city where the person pays taxes;
(8) the state where the person votes; and
(9) where the person's vehicles are registered.

*See Lundquist v. Precision Valley Aviation*, 946 F.2d 8, 11 (1st Cir. 1991). No one factor controls and the list is not exclusive.

Note that a person's domicile can change instantly, a fact that becomes important because what matters is the place of domicile at the time the claim is filed, not the time of the accident. Suppose, for example, that for several years a person clearly was domiciled in New York, but then just before suit was filed he bought a house in and moved his belongings to New Jersey. He then sues a New York citizen: thus, unless he is now domiciled in New Jersey, there is no diversity.

On the other hand, there is a presumption that a long-time domicile continues. Consequently, absent evidence that shows a change of domicile, it would be taken as fact that the person still is a citizen of New Jersey, and so diversity would be lacking. To overcome this presumption, two things are required: "He must take up residence at the new domicile, and he must intend to remain there." *McCann v. Newman Irrevocable Trust*, 458 F.3d 281, 286 (3rd Cir. 2006). To determine whether a party has established a physical presence and intent to stay in a domicile, courts look at the same factors above. *Id.*

*A Special Circumstance: Citizens of the U.S. Domiciled Abroad.* There will never be diversity subject matter jurisdiction over a claim brought by or against citizen of the United States who is domiciled in a foreign country if the opposing party is a citizen of a State. A United States citizen who establishes her domicile abroad cannot sue or be sued in federal court based on diversity of citizenship because she will never be a citizens of different State, since she's a citizen of the foreign country. Thus, there is no diversity under Section 1332(a)(1). *See Coury v. Prot,* 85 F.3d 244 (5th Cir. 1996). Nor will she come within another clause of Section 1332(a)(2), one we will do not focus on, which gives federal courts subject matter jurisdiction over claims between "citizens or subjects of a foreign state." That clause only applies if the suit is between two people who are both citizens of a foreign country, and so while she is a U.S. citizen, the other party is not. *Newman-Green, Inc. v. Alfonzo-Larrain,* 490 U.S. 826, 828 (1989).

### bb. Corporations Are Citizens of Both the State of Incorporation and the State of Principal Place of Business, Which Is Where It Has Its "Nerve Center"

A lot of lawsuits are brought by or against corporations. Corporations do not have "domiciles" since they don't "intend to live" anywhere. Their citizenship is instead defined by Section 1332(c)(1), which provides that, with the exception of certain insurance suits, "a corporation shall be deemed to be a citizen of any State by which it has been incorporated and of the State where it has its principal place of business. . . ." Thus, a corporation may be a citizen of one or two states for purposes of diversity: the state in which it is incorporated (often Delaware) and the state of its principal place of business.

#### States of Incorporation

Determining a corporation's state or states of incorporation is straightforward: to become incorporated, a corporation must file certain documents, including what are called "articles of corporation," with a state agency (typically, the state's Secretary of State). Corporations are typically, but not always, incorporated only by one state. If the corporation is incorporated by more than one state, which is rare, it is a citizen of every state in which it is incorporated. *Lee v. Trans Am. Trucking Serv., Inc.,* 111 F. Supp.2d 135 (E.D.N.Y. 1999); 28 U.S.C. § 1332(c)(1) (a corporation shall be deemed a citizen of "*any* State by which it has been incorporated"). Identifying the states in which a corporation is incorporated is a matter of public record.

*Nerve Center: Where Are the Company's Operational Headquarters?*

Until recently, federal courts had applied competing tests to determine where a corporation had its principal place of business for purposes of Section 1332: (1) "nerve center"; (2) "place of activities" or "locus of operations" test; and (3) "total activities." *J.A. Olson Co. v. City of Winona*, 818 F.2d 401 (5th Cir. 1987) (discussing the tests). Fortunately, the Supreme Court recently held that only the nerve center test determines the citizenship of an active corporation. In *Hertz Corp. v. Friend*, 130 S.Ct. 1181 (2010), the Court held that in determining the state of a corporation's "principal place of business" under Section 1332(c)(1) courts should look to where the corporation's officers direct, control, and coordinate the corporation's activities. Often this will be the corporation's main headquarters. But the inquiry, necessarily, requires comparative analysis, since some corporations may have several plants, many sales offices, and multiple employees located throughout the country. What matters is where the corporate control takes place, even if more "activity" such as sales occurs in a different state, and is more visible to the public.

*Inactive Corporations.* Often corporations become inactive, and so have neither a nerve center nor a place of activity. Yet, the diversity statute requires they be given the citizenship of both the state of incorporation and principal place of business. Does an inactive corporation have a principal place of business? The courts split: (1) it has no principal place of business; (2) the state where it does anything or, if none, the state where it last did some; or (3) a facts and circumstances test. *Holston Investments, Inc. B.V.I. v. LanLogistics Corp.*, 877 F.3d 1068 (11th Cir. 2012).

*Parent, Subsidiary, and Affiliated Corporations Each has its Own Citizenship.* It is common for a corporation to be owned by another corporation (called a parent corporation), or to own a separate corporation (called a subsidiary), or to have "sister" corporations, each owned by a common parent (called affiliated corporations, or sister corporations). Thus, a corporation that is incorporated as a separate entity from its parent, subsidiary, or affiliated corporation has its own principal place of business. *Fitzgerald v. Seaboard System Railroad, Inc.*, 647 F. Supp. 205 (S.D. Ga.1985).

## cc.  Citizenship of Other Business Entities

While Congress has specified which states corporations are deemed to be citizens of, Congress has not defined citizenship for any other form of business entity. Thus, courts have developed common law approaches. This subsection summarizes their holdings.

*Partnerships.* The citizenship of each partner counts for determining diversity. *Chapman v. Barry,* 129 U.S. 677, 682 (1889). So, a partnership of two natural persons will have the citizenship of each natural person; a partnership between a person and a corporation will have the citizenship of (a) the domicile of the natural person; (b) the state of incorporation of the corporation; and (c) the state of the principal place of business of the corporation. (If one partner is a citizen of a foreign country, then as we saw with natural persons, there will not be diversity subject matter jurisdiction because the partnership is not a citizen of any state. *Herrick v. SCS Commun., Inc.,* 251 F.3d 315, 322–23 (2d Cir. 2001)).

*Limited Partnerships.* Limited partnerships have limited partners and at least one general partner. The citizenship of all partners, both general *and* limited, of an LP count for diversity purposes. In *Carden v. Arkoma Assocs.,* 494 U.S. 185 (1990), the Court in a 5–4 decision rejected the holding of the appellate court that only the citizenship of the general partners of the limited partnership mattered, noting that it had "never held that an artificial entity, suing or being sued in its own name, can invoke the diversity jurisdiction of the federal courts based on the citizenship of some but not all of its members." The majority recognized that the general partners are in control of the limited partnership, and that by definition limited partners must be passive, but rejected the dissent's argument that only the citizenship of the "real parties to the controversy" should be counted — that of the limited partnership itself, and the general partner. The impact, obviously, is to make it more difficult for suits by or against limited partnerships to be based on diversity subject matter jurisdiction.

*Limited Liability Partnerships.* An LLP is treated like a partnership, and so has the citizenship of each partner, unless a state statute specifies otherwise. *Belleville Catering Co. v. Champaign Market Place L.L.C.,* 350 F.3d 691 (7th Cir. 2003) ("we have held that limited liability companies are citizens of every state of which any member is a citizen"). LLP's can be comprised of partners who are individuals, partnerships, and corporations.

*Limited Liability Companies.* A Limited Liability Company (LLC) has the citizenship of *each state* of its members. *Wise v. Wachovia Securities, LLC,* 450 F.3d 265, 267 (7th Cir. 2006).

*Unincorporated Associations.* An unincorporated association, such as a trade association or union, is deemed to have the citizenship of each of its members. *United Steelworkers of Am. v. R.H. Bouligny, Inc.,* 382 U.S. 145, 146–50 (1965); *Rose v. Giamatti,* 721 F. Supp. 906 (S.D. Ohio 1989) (major league baseball was an unincorporated association and so had citizenship of each member team).

*Watch for Mixtures.* As briefly noted above, these various business entities can come in tiered forms. For example, in some states a corporation can be a limited partner in a limited liability partnership. Likewise, a partnership might be comprised of two corporations, or a corporation and a person. This can add steps to the citizenship inquiry. For example, if a limited liability corporation has two members—one a natural person and the other a corporation—then it has the citizenship of (1) the domicile of the natural person; (2) the state of incorporation of the corporation; and (3) the principal place of business of that corporation.

### dd.  Representative Actions: Citizenship of Real Party in Interest

Certain persons are not competent to file suit, or for other reasons cannot personally be named as a plaintiff in a suit. For example, infants, incompetent adults, and decedents cannot file suits. Another person as a representative instead brings the suit. Does the citizenship of the representative, or the person she represents, count?

Section 1332(c)(2) provides the answer. It provides that "the legal representative of the estate of a decedent shall be deemed to be a citizen only of the same State as the decedent, and the legal representative of an infant or incompetent shall be deemed to be a citizen only of the same State as the infant or incompetent." Put simply, the state of the real party in interest—the party being represented by the legal representative—controls, not the citizenship of the representative. So, for example, in *Green v. Lake of the Woods County,* 815 F. Supp. 305 (D. Minn. 1993), the father of a boy killed in a car wreck filed suit as trustee of his son's estate filed suit against the driver of the vehicle that killed him. The son and the other driver were citizens of Minnesota, but the father was a citizen of Illinois; even so, the district court held that the son's citizenship controlled and diversity jurisdiction was lacking.

| This Type of Party ... | ... has Citizenship of This or These States |
| --- | --- |
| Natural Person | His State of Domicile |
| Representative of Party | Party's, not Representative's, Citizenship |
| Corporation | State(s) of incorporation *and* State of its nerve center |
| Partnership | Each partner's citizenship |
| Limited Partnership | Each partner's *and* limited partner's citizenship |
| Limited Liability Partnership | Each partner's citizenship |
| Limited Liability Corporation | Each member's citizenship |
| Unincorporated Business Entity | Each member's citizenship |

## ii. Section 1332 Requires More Than $75,000 in Controversy

Not only does Section 1332 require complete, rather than minimal diversity, Congress included a minimum amount in controversy. Article III does not require a minimum amount in controversy. Congress has amended the statute to increase the minimum amount in controversy over the years. Today, it is at $75,000. Thus, even if complete diversity exists there is no diversity subject matter jurisdiction if the amount in controversy, exclusive of interest and costs, does not exceed $75,000. Contrast this with the general federal question statute, which has no minimum amount in controversy.

### (a) When Is the Amount in Controversy Calculated?

The amount in controversy requirement is initially determined by the amount claimed by the plaintiff in its complaint, which "controls if the claim [was] made in good faith." *St. Paul Mercury Indem. Co. v. Red Cab Co.*, 303 U.S. 283, 288–89 (1938). Thus, as with citizenship, the amount in controversy is determined at the time the complaint is filed. *Thesleff v. Harvard Trust Co.*, 154 F.2d 732, 732 n.1 (1st Cir. 1946) ("federal jurisdiction depends upon the facts at the time suit is commenced, and subsequent changes . . . in the amount in controversy [do not] divest it").

But, the defendant's ability to argue that the amount claimed is in bad faith (discussed below) raises some complex issues, and what if the plaintiff does not plead an amount in the complaint, or pleads an amount that is *less* than $75,000? (That latter question gets litigated in removal issues frequently, a topic we'll cover in Chapter 10.) What if the plaintiff in good faith pleads an amount in excess of $75,000, but ends up recovering less from the jury?

### (b) The Legal Certainty Test Applies to the Amount Pled by Plaintiff

A court can dismiss a claim for failure to satisfy the amount in controversy requirement only if it is proven to a legal certainty that the actual amount in controversy is less than $75,000. *Lowdermilk v. U.S. Bank Nat'l Ass'n.*, 479 F.3d 994 (9th Cir. 2007) ("if the complaint alleges damages in excess of the federal amount-in-controversy requirement, then the amount-in-controversy requirement is presumptively satisfied unless it appears to a legal certainty that the claim is actually for less than the jurisdictional amount"). This is an extremely difficult burden: to dismiss because the amount in controversy requirement is not met, "[t]he legal impossibility of recovery must be so certain as virtually to negative the plaintiff's good faith in asserting the claim." *Tongkook Am. v. Shipton Sportswear Co.*, 14 F.3d 781, 786 (2d Cir. 1994). "The court should not consider in its jurisdictional inquiry the legal sufficiency of those claims or whether the legal theory advanced by the plaintiff is probably sound." *Suber v. Chrysler Corp.*, 104 F.3d 578, 583 (3d Cir. 1997). Instead, the court should engage "in only minimal scrutiny of the plaintiff's claims." *Id.; see Coventry Sewage Assocs. v. Dworkin Realty Co.*, 71 F.3d 1, 4 (9th Cir. 1995) (recognizing that although "a federal court should rigorously enforce the jurisdictional limits" of the diversity statute, "preliminary jurisdictional determinations should neither unduly delay, nor unfairly deprive a party from, determination of the controversy on the merits.").

Why is it so hard for a party to prove that the actual amount in controversy really doesn't satisfy the $75,000 requirement? The high standard created by the legal certainty test is designed to avoid pre-trying the case: if a lower standard were used, then to determine if it has subject matter jurisdiction the court would almost have to try the whole case to know if it has jurisdiction to do so. To avoid that problem, it must appear to a legal certainty that the plaintiff *can't* recover more than $75,000 for the court to conclude that the requirement is not met. Thus, the "legal certainty" standard is a minimal check so that the court doesn't have to try the case to determine whether the court has jurisdiction to do so.

In part also to avoid pre-trying the case, the court cannot consider affirmative defenses to "whittle down" the amount in controversy. *Scherer v. Equitable Life Assurance Soc'y of U.S.*, 347 F.3d 394 (2d Cir. 2003) (viewing this also as an aspect of the well-pleaded complaint rule). In *Scherer*, the Second Circuit explained:

> This may seem paradoxical: if it can be said "to a legal certainty" that the defense in question is a winning defense, ought it not be considered for amount-in-controversy purposes? One plausible answer is that because affirmative defenses can be waived, the court cannot at the time of filing be certain that any given affirmative defense will be applied to the case. Given the time-of-filing rule, it follows that waivable "affirmative defenses" are not germane to determining whether the amount-in-controversy requirement has been met.

*Id.* at 398. Likewise, in *St. Paul Mercury Indemnity Co. v. Red Cab Co.*, 303 U.S. 283 (1938), the Supreme Court explained that the plaintiff's inability to ultimately recover the jurisdictional amount does not oust the court of jurisdiction, "[n]or does the fact that the complaint discloses the existence of a valid defense to the claim." *Id.* at 289. Thus, it is somewhat unusual for a court to dismiss where the plaintiff has pled an amount exceeding $75,000, *see, e.g., Danial v. Daniels*, 162 Fed. Appx. 288 (5th Cir. 2006) (affirming dismissal of complaint where plaintiff specifically pled that its damages were less than $7,000); *Nelson v. Kefer*, 451 F.2d 289 (3rd Cir. 1971) (affirming dismissal where medical and property damages in personal injury case came to 1% of amount in controversy requirement), and cases reversing district courts for dismissing a claim for not meeting the amount in controversy are comparatively more common. *See, e.g., Meridian Sec. Ins. Co. v. Sadowski*, 441 F.3d 536 (7th Cir. 2006) (remanding for trial a case that district court had dismissed under the legal certainty test).

This issue may allow for dismissal when there is a substantive rule of law that clearly excludes the type of damages the plaintiff seeks to rely on to meet the $75,000 minimum. Suppose, for example, that a plaintiff brings a breach of contract claim and asserts the damages are more than $75,000 because it suffered emotional distress as a result of the breach. Suppose that under state law, emotional distress damages are not recoverable for breach of contract (that is the general rule, with exceptions relating to disposition of dead bodies and other odd circumstances). In that case, the defendant could establish to a legal certainty that plaintiff would not recover more than $75,000 because the damages sought are not legally recoverable.

*Valuing Injunctive Relief.* Where a plaintiff seeks equitable relief, such as an injunction, how should it be valued? Generally, the amount in controversy requirement is met if the *value of the injunction to the plaintiff* or *the cost to the defendant* meets or exceeds the statutory minimum. *McCauley v. Ford Motor Co.*, 264 F.3d 952, 958 (9th Cir. 2001) (citing *Ridder Bros., Inc. v. Blethen*, 142 F.2d 395, 399 (9th Cir.1944) (the test for determining the amount in controversy is the "pecuniary result to either party which the judgment would directly produce")).

*The Value of the Object Test.* This test is sometimes applied in injunction cases, too, and sometimes in other circumstances. In *Williams v. Kleppe*, 539 F.2d 803 (1st Cir. 1976), for example, the plaintiffs sought to enjoin a statute that prohibited skinny dipping, and applied value of the objective approach and held that the right to skinny dip was probably not worth $10,000 (the amount in controversy requirement at that time).

*Do Attorneys' Fees Count?* The general rule is that attorneys' fees that the plaintiff seeks to recover from the defendant do not "count" for purposes of determining whether the amount in controversy is met. However, there two principal exceptions: (1) where a statute (state or federal) permits their recovery for the claim or (2) for a breach of contract claim, where the plaintiff is entitled to such fees under the terms of the contract in suit. *See Manguno v. Prudential Property & Cas. Ins. Co.*, 276 F.3d 720, 723 (5th Cir.2002) ("[i]f a state statute provides for attorney's fees, such fees are included as part of the amount in controversy."); *Saval v. BL Ltd.*, 710 F.2d 1027, 1033 (4th Cir.1983) (courts consider attorney fees part of the jurisdictional amount in controversy where statutes or contractual provisions transform the fees into substantive rights to which litigants are entitled).

**What if no Amount is Pled in the Complaint?** Where a claim is made for indeterminate or unspecified amount damages, "[the] 'legal certainty test' gives way, and the party seeking to invoke federal jurisdiction bears the burden of proving by a preponderance of the evidence that the claim on which it is basing jurisdiction meets the jurisdictional minimum." *Federated Mut. Ins. Co. v. McKinnon Motors, LLC,* 329 F.3d 805, 807 (11th Cir. 2003). Thus, if a plaintiff or other party *wants* there to be diversity jurisdiction in federal court, it should plead in its complaint that the amount in controversy exclusive of costs and interests exceeds $75,000.

**What About Facts Learned After Filing the Complaint?** What if the plaintiff files suit and in good faith alleges that damages are greater than $75,000, but even before the defendant answers, the plaintiff learns that in fact damages are substantially below the jurisdictional minimum? It doesn't matter: as noted above, the general rule is that federal jurisdiction turns on the facts at the time suit is filed, and so subsequent changes in the amount in controversy are irrelevant. So, for example, in *Coventry Sewage Assocs. v. Dworkin Realty Co.,* 71 F.3d 1 (1st Cir. 1995), the plaintiff in good faith claimed damages in excess of $75,000 but learned before the defendant filed its answer that in fact the actual amount in controversy was about $30,000. The defendant moved to dismiss for lack of subject matter jurisdiction, but the court held that the case fit "well within the rule that once jurisdiction attaches, it is not ousted by a subsequent change of events." *Id.* at 7 (collecting cases).

**What if the Judgment Obtained After Trial is Less Than the Jurisdictional Minimum?** Jurisdiction is unaffected: so long as the complaint met the legal certainty test under the facts at the time of filing—the plaintiff had a good faith basis for believing the amount exceeded $75,000—then jurisdiction attaches and subsequent events are irrelevant. But, under 28 U.S.C. 1332(b), the plaintiff may have to pay certain costs to the defendant, or be denied recovery itself:

> where the plaintiff who files the case originally in the Federal courts is finally adjudged to be entitled to recover less than the sum or value of $75,000, computed without regard to any setoff or counterclaim to which the defendant may be adjudged to be entitled, and exclusive of interest and costs, the district court may deny costs to the plaintiff and, in addition, may impose costs on the plaintiff . . .

Why did the plaintiff in *Coventry* then seek to remain in federal court? Probably because the "costs" that the court can deny to the plaintiff, or impose on it, are typically fairly low, often measuring only a few hundred to a few thousand dollars. *See Coventry,* 71 F.3d at 8 n.1.

### (c) Multiple Claims, Multiple Plaintiffs, and the Amount in Controversy

For a court to have diversity jurisdiction over one claim by a plaintiff against a defendant under Section 1332, the amount in controversy must be satisfied as to that claim. If a plaintiff asserts a claim for $75,001 against a diverse defendant, the amount in controversy is satisfied.

What if a plaintiff has two claims against a single defendant, each of which is for less than $75,000, but when added together—aggregated—the total is more than $75,000? Likewise, what if two (or more) plaintiffs each have a claim against a single defendant, but no one plaintiff's claim exceeds $75,000? Can separate plaintiff's claims be aggregated? Finally, what about one plaintiff with claims against two (or more) defendants, where no one claim exceeds $75,000? (If a plaintiff has a claim against a defendant exceeds $75,000 and has a claim against that defendant, or other defendants, that does not meet the minimum, then the plaintiff could either aggregate them or if aggregation is unavailable, examine whether joinder of the claim for less than $75,000 is proper and whether supplemental jurisdiction exists. *See* Chapter 21.)

### (1) A Single Plaintiff may Aggregate Claims Against a Single Defendant

It is common for a plaintiff to include two (or more) claims against one defendant. The amount of those claims may be aggregated: "in determining whether the amount-in-controversy requirement has been satisfied, a single plaintiff may aggregate two or more claims against a single defendant, even if the claims are unrelated." *ExxonMobil Corp. v. Allapattah Serv., Inc.,* 545 U.S. 546 (2005). Thus, a plaintiff can plead two claims, one for $45,001 and the other for $30,000, and the total amount counts, even if the claims are completely unrelated to each other. This rule holds true for each plaintiff who sues a single defendant: if two plaintiffs sue one defendant, each plaintiff can aggregate its amounts; if two plaintiffs sue two defendants, each plaintiff can aggregate its amounts separately against *each* defendant.

### (2) A Plaintiff Cannot Aggregate Claims Against More Than one Defendant Unless the Defendants are Jointly Liable

In a case by a single plaintiff with claims against more than one defendant, the general rule is that "where a suit is brought against several defendants asserting claims against each of them which are separate and distinct, the test of [the amount in controversy requirement] is the amount of each claim, and not their aggregate." *Jewell v. Grain Dealers Mut. Ins. Co.*, 290 F.2d 11, 13 (5th Cir. 1961). So, if a plaintiff sues one defendant for $65,001, and another for a separate claim for $10,000, the plaintiff does not satisfy the amount in controversy requirement.

There is one fairly large exception to that general rule. Where a plaintiff makes claims against two defendants who are jointly liable to the plaintiff, the amount sought against each defendant can be aggregated (added together) to reach the statutory minimum. *Middle Tenn. News Co. v. Charnel of Cincinnati, Inc.*, 250 F.3d 1077 (7th Cir. 2001). Thus, a plaintiff may aggregate damages claimed against two or more defendants only if under governing state law the defendants are jointly and severally liable to the plaintiff.

If there is no joint and several liability, the plaintiff must satisfy the amount in controversy requirement against at least one individual defendant; if so, there is jurisdiction over that claim, and the question would be whether there is supplemental jurisdiction over the claim against the other, joined defendant. *See* Chapter 21. But, if one or more defendants are not jointly and severally liable and *neither* claim exceeds $75,000, the amount in controversy is not satisfied.

### (3) Multiple Plaintiffs may not Aggregate Their Claims Unless They are Pursuing a Unified Remedy

Suppose more than one plaintiff each signed the same contract with a defendant, say to borrow money, with each plaintiff's damages being less than $75,000, but the total amount they collectively lost exceeding that amount. Can they aggregate their claims to satisfy the amount in controversy?

Almost always the answer is "no": in cases involving multiple plaintiffs, "the separate claims of multiple plaintiffs against a single defendant cannot be aggregated to meet the jurisdictional requirement." *Clark v. State Farm Mutual Auto. Ins. Co.*, 473 F.3d 708 (7th Cir. 2007). So, while the claims of Plaintiff A against Defendant A can be aggregated, the claims of Plaintiffs A and B cannot be. Multiple plaintiffs cannot add their amounts together where their claims are separate and distinct, as in the case of multiple contracts. Each plaintiff must individually satisfy the amount in controversy requirement. *Snyder v. Harris*, 394 U.S. 332, 335 (1969). Thus, if each plaintiff has its own claim against a defendant for breach of contract that resulted in damage to the particular plaintiff, the amounts may not be aggregated even if the two contracts are identical. *Lovell v. State Farm Mut. Auto. Ins. Co.*, 466 F.3d 893 (10th Cir. 2006).

However, there is one fairly narrow exception (and another for federal class actions, a subject discussed in the final part of this book): the amounts can be aggregated when plaintiffs "unite to enforce a single title or right in which they have a common and undivided interest." *Snyder*, 394 U.S. at 335. It is hard to satisfy this "unity of right" requirement:

> Despite pervasive criticism of the "separate and distinct" versus "common and undivided" distinction as arcane and confusing, there appears to be a common thread in the relevant case law-the presence of a "common and undivided interest" is rather uncommon, existing only when the defendant owes an obligation to the group of plaintiffs as a group and not to the individuals severally. *See Eagle v. American Tel. and Tel. Co.*, 769 F.2d 541, 546 (9th Cir.1985) ("[T]he character of the interest asserted depends on the source of plaintiffs' claims. If the claims are derived from rights that they hold in group status, then the claims are common and undivided. If not, the claims are separate and distinct."); *National Org. for Women v. Mutual of Omaha Ins. Co.*, 612 F. Supp. 100, 107 (D.D.C.1985) ("[T]he cases that allow aggregation often speak of the presence of some fund to which a plaintiff class is seeking access[, and] . . . they often involve an attempt to enforce a right that belongs to a group.").

*Friedman v. New York Life Ins. Co.*, 410 F.3d 1350 (11th Cir. 2005). Thus, the general rule that plaintiffs cannot aggregate their claims is broad, and the exceptions are narrow.

# B. Must the Claim be Filed in Federal Court?

## 1. Claims Arising Under Federal Law

There are two significant but counter-intuitive points about federal question jurisdiction.

First, nothing in the Constitution requires Congress to allow *only* federal courts to hear federal question claims: Article III does not say that Congress has to preclude state courts from having concurrent subject matter jurisdiction.

Put another way, Article III allows Congress to enact statutes that permit, but do not require, federal claims to be filed in federal courts. Other portions of the Constitution do give exclusive jurisdiction to federal courts over certain types of claims (*e.g.,* claims between two States can only be brought in the Supreme Court), but Article III does not. Thus, Congress could give federal courts exclusive federal jurisdiction over federal claims (not state claims without, at least, minimal diversity!). But Section 1331does not do so: a claim *may* be filed in federal court under 1331. Unless some other federal statute requires the particular federal claim be filed in federal court, the plaintiff can choose to file in state court. Thus, state courts can "render binding judicial decisions that rest on their own interpretations of federal law." *ASARCO Inc. v. Kadish,* 490 U.S. 605, 617 (1989). *See Testa v. Katt,* 330 U.S. 386 (1947).

The only likely statute that will require a federal claim to be filed in federal court is the statute that creates the claim. There are not many exclusively federal claims, but the common ones include:

- Claims where the United States is a party. Art. III, § 2
- Patent infringement claims. 28 U.S.C. § 1338
- Admiralty and maritime claims. 28 U.S.C. § 1333
- Bankruptcy proceedings. 28 U.S.C. § 1334
- Claims against a foreign state. 28 U.S.C. § 1441(d)
- Federal Tort Claim Act claims. 28 U.S.C. § 1346(b)

But that brings up the second oddity: even if a statute provides that a claim must be filed in federal court, nothing requires a plaintiff to do so. And mistakes do happen. A plaintiff also may make a mistake and file an exclusively federal claim in state court. What happens if a plaintiff files in state court a claim over which the federal courts have exclusive subject matter jurisdiction? If the defendant does not remove the case (*see* Chapter 10), the state court can decide the claim; however, its judgment will be subject to collateral attack. That is, the defendant could later file suit in federal court to challenge the outcome reached by the state court. *See Kalb v. Feuerstein,* 308 U.S. 433 (1940). That may result in the whole state court proceeding being rendered a nullity, and the claim having to be relitigated in a federal forum.

What does the fact that a plaintiff often can file a federal claim in state court, and sometimes may do so even in the rare case when only federal courts have subject matter jurisdiction over the claim? First, the plaintiff may have a choice: it may be that the claim can be properly filed in *either* state or federal court. Filing in state court a claim that is exclusively federal is not a good idea, but it can be done. For the defendant, it means that defense counsel must analyze whether the claim arises under federal law. The plaintiff may have exercised a choice to file in state court a claim that could also be filed in federal court. If the claim does arise under federal law, then the defendant can remove the case to federal court. *See* Chapter 10.

## 2. State Law Claims That Meet Diversity Requirements

Nothing *requires* a plaintiff to file in federal court a claim that meets the requirements of the diversity statute. A plaintiff can file in state court a claim between citizens of different states with an amount in controversy over $75,000. But, the defendant then may "remove" the case to federal court. *See* Chapter 10.

What does the availability of these choices mean for the parties' lawyers? The plaintiff's lawyer can exercise the first option, deciding whether as a practical or strategic matter one forum is more favorable than the other. Generally, lawyers view state courts as more favorable for plaintiffs and federal court more favorable for defendants, although there are many exceptions to that view. If the plaintiff's lawyer chooses to file a claim in state court that meets the requirements of the diversity statute, defense counsel has the power to "remove" the case to federal court. Thus, defense counsel must ascertain whether a claim is "removable," and, if so, decide whether a federal forum would strategically best serve the defendant; if so, defense counsel should remove the case from state to federal court. *See* Chapter 10.

## 3. The Discussion Here Applies to the First Claim and all Other Claims but as to Additional Claims, if There is no Diversity or Federal Question, Supplemental Subject Matter Jurisdiction may be Available

As shown above, the Constitution permits Congress to enact statutes that allow subject matter jurisdiction where federal law is merely an ingredient to a claim, or when there is minimal diversity. In Section 1331 and 1332, Congress chose not to extend federal power to the Constitutional limits.

But there is another statute, 28 U.S.C. § 1367. *See* Chapter 21. It only is available if there is one claim over which the court has subject matter jurisdiction under Section 1331 or 1332, however. We will explore it in detail later. But just because 1332 requires complete diversity and a minimum amount in controversy does not mean that Congress could not enact a statute that requires only minimal diversity or has no amount in controversy. Congress did so in Section 1367, but that statute only applies if there is one claim that fits under

Section 1331 or Section 1332. So, unless there is one claim over which the court has original subject matter jurisdiction under either of those two statutes, Section 1367 is unavailable.

So as to not leave you in suspense, the basic notion behind Section 1367 is this, and it relates to something we talked about at the outset: the same set of facts will give rise to multiple claims. If a plaintiff has a federal claim (say employment discrimination under a federal statute) and, for example, a state law claim that arises out of that same set of facts for breach of contract, why not try those claims in one case? Without Section 1367, unless there was also complete diversity and at least $75,000 in controversy, there would have to be two lawsuits. Section 1367 is designed to allow for efficient resolution of cases already anchored in federal court. That, as you'll see, is the easy part.

## Checkpoints

- Can you identify the three ways that a claim can arise under federal law?
- Can you explain when a plaintiff's state law claim nonetheless arises under federal law?
- Do you know how to determine the citizenship of each type of party?
- Can you calculate when the amount of controversy is satisfied when plaintiff has not simply pled for more than $75,000, including when and when not "aggregation" is proper?
- Can you explain when you will look to Section 1367 and why it may Constitutionally require "less" than Section 1331 or Section 1332?
- If subject matter jurisdiction is lacking, what do you do? *See* Chapter 30.

# Chapter 5

# The Foundations of Personal Jurisdiction

---

### Personal Jurisdiction Roadmap

This chapter explains that the concept of personal jurisdiction arises from a non-resident defendant's right not to be sued in a state where it would be unfair to defend himself, and how that right is balanced against the need for a state to protect its citizens from harm by citizens of some other state.

---

It helps to understand personal jurisdiction to keep in mind that, at their core, civil lawsuits are about obtaining governmental power to coerce resolution of a private dispute: a process we call "adjudication." A person who believes someone has breached a contract, for example, sues to force that person to pay money to compensate for the harm caused by the breach. A court can issue orders that allow the prevailing party to use the government to force the losing party to pay money.

Now, add to that the fact that each state has its own separate government and is sovereign from each other. On the one hand, a state should be able to force a defendant who comes into that state and deliberately hurts one of its citizens to come back to that state and defend a claim arising out of that visit. But, should a state have the power to force a defendant to defend a suit when the defendant has never been to the state and the suit has nothing to do with that state?

Personal jurisdiction is a limit on governmental power. We'll see that some limitations are created by state or federal statute, while others are imposed by the Constitution. Specifically, "long-arm statutes" of the states both create and limit judicial power to force non-residents to defend themselves in a state. Likewise, the Due Process Clauses of the Fifth and Fourteenth Amendments limit the power that federal and state courts have over a person and his property. These limitations on power are expressed by the principle that a court, whether state or federal, must have "personal jurisdiction" over a defendant to enter an order that binds the defendant to pay a money judgment or otherwise be affected by a court's judgment.

Why should a state have any power over non-residents? Why should a court in Arizona have the power to enter a judgment that will require a defendant living in Colorado to pay money to an Arizona resident? Why should the courts of one state be able, *at all*, to force a citizen of another state to defend lawsuits in their state? That question helps to make clear why states do have power to force non-residents to defend claims brought by residents, but also why there are limits on that power.

The power arises from the need of a state to protect its citizens from wrongful acts of out-of-state citizens. Imagine a world where, if a driver from Oregon injured an Arizona resident in a car wreck in Tucson, the Arizona resident must sue the Oregon resident in Oregon. Or, if a citizen of Tennessee bought a defective flat screen TV by mail from a California company, but had to sue in California to get her money back. Many wrongs would go unpunished. Thus, the law recognizes that every state has a "'manifest interest' in providing its residents with a convenient forum for redressing injuries inflicted by out-of-state actors." *Burger King Corp. v. Rudzewicz,* 471 U.S. 462, 474 (1985).

At the same time, this power is not without limits. Some limits are built into "long-arm statutes." Some state long-arm statutes, for example, require that part of the claim have physically occurred in the state. No matter the reach of the long-arm statute, however, the Due Process Clause of the Fourteenth Amendment limits the power of states to force non-residents to be haled into a state to defend themselves. (The Due Process Clause of the Fifth Amendment limits federal courts' power over federal question claim in a similar fashion.)

The law of personal jurisdiction balances the competing concerns of allowing a state to protect its citizens, protecting citizens of another state from defending themselves in another state, and the fact that each state is its own sovereign. *See Pennoyer v. Neff,* 95 U.S. 714 (1877) (recognizing that although "every State possesses exclusive jurisdiction and sovereignty over persons and property within its territory" that principle also means that "no State can exercise direct jurisdiction and authority over persons and proper without its territory").

The limitations on government power that arise from the Due Process Clauses are worth emphasizing. "Even if the defendant would suffer minimal or no inconvenience from being forced to litigate before the tribunals of another State; even if the forum State has a strong interest in applying its law to the controversy; even if the forum State is the most convenient location for litigation, the Due Process Clause, acting as an instrument of interstate federalism, may sometimes act to divest the State of its power to render a valid judgment." *World-Wide Volkswagen Corp. v. Woodson,* 444 U.S. 286 (1980). Think about that: the defendant's constitutional right not to be sued in a forum where "personal jurisdiction" over a claim is lacking outweighs the efficiency interests, the interest of a state of protecting its citizens from harm, and does so even if it would be entirely *convenient* for the defendant to defend itself where suit is filed.

Finding the right balance between these interests—the right of a state to protect its citizens from harm and the right of a citizen not to be haled into foreign courts—is subject to few bright lines. That is why the personal jurisdiction analysis is fact intensive, multi-factored, and often indeterminate.

Personal jurisdiction has many counter-intuitive aspects. Personal jurisdiction can exist even when the defendant has never set foot in the state where he's been sued, for example. Physical connections matter, but they are not controlling. Instead, personal jurisdiction largely turns on whether the defendant has created sufficient contacts with the state where the suit is filed such that it is reasonable for the defendant to defend himself there. Suppose you've never been to Iowa, but an Iowan sues you because, while she was visiting you in the state where you live, you punched her. Should you be required to defend yourself in Iowa when you've never been there, and the wrongdoing didn't occur there? Doesn't sound like you made any connections with Iowa, concerning this claim, does it? You shouldn't be subject to being sued in a state that you haven't made much connection with and which isn't connected to the dispute.

That basic idea—a person should not have to defend himself in a state without having made sufficient contact with that state—underlies personal jurisdiction. "Personal jurisdiction" limits the ability of a state or federal court to force a citizen of another state to defend itself in that state against the threat of a money judgment being rendered that will be enforceable against the person and all his assets. There are three broad principles to remember.

First, a statute must allow the court to assert personal jurisdiction for the claim over the non-resident defendant. These can be state or federal statutes. They are called long-arm statutes because they allow the "long arm" of the state to reach out to grab the non-resident defendant.

Second, personal jurisdiction must be analyzed on a claim-by-claim basis: it is possible that a court will have personal jurisdiction over only some claims in a pleading, not all. Suppose, for example, a Minnesota defendant makes a contract with a Florida resident to build a house in Florida, but builds a defective home. We'll see that it's likely a Florida court would have personal jurisdiction over the defendant on that breach of contract claim because that claim arose directly out of defendant's contacts with Florida. But, what if while in Minnesota visiting friends, the same defendant and same plaintiff happened to get into a fight in a bar; can a Florida court exert personal jurisdiction over a party for claim for battery arising out of a bar fight in Minnesota when the defendant's only connection with Florida is an unrelated contract? No, as we'll see. The point is that each claim must be analyzed separately.

Finally, even if a state or federal long-arm statute literally permits assertion of personal jurisdiction over the claim, the Due Process Clause always limits when any court can force someone to defend himself in another state. The Due Process Clause requires there be "minimum contacts" between the defendant and the forum state, and that it be "fair" for the defendant to be forced to defend itself in that state.

On this third issue, the courts have struggled mightily: when does a defendant have "minimum contacts" and when is it "fair" to require one to come to a state to defend itself? As we'll see, a judgment entered by a court in another state can be brought to the defendant's home state and used by the plaintiff to take away the defendant's property. Allowing a court in another state to enter a judgment that can affect someone who's never been there, or who has only minor connections with that state raises some serious questions. If we make it too easy to do, then defendants will be forced to defend suits in places they have no connection with; if we make it too hard, then the acts of an out-of-state defendant who harms someone may go unpunished, because the victim would have to travel to the defendant's home state to get relief. In the next chapter, we'll see how the law that balances these competing interests is rapidly changing.

## Checkpoints

- What is a long-arm statute?
- Can you articulate the purpose of the Due Process Clause as applied to personal jurisdiction?
- Do you understand whether convenience of the other party, or the court, can outweigh the defendant's Due Process interests?

# Chapter 6

# Personal Jurisdiction: Consent, Long-Arm Statutes, Minimum Contacts, and Fair Play

---

### Personal Jurisdiction Roadmap

This chapter describes the steps to determine whether a court has personal jurisdiction over a claim against a party.

The first step is to determine if the defendant had consented to be sued on the particular claim in the forum state. If so, the analysis is over unless the forum was chosen in bad faith, such as to reduce claims..

The second step requires determining whether a statute — usually a state "long arm" statute — authorizes service of process on the defendant for the claim.

The third step requires looking to see if an individual defendant was "tagged" in the forum state; if so the analysis is at an end unless the defendant was deceived into coming into the forum state in order to serve process on him.

The fourth step requires analyzing whether assertion of personal jurisdiction over the defendant on that claim meets the "minimum contacts" requirements of the Due Process Clause.

The fifth step requires analyzing whether, even though a statute authorizes service of process and minimum contacts are present, assertion of personal jurisdiction would nonetheless violate traditional notions of fair play and substantial justice.

Beyond that, and much in the way that supplemental subject matter jurisdiction under Section 1367 allows a court to decide claims that are closely related to one over which a court has original subject matter, in narrow circumstances *"pendent* personal jurisdiction" allows a court to assert personal jurisdiction over claims closely related to one over which it has "regular" personal jurisdiction.

---

Subject matter jurisdiction is a limitation on federal courts' power over claims. In contrast, personal jurisdiction is a limitation on state and federal courts' power over persons and their property. Like subject matter jurisdiction, personal jurisdiction is determined on a claim-by-claim, defendant-by-defendant basis. Consequently, personal jurisdiction might exist over some, but not all, claims in a particular lawsuit.

As will become clear in this chapter, as a general principle, the Due Process Clause prevents a defendant being subjected to a suit in a state if it would be "unfair" to make the defendant defend himself there. As an easy case, it would be unfair for a defendant with no connection to Colorado to defend herself there against a claim arising out of a car wreck in Georgia. On the other hand, it would be fair to make a defendant who lives in Georgia to defend himself in Georgia against a claim arising out of a Georgia car wreck. But in between those two extremes is an enormous sea of grey. This chapter will shed light on that grey sea.

There are three kinds of personal jurisdiction: *in rem, quasi in rem,* and *in personam*. As their names suggest, the first two are related. They are means by which a court can issue orders that bind specific property of the defendant's — not the defendant's assets in general. *In personam* or "personal" jurisdiction is the more commonly litigated and asserted form of personal jurisdiction. It subjects all of the defendant's assets to satisfaction of any judgment issued against the defendant. *See* Chapters 5, 6 and 7. This chapter addresses *in personam* jurisdiction, and the next chapter addresses *in rem* and *quasi in rem*.

A plaintiff who sues a defendant in a state where the defendant does not have significant presence and seeks to subject all of the defendant's assets to any judgment — and not specific property the defendant has in that state — must establish that the court has *in personam* jurisdiction over the claim against the defendant. *In rem* and *quasi in rem* are not enough to establish unlimited personal liability. Fortunately, as will become clear, the same process to determine whether personal jurisdiction exists is the same, regardless of which type is used.

Analyzing whether personal jurisdiction is proper starts with: did the defendant consent to be sued in the state, whether by operation of law or by agreement? If not, then the analysis requires three steps. First, a statute must authorize service of process on the defendant for the particular claim. These are typically state statutes, and are called "long arm statutes" because the long arm of the state reaches out to a defendant and grabs him. But there are federal long-arm statutes, though they are much less common. Second, the defendant must have "minimum contacts" with the forum (for state law claims, the contacts must be with the state where the federal court sits; for federal claims, the contacts also ordinarily be with the state where the suit is filed, but for a few federal claims,

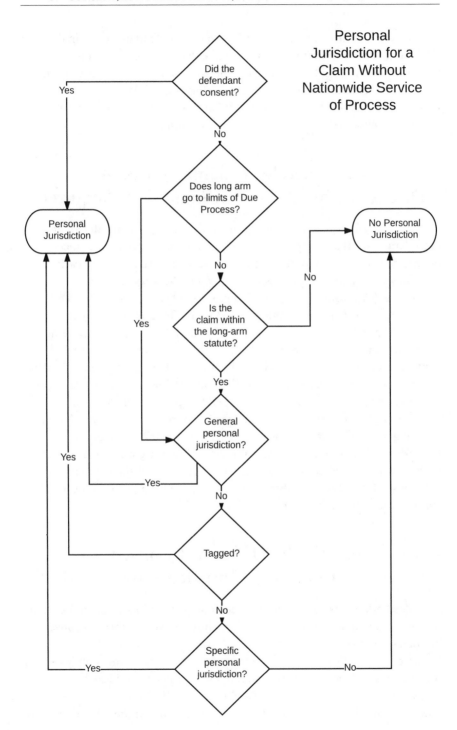

Personal Jurisdiction for a Claim Without Nationwide Service of Process

contacts can be with any state.) Third, even if the defendant is within the long arm statute and has minimum contacts, the defendant can avoid being haled into court by showing that forcing it to defend itself in the state is not "fair."

This chapter addresses personal jurisdiction going from the easiest analysis to the most difficult. Here is a flow chart that captures this chapter and a means to spot and effectively address personal jurisdiction:

## A. Generally a Claim-by-Claim, Defendant-by-Defendant Analysis Is Required

First, analyze personal jurisdiction on a claim-by-claim, defendant-by-defendant basis. If a "complaint contains two [or more] claims . . . there must be an independent basis for the assertion of personal jurisdiction for each claim. Jurisdiction over one claim does not imply jurisdiction over another." *Debreceni v. Bru-Jell Leasing Corp.,* 710 F. Supp. 15, 19 (D. Mass. 1989); *see Druid Group, Inc. v. Dorfman,* 2006 WL 2460553 (N.D. Tex. 2006) ("The Court must conduct the minimum contacts analysis separately for each cause of action asserted, because Plaintiff is obligated to secure jurisdiction over [each defendant] with respect to each claim brought."). So, and just as with subject matter jurisdiction, courts determine personal jurisdiction on a claim-by-claim basis.

However, there is one wrinkle called "pendent personal jurisdiction." A court can sometimes use "pendent" personal jurisdiction to let closely related claims tag along with a claim over which the court has, for lack of a better word, "regular" personal jurisdiction. Further, the same tag along concept that applies to subject matter jurisdiction (and is called "supplemental subject matter jurisdiction, see Chapter 22), and the concept also applies to venue, and is called "pendent venue." *See* Chapter 23.

## B. Did the Defendant Consent to Personal Jurisdiction?

If a defendant has consented to be sued on a claim in a state, for example, then personal jurisdiction will exist. Consent can take two forms: express and by operation of law.

Some of the following apply only to corporations, while others apply to both corporations and individuals, so read carefully. Further, theoretically a state long arm statute could *not* reach these "easy" examples. If a long arm statute somehow, for example, excludes corporations incorporated in the state, then there would be no personal jurisdiction. For that reason, these "easy" points are mentioned again where applicable in the analysis below.

## 1. Did the Parties Contractually Agree the Claim Could or Must be Filed in the Forum State?

Both individuals and corporations can agree by contract that a suit can be filed in a particular state, or that it must be filed there. In fact, many contracts contain "forum selection clauses." Essentially, a forum selection clause is an provision in an agreement that, if a claim is within its scope, the suit can and must be brought in a certain state. So, for example, a contract may state: "The parties to this contract agree that any claim or dispute arising out of or related to this contract must be filed in Fulton, County, Georgia. Further, the parties waive any objection to personal jurisdiction or venue over any suit filed in Fulton County, Georgia."

If the claim is for breach of the contract containing the forum selection clause, and if both the plaintiff and defendant are parties to the contract, then — absent very unusual circumstances — the clause will be enforced. *Carnival Cruise Lines, Inc. v. Shute*, 499 U.S. 585 (1991). Generally, forum selection clauses are enforced unless (1) the existence of the clause was not reasonably communicated to the parties (a minimal standard); (2) the clause was obtained through "fraud or overreaching;" or (3) "enforcement would be unreasonable and unjust." *D.H. Blair & Co. v. Gottdiener*, 462 F.3d 95, 103 (2d Cir. 2006).

If the claim is against a party who did not sign the contract, or if the claim does not fall within its scope — what if the claim has nothing to do with the contract — then ordinarily it will not be covered by the clause. As you can imagine, there is a lot of litigation over what is "close enough" and when someone not a party to a contract can, nonetheless, be covered by it.

## 2. For Corporate Defendants, is the Suit Filed in a State Where a State Statute Required the Corporation to Consent to be Sued Over Any Claim?

This form of consent only applies to corporations. There are two potential ways that a state statute may require that corporations consent to be sued in the state. One is if the corporation is incorporated in the state where the suit is filed, and the other is if the corporation is registered to do business in the state.

If a suit is filed in a state where a corporation is incorporated, the same statute that allows for incorporation almost invariably provides that the corporation agrees that it is subject to be sued in the state by serving process on the state's Secretary of State, or an agent the corporation registers to receive process. Further, as discussed more fully below, the law has long been that a corporation is subject to "general personal jurisdiction" in any state where it is incorporated. Thus, even without a state statute expressly stating that incorporation in a state constitutes consent to be sued in the state, a corporation can be sued in the state for anything. *See Bank of Augusta v. Earle*, 38 U.S. (13 Pet.) 519 (1839) (reasoning that a corporation dwells "in the place of its creation" and so probably are subject to general jurisdiction in the state of incorporation even without a state statute so stating).

As to the second form, many state statutes require corporations that choose to do business in the state to register with the state Secretary of State and provide that by doing so, the corporation agrees to be sued in the state over any claim — even one having nothing to do with the business done by the corporation. The Supreme Court has stated that doing so pursuant to a state registration statute constitutes consent to personal jurisdiction. *See, e.g., Pa. Fire Ins. Co. of Phila. v. Gold Issue Mining & Milling Co.*, 243 U.S. 93, 95 (1917) (corporation consented to personal jurisdiction in Missouri by appointing an agent for service as required by a Missouri statute). That Court emphasized it had "little doubt" that a foreign corporation's appointment of an agent for service of process consented to personal jurisdiction. A few years later, in *Robert Mitchell Furniture Co. v. Selden Breck Const. Co.*, 257 U.S. 213 (1921), the Supreme Court then made clear that a registration statute can support personal jurisdiction, so long as it is broad enough to reach the claim. *See also Neirbo Co. v. Bethlehem Shipbuilding Corp.*, 308 U.S. 165 (1939) (defendant corporation waived its right to contest venue in federal court in New York, by complying with a New York State statute that required it to designate an agent for service of process).

Circuit courts have confirmed this view. *Bane v. Netlink, Inc.*, 925 F.2d 637, 640 (3d Cir.1991) ("[b]y registering to do business in Pennsylvania, [the defendant] purposefully avail[ed] itself of the privilege of conducting activities within the forum State, this invoking the benefits and protections of its laws."); *Knowlton v. Allied Van Lines Inc.*, 900 F.2d 1196, 1199–1200 (8th Cir.1990) (appointment of an agent for service of process conferred "consent to the jurisdiction of Minnesota courts for any cause of action, whether or not arising out of activities within the state."); *Holloway v. Wright & Morrissey, Inc.*, 739 F.2d 695, 697 (1st Cir. 1984). (It is "well-settled that a corporation that authorizes an agent to receive service of process in compliance with the requirements of a state statute, consents to the exercise of personal jurisdiction in any action" within the scope of the agent's authority.)

But it is critical to read the registration statute. If it does not state that consent to be sued over anything, then to avoid a constitutional problem, the statute may be read narrowly. *See Brown v. Lockheed Martin Corp.*, 814 F.3d 619 (2d Cir. 2016) ("although the Connecticut registration statute does not expressly limit the matters as to which an authorized agent may accept service of process, neither does it contain express language alerting the potential registrant that by complying with the statute and appointing an agent it would be agreeing to submit to the general jurisdiction of the state courts").

Despite this long-standing view, after the recent decision in *Daimler AG v. Bauman*, 134 S.Ct. 746 (2014) (discussed below) some corporate defendants are contending these consent-by-registration statutes are unconstitutional. The courts are splitting on whether a registration statute that provides that registering to do business constitutes consent to be sued in a state over any claim violates due process. As one court recently explained:

> Following *Daimler*, courts in our Circuit have reached different outcomes in deciding whether "jurisdiction by consent" contradicts the due process concerns of fair play and substantial justice raised in Daimler. Applying Delaware law, the District of Delaware held *Daimler* "was limited to the conclusion that continuous and systematic contacts, by themselves, were not enough to establish general personal jurisdiction" and "offered no guidance on acceptable criteria for jurisdiction by consent." As a result, the court . . . held a party consents to personal jurisdiction in Delaware "as a result of its compliance with Delaware's business regulation statute." In *Otsuka Pharm. Co. v. Mylan Inc.*, the district court held "it cannot be genuinely disputed that consent, whether by registration or otherwise, remains a valid basis for personal jurisdiction following *International Shoe* and *Daimler*."

*Bors v. Johnson & Johnson*, 2015 WL 517816 (E.D. Pa. Sept. 20, 2016). A court of appeals recently explained:

> In *Daimler*, the Court criticized as "unacceptably grasping" plaintiffs' request that it "approve the exercise of general jurisdiction in every State in which a corporation engages in a substantial, continuous, and systematic course of business." It explained, "If Daimler's California activities sufficed to allow adjudication of this . . . case in California, the same global reach would presumably be available in every other State in which [the subsidiary's] sales are sizable." The Court rejected such an "exorbitant exercise[ ] of all-purpose jurisdiction."
> Brown's interpretation of Connecticut's registration statute is expansive. It proposes that we infer from an ambiguous statute and the mere appointment of an agent for service of process a corporation's

consent to general jurisdiction, creating precisely the result that the Court so roundly rejected in Daimler. It appears that every state in the union—and the District of Columbia, as well—has enacted a business registration statute. States have long endeavored to protect their citizens and levy taxes, among other goals, through this mechanism. If mere registration and the accompanying appointment of an in-state agent—without an express consent to general jurisdiction— nonetheless sufficed to confer general jurisdiction by implicit consent, every corporation would be subject to general jurisdiction in every state in which it registered, and *Daimler's* ruling would be robbed of meaning by a back-door thief.

In *Daimler*, the Court rejected the idea that a corporation was subject to general jurisdiction in every state in which it conducted substantial business. Brown's interpretation of the Connecticut statute could justify the exercise of general jurisdiction over a corporation in a state in which the corporation had done no business at all, so long as it had registered.

Were the Connecticut statute drafted such that it could be fairly construed as requiring foreign corporations to consent to general jurisdiction, we would be confronted with a more difficult constitutional question about the validity of such consent after *Daimler*. Though a defendant may ordinarily, through free and voluntary consent given (for example) in a commercial agreement, submit to jurisdiction a court would otherwise be unable to exercise, we decline to decide here whether consent to general jurisdiction via a registration statute would be similarly effective notwithstanding *Daimler's* strong admonition against the expansive exercise of general jurisdiction. . . . [S]ome of our sister circuits have upheld states' determinations that in their respective states, registration to do business constitutes consent to the exercise of general jurisdiction, and that due process requires no more: That is, personal jurisdiction by consent of a corporate defendant is consistent with due process. Similarly, in an approach emphasizing the amenability to waiver of personal jurisdiction as an individual right, applicable to a defendant corporation without regard to the due process analysis, the Supreme Court has upheld the assertion of personal jurisdiction as a sanction for failure to comply with jurisdictional discovery, holding such failures "may amount to a legal submission to the jurisdiction of the court, whether voluntary or not." Bauxites, 456 U.S. at 704–05. From these sources, it could be concluded that a carefully drawn state statute that expressly required consent to general jurisdiction as a condition on a foreign corporation's doing business in the state, at least in cases brought by state residents, might well be constitutional.

But as the Supreme Court recognized in *Goodyear*, "A state court's assertion of jurisdiction exposes defendants to the State's coercive power, and is therefore subject to review for compatibility with the Fourteenth Amendment's Due Process Clause." The reach of that coercive power, even when exercised pursuant to a corporation's purported "consent," may be limited by the Due Process clause. We need not reach that question here, however, because we conclude that the Connecticut business registration statute did not require Lockheed to consent to general jurisdiction in exchange for the right to do business in the state.

*Brown v. Lockheed Martin Corp.*, 814 F.3d 619 (2d Cir. 2016) (citations omitted). This is an issue that your professor will likely analyze in detail, and so the long quote.

## 3. Operating a Motor Vehicle Consent Statutes

Many states have statutes that provide that, stated very generally, a nonresident person who operates a car in the state consents to personal jurisdiction over claims arising out of the operation of the car. They do this by stating that the nonresident appoints a state agency, such as the Secretary of State, to accept service of process on the nonresident. Here is an example of one:

Any [such] nonresident individual . . . over whom a court may exercise personal jurisdiction [because the nonresident caused harm in the state while in the state], shall be deemed to have appointed the Secretary of the State as its attorney and to have agreed that any process in any civil action brought against the nonresident individual . . . may be served upon the Secretary of the State and shall have the same validity as if served upon the nonresident . . . personally. The process shall be served by the officer to whom the same is directed upon the Secretary of the State by leaving with or at the office of the Secretary of the State, at least twelve days before the return day of such process, a true and attested copy thereof and by sending to the defendant at the defendant's last-known address, by registered or certified mail, postage prepaid, return receipt requested, a like true and attested copy with an endorsement thereon of the service upon the Secretary of the State.

Conn. Gen. Stat. § 52-63. Here is a statute which applies if the owner of the car has registered it in the state, but then left the state after the accident but before suit is filed:

> Any operator or owner of a motor vehicle at the time of issuance of his license or registration shall be deemed to have appointed the Commissioner of Motor Vehicles as his attorney and to have agreed that any process in any civil action against him on account of any claim for damages resulting from his alleged negligence or the alleged negligence of his servant or agent in the operation of any motor vehicle in this state may be served upon the commissioner as provided in this section and shall have the same validity as if served upon the owner or operator personally, even though the person sought to be served has left the state prior to commencement of the action or his present whereabouts is unknown.

Conn. Gen. Stat. § 52-59b.

These statutes will provide personal jurisdiction for claims within their scope. They have been long-held constitutional. *See, e.g., Hess v. Pawloski*, 274 U.S. 352 (1927) (holding that a state could constitutionally adopt a statute which provided that a non-resident consented to personal jurisdiction over accident occurring while driving in the state).

# C. Without Consent: The Three Steps to Evaluate *In Personam* Jurisdiction

## 1. A Long-Arm Statute Must Authorize Service of Process

"Service of a summons is a means of establishing a court's jurisdiction over a defendant." *Cory v. Aztec Steel Building, Inc.*, 468 F.3d 1226, 1229 (10th Cir. 2006). Consequently, Rule 4(k) is the starting place for analyzing personal jurisdiction. That Rule limits effective service of a summons, which must be served along with a copy of the complaint on the defendant. FRCP 4(c).

In addition to two circumstances which relate to specific joinder rules (and so are discussed in connection with joinder), Rule 4(k) provides that if a defendant is served with a summons or files a waiver of service of the summons, the court is authorized to serve process if: (1) the defendant is subject to personal jurisdiction of a state court; (2) service is authorized by a federal statute; or (3) in those cases where the defendant is not subject to personal jurisdiction in any state (*e.g.,* when the defendant is a foreign entity or citizen), where the claim is federal and the defendant has minimum contacts with the United States as a whole.

The first two provisions are the more common ones litigated. This chart summarize those two common prongs of Rule 4(k):

| Federal Claim | State Claim |
| --- | --- |
| State's Long Arm Statute *or* Federal Statute Governing the Claim | State's Long-Arm Statute |

That chart shows that if the claim arises under federal law, then there are two possible sources of authority to serve process: to the extent a state court is authorized to do so by a state statute statute, or as allowed by federal statute. In contrast, a state statute must authorize service of process over state claims. Since the state long-arm statute is common to both state and federal claims, we'll begin with it. Remember that a federal court has authority to serve process over a defendant under the state's long-arm statute for a federal claim. Federal statutes authorizing service of process over federal claims are fairly rare, as we'll see.

### a. State Long-Arm Statutes Apply to Both State and Federal Claims

Rule 4(k)(1)(A) authorizes a federal court to serve process for a state or federal claim as would a state court in that state. Most states have adopted so-called "long-arm" statutes — which authorize the "long arm" of their courts to reach out and assert power over out-of-state defendants. A federal court in the state can do the same thing, to the same extent as a state court in the same state.

No state statute can authorize service beyond the limits of the Due Process Clause of the Constitution. (We'll look at due process later.) So, a state long-arm statute can't — constitutionally — go "further" than due process would allow. But, nothing requires a state to have a long arm statute that goes to the limit of due process; its statute can be "shorter," in that a defendant will have to have "more" connections with a state than the constitution requires.

So, long-arm statutes come in two general types: those that are co-extensive with, and so have precisely the same reach as, the Due Process Clause, and those which have a shorter reach. (The "length" of a particular state long-arm statute is a question of state law, while the question of whether assertion of personal jurisdiction violates Due Process is a matter of federal law, as we'll see.)

Perhaps surprisingly, many state long-arm statutes do not go to the limits of Due Process. Thus, one way to visualize state statutes and the Due Process Clause is as follows:

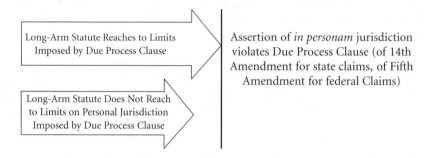

Long-Arm Statute Reaches to Limits Imposed by Due Process Clause

Long-Arm Statute Does Not Reach to Limits on Personal Jurisdiction Imposed by Due Process Clause

Assertion of *in personam* jurisdiction violates Due Process Clause (of 14th Amendment for state claims, of Fifth Amendment for federal Claims)

You should determine the reach of the state long-arm statute and determine whether it requires more contacts than does the Due Process Clause before examining whether asserting personal jurisdiction comports with Due Process: if the state long-arm statute doesn't reach to the limits of Due Process (like the bottom one in the chart above) and under the facts service on the defendant is not authorized by the state long-arm statute, then as a matter of state law there simply is no statute that authorizes service of process, and so no personal jurisdiction. A court would not have to reach the constitutional question of whether asserting personal jurisdiction would comply with Due Process. *See Gust v. Flint*, 356 S.E.2d 513 (Ga. 1987) (holding Georgia's long-arm statute "requires that an out-of-state defendant must do certain acts within the State of Georgia before he can be subjected to personal jurisdiction").

In those states where the statute does not reach the limits of Due Process, service must meet the state statutory requirements *and* assertion of personal jurisdiction must comport with Due Process. You must do both analyses, since it's possible for assertion of jurisdiction over a claim to comply with Due Process, but service not to be authorized by the state long-arm statute because that statute is shorter than the Due Process Clause. For example, New York's long-arm statute does not extend to the limits of Due Process. *Pieczenik v. Dyax Corp.*, 265 F.3d 1329 (Fed. Cir. 2001). If the state statute does not extend to the limits of Due Process and service is not authorized by the statute, then the defendant cannot be forced to defend itself in the state.

It is also possible for a long-arm statute to reach a defendant, but for assertion of personal jurisdiction to violate the Due Process Clause. For example, some state long-arm statutes literally reach any claim over any defendant "engaged in business" in the state. But, as will be seen, it would likely violate

Due Process to assert personal jurisdiction over a claim that has nothing to do with that business, among other things. So, always analyze both the long-arm statute and then, if the conduct is within the long-arm, the Due Process issues.

Statutes that do not extend to the limits of Due Process create interesting interpretive issues. For example, some of these statutes provide that jurisdiction exists if the defendant or its agent "committed a tortious act" in the forum. Courts have reached different interpretations of those words. *Compare Gray v. Am. Radiator & Standard Sanitary Corp.,* 176 N.E.2d 761 (Ill. 1961) (defendant that had manufactured in another state a product that exploded in Illinois committed a "tortious act" in Illinois) *with Feathers v. McLucas,* 209 N.E.2d 68 (N.Y. 1965) (product exploding while on way through the state was not a tort in the state).

Some long-arm statutes go to the limits of, or are "co-terminus" with, Due Process. Thsee come in two types. Some statutes expressly state that they reach to the limits of the Due Process Clause. *E.g.,* Cal. Code Civ Pro. § 410.10 ("A court of this state may exercise jurisdiction on any basis not inconsistent with the Constitution of . . . the United States."). Other long arm statute are not worded so plainly, but have been interpreted by state courts to authorize service to the full extent allowed by the Due Process Clause. *E.g., Wilson v. Belin,* 20 F.3d 644, 648 (5th Cir. 1994) (Recognizing that, even though it does not expressly say so, Texas courts hold that Texas' long-arm statute "authorizes the exercise of personal jurisdiction to the full extent allowed by the Due Process Clause of the Fourteenth Amendment").

In states with statutes that go to the limits of due process, the personal jurisdiction analysis collapses into the single inquiry of whether asserting personal jurisdiction comports with Due Process. By definition, if due process is satisfied, so is the long-arm statute.

Finally, recognize that there is a third type of long-arm statute: one which, when literally applied, allows the court to assert personal jurisdiction over the defendant for the claim, but doing so would violate the due process rights of the defendant. Particularly with this type of statute it is important to always analyze both the statute and due process. This is because even if the defendant is within reach of the state's long-arm statute, you must still address the question of whether assertion of personal jurisdiction violates the defendant's Due Process rights, discussed below.

To sum up, for *every* claim (state or federal), a federal district court is authorized by Rule 4(k) to serve process as allowed by the long-arm statute of the state where that federal court sits. To determine whether service is authorized, the reach of the state long-arm statute first must be determined. If the state long-arm statute does not reach to the limits of due process, then the statute must authorize service under the particular facts *and* assertion of personal jurisdiction must comport with due process. If the statute does reach to the limits of due process, then the only question is whether asserting personal jurisdiction meets the requirements of the Due Process Clause.

### b. Specific Federal Long-arm Statutes Govern Some, but few, Federal Claims

When Congress enacts a statute creating a federal claim, it sometimes — but not often — includes provisions regulating the procedure for adjudicating the new statutory claim, including sometimes providing a specific long-arm statute regulating service of process (and, sometimes, a statute of limitation for the specific claim, and less frequently, even pleading requirements, and other things). For example, when Congress enacted the federal securities statutes, it included a specific statute regulating service of process. The same is true with the antitrust laws and a few other federal claims.

So, it may be that a specific, federal long-arm statute applies to a federal claim. The reach of these federal long-arm statutes varies. Often these statutes have particular requirements that must be analyzed and applied to the facts. *See ESAB Group, Inc. v. Centricut, Inc.,* 126 F.3d 617 (4th Cir. 1997) ("Even for federal claims, the effective territorial authority of the federal court may differ significantly from case to case, depending on the federal statute involved."). Most common, though, are federal long-arm statutes that authorize "nationwide" service of process for the particular claim. *See Cory v. Aztec Steel Building, Inc.,* 468 F.3d 1226 (10th Cir. 2006) (discussing RICO's provision, 18 U.S.C. § 1965).

A particular federal long-arm statute for a specific claim may "go further" than the otherwise applicable state long-arm statute does. Many federal long-arm statutes authorize "nationwide service of process." If so, the a defendant may be sued in any state in the United States if the defendant has minimum contacts *with the United States as a whole* such that assertion of personal jurisdiction does not violate the Due Process Clause of the Fifth Amendment. *See ESAB Group, Inc. v. Centricut, Inc.,* 126 F.3d 617 (4th Cir. 1997). Thus, if a federal statute authorizes nationwide service of process over a particular federal claim, the question becomes one of minimum contacts with the United States, not with the forum state, a subject we'll get to below.

Let's talk about related state law claims for a minute. If there is a federal long-arm statute that authorizes nationwide service, then the doctrine of "pendent personal jurisdiction" may be available to allow a court having personal jurisdiction over the federal claim to also have personal jurisdiction over a related state law claim. Suppose, as is common, a plaintiff includes a related state claim in a complaint along with a federal claim for which Congress has authorized nationwide service of process. Congress empowered federal courts to have personal jurisdiction over the federal claim if the defendant had minimum contacts with the United States as a whole, but that power does not expressly give that power over any state law claims. If a state law claim could not "tag along" with the federal claim, then we'd end up with two suits perhaps in different states. If the state law claim is related to the federal claim, we'd end up with two suits in different states — and maybe one in federal court, the other in state court, in different states — even though the two lawsuits arose out of the same basic set of facts. Pendent personal jurisdiction allows a *related* state law claims to "tag along" with a federal claim that has a "nationwide service of process." *See* Chapter 22.

## 2. If a Claim is Within the Reach of the State's Long-Arm Statute, Assertion of *In Personam* Jurisdiction Must Still Not Violate the Defendant's Due Process Rights

Even if a claim is within a state's long-arm statute, assertion of personal jurisdiction could still violate the Due Process rights of the defendant. The Due Process Clause protects "an individual's liberty interest in not being subject to the binding judgments of a forum with which he has established no meaningful contacts, ties, or relations." *OMI Holdings, Inc. v. Royal Ins. Co. of Canada,* 149 F.3d 1086, 1090 (10th Cir. 1998).

This section next explores how to determine whether assertion of personal jurisdiction over a defendant violates due process. It is organized from the "easier" ways to identify that Due Process has been satisfied to the more difficult ones. Some of the easier ways are not intuitive!

### a. Did the Defendant, Individual or Corporate, "Consent" to Personal Jurisdiction, Either by Operation of Law or by Contract?

As explained above, a person or corporation can consent to be sued in a particular state, sometimes by operation of law and sometimes by agreement. Some of these apply only to corporations, and some only to natural people, however. They are discussed above but this is a reminder to check for consent first.

### b. Was the Individual Defendant "Tagged" with Process While Present in the Forum State After the Suit was Filed?

Most state long arm statutes provide that personal jurisdiction is proper if a person (not a corporation) is served with process after the suit is filed and while the defendant is physically present in the state. In *Burnham v. Superior Court*, 495 U.S. 604 (1990), the Court, based on divided rationales, held that because courts have traditionally held that they have personal jurisdiction over non-residents who are physically present in a state, a plaintiff who serves process on a defendant who is passing through a state satisfies due process. Physical presence in the state is sufficient to establish personal jurisdiction, and it does not violate "fair play and substantial justice" to serve a defendant who happens to be visiting the state on unrelated matters. The Court split on why this was so, but agreed that it was and has long been the case. *See Peabody v. Hamilton*, 106 Mass. 217 (1870) (service effective on defendant who had been served while passing through Boston Harbor on a ship bound for Nova Scotia from New York); *Grace v. McArthur*, 170 F. Supp. 442 (E.D. Ark. 1959) (defendant served while seated in a plane flying over Arkansas airspace).

Thus, a long arm statute that authorizes service on a person who is named as a defendant while physically present in that state is constitutional. And in such a state, personal jurisdiction exists if a person who is a defendant is served with process in a suit arising out of a dispute having nothing to do with Florida while the defendant is actually in Florida. So long as a statute authorizes a "tag you're a defendant" service, it presents no constitutional issues. There are some limits. A plaintiff could render "tag" invalid — what if the plaintiff lured the defendant to the state through deceit — but absent those facts, "tag" if authorized by the long-arm statute creates personal jurisdiction.

### c. Due Process Requires Either Specific or General Personal Jurisdiction Exist

There are two very different approaches to determine whether personal jurisdiction exists. The one you should look for first is "general personal jurisdiction." *See Goodyear Dunlop Tires Operations, S.A. v. Brown*, 1331 S.Ct. 2856 (2011). If general personal jurisdiction exists, then the claim does not have to have anything to do with the forum state. If there is no general personal jurisdiction, then the more difficult steps of "specific personal jurisdiction" have to be addressed. *See Burger King Corp. v. Rudzewicz*, 471 U.S. 462, 472 (1985).

That difference between specific and general jurisdiction is worth emphasizing. Specific jurisdiction requires that the claim be related to the claim. For general jurisdiction, the contacts need not have anything to do with the contacts. Recent cases made is much harder to establish general personal jurisdiction over corporations, but they made the analysis much simpler.

## i. General Personal Jurisdiction

General personal jurisdiction exists only when the defendant has pervasive contacts with the forum sufficient for it to be "at home" in the forum. Luckily, this has become much easier with recent case law developments.

A defendant is a natural person is subject to general personal jurisdiction only in the person's state of domicile. Domicile is determined the same way for personal jurisdiction as it is for determining a person's domicile for purposes of diversity subject matter jurisdiction: it is a person's physical presence coupled with the state of mind to remain for an indeterminate period of time. This issue is discussed in the chapter on diversity subject matter jurisdiction. And again, as noted above, if a person is "tagged" in a state, general personal jurisdiction exists.

Corporations are usually subject to general jurisdiction — a corporation is "at home" in a state and can be sued in that state for any claim whatsoever — in four instances:

First, a corporation is subject to general personal jurisdiction in the state or states where it is incorporated. Most corporations are incorporated only in one state. Some are incorporated in more than one. Determining which state(s) in which a corporation is incorporated is a matter of public record, found on the Internet. Oddly, corporations are deemed to be "at home" in these states merely by the fact of incorporation. Many corporations are incorporated in Delaware but have no real connections to that state; nonetheless, they are "at home" in Delaware and can be sued there over any claim.

Second, a corporation is "at home" and subject to general personal jurisdiction in *the* state where it has its principal place of business. How do you determine a corporation's principal place of business? We don't know. The majority decisions in *Daimler* and *Goodyear* used a proportionality of business test: the majority compared how much business the defendant corporation was doing inside of the state without how much it was doing outside of the state. Clearly, if a majority of a corporation's business is in one state, then that state is its principal place of business. Left unclear is what courts will do when a plurality of business is done in one state, or its business is equally split among many states. The dissent in *Daimler* asserted that the *Hertz* test for principal place of business, which is used for determining a corporation's citizenship for diversity purposes, applies. If that view ends up winning, then the test will be somewhat easier to apply.

The significance of the change in the law that *Daimler* wrought is hard to overstate. It significantly limited the circumstances in which a court can assert general jurisdiction over a foreign corporate defendant. Before *Daimler*, courts routinely asserted general personal jurisdiction over foreign corporations if they engaged in a substantial, continuous, and systematic course of business in the forum state. Now, even doing systematic and continuous business in a forum is not enough. It's important you understand this because some cases still use the "old" rule. Under the "old" rule, a corporation was subject to general personal jurisdiction anywhere where its contacts were sufficiently "continuous and systematic" to be reasonable to be sued there. Thus, there are a lot of cases where—if they were to be filed today—no one would even allege general personal jurisdiction exists. *See, e.g., Helicopteros*, 466 U.S. at 416 (regularly purchasing equipment and training services from the forum, accepting checks drawn on banks from the forum, and sending personnel and officers to the forum to negotiate contracts, insufficient); *Noonan v. Winston Co.*, 135 F.3d 85, 92–93 (1st Cir.1998) (soliciting business in forum, and visiting it to negotiate orders and establish business relationships); *Glater v. Eli Lilly & Co.*, 744 F.2d 213, 217 (1st Cir. 1984) (advertising in the forum, employing sales representatives to distribute information in the forum, and selling products to distributors in the forum); *In re New Motor Vehicles Canadian Export Antitrust Litig.*, 307 F. Supp. 2d 145, 151 (D. Me. 2004) (using an advertising service based in forum, sending officers to attend meetings and train in the forum, purchasing equipment from the forum, manufacturing and selling products that ultimately end up in the market of the forum, and being party to lawsuits in the forum).

Perhaps proving the impact of these cases, if you read *Daimler* and *Goodyear* closely, you'll notice that the lawyers for the one of the defendants—the parent corporation in each case—did not contest personal jurisdiction. This is because under the "old" law, systematic and continuous contacts were "enough" for general personal jurisdiction. Daimler sold a lot of cars in California, and Goodyear shipped a lot of tires into North Carolina. That is no longer enough. But that was not the law before then.

There is one twist to keep in mind. "Principal place of business" doesn't mean "a lot of business." The Supreme Court found general jurisdiction in *Perkins v. Benguet Consol. Mining Co.*, 342 U.S. 437 (1952), where a company operated its office, had bank accounts, held shareholder meetings, and engaged in other business in Ohio, even though the claim concerned activities in the Philippines. In fact, the company was barely operating since its facilities had been taken over by the Japanese. Nonetheless, the court characterized these as "continuous and systematic corporate activities" and found general jurisdiction proper. Thus, even though the corporation was barely doing anything, everything it was doing it was doing it was doing in Ohio. Ohio was as a result its principal place of business.

Third, a corporation is subject to general personal jurisdiction some other state if there are in "exceptional cases." The *Daimler* court left open the possibility that, in addition to the state(s) of incorporation and state of the corporation's principal place of business, there might be an "exceptional" instance where general personal jurisdiction would exist. Again, we will have to wait to see.

If suit is not filed in an individual's domicile, or a corporation's "home" state(s), then the other means to establish compliance with the Due Process Clause is specific personal jurisdiction. We turn there now.

## ii. Specific Personal Jurisdiction: For State Claims and Federal Claims Without Nationwide Service of Process, There Must be Minimum Contacts Between the Forum State and the Defendant; For Federal Claims with Nationwide Service of Process, the Defendant Must Have Minimum Contacts with the United States

Specific jurisdiction exists where the defendant through its acts has created minimum contacts by purposefully availing himself of the laws of the forum state — where the claim is filed — and it would not be unfair to subject it to suit in that forum. *Int'l Shoe Co. v. Washington*, 326 U.S. 310 (1945), is the modern source of this doctrine. In *Shoe,* the plaintiff was the State of Washington. It filed a suit in the state of Washington against the International Shoe Company, which was a Delaware corporation with its principal place of business in Missouri. The claim was that the defendant had employees in the state of Washington but the employee had not paid certain state employment taxes for them. The defendant contested personal jurisdiction. The court held that specific personal jurisdiction was proper.

Under *International Shoe* and subsequent cases, the Due Process Clause is satisfied when three requirements are met: (a) the defendant has "minimum contacts" with the forum through the defendant's purposeful actions; (b) there's a "nexus" between the contacts and the claim (only contacts "related" to the claim "count"); and (c) assertion of personal jurisdiction comports with "fair play and substantial justice." Vague though they surely are, these requirements are the foundations of *in personam* jurisdiction. We now turn to them.

### (a)  Purposeful Availment or Direction by the Defendant Toward the Forum

Perhaps a majority of the courts hold that specific jurisdiction can arise from *either* (1) a showing that the non-resident defendant "purposefully availed" himself or the forum's laws by conducting activities in the forum *or* (2) from an act outside of the forum which was "purposefully directed" at forum residents while they are in the forum. *Pebble Beach Co. v. Caddy,* 453 F.3d 1151, 1155 (9th Cir. 2006). Other courts lump the two together, usually under the "purposeful availment" rubric.

Before we get into the details, make sure you have a firm grasp on this fact: physical presence in the forum that led to the claim isn't required, though it obviously "counts." The question isn't only whether the defendant was "in" the forum but instead whether it had "contacts" "with" the forum. It's possible to have specific jurisdiction over a defendant who has never physically visited a forum.

An example may help. Suppose you stay in your home state but through telephone calls and other communications make an agreement with a Nevada resident to perform several months of work later in Nevada. But, you decide to breach that contract. Does it sound like it would be unfair for the Nevada resident to sue you in Nevada? That's a simple example of both purposeful availment and purposeful direction and a defendant who never set foot in the forum state.

But even with contractual obligations, there is no bright line rule. While it is true that a party who reaches out to another state to create "'continuing relationships and obligations with citizens of another state' are subject to regulation and sanctions in the other State for the consequences of their activities,'" it is also clear that "an individual's contract with an out-of-state party" cannot by itself "automatically establish sufficient minimum contacts in the other party's home forum. . . ." *Burger King,* 471 U.S. at 473 (quoting *Travelers Health Ass'n v. Va.,* 339 U.S. 643, 647 (1950)).

A recent case on specific jurisdiction emphasizes that it is not the knowledge of the defendant that he is interacting with residents of the forum state that matters. It is the defendant's contacts with the forum state. The fact that the plaintiff is connected to the forum state is not enough, and it is still not enough if the defendant knows the plaintiff is headed to the forum state. This is the teaching of the recent case of *Walden v. Fiore,* 134 S.Ct. 1115 (2014), a unanimous case. There, plaintiffs were traveling from Puerto Rico to Nevada by way of Atlanta. The defendant was a TSA agent at Atlanta's Hartsfield International Airport. A guard at the Puerto Rico had alerted the TSA agent that the plaintiffs had almost $100,000 in cash with them. The TSA agent stopped the plaintiffs, and confiscated the money, even though the plaintiffs claimed the money had been gambling winnings and they were professional gamblers. The defendant knew the plaintiffs were headed home to Nevada. He also allegedly drafted a false affidavit after the plaintiffs were back in Nevada in order to justify seizing the money.

The plaintiffs eventually got their money back, and they also sued the TSA agent in Nevada. The Supreme Court held that specific personal jurisdiction was lacking, even as to the claim arising out of the falsified affidavit. The Court emphasized that even with respect to intentional torts, the forum state's exercise of personal jurisdiction "must be based on intentional conduct by the defendant that creates the necessary contacts with the forum."

The Court relied on an earlier case (discussed more fully below), *Calder v. Jones,* stating that "In *Calder,* a California actress brought a libel suit in California state court against a reporter and an editor, both of whom worked for the National Enquirer at its headquarters in Florida." The plaintiff's claims were related to an allegedly libelous article published in a magazine circulated to 600,000 Californians. The Court emphasized that the defendants in writing the article had "relied on phone calls to 'California sources'" for information; "caused reputational injury in California"; and the plaintiff suffered the "brunt" of her injury in California.

But the Court held the *Walden* facts were different. The Court held that Nevada could not exercise personal jurisdiction over Walden, the TSA agent, based on his conduct in Georgia, since he had "approached, questioned, and searched [plaintiffs], and seized the cash at issue, in the Atlanta airport." Walden "never traveled to, conducted activities within, contacted anyone in, or sent anything or anyone to Nevada." Thus, "when viewed through the proper lens—whether the *defendant's* actions connect him to the *forum*—[Walden] formed no jurisdictionally relevant contacts with Nevada." The affidavit itself had never made its way to Nevada, let alone done so by the agent's deliberative acts.

It is also important to distinguish acts of the plaintiff: courts will sometimes call these "unilateral acts" and disregard them. For example, in *Hanson v. Denckla,* 357 U.S. 235 (1958), the plaintiff set up a trust in Delaware with a Delaware bank. Later, the plaintiff moved to Florida. The Court found specific jurisdiction lacking over a claim brought in Florida related to the trust agreement, stating that the "unilateral activity of those who claim some relationship with a non-resident defendant cannot satisfy the requirement of contact with the forum State." *Id.* The fact that the plaintiff moved to Florida did not mean the defendant had minimum contacts with Florida when the events underlying the suit occurred in Delaware while she lived in Delaware.

This concept becomes important in several areas, including products liability claims: is it an act of the defendant if it puts products into the "stream of commerce" knowing that its products will be purchased in or at least be taken to virtually every state? We'll turn back to that question below.

Finally, in part because of the requirement that the claim relate to the contact with specific personal jurisdiction, that analysis can be heavily influenced by the nature of the claim. For example, if someone intentionally travels to Texas to punch someone, chances are personal jurisdiction will exist over a battery claim with just that one connection between the defendant and Texas. If a person makes a product in California, and one happens to wind its way through commerce and negligently injures someone in Texas, probably not. The elements and nature of the claim matters, too. The Supreme Court has stated that the analysis is the same regardless of the claim. While that is true, it is helpful to focus on the claim over which personal jurisdiction is sought to see how the courts have analyzed minimum contacts for each claim, because only the contacts with a "nexus" to the claim "count" for specific personal jurisdiction.

*Breach of Contract Claims.* The Supreme Court found specific jurisdiction in *McGee v. Int'l Life Ins. Co.,* 355 U.S. 20 (1957). There, the Court held that California courts had personal jurisdiction over a defendant insurer who had issued life insurance policy to California resident over claim for breach of the insurance policy, even though the insurer had never solicited a single policy in California besides this one. There, the insurer had been sued in the California state courts, but had not defended, resulting in a default judgment in favor of the insured. When the insured sought to enforce the judgment in Texas, the insurer argued that the California court had lacked personal jurisdiction over it, and so the judgment could not be enforced. The court found specific jurisdiction over the claim for breach of the insurance policy sold to the California resident, and paid for by it while it was in California, to have been proper.

Just a short time later, however, the Court reached the opposite result in *Hanson v. Denckla,* 357 U.S. 235 (1958). There, even though a defendant Delaware trust company had mailed income payments to a Florida resident and had received instructions from a Florida resident on how to implement the trust, the Court found specific jurisdiction lacking over a claim for breach of the trust company's obligations to the trust. The reason? Probably the fact that the Florida residents had, after the contract between them was formed, moved from Delaware to Florida. "The unilateral activity of those who claim some relationship with a non-resident defendant cannot satisfy the requirement of contact with the forum State." *Id.*

In *Kulko v. Superior Court,* 436 U.S. 84 (1978), Ezra and Sharon Kulko lived in New York with their two children. However, they separated and Sharon moved to California. Under the separation agreement they executed in New York, Ezra agreed to pay child support to Sharon in California or anywhere else she designated, and the children were to live in New York during the school year, but stay with Sharon in California over the summers. Their daughter soon wanted to spend the school year in California, and her father agreed and bought her a one-way ticket to California. Their son, with the mother's surreptitious help, also later moved to California. Sharon, then sued Ezra in California, seeking sole custody of their children and an increase in child support. Ezra moved to dismiss for lack of personal jurisdiction, but the California courts held that by allowing the daughter to move to California, he had subjected himself to personal jurisdiction in California over the contract action. The Supreme Court disagreed, rejecting the notion that simply because he obtained an economic benefit from the children being in California — it was less expensive for them to live there — was not enough. The court emphasized that the claim did not arise out of commercial transactions, but from personal domestic relations and that the contract had been negotiated and executed in New York.

Finally, in *Burger King Corp. v. Rudzewicz*, 471 U.S. 462 (1985), the Supreme Court held specific jurisdiction proper where the defendant reached out from its home state to negotiate with a Florida resident, Burger King, to negotiate the purchase of a long-term franchise, but emphasizing that it was because the parties entered into "a 20-year relationship that envisioned continuing and wide-reaching contacts with Burger King in Florida" and so the contacts were neither "fortuitous," "random," or "attenuated." *Burger King*, 474 U.S. at 479–80. In addition, the court noted that the agreements stated that Florida law would govern. *Id*

In sum, courts adopt a "'highly realistic' approach that recognizes that a 'contract' is 'ordinarily but an intermediate step serving to tie up prior business negotiations with future consequences which themselves are the real object of the business transaction.'" *Burger King*, 474 U.S. at 479 (quoting *Hoopeston Canning Co. v. Cullen*, 318 U.S. 313, 316 (1943)). Thus, purposeful availment does not simply turn on the existence of a contract with a forum resident, it turns on "prior negotiations and contemplated future consequences, along with the terms of the contract and the parties actual course of dealing." *Id*. Those facts determine whether the defendant purposefully established minimum contacts with the forum.

***Intentional Tort Claims.*** An act that occurs outside the forum that is "purposefully directed" or "aimed" at the plaintiff in the forum can support personal jurisdiction if it is both aimed at and has effect in that forum. This is often called the "*Calder* effects test," after *Calder v. Jones*, 465 U.S. 783 (1984), which involved the intentional tort of defamation. In *Calder*, National Enquirer employees in

Florida wrote an article about a California Entertainer, Shirley Jones. Jones sued the Enquirer in California. Even through the article had been written in Florida and defendants had few contacts with California, the Court held personal jurisdiction existed because the article was not "mere untargeted negligence" but was intentionally aimed at a California resident, drawn from California sources, and caused professional and reputational harm in California. Other courts have distilled *Calder* to require that the defendant "must have (1) committed an intentional act, which was (2) expressly aimed at the forum state, and (3) caused harm, the brunt of which is suffered and which the defendant knows is likely to be suffered in the forum state." *Bancroft & Masters, Inc. v. Augusta Nat'l, Inc.*, 223 F.3d 1082, 1087 (9th Cir. 2000). *See ESAB Group, Inc. v. Centricut, Inc.*, 126 F.3d 617 (4th Cir. 1997) (applying the *Calder* effects test to claims for intentional interference with contract and related intentional tort claims).

The *Walden* case, discussed above, also involved an intentional act. Recall that beause the TSA agent had not been to or done acts targeted toward forum residents, personal jurisdiction did not exist.

***Negligence and Strict Liability Claims.*** Personal jurisdiction issues have reached the Court twice in products liability cases — where the plaintiff claims she was injured by a product purchased in her state which the defendant had sold "into the stream of commerce" in another state, knowing it might be purchased by a consumer in another state. In first addressing this issue, the Court in *World-Wide Volkswagen Corp. v. Woodson,* 444 U.S. 286 (1980), held that an Oklahoma court could not exercise personal jurisdiction over a non-resident automobile retailer and wholesale distributor whose only connection with Oklahoma was the fact that they had sold a car in New York to a New York resident that later was involved in an accident in Oklahoma. The Court explained that even if it was foreseeable that a car sold in New York could cause injury in Oklahoma, that was an insufficient connection for the defendants to reasonably anticipate being sued in Oklahoma. Foreseeability that the car would end up in the State was not enough.

The Court a few years later again faced this question in *Asahi Metal Indus. Co., Ltd. v. Superior Ct. of Ca.,* 480 U.S. 102 (1987), where a plurality of the Court sought to clarify *World-Wide Volkswagen.* In *Asahi,* a Japanese company made a valve that was then incorporated into a tire by a Taiwanese tire manufacturer. That tire then was installed on a Honda motorcycle that was sold to a California consumer. After an accident in California, the consumer filed a products liability suit naming both Honda and the Taiwanese tire manufacturer as defendants. The tire manufacturer, contending that the valve was the cause of the accident and so the valve manufacturer owed an obligation of indemnity to it, impleaded (*see* Chapter 17) the valve manufacturer. The Supreme Court unanimously held that the valve manufacturer could not be constitutionally required to defend in California.

But in doing so, the Justices used three different tests. Four of the eight participating justices concluded that even had the valve manufacturer introduced the valves into the stream of commerce with awareness that a significant portion of them would be sold in California was insufficient to establish purposeful availment. In a portion of the opinion joined only by the four, Justice O'Connor wrote:

> The placement of a product into the stream of commerce, without more, is not an act of the defendant purposefully directed toward the forum State. Additional conduct of the defendant may indicate an intent or purpose to serve the market in the forum State, for example, designing the product for the market in the forum State, advertising in the forum State, establishing channels for providing regular advice to customers in the forum State, or marketing the product through a distributor who has agreed to serve as the sales agent in the forum State.

*Asahi*, 480 U.S. at 111. This view has become known as the "narrow view" of the stream of commerce doctrine.

A concurring opinion by Justice Brennen took a broader view, and one that has become the second competing view. He wrote: "The stream of commerce refers not to unpredictable currents or eddies, but to the regular and anticipated flow of products from manufacture to distribution to retail sale. . . . A defendant who has placed goods in the stream of commerce benefits economically from the retail sale of the final product in the forum State, and indirectly benefits from the State's laws that regulate and facilitate commercial activity." 480 U.S. at 117.

The third test would evaluate the volume, value and hazardous nature of the goods entering the forum state. *Id.* at 122 (Stevens, J., concurring).

After *Asahi*, the courts remain split on which of the three approaches ought to be applied. The only thing that is clear is that putting a single product into the stream of commerce, without more, will not constitute purposeful availment. In a 2011 plurality decision, *J. McIntyre Mach. Ltd. v. Nicastro*, four justices endorsed the approach of Justice O'Connor. Thus, the split remains in place.

### (b) Relationship Between Claim and Contacts

To have specific jurisdiction, there must not only be "minimum" contacts between the defendant and the forum, but the claim must "arise out of" or "relate to" those contacts. So, for example, in *Burger King* Burger King properly sued the franchisee in Florida for breach of the franchise agreement, but personal jurisdiction in Florida would not have been proper over a claim arising out of conduct unrelated to the contract.

How close must the relationship between the claim and the contacts be? There are few guides to this beyond the statement that the claim must arise out of or be related to the contact. *See Nowak v. Tak How Investments, Ltd.*, 94 F.3d 708 (1st Cir. 1996) (concluding that there are at least three conceptions of "relatedness"). The requirement of relatedness acts as a filter as to which contacts "count" for specific jurisdiction: the more closely the claim must "relate to" the contact, the fewer contacts that will "count" for personal jurisdiction, and the more difficult it will be to establish minimum contacts. As a practical matter, the more contacts a defendant has with a forum, the less the relationship likely has to be between the contacts and the claim. A defendant with a single contact with a forum, therefore, might be subject to specific jurisdiction but only as to claims directly related to that contact. A non-resident defendant with a greater number of contacts with the forum state will be subject to a broader range of claims.

### (c)  Defendant can Show that, Even if There are Minimum Contacts, Assertion of Personal Jurisdiction Would be Unfair

If only specific personal jurisdiction exists over a claim against a defendant, and even if minimum contacts exist, a court must still consider policy and functional issues before concluding whether asserting personal jurisdiction comports with due process. In addition to minimum contacts, the exercise of personal jurisdiction must comport with traditional notions of fair play and substantial justice. *Int'l Shoe*, 326 U.S. at 316. (General personal jurisdiction will never be "unfair.")

Most courts place this burden on the defendant to produce evidence to show that defending the suit in the forum would be unreasonable. The court will consider: (1) the burden on the non-resident defendant; (2) the forum's interest in adjudicating the dispute as compared to the defendant's home forum; (3) the plaintiff's interest in obtaining convenient and effective relief; (4) the judicial system's interest in obtaining the most efficient resolution of controversies; and (5) the shared interest of the several states in furthering substantive social policies. *Burger King Corp.*, 471 U.S. at 477; *World-Wide Volkswagen Corp.*, 444 U.S. at 292.

Some courts have stated that the more contacts a defendant has with the forum, the greater the "unreasonableness" must be. *Ticketmaster-New York, Inc.*

*v. Alioto,* 26 F.3d 201, 210 (1st Cir. 1994) ("the reasonableness prong of the due process inquiry evokes a sliding scale: the weaker the plaintiff's showing on the first two prongs [minimum contacts and relatedness] . . . the less a defendant need shown in terms of unreasonableness to defeat jurisdiction.")

It is quite rare for courts to find that even though a defendant has minimum contacts with a forum, that fair play and substantial justice require finding jurisdiction improper. Further, in *Burger King,* the Court emphasized that "a defendant who purposefully . . . directed his activities at forum residents . . . must present a compelling case that the presence of some other considerations would render jurisdiction unreasonable." *Burger King,* 471 U.S. at 477. Instead, the Court emphasized that other means, such as transferring venue to a more convenient forum, might be the appropriate means to accommodate these considerations. *Id.* Similarly, the court has emphasized that if the defendant purposefully derives economic benefits from interstate activities, "it may well be unfair to allow them to escape having to account in other States for consequences that arise proximately from such activities." *Id.* at 474. In addition, "because 'modern transportation and communications have made it much less burdensome for a party sued to defend himself in a State where he engages in economic activity,' it usually will not be unfair to subject him to the burdens of litigating in another forum for disputes relating to such activity." *Id.* (quoting *McGee v. Int'l Life Ins. Co.,* 355 U.S. 220, 223 (1957)).

# C. Special Issues in *In Personam* Jurisdiction

## 1. Which Contacts by a Corporate Defendant "Count"?

If a defendant is a corporation, obviously its contacts with the forum "count." Do contacts with the forum of related corporations—say the "parent" of the defendant (a corporation which owns all of the defendant's stock) or a subsidiary (a corporation of which the defendant owns all of its stock)—also count? No. The general rule is that contacts by or *in personam* jurisdiction over one corporate entity does not, by itself, count against even wholly owned companies. *Cannon Mfg. Co. v. Cudahy Packing Co.,* 267 U.S. 333 (1925).

There are exceptions that take various forms, however. Some courts permit the contact of a subsidiary to count against a parent, for example, under an "agency theory." "The agency test is satisfied by a showing that the subsidiary functions as the parent corporation's representative in that it performs services that are sufficiently important to the foreign corporation that if it did not have a representative to perform them, the corporation's own officials would undertake to perform substantially similar services." *Doe v. Unocal Corp.,* 248 F.3d 915, 928 (9th Cir. 2001).

Other courts apply a so-called "alter ego" test, holding that if the plaintiff shows that the parent corporation is merely the "alter ego" of its subsidiary, the subsidiary's contacts with the forum "count" against the parent for the purposes of establishing personal jurisdiction. Generally, the plaintiff must prove that the parent controls the business and operations of the subsidiary to succeed on this theory. These factors are relevant to determine whether a parent controls a subsidiary sufficiently to meld the two for minimum contacts purposes:

(1) Whether the parent owns 100% of the subsidiary's stock.
(2) Whether the two corporations maintain separate headquarters.
(3) Whether the parent and subsidiary share common officers and directors.
(4) Whether corporate formalities are observed.
(5) Whether separate accounting systems are maintained.
(6) Whether the parent exercises complete authority over general policy.
(7) Whether the subsidiary exercises complete authority over daily operations, including research and development, marketing, and supply.

*Dalton v. R & W Marine, Inc.,* 897 F.2d 1359, 1363 (5th Cir.1990). Although "alter ego" is also relating to "piercing the corporate veil" for purposes of imposing liability on one corporation for the acts of another, "the alter ego test for attribution of contacts, i.e., personal jurisdiction, is less stringent than that for liability." *Stuart v. Spademan,* 772 F.2d 1185, 1198 n. 12 (5th Cir.1985).

## 2.  Does an Internet Website Count?

The Internet creates some interesting personal jurisdiction issues. Is a website "in" every forum? How do we know if a defendant with a website "targeted" citizens of a particular forum—does the fact that the plaintiff placed an order through the site establish that? These are recent questions for courts, and yet some consistency is emerging.

With respect to general jurisdiction, the existence of a web page seems irrelevant. If a court were to deem the existence of a web page pertinent to general jurisdiction, then it would be pertinent everywhere, since web pages are accessible throughout the United States (and world, obviously). *See Bird v. Parsons,* 289 F.3d 865 (6th Cir. 2002) ("the fact that [defendant] maintains a website that is accessible to anyone . . . is insufficient to justify general jurisdiction.").

However, web pages can play a role in specific jurisdiction, depending in large part on the nature and element of the claim. *See Zippo Mfg. Co. v. Zippo*

*Dot Com, Inc.,* 952 F. Supp. 1119 (W.D. Pa. 1997) (posting of web page that allowed for interactivity with forum residents and targeted to Pennsylvania).

An appellate decision reveals how courts currently address the role of the Internet in the specific jurisdiction analysis. In *Pebble Beach Co. v. Caddy,* 453 F.3d 1151 (9th Cir. 2006), a resident of a foreign country used the name "Pebble Beach" in a website domain name even though it is the trademark of the famous California golf course. The fact that California residents could access the site and the defendant knew that the golf course was in California was not enough to show that the defendant had purposefully directed his activities in California. The court emphasized that a passive website, even one with obvious connections to California, was insufficient: there must be "something more" than just a foreseeable effect in the forum state, and owning a passive website was not enough. *Id.* at 1158. In so holding, the *Pebble Beach* court distinguished cases where the website owners engaged in active contact, such as through e-mail, interactive website communications or similar electronic contacts with California residents. In fact, where there is interactivity, and not just a passive website, specific jurisdiction can arise. *See, e.g., Compuserve, Inc. v. Patterson,* 89 F.3d 1257 (6th Cir. 1996) (specific jurisdiction found where Texas resident sold shareware through CompuServe, located in Ohio); *See Cybersell, Inc. v. Cybersell, Inc.,* 130 F.3d 414 (9th Cir. 1997) (no purposeful activity arising from "essentially passive nature . . . in posting a home page"); *Revell v. Lidov,* 317 F.3d 467 (5th Cir. 2002) (affirming dismissal of defamation claim brought by Texas resident against Columbia professor and Columbia University over article posted on Columbia University's website).

On the other hand, specific jurisdiction over intentional tort claims can based on Internet activities if those activities are the basis of the claim. For example, in *Panavision Int'l, L.P. v. Toeppen,* 141 F.3d 1316 (9th Cir. 1998), Panavision sued an alleged "cyber pirate" who obtained domain names using Panavision trademarks and offered to sell them to Panavision at a price. The court held personal jurisdiction was present because the tort was intentional and was expressly aimed at a California corporation, and the "brunt" of the harm was felt in California. "Toeppen engaged in a scheme to register Pan-a-vision's trademarks as his domain names for the purpose of extorting money from Panavision. His conduct, as he knew it likely would, had the effect of injuring Panavision in California. . . ."

## 3. Rule 4(k)(2) and Foreign-Country Defendants

Rule 4(k)(2) is often called the "federal long-arm statute" since it authorizes a federal court to assert personal jurisdiction over a defendant so long as

(1) the claim arises under federal law; (2) the defendant is beyond the reach of any state court of general jurisdiction (*i.e.,* personal jurisdiction cannot be imposed under any state long-arm statute); and (3) assertion of personal jurisdiction comports with Due Process. *See U.S. v. Swiss Am. Bank, Ltd.,* 191 F.3d 30, 38 (1st Cir. 1999). This rule was adopted to eliminate a gap: a foreign defendant "who lacked single-state contacts sufficient to bring them within the reach of a given state's long-arm statue (whether by reason of the paucity of the contacts or of limitations built into the statute itself) ... could evade responsibility for civil violations of federal laws that did not provide specifically for service of process." *Id.* Now, so long as the defendant has sufficient contacts with the United States as a whole, a plaintiff may assert a federal claim against him. Thus, it fills a gap left when there is no state long-arm statute or federal statute that would authorize service of process, but the defendant's contacts with the United States as a whole made it Constitutionally subject to suit—in the United States.

Courts have disagreed on who has the burden of proof under this rule. Even though a plaintiff has the burden to plead and prove personal jurisdiction, courts believe the rule requires a different approach.

On the one hand, some courts hold that the plaintiff must establish a prima facie case that personal jurisdiction is not available in any state, and that asserting personal jurisdiction would be constitutional. Then the defendant must produce evidence, which would show either that it could be sued in at least one state *or* its contacts with the U.S. as a whole are insufficient to constitutionally assert personal jurisdiction. *Id.* at 41–42. If a defendant relies on the first option—showing it could be sued in a particular state—then either the plaintiff can negate that showing, or the case can be transferred to that state. If the defendant relies on the second option and shows it lacks minimum contacts with the U.S. as a whole, then the plaintiff must show that the court may constitutionally assert personal jurisdiction. *Id.*

On the other hand, other courts hold that the defendant can avoid the reach of this Rule only if it designates a state in which the plaintiff could have filed suit. *Touchcom, Inc. v. Bereskin & Parr,* 574 F.3d 1403, 1414 (Fed. Cir. 2009) (discussing split in the case law). This avoids the plaintiff from having to prove a negative—that the defendant can't be sued in any particular state, and so the plaintiff should be permitted to rely on this gap-filling rule.

Under both approaches, "'due process demands [a showing of minimum contacts with the United States] with respect to foreign defendants before a court can assert personal jurisdiction.'" *Go-Video, Inc. v. Akai Elec. Co., Ltd.,* 885 F.2d 1406, 1416 (9th Cir. 1989).

## 4. The Few Federal, Claim-Specific Long-Arm Statutes

As discussed above, the question is minimum contacts between the defendant and the forum. But what constitutes the "forum" depends on the statute that authorizes service of process over the claim. If no federal statute authorizes nationwide service of process (*i.e.,* if it's a state law claim or a federal claim that does not have a specific statute authorizing service of process), then the "forum" is the state in which the district court sits. The defendant must have "minimum contacts" with that state.

If a specific federal statute authorizes nationwide service of process on the federal claim in the suit, then the "forum" with which there must be "minimum contacts" is the United States as a whole. The Due Process Clause of the Fifth Amendment requires minimum contacts for federal claims only with the United States as a whole. *See Pinker v. Roche Holdings, Ltd.,* 292 F.2d 361, 369 (3d Cir. 2002) ("We too are persuaded by the reasoning of our prior opinions on the subject, and, consistent with several of our sister courts of appeals, hold that a federal court's personal jurisdiction may be assessed on the basis of the defendant's national contacts when the plaintiff's claim rests on a federal statute authorizing nationwide service of process."); *U.S. v. Union Pacific R.R.,* 98 U.S. 569, 604 (1879) ("nothing in the Constitution . . . forbids Congress" from enacting a statute allowing for nation-wide service of process).

The chart below summarizes these points. Note that in both instances even if there are minimum contacts, the assertion of personal jurisdiction must also still be "fair." (In addition, a few federal statutes authorize worldwide service of process even over foreign citizens not present in the United States. *E.g.,* 1934 Exchange Act, 15 U.S.C. § 78aa. Under those statutes, courts analyze (1) whether the defendant had constitutionally sufficient minimum contacts with the United States as a whole (in terms of the Due Process Clause of Fifth Amendment) and (2) whether the exercise of personal jurisdiction is reasonable, i.e., consistent with "traditional notions of fair play and substantial justice." *Pinker v. Roche Holdings Ltd.,* 292 F.3d 361, 369–71 and n. 2 (3d Cir. 2002).)

| Claim | Contacts with this "Forum" Count |
|---|---|
| State claim | Only the state where the court sits |
| Federal claim | Only the state where the court sits |
| Federal claim created by statute authorizing nationwide service of process | The United States as a whole |

This chart shows that when analyzing minimum contacts, "forum" means the United States if a statute allows nationwide service of process; otherwise, "forum" means the state where the federal court in which the suit has been filed is located.

### ii.  Specific Jurisdiction: "Sufficient" Contacts, a Relationship between the Claim and the Contacts, and Fairness

There are three steps to determine whether specific personal jurisdiction exists of a claim:

(A) whether the defendant has minimum contacts with the forum because it either purposely directed its activities toward the forum state or purposefully availed itself of the privileges of conducting activities in the forum;

(B) whether the plaintiff's cause of action is related to the defendant's contacts; and

(C) whether, if the first two elements are satisfied, the defendant can show that the exercise of personal jurisdiction would not be fair and reasonable.

---

### Checkpoints

- Can you identify when a state statute extends to the limits of due process, and when it does not, and explain the impact that has on a personal jurisdiction analysis?
- Can you explain how to determine whether specific jurisdiction exists? General? Consent? Tag?
- Can you articulate when a court may find that traditional notions of fair play and substantial justice are violated?
- If personal jurisdiction is lacking, what do you do? *See* Chapter 31

Chapter 7

# *In Rem* and *Quasi In Rem* Jurisdiction

---

### *In Rem* and *Quasi In Rem* Jurisdiction Roadmap

This chapter identifies the forms of *in rem* jurisdiction and explains how to determine whether a court has personal jurisdiction.

---

As we saw in Chapter 6, personal jurisdiction is proper if a statute authorizes service of process and the assertion of personal jurisdiction comports with due process. The benefit of having *in personam* personal jurisdiction is that the court has jurisdiction over the person — and thus all the defendant's assets. The plaintiff, if it prevails, can recover money to satisfy any award entered against the judgment by accessing all the defendant's assets.

"*In rem*" means "against the thing." A judgment obtained based upon *in rem* personal jurisdiction applies only to certain property; it does not give the plaintiff the ability to execute on all of the defendant's assets, wherever they may be.

## A. The Three Types of *In Rem* Jurisdiction

A recent case summarized the three types of *in rem* jurisdiction:

> The first, usually called "*in rem*" or "true *in rem*," arises when the court adjudicates the property rights corresponding to a particular *res*, or thing, for every potential rights holder, whether named in the proceeding or not. Examples of this type of true *in rem* proceeding are forfeiture, condemnation, probate and arrests of vessels in admiralty.
>
> A second class of *in rem* proceeding is called "*quasi in rem*," or more specifically "*quasi in rem* type I," which allocates property rights as against particular named persons. Examples of this type of proceeding are actions to remove a cloud on title to land or actions that seek to quiet title against a particular rival's claim.

A third type of *in rem* proceeding is sometimes considered a subcategory of the second, and is consequently called a *"quasi in rem* type II" proceeding; it may be also called an "attachment" or "sequestration" proceeding. This type of action concerns the rights of a particular person or persons in a thing, but is distinguished from type I *quasi in rem* proceedings because the claim against the person that gives rise to the action is not related to the *res* that provides jurisdiction. That is, the plaintiff does not dispute the property rights of the owner of the *res*, but seeks to obtain the *res* in satisfaction of some separate claim.

*FleetBoston Fin. Corp. v. FleetBostonFinancial.com,* 138 F. Supp. 2d 121 (D. Mass. 2001).

We will explore these distinctions a little bit more before turning to the personal jurisdiction analysis.

## 1. True *In Rem*

In a true *in rem* proceeding the federal court is adjudicating title to property in the state as to all people, not just the named parties to the suit. A typical *in rem* case involves a dispute over who of several claimants owns a parcel of land. A court in the state where the land is located has power to decide who owns it, for example, regardless of where claimants reside. A judgment entered *"in rem"* binds the world, and not just particular parties, but it only affects the property in the forum state. In effect, the court's power is over the "thing" not the persons. For example, in *Marex Titanic, Inc. v. Wrecked and Abandoned Vessel,* 2 F.3d 544 (4th Cir. 1993), a party who had salvaged parts from The Titanic and brought suit—actually naming the property as the "defendant" and sought an order that the party was its rightful owner.

The practical limitations arise from the fact that the property must be in the state. Although often *in rem* actions can be brought to resolve disputes over even intangible property (such as stocks and bonds), the property must be in the state. There are only a few claims that are true *in rem* actions, including actions to quiet title, certain probate actions, and some actions in admiralty or bankruptcy. They are rare but important.

In one case, *Harris v. Balk,* 198 U.S. 215 (1905), Harris owed $180 to fellow North Carolinian Balk, who in turn owed $300 to Epstein, a resident of Maryland. When Harris went to Maryland to visit Epstein, Epstein used a state court proceeding to "attach" Harris's debt to Balk. In response, Harris paid to Balk the $180 Harris owed to Epstein, and a Maryland state court in favor of Epstein entered a final judgment. When Harris got back to North Carolina,

Balk sued him for the $180 debt—which Harris had just paid to Epstein. Harris in defense argued that the Maryland judgment barred recovery of the $180 from him. The North Carolina state courts held that the Maryland courts had not had jurisdiction to attach the debt Harris owed to Balk, and ordered Harris to pay the $180 to Balk. Harris balked at paying twice, and appealed to the Supreme Court. The Supreme Court held that because Harris had physically been present in Maryland, its courts had power over his person, and the fact that the debt from Harris to Balk originated in North Carolina was immaterial. "The obligation of the debtor to pay his debt clings to and accompanies him wherever he goes." *Id.* Notice that the court did not hold that *all* of Harris' property was subject to judgment, just the $180 debt, which was "property" that was "with" him while he was in Maryland. *Cf. Burnham v. Superior Court of Cal.*, 495 U.S. 604 (1990) (state statute that authorizes *in personam* jurisdiction to arise by service on a defendant who is only temporarily in a state satisfied Due Process).

## 2. *Quasi In Rem*

In general, *quasi in rem* jurisdiction is used where the dispute is not over title to the property, but, instead, a party has previously obtained a judgment against a party who owns property, and wants an order from a court that gives title to property to the judgment-winner to satisfy the judgment. *Quasi in rem* jurisdiction is useful where, for example, the defendant lives in some other state and is not subject to personal jurisdiction in the state where the defendant owns a piece of property, but the plaintiff wants a court in the state where the defendant owns the property to issue a judgment affecting ownership of, or title to, that property. So, a plaintiff in Iowa can seek a judgment from an Iowa court concerning land in Iowa, even if the defendant lives in Florida and is not subject to personal jurisdiction in Iowa.

### a. Quasi In Rem *Type 1*

These forms of *quasi in rem* jurisdiction have special uses, and in those instances when the defendant has significant property in the jurisdiction, one or the other may be sufficient. For example, one federal statute creates *quasi in rem* type 1 jurisdiction for disputes over domain names: a suit to force forfeiture, cancellation, or transfer of an Internet domain name can, under some circumstances, be filed in jurisdictions where the domain name is registered. 15 U.S.C. § 1125(d)(2) (part of the Anti-cybersquatting Consumer Protection Act, or "ACPA").

### *b.* Quasi In Rem *Type 2*

*Quasi in rem* Type 2 jurisdiction is distinct in that the claim has nothing to do with the property that is being sought by the plaintiff. This form of jurisdiction is often utilized to "attach" specific property due to a prior judgment obtained by the plaintiff against the property owner. "Tormented souls of first-year civil procedure will recognize . . . *quasi in rem* type II, where 'the plaintiff seeks to apply what he concedes to be the property of the defendant to the satisfaction of a claim against him.'" *Glencore Grain Rotterdam B.V. v. Shivnath Rai Harnarain Co.*, 284 F.3d 1114 (9th Cir. 2002) (quoting *Hanson v. Denckla*, 357 U.S. 235, 246 n. 12 (1958)). The plaintiff must identify the defendant's property in the jurisdiction and allege that it is subject to attachment or seizure. *Glencore Grain*, 284 F.3d at 1128.

# B. The Same Standards for *In Personam* Jurisdiction Apply to *In Rem* Jurisdiction

In *Shaffer v. Heitner*, 433 U.S. 186 (1977), the plaintiff filed a shareholder's derivative suit in Delaware on behalf of a corporation against some of its present and former officers and directors. (Not the corporation itself!) The plaintiff alleged that the individual defendants had engaged in activities that subjected the corporation to liability in Oregon, and sought sequestration of their property—shares of the corporation's stock—that were present in Delaware (because a Delaware statute said that shares of Delaware corporations were constructively present in Delaware). Although the lower courts had held that assertion of *in rem* jurisdiction was constitutional, the Supreme Court reversed and held that the rubric of *International Shoe* applied to *in rem* actions.

Thus, the same standard for personal jurisdiction applies to all kinds of *in rem* jurisdiction:

> *Shaffer* . . . eliminated all doubt that the minimum contacts standard in *International Shoe* governs *in rem* and *quasi in rem* actions as well as *in personam* actions. Shaffer, 433 U.S. at 207–12. The Court held that "in order to justify an exercise of jurisdiction in rem, the basis for jurisdiction must be sufficient to justify exercising jurisdiction over the interests of persons in a thing." *Id.* at 207. And "[t]he standard for determining whether an exercise of jurisdiction over the interests of persons is consistent with the Due Process Clause is the minimum-contacts standard elucidated in International Shoe." *Id.*

*Base Metal Trading, Ltd. v. OJSC "Novokuznetsky Aluminum Factory,"* 283 F.3d 208 (4th Cir. 2002).

Obviously the existence of property in the state matters. Indeed, if the property is present and the claim relates to the property, then it will be rare that personal jurisdiction does not exist. The two steps to apply *International Shoe* to *in rem* proceedings are:

First, does the claim relate to the property in the state? If so, and even though the *Shoe* analysis must be made, the Supreme Court in *Shaffer* stated that "when claims to the property itself are the source of the underlying controversy between the plaintiff and the defendant, it would be unusual for the State where the property is located not to have jurisdiction." That was not the case in *Shaffer*, however: the ownership of stock by the defendant directors had nothing to do with whether they were liable to the corporation for their wrong-doing.

Second, if the claim does not relate to the property, then a careful application of the minimum contacts analysis of *Shoe* is required. The presence of the defendant's property in the state obviously matters to that analysis:

> Of course, the presence of property in a state may have an impact on the personal jurisdiction inquiry .... Yet, when the property that serves as the basis for jurisdiction is completely unrelated to the plaintiff's cause of action, the presence of property alone will not support jurisdiction. While, "the presence of the defendant's property in a State might suggest the existence of other ties among the defendant, the State, and the litigation," when those "other ties" do not exist, jurisdiction is not reasonable. *Id.*

*Base Metal,* 283 F.3d at 213.

# C. How Is Notice Given?

When the action is against the world as in a true *in rem* proceeding, a state statute typically authorizes notice by publication of the filing of the lawsuit. *See, e.g., Ehorn v. Sunken Vessel Known as "Rosinco,"* 294 F.3d 856 (7th Cir. 2002) (describing plaintiff's posting of ads in two newspapers and posting notice in federal court house). This publication is called "constructive" service of process.

Where the proceeding is quasi *in rem*, a statute must authorize service of process. The requirements vary by state, some permitting service of process, while others allow for constructive service. *See Monahan v. Holmes,* 139 F. Supp. 2d 253 (D. Conn. 2001).

## Checkpoints

- Can you articulate the differences between true *in rem* and the two types of *quasi in rem* jurisdiction?

- What difference does whether the claim relates to the property make in the analysis?

- When will either *in rem* or *quasi in rem* jurisdiction be sufficient, as a practical matter, for a plaintiff?

# Chapter 8

# The Foundations of Venue

---

### Venue Roadmap

This chapter describes the law of venue, which determines, in states that have more than one federal district court, which district is a proper place to file a particular claim. While subject matter jurisdiction tells us whether a claim can be filed in federal court, and personal jurisdiction tells us which state or states a claim can be filed in, venue tells us which district within a state a claim can properly be filed in. We will also see that even though suit has been filed in a proper venue, the case may be transferred to a more convenient, proper venue. Finally, we'll see that — much like supplemental jurisdiction expands the basic subject matter jurisdiction of federal courts, and pendent person jurisdiction expands the basic reach of long-arm statutes — "pendent venue" expands venue to let related claims "tag along" under some circumstances.

---

The word "venue" is commonly used in real life in much the same way that it is used in civil procedure. When someone says, "that was a great venue for that concert," he's saying that the show worked well in the place: it fit. The same thing is true with "venue" in civil lawsuits: when a court is a proper venue, it means that the district where the court is located is a good fit under the circumstances. This chapter explores the issue of why a court in a particular state, even if it has personal and subject matter jurisdiction, may not be the best place in a particular state for the show. The question of which federal court, when there is more than one in a particular state, should hear a case largely turns on efficiency and convenience, but is influenced by other factors such as the plaintiff's choice of forum.

Venue is related to, but distinct from, personal and subject matter jurisdiction. A court can have personal jurisdiction over a claim against defendant, for example, but venue over that claim may be improper. Keep the analyses separate.

Why, if subject matter jurisdiction and personal jurisdiction are proper, do federal statutes further restrict which federal district court in a state with more than one district can hear a claim? Because subject matter jurisdiction refers to the power of the court to hear the dispute, and personal jurisdiction is the court's power over the defendant. Neither of them tells us whether the particular court in that state is a convenient place for trial, as those concepts are concerned with power in terms of power of the court to hear a claim or power of the court to force the non-resident defendant to defend itself in the forum state.

Specifically, "subject matter jurisdiction" simply means either that the claim arises under federal law or the parties are diverse and the amount in controversy is satisfied. Likewise, "personal jurisdiction" means that a defendant has sufficient contacts with a state. But, simply because a claim meets the requirements of diversity or presents a federal question, doesn't tell us where in that state the suit should for the sake of convenience be tried. Further, simply because a defendant is subject to personal jurisdiction in a particular state doesn't even mean that the case should be tried in that state — it may just mean, for example, that the defendant is subject to general personal jurisdiction in that state. That fact doesn't tell us where the witnesses and documents are located or, necessarily, where the events that led to the claim occurred. Personal and subject matter jurisdiction do not tell us anything about convenience or efficiency.

In contrast, venue doesn't relate to power of the court over the claim or the person, but instead relates to the convenience of the court, the parties, and the witnesses. *Leroy v. Great W. United Corp.*, 443 U.S. 173, 180 (1979) (noting that venue "is primarily a matter of choosing a convenient forum"). Venue is not about limiting power of the courts in a forum over a defendant, but is instead about convenience and efficiency of federal courts *within a forum that does have power over the defendant.*

The need for venue statutes arises from the fact that most states are divided into more than one federal district. Texas, for example, has several districts, ranging from the Eastern District covering the areas generally east of Houston, to the Northern District, covering Dallas and areas northward, the Western District, covering Austin to El Paso, and the Southern District, covering essentially Houston to the Rio Grande Valley. So to say that personal jurisdiction is proper "in Texas" doesn't tell us which district in Texas is a proper venue to try the case. A determination that a defendant has minimum contacts with "the United States" likewise doesn't say anything about where it would cheap and easy to try the claim. Even if a defendant is subject to personal jurisdiction in a state, there may be a much better (more convenient and efficient) state in which to try the claim.

The propriety of venue is determined by examining connections between the facts that led to the claim and the district in which the suit is filed. Thus, if you know that a defendant has minimum contacts with Texas, you know that personal jurisdiction is proper in the Lone Star State; you still need to analyze which district or districts, if any, will have proper venue over the claim. (Again, some small states have only one district, and so the only district that might have venue over the case is the one district in the state. That is the exception, not the rule.)

Why does the location of witnesses or evidence matter? Trials require that juries hear testimony and see evidence. Evidence is either testimonial (eye witness testimony to a car wreck, for example) or tangible (*e.g.*, documents evidencing a breached contract to sell land). Given that reality, some districts will be more convenient and efficient to try the claim than others because more of the witnesses, documents, or both, are located in that district. The broad goal of the rules and statutes governing venue is to have trial occur in a district that's generally more convenient than others given the facts underlying the claim.

What this chapter shows is that federal venue statutes set a rough limit on where venue is *proper*: Congress made some pretty high-level determinations as to which districts will likely be relatively convenient places to try a claim. As we'll see, Congress realized that as a general rule it ought to be *proper* to file a claim where the defendant lives, the plaintiff lives, or the incident giving rise to the claim occurred. That's not a bad guess as to where, most of the time, trial of a claim would be convenient, at least as compared to the many places where neither of the parties live and none of the events occurred, and filing it in those venues is *improper*.

Second, in Chapter 39 we'll deal with the refinements available to the rough cut of "proper" versus "improper" venue. We'll see that Congress recognized that the rough pass of "proper" versus "improper" venue might not lead a case to be filed in what, given all the circumstances, is a much more *convenient* venue. Suppose, for example, the plaintiff files in a proper venue, but there's another proper venue where there are more witnesses, more documents, and in which trial will generally be more convenient. For instance, what if the accident occurred in Minnesota, but now the parties and witnesses live in other states. Venue might be proper in Minnesota under the "rough first pass" approach, but does it really make sense to try the suit in Minnesota? As we'll see, parties can move to transfer even a case filed in a *proper* venue to one that's both proper and *more convenient* for the parties and witnesses. A number of circumstances are relevant to determining convenience, and convenience is weighed against the plaintiff's choice of a proper venue. While a court will readily transfer or dismiss a claim filed in an *improper* venue, transferring a claim from a *proper* venue to a "more convenient one" overrides a legitimate choice by the plaintiff, and so is done only with some reluctance by the courts. But it is done.

That broad background raises a number of distinct concepts you should grasp early on. We'll fill in the details below.

First, venue is determined by district. Although a few states have only one federal district court, most states have more than one district. Thus, venue generally is not determined on a state-level, as with personal jurisdiction, but on a district (and sometimes, intra-district or "divisional" level). So, personal jurisdiction over a claim might be proper in Texas, but it's seldom correct to say that venue is proper "in Texas": venue might be proper in the Northern District of Texas (around Dallas) or the Southern District (Houston), or the Eastern District (Marshall), but usually not "Texas" as a whole.

Second, this is a black and white issue: venue is either proper or improper. Federal statutes define where venue is proper; if it's not filed in a proper district, then it's improper. As noted above, there are general federal venue statutes that apply to most claims. In addition, some federal statutes have specific venue provisions that identify the criteria for determining the venues in which a particular claim, say patent infringement, can be properly filed.

Third, venue is often proper in more than one district in a given state. That is, a plaintiff can often choose which district to file in. Obviously, the plaintiff has the first choice of proper venues to file in.

Fourth, if venue is improper in a district, then, if a defendant timely moves to change venue, the court *must* do so. While the plaintiff's choice of a proper venue carries weight, filing in an improper venue gives the defendant the ability to move to transfer venue to a proper district.

Fifth, "proper" venue doesn't mean "best" or "most convenient." It means only that by the terms of the federal venue states, venue is proper, not that the district is the best district for trial. Even so, because often venue will be proper in more than one district, the defendant can move to transfer venue to another forum for convenience of the parties and witnesses, even though venue is proper where the case was filed. One district may be a proper venue, but that court may conclude that another district with proper venue would be more convenient, and so it may order the case transferred to another proper, and more convenient, district. That's the topic we'll deal with in a Chapter 39.

Sixth — and this is some good news — some claims, including counterclaims, aren't subject to venue requirements. *See* Chapter 23. The venue requirements do apply, however, to every claim by a plaintiff against a defendant, though "pendent venue" expands the venue statutes slightly if there is one claim in a case for which venue is proper. *See* Chapter 23. With that background, let's get started with determining what makes a venue proper, or not.

## Checkpoints

- Do you understand that the district, and not the state, is the measuring unit for venue?

- Do you understand the difference between proper and improper venue, as compared to a more convenient and proper venue?

# Chapter 9

# Proper and Improper Venue

---

### Proper and Improper Venue Roadmap

This chapter identifies the statutory venue requirements and explains how they promote convenience by, generally, requiring that a claim be filed either where a party "resides" or a substantial part of the claim occurred.

The chapter explains how to determine both where a party resides for purposes of venue and where a substantial part of the claim occurred, and when those facts can render venue proper.

---

## A. Determining *Proper* Venue

Congress has enacted specific statutes that define where venue is proper for particular federal claims. When Congress enacts a statute that creates a federal claim, it sometimes also enacts a provision that addresses where venue over those claims is proper. So, to identify the proper venue(s), you first have to look at the complaint to determine whether it's a federal claim that has its own specific venue statute. If so, that specific statute controls. (We'll talk about some specific venue statutes below.) If, as is usually the case, there is no specific venue statute for the claim, then venue turns on the general federal venue statute.

The general federal venue statute, 28 U.S.C. § 1391, identifies which districts are *proper* venue for a claim. This statute was heavily amended (and simplified, they say!) in 2011. The key parts of the statute defining proper venues are:

(b) **Venue in General.** — A civil action may be brought in —
  (1) a judicial district in which any defendant resides, if all defendants are residents of the State in which the district is located;
  (2) a judicial district in which a substantial part of the events or omissions giving rise to the claim occurred, or a substantial part of property that is the subject of the action is situated; or
  (3) if there is no district in which an action may otherwise be brought as provided in this section, any judicial district in which any

105

defendant is subject to the court's personal jurisdiction with respect to such action.

Thus, there are three possible categories of proper venues (and there may be many districts which fall within one or more of those categories. We'll go through each one next.

## 1. The Three Possible *Proper* Venues Under the General Venue Statute

Put in order of easiest to hardest, the potential proper venues are these:

(a) a judicial district in which a substantial part of the events or omissions giving rise to the claim occurred, or a substantial part of the property that is the subject of the action is situated;

(b) a judicial district where any defendant resides if all defendants reside in the forum State; or

(c) if there is no district in which the action may otherwise be brought, a judicial district in which *any* defendant is subject to personal jurisdiction at the time the action is commenced.

Notice that the final option applies only if venue is not proper under either of the first two subsections. That's why it's the hardest subsection to apply: you have to analyze the first two to figure out if you can use the third one. Bear in mind that even if suit is filed in a "proper" venue in terms of Section 1391, there may be a more convenient venue to which it can be transferred under Section 1404. Section 1391 only defines which districts are proper or improper venues.

### (a) A district in which a substantial part of the events or omissions giving rise to the claim occurred

Venue is proper where "a substantial part of the events or omissions giving rise to the claim occurred." There are two requirements to the first part of this prong: there must have occurred in the district (1) a substantial part (2) of the events or omissions giving rise to the claim. We'll take the two elements required to establish proper venue under this subsection in reverse order, since it's easier to understand that way.

## 1. Substantial Part of the Events or Omissions

To determine whether the events or omissions relied upon to establish venue were "part of the events giving rise to the claim," the elements of the claim must be analyzed to determine what acts or omissions form the claim. Only those acts or omissions that form "part of the historical predicate" for the claim count. *Uffner v. La Reunion Francaise, S.A.*, 244 F.3d 38, 42 (1st Cir. 2002). They must "have more than some tangential connection to the claim." *Lomano v. Black*, 285 F. Supp. 2d 637, 640 (E.D. Pa. 2003). They do not need to be disputed or have directly led to the filing of the action. *Mitrano v. Hawes*, 377 F.3d 402 (4th Cir. 2004). Rather, what counts is "the entire sequence of events underlying the claim." *Uffner.*, 244 F.3d at 42.

Why are the acts or omissions the focus? Because the events that led to the claim will indicate where witnesses and tangible evidence will be found, and having suit filed there furthers the purpose of venue. Thus, the test for determining whether venue is proper under this prong does not turn on "the defendant's 'contacts' with a particular district, but rather the location of those 'events or omissions giving rise to the claim.'" *Cottman Transmission Sys., Inc. v. Martino*, 36 F.3d 291, 294 (3d Cir. 1994).

## 2. What Does "Substantial Part" Mean?

To determine whether the events were a "substantial part" of the claim," there's both a qualitative and a quantitative aspect. First, to "count," the event or omission must have a close nexus to the claim. *Daniel v. Am. Bd. Of Emergency Med.*, 428 F.3d 408, 433 (2d Cir. 2005). Second, there must be "enough" of these closely related events or omissions to justify characterizing the connection as being "substantial." *Id.*

So, for example, venue over a claim alleging fraud would be proper in the district where a document containing the fraudulent misrepresentation was sent. *Moore v. Dixon*, 2006 WL 3091142 (E.D. Wis. 2006) (collecting cases). In one case, the defendants allegedly sent documents containing false statements concerning the sale of a hockey team to the plaintiff in Illinois. The court held venue proper in Illinois because the letter was mailed into the district where suit was filed and "in reaching its decision to purchase [the hockey team, the plaintiff] relied on [defendants'] misrepresentations" in the district. *Mercantile Capital Partners v. Agenzia Sports, Inc.*, 2005 WL 351926 (N.D. Ill. 2005).

"Substantial" doesn't mean "most" or "more than other districts"—it means only that a substantial part of the events that led to the claim occurred in the district. The test isn't whether a majority of the events occurred in the district. Under a former version of the venue statute, but not the existing one, courts had to determine where the "weight of the contacts" occurred—but "most" is no longer the test, "substantial" is. *Mitrano v. Hawes*, 377 F.3d 402 (4th Cir. 2004). Accordingly, venue can be proper in multiple districts: "There may be several districts that qualify as a situs of such 'substantial' activities . . . However, if the selected district's contacts are 'substantial,' it should make no difference that another's are more so, or the most so." *Rich-Mix Products, Inc v. Quickrete Companies, Inc.,* 1999 WL 409946 (N.D. Ill. 1999).

For example, in *First of Michigan Corp. v. Bramlet,* 141 F.3d 260 (6th Cir. 1998), the plaintiffs brought a fraud claim against the defendant based on investment advice. The plaintiffs began receiving the allegedly bad advice while they lived in Michigan, but soon moved to Florida, and received most of the advice and suffered most of the harm while living in Florida, not Michigan. The district court dismissed for improper venue, but the appellate court reversed, holding that because a substantial part of the events happened in Michigan, venue was proper, whether or not substantial events, or more events, also happened in Florida.

Another example is *PKWare v. Meade,* 79 F. Supp. 2d 1007, 1018 (E.D. Wis. 2000), where the plaintiff brought a breach of contract claim. The district court held "substantial parts" of a contract claim included where the conduct underlying the breach occurred, where performance was to have occurred, and where the delivery or non-delivery of goods or payment or non-payment occurred. Thus, in a typical contract action venue might be proper in several districts. *See also Bates v. C&S Adjusters, Inc.,* 980 F.2d 865 (2d Cir. 1992) (weight of contacts for Fair Debt Collection Practices Act claim was in district where collection notice that violated act had been received).

Consequently, there may be more than one district—indeed, more than one state—in which a substantial part of the events or omissions occurred. In other words, there can be more than one proper venue under this subsection. It doesn't matter if *more* events occurred in another district than in the one which plaintiff filed the claim: so long as "substantial" events or omissions occurred in that district, venue is proper there even if "more" occurred elsewhere. (We'll see that it may be that venue can be transferred to that district if it is more convenient, but venue is not improper in a district where a substantial part of the activities or omissions occurred, even if the majority of them occurred in another district.)

### (b) A judicial district where any defendant resides if all defendants reside—or the only defendant resides— in the forum state.

If the claim is not filed in a state where a substantial part of the cause of action occurred, then venue can be proper in a district where a defendant "resides" if all reside in the forum state.

First, one odd thing about this subsection: it applies to single-defendant cases. So, if there is only one defendant, then venue will be proper in the district where that defendant "resides." In multiple defendant cases where all defendants "reside" in the forum state, then venue will be proper where any single defendant "resides." But, if one defendant "resides" in Texas, and the other in Louisiana, venue cannot be based on this subsection. It's only available if every defendant—all of them, whether one or more—resides in the forum state.

The meaning of "reside" is obviously the determinative issue. Luckily the statute defines "residency" by the type of defendant. Also luckily, it's relatively straightforward with respect to natural persons who are defendants. The statute provides that "a natural person, including an alien lawfully admitted for permanent residence in the United States, shall be deemed to reside in the judicial district in which that person is domiciled." Thus, if the defendant is a natural person, the defendant resides in the district of the person's domicile. This is determined just as with subject matter and personal jurisdiction, though on a district level: which district does the defendant have a physical presence coupled with an intent to remain for an indeterminate period of time? *See* Chapter 4. Accordingly, it is the individual's domicile that determines where the person "resides." *Henshell Corp. v. Childerston*, 1999 WL 549027 (E.D. Pa. 1999).

**Things are not so easy with respect to business entities like partnerships or corporations.** Entities have no "home" as such, and "they" don't have any intent to live somewhere, since they're not real. Unfortunately, the statute divides business entities into two categories: corporate and non-corporate.

First, be sure that you understand that "corporation" is not the same thing as a "partnership" or a "business." The word "corporation" means a specific form of business, meaning an artificial person that has been incorporated under state law. So, if you read the following carefully, you will see that subsection 1391(d) only applies to corporations, not other business entities. Further still, subsection 1391(c) and (d) each addresses where a "corporation" "resides" for venue purposes, with the former applying to single-district states and the latter to multi-district states:

(c)  **Residency.**—For all venue purposes— ...

(2) an entity with the capacity to sue and be sued in its common name under applicable law, whether or not incorporated, shall be deemed to reside, if a defendant, in any judicial district in which such defendant is subject to the court's personal jurisdiction with respect to the civil action in question and, if a plaintiff, only in the judicial district in which it maintains its principal place of business; ...

(d) **Residency of Corporations in States With Multiple Districts.**— For purposes of venue under this chapter, in a State which has more than one judicial district and in which a defendant that is a corporation is subject to personal jurisdiction at the time an action is commenced, such corporation shall be deemed to reside in any district in that State within which its contacts would be sufficient to subject it to personal jurisdiction if that district were a separate State, and, if there is no such district, the corporation shall be deemed to reside in the district within which it has the most significant contacts.

That's a lot of words, but it turns on two variables: whether the entity is a corporation and whether the state in which it is subject to personal jurisdiction has more than one district:

| Type of Entity | If subject to personal jurisdiction in a single-district state, residency is in: | If subject to personal jurisdiction in a multi-district state, residency is in |
|---|---|---|
| Corporate defendant | • the forum's district | • if there is a district which—if the district were treated as a separate state the corporation would be subject to personal jurisdiction in it—then that district(s); but if there is no such district then<br>• in the district where the corporation has its most significant contacts. |
| Non-corporate entity defendant | • the forum's district | • if there is a district which—if the district were treated as a separate state the entity would be subject to personal jurisdiction in it—then that district(s). |

So, the first step to determine where a corporation "resides" is to determine whether it is subject to personal jurisdiction in a state. If so, and if the state has one district, you're done. (If the corporation is a plaintiff, it is deemed to reside in the district with this principal place of business. There are very few statutes where the plaintiff's residence matters, however, and it does not matter for the general venue statute, Section 1391.)

If the state has more than one district, you need to pretend that each district is its own state and ask whether each district, were it a state, would have personal jurisdiction over the defendant. If one or more districts in the state would have personal jurisdiction, then you're done: the corporation "resides" in *each* of those districts. One weird question: do you look at the long-arm statute, or just the due process case law? This would matter if the state long arm statute is more restrictive than due process requires. The courts are splitting on that issue.

If the defendant is subject to personal jurisdiction in the state, but there's no single district that would have personal jurisdiction as if it were a separate state, then you need to identify the *one* district with which the defendant has the most significant contacts. That district is where the corporate defendant "resides."

There's one more weird thing left.

Read Section 1391(c) closely. Unlike Section 1391(b), it is limited to corporations, not entities that can sue in their own name (*e.g.*, partnership). Instead, on its face, Section 1391(c) only applies to the residence of "corporations." What of other business entities, such as partnerships or limited partnerships? The text of the statute would not cover unincorporated entities such as these. Nonetheless, the Supreme Court has construed Section 1391(c) to apply to labor unions. *See Denver & R.G.W.R. Co. v. Brotherhood of R.R. Trainmen*, 387 U.S. 556, 562 (1967). Since then, some lower courts have construed Section 1391(c) to define the residences of partnerships. *See, e.g., Penrod Drilling Co. v. Johnson*, 414 F.2d 1217 (5th Cir. 1969) (applying Section 1391(c) to partnership); *Injection Research Specialists v. Polaris Indus., L.P.*, 759 F. Supp. 1511, 1515 (D. Colo. 1991) (holding that partnership should be treated like a corporation for this purpose). *See also Pepsico, Inc., v. Board of Trustees of the W. Conference of Teamsters Pension Trust Fund*, 1988 WL 64869, *2 (S.D.N.Y. 1988) (holding that Section 1391(c) covered an unincorporated association).

Other courts have rejected a broad reading, however, and have deemed partnerships to reside where both the partnership and each of its individual partners resides. *See Muenzberg v. Barnes*, 1998 WL 61207, *2 (N.D. Cal. 1998) (refusing to expand "the already expansive judicial interpretation of 'corporation' under 1391(c)" to include public entities, such as state subdivisions); *Blue Compass Corp. v. Polish Masters of Am.*, 777 F. Supp. 4, 5 (D. Vt. 1991) (rejecting argument that Section 1391(c) covers a sole proprietorship).

Suppose a sole proprietor starts up a pizza shop. It becomes quite popular, and soon he branches out and establishes other franchises throughout the country. He forms a partnership, but does not incorporate. Should Section 1391(c) define the residency of this partnership? That turns on whether the courts will look at the plain text of the statute—in which case partnership is not a corporation—or toward the purpose of the statute, which arguably was to allow venue over claims against business entities to be proper in more circumstances.

### (c)  Venue Based on the Catch-All Subsection

The third clause of Section 1391 can be used to support proper venue only if no other district has proper venue under either of the first two subsections. It is designed to identify venue in multi-defendant cases where virtually all of the events underlying the claim did not occur in any district, and no defendant resides in any district. It's largely going to apply when a foreign defendant—one who lives overseas—committed a wrong through acts that occurred almost entirely, if not entirely, overseas. It's a narrow catch-all that will ordinarily not apply in common suits among citizens of the United States or corporations incorporated in the United States.

## 2. Establishing Proper Venue Based on Specific Federal Venue Statutes

The introductory clause of Section 1391 provides that venue is proper "as otherwise provided by law." So, if a federal statute makes venue proper for a particular claim in certain districts, that statute controls over the general federal venue statute. *See, e.g., Hodgson v. Gilmartin,* 2006 WL 2707397 (E.D. Pa. Sept. 18, 2006). A number of federal statutes create federal claims and, further, provide specific venue statutes for those claims. The problem is that these statutes differ from the general federal venue statute, and some of them replace its rules about proper venue—venue is proper *only* under the specific statute—while others supplement it, allowing venue to be proper under the general statute *or* the specific one. Because the scope of those statutes is claim-specific, we'll not focus on them. They can create problems that courts address by the doctrine of "pendent venue," a point will touch on next and also later on. *See* Chapter 23.

## 3. There Must be Proper Venue, or Pendent Venue, Over Each Claim of a Plaintiff

Venue is determined on a claim-by-claim basis for each claim by a plaintiff. Consequently, venue must be proper over each claim by a plaintiff against each defendant. *New York v. Cyco.net, Inc.,* 383 F. Supp. 2d 526, 543 (S.D.N.Y. 2005); *Salpoglou v. Schlomo Widder,* 899 F. Supp. 835, 839 (D. Mass. 1995). The fact that venue must be proper over each claim of a plaintiff against a defendant is particularly important where one claim is covered by a specific venue statute, and another is covered by the general federal venue statute. For example, in *Dobrick-Peirce v. Open Options, Inc.,* 2006 WL 2089960 (W.D. Pa. 2006), in addition to two state law claims, the plaintiff included a federal discrimination claim under Title VII. The court held that venue was proper over the Title VII claim because Congress included in Title VII a specific venue provision that was quite broad. Nonetheless it recognized that the "fact that venue is proper for the Title VII claim does not necessarily mean that venue is proper for the two tort claims," which were instead covered by the general federal venue statute, and, more specifically, Section 1391(b). It then held that venue was *improper* as to the two state law claims. Similarly, in *PKWare v. Meade,* 79 F. Supp. 2d 1007 (E.D. Wis. 2000), the court refused to allow pendent venue where venue was based, not on the general federal statute, but on a venue statute specific to patent infringement claims, 28 U.S.C. § 1400(b).

We'll see below how the *Dobrick-Peirce* court resolved this issue: it transferred the entire case to a district where all of the claims could have been brought. Sometimes, however, courts invoke a doctrine known as "pendent venue" to accept venue over a any claim that is closely related to a claim over which venue is proper. *See* Chapter 23.

---

## Checkpoints

- Can you identify the way in which venue is determined where the complaint contains a federal claim? Contains only state law claims?
- Do you know how to identify the "residence" of each type of party?
- If venue is improper, what do you do? *See* Chapter 32.

# Chapter 10

# Removal: What Can the Defendant do if the Plaintiff Filed in State Court a Claim over Which a Federal Court Would Have Subject Matter Jurisdiction?

---

### Removal Roadmap

This chapter explains when it is proper for a defendant to move to remove to federal court a case (not a claim, but the entire case) filed by a plaintiff in state court.

This chapter explains the procedure for a defendant to remove a case from state to federal court.

This chapter also explains when and how a party can move the federal court to "remand" some claims in, or the entire removed case, back to state court.

---

Nothing requires a plaintiff with a claim that exceeds $75,000 against a diverse defendant to file that claim in federal court. Likewise, federal subject matter jurisdiction statutes usually give state and federal courts "concurrent" subject matter jurisdiction over federal claims, allowing a federal claim to be filed in either state or federal court. Further, sometimes plaintiffs mistakenly file in state court claims over which the federal courts have exclusive subject matter jurisdiction (though such claims are rare).

Various circumstances could give a plaintiff an advantage in state court. For example, sometimes it takes less time to get to trial in state court, or sometimes state court judges, or the particular state court judge to whom the case was assigned, are perceived as more "plaintiff friendly." The number of jurors may vary between state and federal court, and the pool from which jurors are selected may also be different. These and other factors can have a substantial impact on the perceived value of a case.

In short, choice of forum can matter greatly. That is why plaintiffs sometimes file claims in state court that could be filed in federal court. If the requirements for removal are present, the defendant can remove a case state to federal court. Any time a case is filed in state court, defense counsel must determine if the case is removable, and, if so, whether as a strategic matter the case should be removed to federal court in order to deny the plaintiff's choice of a state court forum. A defendant who removes a case from state to federal court may severely reduce the settlement value, or likely verdict, in a particular dispute.

One preliminary note: a plaintiff who files in state court may not remove the case even after the defendant asserts a counterclaim in state court that is removable. *Shamrock Oil & Gas Corp. v. Sheets,* 313 U.S. 100 (1941). The plaintiff chose state court, and removal is determined from the complaint, not the answer and counterclaims.

## A. The Foundations of Removal

Suppose a plaintiff serves on a defendant process for a suit that the plaintiff has filed in state court, and the complaint includes a federal claim or a state claim between citizens of different states for more than $75,000. Under those circumstances, the defendant may be able to remove the case from state to federal court. The defendant must act quickly (generally within 30 days of receipt of a paper that shows the case is removable, and, where diversity is the basis of removal, there is a one-year bar that also applies) by obtaining consent from all properly joined defendants to file a notice of removal with the federal court for the district and division where the state suit is filed, and also to notify the state court of the removal of the case.

A plaintiff who believes that a case has been improperly removed to federal court must file a motion to remand the case back to state court. Unless the defect is subject matter jurisdiction, the plaintiff must file the motion to remand within 30 days of removal. In some instances, only part of the case—that is, some of the claims—will be remanded to state court.

## B. When Is a Case Removable?

A case may become removable at almost any time, but once it becomes so, it is removable only for a limited time. There are two time limitations.

First, regardless of whether the case is removable because of the presence of a diversity-type or federal question claim, the notice of removal must be filed (a) within 30 days of service of the initial pleading if it shows that a claim was removable; or (b) if not, within 30 days of receipt of a paper showing it is removable. 28 U.S.C. § 1446(b)(1) & (3). As recently amended, if there is more than one defendant, each defendant gets 30 days from its receipt of a paper to remove, but consent from other defendants is required, as discussed more fully below. For now, just note that a defendant must look at the first pleading to see if there's a removable claim; if not, it must monitor to see if it receives a paper that makes the case removable. Either circumstance gives the defendant only 30 days to remove the case from state to federal court.

Second, there is a one-year bar for removal based on diversity. If more than one year has passed from filing the suit then, absent bad faith by the plaintiff, a case cannot be removed unless a federal question has been added. So, for example, if 13 months after filing suit, the plaintiff dismisses a non-diverse defendant, or makes it clear that the amount in controversy in a case with diversity exceeds $75,000, the case cannot be removed or, if removed, should be remanded on motion of the plaintiff.

# C. What Claims and Circumstances Make a Case Removable?

Removability is determined by the pleadings at the time of removal. *Pullman Co. v. Jenkins,* 305 U.S. 534, 537 (1939). Thus, often removal turns on the allegations in the plaintiff's state court pleading (which can be called a complaint, a petition, or some other name, but which essentially serves the same purpose as does a complaint filed in federal court). A case is removable if either:

> the plaintiff's state court pleading asserts a claim that arises under federal law (and so presents federal question subject matter jurisdiction) *or* the plaintiff's state court pleading asserts a claim (a) between citizens of different states but excluding the citizenship of any "fraudulently joined" or fictitiously named defendants; (b) involves an amount in controversy greater than $75,000; *and* (c) no properly joined and served defendant is a citizen of the forum state (again, excluding the citizenship of any "fraudulently joined" or fictitious defendants).

The complaint must contain at least one claim that either arises under federal law or meets the narrower diversity-like requirements in the removal statute.

If there is one such claim, then the case may be removed even if there are other claims that do not meet either requirement. We'll discuss below what happens when a case is removed but has a claim (or claims) that do not meet the requirements for removal. But *cases* are removed, not claims.

Finally, removal must be considered in light of the policy against removal: "In light of the congressional intent to restrict federal court jurisdiction, as well as the importance of preserving the independence of state governments, federal courts construe the removal statute narrowly, resolving any doubts against removability." *Fed. Ins. Co. v. Tyoco Int'l, Ltd.*, 2006 WL 728400 (S.D.N.Y. 2006). In addition, a defendant seeking to remove a case bears the burden to establish that removal is proper. *Boyer v. Snap-on Tools Corp.*, 913 F.2d 108, 111 (3rd Cir. 1990). Likewise, all disputed questions of law are resolved against the party seeking removal. *Burden v. Gen'l Dynamics Corp.*, 60 F.3d 212, 217 (5th Cir. 1995).

This chapter addresses only the general removal statutes. Other statutes may allow certain defendants, such as governmental entities, to remove under different circumstances.

# 1. Removal on the Basis of Federal Question

## a. Single Federal Claim in a State Court Complaint

As explained in Chapter 4, federal question subject matter jurisdiction largely turns on the well-pleaded complaint rule, and, most of the time, exists only if the plaintiff has pled a claim for relief created by a federal statute. Those same principles apply to determine whether a complaint filed in state court states a claim that arises under federal law. Here, this means that a defendant generally cannot remove the case unless the federal claim is in the complaint; there are limited exceptions such as preemption of state law. However, those exceptions are quite narrow.

## b. Federal Claim Joined with Non-Removable State Claim in the State Court Complaint

If a state court pleading includes a federal question claim and a state law claim "not within the original or supplemental jurisdiction of the district court or a claim that has been nonremovable by statute," then the entire case can be removed "if the action would be removable without the inclusion of" such claim(s). 28 U.S.C. § 1441(c)(1). Thus, if there is a removable federal claim (in rare instances, a federal statute makes federal claims filed in state court non-removable), then the entire case is removable even if there are state law claims and no diversity, or state law claims that are outside 28 U.S.C. § 1367's grant of supplemental jurisdiction. Supplemental jurisdiction exists over state law claims by a plaintiff if the state law claim is part of the same "case or controversy" as the federal claim. Usually courts will say that the federal claim is "separate and independent" from the state claims, even though the statute no longer uses that language.

Once the case is removed, then the district court must sever and remand those claims that are not (a) federal claims; (b) diverse claims; or (c) within the scope of Section 1367. The net effect? State law claims that arise out of the same case or controversy as the federal claim will remain in federal court, as will any state law claims that were removable based upon their own independent jurisdictional basis for removal.

## 2. Removal on the Existence of a Removal-Type Diversity Claim

Congress chose not to allow cases to be removed even if there is complete diversity and the amount in controversy is met. Instead, those requirements must be met *and* no defendant properly joined and served can be a citizen of the state in which the suit was filed. 28 U.S.C. § 1441(b)(2). This is called the "no forum defendant rule." Thus, it is clear that a case may be removed if there is complete diversity, the amount in controversy for the claim exceeds $75,000, *and* no defendant is a citizen of the forum state. Because most states do not require pleading of citizenship, some research may be required to determine whether a particular case meets these criteria.

But there are issues beyond the simple fact patterns. For example, it may be that a state court pleading which, on its face, is not removable may in fact be removable. This can happen in at least two ways.

First, removal maybe available even if the amount of damages sought by the plaintiff is at or below $75,000. Suppose, for example, the plaintiff does not plead an amount in controversy (it is not required by all state court systems) or pleads an amount below $75,000. But, the facts are that in reality much more than $75,000 is in controversy. That case may be removable; otherwise, a plaintiff could have a million dollar claim but plead an amount below $75,000 and avoid removal.

Second, a claim can be removable even without complete diversity, or even if a named defendant is a citizen of the forum state. Suppose the plaintiff joins more than one defendant, or joins one or more additional parties as plaintiffs, and the additional party destroys complete diversity or is a forum-defendant. But, in reality either (a) it does not appear that the non-diverse plaintiff has any claim, or (b) the claim against the non-diverse defendant is frivolous. If removal was not possible simply because the plaintiff joined a non-diverse party, or a forum defendant, who had no real claim or against whom no real relief would be sought, then plaintiffs could easily make a case non-removable for those reasons.

To avoid gamesmanship, sometimes the defendant can remove cases where either the amount in controversy does not seem satisfied or there is a lack of complete diversity or a forum-state defendant is joined to the suit. For these reasons, determining removability requires additional steps than does analysis under the diversity statute. First, not every party's citizenship necessarily counts. Specifically, if a party has been "fraudulently joined" their citizenship does not count. Second, the amount in controversy must be examined in a different manner than under the diversity statute. We turn to these two steps next.

### a. Citizenship of Fraudulently Joined Defendants Is Ignored

In addition to ignoring "John Doe" defendants, 28 U.S.C. § 1441(b)(2), the citizenship of defendants who are not "properly joined and served" is ignored. This is called the "fraudulent joinder" doctrine. It is extremely difficult to establish that a defendant's citizenship should be ignored because that defendant has been "fraudulently" (or "improperly") joined.

This question — of whether the federal court should ignore the citizenship of a defendant — typically gets litigated when a plaintiff moves to remand a case to state court that the defendant previously removed. (See below.) However, the defendant must examine these questions before seeking to remove it: if the case is removable because of fraudulent joinder, for example, the defendant must act promptly. Consequently, defense counsel typically must look at the complaint when filed and, even if it does not show on its face that the case is removable, must examine at that time whether there's a reasonable basis for arguing that the citizenship of non-diverse parties or a forum-state defendant should not count. If so, the defendant can remove the case.

If the defendant removes the case, the question of whether the citizenship of non-diverse or forum-state defendant should "count" will be determined by the court, — but only if the plaintiff moves to remand the case back to state court. Motions to remand are discussed below. To assess the citizenship of parties for the purposes of removal, a district court is permitted to look beyond the pleadings and examine affidavits and other forms of evidence typically offered in summary judgment motions, including deposition transcripts. *Morris v. Princess Cruises, Inc.*, 236 F.3d 1061, 1067 (9th Cir. 2001).

There are two common types of fraudulent joinder, and a third type that is less common. The first one is somewhat easy to detect and prove, and the other two much more difficult on both counts. The easy one first.

### i. Fraudulent Jurisdictional Allegations

Suppose a plaintiff alleges that a defendant shares citizenship with the same state as the defendant, but it's simply incorrect or false: in fact, the parties are diverse. Or the plaintiff alleges that one defendant is a citizen of the forum, thus precluding removal. Under these circumstances, whether the plaintiff made the allegations through fraud or simple mistake, the false or incorrect allegations do not control. *Triggs v. John Crump Toyota, Inc.,* 154 F.3d 1284, 1287 (11th Cir. 1998). In the notice of removal (*see* below), the defendant would by affidavit establish the true facts.

### ii. No Possibility of Recovery

Suppose the plaintiff has joined a defendant who is a citizen of the same state as the plaintiff or a forum-state resident, but against whom the plaintiff has no possibility of recovery. If the citizenship of such defendants counted, then a plaintiff could always destroy diversity jurisdiction by naming a non-diverse defendant, *albeit* one from whom the plaintiff will never actually recover a dime. A plaintiff's lawyer could sue his secretary if she was a forum resident with the understanding he'd never actually pursue the claim, and by doing so defeat removal. Plaintiffs' lawyers thought of this tactic, and the courts reacted to the cries of "foul" from defense counsel, eventually creating the doctrine of "fraudulent joinder." Under that doctrine, the citizenship of a defendant does not count if the removing party establishes that it has been "fraudulently joined" to the suit.

To succeed in having the court ignore the citizenship of a defendant under the doctrine of fraudulent joinder, the party seeking to must establish by clear and convincing evidence that the plaintiff has no reasonable possibility of recovering against that defendant. *In re Rezulin Prods. Liab. Litig,* 133 F. Supp. 2d 272, 280 n.4 (S.D.N.Y. 2001). Although courts sometimes state that the removing party must show there is "no possibility" of recovering, obviously it cannot be taken that literally, since there's always a possibility: it turns on a reasonable basis. *Id.* In addition, even though the doctrine refers to fraudulent intent, the intent of the plaintiff is irrelevant: what counts is whether there is no reasonable possibility of recovering. *Id.* This is an extremely high standard. Whether a plaintiff has a possibility of recovery turns on state substantive law — whether there is no possibility the removal-defeating defendant could be liable to the plaintiff for the claim pled.

The same circumstance can arise if the plaintiff joins another plaintiff, who destroys diversity, but who clearly has no possibility of recovering against the defendant. These cases are rarer, but as a general rule the courts use the same approach for determining whether a diversity-defeating plaintiff has been fraudulently joined as they do with diversity-defeating defendants.

### iii. Fraudulent Procedural "Misjoinder"

Suppose a plaintiff files a complaint in state court that includes a claim against a defendant for breach of contract, and expressly states that it seeks recovery for less than $75,000. On its face that claim is not removable. In addition, however, the plaintiff joins with that non-removable claim an unrelated claim against an unrelated defendant, and that claim presents a federal question, or is a claim that meets the diversity requirements. Clearly, that claim is removable.

Suppose the claim against the non-diverse defendant is one that the plaintiff intends to pursue and has a reasonable shot of winning, and so it's not fraudulently joined in the sense we just discussed, but the plaintiff has pled in one state court pleading two completely unrelated claims. Is there anything the diverse defendant can do, or does the citizenship of the other defendant count since there is no fraudulent joinder. Notice that this claim cannot be removed under Section 1441(c) because two *parties* are joined, not two *claims*.

Some courts recognize a doctrine called "fraudulent misjoinder" or "procedural misjoinder" that applies where the plaintiff names two or more defendants in one suit but the claims against them do not arise out of the same basic set of facts. The doctrine is aimed at efforts "to defeat removal by joining together claims against two or more defendants where the presence of one would defeat removal and where in reality there is no sufficient factual nexus among the claims to satisfy the permissive joinder standard." *Conk v. Richard & O'Neil LLP,* 77 F. Supp. 2d 956, 971 (S.D. Ind. 1999).

But, the fact that removability is strictly construed means that it is *not* enough that the claims against two defendants are unrelated: instead, it must be an "egregious" a case of joining together unrelated claims. How far apart the claims must be from each other to be "egregious" is not clear. *A. Kraus & Son v. Benjamin Moore & Co.,* 2006 WL 1582193 (E.D.N.Y. 2006) (collecting cases that conclude there's no clear definition of what is, and is not, egregious enough). Some courts hold that there must be bad faith by the plaintiff in joining the parties, not just "unrelated" claims. *Coleman v. Conseco, Inc.,* 238 F. Supp. 2d 804, 817 (S.D. Miss. 2004). Further, some courts have reasoned that the fraudulent misjoinder should allow removal, if at all, only to federal question claims joined with a separate and independent state claim against a non-diverse defendant. *See Bird v. Carteret Mortgage Corp.,* 2007 WL 43551 (S.D. Ohio 2007). Finally, other courts have rejected "fraudulent misjoinder" as not a proper basis to ignore the citizenship of non-diverse defendants. *E.g., Rutherford v. Merck & Co.,* 428 F. Supp. 2d 842, 851 (S.D. Ill. 2006) ("whether viable state-law claims have been misjoined—even egregiously—is a matter to be resolved by a state court.").

In sum, it is unclear when fraudulent misjoinder applies, if at all. If it does, it may only permit federal courts to ignore the citizenship of non-diverse parties where a federal question claim is egregiously joined with an unrelated state claim against a removal-defeating defendant, or it may permit those citizenships to be ignored in all cases of egregious joinder.

### iv.  The Trump Card: The No Forum-Defendant Rule

Since fraudulent joinder doctrines permit a court to ignore the citizenship of some parties, in that respect removal is broader than diversity subject matter jurisdiction. However, in one key respect removability is much narrower than diversity subject matter jurisdiction: removal is improper if any party properly joined and served as a defendant is a citizen of the state where the suit is filed. 28 U.S.C. § 1441(b)(2). Thus, if suit is filed in Texas state court, and a non-fraudulently joined defendant is a citizen of Texas, the case cannot be removed, even if the plaintiff is from Illinois.

Why? The short answer: the statute says so. *See id.* (A claim that does not arise under federal law "may not be removed if any of the parties in interest properly joined and served as defendants is a citizen of the State in which such action is brought.")

Why does the statute say so? Remember that one reason for diversity jurisdiction is that states were afraid that their citizens would be treated unfairly if sued in the state courts of another state, so a federal forum was viewed as neutral. Where the defendant is a citizen of the state, this concern does not arise, and Congress reasoned that if *one* defendant was a citizen of the forum state, that would reduce any bias such that the case should not be removed given the impact on federal dockets and the intrusion by federal courts into deciding matters of state law that occurs when a case is removed. Again, though, the citizenship of a fraudulently joined defendant does not count. *See* above. A forum-defendant who is fraudulently joined does not prevent removal.

Finally, courts split on whether the forum-defendant rule is procedural, not jurisdictional. If it is merely a procedural requirement that no forum-defendant be present, then the failure to raise the issue as a basis to remand can waive it. If it is jurisdictional, then a party cannot waive it. In those jurisdictions where the presence of a forum defendant is merely procedural, a plaintiff must move to remand a case within 30 days, or the objection is waived.

## b. Determining the Amount in Controversy

Various issues can arise concerning the amount in controversy requirement. The general rule is that the "sum demanded in good faith in the initial pleading shall be deemed to be the amount in controversy . . . ." 28 U.S.C. § 1446(c)(2). So, if the plaintiff pleads in the state court pleading that the amount in controversy exceeds $75,000, then obviously the amount in controversy requirement is satisfied. *S.W.S. Erectors, Inc. v. Infax, Inc.*, 72 F.3d 489, 492 (5th Cir. 1996).

What, however, if the plaintiff pleads no specific amount (not all court systems require pleading an amount in controversy), or expressly pleads that the amount in controversy is less than $75,000? What if the plaintiff seeks injunctive relief, and not money damages? We'll now explore those issues.

### i. Plaintiff Pleads no Specific Amount

If the plaintiff has pled no specific amount in its state court pleading, the defendant in the notice of removal must aver that it exceeds $75,000 and the if that is contested, the defendant must establish by preponderant evidence that the amount in controversy exceeds $75,000. 28 U.S.C. § 1441(c)(2). How can the defendant do this? Among other things the defendant may rely on: (i) an estimate of the potential damages from the allegations in the complaint; (ii) other documentation to provide a basis for determining the amount in controversy, such as interrogatories obtained in the state court before removal, affidavits, or other evidence submitted in federal court afterward; and (iii) the plaintiff's proposed settlement amount if it appears to reflect a reasonable estimate of the plaintiff's claim, because the plaintiff's own estimation of its claim is a proper means of supporting the allegations in the notice of removal. *Aguayo v. AMCO Ins. Co.*, 59 F. Supp. 3d 1225, 1243 (D.N.M. 2014).

### ii. Plaintiff Pleads Less Than $75,000 in its State Court Pleading

If the plaintiff expressly pleads in state court pleading an amount less than $75,000 is in controversy, the defendant can still remove the case if the state court from which removal is taken permits plaintiffs to recover more than the amount pled and the defendant (through procedures similar to those above) establishes that more than $75,000 is in play in the suit. 28 U.S.C. 1441(c)(2)(A)(ii).

The plaintiff can move to remand the case. The plaintiff can still show in its motion to remand that the defendant has not carried its burden. *De Aguilar v. Boeing Co.*, 47 F.3d 1404, 1412 (5th Cir. 1995). The plaintiff can do this either by (1) showing that state law that prohibits recovering more than $75,000 or (2) filing a binding stipulation or agreement with their state court complaint that precludes recovery in excess of $75,000. *See id.* If you're following this, you realize that the plaintiff in seeking to remand the case back to state court will be arguing that it's entitled to recover *less* than the defendant says it is. "We recognize that requiring a defendant to show to a legal certainty that the amount in controversy exceeds the statutory minimum may lead to somewhat bizarre situations." *Samuel-Bassett v. KIA Motors Am., Inc.,* 357 F.3d 392, 398 (3rd Cir. 2004).

### iii. Plaintiff Seeks Injunctive Relief

What if the plaintiff only seeks injunctive relief? The defendant may state the value in its notice of removal, and the question becomes whether the cost, benefit, or either or both of those of complying with the injunction exceeds $75,000. *See* 28 U.S.C. § 1441(2)(c)(A)(i). For example, the Tenth Circuit follows what is called the "either viewpoint rule" which considers either the value to the plaintiff or the cost to defendant of relief as the measure of the amount in controversy. *Justice v. Atchison, Topeka and Santa Fe Ry. Co.,* 927 F.2d 503, 505 (10th Cir. 1991). Some courts rely only on the cost to the defendant, and others the value of the injunction to the plaintiff. *See id.*

# D. Deadlines, Waiver by Conduct, and Procedure for Removal

## 1. Deadlines

As noted above, there are two deadlines: a 30-day deadline runs from the date that the case becomes removable; the other, a one-year deadline, from the date the case is filed in state court.

### a. The 30-Day Deadline

As a general rule, a defendant has 30 days from the day it receives a paper showing a case is removable. That paper may be the first pleading served by the plaintiff, or something received later. So, if the initial complaint is removable, the defendants have 30 days within receipt of it "through service or otherwise" to act. 28 U.S.C. § 1446(b)(1). If the initial complaint was not removable, but the defendant later "receives" a "paper" showing the case is removable (*e.g.,* an answer to an interrogatory or an amended complaint), the 30 days runs from "receipt by the defendant, through service or otherwise" of that paper. 28 U.S.C. § 1446(c)(3). But if the initial pleading was removable, once thirty days have passed, the case is not removable even if some "new" basis for removal arises in a "paper."

### i. Initial Pleading: What Is "Receipt Through Service or Otherwise"?

For a while, it was unclear what constituted receipt of a state court pleading "through service or otherwise." (Chapter 25 discusses what service is, but with respect to a complaint, service essentially means some sort of formal and memorialized delivery of summons and the complaint.) Suppose, for example, that the plaintiff did not formally serve the pleading, but simply faxed it to the defendant. For a long time, it was unclear whether receipt, without formal service, counted. The Supreme Court answered that question in 1999: the 30-day deadline for removal begins once a defendant is formally served with the summons and complaint, and not a "mere receipt of the complaint unattended by any formal service." *Murphy Bros., Inc. v. Michetti Pipe Stringing, Inc.*, 526 U.S. 344, 348 (1999). In addition, the last clause of the first paragraph of § 1446(b) makes it clear that, if the state does not require that the complaint be served with the summons, then the 30 days runs from the date the summons or complaint was served, whichever is shorter. *Id.* Thus, if state law requires formal service of the summons and complaint, the 30-day deadline begins to run only when that occurs; otherwise it runs from service of summons or the complaint.

As we saw, removability turns on whether there is a federal question or a diversity claim without a forum-defendant. A state court complaint may state a federal claim, or one between citizens of different states without a forum state defendant and for an amount exceeding $75,000. In either case, the 30-day window begins to run. Similarly, the state court pleading may show that the non-diverse or forum-defendant has been fraudulently joined. Again, the 30-day deadline begins to run at that point if the defendant learns that the plaintiff has no reasonable possibility of recovering against a defendant whose joinder defeats removability.

A common problem is how to determine when the 30 days begins to run when there are multiple defendants: suppose one defendant is served with the complaint on January 1; a second on January 29; and the third on February 14. Does each defendant get 30 days, or does the 30 days begin to run when the first defendant is served, in which case here the second-served defendant has a day to act, and the third defendant has no opportunity to remove?

The courts had split but Congress clarified the issue in 2011. Under § 1446(b)(2(B), each defendant has 30 days from receipt or service of the initial complaint to file a notice of removal, and if defendants are served at different times, "and a later-served defendant files a notice of removal, any earlier-served defendant may consent to the removal even though that earlier-served defendant" had not tried to remove the case. 28 U.S.C. § 1446(b)(2)(B) & (C).

## ii. Subsequent Papers: "Receipt"

Even if the initial pleading is not removable, subsequent papers received by the defendant may make the case removable. A "paper" can be a lot of things, some of which we have not studied yet, and the meaning of which you won't fully grasp until later. This is a non-exclusive list of post-filing papers that have been held to satisfy the "paper" requirement and thus render the case removable within 30 days of receipt:

- An amended pleading served by the plaintiff that makes the case removable by dismissing claims against the non-diverse defendants or adding a federal question;
- A demand letter from the plaintiff that shows that the amount in controversy exceeds $75,000;
- An interrogatory answer from the plaintiff revealing that the case is removable (because, for example, it reveals that citizenship is diverse or the amount exceeds $75,000); or
- The taking of a deposition (as opposed to receiving the transcript of it) revealing the case is removable.

*See generally, Norris v. Wal-Mart Stores, Inc.,* 2006 WL 1476045 (W.D. La. 2006). Put simply, "paper" is generally broadly construed.

First, a defendant cannot rely on a paper it received prior to filing suit to argue that a case that was not initially removable became removable later. In general, papers received prior to filing of the suit do not count in determining whether a case subsequent to filing became removable. At most, pre-filing papers may show that the amount in controversy does, in fact, exceed $75,000, but a defendant cannot use a paper that it received before suit was filed to show that the suit has "later" become removable.

In that regard, remember that if the case was removable when the initial pleading was received, the defendant had 30 days to remove it. This principle simply prevents a defendant from arguing that information it had when it received the initial pleading only counted later.

Second, a paper that results from an involuntary act of the plaintiff does not count. What's that mean? If a plaintiff serves an amended state court complaint that adds a federal question, or voluntarily dismisses all claims against the non-diverse defendant, or amends its state court complaint to specifically state the amount in controversy exceeds $75,000, then the plaintiff acted voluntarily. Those acts count, and when the defendant receives the paper showing them, then the 30-day period is triggered.

In contrast, though, suppose the non-diverse defendant moves to dismiss the claim against it, or moves for summary judgment on the claim against it, and the district court grants that motion, leaving only diverse parties in the suit. Can they remove? No, because the action was not a voluntary one by the plaintiff. The voluntary-involuntary principle holds that only a voluntary action by the plaintiff, such as the voluntary dismissal of a diversity-defeating defendant, can make a case removable. *See Great N. Ry. Co. v. Alexander*, 246 U.S. 276, 281 (1918) ("[C]onversion [of an action from nonremovable to removable in diversity] can only be accomplished . . . where the case is not removable because of joinder of defendants, by the voluntary dismissal or nonsuit by [a plaintiff] of a party or of parties defendant."); *Poulos v. Naas Foods, Inc.*, 959 F.2d 69, 71–72 (7th Cir.1992) ( "[C]ases with non-diverse parties [do] not become removable just because a non-diverse defendant [is] dismissed from the case. . . . Instead, . . . such suits [are] removable only if the plaintiff voluntarily dismissed a non-diverse defendant.").

There are two policies served by the voluntary-involuntary rule, one practical, and one quite fundamental.

As a practical matter, the fact that the non-diverse defendant manages to get the claim against it dismissed does not mean state court action against that defendant is over. For example, the plaintiff could appeal the state court's dismissal of the non-diverse defendant. "An involuntary dismissal of [a] non-diverse party in a state court action should not lead to removal of the action to federal court if the complete diversity just created by the dismissal might be destroyed by an appeal and reversal of the state court's decision." *Atlanta Shipping Corp. v. International Modular Hous., Inc.*, 547 F. Supp. 1356, 1360 n. 8 (S.D.N.Y.1982). But if the plaintiff voluntarily dismisses the claims, it cannot appeal them, and so finality does occur. *Burke v. General Motors Corp.*, 492 F. Supp. 506, 508 (N.D. Ala.1980) (the voluntary-involuntary rule "is premised upon the assumption that voluntary actions of the plaintiff which remove a party from a case are final" and thus not subject to reversal on appeal so as to divest a federal court of jurisdiction on removal); *Ennis v. Queen Ins. Co. of Am.*, 364 F. Supp. 964, 966 (W.D. Tenn. 1973) ("The reason for the 'voluntary dismissal' rule is based on judicial efficiency. The voluntary dismissal of a resident defendant is not appealable. Such a dismissal finally determines who are the parties to the action in a state court proceeding immediately prior to removal to a federal court. The involuntary dismissal of a resident defendant, however, is appealable. Thus, an involuntary dismissal would involve the possibility of duplication and expense of an appeal being heard in state courts and the same proceeding being before the federal courts at the same time, if such a case could be removed to the federal courts.").

The rule that only voluntary acts of the plaintiff count also has a broad, fundamental purpose: it protects the plaintiff's right to choose the forum. The more fundamental purpose of the voluntary-involuntary rule is "to protect plaintiff's choice of forum as long as [the plaintiff] wants it protected." *Ford Motor Credit Co. v. Aaron-Lincoln Mercury*, 563 F. Supp. 1108, 1117 (N.D. Ill. 1983). *See also Ushman v. Sterling Drug, Inc.*, 681 F. Supp. 1331, 1337 (C.D. Ill.1988) ("the purpose of the rule is to protect plaintiff's forum"); *Jenkins v. National Union Fire Ins. Co. of Pa.*, 650 F. Supp. 609, 614 (N.D. Ga. 1986) ("What emerges from an examination of the Supreme Court cases on the voluntary-involuntary rule is the conclusion that the rule is not based upon an appealability/finality rationale but upon a policy of favoring the plaintiff's power to determine the removability of his case.").

### b. One-Year Deadline for Diversity-Type Removal

The second deadline only applies to diversity-type removal. A case that has been on file for more than one year cannot be removed, even if the defendant receives a paper showing the case has become removable, if the basis for federal subject matter jurisdiction after removal is diversity. Under Section 1446(c), unless the plaintiff has acted in bad faith to prevent removal, a case may not be removed on the basis of diversity jurisdiction "more than 1 year after commencement of the action . . . ."

What is bad faith? The statute specifically states that it includes the plaintiff deliberately failing to disclose the actual amount in controversy to prevent removal. 28 U.S.C. 1446(c)(3)(B). Beyond that, the law in this area is just developing. Courts have stated, however, that bad faith can be ferreted out by this two-part test:

> First, the Court inquires whether the plaintiff actively litigated against the removal spoiler in state court: asserting valid claims, taking discovery, negotiating settlement, seeking default judgments if the defendant does not answer the complaint, et cetera. Failure to actively litigate against the removal spoiler will be deemed bad faith; actively litigating against the removal spoiler, however, will create a rebuttable presumption of good faith. Second, the defendant may attempt to rebut this presumption with evidence already in the defendant's possession that establishes that, despite the plaintiff's active litigation

against the removal spoiler, the plaintiff would not have named the removal spoiler or would have dropped the spoiler before the one-year mark but for the plaintiff's desire to keep the case in state court. The defendant may introduce direct evidence of the plaintiff's bad faith at this stage—e.g., electronic mail transmissions in which the plaintiff states that he or she is only keeping the removal spoiler joined to defeat removal—but will not receive discovery or an evidentiary hearing in federal court to obtain such evidence.

*Aguayo v. AMCO Ins. Co.*, 59 F. Supp. 3d 1225, 1262-63 (D.N.M. 2014).

Absent bad faith, however, removal based upon diversity becomes barred one year after commencement of the action, even if the paper initially showing the case is removable on that grounds comes on the 366th day of the case. Again, the one-year bar does not apply to removal based upon federal question; but the 30-day deadline does.

## 2. Waiver by Conduct of Right to Remove

In addition to the 30-day and one-year deadlines, a defendant can waive its right to remove a case by defending the merits of the suit in state court. To determine whether a defendant has by conduct waived the right to remove, the court must examine "whether the actions taken by the defendant in state court were for the purpose of preserving the status quo," or whether they manifested "an intent to litigate on the merits in state court." *Haynes v. Gasoline Marketers, Inc.*, 184 F.R.D. 414, 416 (M.D. Ala. 1999); *see Beighley v. Federal Deposit Ins. Corp.*, 868 F.2d 776, 782 (5th Cir.1989) (The "right of removal is not lost by action in the state court short of proceeding to an adjudication on the merits."). Defendants' acts must express "clear and unequivocal intent to waive the right to remove." *Id.* Waiver has been found, for example, in these circumstances:

- The defendant had agreed in the contract in suit that any dispute would be filed in state court;
- The defendant filed a motion to dismiss in state court *and* sought a hearing on the motion;
- The defendant moved in the state court to transfer venue;
- The defendant filed a motion for summary judgment; or
- The defendant files permissive counterclaims or other claims.

*See, e.g., Johnson v. Heublein Inc.*, 227 F.3d 236 (5th Cir. 2000) (motion to dismiss and summary judgment filed in state court); *Moore v. Permanente Med.*

*Group, Inc.,* 981 F.2d 443 (9th Cir. 1992) (state court motion to transfer venue); *Global Satellite Commun. Co. v. Starmill U.K. Ltd.,* 378 F.3d 1269 (11th Cir. 2004) (contractual forum selection clause).

On the other hand, courts have found no waiver where the defendant only filed an answer with affirmative defenses. *See Miami Herald Pub. Co. Div. of Knight-Ridder Newspapers, Inc. v. Ferre,* 606 F. Supp. 122 (S.D.Fla.1984) (filing answer and affirmative defenses not clear intent to waive removal rights); *Rose v. Giamatti,* 721 F. Supp. 906, 922 (S.D. Ohio 1989) (no clear intent to litigate in state court where defendant sought discovery for an appeal of a temporary restraining order).

Obviously, a defendant who wants to remove should engage in as little conduct in state court as is possible before filing the notice of removal.

## 3. Procedure for Removal

### a. Consent of All Properly Joined and Served Defendants

If there is more than one defendant, then Section 1446(b)(2)(A) generally requires that each defendant consents or join in the notice of removal. If one properly served and joined defendant refuses to consent, then removal is improper and, if the plaintiff seeks remand, the case should be remanded, *unless* the defendant who failed to join or consent falls within an exception. *Doe v. Kerwood,* 969 F.2d 165, 167 (5th Cir. 1992).

The exceptions are narrow, however. Specifically, consent is not required from a defendant who: (1) was fraudulently joined; (2) is a "Doe" or nominal defendant; or (3) was not served at the time of the filing of the notice of removal. *See id.* In addition, statutes give certain defendants or foreign sovereigns the right to remove even if other defendants do not consent.

Consent may be indicated either by having counsel for each defendant sign the notice of removal (discussed next) or by filing with the federal district court a separate document evidencing the defendant's consent to removal. Each defendant must comply with the 30-day deadline, or removal is untimely.

For example, in *McCurtain County Production Corp. v. Cowett,* 482 F. Supp. 809 (E.D. Okla. 1978), several defendants were sued in state court, but only defendant Deere signed the notice of removal. The plaintiff moved to remand, but Deere argued that consent of the other defendants was not necessary because the court lacked personal jurisdiction over them. The district court remanded to state court because none of the exceptions applied. It also emphasized that a party who removes a case to federal court does not waive any objection, including one that the court lacks personal jurisdiction. *Id.*

Significantly, nothing prevents a defendant from removing *before* anyone is served. If a defendant files notice of removal before anyone is served, can the case be removed even if there is a forum defendant (obviously, if there is no diversity or federal question, the case has to be dismissed). The courts split on this question. Perhaps a majority of courts hold that the statute permits removal as long as no in-state defendant has been served. In that regard, many courts have held that a *non-forum* defendant can remove before service of any forum-defendant. *See, e.g., Regal Stone Ltd. v. Longs Drug Stores California LLC,* 881 F. Supp. 2d 1123 (N.D. Cal. 2012). That approach abrogates the "no forum defendant" rule.

### b. Required Filings

The defendant must file with the federal district court for the district in which the state court sits a notice of removal with certain attachments., and serve it on all parties. The notice of removal must be "signed pursuant to Rule 11 of the Federal Rules of Civil Procedure" and must contain "a short and plain statement of the grounds for removal." 28 U.S.C. § 1446(a). The notice must also attach as exhibits any "process, pleadings, and orders served upon such defendant or defendants" while the matter was pending in state court. *Id.* The removing party's lawyer must also file the notice, without attachments, in state court to notify the state court that it has lost jurisdiction over the case. The receipt by the state court of the notice of notice of removal ends its power over the case.

# E. Plaintiff's Motion to Remand to State Court

Section 1447(c) provides a time frame for raising certain objections to removal, while allowing lack of subject matter jurisdiction to be raised at any time:

> A motion to remand the case on the basis of any defect other than lack of subject matter jurisdiction must be made within 30 days after the filing of the notice of removal under section 1446(a). If at any time before final judgment it appears that the district court lacks subject matter jurisdiction, the case shall be remanded. . . .

Within the first 30 days after removal, then, a case can be remanded for a variety of reasons, all of which are conditions of removal or of subject matter jurisdiction:

- There is no diversity jurisdiction, either because of citizenship or lack of sufficient amount in controversy;
- A defendant is a citizen of the forum state in diversity;
- There is no federal question under the well-pleaded complaint rule;
- The notice of removal was not filed within 30 days;
- The notice of removal was filed more than one year after the state case was filed and jurisdiction is based on diversity, and plaintiff did not act in bad faith;
- An involuntary act of plaintiff created removability;
- All defendants did not consent; or
- The defendant waived its right to remove by conduct in the state court.

If the motion to remand is based upon anything other than lack of subject matter jurisdiction, the plaintiff must file it within 30 days of removal. 28 U.S.C. § 1447(c). Thus, for example, if a defendant removes a case even though one defendant is a citizen of the forum state, if the plaintiff does not seek to remand within 30 days, that objection is waived. *Hurley v. Motor Coach Indus., Inc.*, 222 F.3d 377, 380 (7th Cir. 2000). Put another way, subsection (c) limits the ability of district courts to remand cases: remand can only be made for "defects other than lack of subject matter jurisdiction" during the first 30 days; after that time, only the lack of subject matter jurisdiction permits remand. *Lively v. Wild Oats Markets, Inc.*, 456 F.3d 933, 937 (9th Cir. 2006).

## 1. Attorneys' Fees and Costs

A plaintiff who succeeds in remanding a case to state court may move the federal court to award it the costs and attorneys' fees it incurred in having done so. Specifically, § 1447(c) gives district courts that decide to remand a case to state court discretion to "require payment of just costs and any actual expenses, including attorney fees, incurred as a result of the removal." *See also Valdes v. Wal-Mart Stores, Inc.*, 199 F.3d 290, 293 (5th Cir. 2000) (district court's decision under Section 1447(c) is reviewed for abuse of discretion).

An award is not automatic. Essentially, whether costs and expenses should be awarded to a plaintiff who succeeds in having a case remanded turns on the reasonableness of the defendant's removal. Absent "unusual circumstances," if the removing party had an objectively reasonable basis for seeking removal, then an award should be denied. *Martin v. Franklin Capital Corp.*, 546 U.S. 132 (2005).

# F. Removed or Remanded: What Next?

Once removed, litigation in the state court is automatically stayed. The Rules apply once a case is removed. Rule 81(c). The time for the defendant to file an answer (or move under Rule 12, *see* Chapter 29), if it did not answer in state court, is 20 days after it received the state court pleading, or 5 days after it filed the notice of removal, whichever is longer. Rule 81(c).

If the plaintiff's motion to remand is granted by the district court, then the case is returned to the state court for adjudication. State rules govern from that point onward. A federal district court may only either keep the case or remand it to state court; it may not *dismiss* the case. *Bromwell v. Mich. Mut. Ins. Co.*, 115 F.3d 208, 214 (3rd Cir. 1997).

# G. Post-Removal Actions That Destroy or Create Subject Matter Jurisdiction

Suppose after the case is properly removed, the plaintiff seeks to join to the suit a non-diverse defendant, or one against whom it does not seek more than $75,000. What then? Section 1447(e) answers this question:

If after removal the plaintiff seeks to join additional defendants whose joinder would destroy subject matter jurisdiction, the court may deny joinder, or permit joinder and remand the action to the State court.

If the district court concludes that the non-diverse defendant is an "indispensable party" in terms of Rule 19, *see* Chapters 17 and 35, then it must allow joinder of the defendant and remand the case. *Steel Valley Auth. v. Union Switch & Signal Div.*, 809 F.2d 1006, 1010–11 (3d. Cir.1987) ("[W]hen a non-diverse party is added to a federal proceeding and that party's presence is indispensable to the furnishing of complete relief, remand is mandated where federal subject matter jurisdiction depends on diversity jurisdiction, even though removal was originally proper.").

If, however, the defendant is not indispensable in terms of Rule 19, then the court has discretion on how to proceed. In determining whether to allow the amendment, "the court should examine the following factors: (1) the extent to which the purpose of the amendment is to defeat federal jurisdiction, (2) whether the plaintiff has been dilatory in asking for the amendment, (3) whether the plaintiff will be significantly injured if the amendment is not allowed, and (4) any other factors bearing on the equities." *Weathington v. United Behavioral Health*, 41 F. Supp. 2d 1315, 1318 (M.D. Ala. 1999).

The opposite facts also raise an interesting question. What happens if the plaintiff's motion to remand is incorrectly denied, but before the case goes to final judgment in federal court the non-diverse party is dismissed, and so the court "then" has subject matter jurisdiction? In *Caterpillar Inc. v. Lewis*, 519 U.S. 61 (1996), the defendants removed the case even though complete diversity was lacking, but before the case was tried the non-diverse defendants settled and were dismissed as parties. The court held that so long as the federal court had subject matter jurisdiction at the time of judgment, it did not need to remand the case to state court. The court found as the "overriding considerations" of "finality, efficiency, and economy" were "overwhelming" since the case had been tried to verdict.

# H. Limited Appealability of Orders Granting or Denying Remand

Congress has almost eliminated appeals of orders granting or denying motions to remand cases to state court, at least before a final judgment is entered in the case. Unless an interlocutory appeal is allowed, in other words, any error in keeping a case in federal court must await final judgment, and any error in remanding a case will not be examined by an appellate court.

## 1. Orders Granting Remand

With very narrow exceptions, an order granting remand cannot be appealed. Thus, even if the district court erroneously concludes that it lacks subject matter jurisdiction, appellate review is unavailable. "The policy of Congress opposes 'interruption of the litigation of the merits of a removed cause by prolonged litigation of questions of the jurisdiction of the district court to which the cause is removed.'" *Kircher v. Putnam Funds Trust*, 126 S.Ct. 2145, 2152 (2006) (quoting *U.S. v. Rice*, 327 U.S. 742, 751 (1946)). As a result, attempts to obtain appellate review through interlocutory appeals and mandamus (*see* Chapter 57), have failed. *See In re Briscoe*, 448 F.3d 201, 216 (3rd Cir. 2006) (noting that the Supreme Court long ago "rejected the general availability of mandamus as a means of reviewing the actions of a district court in denying a motion to remand a case of the state court from which it had been removed.").

## 2. Orders Denying Remand

An order denying a motion to remand cannot be appealed until after any final judgment is entered. *Caterpillar Inc. v. Lewis,* 519 U.S. 61, 74 (1996). Nor is mandamus available. *In re Briscoe,* 448 F.3d at 216. *See* Chapter 57.

# I. Removal by Parties Other Than Defendants

As noted above, a plaintiff cannot remove a case even if the defendant asserts a compulsory counterclaim that arises under federal law or is between citizens of different states with an amount in controversy exceeding $75,000. A counterclaim cannot be the basis of federal jurisdiction. *Holmes Group, Inc. v. Vornado Air Circulation Sys.,* 535 U.S. 826, 830 (2002).

In Chapter 17 we will examine impleader under Rule 14(a). Essentially, impleader allows a party that has been sued to join to the suit a non-party who may be liable to that party if it is liable on the claim asserted against it. A defendant, typically, can "implead" a non-party where that non-party owes contribution or indemnity to the defendant on the claim asserted against it. The defendant is called a "third-party plaintiff" and the party it sues, the "third-party defendant."

May a third-party defendant who is joined under state versions of Rule 14(a) remove a case? The majority of the courts limit the right to remove to "defendants," not third-party defendants. *See Foster Poultry Farms, Inc. v. Int'l Bus. Mach. Corp.,* 2006 WL 2769944 (E.D. Cal. 2006) (collecting cases on the split).

---

### Checkpoints

- Can you describe the time frames for removal, both how long and when the clock starts to run?

- Can you describe when a federal claim is removable? When a case with state law claims is removable? Why non-removable claims can be removed if they relate to a federal question?

- Can you define when a defendant will be deemed to be "fraudulently joined" and the consequences of that conclusion?

- Do you know how to determine the amount in controversy for removal?

- Do you understand the procedure for removing a case, and seeking remand?

# Part B

## Judicial Resolution of (1) Personal and Subject Matter Jurisdiction and Venue; (2) the Merits of a Dispute Without Discovery, with Discovery but Without Trial, and only After Discovery and Trial; and (3) Appeals

# Chapter 11

# A Preview of Part B of This Book

Part A of this book addressed the three requirements for a claim to be properly filed by one party against another in federal court: subject matter jurisdiction, personal jurisdiction, and venue. It also described how a defendant can remove a case from state to federal court. We thus know what a plaintiff must do to file a case in federal court, and what a defendant can do if the plaintiff files, in state court, a case that can be removed to federal court. It is important to bear in mind that—except for a very few federal claims which have exclusive federal subject matter jurisdiction (like patents, for example)—the plaintiff can choose state court, and—again absent those few claims—the defendant can leave the case in state court. Which system either party would want the case to be in is a matter of strategy that turns on the facts. Choice of court system is not, usually, driven by the law.

Part B of this book addresses how a plaintiff starts a lawsuit by filing a complaint in federal court. It explains how plaintiff's counsel drafts a complaint that asserts at least one claim and complies with the Rules' requirements for investigating, filing, serving, and properly formatting a pleading. It then turns to how defense counsel responds to that complaint, including the requirements that defense counsel investigate before responding to the complaint, and the various options that defense counsel may have.

After that, we'll return to what Chapter 1 emphasized: it's common for a party to have multiple claims that arise out of the same basic set of facts. The same set of facts that create a breach of contract claim might, for example, present a fraud or negligent misrepresentation claim. The same set of facts that demonstrate a federal employment law claim might also support a state law claim for intentional infliction of emotional distress. How do you analyze the joinder of an additional claim in the complaint or the assertion of a claim by the defendant, or even the joinder of a party by a plaintiff (say, another plaintiff or another defendant) or the defendant (can a defendant even join parties?). This Part of this book answers these questions as well.

Admittedly those topics fit nowhere perfectly. Let me explain to you why I, after a lot of thought and after using several other organizational structures, put it here. It'll help you to understand the next part of this book (or whatever part of your course you're covering this in) as something other than esoteric abstractions.

Some civil procedure casebooks, and some courses, go all the way through the course or book using a one-plaintiff-versus-one-defendant-with-one-claim before turning to cases involving multiple claims, multiple parties, or both. I have found it confuses a many students to wait to study joinder of claims and parties. For example, we've seen that diversity subject matter jurisdiction requires both "complete diversity" and more than $75,000 "in controversy." That's only half the story, however, because another statute, Section 1367, creates numerous exceptions to that rule. Likewise, we have seen that "pendent venue" and "pendent personal jurisdiction" perform roles similar to supplemental subject matter jurisdiction, when there is a federal statute authorizing nationwide service of process over a federal claim with "tag along" state law claims.

More fundamentally, a lawyer investigating whether a suit can be filed in federal court, or whether one can be structured to prevent removal to federal court, or removed from state court, or whether a suit has properly been filed in federal court, almost invariably must consider the impact of the federal joinder rules and the supplemental jurisdictional statute. Likewise, many suits involve multiple claims, and a significant number involve multiple parties, and a substantial number involve both. Consequently, a lawyer must consider the joinder rules at the outset of a lawsuit, not at its end. I think you will learn this subject better if you learn the issues in the context in which they arise, and not in an artificial one.

Having said that, though, this book is structured to work no matter how your professor teaches the course. If you get to the joinder rules covered in Part B of this book at the end of the course, read it then, but if you're reading this near the end of your course, when you've studied pretty much all of the subjects, I'd tackle it in the order it's presented here. I think it makes more sense that way.

# Chapter 12

# The Plaintiff's Pre-Suit Investigation Required by Rule 11

---

### Plaintiff's Pre-Suit Investigation Roadmap

This chapter explains why plaintiff's counsel is required to investigate the law and facts prior to filing a lawsuit in federal court.

---

Rule 11 is in the background of virtually all aspects of civil lawsuits (except for discovery, where other rules control sanctions. *See* Chapter 51.) Even before a lawsuit is filed, Rule 11 comes into play since it requires plaintiff's counsel to investigate the legal and factual merits of the anticipated litigation, both substantive (*e.g.*, does the plaintiff have a reasonable basis to sue someone?) and procedural (*e.g.*, can this case be filed in federal court?).

If the plaintiff violates Rule 11, then in response to the filing of the complaint, a defendant can seek sanctions. This chapter describes what Rule 11 requires of plaintiffs' counsel before suit is filed. Chapter 37 analyzes obligation of defense counsel in drafting an answer or other response, and also completes the discussion of how Rule 11 motions are adjudicated.

## A. The Purpose of Rule 11 Is to Eliminate Frivolous Legal and Factual Assertions in Filed Court Papers

"The central purpose of Rule 11 is to deter baseless filings in district court and thus . . . streamline the administration and procedure of the federal courts." *Cooter & Gell v. Hartmarx Corp.*, 496 U.S. 384, 393 (1990). It does this by requiring litigants to certify that papers filed with the court are well founded both in fact and in law. *Bus. Guides, Inc. v. Chromatic Communs. Enterp., Inc.*,

498 U.S. 533, 542 (1991). That means that, before filing a complaint a plaintiff must investigate both the law and the facts supporting the complaint.

Rule 11 may at first seem counter-intuitive if have heard much of the "duty of zealous advocacy" and a lawyer's obligation to put a client's interests ahead of all others. Rule 11 limits a lawyer's ability to zealously represent a client by permitting courts to impose monetary and other sanctions if, boiled down, counsel makes a "frivolous" legal argument or assertion of fact. The Rule in effect penalizes lawyers who go too far in representing their clients. But, we'll see that they have to go way too far to be sanctioned under Rule 11.

# B. Every Document Signed and Filed with a Court, Including the Complaint, Is Covered by Rule 11

Every document filed with a court must be signed. Specifically, Rule 11 requires that at least one attorney or, in *pro se* cases, the party, sign each document filed with the district court. FRCP 11(a). In addition to being signed, the paper must state the signer's address and telephone number. The court should strike papers filed without signature, unless promptly corrected. *Id.* The requirement that a document be signed is broad and inclusive. *See* Chapter 38. It clearly covers a complaint. *See* FRCP 11(d).

# C. The Representations Implied by Rule 11

## 1. The Implied Representation of Reasonable Inquiry

Rule 11 states that a signature on a paper constitutes a certification "that to the best of the person's knowledge, information, and belief, *formed after an inquiry reasonable* under the circumstances" the filing does not violate four subsections of Rule 11(b). Thus, the basic obligation is to conduct an "inquiry reasonable under the circumstances." The amount and quality of investigation necessary to be "reasonable under the circumstances" turns on all the circumstances. *Donaldson v. Clark*, 819 F.2d 1551, 1556 (11th Cir. 1987). Factors courts consider include the time available for investigation, whether the attorney had to rely on information from the client, and the general plausibility of legal arguments. *Id.* The test is objective, not subjective. *Lieb v. Topstone Indus. Inc.*, 788 F.2d 151, 157 (3rd Cir. 1988). The objective standard is intended discourage submissions "without factual foundation, even though the paper was not filed in subjective bad faith." *Bradgate Assocs. Inc. v. Fellows, Read & Assocs.,*

*Inc.*, 999 F.2d 745, 749 (3rd Cir. 1993). The objective standard eliminated any "empty-head pure-heart" justification for frivolous filings. FRCP 11 advisory committee note.

The attorney who signs the document doesn't have to do all of the investigation himself. He can rely on information from other persons. "For example, no one could argue fairly that it would be unreasonable for an attorney to rely on witnesses to an accident before bringing a personal injury action. After all, the accident hardly can be reconstructed for the benefit of a plaintiff's attorney." *Garr v. U.S. Healthcare, Inc.*, 22 F.3d 1274, 1278 (3rd Cir. 1994). Thus, attorneys can rely on their clients' objectively reasonable representations about the facts. *Hadges v. Yonkers Racing Corp.*, 48 F.3d 1320, 1329–30 (2d Cir. 1995).

With respect to the duty to investigate and Rule 11 generally, all doubts are resolved against sanctions and in favor of the person who signed the paper. *Rodick v. City of Schenectady*, 1 F.3d 1341, 1350 (2d Cir. 1993). The reason for the hesitation to impose sanctions is that Rule 11 "must be read in light of concerns that it will . . . chill vigorous advocacy." *Cooter & Gell v. Hartmarx Corp.*, 496 U.S. 384, 393 (1990). Other courts emphasize that "judges should always reflect seriously upon the nuances of the particular case, and the implications the case has on the nature of the legal representation, before imposing sanctions." *Thompson v. Duke*, 940 F.2d 192, 195 (7th Cir. 1991).

Also important to the reasonable inquiry analysis is the "snapshot rule." Rule 11 can be violated only if the duty of inquiry was breached "at the moment of filing." *Skidmore Energy, Inc., v. KPMG*, 455 F.3d 564, 570 (5th Cir.), *cert. denied*, 127 S.Ct. 524 (2006). Thus, the focus is on the signing attorney's conduct "by inquiring what was reasonable to believe at the time the pleading" was submitted. *Donaldson v. Clark*, 819 F.2d 1551, 1555–56 (11th Cir. 1987). "Like a snapshot, Rule 11 review focuses upon the instant when the picture is taken—when the signature is placed on the document." *Thomas v. Capital Security Serv., Inc.*, 836 F.2d 866, 874 (5th Cir. 1988). Thus, hindsight cannot be used to find that a paper, though proper when filed, violated Rule 11 because of subsequently gained knowledge or events.

Underlying all of Rule 11 is this duty of reasonable inquiry. In filing any written document, counsel represents to the court that he has conducted a reasonable inquiry. A reasonable inquiry into what?

## 2. The Other Four Implied Representations

### a. No Improper Purpose

Rule 11 prohibits filing of papers that are "presented for any improper purpose, such as to harass or to cause unnecessary delay or needless increase in the cost of litigation." FRCP 11(b)(1). Most courts view this as closely related to having legal and factual support: if a complaint has legal and factual support, then it has not been filed for an improper purpose. As a result, the subjective intent of the party or attorney is irrelevant. *Intamin Ltd. v. Magnetar Tech., Corp.*, 2007 WL 1138489 (Fed. Cir. 2007) ("complaints are not filed for an improper purpose if they are non-frivolous"). The Constitution probably requires this: citizens have a First Amendment right to bring non-frivolous litigation, even if they do so with "bad" intent. *Professional Real Estate Investors, Inc. v. Columbia Pictures Indus., Inc.*, 508 U.S. 49 (1993).

### b. No Frivolous Legal Arguments, Claims, or Defenses

Rule 11 prohibits frivolous legal arguments. Specifically, claims, defenses, and other legal contentions must be "warranted by existing law or by a nonfrivolous argument for extending, modifying, or reversing existing law or for establishing new law." FRCP 11(b)(2). A legal argument violates Rule 11(b)(2) when "in applying a standard of objective reasonableness, it can be said that a reasonable attorney in like circumstances could not have believed his actions to be legally justified." *Hunter v. Earthgrains Co. Bakery*, 281 F.3d 144, 153 (4th Cir. 2002). "The legal argument must have absolutely no chance of success under the existing precedent" to violate the rule. *Id.*

For example, in filing a complaint, plaintiff's counsel certifies she has conducted reasonable inquiry into the law. For each claim asserted in the complaint, plaintiff's counsel certifies that she has a non-frivolous legal argument that applicable law supports or reasonably could support. *Arons v. Lalime*, 3 F. Supp. 2d 314 (W.D.N.Y. 1998).

### c. No Unfounded Allegations

Rule 11 prohibits filing papers that make "allegations and other factual contentions" that lack "evidentiary support" unless the allegation is specifically identified as likely to "have evidentiary support after a reasonable opportunity for further investigation or discovery." FRCP 11(b)(3). The standard for imposing sanctions is "reasonableness under the circumstances." *Landon v. Hunt*, 938 F.2d 450, 453 n.3 (3rd Cir. 1991). If, for example, the plaintiff claims the defendant breached a contract, plaintiff's counsel must reasonably investigate whether there was a contract, whether it was breached, and whether it caused damage. Unless a federal question is presented, the lawyer must reasonably investigate the citizenship of the parties, the amount in controversy, and the facts supporting personal jurisdiction and venue.

A lawyer can properly file suit without having support for every allegation. However, a specific process is required to avoid violating Rule 11 when the lawyer does not have a reasonable basis in hand for an allegation. If plaintiff's counsel cannot find evidentiary support for an allegation, whether because of the press of time or inaccessibility to evidence that would support the allegation, the lawyer must identify in the complaint that allegation as being one likely to have evidentiary support after a reasonable opportunity for further investigation.

For example, if a pleading must be filed quickly due to an approaching statute of limitations, sanctions may be less appropriate than when an attorney has the usual amount of time to make a pre-suit investigation. *Garr*, 22 F.3d at 1279. On the other hand, absent exigent circumstances, an attorney who relied solely on a newspaper article to form the allegations of a securities fraud complaint violated Rule 11. *Id.* at 1280. Sometimes lawyers state "based on information and belief," an allegation is true. At other times, they mimic the language of the rule, stating that the lawyer believes the allegation "will have evidentiary support after reasonable investigation."

### d. No Unfounded Denials of Allegations

Rule 11 prohibits denying a factual contention made by another party unless "warranted on the evidence" unless the denial is specifically and reasonably identified as "based on belief or lack of information." FRCP 11(b)(4). Rule 11(b)(4) will not apply very often to a complaint; it mostly applies to defense counsel and their preparation of an answer.

### e. What Must be Investigated?

Plaintiff's counsel must investigate the facts necessary to support jurisdiction (personal and subject matter) and venue. In addition, the lawyer must conduct reasonable legal research into the claim and reasonable investigation into as to whether the allegations that the law requires be made have "evidentiary support."

### f. Examples With Explanations

What Rule 11 means for counsel filing a complaint is that the lawyer must reasonably investigate the law and facts to be certain not to violate the implied representations in Rule 11. *See Morris v. Wachovia Sec., Inc.,* 448 F.3d 268 (4th Cir. 2006). So, for example, in *Walker v. Norwest Corp.,* 108 F.3d 158 (8th Cir. 1996), the plaintiff alleged that the plaintiff was a citizen of a different state than "some of the defendants." Defense counsel raised the lack of subject matter jurisdiction in a letter to plaintiff's counsel, but he refused to dismiss. Ultimately, the district court dismissed for lack of subject matter jurisdiction and imposed $4,800 in sanctions on plaintiff's counsel. The appellate court affirmed, finding no abuse of discretion even though the plaintiff's lawyer argued that it had not alleged each defendant's citizenship because it "would be more trouble than [plaintiff] should be expected to take."

Similarly, in *Christian v. Mattel, Inc.,* 286 F.3d 1118 (9th Cir. 2003), the plaintiff filed suit against Mattel, claiming it had stolen his idea for a Barbie doll and seeking $2.4 billion (yes, billion) in damages. The problem was that Mattel had been selling its doll for nearly six years before the plaintiff allegedly thought of his doll, and that fact could have been easily discerned by plaintiff's counsel since that date was stamped on the back of each Mattel Barbie's head. Although holding that the district court erred in awarding Rule 11 sanctions for various oral arguments made by plaintiff's counsel because Rule 11 only applies to filed documents, the appellate court remanded for the district court to determine the appropriate sanction for filing the suit based upon inadequate investigation.

The fact that these courts imposed sanctions is fairly uncommon. In part, this is because "any and all doubts must be resolved in favor of the signer." *Eastway Const. Corp. v. City of New York,* 762 F.2d 243, 254 (2d Cir.1985); *see also Rodick v. City of Schenectady,* 1 F.3d 1341, 1350 (2d Cir.1993) ("When divining the point at which an argument turns from merely losing to losing and sanctionable . . . we have instructed the district courts to resolve all doubts in favor of the signer."). But it is also because litigation is expensive, and plaintiff's counsel—who often are not paid unless their clients recover money—have clear financial self-interest to not bring suits that lack merit.

---

### Checkpoints

- Can you identify the representations that come with filing a signed paper?
- Which one is not likely to be implicated in preparing a complaint?

# Chapter 13

# Pleadings: The Complaint

---

### Complaint Roadmap

This chapter summarizes the evolution of the role of pleadings in civil litigation, identifies the pleadings that are authorized by the Rules, and describes their purpose.

This chapter describes the central requirement that a complaint provide notice to the defendant of the claim by including assertion of facts plausible facts which, if true, state a claim upon which relief can be granted, as well as the few other substantive and "technical" requirements of pleadings.

---

Rule 3 makes clear that a federal lawsuit commences with the filing of a complaint. But as we saw in Chapter 12, the work of the plaintiff's lawyer began earlier, as Rule 11 requires a plaintiff's lawyer investigate the law and facts and before filing the complaint.

After summarizing the history and current general role of pleadings under the Rules, this chapter describes the requirements for complaints. They have changed, radically, in just the past few years.

The next chapter looks at the defendant's responses to the filing of a complaint. There is a close relationship between that chapter and this one. First, keep in mind that the key audience for the complaint is defense counsel — not the judge or jury, neither of whom will likely see it. The complaint will also set many of the boundaries for the suit, including the scope of discovery and of any trial. More immediately, if the complaint fails to state a claim upon which relief can be granted, the defendant can move under Rule 12(b)(6) to dismiss the complaint. Thus, after you read about the defendant's responses, come back and re-read the latter portion of this chapter to master the subject matter. (Yes, that was intentional.)

## A. Historical Role of Pleadings

In the not-too-distant past, pleadings were the dominant form of communication between the parties prior to trial. Back then, pleadings were the way that the parties exchanged information about their positions on the law and facts. A plaintiff would write a pleading; the defense would write a response to it; the plaintiff would write a reply to that; and so on. A goal of the pleading system was to use rounds of pleadings to identify one issue that could resolve the parties' dispute. The rounds of pleadings were used to identify that issue and to determine whether the issue was one that had to be decided by a judge or by a jury. Parties exchanged principally only papers called "pleadings."

The parties were unable to ask questions of each other about their positions or the underlying facts that led to the suit being filed. What would a witness say at trial? Unless the rules of pleading required it to be disclosed, it could remain a secret until trial.

## B. The Modern Limited Role of Pleadings

The role of pleadings under the Rules is much more limited. There are fewer pleadings and for all but a very few, there is just one responsive pleading to another party's pleading. The Rules limit "pleadings" to six types that are permitted as a matter of course, and two types that can be filed only with court permission:

| Name of Pleading | Who Typically Files It | Comments |
|---|---|---|
| Complaint | Plaintiff | Typically the only pleading filed by a plaintiff. |
| Answer | Defendant | Typically the only pleading filed by a defendant. A defendant can include in its answer a "counterclaim" pursuant to Rule 13 against the plaintiff. If so, the plaintiff must file a reply. See below. A counterclaim is the way the defendant "sues" the plaintiff. |
| Reply to Counterclaim | Plaintiff | If the defendant includes a counterclaim (see above), the plaintiff must file a reply to it. A reply serves the same purpose as a defendant's answer. |
| Reply to Answer | Plaintiff | A court may order a plaintiff to file a reply to a defendant's answer, but otherwise it is not permitted. |
| Answer to Crossclaim | Defendant (typically) or plaintiff (less common) | If there is more than one defendant, this is how one defendant can "sue" another. (The same is true if there is more than one plaintiff.) *See* FRCP 13(g) |
| Third-Party Complaint | Defendant | A defendant who believes that, if it is liable to the plaintiff a non-party is liable to it, can "sue" that person under Rule 14(a). |
| Third-Party Answer | Third-Party Defendant | The third party "sued" by the defendant through a third-party complaint (see above) must answer the defendant's complaint. |
| Reply to a Third-Party Answer | Defendant | If allowed by the court, the party who filed a third-party complaint under Rule 14(a) can file this in response to the Third-Party Defendant's Third-Party Answer. |

Rule 7(a) states that these, and only these, are "pleadings." *No* other paper involved in a lawsuit is a "pleading." *Id.* It will clear a lot of clutter away if you understand that the word "pleading" is a term of art. Do not give the word "pleading" any broader meaning or you will get completely confused. Motions are not pleadings, for example.

As the chart shows, there no longer are rounds of pleadings. Instead, typically one pleading states at least one claim (with different names, such as claim, counterclaim, crossclaim and third-party claim) and another pleading responds to that pleading. In a few instances, a third round may be allowed. Viewed functionally, therefore, the required pleadings look like this:

| Plaintiff's Claims | Responsive Pleading |
| --- | --- |
| Complaint | Answer (by defendant) |
| Crossclaim | Answer to Crossclaim (by co-plaintiff) |
| **Defendant's Claims** | **Responsive Pleading** |
| Counterclaim (against plaintiff) | Reply to Counterclaim (by plaintiff) |
| Crossclaim | Answer to Crossclaim (by co-defendant) |
| Third-Party Complaint | Third-Party Answer (by third-party defendant) |

# C. Requirements for Pleadings

## 1. Technical Requirements

While the focus of this Section is on the complaint, some requirements from Rules 8, 10 and 11(a) apply to all pleadings. Though somewhat mechanical, they are important for you to know, since if you do it wrong, it shows opposing counsel you don't know what you're doing:

- Include the name of the court;
- Name every party (as the "title") in the caption;
- Include a blank for the judge's name (will be randomly assigned by the court);
- Include a blank for case number (will be sequentially assigned by the court);
- Give it a "designation" (*i.e.,* the complaint has to be titled "complaint").
- Separately number each paragraph, each limited to one topic;

- Separately identify each "count" ("count" means "claim") as "Count 1," "Count 2" and so on;
- A lawyer must sign it and include her name, address, and phone number.

## 2. Substantive Requirements

It may surprise you how little substance the Rules require, at least on their face. Because a complaint is a pleading that sets forth a claim for relief it must comply with Rule 8(a) (why?) and so must contain: (a) a short and plain statement of the grounds for the court's jurisdiction, unless the court already has jurisdiction and the claim needs no new jurisdictional support [which will never be the case with a complaint], (b) a short and plain statement of the claim showing that the pleader is entitled to relief, and (c) a demand for judgment for the relief the pleader seeks. FRCP 8(a).

### a. Short and Plain Statement of the Court's Jurisdiction

A complaint must include a short and plain statement of the court's jurisdiction. Typically this is accomplished in a short paragraph or two, where the plaintiff asserts the basis for subject matter jurisdiction. The example below shows two typical examples, one invoking diversity jurisdiction and the other federal question. Notice that each makes the broad allegation that subject matter jurisdiction exists, but also states the facts (in a very general sense) that support that allegation.

If jurisdiction is based on diversity, citizenship and amount in controversy must be alleged. So, for example, a plaintiff must allege the citizenship of a corporation by alleging these specific facts—its state of incorporation and the state of its principal place of business (*i.e.*, the location of its "nerve center"). *Randazzo v. Eagle-Picher Indus., Inc.*, 117 F.R.D. 557 (E.D. Pa. 1987) (deriding counsel who failed to make these specific allegations but instead alleged where the business operated, not the exact words "principal place of business" and "state of incorporation"). Do it *exactly* the way it needs to be done or you'll look like you don't know what you're doing, in other words.

Although not required, lawyers include allegations as to why venue is proper. For example, a complaint might aver: "Venue is proper in the district because a substantial part of the events or omissions giving rise to the claim occurred in this judicial district."

### b. Short and Plain Statement of the Claim

Not that long ago in federal court, pleadings had to include not just a plain statement of the claim, but evidence and detailed factual allegations. Remember that pleadings were the way parties exchanged information.

There was a massive shift when the Rules were adopted, which reduced the role of pleadings in information exchange and replaced it with what is called "discovery," which we'll get to later. With only the exception in Rule 9(b), which we will get to, the Rules require that pleading stating a claim need only give notice of the claim asserted. "The function of a complaint . . . is to afford fair notice to the adversary of the nature and basis of the claim asserted and a general indication of the type of litigation involved." *Lewis v. U.S. Slicing Mach. Co.,* 311 F. Supp. 139 (W.D. Pa. 1970). What is "fair notice?" That changed in the last few years.

Your professor may spend a lot of time on two cases — *Bell Atlantic Corp. v. Twombly,* 550 U.S. 544 (2007) and *Ashcroft v. Iqbal,* 129 S.Ct. 1937 (2009) — because they overruled a case — *Conley v. Gibson,* 355 U.S. 41 (1957) — that had for fifty years provided a simple, bright line test for "how much" detail needs to be in a complaint to give "notice" under Rule 8(a). Sounds like a minor detail? Not so: increasing what Rule 8(a) required plaintiffs to allege will reduce the filing of complaints and make it easier for defendants to dismiss a complaint because it fails to give "enough" notice to state a claim upon which relief can be granted. *See* FRCP 12(b)(6). Let's understand the old standard, then understand what is now required under *Twombly* and *Iqbal,* and then be sure to understand the significance.

*Conley v. Gibson* was a race discrimination case. To make this "how much is enough" issue more concrete, here is the Court's summary of the complaint:

> Petitioners were employees of the Texas and New Orleans Railroad at its Houston Freight House. Local 28 of the Brotherhood was the designated bargaining agents under the Railway Labor Act for the bargaining unit to which petitioners belonged. A contract existed between the Union and the Railroad which gave the employees in the bargaining unit certain protection from discharge and loss of seniority. In May, 1954, the Railroad purported to abolish 45 jobs held by petitioners or other Negroes, all of whom were either discharged or demoted. In truth, the 45 jobs were not abolished at all, but instead filled by whites as the Negroes were ousted, except for a few instances where Negroes were rehired to fill their old jobs, but with loss of seniority. Despite repeated pleas by petitioners, the Union, acting according to plan, did nothing to protect them against these discriminatory discharges and refused to give them protection comparable to that given white employees. The complaint then went on to allege that the Union had failed in general to represent Negro employees equally and in good faith. It charged that such discrimination constituted a violation of petitioners' right under the Railway Labor Act to fair representation from their

bargaining agent. And it concluded by asking for relief in the nature of declaratory judgment, injunction and damages.

355 U.S. at 43. The Court stated these allegations gave notice of a claim under the Railway Labor Act:

> In appraising the sufficiency of the complaint, we follow, of course, the accepted rule that *a complaint should not be dismissed for failure to state a claim unless it appears beyond doubt that the plaintiff can prove no set of facts in support of his claim which would entitle him to relief.*
>
> Here, the complaint alleged, in part, that petitioners were discharged wrongfully by the Railroad and that the Union, acting according to plan, refused to protect their jobs as it did those of white employees or to help them with their grievances all because they were Negroes. If these allegations are proven, there has been a manifest breach of the Union's statutory duty to represent fairly and without hostile discrimination all of the employees in the bargaining unit. [D]iscrimination in representation because of race is prohibited by the Railway Labor Act.

355 U.S. at 46 (emph. added). The kind of pleading allowed by *Conley* was known as "notice pleading": it was enough if the complaint gave notice of the claim and a set of facts could support it. At that point, the role of pleadings in the exchange of information was over, and the parties were left to discovery.

There's a lot you can learn about how to analyze the issue of stating a claim from that passage. Start with the last sentence: a statute creates a claim for those discriminated against on the basis of race in union representation. What did they allege? That they were union members who were discriminated against on the basis of race. Allegations to support each element of the claim were made (apparently damages were not a required element). At that generalized level, the approach remains exactly the same today, but "more" notice in the complaint is required.

*Twombly* was a federal antitrust case, brought under a statute that gave a claim to anyone injured as a result of any "contract, combination . . . or conspiracy, in restraint of trade or commerce." 15 U.S.C. 1. The statute gave a claim to those injured by contract, combinations, or conspiracies, but not to merely "parallel conduct" that sometimes happens when two actors engage in independent, but still identical behavior. (Think about when one gas station raises its price a penny, and the one across the street then follows suit: could be a conspiracy, but could also be independent but parallel conduct.) Now put yourself in a potential plaintiff's counsel's shoes: suppose you believe it's a conspiracy: to allege it, you have to have a Rule 11 basis to do so.

In *Twombly*, the plaintiff alleged "upon information and belief" that a contract, combination, or conspiracy existed among certain Internet and local phone service providers based the fact that the defendants did not compete with each other in each other's markets and various other facts and circumstances. The district court held the allegations were insufficient to state a claim upon which relief could be granted because the pled "factual matter (taken as true)" did not "suggest that an agreement" had been made. The complaint must contain "enough fact to raise a reasonable expectation that discovery will reveal evidence of illegal agreement," or "plausible grounds to infer an agreement." Because the factual matter of the *Twombly* complaint did not plausibly suggest a conspiracy, but instead was more likely explained by lawful, parallel conduct, the Court held the complaint did not state a claim upon which relief could be granted.

At first many thought *Twombly* was merely an narrow application of the pleading rule to the context of expensive antitrust cases, where getting past the pleading stage often meant, as the Court noted, high discovery costs and thus created significant settlement value. But in reaching its conclusion the Court criticized *Conley's* "no set of facts" standard as being "best forgotten as an incomplete, negative gloss on an accepted pleading standard: once a claim has been stated adequately, it may be supported by showing any set of facts consistent with the allegations in the complaint."

Nonetheless, the Court re-iterated that detailed factual allegations were not necessary, but the plaintiff had to provide "the grounds" that entitle it to relief, which required "more than labels and conclusions" and emphasized that a mere "formulaic recitation of the elements of a cause of action will not do." *Id.* Instead, the court held that though basic the "factual allegations must be enough to raise a right to above the speculative level." *Id.* Although *Twombly* did not articulate the new standard precisely, the Court seems to indicate that a complaint must "contain either direct or inferential allegations respecting all the material elements necessary to sustain recovery under *some* viable legal theory." *Id.*, quoting *Car Carriers, Inc. v. Ford Motor Co.*, 745 F.2d 1101, 1106 (7th Cir. 1984).

*Iqbal* made it clear that *Twombly* was not a narrow exception. The complaint in *Iqbal* alleged that Iqbal was a Muslim, Pakistani citizen who had been unlawfully detained after the attacks of September 11, 2001. He sued several defendants, including Ashcroft, who had been the Attorney General of the United States at the time of his arrest, and Mueller, who had been Director of the FBI. The complaint alleged misconduct by lower level officials in a way that satisfied Rule 8(a): he was kept in maximum security lockdown 23 hours a day, was often in chains, and was kicked in the stomach and punched in the face without provocation. He plead guilty, served his time, then sued the guards, some other administrators, and Ashcroft and Mueller.

Lawyers for Ashcroft and Mueller—but not the guards and administrators—moved to dismiss the complaint for failing to state a claim. The Court emphasized that the complaint did not allege that those two men had kicked or beaten Iqbal, but that each had approved of policies of holding men of certain races following the September 11 attacks and that, allegedly, they had done so because of Iqbal's race, religion, or national origin.

It explained how to apply *Twombly:* First, legal conclusions are not "factual matter" and so are not entitled to be presumed as true: thus, the bare allegation in *Twombly* that there was an agreement or conspiracy did not "count" as factual matter. So, legal conclusions are ignored. Once that is done, the remaining "factual matter" is taken as true and the court must determines whether the remaining allegations plausibly states a claim upon which relief can be granted.

In *Iqbal* the court held these allegations were "legal conclusions" and so not entitled to any weight: that the defendants condoned subjecting him to harsh conditions because of his race and that Ashcroft was the architect of the policy and Mueller was instrumental in executing it. The remaining "factual matter" the Court held stated a claim but was subject to "more likely explanations" than race discrimination. Because it was as plausible that the men acted with the purpose of keeping "suspected terrorist in the most secure conditions available" until they could be cleared, the allegations did not state a claim for discrimination because of race, religion, or national origin.

First the good news: Although *Twombly* and *Iqbal* overruled *Conley* and said more detail was needed in pleadings, lawyers had already and for a long time been doing pretty much what those cases require. *Twombly* and *Iqbal* mean, at one level, that courts can require what had been often already been the practice. So, in some ways, "big deal."

But, the bad news comes first because lawyers must now distinguish between "legal conclusions" and "factual matter," and only the latter "counts" and is assumed true, and even then the claim must still be "plausible" in light of those allegations.

Second, *Twombly* and *Iqbal* did overrule a long-standing case, and secondly because at the margins, the new standard can be very significant. What do I mean by at the margins? In a car wreck case where someone ran a red light, is the new standard gong to matter? No. But what in those cases where, for example, the evidence to support an allegation is in the defendant's sole possession, and so plaintiff's counsel can't get to it. What about where intent is an element of the tort and the facts are weak about inferring intent—plaintiff's counsel can't know what is going on in someone's head. Marginal cases will be affected: there will be fewer filings and more dismissals on the pleadings under the new standard.

Third, *Twombly* and *Iqbal* were in the eyes of many inconsistent with the very conclusory official pleading forms that, until 2015, were in an appendix to the Rules. Here is Form 9, which was until 2015 effective to plead negligence:

---

1.        [Allegation of jurisdiction.]

2.        On June 1, 1936 in a public highway called Boylston Street in Boston, Massachusetts, defendant negligently drove a motor vehicle against plaintiff who was then crossing said highway.

3.        As a result plaintiff was thrown down and had his leg broken and was otherwise injured, was prevented from transacting his business, suffered great pain of body and mind, and incurred expenses for medical attention and hospitalization in the sum of one thousand dollars.

> Wherefore plaintiff demands judgment against the defendant in the sum of ____ dollars and costs.

---

These forms are no longer automatically sufficient after December 2015.

Fourth, there's tension between *Twombly* and *Iqbal* and another rule about pleadings. Courts often say that the plaintiff pled *too much*. *Viacom, Inc. v. Harbridge Merchant Servs., Inc.*, 20 F.3d 771, 775–76 (7th Cir. 1994). Pleadings that are confusing or contain too much detail or which plead evidence violate Rule 8, in other words. *See Conley v. Gibson*, 355 U.S. 41, 47 (1957), *abrogated on other grounds, Bell Atlantic Corp. v. Twombly*, 127 S.Ct. 1955 (2007). Some pleadings have too little, some too much, and others, just right. *See Matrixx Initiatives, Inc. v. Siracusano*, 2011 WL 977060 (March 22, 2011) (holding complaint stated claim under *Twombly* and *Iqbal*).

One final note: Lawyers plead cases in slightly different ways in federal courts throughout the country. Be sure you get a feel for what your professor thinks is "right" and in practice learn what local custom expects.

### i. Inconsistent Claims (or Defenses)

A party may assert inconsistent claims in the pleading. Rule 8(d)(2) provides:

> A party may set out 2 or more statements of a claim or defense alternatively or hypothetically, either in a single count or defense or in separate ones. If a party makes alternative statements, the pleading is sufficient if any one of them is sufficient.

Likewise, Rule 8(d)(3) permits a party to "state as many separate claims or defenses as it has, regardless of consistency." A plaintiff may, therefore, plead that the defendant is subject to strict liability, and was negligent, and committed fraud, and so on.

Why do the Rules allow this? Remember that the plaintiff's lawyer will not know all the facts when drafting the complaint. He will not, for example, likely have had access to any information known only to the defendant. (It's generally unethical for a lawyer to talk to a person who is represented by counsel in a matter, and even if the person is not represented, a lawyer has significant restrictions on how he can conduct pre-suit investigations of people who his client intends to sue. These are subjects you'll cover in your Professional Responsibility class.) For these reasons, lawyers are given some freedom, limited by Rule 11, to plead alternative claims and theories.

### ii. Pleading Unsupported Allegations

A lawyer must specifically identify any allegation that the lawyer does not know has evidentiary support. *See* Rule 11. As we saw, this is permitted where, for example, the suit had to be filed quickly. *See* Chapter 12.

### iii. Rule 9(b) as an Exception

The only exception in the Rules to the requirement that a pleading must only give notice is Rule 9(b). Rule 9(b) requires a party to "state with particularity the circumstances constituting fraud or mistake." This "particularity" requirement has generally been construed to require that the plaintiff must plead "the statements contended to be fraudulent, identify the speaker, state when and where the statements were made, and explain why the statements were fraudulent." *Southland Sec. Corp. v. Inspire Ins. Solutions, Inc.,* 365 F.3d 353, 362 (5th Cir. 2002).

Meeting this requirement is especially intricate when the fraud claim is made against a business entity: it is not sufficient to allege that "the corporation" made a false statement, or that "an agent" of it did so; the person must be identified.

Cases illustrate how much more "particularity" requires than a "short and plain statement." For example, in *Stradford v. Zurich Ins. Co.,* 2002 WL 31027517 (S.D.N.Y. 2002), the plaintiff insured brought a claim against the insurance company for an unpaid claim, and the defendant insurer filed a counterclaim for fraud. The defendant alleged only that the plaintiff had "knowingly and willfully devised a scheme and artifice ... to defraud defendants and obtain money by false pretenses and representations." The district court held this was insufficient under Rule 9(b) because it did not disclose the "time, place, and nature of the alleged misrepresentations." *Id.*

Why is more required in cases of fraud or mistake? Courts offer various justifications for the rule, and some say it should not exist at all. One common justification is that both fraud and mistake can be used to avoid contractual obligations; if a party is seeking to avoid contractual obligations, it should be required to explain why the contract should not be enforced with more detail. Likewise, fraud claims can result in tort damages (which, generally, are greater than contract damages) and punitive damages (which generally are not available for breach of contract); so, if the party believes that it is entitled to more than what the contract it has with the other party would allow, it should be required to explain why in more detail.

Rule 9(b) has other limitations: "[m]alice, intent, knowledge, and other conditions of a person's mind may be alleged." FRCP 9(b). The last sentence of Rule 9(b) means that while the facts that constitute fraud must be pled with particularity, "the requisite intent of the [person who committed the alleged fraud] need not be alleged with specificity." *Wight v. Bankamerica Corp.*, 219 F.3d 79, 91 (2d Cir. 2000).

Courts should not interpret Rule 9(b) to require parties to plead anything other than fraud or mistake with particularity. *Swierkiewicz v. Sorema*, 534 U.S. 506, 51 (2002); *Leatherman v. Tarrant County Narcotics Intell. & Coord. Unit*, 507 U.S. 163 (1993) ("In the absence of [an amendment allowing federal courts to require particularity in other cases] federal courts and litigants must rely on summary judgment and control of discovery to weed out unmeritorious claims sooner rather than later."). Nonetheless, a few courts particularly in "civil rights cases" require more than Rule 8. *See generally, Kyle v. Morton High School*, 144 F.3d 448 (7th Cir. 1998) (appellate court split on whether this practice was still appropriate after *Leatherman*). Finally, certain statutes, such as the Private Securities Litigation Reform Act, may require more detail than does Rule 8. *See In re Advanta Corp. Securities Litig.*, 180 F.3d 525 (3rd Cir. 1999).

### c. Demand for Relief

A plaintiff must include a demand for all the relief that it seeks. Thus, if a plaintiff seeks both money damages and injunctive relief (including specific performance), it should include a demand (often called a "prayer for relief") that mentions these remedies.

Despite the requirement of a demand, the plaintiff generally need not specify the amount of damages sought. Although a plaintiff is required to demand relief, as a general rule the plaintiff is not required to plead a specific dollar amount. *Avita v. Metropolitan Club*, 49 F.3d 1219, 1226 (7th Cir. 1995).

However, there is an exception: if the plaintiff seeks special damages, it must identify those damages. The dividing line between general and special damages varies, depending on whether the claim is in contract or tort, and states do not uniformly divide damages into the same category. However, generally speaking "general damages"—those that need not be specifically pled—are those that flow naturally and necessarily from the defendant's wrongdoing. *M.F. Patterson Dental Supply v. Wadley,* 401 F.2d 167, 172 (10th Cir. 1968). On the other hand, "special damages"—which must be pled—are those that the defendant caused, but that are not normally caused by the claim alleged against the defendant. *PdP Parfums de Paris v. Int'l Fragrances,* 901 F. Supp. 581, 585 (E.D. N.Y. 1995).

Finally, related to the demand for relief is a demand for a jury trial. The plaintiff may demand a jury trial by simply including it in its complaint by stating "Plaintiff demands a trial by jury" somewhere in the complaint. *See* FRCP 38(b) (1); Chapter 54.

# D. Who Must Be a Named Plaintiff and a Named Defendant?

Rule 17 requires that a claim be prosecuted in the name of the "real party in interest," unless the plaintiff is a minor, is incapacitated, or for some other reason the plaintiff who must bring the action must do so as a "representative" of the real party in interest. So, for example, normally a person who is injured in a car wreck must be named as a plaintiff to recover for damages caused to that person by the wreck. However, where a minor is injured, or the person who is injured is incapacitated or killed in the wreck, then suit can be brought by a representative on behalf of the real party in interest.

The question of when a representative must be appointed, and of when a parent is the real party in interest to recover for damages caused to a minor child are generally governed by state law, and are not the focus of the Rules. Rule 17 requires that the real party in interest be the named plaintiff, unless for some other reason it is proper for the suit to be prosecuted by a representative. *See Green v. Daimler Benz, A.G.,* 157 F.R.D. 340 (E.D. Pa. 1994). So, for example, in *Naghiu v. Inter-Continental Hotels Group, Inc.,* 165 F.R.D. 413 (D. Del. 1996), the plaintiff while in Zaire staying in the defendant's hotel was beaten up and $146,000 in cash that belonged to his employer was stolen. The court held that because the plaintiff had no legal interest in the money, his employer was the real party in interest. The court concluded that he was not a bailee of the money, but simply an employee, and so he had no legal interest in the money.

As for defendants, the capacity of a defendant to be sued is also generally determined under state law. *See* FRCP 17(b). As a general matter, the question of which is the right defendant to sue is a matter of substantive, not procedural, law, with the exception of incapacitated defendants and certain business forms, such as unincorporated divisions and associations.

If after suit is filed a named party dies or becomes incapacitated, Rule 25 permits substitution of a party to replace the now-deceased or incapacitated party.

# E. Examples and Forms

Below is a very simple complaint, but one that complies with the Rules and is typical of how a lawyer would draft it. Notice that the Cause Number ("Civ. A. No.") and "Judge" are blank: the clerk will fill in that information after the complaint is filed.

---

IN THE UNITED STATES DISTRICT COURT FOR
THE WESTERN DISTRICT OF TEXAS

Mangia Pizza, Co.              Civ. A. No. _____
   Plaintiff,

v.

Bob Smith, LP                  Judge _____
   Defendant

### COMPLAINT

#### PARTIES

1.      Plaintiff Mangia Pizza Company is a Texas Corporation with its principal place of business in Austin, Texas.

2.      Defendant Bob Smith, LP is a limited partnership which is a citizen of the State of Illinois.

#### JURISDICTION AND VENUE

3.      This Court has subject matter jurisdiction under 28 U.S.C. § 1332(a) because the parties are citizens of different states and the amount in controversy exceeds $75,000 exclusive of costs and interest.

4.      Venue is proper in this district under 28 U.S.C. § 1391(a) because a substantial part of the events or omissions giving rise to the claim occurred in this district.

#### BACKGROUND FACTS

5.      Defendant agreed to sell to plaintiff in Austin, Texas pizza boxes that met performance standards set forth in an agreement between them dated August 5, 2007. A true and correct copy of that agreement is attached as Exhibit A.

6. In violation of that agreement, Defendant delivered boxes that did not comply with the contractual or statutory specifications.

7. As a result of Defendant's actions, plaintiff was damaged.

## COUNT I
### BREACH OF CONTRACT

8. Plaintiff incorporates paragraphs 1 to 7 by reference.

9. Plaintiff had a valid contract with defendant, which defendant breached by delivering pizza boxes to plaintiff in Austin, Texas that failed to meet the specifications set forth in the contract.

10. As a result, plaintiff has been damaged in an amount exceeding $100,000.

### PRAYER FOR RELIEF

11. Plaintiff prays that this Court award its actual damages and for all other relief to which it is justly entitled.

Respectfully submitted,

_____

David Hricik
Fed. I.D. No. 123
Tex. St. B. 12345
Lawfirm, LLP
909 Fannin St. Ste. 3600
Houston, TX 77010
(713) 632-8000
(713) 632-8002 (fax)
Hricik_d@law.mercer.edu

Be sure you realize that an allegation is just that: it does not mean jurisdiction necessarily exists, or that the plaintiff will "win" its claim and receive the relief it demanded. Plaintiff is required to make allegations which, if proven, means (a) the court has subject matter jurisdiction; and (b) the court will award relief to the plaintiff. The defendant has not even had a turn, yet.

# F. Corporate Disclosure Statement and Civil Cover Sheet

The first time a non-governmental corporate party (*e.g.,* a corporation) files any motion, pleading, or other document in a case, it must also file a "Disclosure Statement." FRCP 7.1. This form requires lawyers representing corporate parties to list for the court any parent corporation of the party, or any corporation that owns more than 10% of the stock of the party, or to state that there are no such parties. The purpose of the disclosure is to aid the judges of the court to determine whether anyone owns any disqualifying financial interest in a party. Thus, a non-governmental corporate plaintiff typically files a Rule 7.1 statement along with the complaint, and a non-governmental corporate defendant, along with its answer or Rule 12 motion.

Another form that must be filed along with the complaint is a "Civil Cover Sheet." The government uses the forms to collect data on civil filings. It is available on the website of each district court, and is often in a PDF form that can be completed on-line and then printed.

# G. Conclusion

What remains to be seen is whether the plaintiff can support its allegation: it may be that the facts do not support the allegations of subject matter jurisdiction, or the facts alleged in support of a claim are untrue (or can't be proven), or the defendant has an "affirmative defense" which means that, even if the plaintiff proves every allegation of a claim, the plaintiff still will not recover.

The defendant's pleading and then the process of discovery are the means by which parties uncover the facts. Summary judgment and trial are the vehicles by which the court, or a jury, determines whether a party can prove the allegations: can the plaintiff prove each element of its claim? Can the defendant prove each element of its affirmative defense? We will turn to those procedures shortly.

But first, we'll look at a matter that often is not addressed until the end of a civil procedure course, but which counsel for plaintiff and defendant must confront early on: joinder of claims and parties. Some professors will cover this material only at the end of the course, while others (me included) deal with it where it belongs: at the outset of the suit, when lawyers must make decisions about what claims can, and must be brought, and who can, must, and cannot be joined with the suit.

## Checkpoints

- Can you list each pleading and its function?
- Can you explain what is required by a "short and plain" statement of a claim?
- Can you identify when something is a "legal conclusion," and the significance of that conclusion?
- When does Rule 9(b) apply and what more does it require? Why?

# Chapter 14

# Preview of the Four Steps to Analyze Joinder of Claims and Parties

As we saw, a federal court must have subject matter jurisdiction over each claim. It must also have personal jurisdiction and, for claims asserted by a plaintiff, venue must be proper. We learned earlier about original subject matter jurisdiction—federal question and diversity—personal jurisdiction, and venue. There must be original jurisdiction, "regular" personal jurisdiction, and "regular" venue over a claim for a case to be anchored in federal court.

In this chapter, we'll learn that—once there is an anchoring claim—then doctrines expand original or regular subject matter jurisdiction, personal jurisdiction, and venue to permit a claim that is related to the anchor claim to "tag along"—even if, strictly speaking, there is no diversity or federal question, or there is no personal jurisdiction, or venue is technically improper, or all three are lacking—over that *additional* claim.

Be sure you understand that supplemental subject matter jurisdiction, pendent personal jurisdiction, and pendent venue are only available for additional claims beyond the anchor claim. Put more precisely: if there is no claim over which the court has all three—original subject matter jurisdiction (federal question or diversity), venue, and personal jurisdiction—or if the defendant fails to recognize and properly take action and waives any objection to venue or personal jurisdiction—then these doctrines are unavailable. Put another way, they can only be used if there is a claim that has proper subject matter jurisdiction and *either* (a) personal jurisdiction and venue or proper or (b) the defendant failed to object to any defects with them.

We'll see over the next several chapters that in addition to the two forms of *original* subject matter jurisdiction we've seen, a federal statute creates "supplemental" subject matter jurisdiction. Likewise, we'll see that judges have in addition to the regular forms of personal jurisdiction developed "pendent personal jurisdiction" and, in addition to venue defined by statute, developed "pendent venue." All three are intended to help efficiently adjudicate claims closely related to an anchor claim.

Why are these doctrines necessary? Remember that often the same set of facts gives rise to more than one claim. It is common, for example, for a plaintiff to plead more than state law claim, or to combine a state law claim with a federal claim. For example, suppose you live in Texas but travel to California, where you sell your car to a California resident. If the Californian believes you breached the contract by selling him a defective car, he could sue you for breach of contract. In addition, he might combine with that a claim for fraud, alleging that you deliberately misrepresented the car's quality. One set of facts might give rise to two or more state law claims, or combinations of state and federal claims, if for example a federal statute gave a civil cause of action to someone who bought a car in reliance on a misrepresentation.

Similarly, a complaint may make claims against more than one defendant, or more than one plaintiff may assert claims against a single defendant. For example, a patient injured during back surgery may sue both the doctor who operated and the manufacturer of an artificial disc that the doctor implanted. Or, a husband and wife injured in a car wreck may sue the other driver.

One plaintiff, at least, must have one anchor claim that meets all the basic requirements discussed in Part A of this book: subject matter, personal jurisdiction, and venue. As to each additional claim by that plaintiff against that defendant, and even by other parties against each other, the same requirements exist—subject matter jurisdiction, personal jurisdiction and venue—but the ways to meet those requirements for each additional claim relaxes a bit. A party can still show subject matter jurisdiction exists by establishing diversity or federal question, and can still show that the traditional minimum contacts test is met and that the general federal venue statute or a specific statute is met. In addition, however, each additional claim can also be proper under supplemental subject matter jurisdiction, pendent personal jurisdiction, and pendent venue.

This chapter focuses on the steps that must be undertaken for every additional claim beyond the anchor claim that the plaintiff makes against each defendant to properly anchor the dispute in federal court. The analysis applies to all claims "joined" with that first, anchor claim, whether "joined" in the initial complaint or after suit is filed.

To reiterate the point made above, which is counter-intuitive: "Join" sometimes misleads some students. The word sounds like it applies only after the complaint is filed. That's not right. The Rules governing joinder apply always. For example, they apply if the plaintiff has included more than one claim against a defendant, either originally or in an amended pleading (we'll get there), and also if the plaintiff joins two defendants in the original complaint, or at first sues only one and then joins another defendant later through an amended complaint. The rules apply from the original complaint onward.

# A. The Anchor Claim

We saw in Chapter 13 that the Rules require a complaint to state a claim for relief against a defendant over which the court has subject matter jurisdiction, either diversity or federal question, and over which venue is proper (or any objection to personal jurisdiction or venue is waived by the defendant, or the court and the parties fail to recognize any defect with subject matter jurisdiction). This is the "anchor claim." There must be one claim that anchors the case in federal court, or the suit can be dismissed upon motion of the defendant: if there is no single claim in the complaint that has all three—venue is improper, personal jurisdiction exists, and subject matter jurisdiction exists—defense counsel can move to dismiss the complaint; or, in the case of subject matter jurisdiction, upon the motion of any party or by the court.

We've also seen that in some circumstances a plaintiff can aggregate its claims against a single defendant to attain the minimum amount in controversy, and also that a plaintiff can aggregate its claims against multiple defendants if the defendants are jointly and severally liable to the plaintiff. Those claims, too, can anchor a case in federal court, creating a diversity anchor claim.

There can be more than one anchor claim: a plaintiff can include in the complaint two claims, both of which are federal questions and over which venue and personal jurisdiction proper. But there must be at least one claim by one plaintiff against one defendant that meets all three requirements or the entire case is subject to dismissal by motion of the defendant (or, if subject matter jurisdiction is lacking, by the court, as we'll see), because no one claim anchors the dispute in federal court. If there is more than one claim against a defendant that does so, then *each* can serve the purpose of "anchoring" additional claims.

To put it graphically, and *assuming* the court lacks subject matter jurisdiction, personal jurisdiction, and/or venue, here is the analysis to determine whether a claim can serve as an anchor claim:

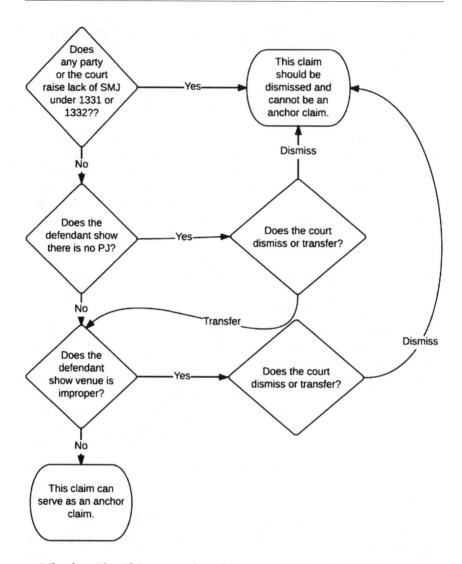

Why does identifying an anchor claim matter? If a well-pleaded complaint contains either a diversity or federal question claim, a court "beyond all question has original jurisdiction over that claim." *ExxonMobil Corp. v. Allapattah Serv., Inc.,* 125 S.Ct. 2611, 2620 (2005). Thus, if a court has original jurisdiction "over a single claim in the complaint, the court has original jurisdiction over a 'civil action' within the meaning of § 1367(a) [the statute governing supplemental subject matter jurisdiction], even if the civil action over which it has jurisdiction comprises fewer claims than were included in the complaint." *Id.* at 2620. Once a civil action is properly anchored in federal court, then the court "can turn to the question whether it has a constitutional and statutory basis for exercising supplemental jurisdiction over the other claims in the action." *Id.* at 2621. Thus, if there is at least *one* anchor claim, then the court has subject matter jurisdiction over the civil action, and the issue turns to whether it has subject matter jurisdiction over each other claim in that civil action. That and the related requirements of personal jurisdiction and venue, is where we turn to next.

## B. The Four Steps for Analyzing Joining Each Additional Claim Against Each Party

As to each additional claim made by a party — whether included in the original pleading or added later through amendment — there must be:

> *authority* by a Rule to add the claim or party: there must be a Rule that authorizes the claim to be joined with the anchor claim(s) or to join a person as party (*see* Chapters 15 to 18);
> *original* or *supplemental subject matter jurisdiction*: there must be *either* original jurisdiction (diversity or federal question) *or* supplemental jurisdiction under 28 U.S.C.§ 1367 for each additional claim (*see* Chapter 21);
> *personal jurisdiction*: if a separate basis for personal jurisdiction is required over the claim (sometimes it is not) there must be *either* actual *or* pendent personal jurisdiction for each additional claim (*see* Chapter 22); *and*
> *venue*: if a separate basis for venue is required over the claim (sometimes it is not), venue must be proper under the general federal venue statute, or under any applicable federal statute specific to that claim *or* there must be pendent venue over the additional claim (*see* Chapter 23).

We'll see that sometimes the rules give broad authority to add certain claims, but the subject matter jurisdiction statutes exclude many of them. Conversely, sometimes the Rules give very little authority to add claims, but there will almost always be subject matter jurisdiction over them. Each inquiry is independent and required. Likewise, venue and jurisdiction must be analyzed for each claim.

One last word, but it's important: before Congress had enacted the supplemental jurisdiction statute, 28 U.S.C. § 1367, federal courts had developed common law doctrines called "ancillary" and "pendent" subject matter jurisdiction. They did, basically, the same thing that Section 1367 does. But, they're gone: "Nothing in § 1367 indicates a congressional intent to recognize, preserve, or create some meaningful substantive distinction between the jurisdictional categories [the Court has] previously labeled pendent and ancillary." *ExxonMobil Corp. v. Allapattah Serv., Inc.,* 125 S.Ct. 2611, 2621 (2005). In other words, Section 1367(a) did not adopt this law; the statute replaces that judge-made law and expresses Congress' controlling view of when federal courts have supplemental subject matter jurisdiction. Section 1367, controls. *See id.* (distinguishing pre-Section 1367 case law from Section 1367).

# Chapter 15

# Joinder Step One: Authority in a Rule for Joining the Party or the Claim

If a Rule does not give authority for a claim or party to be joined to a civil action, then a party can object to joining the claim even if subject matter and personal jurisdiction and venue are all present. Thus lack of authority by itself is a basis to dismiss a claim: you must learn to identify which Rule, if any, authorizes joinder of the party or claim. The identity of the Rule that authorizes joinder serves a second purpose: we will see that whether a separate basis for personal jurisdiction is required, or whether a separate basis for venue is required, and how to determine whether supplemental jurisdiction under Section 1367 exists, each turns in part on which Rule authorizes joinder of the claim or party. Correctly identifying which, if any, Rule authorizes joinder of the claim or party is the critical first step. Get it wrong, and you're toast.

## A. Introduction to the Concept of Authority

There must be authority in a Rule to join a party or claim. A Rule must give a plaintiff authority to join an additional claim against a defendant, for example, and a Rule must give a defendant authority to join a claim — called a counterclaim — against a plaintiff. Likewise, if a party wants to make a claim against a person who is not yet a party, a Rule must authorize that party to join that person as a party to the suit and to assert a claim against it.

There's a big picture that will help to give you some intuition about joinder, but the details will always control: the joinder rules are designed to allow all of the claims that arise out of the same incident and which involve all of the parties to that incident to be litigated in one case. But it's not that simple, because cutting against that principle is that the joinder rules also to a large degree permit the plaintiff to determine who to sue, and over what. The plaintiff is the "master" of the lawsuit. As a result, a defendant, we will see, often has less ability to compel efficient resolution of a dispute than intuition might suggest should be the case. (Further, the subject matter jurisdiction, personal jurisdiction, and venue requirements of federal courts also at times operate to eliminate efficient resolution of disputes, as we'll see.)

The joinder rules are not that many, but they are quite specific. Be sure that when you are determining whether joinder of a claim or party is authorized, that you identify the correct Rule. Being correct — what type of party (*e.g.*, plaintiff or defendant) is seeking to join the claim or party, and on what basis is it doing so — is critical. To help, these tables summarize what we'll explore next, and may be used to identify which Rule applies to joinder by a specific party:

### JOINDER OF CLAIMS BY A PLAINTIFF

| JOINDER OF A CLAIM BY A PLAINTIFF AGAINST A PERSON WHO IS ALREADY A ... ||
|---|---|
| DEFENDANT | Rule 18(a) |
| CO-PLAINTIFF | Rule 13(g) |
| THIRD-PARTY DEFENDANT | Rule 14(a)(3) |

### JOINDER OF PARTIES BY A PLAINTIFF

| A PLAINTIFF CAN JOIN A PERSON AS A ... ||
|---|---|
| CO-PLAINTIFF | Rule 20(a); 19 |
| CO-DEFENDANT | Rule 20(a); 19 |
| PARTY TO A CROSSCLAIM AGAINST AN EXISTING PARTY | Rule 13(h); 19 |
| THIRD-PARTY DEFENDANT TO A COUNTERCLAIM MADE AGAINST THE PLAINTIFF | Rule 14(b) |

### JOINDER OF CLAIMS BY A DEFENDANT

| JOINDER OF A CLAIM BY A DEFENDANT AGAINST A PERSON WHO IS ALREADY A ... ||
|---|---|
| CO-DEFENDANT | Rule 13(g) |
| PLAINTIFF | Rule 13(a) and (b) |
| THIRD-PARTY DEFENDANT | Rule 14(a)(2) |

### JOINDER OF PARTIES BY A DEFENDANT

| A DEFENDANT CAN JOINT A PARTY AS A ... ||
|---|---|
| PARTY TO A COUNTERCLAIM AGAINST PLAINTIFF | Rule 13(h) |
| THIRD-PARTY DEFENDANT | Rule 14(a)(5) |
| PARTY TO A CROSSCLAIM ASSERTED BY AN EXISTING DEFENDANT | Rule 13(h) |

We will start with joinder of claims, since in many schools students study that first. The issue is: when can the plaintiff who has one claim anchored in federal court join claims against that one defendant, or when can a defendant assert a counterclaim against an existing plaintiff? Then, we, as likely will your professor, move on to joining additional parties—not just one plaintiff and one defendant.

# Chapter 16

# Authority to Join Claims

---

### Authority to Join Claims Roadmap

This chapter identifies the Rules that authorize the joinder of claims by a plaintiff or defendant already anchored in federal court

This chapter also explains when a plaintiff or defendant may, or must, join a claim against an opposing party.

---

Over the next few chapters, we will explore how the underlying policy of the Rules and statutes is to permit parties to resolve in one suit all claims involving all parties that arise out of the same basic set of facts, while still giving the plaintiff some control over the scope of the suit. The Rules and statutes balance these interests and others.

## A. Joinder of Claims by a Plaintiff

While one-plaintiff-asserting-one-claim-against-one-defendant litigation is not uncommon, a significant amount of federal litigation involves more than one plaintiff or defendant, more than one claim, and to a lesser extent, "third-party practice." In this chapter, we'll examine the extent to which a plaintiff may properly join additional claims against a defendant, and then when a defendant may assert claims against the plaintiff. (We'll explore crossclaims later, since more than one plaintiff or defendant must be properly joined to make those claims. Likewise, we'll explore joining parties to a counterclaim or crossclaim, or through "third-party practice" later, since they turn on the existence of a pending or proposed claim.)

Remember that identifying the authority in a Rule to join a claim is one step in the process of determining whether a claim or party can be joined: there must be a claim that anchors the case in federal court, and for each additional claim, there must be either original subject matter or supplemental jurisdiction, as well as for some claims a separate basis for personal jurisdiction and venue. To determine whether supplemental subject matter jurisdiction exists, a key step is identifying which Rule authorizes joinder of the claim or party. This chapter, therefore, not only begins our examination of the scope of authority of each Rule to join a claim or party, it also provides the details of one step that you must apply when determining whether a court has supplemental jurisdiction over the claim.

# 1. Joinder of a Claim by an Existing Plaintiff Against an Existing Defendant

The following table lists *every* circumstance in which a plaintiff is authorized to join a claim against an existing defendant where there are no claims by the defendant (if the defendant has asserted a counterclaim or joins a third party, see below):

JOINDER OF CLAIMS BY A PLAINTIFF

| JOINDER OF A CLAIM BY A PLAINTIFF AGAINST A PERSON WHO IS ALREADY A ... | |
|---|---|
| Defendant | Rule 18(a) |

### a. Permissive Joinder

Once a plaintiff has an anchor claim against a defendant, Rule 18(a) gives that plaintiff authority to join every additional claim it has against that defendant, even if the claim has nothing to do with the anchor claim. "A party asserting a claim ... may join as independent or as alternative claims as many claims ... as it has against the opposing party." FRCP 18(a). It allows the plaintiff to throw in the kitchen sink.

So, for example, a plaintiff anchors a case in federal court with a federal claim for employment discrimination has authority in Rule 18(a) to join a totally unrelated claim arising out of a car wreck between those parties. There's authority in Rule 18(a) for the plaintiff to join any claim—related or not to an anchor claim. So, in the example below the complaint joins two claims in the hypothetical Mangia Pizza versus Bob Smith, LP complaint we saw above, with a new federal claim joined with the state law breach of contract action:

## IN THE UNITED STATES DISTRICT COURT FOR
## THE WESTERN DISTRICT OF TEXAS

Mangia Pizza, Co.          Civ. A. No. _____
  Plaintiff,

v.

Bob Smith, LP              Judge _____
  Defendant

### COMPLAINT
### PARTIES

1.      Plaintiff Mangia Pizza Company is a Texas Corporation with its principal place of business in Austin, Texas.

2.      Defendant Bob Smith, LP is a limited partnership which is a citizen of the State of Illinois.

### JURISDICTION AND VENUE

3.      This Court has subject matter jurisdiction under 28 U.S.C. § 1332(a) because the parties are citizens of different states and the amount in controversy exceeds $75,000 exclusive of costs and interest. This court also has subject matter jurisdiction under 28 U.S.C. § 1331 of Count II of this complaint because that claim arises under the laws of the United States; specifically, 35 U.S.C. § 8100(a)(1).

4.      Venue is proper in this district under 28 U.S.C. § 1391(a) and (b) because a substantial part of the events or omissions giving rise to the claims occurred in this district.

### BACKGROUND FACTS

5.      Defendant agreed to sell to plaintiff in Austin, Texas pizza boxes that met performance standards set forth in an agreement between them dated August 5, 2007.

6.      Those standards were identical to the federal standards for pizza boxes set forth in 35 U.S.C. § 81000(a)(1).

7.      In violation of that agreement, Defendant delivered boxes that did not comply with the contractual or statutory specifications.

8.      As a result of Defendant's actions, plaintiff was damaged.

## COUNT I
## BREACH OF CONTRACT

9.      Plaintiff incorporates paragraphs 1 to 8 by reference.

10.     Plaintiff had a valid contract with defendant, which defendant breached by delivering pizza boxes to plaintiff in Austin, Texas that failed to meet the specifications set forth in the contract.

11.     As a result, plaintiff has been damaged in an amount exceeding $100,000.

## COUNT II
## VIOLATION OF 35 U.S.C. § 81000(a)(1)

12.     Plaintiff incorporates by reference paragraphs 1 to 8.

13.     Defendant violated 35 U.S.C. § 81000(a)(1) by delivering to plaintiff in the United States boxes intended for transportation and intermediate storage of pizza that were less than .001 inches thick.

14.     As a result, plaintiff has been damaged in an amount exceeding $100,000.

## PRAYER FOR RELIEF

15.     Plaintiff prays that this Court award its actual damages and for all other relief to which it is justly entitled.

Respectfully submitted,

_____

David Hricik
Fed. I.D. No. 555
Tex. St. B. 100129100
Yetter & Warden, LLP
909 Fannin St. Ste. 3600
Houston, TX 77010
(713) 632-8000
(713) 632-8002 (fax)
dhricik@yetterwarden.com

It is unlikely that two private individuals who have a dispute with each other will have multiple unrelated disputes. If Bob and Susie get in a car wreck, it's unlikely they also have a claim arising out of some contract. Any claims each has against the other will all likely arise out of the car wreck. But the unfettered authority to join claims can create problems. Think about what Rule 18(a)'s broad grant of authority means when two large companies that do a lot of business with each other and have many disputes get into a lawsuit.

Fortunately these potential monster disputes are limited by other concepts: simply having authority to join a claim doesn't end the analysis: there must also be subject matter and personal jurisdiction over each claim, and venue for a claim must be proper (at least for all claims by plaintiffs). Those principles will limit the plaintiff's practical ability to add claims to a suit. In addition, we will explore tools — severance and separate trial — that allow courts to reduce the number of parties and claims in a particular suit as it progresses, or only at trial. *See* Chapter 18.

### b. Mandatory Joinder of Claims by Plaintiffs

Nothing in Rule 18(a) (or any other Rule) *requires* a plaintiff to join any additional claim. Rule 18(a) is purely permissive. But, we'll see in Chapter 60 that common law doctrines of *res judicata* (now called "claim preclusion") require plaintiffs to join certain claims; the Rules, however, do not.

## B. Joinder of Claims by a Defendant Against an Existing Plaintiff

Early in a suit, defense counsel must make analyze whether the defendant has any claims that it can, or must, bring against any existing party to the suit: a plaintiff or a co-defendant already joined by the plaintiff. The Rules more closely limit the ability of a defendant to assert claims against existing parties, however. The only Rules that permit a defendant to make a claim against an existing plaintiff are in this chart:

| JOINDER OF A CLAIM BY DEFENDANT AGAINST A PERSON WHO IS ALREADY A … | |
|---|---|
| PLAINTIFF | Rule 13(a), (b) |

Suppose defense counsel concludes that the defendant has a claim against the plaintiff. This is quite common. For example, in a car wreck, the plaintiff may sue the defendant, alleging the defendant was at fault, while the defendant may believe the plaintiff was at fault and should pay for the defendant's injuries and damages. Or, in a business dispute, the plaintiff may believe that the defendant breached the contract, but the defendant believes it was the victim of the breach. This section describes the authority for a party who was already joined as a defendant by the plaintiff to join a claim against a party already joined as a plaintiff.

A defendant can make only one claim against a plaintiff: a counterclaim. Rule 13 authorizes two types of counterclaims: (1) compulsory and (2) permissive. As their names sound, a defendant *must* assert a compulsory counterclaim, or it will be barred from doing so in a later suit; in contrast, the Rules authorize but do not require a defendant to file permissive counterclaims. *See* Chapter 60.

## 1. Compulsory Counterclaims

A defendant *must* assert any claim that is a "compulsory counterclaim" or it is barred. If you keep in mind that one goal of the law is to resolve all claims that arise out of the same dispute that is anchored in federal court, then the compulsory counterclaim rule is fairly intuitive.

Read Rule 13(a), which defines what is and what is not a compulsory counterclaim. No matter how related it is to a claim by the plaintiff, a claim is *not* a compulsory counterclaim if:

(a)  when the lawsuit against this defendant was filed, its would-be counterclaim was pending in another suit;

(b)  the plaintiff brought suit by attachment or other process resulting only *in rem* or *quasi in rem* jurisdiction and defendant has not filed a counterclaim;

(c)  including the counterclaim requires joining a party over whom the court lacks jurisdiction; or

(d)  the defendant did not have the would-be counterclaim—because it did not yet exist—when defendant served its answer.

FRCP 13(a); *Baker v. Gold Seal Liquors, Inc.,* 417 U.S. 467 (1974). So, for example, if Bob has sued Susie over a car wreck in state court, and then Susie sues Bob in federal court over that same wreck, Bob doesn't need to bring a "counterclaim" against her. (See (a) above.) Likewise, a defendant is not required to include in its answer a claim that it can't yet bring!

What *is* a compulsory counterclaim? It is one that does not fall in any of the four categories above *and* which "arises out of the transaction or occurrence that is the subject matter of the opposing party's claim." Four inquiries help determine whether a counterclaim "arises out of the same transaction or occurrence" as a claim against the defendant:

(a)  whether the issues of fact and law in the claim and counterclaim are essentially the same;

(b) whether *res judicata* would bar a subsequent suit on the counterclaim absent the compulsory counterclaim rule;

(c) whether the same evidence would support or refute the claim and the counterclaim; *or*

(d) whether there is a logical relationship between the claim and the counterclaim.

*Q Int'l Courier, Inc. v. Smoak*, 441 F.3d 214, 219 (4th Cir. 2006); *see Iglesias v. Mut. Life Ins. Co.*, 156 F.3d 327 (1st Cir. 1998). These are not elements: the court "need not answer all these questions in the affirmative for the counterclaim to be compulsory." Instead, these inquiries work "less like a litmus" test and "more like a guideline." *Id.* The tests are fact-intensive and often the answer turns on the broader question of whether trial would be efficient if the counterclaim were joined with the plaintiff's claim.

For example, the plaintiff in *Iglesias* brought employment discrimination and breach of contract claims against the defendant. The defendant filed a counterclaim seeking restitution from the plaintiff for amounts the plaintiff had "padded" his expense account with. The court held that the counterclaim was not compulsory, emphasizing that the facts that gave rise to the counterclaim rested on different sets of facts, and that the counterclaim did not depend on the success or failure of plaintiff's claim against the defendant. In other words, the plaintiff's claim turned on proving discrimination; the defendant's counterclaim turned on whether plaintiff padded his expense account. Ask whether the same would be true if the defendant asserted a claim for padding the expenses, but also asserted that it had fired the plaintiff for having done so, not because of discrimination. The facts matter.

Leading casebooks often discuss two cases that reach different results on similar facts. On the one hand, in *Plant v. Blazer Financial Services*, 598 F.2d 1357 (5th Cir. 1979), the court held the logical-relationship test was satisfied where the plaintiff brought a truth-in-lending claim and the defendant filed a counterclaim for payment, and both claims arose out of the same note. The plaintiff's claim was based on the defendant creditor's failure to disclose terms regarding an after-acquired security interest, while the counterclaim was based on the plaintiff debtor's failure to make any payments on the note. The court reasoned that resolution of the counterclaim would impose little burden in fact because the only additional finding to be made is simply "how much the plaintiff has paid." Further, the court explained that if the creditor was not allowed to assert his delinquent-payment counterclaim against the defaulting debtor, the creditor "could be forced to satisfy the debtor's truth-in-lending claim without any assurance that his claims against the defaulting debtor arising from the same transaction will be taken into account or even that the funds he has been required to pay will still be available should he obtain a state court judgment in excess of the judgment on the truth-in-lending claim." Thus, the court concluded that where a delinquent-payment counterclaim and a failure-to-disclose claim arose from the same note, they were logically related, notwithstanding that the reasons for the delinquent payment had nothing to do with the reasons for the failure to disclose.

On the other hand, in *Hart v. Clayton-Parker and Assocs., Inc.*, 869 F. Supp. 774 (D. Ariz. 1994), the plaintiff brought a claim for violation of a related federal statute governing debt collectors (the Fair Debt Collection Practices Act, or "FDCPA"). The creditor counterclaimed for the unpaid balance. The district court noted that *Plant* represented a minority view under the truth-in-lending statute and that all of the courts applying the FDCPA had held that a claim for the unpaid balance was not a compulsory counterclaim to an FDCPA claim. The court reasoned that "plaintiff's FDCPA claim relates to the alleged use of abusive debt collection practices, while the defendant's counterclaim" related to a state law debt; one turned on written demand letters made during collection efforts, the other statements in loan documents.

This flow chart summarizes the steps to determine if a claim is a compulsory counterclaim, or not (again assuming no party must be joined):

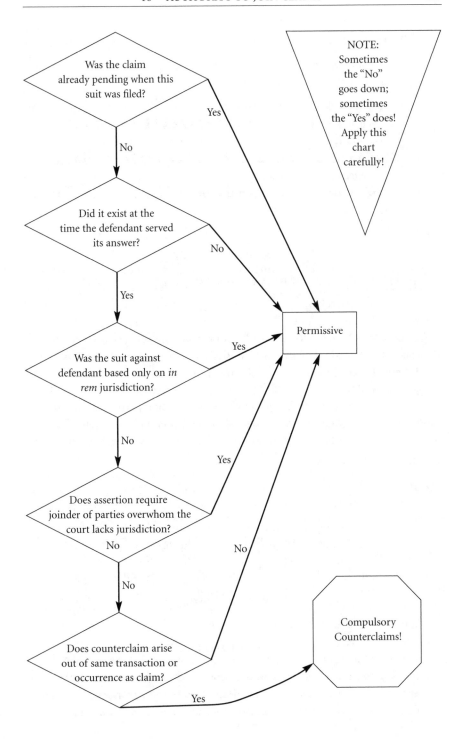

Was the claim already pending when this suit was filed?

Yes

No

NOTE: Sometimes the "No" goes down; sometimes the "Yes" does! Apply this chart carefully!

Did it exist at the time the defendant served its answer?

No

Yes

Permissive

Was the suit against defendant based only on *in rem* jurisdiction?

Yes

No

Yes

Does assertion require joinder of parties overwhom the court lacks jurisdiction?

No

No

No

Does counterclaim arise out of same transaction or occurrence as claim?

Yes

Compulsory Counterclaims!

## 2. Permissive Counterclaims

A counterclaim is permissive if it is not compulsory. FRCP 13(b). In other words, a claim "may," but need not be, brought if it:

- Does not arise out of the same transaction or occurrence as the claim;
- Does not exist at the time the defendant serves its answer;
- Was already the subject of a pending suit when the action was filed;
- Is in a case where jurisdiction is based on *quasi in rem* or *in rem*, but not *in personam* jurisdiction; or
- Requires for its adjudication the joining third parties of whom the court lacks jurisdiction.

If a defendant *chooses* to file a permissive counterclaim, the court *must* permit it to be filed. The word "may" in Rule 13(b) does not give discretion to the court to deny the timely filing of a permissive counterclaim; rather, it gives the defendant the choice either to join it. Rule 13(b) gives a defendant the right to have a permissive counterclaim determined along with the claims of the plaintiff. *Montecatini Edison, S.P.A. v. Ziegler,* 486 F.2d 1279, 1282 (D.C. Cir. 1973).

Again, remember that Rule 13 only *authorizes* joining a counterclaim. Subject matter and personal jurisdiction and venue remain as requirements. If you recall the goal—to litigate related claims in one suit—your intuition should tell you that the law will likely allow compulsory counterclaims to be adjudicated in one suit, but may not permit permissive counterclaims that do not arise out of the same transaction or occurrence to be litigated.

## 3. Impact of Rule 18(a)

If the defendant can properly assert a counterclaim against a plaintiff, then Rule 18(a) authorizes the defendant to join all other claims it has against the plaintiff, whether related to the counterclaim, or not. "A party asserting a claim to relief as . . . a counterclaim . . . may join, either as independent or as alternative claims as many claims . . . as the party has against an opposing party." Rule 18(a). Thus, a defendant has the same unfettered authority that as a plaintiff to add additional claims *once it asserts a permissive or compulsory counterclaim that is properly anchored in federal court.* There is no requirement that an *additional* counterclaim arise out of the same set of facts as the first counterclaim, for example.

But, before the defendant can take advantage of Rule 18(a)'s broad authorization to join even completely unrelated claims, the defendant must first have authority under Rule 13(a) or (b) to join at least one counterclaim against the plaintiff *and* subject matter jurisdiction must exist and the parties must examine whether independent bases for personal jurisdiction or venue are required.

# C. Procedure for Joining Claims or Counterclaims

As illustrated above, a plaintiff exercises the authority granted by Rule 18(a) by joining in its complaint any additional claims it has. A plaintiff may also amend its original complaint to join claims later. *See* Chapter 42.

A defendant can include in its answer any counterclaim that it has against the plaintiff by pleading it, in form much like the plaintiff's complaint. Typically, at the end of its answer the defendant will include a statement of each counterclaim, generally following the format of a complaint. If a defendant files an answer without including either form of counterclaim, the defendant may have to seek leave to amend its answer. *See* Chapter 41.

---

## Checkpoints

- Can you explain when the Rules authorize a plaintiff to join a claim? When they require joinder?

- When can a defendant join a claim against a plaintiff? What is that called? Against a defendant? What is that called?

- When must a defendant join a claim against a plaintiff?

# Chapter 17

# Authority to Join Parties

---

### Party Joinder Roadmap

This chapter identifies the Rules that authorize joinder of a *party* to a suit, including as a plaintiff, defendant, crossclaim defendant, counter-claim defendant, or third-party defendant.

This chapter also describes the narrow circumstances when Rule 19 requires that a party be joined, or the claim be dismissed, and explains the process for making that determination.

---

This chapter explores joinder of parties. As you have seen and will see further, although the Rules do circumscribe joinder, circumstances could lead to a huge suit with many parties joining completely unrelated claims that could be unmanageable. Consequently, even if joinder of claims or parties is proper, a district court has discretion to sever claims completely (putting them in distinct lawsuits), or to order separate trials (keeping them together for pre-trial purposes, but then holding separate trials). *See* Chapter 18.

## A. Joinder of Parties by Plaintiffs

### 1. Permissive Joinder of Parties by Plaintiffs

This first paragraph may sound silly but it is important. There is no rule about joining or "being" the first plaintiff, or the first defendant. Someone just "is" the first plaintiff and is the first defendant, at least so far as the rules go. One rule, Rule 17 bears only a little on this issue. The real law about who must be a plaintiff, and who must be a defendant, comes from substantive law: third party beneficiary contract law explains, for example, who may sue when a contract is breached; foreseeability doctrine in tort law limits who can sue. Likewise, a defendant's duty—whether arising in tort, contract, or by statute—generally governs who may be sued. Those are not procedural rules, however.

Rule 20(a) is the primary source of authority for two or more plaintiffs to agree to file a suit together, to for one or more plaintiffs to agree to bring one civil action against one or more defendants. That Rule permits a person to join a suit as an additional plaintiff if the person's claim arises out of the same basic set of facts as an existing plaintiff. Similarly, Rule 20(a) also permits a plaintiff to join an additional defendant if the claim against that person arises out of the same basic set of facts as the claim against another defendant. In other words, the Rules generally permit: (A) everybody who has a claim arising out of the same basic set of facts to join as a plaintiff in one suit, and (B) joining as a defendant everyone who might be liable to a plaintiff for what happened in that same basic set of facts. A district court's decision granting or denying joinder of parties under Rule 20(a) will be reversed only for abuse of discretion, and those instances are difficult to find. *Watson v. Blankinship,* 20 F.3d 383 (10th Cir. 1994) (finding district court had improperly permitted joinder of defendant against whom plaintiff asserted an assault claim with a defendant against whom the plaintiff asserted a tortious interference with contract claim).

In addition to Rule 20(a), if a defendant asserts a counterclaim against an existing plaintiff, then that plaintiff may join a party as a third-party defendant under Rule 14(b). Rule 14 is discussed below.

### a. Permissive Joinder of One or More Co-Plaintiffs by a Plaintiff

Rule 20(a)(1) describes when a party *may* join a party as a co-plaintiff. Rule 20(a)(2) describes when a plaintiff may join a party as a co-defendant. Rule 19 describes when a party *must* be joined — as either a plaintiff or defendant. We'll tackle Rule 20 first.

When *can* an existing plaintiff join a party as a co-plaintiff? "Persons may join in one action as plaintiffs if (A) they assert any right to relief jointly, severally, or in the alternative with respect to or arising out of the same transaction, occurrence, or series of transactions or occurrences; *and* (B) any question of law or fact common to all plaintiffs will arise in the action." FRCP 20(a)(1). Thus, there are two requirements: (A) the person to be joined as a co-plaintiff must assert a right to relief with respect to the same transaction as another plaintiff *and* (B) there must be a question of law or fact in common among their claims. Two plaintiffs do not need to seek identical relief to be joined. FRCP 20(a)(3). Also realize that if one plaintiff wants to sue alone, someone can't use Rule 20 to force themselves to be a plaintiff; courts cannot use Rule 20 to "bring in" people to be plaintiffs.

### i. What Is the "Same Transaction or Occurrence"?

To determine whether a particular factual situation constitutes a transaction or occurrence for purposes of Rule 20, courts consider whether a "logical relationship" exists between the claims. *See Mosley v. General Motors Corp.*, 497 F.2d 1330, 1333 (8th Cir. 1974) ("'Transaction' is a word of flexible meaning. It may comprehend a series of many occurrences, depending not so much upon the immediateness of their connection as upon their logical relationship."). Figuring out what that means is aided by the purpose of Rule 20(a): "to promote trial convenience and expedite the final determination of disputes, thereby preventing multiple lawsuits." *Mosley*, 497 F.2d 1330, at 1332. "Under the Rules, the impulse is toward entertaining the broadest possible scope of action consistent with fairness to the parties; joinder of claims, parties and remedies is strongly encouraged." *United Mine Workers of America v. Gibbs*, 383 U.S. 715, 724 (1966). Thus, courts have defined "series of transactions or occurrences" broadly in applying this Rule. *See Mosley*, 497 F.2d 1330.

For example, in *Mosley*, plaintiffs were African-American employees of GM who alleged that GM had a general policy of discrimination against African-Americans. *Id.* at 1331–33. Plaintiffs brought various claims, and sought injunctive relief, back pay, and other relief for purported instances of discrimination. The *Mosley* court held that the trial court had abused its discretion in denying plaintiffs the opportunity to join together in one action. The court recognized that joinder should be permitted of "all reasonably related claims for relief by or against different parties" and that "[a]bsolute identity of all events is unnecessary." *Id.* at 1333. Applying that law, the court held that the claims relating to "a company-wide policy purportedly designed to discriminate against blacks in employment" arise out the same series of transactions or occurrences, even though many of the facts alleged in support of each plaintiff's claims were quite distinct. (The court further concluded that the "discriminatory character of the defendants' conduct" created a common question of fact sufficient to satisfy the rule's second prong, discussed below.) *See Puricelli v. CAN Ins. Co.*, 185 F.R.D. 139 (N.D.N.Y. 1999) (similar fact pattern as *Mosley*). In contrast, where a policy is not alleged and the claims arise out of different employment circumstances, courts have found joinder improper. *See Sheets v. CTS Wireless Components, Inc.*, 213 F. Supp. 2d 1279 (D. N.M. 2002).

## ii. What is a "Common Question of Law or Fact"?

This requirement is minimal: there need be only a common question of law or fact, not identity of legal and factual issues among the parties. *See Anderson v. Docuport, Inc.*, 2007 WL 485342 (S.D.N.Y. 2007). If a logical relationship between the plaintiffs' claims exists, almost invariably there will be a common question of law or fact.

### b.  Permissive Joinder of Co-Defendants by a Plaintiff

Rule 20(a)(2) describes when a plaintiff may join a party as an additional defendant. In parallel with the first sentence of Rule 20(a), the second sentence provides: "Persons . . . may be joined in one action as defendants if (A) any right to relief is asserted against them jointly, severally, or in the alternative with respect of or arising out of the same transaction, occurrence, or series of transactions or occurrences, and (B) any question of law or fact common to all defendants will arise in the action." Thus, there are two requirements: (A) a right to relief must be asserted by a plaintiff against the additional defendant with respect to the same transaction as the claim against an existing defendant *and* (B) a question of law or fact in common must exist between the claims. It is not necessary that the defendant assert all, or the same, defenses as the other defendants. FRCP 20(a)(3).

These terms have the same meaning as under Rule 20(a)(1) concerning plaintiffs: there must be a logical relationship between the claims and at least one common question of law or fact.

## 2.  Mandatory Joinder of Parties: Rule 19 as a Narrow Exception to Party Autonomy

### a.  How Rule 19 Typically Gets Litigated

Rule 19 has some unusual aspects to it, and it's probably the densest of any of the Rules, but luckily it's narrower than it sounds. We will break it down into steps to master it. This section concludes with a flowchart to help you pull the analysis together.

Why is it rare? Normally, a plaintiff is going to sue everyone who ought to be sued so the plaintiff can obtain the full relief it wants and is entitled to. If a plaintiff can make more money by suing two defendants rather than one, more likely than not the plaintiff will sue them both. That's pretty obvious.

Suppose, though, that a plaintiff doesn't (because it wants to avoid joining a defendant who would destroy diversity), or can't join a person as a defendant (because the court lacks personal jurisdiction over the defendant, or venue would be improper over the claim against the additional defendant), and not only is that person someone who "should" be a defendant, but the court as a practical matter can't adjudicate the particular claim without that person being joined as a party. What if, for example, there's a dispute over who owns a painting. Bob claims title to the painting. Susie and Ernie, jointly as husband and wife, also claim title to it. Bob obviously ought to sue both Susie and Ernie. Most of the time, as noted above, Bob will: why shouldn't he, if what he wants is an order from the court giving him clear title to the painting?

But what if Bob doesn't, or can't sue both? Suppose, for example, that Bob's lawyer realizes that the court lacks personal jurisdiction over Susie, so suit is filed only against Ernie. Susie's not a party, and can't be made one, but she says she has an interest in the painting at issue. A court can't decide what she owns without her being a party. What happens?

Or, suppose Bob does sue both Ernie and Susie, but then Susie moves to dismiss for lack of personal jurisdiction, and is dismissed from the case. Can the case proceed against only Ernie? Often, the plaintiff *does* join every defendant who really ought to be a party, but then one obtains dismissal of claims against it for lack of personal or subject matter jurisdiction, or for improper venue. The remaining defendants then move to dismiss the claims against them under Rule 12(b)(7) for failure to join an indispensable party—namely, the defendant that just got itself dismissed! *See, e.g., Great-West Life Annuity Ins. Co. v. Woldemicael,* 2006 WL 1638497 (W.D. Wash. 2006) (after one defendant was dismissed for lack of personal jurisdiction, other defendants moved to dismiss for failing to join an indispensable party). Thus, a motion to dismiss for failure to join an indispensable party often follows the dismissal for lack of personal or subject matter jurisdiction, or for improper venue, of claims against one defendant in a multiple defendant case. That's a typical way that the question of whether someone who hasn't been joined to the suit must be joined.

Rule 19 is concerned with the problem of a suit lacking a party who "really, really ought" to be there, whether the party was omitted by the plaintiff or was named as a defendant but has been dismissed from the case. Combined with Rule 12(b)(7), *see* Chapter 35, Rule 19 allows a party to dismiss a claim when not everyone who "really, really ought" to be a party isn't one and can't be joined as one.

With that background, we will break down Rule 19 to grasp its unintuitive terminology and, in doing so, learn what the Rule means. Along the way, we'll pull the whole thing together with a flow chart and other visual aids that will help you master this rule.

A brief word on service of process and Rule 19. Rule 4(k)(1)(B) allows, in addition to service under applicable long-arm statutes, service on a Rule 19 defendant within 100 miles of the court house, whether the defendant is within the same state, or not. This "100 mile bulge" extends from a court into an adjoining state if the defendant is joined under Rule 19.

### b. Rule 19: Three Steps with a Venue-Related Twist

Rule 19 requires three-steps to determine what, if anything, should be done to decide a motion to dismiss under Rule 12(b)(7). In addition, the Rule takes an unusual twist about venue. The three steps to determine what impact an absent defendant has on a claim are:

1. If the absentee is not even a "necessary" party, deny the motion and proceed with litigation.
2. If the absentee is a "necessary" party, order the person joined if personal and subject matter jurisdiction are proper, without regard to venue.
3. If personal and subject matter jurisdiction are not proper, or if the person objects to venue after being joined and the claim cannot be transferred to a place with proper venue, determine whether the claim can proceed without the person. If so, proceed without joining the person; if not, dismiss the claim or, if possible, transfer it to a proper venue.

### i. Is the Person a "Necessary" Party?

The first step is to determine whether the missing person is even a "necessary" party. Often this will end the inquiry because "necessary" has been construed *very* narrowly. Rule 19(a) defines necessary parties. There are two, and only two, types of necessary parties:

| Two Types of Necessary Parties Under FRCP 19(a) | |
|---|---|
| (1) in that person's absence, the court cannot accord complete relief among existing parties; | (2) the person claims an interest relating to the subject of the action and is so situated that the disposition of the action in the person's absence may (i) as a practical matter impair or impede the person's ability to protect that interest or (ii) leave an existing party subject to a substantial risk of incurring double, multiple, or otherwise inconsistent obligations because of the interest ... |

These two types are *much narrower than you probably think*. I can't say it enough though: it's rare that a party is "necessary." "If understood in its ordinary sense, 'necessary' is too strong a word, for it is still possible under Rule 19(b) for the case to proceed without the joinder of the so-called 'necessary' absentee." *E.E.O.C. v. Peabody West. Coal Co.*, 400 F.3d 774, 779 (9th Cir. 2005). Instead of some intuitive meaning of "necessary," Rule 19(a) "defines the person whose joinder in the action is *desirable* in the interests of just adjudication." *Id.*

### (a) Parties Who Are Necessary to Accord Complete Relief to Existing Parties

The first type of Rule 19(a) necessary parties are those in whose absence complete relief cannot be accorded among those who are already parties. It means only what it says, and is narrower than it sounds.

Suppose a plaintiff is injured by a defective product, and sues only the retailer of the product, not the ultimate manufacturer. Is the manufacturer a necessary defendant? Or, what if a plaintiff brings a claim arising out of a conspiracy, but sues only one of the alleged conspirators. Are other conspirators necessary defendants? Put broadly, is one joint tortfeasor a necessary party to a suit against another?

The answer is "no." Joint tortfeasors are *never* even necessary parties. For example, in *Temple v. Synthes Corp., Ltd.*, 498 U.S. 5 (1990), plaintiff was injured after a device that had been implanted in his spine during surgery broke inside his body. The plaintiff filed a federal diversity suit against the manufacturer and also filed a state court negligence suit against the hospital and doctor who had performed the operation. The manufacturer moved the federal court to dismiss under Rule 12(b)(7) for failure to join indispensable parties—the hospital and doctor. The district court held that they were necessary parties. The Supreme Court reversed for abuse of discretion. It held that as a matter of law joint tortfeasors are not even "necessary" parties: "it is not necessary for all joint tortfeasors to be named as defendants in a single lawsuit." *Id.* Because the absentee defendants were not even "necessary" parties in terms of Rule 19(a), the Court concluded that "no inquiry under Rule 19(b) [was] necessary, because the threshold requirements of Rule 19(a) [had] not been satisfied." *Id.*

The Court's holding is in line with the literal language of Rule 19(a)(1)(A): a plaintiff can obtain complete relief against one of two joint tortfeasors. The fact that one then may have a claim for contribution or indemnity against a non-party does not mean the plaintiff can't obtain the relief it is entitled to against the one defendant; it means that the one defendant may have a claim against the non-party. (Nor, obviously, does a party who might be liable to a plaintiff claim an interest in the suit—just the opposite!) Other examples of this type of "necessary" parties include co-obligees on a contract. *Dickson v. Murphy,* 2006 WL 2847238 (3rd Cir. 2006). Again, the term "necessary" is much narrower than it sounds.

## (b) Parties Who Claim an Interest and Are Necessary to Join

The second type of necessary party is someone who claims "an interest relating to the subject of the action and is so situated that the disposition of the action in the person's absence may (i) as a practical matter impair or impede the person's ability to protect that interest or (ii) leave any existing party subject to a substantial risk of incurring double, multiple, or otherwise inconsistent obligations because of the claimed interest . . ." Rule 19(a)(1)(B). Whether a person is an indispensable party must be determined on a case-by-case basis and depends on the facts and circumstances. *Helzberg's Diamond Shops, Inc. v. Valley West Des Moines Shopping Center, Inc.,* 564 F.2d 816 (8th Cir. 1977).

One example of this type necessary party arises when two people jointly hold title to property, but only one is a named party to a suit over title to that property. For example, in *Broussard v. Columbia Gulf Transmission Co.,* 398 F.2d 885 (5th Cir. 1968), the court held that the owner of a small interest in real property was a necessary party to a suit to invalidate an easement over that property. Likewise, as a general rule, if litigation of a claim will result in a judgment that determines a non-party's rights under a contract, that non-party is a necessary party. *See Peregrine Myanmar Ltd. v. Segal,* 89 F.3d 41, 48 (2d Cir. 1996). But the suit must determine the non-party's rights.

A case used in casebooks to illustrate this type of necessary party is *Haas v. Jefferson Nat'l Bank,* 442 F.2d 394 (5th Cir. 1971). There, Haas sued the bank, contending that even though the bank had known of an agreement between Haas and Glueck whereby they agreed to jointly acquire some stock in that bank, the bank had issued all of the shares and had paid dividends only to Glueck. Haas sought an order compelling the bank to issue 50% of the shares to him, or to pay him damages equal to that amount. The bank argued that Glueck was an indispensable party, and the district court ordered that he be joined. However, joinder destroyed subject matter jurisdiction (Glueck was a citizen of the same state as Haas) and so the court dismissed the complaint without prejudice. The appellate court held that Glueck was a necessary party since he claimed an interest in the stock and if he was not added as a party, the Bank might as a practical matter face inconsistent obligations, since even if in this suit Haas was awarded some of the stock, that would not preclude Glueck from being awarded that same stock if he brought suit later.

## ii. If the Person Is Necessary, Joinder Must Be Ordered if Personal and Subject Matter Jurisdiction Exist

A party who is "necessary" *must* be joined. Thus, if an absentee is "necessary" then joinder is required. If the absentee can be joined as a party—if there is authority for the claim, subject matter jurisdiction exists, venue is proper, and the court has personal jurisdiction—then the party is joined and off everyone goes.

But, what does a court do if the absentee cannot be joined because the court lacks subject matter jurisdiction over the claim, or personal jurisdiction over the absentee?

Here's the counter-intuitive part of Rule 19: the court doesn't have to dismiss even if it lacks personal or subject matter jurisdiction over a claim involving a person who is "necessary." The word "necessary" may import to you too much significance, and may lead you to counter-intuitive result. Suit can proceed without joining a "necessary" party. "If understood in its ordinary sense, 'necessary' is too strong a word, for it is still possible under FRCP 19(b) for the case to proceed without the so-called 'necessary' absentee. In fact, FRCP 19(a) 'defines the persons whose joinder in the action is desirable in the interests of just adjudication." *Equal Employment Opp'y Comm'n. v. Peabody Western Coal Co.*, 400 F.3d 774, 779 (9th Cir. 2005).

Instead, "necessary" means only that the analysis proceeds to the next step: the court must determine whether the "necessary" person is "indispensable." That's what FRCP 19(b) defines. If the necessary person indispensable, then, and only then, might the court have to dismiss if it can't join the person as a party. Before we get there, though, you need to appreciate the following: the venue twist.

### (a) Joinder Can't be Ordered if Personal or Subject Matter Jurisdiction is Lacking, but Must be Ordered Even if Venue is Improper

To determine whether a necessary person can be joined, there need only be subject matter and personal jurisdiction. If either or both are lacking, then the court must determine whether the necessary person is "indispensable" under Rule 19(b).

The Rule treats venue differently. If the court has personal and subject matter jurisdiction over a claim against the necessary absentee, that absentee must be joined. If, after joinder, the necessary absentee objects to venue and it's in fact improper, then the case proceeds—but without that party. This comes from Rule 19(a)(3) which says: "If a joined party objects to venue and the joinder would make venue improper, the court must dismiss that party." Thus, the person is joined, but if he objects to venue, then claims against that party over which venue is improper must be dismissed. *Patterson v. MacDougall*, 506 F.2d 1, 5 (5th Cir. 1971) (courts will not pre-determine whether necessary party will object to venue); *Turner v. CF&I Steel Corp.*, 510 F. Supp. 537, 546–47 (E.D. Pa. 1981) (joining necessary party to see if it raises improper venue as an objection). Put another way, a necessary party must be joined without a court determining whether or not venue would be proper. But, not all courts recognize this, and some hold that improper venue is a basis to deny joinder. *E.g., Dickson v. Murphy*, 2006 WL 2847238 (3rd Cir. 2006). However, that's not what Rule 19(a)(3) says: it says dismiss that party. A court doesn't dismiss someone who has never been made a party.

Once the absentee is joined as a party, then it can object if venue is improper, and must do so under Rule 12(b)(3) and seek dismissal or transfer under 28 U.S.C. § 1406(a) if venue is improper. *See* Rule 19(a)(3); Chapter 32. If venue is improper, then the court must dismiss or transfer. But what joining the necessary party allows the court to do is to determine whether there is a district to which the case can be transferred where venue, subject matter jurisdiction, and personal jurisdiction will be proper. If there is no such district or the court deems that the interests of justice do not warrant transfer, then the court must grant the motion to dismiss for improper venue by dismissing the necessary party after joining it. So, if personal or subject matter jurisdiction are lacking, or if the party is joined but then dismissed because it objects to improper venue, then the court must analyze the next step.

### iii. Determining Whether a Necessary Person Is Indispensable

Rule 19(b) defines "indispensable parties." Indispensable parties are a narrower subset of the already narrow category of necessary parties. The question of indispensability only comes up if the court can't join a necessary party or joins them but they object to venue and the court can't transfer the claim but instead must dismiss.

A court faced with a necessary party that cannot be joined or after being joined objects to venue and the claim can't be transferred must consider the four factors in Rule 19(b) to determine whether that necessary party is also "indispensable":

(1) the extent to which a judgment rendered in the person's absence might prejudice that person or existing parties;

(2) the extent to which any prejudice could be lessened or avoided by protective provisions in the judgment, shaping the relief, or other measures;

(3) whether a judgment rendered in the person's absence would will be adequate; and

(4) whether the plaintiff would have an adequate remedy if the action were dismissed for non-joinder.

Based upon these and any other pertinent factors, the court must determine whether it can "in equity and good conscience" proceed without joining the necessary person or, instead, should dismiss the claim. *Gardiner v. V.I. Water & Power Auth.*, 145 F.3d 635, 640–41 (3rd Cir. 1998) (Rule 19(b)'s factors are the most important but not the exclusive factors in assessing indispensability).

The first factor "overlaps considerably with the Rule 19(a) analysis." *Gardiner v. V.I. Water & Power Auth.*, 145 F.3d 635, 641 n. 4 (3rd Cir. 1998). Courts consider whether, as a practical matter, the absent party's interests will be protected. *Merrill Lynch, Pierce, Fenner and Smith, Inc. v. ENC Corp.*, 464 F.3d 885, 892 (9th Cir. 2006). The second factor considers whether the court can shape the judgment or relief sought to lessen the prejudice arising from non-joinder. The third factor notes the interest of the public in having a dispute completely, consistently, and efficiently resolved. *Provident Tradesmens Bank & Trust Co. v. Patterson*, 390 U.S. 102, 111 (1968). The fourth factor considers whether, if the claim is dismissed, it could be litigated in another state or federal court. *See Bank of Am. Nat'l Trust & Savs. Asss'n. v. Nilsi*, 844 F.3d 1050, 1055 (3rd Cir. 1988). These factors are not exclusive, and the entire inquiry is based on "the balancing of competing interests" and is "steeped in pragmatic considerations." *Mattel, Inc. v. Bryant*, 446 F.3d 1011 (9th Cir. 2006). *See Provident Tradesmen's Bank & Trust Co. v. Patterson*, 390 U.S. 102 (1968) (engaging in lengthy analysis of practical consequences of proceeding without joining a person).

Several casebooks include the *Helzberg* case. There, Valley West Mall leased a space to Helzberg's, a full line jewelry story. A provision in the lease stated that the Mall would not lease spaces to more than two other full line jewelry stores. It leased two other spaces to full line jewelry stores, and leased a space to Lord's Jewelers, but the lease provided that Lords would not run a full line jewelry store. Even so, Lords intended to operate a full line jewelry store in its space. Naturally, Helzberg filed suit, but it named only Valley West Mall as the defendant, not Lords, even though it sought as relief for its breach of contract claim an injunction to order Valley West Mall not to permit Lords, or any one else, to operate a fourth full line jewelry store in the mall.

Valley West Mall moved to dismiss for failure to join an indispensable party. The district court held that Lords was a necessary party under Rule 19(a), since the injunction would prevent Lords from operating its jewelry store in the mall. However, the district court held that Lords was not indispensable. The appellate court affirmed. It reasoned that Lord's rights under its lease would not be adjudicated in the case between Helzberg and Valley West Mall, since Lords was not a party to that case. The court also held that, even if Valley West Mall might be subject to inconsistent obligations as a result of the case, those inconsistent obligations were not the result of the litigation, but the result of Valley West Mall entering into potentially inconsistent lease agreements. It also reasoned that because the district court had offered to let Lords intervene, the district court had taken steps to protect Lord's interest. Finally, it held that any potential for inconsistent obligations were merely speculative, since there was no indication that Lords was about to sue Valley West Mall, nor that a court would give its lease with Valley West Mall a reading inconsistent with the district court's order here. Accordingly, although Lords was a necessary party, it was not indispensable. The fact that it could not be joined did not preclude the court from proceeding to judgment.

Another case from casebooks is *Haas v. Jefferson Nat'l Bank*, 442 F.2d 394 (5th Cir. 1971), which reached a different conclusion. In that case, Haas alleged that the defendant bank had issued stock to Glueck that should have been issued to him, and the bank knew it. The court not only held that Glueck was a necessary party, as noted above, it held he was indispensable under Rule 19(b) because without joining Glueck the bank would likely face a second suit from Glueck over ownership of the shares, and it could result in inconsistent obligations owed by the bank; a jury could hold in the first case that Haas owned the stock, but in the second case that Glueck did. Finally, it realized that Haas could join Glueck as a party in state court, and resolve all the parties' ownership claims there.

If a court concludes it cannot proceed without the person joined as a party, then the person is indispensable: the court must join the person if it can do so without destroying subject matter jurisdiction, and it must obviously have personal jurisdiction. If it cannot join the party for either or both of those reasons, then the claim must be dismissed for failure to join an indispensable party. If the party can be joined, but after joinder raises a venue objection and venue is improper, then the court must dismiss the claims against that party if it cannot transfer the case to a district is proper. *Curtis Management Group, Inc. v. Academy of Motion Picture Arts & Sciences*, 717 F. Supp. 1362, 1374 (S.D. Ind. 1989) (recognizing court could transfer a case under 28 U.S.C. § 1406(a) where venue was improper over claim against necessary party). For a discussion of transfer of venue, see Chapter 39.

Finally, note that Rule 19 allows for joinder of a person not just as a defendant, but also as an "involuntary plaintiff." Suppose some but not all of the members of a homeowners' association file suit, and the plaintiffs want to join those homeowners who have not joined because they all have an interest in the suit and meet the definition of necessary parties, and can be joined. The existing plaintiffs can serve them with process and the court will align them as plaintiffs to reflect their interests.

**A Flow Chart for Rule 19**

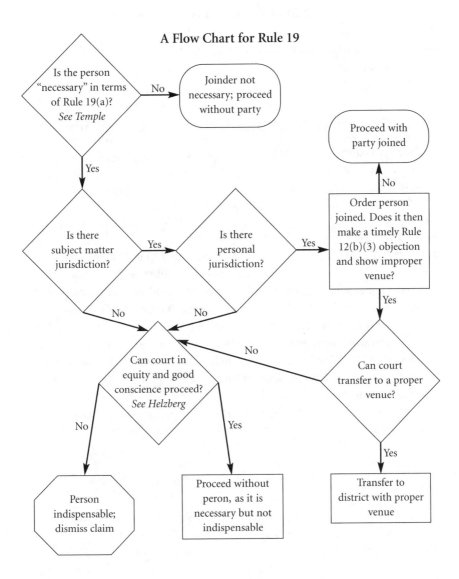

# B. Joinder of Parties by Defendants

The following table shows the only circumstances in which a defendant has authority to join a party. As we'll see, the first two are identical grants of authority that apply in slightly different circumstances.

| A Defendant Can Join a Person as a ... | |
|---|---|
| Party to a cross-claim asserted by it. | Rule 13(h) |
| Party to a counterclaim asserted by it. | Rule 13(h) |
| Third-party defendant | Rule 14(a)(5) |

## 1. Joining a Party to a Counterclaim or Crossclaim

Rule 13(h) doesn't have the meaning you might give it on first read. It sounds like it permits a defendant to join a non-party and make a claim *only* against it. Rule 13(h) is narrower than that.

A key point first. To take advantage of party joinder under Rule 13(h), the defendant must have a counter- or crossclaim pending against an existing party *or* must be making one in the pleading that seeks to join the additional party as a counterclaim or crossclaim defendant, pursuant to Rule 13(h). "Rule 13(h) only authorizes a court to join additional persons to adjudicate a counterclaim or cross-claim that is already in a filed pleading filed or that is being filed at the same time joinder of the non-party is sought. A counterclaim or crossclaim may not be directed solely against persons who are not already parties to the original action, but must be against at least one existing party." *F.D.I.C. v. Bathgate,* 27 F.3d 850, 873–74 (3d Cir. 1994). So, a defendant cannot under Rule 13(h) simply add a plaintiff to assert a counterclaim against it without making a counterclaim against an existing plaintiff:

| Proper Use of 13(h) | Improper Uses of 13(h) |
|---|---|
| 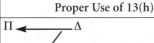 The defendant asserts a counterclaim against the plaintiff and joins the counterclaim-defendant; joinder of the counterclaim-defendant must be proper under Rules 19 or 20 (*i.e.*, at minimum the defendant asserts a claim against them that involves joint, several, or alternative liability and arises from a common question of law or fact. Suppose, for example, that in a suit for breach of contract, the defendant asserts in its counterclaim that the plaintiff breached the contract by conspiring with the counterclaim defendant. |  This is improper because defendant cannot use 13(h) to join a counterclaim defendant without also asserting a counterclaim against an existing plaintiff (and, even joinder of the counterclaim defendant must comply with Rule 19 or 20). |
| |  If the counterclaim against the counterclaim defendant neither meets Rule 19 or 20, then joinder of the counterclaim defendant is improper. Suppose, for example, the defendant asserts a counterclaim against the plaintiff and tries to assert a completely unrelated claim against the counterclaim defendant. It would be hard to envision how that circumstance could meet the requirements of either Rule 19 or 20. |

The table should make the text of Rule 13(h) clear to you in its central limitation: "Rules 19 and 20 govern the addition of a person as a party to a counterclaim or cross-claim." FRCP 13(h). Thus, a party can be joined if a counterclaim or cross-claim is asserted against an existing party *and* joinder of that additional party is proper under Rules 19 or 20. *See, e.g., Schoot v. U.S.,* 664 F. Supp. 293 (N.D. Ill. 1987).

Rule 13(h) allows joinder to parties as counterclaim plaintiffs or counter-claim defendants. The additional party must be authorized to make a claim, or have a claim made against it, under Rule 20 or 19. The same analysis above about the operation of Rule 19 applies when a defendant is acting like a plaintiff in asserting a counter- or crossclaim. A party asserting a claim against two parties can join them either (1) under Rule 20 as defendants to a claim if *both* (a) the two parties allegedly are liable for a claim arising out of the same circumstances *and* (b) a common question of law or fact will exists *or* (2) under Rule 19 if the person is either (a) a "necessary" *or* (b) "indispensable" party.

## 2. Impleader of Third-Party Defendants

### a. Scope of Rule 14(a)(1)

Rule 14(a)(1) is in some ways broader and other ways narrower than Rule 13(h). Specifically, Rule 14(a)(1) does allow a defendant to join a party without having to also assert a counter-claim or crossclaim against an existing party, and so in that respect it is broader than Rule 13(h). Rule 14 is the only Rule that permits a defendant to join a party without asserting a claim against an existing party. (If a defendant asserts a counterclaim against a plaintiff, the plaintiff may rely on Rule 14 to implead a third party. *See* Rule 14(b).)

However, Rule 14 is narrower than Rule 13(h) in that it allows the joinder of a third-party defendant only where that person "is or may be liable to [the existing defendant who is seeking to join the person under Rule 14] for all or part of the plaintiff's claim against" that existing defendant. FRCP 14(a)(1). The existing defendant, as a "third-party plaintiff" files a "third-party complaint" naming the non-party as a "third-party defendant" and serves it on the other parties, and obtains service of process on the non-party that it is seeking to join. This is called impleader.

Impleader is proper only when the basis for the claim by the third-party plaintiff (the existing defendant) is that the third-party defendant is or may be liable to the third-party plaintiff for all or a part of an existing plaintiff's claim. That's a narrow: typically, impleader will be proper where the defendant has a claim against the non-party should indemnify or at least contribute to any judgment the plaintiff obtains against the defendant. So, for example, impleader is proper where the defendant has a contractual claim for indemnification against a non-party, or a claim for contribution or indemnity arising under state or federal law. *See, e.g., Price v. CTB, Inc.,* 168 F. Supp. 2d 1299 (M.D. Ala. 2001) (impleading party authorized where state law recognized an implied claim for indemnity on behalf of defendant, against whom claims arising out of sale of defective chicken coops, against non-party who had allegedly sold the defendant components for the chicken coops). These are claims where the defendant can essentially allege: "if I'm liable to the plaintiff, you, non-party, are liable to me."

For these reasons, impleader is appropriate only when the third-party defendant's liability to the third-party plaintiff is "dependent upon the outcome of the main claim" or the third-party defendant is "potentially secondarily liable as a contributor to the defendant." *Kenneth Leventhal & Co. v. Joyner Wholesale Co.*, 736 F.2d 29, 31 (2d Cir. 1984). Impleader may be used only "when the third-party defendant's potential liability is dependent upon the outcome of the main claim" but cannot be used otherwise, even if the claim "arises out of the same general set of facts as the main claim." *Am. Express Travel Related Serv. Co., Inc. v. Beaumont*, 2002 WL 31298867 (N.D. Tex. 2002).

So, for example, in one typical casebook case, *Markvicka v. Broadhead-Garrett Co.*, 76 F.R.D. 205 (D. Neb. 1977), a machine injured a student during woodworking class. When the parents brought a products liability claim against the machine's manufacturer, it filed a third-party complaint against the school district, alleging that the school district owed contribution to the manufacturer for any liability it had to the plaintiff because the school district had improperly maintained the machine and had failed to supervise the student. The court denied the school district's motion to dismiss because under Nebraska law there was a right of contribution among joint tortfeasors.

In contrast, joinder under Rule 14 is not proper where the defendant is effectively alleging, "the plaintiff sued the wrong person, non-party: it's all the non-party's fault." Those claims are not within Rule 14(a) — the non-party not someone who "is or may be liable to [the existing defendant] for all or part of *the plaintiff's claim against the*" defendant. *See, e.g., Watergate Landmark Condo. Unit Owner's Ass'n v. Wiss, Janey, Elstner Ass'n.*, 117 F.R.D. 576, 578 (E.D. Va. 1987) ("a third-party claim is not appropriate where the defendant and putative third-party plaintiff says, in effect, 'It was him, not me.'"). Put the other way, a defendant cannot use Rule 14(a) to join a party who may be liable *to the plaintiff. Barab v. Menford*, 98 F.R.D. 455, 456 (E.D. Pa. 1983); *Allstate Ins. Co. v. Hugh Cole Builder, Inc.*, 187 F.R.D. 671 (M.D. Ala. 1999); *Walkill 5 Assocs. II v. Tectonic Eng'r, P.C.*, 1997 WL 452252 (D.N.J. 1997).

So, for example, in a case the course books cover, *Barab v. Menford*, 98 F.R.D. 455 (E.D. Pa. 1983), the plaintiff sued a hotel after tripping over a doormat. The hotel properly impleaded Channel, the party that had sold the doormat to the hotel, alleging that the doormat was defective and so if the hotel was liable to the plaintiff, the manufacturer had to indemnify the hotel. Channel, in turn, relied on the language then in Rule 14(a) providing that a "third-party defendant may proceed under this rule against any person not a party to the action who is or may be liable to the third-party defendant for all or a part of the claim made in the action against the third-party defendant." However, what the third-party defendant claimed was not that the fourth party defendant had sold the doormat to it, and so was liable to it if it was liable to the plaintiff, but instead alleged that the fourth party defendant had, in fact, sold the doormat directly to the plaintiff. The district court as a result denied the motion for leave to implead the fourth party defendant.

Why the rule and its limitations? The purpose of this rule is to promote efficiency by eliminating the need for the defendant to bring a separate lawsuit against a third party for contribution or indemnity where that claim arises out of the same occurrence as a plaintiff's claim against the defendant. Where that efficiency is lacking, then the purpose of the Rule is not met, and joinder is not authorized. In that regard, a district court has discretion to permit or reject the joinder of even an appropriate third-party claim. *Walkill 5 Assocs. II v. Tectonic Eng'r, P.C.*, 1997 WL 452252 (D.N.J. 1997).

### b. Time for Filing and Serving

A defendant has the right to file and serve a third-party complaint so long as it is filed within 14 days of serving its original answer. FRCP 14(a)(1). Otherwise, the third-party plaintiff must seek leave from the court to file the third-party complaint. *Id.* The courts generally consider these factors in deciding whether to grant leave to file when sought after the 14 day period:

> (i) whether the movant deliberately delayed or was derelict in filing the motion; (ii) whether impleading would unduly delay or complicate the trial; (iii) whether impleading would prejudice the third-party defendant; and (iv) whether the third-party complaint states a claim upon which relief can be granted. The court must balance the benefits derived from impleader — that is, the benefits of settling related matters in one suit — against the potential prejudice to the plaintiff and third-party defendants.

*Too, Inc. v. Kohl's Dept. Stores, Inc.*, 213 F.R.D. 138, 140 (S.D.N.Y. 2003). *See, e.g., Sovereign Sales, L.L.C. v. New York Accessory Group, Inc.*, 2005 WL 289577 (S.D.N.Y 2005) (denying motion for leave to file third-party complaint sought two years after suit had been filed and where suit for contribution could still be separately filed); *Southern Boston Mgmt. Corp. v. BP Prods. N. Am. Inc.*, 2004 WL 2624891 (Nov. 18, 2004) (filing permitted where parties had not yet begun discovery).

### c. Service of the Third-Party Complaint

While the long-arm statute may also be used, Rule 4(k)(1)(B) authorizes service of a party joined under Rule 14 who is served "within a judicial district of the United States and not more than 100 miles from the place from which the summons issues." Thus, in addition to service under long-arm statutes, service on a third-party defendant within 100 miles of the courthouse, whether the third-party defendant is within the same state or not, is proper if the third-party defendant has minimum contacts with that "bulge" area. *Flight Extenders, Inc. v. Lakewood Aircraft Serv., Inc.*, 90 F.R.D. 676 (E.D. Pa. 1981). The third-party defendant, however, must be served within the 100-mile bulge; it is not enough if it has minimum contacts with the bulge, but is served elsewhere. *Langsam-Borenstein Partnership by Langsam v. NOC Enterp., Inc.*, 137 F.R.D. 217 (E.D. Pa. 1990).

## 3. Joinder of Additional Claims Under Rule 18(a)

If a defendant has one claim authorized by Rule 14(a) against a third-party defendant over which the court has subject matter and personal jurisdiction, then that claim can serve as an anchor claim for additional claims under Rule 18(a). (Venue is not required over claims under Rule 14 by defendants, but it will almost inevitably be proper.) Consequently, the defendant as a third-party plaintiff may join against the third-party defendant all claims that the third-party plaintiff has to assert under Rule 18(a), whether or not related to the claim authorized by Rule 14(a). Again, the district court may sever the claims or order separate trials.

---

### Checkpoints

- Can you describe when a plaintiff may be join a co-plaintiff? A co-defendant?
- What is a necessary party under Rule 19? What happens if that necessary party cannot be joined? If a party that cannot be joined indispensable?
- Can you describe when a defendant may join a party to a cross-claim? Counterclaim? By way of impleader?

# Chapter 18

# Multiple Parties and Joinder

---

### Multiple Parties Roadmap

This chapter discusses some of the additional claims that can be brought once a party is properly joined to a suit. Then it describes severance and separate trials — the two means by which a court can simplify even the most convoluted cases for the entire litigation or just for trial.

---

## A. Crossclaims against Co-Parties and Joinder of Parties to Crossclaims

Rule 13(g) authorizes a party—plaintiff or defendant—to bring a "crossclaim" against a co-party, that is, a party who is already, too, named as a plaintiff or defendant. So, a plaintiff can bring a crossclaim against a party already joined as a plaintiff, and a defendant can do so against a party already joined as a defendant. This is joining claims against existing parties.

So, if two plaintiffs are properly joined as plaintiffs, one of them may under Rule 13(g) assert a crossclaim against the other so long as the crossclaim arises "out of the transaction or occurrence that is the subject matter of the original action or of a counterclaim, or if the claim relates to any property that is the subject matter of the original action." FRCP 13(g). A crossclaim "may include a claim that the co-party is or may be liable to the crossclaimant for all or part of a claim asserted in the action against the crossclaimant." *Id.; cf.* FRCP 14(a). Crossclaims are permissive, not compulsory, under the Rules.

So, for example, in *Harrison v. M.S. Carriers, Inc.,* 1999 WL 195539 (E.D. La. 1999), a driver and passenger as plaintiffs sued another driver in negligence arising out of a car wreck. The passenger then filed a crossclaim against her fellow plaintiff, who was driving the car she was riding in. The court held that the crossclaim was proper since it was against a co-party and arose out of the same transaction or occurrence as the original claim.

Rule 18(a) applies once a crossclaim is properly asserted. Thus, a party who asserts a crossclaim against a party can use Rule 18(a) to join even unrelated claims against that same party.

The rules also allow joining a party to a crossclaim asserted against an existing party. Specifically, Rule 13(h) allows a party who asserts a crossclaim against an existing party to join a party to that crossclaim, either as a cross-claim defendant or cross-claim plaintiff. But Rule 13(h) cannot be used unless there is already an existing co-party against whom the crossclaim is asserted, as is the case with counterclaims as we saw in the earlier chapter.

What about compulsory counterclaims when a crossclaim is asserted? Suppose Bob and Susie sue Jill for breach of contract. Bob also makes a crossclaim against Susie. What if Susie has a claim that arises out of the same transaction or occurrence as Bob's crossclaim against her? Does Susie simply have a permissive crossclaim, or is Bob now an "opposing party" and so the compulsory counterclaim rule applies? The courts split. *Rainbow Mgmt. Group., Ltd. v. Atlantis Submarines Hawaii, L.P.,* 158 F.R.D. 656 (D. Haw. 1994). If, however, the crossclaim is merely one for indemnity or contribution, courts hold that the parties do not become "opposing parties" and trigger the compulsory counterclaim rule. *See Hemme v. Bharti,* 183 S.W.3d 593 (Mo. 2006).

# B. Rule 14: Fourth-Party Defendants and Beyond

Rule 14 is dense. Among the options it presents is the ability of the third-party defendant to "assert against the plaintiff any claim arising out of the transaction or occurrence that is the subject matter of the plaintiff's claim against the third-party plaintiff." FRCP 14(a)(2)(D). So, a third-party defendant can bring a claim against the party who impleaded it if the claim arises out of the transaction or occurrence. Rule 18(a) does not permit the third-party defendant to join any additional claims, however.

Similarly, Rule 14(a)(5) permits the third-party defendant to "proceed under this rule against a non-party who is or may be liable to the third-party defendant for all or a part of any claim against it." So, the third-party defendant can file its own third-party complaint against a fourth-party defendant, arguing that if the third-party defendant is liable to the third-party plaintiff, the fourth-party defendant is liable to the third-party defendant. The caption might look something like this:

Bob,
Plaintiff v.
Susie,

Defendant/Third-party plaintiff v.

Jill,

Third-party Defendant/Fourth-party plaintiff v.

Ernie,

Fourth-party Defendant

Finally, if a counterclaim is made against the plaintiff, the plaintiff is authorized to bring a third-party complaint to the same extent as is a defendant. FRCP 14(b). An interesting example of this arose in *Guaranteed Sys., Inc. v. Am. Nat'l Can Co.*, 842 F. Supp. 855 (M.D.N.C. 1994). The defendant filed a counterclaim against the plaintiff in a case where subject matter jurisdiction was based on diversity. The plaintiff then used Rule 14(b) to implead a third-party defendant who would be liable to the plaintiff if the plaintiff were liable to the defendant on the counterclaim. The court held the plaintiff had authority to join the third-party defendant. However, for reasons we will see later, the court recognized that there was no original jurisdiction over the claim and the supplemental jurisdiction statute excluded a claim by a plaintiff against a party joined under Rule 14. *See* Chapter 21.

## C. Misjoinder, Severance, and Separate Trials

Rule 21 provides that misjoinder of a claim or party is not grounds for dismissal. Instead, the court may on its own or upon motion of a party drop a claim or a party. FRCP 21. Thus, if joinder of a claim or party is improper, the party or claim is dismissed, not the whole lawsuit.

In addition, as we've seen with respect to other joinder rules, rules allow courts to sever claims from a lawsuit—they proceed as a separate suit—or to order the claims remain together in one "suit" but for claims to be tried separately to different juries.

---

### Checkpoints

- Can you identify a crossclaim and when it is proper to join a party to a crossclaim?
- Do you understand how Rule 14(a) permits the third-party defendant to bring claims against the plaintiff? To join fourth-party defendants?
- Can you describe the likely impact of improper joinder?

# Chapter 19

# Interpleader: A Non-Party Creates a Suit between Two Parties

---

### Interpleader Roadmap

This chapter describes the two types of interpleader, both of which allow a person who holds property but claims no interest in it to force two or more others who do claim an interest in that property to litigate their claims to that property.

---

The Rules authorize a person to file a proceeding that does not fit neatly in any other chapter. Lawsuits often are between two parties, each of whom claims it owns certain property or is entitled to certain rights. What if a person possesses property, but *doesn't* believe he owns it, but two or more other people have competing claims to the property, but the person who possesses the property doesn't know which of them in fact is the rightful owner? If the person keeps the property, he's going to get sued by two parties; if he gives it to one of them, he may get sued by the other.

Interpleader allows a person in possession of property—called the "stakeholder"—to settle the competing claims in one lawsuit by forcing the people who claim to own the property to litigate the question of ownership. It lets the stakeholder get out of their way, but he can seek attorneys' fees and costs. *Interstate Life Assurance Co. v. Sedlak,* 1985 WL 1595 (N.D. Ill. 1985) ("federal courts have exercised their discretion to award fees as a matter of course to disinterested stakeholders who are forced to commence litigation through no fault of their own").

## A. What the Two Kinds of Interpleader Share

There are two types of interpleader: (1) "rule interpleader" under Rule 22; and (2) "statutory interpleader" under 28 U.S.C. §§ 1335, 1397 and 2361. We will address their many similarities first.

First, there must be a single and identifiable property, fund, or right. *See State Farm Fire & Cas. Co. v Tashire,* 386 U.S. 523 (1967). Second, the stakeholder must not claim an interest in the property, fund, or right. Third, more than one claimant must assert claims to the property, fund, or right. *See Morongo Band of Mission Indians v. Ca. St. Bd. of Equalization,* 858 F.2d 1376, 1381 (9th Cir. 1998). Fourth, the stakeholder must demonstrate a real, reasonable fear of inconsistent liability. *Indianapolis Colts v. Mayor & City Council of Baltimore,* 741 F.2d 954, 957 (7th Cir. 1984). Finally, fifth, the stakeholder must timely file the interpleader action. *Mendez v. Teachers Ins. & Annuity Ass'n,* 982 F.2d 783, 788 (2d Cir. 1992) (11 month delay after receiving notice of claims was untimely).

After filing an interpleader action, the competing claimants—who, unlike the stakeholder, do claim an interest in the property—litigate who should be awarded title to the property. *See Commercial Nat'l Bank v. Demos,* 18 F.3d 485, 487 (7th Cir. 1994).

# B. Statutory Interpleader

Statutory interpleader has several benefits over rule interpleader. First, Section 1335(a) creates subject matter jurisdiction more broadly than the general diversity statute. Rather than requiring complete diversity and an amount in controversy exceeding $75,000, subject matter jurisdiction exists where: (a) two of the claimants have diverse citizenship, without regard to the citizenship of the stakeholder, *Truck-a-Tune, Inc. v. Re,* 23 F.3d 60, 62 (2d Cir. 1994), *and* (b) the value of the property exceeds $500. *See* 28 U.S.C. § 1335(a). Second, venue is proper in any district where at least one claimant resides. 28 U.S.C. § 1397. Third, the stakeholder can rely on nationwide service of process. 28 U.S.C. § 2361. However, unlike rule interpleader, the stakeholder must deposit the property with the court. 28 U.S.C. § 1335(a)(2). On the other hand, venue is not available under the general venue statute for statutory interpleader. *See New Jersey Sports Prods., Inc. v. Don King Prods., Inc.,* 15 F. Supp. 2d 534 (D. N.J. 1998).

# C. Rule Interpleader

Because it is a rule, not a statute, Rule 22 does not create any subject matter jurisdiction. Instead, there must be either diversity or federal question jurisdiction. Further, rule interpleader does not require that the stakeholder deposit the property with the court, but a court can require that it be deposited, and the stakeholder can ask the court to take possession of it. *See John v. Sotheby's Inc.,* 141 F.R.D. 29, 34 (S.D.N.Y. 1992).

# D. Adjudication of Interpleader Actions

Interpleader actions generally involve two separate trials: in the first, the parties try the issue of whether the stakeholder meets the conditions for interpleader; if interpleader is proper, then in the second, the court will determine which claimant should be awarded title to the property. *NYLife Distribs., Inc., v. Adherence Group, Inc.,* 72 F.3d 371, 375 (3rd Cir. 1995).

As an example of the first, in a case used in the casebooks, *Don King Productions,* a New Jersey boxing promoter had possession of a $3 million guaranteed minimum that ostensibly belonged to the loser of a boxing match. It was unclear who should be paid the prize, however, because of controversy over how the boxing match had ended. It could be that the prize money belonged to various entertainment interests, or to the losing boxer, or to other parties. The promoter therefore filed an interpleader action, showing that there were adverse claims to the monies, and that it faced inconsistent or multiple obligations if interpleader were not allowed.

If the court holds interpleader is improper and dismisses the case, the order is immediately appealable, but if the court finds interpleader proper, appeal cannot take place until after the second trial is held. *Diamond Shamrock Oil & Gas v. Comm'r of I.R.S.,* 422 F.2d 532, 534 (8th Cir. 1970).

---

## Checkpoints

- Can you describe when interpleader is proper?
- Can you describe the similarities and differences between statutory and rule-based interpleader?

# Chapter 20

# Intervention: The Only Way for Someone to Force Himself into a Lawsuit

---

### Intervention Roadmap

This chapter discusses the rare circumstances when a non-party may, or must be permitted to, intervene in a lawsuit already pending between other parties.

---

What if a suit is pending and a person hasn't been joined as a party, but if he is not joined, there will likely have to be another suit over, essentially, the same issues? While normally the plaintiff and defendant control who is joined to a suit, Rule 24 allows a person—called an "applicant"—to voluntarily seek court permission to join a pending lawsuit even though neither the defendant nor plaintiff sought to join it and even if all existing parties in fact object to joinder. The purpose is to prevent the need for more than one suit over the same basic set of facts.

However, the Rules do not permit a person to "crash" a lawsuit simply because there might be multiple suits. Instead, the ability of an applicant to intervene is *very* limited.

Why, you ask, would anyone want to be joined in a lawsuit? There are many instances. Suppose, for example, that a plaintiff has sued a defendant, and the defendant is about to disclose information to the plaintiff that a third party believes is privileged. The plaintiff may want to intervene in that suit to prevent the disclosure of the privileged information.

## A. Intervention

There are two types of intervention: (1) intervention as of right; and (2) permissive intervention. For either type, the applicant serves on the original parties and files with the court a motion to intervene that explains the basis for intervention and the claim or defense in which the applicant wants to intervene. FRCP 24(c). The applicant should also include with that motion a copy of the pleading—typically a complaint or an answer—on which it seeks to intervene. Both types of intervention also have two types, as summarized by this chart:

| Intervention as of Right | Permissive Intervention |
| --- | --- |
| Must be allowed if a federal statute gives the applicant an unconditional right to intervene. | May be allowed if a federal statute gives the applicant a conditional right to intervene. |
| Must be allowed if the applicant (a) claims an interest relating to the property or transaction which is subject of the pending action and (b) is so situated that disposing of the action may as a practical matter impair or impede the movant's ability to protect that interest, *unless* the existing parties adequately represent that interest. | May be allowed if the applicant's claim or defense and the pending action have a question or law or fact in common, taking into consideration whether allowing the applicant to intervene will unduly delay or prejudice adjudication of the rights of the original parties to the pending action. |

# 1. Intervention as of Right

There are two types: (a) statutory and (b) by rule. Where intervention is as of right, the applicant does not need to establish an independent basis for subject matter jurisdiction over its claim. *Smith Pet. Serv. Int'l v. Monsanto Chem. Co.,* 420 F.2d 1103, 1115 (5th Cir. 1972).

### a. Rule 24(a)(1): Unconditional Statutory Right

Statutes that give private parties the unconditional right to intervene are uncommon, but those that permit the federal government to intervene in certain disputes are common. For example, if the constitutionality of a federal statute is at issue, the federal government has the right to intervene.

### b. Rule 24(a)(2): Rule-Based Right

Intervention as of right requires proof by the applicant of three elements: (1) it timely filed an application to intervene in which it (2) claims an interest relating to the property or transaction which is subject of the suit and (3) shows that it is so situated that disposing of the action may as a practical matter impair or impede the movant's ability to protect its interest, unless existing parties adequately represent that interest. FRCP 24(a).

Timeliness is a flexible determination that examines whether the applicant knew of the dispute but delayed, and considers the prejudice to the parties as well as to the party seeking to intervene. *Cohen v. Republic of the Philippines,* 146 F.R.D. 90 (S.D.N.Y. 1993). With respect to the second element, the applicant need not be interested in every aspect of the case, but must claim an interest in subject matter involved in the suit. It is sufficient if the litigation could result in an injunction that will affect the intervener's interest. *Daggett v. Comm. on Gov'tal Ethics & Election Practices,* 172 F.3d 104, 110–11 (1st Cir. 1999). With respect to the third element, the applicant must show that its ability to protect the interest as a practical matter will be impaired or impeded if it is denied intervention. For example, it is sufficient if the relief sought in the suit will affect the proposed intervenor's contractual rights. *B. Fernandez & HNOS, Inc. v. Kellogg USA, Inc.,* 440 F.3d 541, 545 (1st Cir. 2006).

A case cited in the casebooks and applying these principles is *Cohen v. Republic of the Philippines,* 146 F.R.D. 90 (S.D.N.Y. 1993), where Imelda Marcos (wife of the former dictator of the Philippines) moved to intervene in an interpleader action between the government of the Philippines and Cohen over which of the two owned certain valuable paintings. Marcos claimed that neither of them owned them; she did. The court granted her motion to intervene because she had moved to intervene within five months of learning of the dispute and without great prejudice to the parties, who knew she claimed and interest in the paintings. She supported her claim to the paintings with an affidavit explaining how she acquired them with her own money. Finally, she showed that the existing parties did not represent her interest, since her interest was contrary to both of their interests.

## 2. Permissive Intervention

An applicant seeking permissive intervention must establish an independent basis for subject matter jurisdiction over its claim, unlike intervention as of right.

### a. Rule 24(b)(1)(A): Conditional Statutory Right

Federal statutes may give a private party or the federal government a conditional right to intervene in a suit. These are not common but obviously control when applicable.

### b. Rule 24(b)(1)(B): Rule-Based Conditional Right

Under Rule 24(b)(1)(B), the applicant may be allowed to intervene if it has a claim or defense that shares a common question of law or fact with the pending case. This is narrower than it sounds, however: the "an applicant must

(1) timely file an application, (2) show an interest in the action, (3) demonstrate that the interest may be impaired by the disposition of the action, and (4) show that the interest is not protected adequately by the parties to the action." *In re Bank of N.Y. Derivative Litig.*, 320 F.3d 291, 300 (2d Cir. 2003). "Failure to satisfy any one of these [four] requirements is a sufficient ground to deny the application." *Id.*

## C. Impact of Intervention on Subject Matter Jurisdiction

Where jurisdiction is founded on diversity, the intervention of a non-diverse party will not destroy subject matter jurisdiction unless the intervenor is indispensable under Rule 19 *Freeport-McMoRan, Inc. v. KN Energy, Inc.,* 498 U.S. 426, 428–29 (1991) (presence of a non-diverse and not indispensable defendant intervenor does not destroy complete diversity under Section 1332). Even if the intervenor's presence destroys complete diversity because it is indispensable, there may be supplemental jurisdiction. *See* Chapter 21.

## D. Appellate Review

Appellate courts review the denial of a motion to intervene for abuse of discretion. *B. Fernandez & HNOS, Inc. v. Kellogg USA, Inc.,* 440 F.3d 541, 544 (1st Cir. 2006). Thus, "even [where] there is common question of law or fact, or the requirements of 24(b) are otherwise satisfied," a district court may deny permissive intervention if such would "unduly delay or prejudice the adjudication of the rights of the original parties." *Kneeland v. Nat'l Collegiate Athletic Ass'n,* 806 F.2d 1285, 1289 (5th Cir.1987).

---

### Checkpoints

- Can you describe when intervention is permitted?
- Can you describe when intervention is mandatory?

# Chapter 21

# Joinder Step Two: Original or Supplemental Subject Matter Jurisdiction Must Exist

---

### Joinder Step Two Roadmap

This chapter explains the second step for determining whether a claim or party can be joined to a suit — whether from the beginning or after it is filed by amendment of a pleading.

This chapter explains that either original subject matter jurisdiction or supplemental subject matter jurisdiction must exist over every claim by a party, and explains the process to determine if supplemental jurisdiction exists.

---

A federal court must have subject matter jurisdiction over each claim. In Chapter 4 we studied the two forms of original subject matter jurisdiction, diversity and federal question. There must be at least one claim over which the court has original subject matter jurisdiction, personal jurisdiction, and venue (or, with respect to the latter two requirements, if lacking or improper, the defendant does not object). Not all claims have to have original subject matter jurisdiction (or personal jurisdiction or venue — matters we will get to later).

With respect to subject matter jurisdiction, Congress gave federal courts power in 28 U.S.C. § 1367 to resolve additional claims, even without original jurisdiction, so long as they are closely related to a claim over which district courts do have original jurisdiction and the additional claims meet other requirements in that statute. The power of federal courts to adjudicate related claims is now determined solely by § 1367. If the case is anchored in federal court by one claim, subject matter jurisdiction can — for additional claims — come from Sections 1331, 1332 *or* 1367.

# A. Is There Original Subject Matter Jurisdiction Over the Additional Claim?

If the additional claim arises under federal law or satisfies the diversity statute, then original subject matter jurisdiction exists. In addition, if the claim is one that can be aggregated with another claim for diversity purposes, then original diversity subject matter jurisdiction over that claim exists. *See* Chapter 4. Even if there is no original subject matter jurisdiction, there still may be "supplemental" jurisdiction over an additional claim. We next turn to that issue.

# B. Is There Supplemental Jurisdiction Over the Additional Claim?

Supplemental jurisdiction is now codified in § 1367. That statute arose after case law had confronted the fact that often a court will have original subject matter jurisdiction over one claim (the claim that anchors the case in federal court), but not original subject matter jurisdiction over closely related claims even though, as a matter of efficiency, the additional claims ought to be tried along with the anchor claim. Often, for example, a plaintiff would assert a federal question claim and closely related state law claims: if there was no diversity jurisdiction over the state law claims, then without some way to keep those additional claims in federal court, it might hear the federal claim but a state court might have to hear the state claims, even though they arose out of the exact same set of facts and involve the same parties. Cases, including *United Mine Workers v. Gibbs*, 383 U.S. 715, 725 (1966) and *Owen Equip. & Erection Co. v. Kroger*, 437 U.S. 365 (1978), gave federal courts power over "ancillary" and "pendent" parties and claims to enhance the efficiency of litigation that, nonetheless, stayed within statutory and constitutional limitations on federal power.

In response to case developments, Congress adopted § 1367 to replace "pendent" and "ancillary" jurisdictional constructs with what it called "supplemental jurisdiction." Section 1367 is still relatively new, and substantial litigation has occurred over its meaning. Some people think it is not a well drafted statute. Even so, the Court has emphasized that ordinary statutory rules of interpretation apply to Section 1367 and that it is important to analyze its "text in light of context, structure, and related statutory provisions." *ExxonMobil Corp. v. Allapattah Serv., Inc.*, 545 U.S. 546 (2005). Consistent with its general approach to statutory interpretation, the Court has given § 1367 its plain meaning. *Id.*

One goal of § 1367 was to allow federal courts to efficiently resolve all of the claims that were part of the same "case or controversy" giving rise to an anchor claim, but, at the same time, to prevent parties from structuring lawsuits to get into federal court on a claim that could not originally have been brought in federal court if all of the parties had been properly joined. For example, Congress did not want a plaintiff to name one diverse defendant when, to effectively resolve the claim, a non-diverse defendant was a necessary party to the suit. The plaintiff shouldn't be allowed to sue one defendant who was diverse, but then after that defendant joins the non-diverse defendant, the plaintiff then makes a claim against it, thereby obtaining relief in federal court when it could not have brought the claim originally.

Whether § 1367 succeeded in achieving that goal is another matter. We'll see some very difficult issues Section 1367 creates, many of which are counterintuitive to both principles that apply to the diversity statute and to efficient resolution of litigation. The courts struggle with this statute and will continue to do so during your career as a lawyer.

You should use three steps to determine whether supplemental jurisdiction exists. Each step has sub-parts. Fortunately, once you master the three steps, they collapse into the very simple two-part chart that appears below. It won't make sense to you now, but come back to it and you'll see its utility. There's also a long flowchart later.

FEDERAL QUESTION ANCHOR CLAIM

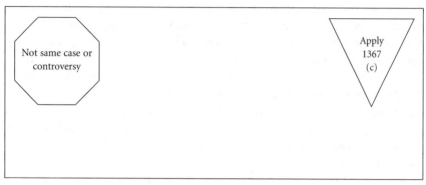

ONLY DIVERSITY ANCHOR CLAIM(S)

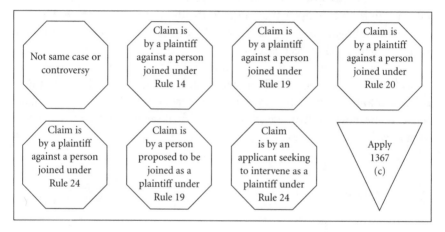

## 1. Step One: Is the Additional Claim Part of the Same "Case or Controversy" as an Anchor Claim?

Boiled down, the first subsection of § 1367 is designed to give district courts additional — "supplemental" in that sense of the word — subject matter jurisdiction over claims that are closely enough related to an anchor claim to be considered part of the same case or controversy. (We'll see that § 1367(b) is designed to avoid allowing parties to structure cases to get federal jurisdiction when it "shouldn't" be allowed, and § 1367(c) is designed to promote federalism concerns.) Section 1367(a) accomplishes this goal of giving federal courts supplemental jurisdiction over related claims by providing:

Except as provided in subsections (b) and (c) or as expressly provided otherwise by federal statute, *in any civil action of which the district courts have original jurisdiction, the district courts shall have supplemental jurisdiction over all other claims that are so related to claims in the action within such original jurisdiction that they form part of the same case or controversy* under Article III of the United States Constitution. Such supplemental jurisdiction *shall include claims that involve the joinder or intervention of additional parties.*

This section gives federal courts over a claim that is part of the case or controversy involved in the claim over which the court has original subject matter jurisdiction. It would allow, for example, a federal district court to hear a non-diverse state law claim that is related to a plaintiff's federal question claim. The district court would have original subject matter jurisdiction over the federal question claim, and assuming the additional claim is related "enough" to form part of the same case or controversy, it would have supplemental jurisdiction over the non-diverse state law claim.

So, the first inquiry is whether the additional claim is "so related to claims in the action within such original jurisdiction that they form part of the case or controversy under Article III of the United States Constitution." Put in pragmatic terms: is the additional claim so closely related to an anchor claim (remember, too, that a case can have multiple anchor claims) that the additional claim should be treated as part of the same case?

In a case the casebooks discuss but which was decided prior to enactment of Section 1367, the Court had reasoned that claims that "derive from a common nucleus of operative fact" are part of the same case or controversy. *United Mine Workers of Am. v. Gibbs*, 383 U.S. 715 (1966). Some courts hold that the "case or controversy" language in Section 1367(a) means the same thing as *Gibbs'* "common nucleus" test. *See Achtman v. Kirby, McInerney & Squire, LLP*, 464 F.3d 328, 335 (2d Cir. 2006) (explaining that the *Gibbs* test applies under 1367(a)). Other courts, however, have concluded that Section 1367(a) goes farther. *Jones v. Ford Motor Credit Co.*, 358 F.3d 205, 212 n.5 (2d Cir. 2004). The issue is this: does *Gibbs'* statement of "common nucleus of operative facts" define "case or controversy" or does it define something less than that, and so "case or controversy" is broader? *See Jones*, 358 F.3d at 213 (concluding that Section 1367(a) is likely broader than *Gibbs*). Whether Section 1367(a) extends supplemental jurisdiction beyond the scope of claims with a "common nucleus of operative facts" remains for the Court to answer.

Until then, whether a claim arises from the same case or controversy as an anchor claim likely will continue to turn on *Gibbs'* common nucleus of operative facts test. Under that test, one claim shares a common nucleus of operative facts with another if the facts underlying one claim substantially overlap with the facts underlying the other claim. *Achtman,* 464 F.3d at 335. Would you expect them to be litigated together? *See Gibbs,* 383 U.S. at 725; *Lindsay v. Gov't Employees Ins. Co.,* 448 F.3d 416, 424 (D.C. Cir. 2006) (collecting cases holding that if the facts necessary to prove one claim are practically the same as those necessary to prove another, then they form the same case or controversy).

A casebook case is *Jin v. Ministry of State Security,* 254 F. Supp. 2d 61 (D. D.C. 2003). There, the defendant argued that the court lacked supplemental jurisdiction over a state law claim for defamation because it did not arise out of a "common nucleus of operative facts" as the plaintiffs' federal civil rights claim. The court reasoned that "the facts supporting the defamation claims are linked to the facts supporting the remaining claims because they form a key part of an alleged overarching campaign to abridge and nullify the plaintiffs' rights and liberties" and so would be expected to be tried together.

There's one very difficult issue that concerns diversity jurisdiction and joinder that needs emphasizing. Luckily, it arises only when the only basis for original jurisdiction is diversity, and only when party, as opposed to claim, joinder is at issue. Here's the issue: Section 1332, as we saw, requires "complete diversity." What happens if a diverse plaintiff making a claim for more than $75,000 joins a second plaintiff, and either the amount in controversy does not exceed $75,000 or the second plaintiff is a citizen of the same state as the defendant?

One way to look at it—and, frankly, I think the right way—is that the court has original jurisdiction over the claim by the diverse plaintiff that exceeds $75,000, and to then turn to the supplemental jurisdiction statute to determine whether there is subject matter jurisdiction over the second plaintiff's claim. That would be consistent with the approach to federal question jurisdiction, and it would also be consistent with the way venue, personal jurisdiction, and virtually all aspects of civil litigation are determined.

But, the Court in *Exxon Mobil Corp. v. Allapattah Serv., Inc.,* 125 S.Ct. 2611 (2005) rejected that approach—at least in part, but only in *dicta.* The Court held, first, that the claim-by-claim approach does apply where the diversity jurisdictional defect is due to the amount in controversy: so, if one diverse plaintiff asserts a claim for more than $75,000, and a second diverse plaintiff asserts a claim for less than that amount, the court has original jurisdiction over the first claim, and whether it has jurisdiction over the second turns on whether supplemental jurisdiction exists. (Obviously, if the plaintiffs can aggregate, then there would be original jurisdiction.)

However, in very strong *dicta,* the Court said that citizenship is different from amount in controversy: if a diverse plaintiff joins a non-diverse plaintiff in a suit, the lack of complete diversity "contaminates" the entire case, and there is no "original jurisdiction" at all—and so nothing for any additional claim to anchor to. As the Court viewed it, "[i]ncomplete diversity destroys original jurisdiction with respect to all claims, so there is nothing to which supplemental jurisdiction can adhere." *Id.* As a result, if one diverse plaintiff joins one non-diverse plaintiff to each assert a claim for more than $75,000, a court will lack subject matter jurisdiction over the entire case, at least according to the *ExxonMobil dicta. E.g., Picciotto v. Continental Cas. Co.,* 512 F.3d 9 (1st Cir. 2008) (at least where the non-diverse plaintiff is indispensable in terms of Rule 19, joinder destroys diversity jurisdiction over entire case). It may be that "contamination" occurs only if the non-drivers plaintiff is indispensable under Rule 19, but that remains an open issue, except it is inconsistent with the *ExxonMobil dicta.* (But I think that's right.)

If an additional claim does arise out of the same "case or controversy," the district court *must* exert jurisdiction over the claim, unless it is excluded by operation of either Section 1367(b) or 1367(c). Put the other way, a court has *no discretion* under Section 1367(a) to decline to exercise supplemental jurisdiction over a claim that is part of the same case or controversy as a claim over which it has original jurisdiction. *Lindsay v. Gov't Employees Ins. Co.,* 448 F.3d 416, 421 (D.C. Cir. 2006) (collecting cases). This is because Section 1367(a) states that the courts "shall have" supplemental jurisdiction over such claims. *See id.*

Be sure you understand that a claim against one defendant can be part of the same case or controversy as a claim against another defendant; likewise, a claim by one plaintiff against one defendant can be part of the same case or controversy as a claim by another plaintiff against a different defendant. The last sentence of Section 1367(a) makes this clear: "Such supplemental jurisdiction shall include claims that involve the joinder or intervention of additional parties." So long as the claim arises from the same common nucleus of operative facts, it doesn't matter if the plaintiff bringing the claim is distinct from another plaintiff, or the claim is against a different defendant.

The next two steps—lengthy as they are—each arises from a few words at the beginning of § 1367 (a): "Except as provided in subsections (b) and (c). . . ."

## 2. Step Two: Even if it is Part of the Same "Case or Controversy" and is not "Contaminated" does Section 1367(b) Preclude Supplemental Jurisdiction Over the Additional Claim?

The second step of determining whether supplemental jurisdiction exists occurs only if Section 1367(a) is satisfied—the additional claim is part of the same "case or controversy" as an anchor claim. Subsection (b) provides the second step. It is best to break Section 1367(b) into two sub-steps. The first one is easy and can mean skipping the harder, second step.

### a. Is the Additional Claim Anchored by a Federal Question Claim?

If there is at least one anchor claim based on federal question subject matter jurisdiction, then there will be supplemental jurisdiction over a non-diverse state law claim related to it. If so, then you can skip to the third step. Why can you stop there? The lead in clause to Section 1367(b) is a condition for all the rest of that subsection: if the civil action is *not* founded solely on diversity, then the rest of subsection § 1367(c) doesn't matter. So, if there is one federal question anchor claim, under Section 1367(a), there will be supplemental jurisdiction over all other claims that arise out of the same case or controversy, and Section 1367(b) excludes none of them. *Lindsay v. Gov't Employees Ins. Co.*, 448 F.3d 416, 421 (D.C. Cir. 2006) (explaining that subsection (b) "relates to diversity jurisdiction only").

Now look back at the charts. The chart labeled "Federal Question" has only one "stop sign" in it (*i.e.*, if federal question is the anchor claim, there's only one way there's no supplemental jurisdiction over a related claim): if the additional claim is not part of the same case or controversy as the federal claim. (We'll get to § 1367(c) when we get to the third step; to be very precise, however, § 1367(c) does not exclude claims, since the court *has* supplemental jurisdiction, but § 1367(c) gives the court discretion not to exert that power. That's why § 1367(c) is represented on the charts as a yield sign, not a stop sign.)

However, if there is no federal question claim, that brings us to the second sub-step. The words of § 1367(b) are very important:

> (b) In any civil action of which the district courts have original jurisdiction founded solely on section 1332 of this title, the district courts hall not have supplemental jurisdiction under subsection (a) over claims by plaintiffs against persons made parties under Rule 14, 19, 20, or 24 of the Federal Rules of Civil Procedure, or over claims by persons proposed to be joined as plaintiffs under Rule 19 of such rules, or seeking to intervene as plaintiffs under Rule 24 of such rules, when exercising supplemental jurisdiction over such claims would be inconsistent with the jurisdictional requirements of section 1332.

Section 1367(b) presents a thicket, but one not as dense as it seems. There are three ways that we'll learn it: by text, flow chart, and a graphic.

# i. What's Not Excluded by Section 1367(b)?

## (a) No Claim Is Excluded if There is at Least one Federal Question Anchor Claim

To make clear what we just went through in the first sub-step, the first clause of subsection 1367(b) limits its applicability to only those civil actions where original jurisdiction is founded solely on diversity. Accordingly, nothing is excluded by subsection 1367(b) if there's at least one federal question in the complaint.

## (b) No Claim by a Defendant or a Party Sought to be Joined as a Defendant is Excluded

Subsection 1367(b) only affects claims by plaintiffs or parties sought to be joined as plaintiffs. *See Hartford Steam Boiler Inspection & Ins. Co. v. Quantum Chem. Corp.,* 1994 WL 494776 (N.D. Ill. 1994). Specifically, where jurisdiction is founded solely on diversity, subsection 1367(b) excludes even a claim that is part of the same case or controversy of an anchor claim if that claim:

- Is by a plaintiff against person joined under Rule 14;
- Is by a plaintiff against person joined under Rule 19;
- Is by a plaintiff against person joined under Rule 20;
- Is by a plaintiff against person joined under Rule 24;
- Is by a person proposed to be joined as plaintiff under Rule 19; *or*
- Is by an applicant seeking to intervene as a plaintiff Rule 24.

## (c) No Claim by a Single Plaintiff against a Single Defendant is Excluded

If a single plaintiff is seeking to add a claim against a single defendant, *no claim is excluded by subsection 1367(b).* Although the claim is by a plaintiff, neither the plaintiff nor the defendant is "joined" under any of the listed rules. (Recall that the first plaintiff and first defendant are not "joined" in any term in the rule, except to a limited extent by Rule 17.)

Further, Rule 18(a) authorizes a plaintiff to join an additional claim — and Rule 18(a) is not mentioned in subsection 1367(b). Thus, if an additional claim by a plaintiff against a defendant forms part of the same case or controversy as an anchor claim by that plaintiff against that defendant, subsection 1367(b) will never exclude that claim.

Think of the big picture: the combined effect of Rule 18(a) and subsections 1367(a) and (b) is to permit each plaintiff to join in a suit all claims it has against a defendant that arise out of the same case or controversy as an anchor claim — a claim that will be in federal court — that the plaintiff has against that defendant.

The goal of efficiency is met, and because the additional claim is related to an anchor claim that the federal court must address anyway, the plaintiff is not avoiding limitations on federal subject matter jurisdiction.

### ii.  What is Excluded?

Where jurisdiction is founded solely on diversity, subsection 1376(b) excludes even a claim that is part of the same case or controversy of an anchor claim if that claim:

- Is by a plaintiff against person joined under Rule 14;
- Is by a plaintiff against person joined under Rule 19;
- Is by a plaintiff against person joined under Rule 20;
- Is by a plaintiff against person joined under Rule 24;
- Is by a person proposed to be joined as plaintiff under Rule 19; *or*
- Is by an applicant seeking to intervene as a plaintiff Rule 24.

This is why it is important to identify the authority *in a rule* to join the claim or party. *See* Chapters 14 to 20. You have to identify the rule that authorizes joining the claim or party to know whether subsection 1367(b) takes away supplemental jurisdiction. This next step is simply mechanical: since you've identified what rule authorizes joinder of the claim or party, simply see if it is excluded by subsection 1367(b).

Now look back at the chart in the prior chapter concerning cases where there is no federal question jurisdiction. Notice that it has a 'stop sign' for each of these exclusions: the district court cannot exert supplemental jurisdiction over a claim that is not within subsection 1367(a) or is excluded by subsection 1367(b) (and *may* choose not to exert jurisdiction under subsection 1367(c), which we'll get to). If a claim is excluded under subsection 1367(b), then the court *must* dismiss that claim for lack subject matter jurisdiction.

Dismissal is not required with the third step: if the court has subject matter jurisdiction over the additional claim because it's within subsection 1367(a) and is not excluded by subsection 1367(b), the district court *may* nonetheless decline to exercise subject matter jurisdiction over the additional claim. We turn there now.

## 3.  Step Three: Does the District Court Have Discretion to Decline to Exercise Supplemental Jurisdiction Over the Additional Claim?

Courts *must apply* subsection 1367(c) even if the claim is part of the same case or controversy as an anchor claim and is not excluded by subsection

1367(b). With respect to such claims, the court *has supplemental jurisdiction* but subsection 1367(c) gives the court discretion under certain circumstances to decline to exert supplemental jurisdiction over that additional claim. Notice that both charts have a 'yield sign' for subsection 1367(c). But even if the additional claim "fits in" a subsection of subsection 1367(c), the court has discretion to keep the claim.

Subsection 1367(c) codifies Congressional concern over unnecessarily intruding into matters of state law. It gives district courts discretion to decline to exercise supplemental jurisdiction where Congress concluded that the federal interest in the type of dispute was slight. That subsection provides:

> (c) The district courts may decline to exercise supplemental jurisdiction over a claim under subsection (a) if—
>> (1) the claim raises a novel or complex issue of State law;
>> (2) the claim substantially predominates over the claim or claims over which the district court has original jurisdiction;
>> (3) the district court has dismissed all claims over which it has original jurisdiction; or
>> (4) in exceptional circumstances, there are other compelling reasons for declining jurisdiction.

Notice how subsection 1367(c) operates: it gives the district court discretion to dismiss a claim, but that discretion arises only if one of the four circumstances in subparagraphs (1) to (4) are present. If one of those circumstances is *not* present, then the district court *must* exert jurisdiction. *Lindsay v. Gov't Employees Ins. Co.*, 448 F.3d 416, 421 (D.C. Cir. 2006); *Schwarm v. Craighead*, 233 F.R.D. 655, 658 n. 4 (E.D. Cal. 2006) (collecting cases holding that, unless one of the predicates in subsection 1367(c) is present, a court cannot decline to assert supplemental jurisdiction); *Tinius v. Carroll County Sheriff Dept.*, 255 F. Supp. 2d 971, 977 (N.D. Iowa 2003) ("The statute plainly allows the district court to reject jurisdiction over supplemental claims only in the four instances described therein."). We'll now explore each circumstance that *must* be present before the court *may* decline to exercise supplemental jurisdiction.

### a. The Four Triggers to Exercise of Discretion in the Subparagraphs of Subsection 1367(c)

Again, the triggers listed in subsection 1367(c) are the only four circumstances that permit a district court to exercise its discretion to dismiss claims over which the court has supplemental jurisdiction. *Executive Software N. Am., Inc. v. U.S. Dist. Ct.*, 24 F.3d 1545, 1556 (9th Cir. 1994).

### i. Dismissal of an Additional Claim That Raises a Novel or Complex Issue of State Law

Subparagraph 1367(c)(1) codifies the policy of avoiding federal court involvement in novel or complex issues of state law. The federal court may "guess" wrong about what state law means, and as a result interfere with the development of state law, as well as do injustice to the parties before it. But the exception is is narrow: it is not enough for the issue to be simply one that on which there is no case precisely on point. Instead, courts have found this subparagraph met when the claim raises "issues of first impression that are numerous or of [state] constitutional magnitude." *Schwarm v. Craighead*, 233 F.R.D. 655, 658 (E.D. Cal. 2006) (finding discretion not triggered even though the claim presented a novel, but "unexceptional" question of interpreting a state statute); *see Jin v. Ministry of State Security*, 254 F. Supp. 2d 61 (D.D.C. 2003) ("The court is reluctant . . . to equate difficulty with complexity.").

### ii. Dismissal of an Additional Claim That Substantially Predominates Over the Claim or Claims Over Which the District Court has Original Jurisdiction

This subparagraph gives another reason why a federal court, with original jurisdiction over one claim, *may* dismiss a state law claim that is so closely related to that claim that they form the same case or controversy. A district court pointed to the divided nature of government as the basis for this exception:

> Litigation in the federal courts involving both federal law claims and supplemental state law claims has caused procedural and substantive problems. Even if the federal and state claims in this action arise out of the same factual situation, litigating these claims together may not serve judicial economy or trial convenience. Federal and state law each have a different focus, and the two bodies of law have evolved at different times and in different legislative and judicial systems. Because of this, in almost every case with supplemental state claims, the courts and counsel are unduly preoccupied with substantive and procedural problems in reconciling the two bodies of law and providing a fair and meaningful proceeding.
>
> The attempt to reconcile these two distinct bodies of law often dominates and prolongs pretrial practice, complicates the trial, lengthens the jury instructions, confuses the jury, results in inconsistent verdicts, and causes post-trial problems with respect to judgment interest and attorney fees. Consequently, in many cases the apparent judicial economy

and convenience of the parties' interest in the entertainment of supplemental state claims may be offset by the problems they create.

*Karibian v. Village Green Mgmt. Co.*, 2006 WL 3333099 (E.D. Mich. 2006) (declining to exercise supplemental jurisdiction under subparagraph (c)(2)).

### iii. Dismissal of the Additional Claims After the District Court has Dismissed all Claims Over Which that Court had Original Jurisdiction

Subparagraph 1367(c)(3) is the only subparagraph that presents a bright line: if the district court dismisses all claims over which it had original subject matter jurisdiction, it may dismiss any remaining claims. So, if a case is anchored in federal court by a federal question claim, and the district court had supplemental jurisdiction over non-diverse state law claims arising out of the same case or controversy, if the district court dismisses the federal claim, it may dismiss the related state law claims. *See Acri v. Varian Assocs., Inc.*, 114 F.3d 999 (9th Cir. 1997) (a district court *must consider* whether to dismiss when the claims with original jurisdiction are dismissed, but is not *required* to dismiss them).

### iv. Dismissal of an Additional Claim When, in Exceptional Circumstances, There are Other Compelling Reasons for Declining Jurisdiction

The "catch-all" in subparagraph 1367(c)(4) requires a showing much like those described by the first three subparagraphs. The "'compelling reasons' for the purposes of subsection (c)(4) should be those that lead a court to conclude that declining jurisdiction 'best accommodate[s] the values of economy, convenience, fairness, and comity.'" *Executive Software N. Am., Inc. v. U.S. Dist. Ct.*, 24 F.3d 1545, 1556 (9th Cir. 1994) (quoting *Carnegie-Mellon Univ. v. Cohill*, 484 U.S. 343, 351 (1988)). Its requirements have been found met where, for example, a parallel state suit was pending and so adjudication of the same state claim in federal court would "be a pointless waste of judicial resources." *Hays County Guardian v. Supple*, 969 F.2d 111 (5th Cir. 1992).

### b. If One Subparagraph is Met, What Informs the District Court's Discretion?

If the court finds that one of the circumstances in subsection 1367(c) is present, and so it has discretion to dismiss or keep an additional claim, what informs its exercise of discretion? District courts balance "factors such as judicial economy, convenience, fairness and comity . . ." *Quinn v. Owen Fed. Bank*

*FSB*, 470 F.3d 1240, 1249 (8th Cir. 2006) (holding trial court did not abuse its discretion in dismissing state claims after it had dismissed federal claims). How these factors apply in part turns on which of the four predicates in subsection 1367(c) was found to be present.

If the federal court litigation is going to continue — if the court has not dismissed the anchor claim under subparagraph 1367(c)(4) — then obviously the fact that dismissing the claims will increase litigation and costs is an important factor. *Schwarm*, 233 F.R.D. at 659 ("economy and convenience are best served in the maintenance of a single suit"). Militating against that, however, is the impact of a federal court needlessly intruding on state law. *Id.*

On the other hand, if under subparagraph 1367(c)(4) the court dismisses all anchor claims early in the suit, some courts hold it is an abuse of discretion to exert supplemental jurisdiction over an additional claim. *Certain Underwriters at Lloyds, London v. Warrantech Corp.*, 461 F.3d 568, 578–79 (5th Cir. 2006) ("if the federal claims are dismissed before trial, even though not insubstantial in a jurisdictional sense, the state claims should be dismissed as well."). On the other hand, "the substantial investment of judicial time and resources in the case . . . justifies the exercise of jurisdiction over the state claim, even after the federal claim has been dismissed." *Pioneer Hi-Bred Int'l v. Holden Found. Seeds, Inc.*, 35 F.3d 1226, 1242 (8th Cir. 1994). In sum, what constitutes abuse of discretion turns on all the facts, including balancing the costs to the parties with the risk of intruding into matters of state law.

# B. What Happens if the Court Dismisses the Additional Claim?

We will later see that a dismissal for lack of subject matter jurisdiction is "without prejudice," meaning that it can be refiled. If the district court does dismiss the claim, subsection 1367(d) gives the party who had asserted the dismissed claim at least 30 days to re-file it before the dismissed claim can become barred by a statute of limitation:

> (d) The period of limitations for any claim asserted under subsection (a), and for any other claim in the same action that is voluntarily dismissed at the same time as or after the dismissal of the claim under subsection (a), shall be tolled while the claim is pending and for a period of 30 days after it is dismissed unless State law provides for a longer tolling period.

## Checkpoints

- Can you describe when a claim falls within subsection 1367(a)?

- Can you list the claims that are excluded by subsection 1367(b)? Those that are not?

- Can you explain why a court, though having supplemental jurisdiction over a claim, nonetheless can decline to exercise jurisdiction under subsection 1367(c)?

# Chapter 22

# Joinder Step Three: Personal or Pendent Personal Jurisdiction Must Exist Over Most Claims

---

### Joinder Step Three Roadmap

This chapter explains when there must be personal jurisdiction — either "regular" or "pendent" — over each claim by a plaintiff against a party, and for some other claims.

This chapter also explains when "pendent personal jurisdiction" is available, and how to determine whether it exists.

---

As we saw in Chapters 6 and 7, a court must have personal jurisdiction over each claim by a plaintiff against each defendant. While an anchor claim must have "regular" personal jurisdiction (as we studied in Part A of this book), an additional claim can have *either* regular personal jurisdiction (as we discussed in Chapters 6 and 7) *or* "pendent personal jurisdiction." (Remember that if personal jurisdiction is lacking, nothing will happen unless the party against whom the claim is asserted promptly and properly moves to dismiss or transfer for lack of personal jurisdiction.)

In some ways, pendent personal jurisdiction is analogous to supplemental subject matter jurisdiction because both give federal courts greater power to decide additional, related claims than they do to decide an anchor claim itself. (We'll see the same thing with pendent venue in the next chapter.) Thus, step three of determining whether joinder of a claim against a party is proper is to examine whether there is either "regular" personal jurisdiction, or "pendent" personal jurisdiction. Generally, pendent personal jurisdiction will be available only if a federal claim allows for nationwide service of process, and the plaintiff brings related state law claims, too, that do not meet the requirements of state long arm statutes or due process.

While a court must have personal jurisdiction over a claim by every plaintiff against each defendant, the same is not true for every other claim and party. The first section below explores that issue further.

# A. Must There be, and if so is There, Regular Personal Jurisdiction Over the Additional Claim?

The first part of this step is to determine whether the court has "regular" personal jurisdiction for each claim by a plaintiff against defendant for each additional claim. *See* Chapters 6 and 7. If so, then there is regular personal jurisdiction and the analysis ends. If not, there may be pendent personal jurisdiction. But pendent personal jurisdiction exists only if (a) there is an anchor claim that is a federal question for which (b) a statute authorizes nationwide service of process that provides that national contacts "count" for personal jurisdiction. We'll see below why both are required before pendent personal jurisdiction is available for an additional claim.

Personal jurisdiction is not required for some claims. Specifically, a plaintiff may not object to personal jurisdiction for any counterclaim — permissive or compulsory — filed by a defendant against it. *See* 6 Charles A. Wright, Arthur R. Miller & Mary Kay Kane, *Federal Practice and Procedure* §§ 1416, 1424 (2015). The idea is that by filing suit the plaintiff has submitted itself to the jurisdiction of the court: "Typically of course, obtaining [personal] jurisdiction on a crossclaim is no problem when the crossclaim defendant shows up to defend the principal suit [as] his presence removes any objections to jurisdiction on the crossclaim." *Cincinnati Ins. Co. v. Belkin Corp.*, No. CIV A 07-0615-WS-C, 2008 WL 4949783, at *15 (S.D. Ala. Nov. 14, 2008) (internal quotations and citation omitted). On the other hand, there must be personal jurisdiction for claims by defendants as third party plaintiffs against third party defendants, but there need not be for claims by plaintiffs against third party defendants. Also, there must be personal jurisdiction over a party joined to a counterclaim. *See Calista Enterprises Ltd. v. Tenza Trading Ltd.*, No. 3:13-CV-01045-SI, 2014 WL 3670856, at *3 (D. Or. July 23, 2014) (collecting cases). Thus:

| Personal Jurisdiction Needed | Personal Jurisdiction Not Needed |
|---|---|
| Claims by plaintiffs against defendants. | Counterclaims by defendants against plaintiffs. |
| Claims by third-party plaintiffs against third party defendants. | Cross-claims, if the party defending the cross-claim has appeared. |
| Claims by an existing party against a party joined to a counterclaim. | Claims by plaintiffs against third-party defendants. |

## B. If Needed but There is no Regular Personal Jurisdiction, is There Pendent Personal Jurisdiction Over the Additional Claim?

Under pendent personal jurisdiction, a court may assert personal jurisdiction over a defendant with respect to a claim for which there is no other source of personal jurisdiction so long as that claim arises out of a common nucleus of operative facts as a claim over which the court does have personal jurisdiction. *U.S. v. Botefuhr*, 309 F.3d 1263, 1272 (10th Cir. 2002). Normally, of course, if two claims are part of the same case or controversy, there will likely be personal jurisdiction over both: if a plaintiff pleads two claims arising out of a breach of contract, for example, it's difficult to imagine circumstances where each claim won't satisfy regular personal jurisdiction.

But sometimes a federal statute allows personal jurisdiction to be proper for federal claims to be based upon contacts, not with a state, but with the country as a whole. Pendent personal jurisdiction allows federal courts to assert personal jurisdiction over an additional claim that arises out of the same case or controversy as a federal anchor claim for which a statute creates nationwide service of process. We saw in Chapter 4 that some — a few — federal statutes authorize nationwide service of process, permitting a defendant to be sued in much broader circumstances than would typically be possible under normal state long-arm statutes, and allowing personal jurisdiction to be based upon contacts with the United States as a whole, not the particular state where the district court sits.

The availability of nationwide service of process based on national minimum contacts gives rise to the practical need for pendent personal jurisdiction: if a defendant is subject to suit in any state over a federal claim because nationwide service of process, but the complaint includes a related claim (under state or federal law) for which no statute authorizes nationwide service of process based on national contacts, a court in a state with personal jurisdiction over the nationwide federal claim wouldn't have personal jurisdiction over the defendant on the related claim. Although the Supreme Court has never expressly approved its use, many circuits have done so. *See Action Embroidery Corp. v. Atlantic Embroidery, Inc.,* 368 F.3d 1174 (9th Cir. 2004) (collecting cases).

Thus, pendent personal jurisdiction will matter when Congress has created a federal statute to authorize nationwide service of process for a federal claim that anchors the case, and the plaintiff pleads a related law claim. Not many federal claims have nationwide service of process based on the defendant's contacts with the entire country, and no federal statute authorizes nationwide service of process for any state law claim. Thus, pendent personal jurisdiction fills a gap. Specifically, without pendent personal jurisdiction, there may have to be two lawsuits *or* Congress' desire to authorize nationwide service of process would as a practical matter be nullified. If suit had to be filed in a state where personal jurisdiction over the related state law claim existed, then Congress's decision to permit nationwide service of process based upon national contacts for the federal claim would be neutered: the plaintiff would either have to forego the related state law claims or file the suit where assertion of personal jurisdiction over the state law claims was proper. Or the plaintiff would have to file two suits.

To avoid frustrating Congressional intent, courts developed the doctrine of pendent personal jurisdiction. For pendent personal jurisdiction to be proper, the claim lacking personal jurisdiction must be so closely related to the claim with personal jurisdiction that it forms part of the same "case or controversy." *See ESAB Group, Inc. v. Centricut, Inc.,* 126 F.3d 617 (4th Cir. 1997) ("When a federal statute authorizes a federal district court to exercise personal jurisdiction over a defendant . . . we can find little reason not to authorize the court to adjudicate a state claim . . . so long as the facts of the federal and state claims arise form a common nucleus of operative fact."). Under that circumstance, the state law claim can piggyback on the federal one, even though no statute authorizes service of process under the circumstances and even if the defendant lacks minimum contacts with the particular state.

To sum up, if a court has personal jurisdiction over a defendant for one claim, the plaintiff may 'piggyback' onto that claim other claims for which there is no independent basis for asserting personal jurisdiction, but only to the extent that each additional claim arises from the same facts as the claim over which the court has personal jurisdiction. Ordinarily, this only matters if a related claim is brought that can be filed in any state if the defendant has minimum contacts with the country.

# C. Assertion of Pendent Personal Jurisdiction Must Comport with Due Process

Even if a court has pendent personal jurisdiction over a claim, assertion of pendent personal jurisdiction must still comply with the Due Process Clause. *See Stelax Indus., Ltd. v. Donahue*, 2004 WL 733844 (N.D. Tex. 2004) (court could not rely on pendent personal jurisdiction where assertion violated the Due Process Clause). However, the "forum" for minimum contacts analysis is the United States, not the forum state: the rationale for that is that "when a federal court exercises jurisdiction pursuant to a national service of process provision, it is exercising jurisdiction for the territory of the United States and the individual liberty concern is whether the individual over which the court is exercising jurisdiction has sufficient minimum contacts with the United States." *Med. Mut. of Ohio v. de Soto*, 245 F.3d 561, 567–568 (6th Cir. 2001).

---

### Checkpoints

- Can you explain why courts developed pendent personal jurisdiction?
- Can you explain when it is available?
- Can you explain what is required to take advantage of it?
- Can you explain why it will not ordinarily be necessary unless one claim is based upon nationwide service of process?

# Chapter 23

# Joinder Step Four: Venue or Pendent Venue Must Exist Over Some Claims

---

### Joinder Step Four Roadmap

This chapter explains that venue, or pendent venue, must exist over most claims.

This chapter also explains when pendent venue is available, and how to determine whether pendent venue is proper.

---

As we saw in Chapters 8 and 9, venue must be proper over each claim by plaintiff against each defendant. Thus, for each claim by a plaintiff is to determine if venue is proper under the general federal venue statute or another applicable claim-specific federal statute. If so, then venue is proper. There must be one claim for which venue is proper. If so, for additional claims, venue can be proper under either the regular statutes or by pendent venue. Like pendent personal jurisdiction, courts developed this doctrine to allow venue to be proper over all claims that are closely related to a claim over an anchor claim. Like pendent personal jurisdiction, pendent venue slightly relaxes "regular" venue requirements.

Claims other than by a plaintiff against a defendant sometimes require venue, but some do not, as we will see in this chapter. Pendent venue is available for these claims as well, when venue is required.

## A. Is Venue Proper Under the "Regular" Analysis?

If the "regular" venue analysis reveals that venue over an additional claim is proper, then the analysis need go no further. But, for each claim beyond the anchor claim — over which the venue must be proper (or the defendant waives any objection to it) — a party may also establish that there is "pendent venue."

# B. Is Proper Venue Unnecessary Over the Claim?

In several circumstances, proper venue is not required. Note that in each circumstance, if a party nonetheless objects to venue, then the other parties must point out that that objection is not well founded.

### a. Venue is not Required for a Counterclaim Against an Existing Plaintiff

A plaintiff cannot object to venue over a permissive or compulsory counterclaim. *General Elec. Co. v. Marvel Rare Metals Co.*, 287 U.S. 430 (1932).

### b. Venue is not Required for a Counterclaim Against a Party Joined as a Counterclaim Defendant Under Rule 13(h)

A party joined as a counterclaim defendant under Rule 13(h) may not object to venue. *Lesnik v. Public Industrials Corp.*, 144 F.2d 968 (2d Cir. 1944).

### c. Venue is not Required for a Claim Against a Third-Party Defendant Joined Under Rule 14(a)

A defendant impleaded under Rule 14(a) cannot object to venue, whether the claim is by the third-party plaintiff or the original plaintiff: if venue is proper for the original action, an independent basis of venue for a third-party claim is not required. *One Beacon Ins. Co. v. JNB Storage Trailer Rental Corp.*, 312 F. Supp. 2d 824, 828 (E.D. Va. 2004); 6 Wright, Miller & Kane, Federal Practice and Procedure: Civil 2d § 1445, at p.353 ("[V]enue over a claim by plaintiff against the third-party defendant should be held to be ancillary if the court has subject-matter and personal jurisdiction over it."). Thus:

Venue Needed Unless

Counterclaim against existing plaintiff

Counterclaim against counterclaim defendant joined under Rule 13(h)

Claim by third-party plaintiff against third-party defendant under Rule 14(a)

## 2. All Other Claims Require Proper Venue or Pendent Venue

If "regular" venue is not available, "pendent venue" may allow a related claim to "tag along" with an anchor claim. *Beattie v. U.S.*, 756 F.2d 91, 103 (D.C. Cir. 1984). Much like both pendent personal jurisdiction and supplemental subject matter jurisdiction, the claim must "arise out of the same core of operative facts" as a claim over which the court has proper venue. *Id.* Whether to apply pendent venue is left to the discretion of the district court. *Id.* The factors that a court should consider include judicial economy, convenience of the parties and witnesses, avoiding piecemeal litigation, and fairness. *Id.; Bishop v. Okla.*, 447 F. Supp. 2d 1239, 1254–55 (N.D. Okla. 2006).

Pendent venue can apply in different circumstances than pendent personal jurisdiction. For example, it can allow a claim that is covered by the general federal venue statute to tag along with a claim governed exclusively by a specific venue statute. So, for example, if a claim against a defendant over which venue is proper under the general federal venue statute is joined with a claim that arises under a federal statute covered by its own venue provision, a court could exercise pendent venue and keep all of the claims if the claim over which venue was improper arose out of the same set of facts as the anchor claim. *Taylor v. CSX Transp., Inc.*, 2006 WL 2550021 (N.D. Ohio 2006).

Pendent venue also applies when state claims subject to the general federal venue statute are joined with a federal claim subject to a specific venue statute. For example, in *PKWare v. Meade*, 79 F. Supp. 2d 1007, 1018 (E.D. Wis. 2000), the plaintiff pled both a state law contract claim and a claim under federal law for patent infringement. The court held that it had venue over the contract claim, but recognized that specific statute covers venue in patent infringement, 28 U.S.C. § 1400(b). Venue was improper as to the patent claim under that statute. The court, though noting that pendent venue might be proper, rejected applying it because Section 1400(b) narrowed the available venues for patent infringement. Thus, allowing the patent infringement claim to have venue pend from the contract claim was "inconsistent with the specific requirements" of Section 1400(b). Thus, it dismissed the patent infringement claim for improper venue.

In another case, the court confronted state law claims that were related to each other, but over which venue was improper as to some of them. The plaintiff's claim over which venue was proper was a fraud claim: plaintiff claimed defendant defrauded it in part through representations made in letters mailed into the district. The court found venue proper on that claim, concluding that the letters constituted acts that occurred in the district that formed a substantial part of the fraud claim. *Moore v. Dixon,* 2006 WL 3091142 (E.D. Wis. 2006). The plaintiff also pled two other claims: breach of fiduciary duty and breach of contract. The letters were not pertinent to those claims, since they both related to events that occurred later. Nonetheless the court found that the two claims shared "a common nucleus of operative fact with the plaintiff's misrepresentation claim" and so found pendent venue proper. *Id.*

The doctrine of pendent venue is not fully developed. The reason may be that it doesn't get raised a lot: a defendant who is going to face a claim in a particular court might as well deal with all of the claims then and there, rather than facing multiple suits in different forums. But, sometimes one claim doesn't provide the same relief that another claim might, and so there will remain reasons to analyze venue on a claim-by-claim basis, and to look for pendent venue if "regular" venue is unavailable.

---

## Checkpoints

- Can you explain when pendent venue is available to support venue over a claim?
- Can you describe what is required to meet the doctrine?

# Chapter 24

# A Recap and Flow Chart of the Four Steps for Adding Claims or Parties

We saw that for each additional claim asserted by a party and for joining a party there must be authority to join the claim under a Rule, subject matter jurisdiction, personal jurisdiction, and venue. This chapter recaps Section 1367 and applies the four steps to common fact patterns. The big picture is that Congress wanted to allow claims that arise out of the same case or controversy to be tried in one suit, but not to let the original plaintiff maneuver "a non-federal claim into federal court by initially filing claims against only diverse parties, and then later seeking to add [claims against] non-diverse parties, whose presence, had plaintiff included them in its original complaint, would have destroyed diversity." *Hartford Steam Boiler Inspection & Ins. Co. v. Quantum Chem. Corp.*, 1994 WL 494776 (N.D. Ill. 1994).

## A. A Flow Chart for Applying Section 1367

If there is one claim over which the court has original jurisdiction, then as to any joined party or claim, the flow chart on the next page controls:

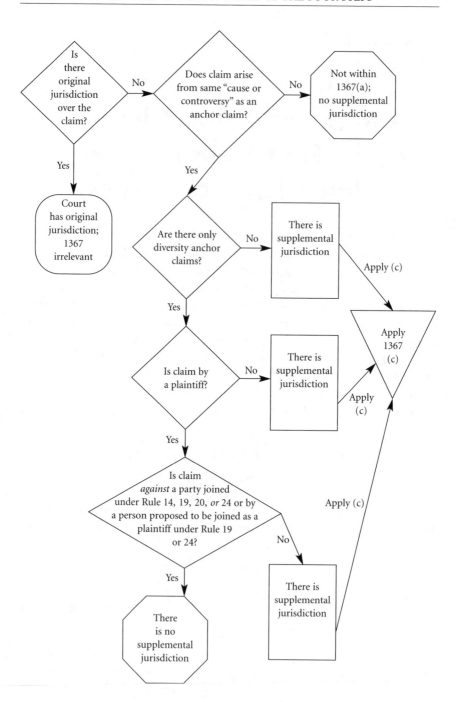

# B.  The Charts Revisited

With any luck, these charts now make absolute sense to you:

ONLY DIVERSITY ANCHOR CLAIM(S)

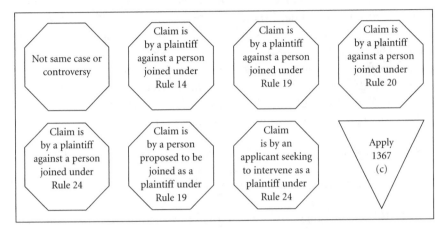

FEDERAL QUESTION ANCHOR CLAIM

# C.  Some Examples with Explanations

I strongly recommend using the flow chart or the graphics before you do this analysis or, at minimum, use them afterwards to double check. My students have told me that these study aids work.

# 1. Compulsory Counterclaims

Suppose the defendant includes in its answer a compulsory counterclaim. We'll see here that there will always be authority, subject matter jurisdiction, personal jurisdiction, and no need for venue over that claim regardless of what the subject matter jurisdiction exists over the anchor claim in plaintiff's complaint. (Remember: Venue is not needed even over permissive counterclaims. Likewise, a plaintiff may not object to personal jurisdiction over a compulsory counterclaim.) The reason why subject matter jurisdiction will exist is because a compulsory counterclaim will by definition form part of the same case or controversy as the plaintiff's claim — so it will be within subsection 1367(a) — and subsection 1367(b) does not exclude claims by defendants. *See Hartford Steam Boiler Inspection & Ins. Co. v. Quantum Chem. Corp.,* 1994 WL 494776 (N.D. Ill. 1994).

If the anchor claim is federal question, the four step analysis is as follows:

(1) The authority to assert a compulsory counterclaim comes from Rule 13(a).

(2) If the court does not have original jurisdiction over the additional claim, the claim nonetheless will be within Section 1367(a): in order to be a compulsory counterclaim under Rule 13(a) the claim must arise out of the same transaction or occurrence as the plaintiff's claim, and by a claim that arises out of the same transaction or occurrence is invariably within the "case or controversy" required by Section 1367(a).

(3) The claim is not excluded by 1367(b) because it only applies when the anchor claim is only diversity. (Even if it did apply, it wouldn't here because the claim is by a defendant.)

(4) The court would have discretion to dismiss the claim if one of the circumstances in Section 1367(c) is present.

If instead subject matter jurisdiction is based solely on diversity, then the only change is with respect to step (3): subsection 1367(b) will apply because federal question is not an anchor claim. However, subsection 1367(b) does not exclude claims by defendants, and so the counterclaim is not excluded.

The net effect? There will always be subject matter jurisdiction over compulsory counterclaims. Personal jurisdiction will also always be present since the filing of a suit waives personal jurisdiction objections as to compulsory counterclaims. Likewise, venue will be proper because venue statutes do not apply to counterclaims. Think of the big picture: we want courts to efficiently adjudicate all claims arising out of the same basic set of facts. They do so here.

## 2. Certain Permissive Counterclaims

Contrary to a lot of hornbooks and *dicta* from cases, not all permissive counterclaims are the same. Permissive counterclaims come in different forms, and the answers to whether they can be joined in a suit can vary depending on the reason why the counterclaim is permissive. It is important that you be careful: a lot of cases and even casebooks say that permissive counterclaims *must* have an independent jurisdictional basis; that's not always true. For example, if the only reason the claim is permissive is because it was pending in another suit, it will *not* need an independent jurisdictional basis if it arises out of the same claim or transaction, and so the same case or controversy, as the plaintiff's claim, but just happened to be filed in another suit before the civil action making it a counterclaim was filed.

The most common reason why a counterclaim is permissive is because it does not arise out of the same transaction or occurrence as a claim by the plaintiff. Suppose, for example, that the plaintiff sues the defendant for breach of contract, and the defendant counterclaims over an unrelated tort action. What is the analysis (we'll see it's the same whether the anchor claim is a federal question or not):

(1) Authority for permissive counterclaims comes from Rule 13(b).

(2) If the court does not have original subject matter jurisdiction over the permissive counterclaim, the question first would be whether the counterclaim is part of the same "case or controversy" as the anchor claim, and so is within subsection 1367(a). If the counterclaim is not part of the same case or controversy, then it would not be within subsection 1367(a) and the court would lack subject matter jurisdiction. If it does arise out of the same case or controversy, then the claim is within subsection 1367(a), and the analysis proceeds to subsection 1367(b). (Recall that a counterclaim is permissive not just if it does not arise out of the same transaction or occurrence as the plaintiff's claims but also for other reasons, including if it was already pending in another court.)

(3) Regardless of whether the anchor claim is federal question or diversity, permissive counterclaims are not excluded by subsection 1367(b) because the counterclaim is by a defendant, and that subsection does not exclude any claims by defendants.

(4) The court always has discretion to dismiss but only if at least one of the circumstances in subsection 1367(c) exists.

Personal jurisdiction need not exist, since a plaintiff waives objection to any counterclaim. A plaintiff cannot object to venue over a counterclaim. Thus, the net effect is that a permissive counterclaim must have an independent basis for subject matter jurisdiction *only* if the reason why it's permissive is because it does not arise out of the same case or controversy as a plaintiff's claim. Subsection 1367(b) will never exclude counterclaims, as they're made by defendants.

## 3. Joinder of Plaintiffs Under Rules 19 and 20

As discussed Chapter 20, the *ExxonMobil* Court took the view that if a diverse plaintiff making a claim for more than $75,000 joins a second plaintiff, supplemental jurisdiction can exist only if the second plaintiff is diverse from each defendant. Thus, the supplemental jurisdiction statute can be used where there is no federal question jurisdiction only if there is complete diversity of citizenship. Absent complete diversity, there is no "original jurisdiction" due to "contamination" of the entire case by a nondiverse party. As noted in Chapter 20, however, this *may be* the rule only if the non-diverse plaintiff is indispensable in terms of Rule 19. The rest of this section assumes there is original jurisdiction that anchors the case in federal court; that there is no contamination.

Suppose two parties each have claims against a single defendant: a driver and passenger in a car wreck, for example, sue the other driver. The analysis for joinder of each plaintiff is as follows. You will see that the answer to the first step — what rule authorizes joinder — is critical where the anchor claim is diversity. This is because if the plaintiff is being joined is a necessary party in terms of Rule 19, then the court will not have supplemental subject matter jurisdiction because joinder will be improper under subsection 1367(b).

(1) The authority for a plaintiff to join a co-plaintiff comes from *one* of two places. Permissive joinder is authorized by the first sentence of Rule 20(a): the plaintiff can be joined if it assert a claim arising out of the same transaction or occurrence against the defendant and assert join, several, or alternative liability. Rule 19 authorizes — indeed, requires — joinder of a plaintiff in whose absence complete relief cannot be afforded to the existing parties, *or* who claims an interest in the subject matter, *and* whose non-joinder will impact the parties. *See* Chapter 17. If a plaintiff is a necessary party — which, again, will be rare — then the authority to join the party is Rule 19; otherwise, it is Rule 20. The answer to that inquiry becomes important in the third step.

(2) If joinder is proper under either Rule 19 or 20 that would almost invariably mean that the additional plaintiff's claim arises from the same case or controversy as the anchor plaintiff's claim. Thus, joinder would be within subsection 1367(a) if the plaintiff is joined under either Rule 20 or 19.

(3) Whether joinder is precluded by subsection 1367(b) requires more thought. First, if the anchor claim(s) include a federal question, then subsection 1367(b) would not exclude joinder since it applies if only diversity claims anchor the case in federal court. Thus, if there is a federal question claim, then nothing is excluded by subsection 1367(b). If there is no federal question anchor claim, then the determinative issue under subsection 1367(b) is whether the plaintiff is joined under Rule 20 (permissively) or under Rule 19 (necessarily). Why is that? If the plaintiff is joined under Rule 20, then the claim is not excluded; if the plaintiff is joined under Rule 19, then the claim is excluded. That sounds backwards: if the plaintiff *has to* be part of the case, then the court lacks jurisdiction. Why does that make sense? If the plaintiff is a necessary party in terms of Rule 19, then allowing the case to proceed in federal court will allow a case to proceed where the additional plaintiff is a necessary party. In other words, Congress in subsection 1367(b) decided to allow a plaintiff to join with another plaintiff, so long as it was merely permissive, and not necessary, the plaintiff to be a party. Allowing a necessary party to join would allow a claim that should not be brought in federal court to be brought when it *should be dismissed* under Rule 19 since joinder destroys diversity; allowing a permissively joined plaintiff simply lets a federal court resolve related claims in one proceeding without violating Rule 19 or allowing a party to bring a claim in federal court where a party that *should* be joined defeats diversity. Accordingly, if the anchor claim(s) are only diversity, and if the plaintiff is necessary in terms of Rule 19, there is no supplemental jurisdiction. (Note: under the *ExxonMobil* contamination approach, the presence of a nondiverse plaintiff would mean there is no original subject matter jurisdiction; as mentioned, my view is that there is original subject matter jurisdiction but the wording of subsection 1367(b) ensures that if joinder of the plaintiff is required by Rule 19 the case will be dismissed and cannot be refiled by one plaintiff alone.)

(4) If the claim is not excluded by subsection 1367(b), the court still has discretion to dismiss if one or more circumstances in subsection 1367(c) exists.

Note that the additional plaintiff must still establish that personal jurisdiction exists and that venue is proper over each claim it has against the defendant.

So, for example, in *ExxonMobil Corp. v. Allapattah Serv., Inc.,* 125 S.Ct. 2611 (2005), one plaintiff brought a diversity claim, and joined a co-plaintiff who, while diverse in citizenship from the defendant, did not assert an amount in controversy that exceeded the minimum jurisdictional amount. The Court held that there was supplemental jurisdiction over the claim because the two claims arose out of the same case or controversy and Section 1367(b) "does not withdraw supplemental jurisdiction over the claims of the additional parties at issue here." An interesting question that is addressed at length in *dicta* in *ExxonMobil* is whether the same result would apply if the co-plaintiff had met the minimum amount, but was from the same state as the defendant. The text of subsection 1367(b) would seem to allow that claim to be brought, but the *ExxonMobil* Court strongly suggested that might not be the case. Stay tuned to how this develops in the law.

## 4. Joinder of Defendants Under Rules 19 and 20

Suppose a plaintiff wants to sue two defendants: say a plaintiff injured in back surgery wants to sue the doctor who implanted a surgical device along with the manufacturer of that device. Is joinder proper? The result that emerges is that there will be no supplemental jurisdiction over such claims unless the anchor claim is federal question:

(1) Authority to join defendants comes from Rule 20(a) or Rule 19. Unlike joinder of plaintiffs, the characterization of the defendant as merely a proper or necessary party will have no effect, as we'll see in step three. Under Rule 20(a), a defendant may be joined if the claim asserted against it asserts joint, several, or alternative liability and arises out of the same transaction or occurrence; under Rule 19, a defendant must be joined as a party if it falls within the definition of "necessary party."

(2) If the claim is authorized by either Rule 19 or 20, it would very likely also meet the "same case or controversy" requirement of subsection 1367(a).

(3) If the anchor claim is federal question, then subsection 1367(b) will not exclude anything. However, if the anchor claims are only diversity, then subsection 1367(b) will exclude the additional claim since it is a claim against a party joined under Rule 19 or under Rule 20. The net effect is that a plaintiff may only join a non-diverse defendant to assert a state law claim that is related to a federal claim against another defendant. That reflects a judgment: if there's a federal claim involved, the other defendant can be joined because federal litigation is likely to proceed anyway; but if not, then the plaintiff must file another suit in state court even though that claim is closely related to a diversity claim

that properly could be tried in federal court. If the plaintiff wants to have one suit, the one suit must be in state court.

(4) Even if the claim is not excluded by subsection 1367(b), the court will have discretion to decline to exercise supplemental jurisdiction if one of the conditions in subsection 1367(c) exists.

Venue and personal jurisdiction, of either the original or pendent variety, must exist over each claim against the joined defendant.

## 5. Joinder of a Counterclaim Defendant to a Counterclaim Against and Existing Plaintiff Under Rule 13(h)

We saw in Chapter 17 that if a defendant asserts or has asserted a counterclaim against an existing plaintiff, that defendant may join a person who was not yet a party as a counterclaim defendant. For example, suppose a plaintiff sues a defendant for breach of contract. If the defendant believes that the plaintiff along with another person conspired to fraudulently induce the defendant to enter into that contract, the defendant may want to bring a counterclaim against the plaintiff and join the co-conspirator to that counterclaim. The defendant would file an answer with a counterclaim naming the existing plaintiff as, and joining that other person as, "counter-claim defendants." We will now analyze joinder of that other person as a counterclaim defendant and will see that there will always be supplemental jurisdiction over joinder of a party to a counterclaim whether the counterclaim against the existing plaintiff is based on diversity or federal question:

(1) The authority to join a party to a counterclaim is Rule 13(h).

(2) Because a party can be joined under Rule 13(h) only if the claim against it arises out of the same transaction or occurrence as the counterclaim against the existing party, almost invariably that claim will arise out of the same case or controversy and so be within subsection 1367(a).

(3) Subsection 1367(b) does not exclude claims by defendants regardless of the basis of subject matter jurisdiction of the counterclaim.

(4) Subsection 1367(c) must always be examined.

## 6. Third-Party Practice Under Rule 14

Every casebook includes *Owen Equipment & Erection Co. v. Kroger*, 437 U.S. 365 (1978) in its discussion of supplemental jurisdiction. Be careful because this case was decided before enactment of Section 1367 and so uses terminology and analysis different from that which we now use under Section 1367. And, again, be careful: the *only* source of supplemental subject matter jurisdiction is Section 1367. The doctrines of "pendent party" and "ancillary claim" are gone.

In *Owen,* an Iowa citizen, Mrs. Kroger, brought a wrongful death claim against a Nebraska utility ("OPPD") after her husband was killed when the crane he was working in made contact with a power line owned by OPPD. OPPD, in turn, impleaded under Rule 14(a) the manufacturer of the crane, Owen, asserting that if OPPD was liable to the plaintiff, OPPD had a right of contribution against Owen as joint tortfeasors under applicable state tort law.

Then Mrs. Kroger amended her complaint to assert a claim against Owen that sought more than the minimum jurisdictional amount at the time. She alleged in the amended complaint, and Owen admitted in its answer, that it was a Nebraska corporation with its principal place of business in Nebraska. Thus, ostensibly there was diversity. OPPD then obtained summary judgment on Mrs. Kroger's claim against it. Much later, on the third day of trial in fact, it came out that Owen's principal place of business was not in Nebraska, but was instead in Mrs. Kroger's home state of Iowa. Thus, at that time the claim was between two citizens of Iowa.

Owen then moved to dismiss for lack of subject matter jurisdiction. The district court refused, and the appellate court affirmed. The Supreme Court reversed. It emphasized that this was *not* a claim by a defendant against a party joined under Rule 14(a), but instead was a claim by a plaintiff, and so the non-diverse claim was not asserted by a party "haled into court against his will." A plaintiff cannot complain if ancillary jurisdiction does not encompass all of his possible claims in a case such as this one, since it is he who has chosen the federal rather than the state forum and must thus accept its limitations." *Id.*

How does third-party practice work under Section 1367? Let's look first at the defendant's (*i.e.,* the third-party plaintiff's) claim against the third-party defendant, then claims by the plaintiff against the third-party defendant (the latter being the problem in *Kroger*).

First, with respect to the claim brought by the third-party plaintiff, there will always be supplemental jurisdiction:

(1) Rule 14(a) authorizes the claim.
(2) Because a claim authorized under Rule 14(a) can only be brought if the third-party defendant will be liable for some or all of the third-party plaintiff's liability to the plaintiff, it will invariably arise out of the same case or controversy as a claim by the plaintiff against the third-party plaintiff, and so will be within subsection 1367(a).

(3) Claims by defendants are not excluded by subsection 1367(b).

(4) Subsection 1367(c) must always be analyzed.

What if the plaintiff joins a claim against the third-party defendant? If the plaintiff's claim against the defendant is based on diversity, then there will not be supplemental jurisdiction over the claim.

(1) Rule 14(a) authorizes a plaintiff to bring a claim against a party joined under Rule 14(a). (It's buried in that Rule.)

(2) If the claim does not arise out of the same case or controversy as plaintiff's claim against the defendant, the claim will not be within subsection 1367(b). If it does, then it will be within that section.

(3) If there is a federal question anchor claim, then subsection 1367(b) will not exclude the plaintiff's claim. However, if there is not a diversity anchor claim, then the claim by a plaintiff against a party joined under Rule 14(a) is excluded by subsection 1367(b). There will never be supplemental jurisdiction over a claim by a plaintiff against a party joined under Rule 14(a) unless there is a federal question anchoring the plaintiff in federal court.

(4) Subsection 1367(c) must always be applied.

What's the net effect of this? The result in *Kroger* would be exactly the same: the claim against Owen arose out of the same case or controversy as the claim against OPPD; without a federal question anchor claim, the claim against Owen, though within subsection 1367(a), is excluded by subsection 1367(b).

## 7. Rule 18(a) Joinder of Claims

We saw that Rule 18(a) authorizes a party to join even completely unrelated claims once it anchors a claim in federal court. However, remember that *authority* is only one of the steps. If the claim is unrelated to an anchor claim, it will have to have an independent—original—basis for subject matter jurisdiction. Let's see why.

(1) The authority to join the claim is Rule 18(a).

(2) If the claim does not arise out of the same case or controversy as an anchor claim, it will not be within subsection 1367(a). If it does, then it will be.

(3) No claim by defendants or plaintiffs joined under Rule 18(a) is excluded by subsection 1367(b).

(4) Subsection 1367(c) must always be examined.

Thus, the net result is that if a claim joined under Rule 18(a) arises from the same case or controversy, there will be supplemental jurisdiction over it, no matter who asserts it. This fits within the goal of allowing all claims that arise out of the same case or controversy to be tried together. It also illustrates, however, that often authority is broader than the real ability to litigate claims: unrelated claims joined under Rule 18(a) that lack original jurisdiction will be subject to dismissal because they will not be within subsection 1367(a).

# Chapter 25

# Notifying the Defendant of the Filing of Suit through Service, Waiver of Service of Process, or Substituted Service

---

### Notifying the Defendant Roadmap

This chapter explains the steps that plaintiff's counsel must take to initiate a civil lawsuit.

---

Once the plaintiff has drafted the complaint, the next step is filing it, the civil cover sheet, and the Rule 7.1 disclosure form with the district court. The act of filing the complaint "commences" the civil action. FRCP 3. Then the plaintiff must properly notify the defendant that a civil action has been filed against it, either through actual or, if that is unavailable, constructive service.

## A. Formal Service or Request for Waiver of Formal Service

"An elementary and fundamental requirement of due process in any proceeding which is to be accorded finality is notice reasonably calculated, under all the circumstances, to apprise interested parties of the pendency of the action and afford them an opportunity to present their objections." *Mullane v. Central Hanover Bank & Trust CO.*, 339 U.S. 306 (1950). Importantly, it is not *actual notice* that is required but instead reasonable efforts to apprise interested parties. *Dusenberry v. U.S.*, 534 U.S. 161 (2002).

The plaintiff has a choice: either use personal service—which requires the plaintiff to pay someone to find the defendant and personally provide him with the required documents—or instead mail a request to the defendant asking that it waive service. (Personal service is required if the defendant is a a governmental entity, infant, or incompetent person to do so. FRCP 4(d)(1); 4(g); 4(h).)

# 1. Formal Service of Process

Formal service requires the plaintiff have the defendant served with both a summons and a copy of the complaint. Together, the summons and the complaint are often referred to as "process." By validly serving process, (a) the defendant is notified of the suit; (b) the court acquires personal jurisdiction over the defendant (subject to any objection he may have); and (c) the defendant is given an opportunity to defend. *Henderson v. U.S.,* 517 U.S. 654, 672 (1996); *Omni Capital Int'l, Ltd. v. Rudolf Wolff & Co.,* 484 U.S. 97, 104 (1987). There are five steps involved in effecting service.

### a. Plaintiff's Counsel Fills Out the Forms

First, the plaintiff's lawyer is required to complete the summons form. A form of summons is available on-line in PDF format, and an example is below. The summons must contain:

- The identity of the court;
- The name of each plaintiff;
- The name of plaintiff's counsel;
- The name of each defendant;
- The identity of any agent for service of process of the defendant (see below);
- A statement of when the defendant is required to respond;
- The clerk's signature and the seal of the court.

### b. The Court Clerk Signs and Seals the Forms

Second, the plaintiff's lawyer must submit the summons to the clerk of the court to have it signed and sealed. FRCP 4(a), (b). If the summons is in proper form, the clerk signs and seals it, then returns it to the plaintiff.

### c. Plaintiff's Lawyer has Process Properly and Timely Served

The plaintiff's lawyer must have the summons and certain other documents served on the defendant, and do so in a timely fashion. If service is done by personally delivering summons, it must be done by a person who is not a party and who is at least 18 years old. FRCP 4(c)(2). In some circumstances, service by a U.S. Marshall is required. FRCP 4(c)(3).

The proper way to effect service depend on the type of defendant:

*Competent Adults.* Rule 4(e) gives the plaintiff two options on serving competent adults: (a) service may be effected under Rule 4(e)(1) according to state law of either the state where the suit is filed or where the defendant resides; or (b) service may be effected by "delivering" process in terms of Rule 4(e)(2). Either is sufficient; both may be used; and neither is favored under the Rules.

*Service According to State Law.* Although it varies some, most states permit service of process by: first class mail; in-person delivery; publication; or by "long-arm" statute where the defendant does not reside in the state. Rule 4(e)(2) permits service by in-person delivery; leaving process at the individual's dwelling house or usual place of abode with an appropriate person; or delivering process to an authorized agent. A person may have more than one "dwelling house or usual place of abode." For example, in *Nat'l Dev. Co. v. Triad Holding Corp.*, 930 F.2d 253 (2d Cir. 1991), the court held service proper so long as the defendant was actually living in the dwelling at the time of service, even if he spent other time living in other dwellings. Courts have tended to give the term a flexible meaning, focusing more on whether notice was likely received than the rigid meaning of the term.

*Infants and Incompetent Natural Persons.* Service must be performed as authorized by the law of the state in which the district court where suit has been filed is located. FRCP 4(g).

*Business Entities.* Rule 4(h) permits service on business entities either according to state law (*see* above) or by serving process on an officer, managing or general agent, or any other agent authorized by law or appointment to receive process. Often, state statutes require corporations to designate an agent for service of process.

*Governmental Entities.* To effect service on a state governmental entity, see FRCP 4(j)(2). To effect service on a federal governmental entity, see FRCP 4(i).

*Time to Serve.* The amount of time to effect service is fairly short. Unless the defendant is outside the U.S., the deadline is 90 days after the complaint is filed, shortened in 2015 from 120 days. FRCP 4(m). If a plaintiff does not have the defendant served within that time period, the court may dismiss the suit, without prejudice (meaning it can be refiled, subject to the statute of limitations running on the claims), unless (1) the plaintiff files a motion to extend the time and establishes good cause for not having timely served it; or (2) the court in its discretion, and even without a showing of good cause, extends the time. *See Henderson v. U.S.*, 517 U.S. 654, 662 (1996) (court must grant extension if good cause shown); *Espinoza v. U.S.*, 52 F.3d 838, 841 (10th Cir. 1995) (court may grant extension even if no good cause shown). "Good cause" in this context is limited to valid reasons for delay, but includes the fact that the defendant actively sought to evade service. *Coleman v. Milwaukee Bd. of School Directors*, 290 F.3d 932, 934 (7th Cir. 2002).

### d. The Process Server Completes Proof of Service

The second page of the summons shown above consists of a form that must be completed, and a declaration attested to, showing how process was served. The person who served process must complete it.

### e. Plaintiff Files the Proof of Service

Plaintiff counsel's last step is to file the completed summons and proof of service form with the court. FRCP 4(l). The entire process is not a mere technicality, but instead is a part of the fundamental process of obtaining personal jurisdiction over the defendant: "Absent consent, . . . there must be authorization for service of summons on the defendant." *Omni Capital Int'l v. Rudolf Wolff & Co.*, 484 U.S. 97, 104 (1987). Thus, compliance with the Rules is required, unless the defendant waives formal service.

## 2. Request for Waiver of Service of Process

Rule 4(d)(1)(A) lists what must be included in a request for waiver of service of process, and as of 2015 following Rule 4 is an "official" form. Usually the district court will have posted on line interactive pdf files that can be completed online, printed, and then mailed. The defendant must be given two copies of the notice and request; a pre-paid means to mail a response (*e.g.,* a stamped returned envelope); and a copy of the complaint. FRCP 4(d)(1)(C). Although first class mail is sufficient, "reliable means" can be used. FRCP 4(d)(1)(G).

The rules (and form following Rule 4) give the defendant a choice. The defendant is encouraged to waive formal service comes in several ways. First, the defendant does not waive any defense by waiving service of process. FRCP 4(d)(5). Second, the defendant is given more time to respond to the complaint, generally giving a defendant who waives service 60 days to answer, while a defendant who does not waive service is given only 20 days. FRCP 12(a)(1)(B); FRCP 4(d)(3). Third, a defendant who chooses not to waive process without good cause must pay the costs of obtaining formal service. FRCP 4(d)(2). In fact, the plaintiff may be able to recover not just the costs of formal service, but also the cost of any motion it has to file to collect them, along with reasonable attorney fees for filing that motion. FRCP 4(d)(2).

The defendant must be given a reasonable time to respond to the request, which is 30 days for a request mailed to an address within the United States. FRCP 4(d)(1)(F); *see id.* (60 days for defendants with addresses outside the U.S.). If the defendant waives service of process, the plaintiff must file with the court the waiver it receives from the defendant, FRCP 4(d)(4), and the suit proceeds as if the defendant had been formally served. FRCP 4(d)(1). If the defendant does not waive service, then the plaintiff must formally serve the defendant with process. That brings us to the often waived second step.

## B. Constructive Service of Process as an Alternative to Formal Service or Waiver of Formal Service

If personal service or waiver of it is not successful, a plaintiff may move the court for permission to use alternatives to personal service. Other forms of notice are available in "constructive" form, such as putting an advertisement about the lawsuit in newspapers, are difficult to sustain. (Many newspapers regularly contain columns of such notices, however.) In several cases, the Court has held that absent unusual circumstances personal notice is required, not merely posting a flyer or advertising the suit in the newspaper. *E.g., Mennonite Bd. of Missions v. Adams,* 462 U.S. 791 (1983). Due process may be satisfied, however, if enough advertising or other notice occurs. *Smith v. Islamic Emirate of Afghanistan,* 2001 U.S. Dist. Lexis 21712 (S.D.N.Y. 2001) (holding that notice to Osama bin Laden could be accomplished by advertising a suit on CNN, al Jazeera, and in Afghani and Pakistani newspapers).

Why is constructive service the last resort? Because it's constructive-only, meaning that the defendant will be bound by the court's action even if it never actually gets notice of the suit.

Generally, courts will not allow substituted service unless the plaintiff in its motion demonstrates that it has taken reasonable efforts to personally serve the defendant, but has been unsuccessful. State law dictates how to accomplish substituted service (how often and where a notice must be published, for example).

A recent issue is whether notice of a suit can be given through Facebook or by email, rather than through newspaper advertisements. Generally, courts are requiring proof from the plaintiff that the defendant regularly accesses email or Facebook before approving of those methods for substituted service. The cases, as of now, are about evenly split.

## C. What's Next?

The ball is now in the defendant's court. The defendant has several options after it has either chosen to waive service, or has been formally served. That's where we go next.

## Checkpoints

- Can you describe how a plaintiff must initiate a lawsuit?
- Why would a defendant choose to waive service of process?
- Does a defendant waive any defenses or objections by waiving service of process?

# Chapter 26

# Preview of the Defendant's Options in Response to Receiving a Federal Court Complaint

As we have seen, the plaintiff in its complaint is required to give notice of circumstances which, which if plausible and true, show that the court has both personal and subject matter jurisdiction over each claim and state one or more claims upon which relief can be granted. (The rules do not require the plaintiff to plead how venue over each claim is proper, but many lawyers do so.) Plaintiff's counsel then notifies the defendant of the suit.

What must the defendant do? Before we see the answer, think about the possibilities. The Rules could give only one option: require a defendant to respond to each of plaintiff's allegations and to include any defenses to the claims asserted. Or, the Rules could assume that the defendant denies everything that the plaintiff alleges, and so require no formal response of any kind, and even let the defendant later prove any sort of "defense" that it may have to the claim without providing any notice to the plaintiff of what that defense might be.

Or, the Rules could do what they do, which is give defendants options. The defendant can choose to only address preliminary procedural matters—such as the lack of subject matter jurisdiction, personal jurisdiction, or venue—without having to respond to the substance of the allegations of plaintiff's complaint. Or, the defendant can elect to respond to the allegations on the merits *and* address any objections to personal jurisdiction, venue, and subject matter jurisdiction. If the defendant responds to the merits, we'll see that it has to admit or deny the allegations made by the plaintiff, and plead any "affirmative defenses."

Why not just assume everything's denied and move to the next phase? The short answer is that this approach would not help to narrow the issues. Suppose, for example, plaintiff sues the defendant for breach of contract. Defendant did breach the contract, but believes the breach caused plaintiff no damage. If the defendant isn't required to respond to the merits of plaintiff's complaint *or* everything alleged by the plaintiff is presumed to be denied, then the plaintiff will waste time (and money, and likely the court's time, too) learning that the dispute is over causation of damages, not breach. Likewise, suppose the defendant in that same case even believed that it breached the contract *and* the plaintiff was damaged, but that the claim is barred by something else — the statute of limitations or the statute of frauds, for example. Even though the defendant has notice of plaintiff's claim, the plaintiff won't know what the defendant's "affirmative defense" will be, even though the defendant will know what plaintiff's claim is.

So, we require the defendant to respond in a way that helps to narrow down the issues and to provide notice to the plaintiff of what really is in dispute, but permit the defendant to raise procedural objections without addressing the merits of the claim if it so chooses.

Why do the Rules allow the defendant to raise preliminary procedural objections, such as venue, even before providing notice about its positions in the suit? After all, that seems like an extra step: why not require anything that might constitute a flaw or reason not to allow the suit to proceed to be put in the answer? To save money. Recall that lawyers are required to investigate under Rule 11 before filing signed papers. Thus, before defense counsel can take a position in a paper filed with the court on whether each allegation in the complaint is true or not, defense counsel must reasonably investigate. Likewise, we'll see that the defendant *must* plead "affirmative defenses" in Rule 8(c) and we've seen that he *must* plead "compulsory counterclaims" in Rule 13(a). To determine if the defendant has an affirmative defense or a compulsory counterclaim (or a permissive one, for that matter), defense counsel must investigate the law and the facts. In some circumstances, and that investigation can be expensive.

Now imagine that a plaintiff has filed suit in a federal court where personal jurisdiction is lacking, venue is improper, or where the court lacks subject matter jurisdiction. Not only are those issues largely separate from the merits of the claim that the lawyer will need to investigate if she has to respond to the substantive allegations, they are likely comparatively cheap to investigate. (Where do the parties reside? Does the defendant have contacts with the forum? Where did most of the events that led to the lawsuit occur?) Shouldn't we allow the defendant to raise these preliminary objections — ones that are essentially separate from the merits, the question of whether the defendant should pay money to the plaintiff — but which would require the court to dismiss the claim and avoid or at least delay defendants' cost to investigate the merits?

To make litigation more efficient for both courts and parties, the Rules require defendants to respond to allegations and give the plaintiff notice of affirmative defenses, but the Rules also allow defendants to raise objections apart from the merits—typically that the suit either should not proceed in federal court (*e.g.,* subject matter jurisdiction is lacking) or at least in this particular federal court (*e.g.,* venue is improper or personal jurisdiction is lacking)— before filing an answer that takes positions on the merits. The Rules permit defendants to raise these "this is the wrong court" type of objections without addressing the merits of the allegations.

But, the Rules also permit—with very narrow exceptions—the defendant to do all of the above at once: it can respond to the plaintiff's allegations, plead its affirmative defenses, *and* make "wrong court" objections, all in one paper. Why this last option? If, after all, the court lacks subject matter or personal jurisdiction, or venue is improper, the court will have to dismiss (or transfer) the claim, so why not require the defendant to raise those objections before dealing with the merits?

The defendant has a choice: it can file a motion that contains preliminary objections to the suit, or it can file an answer responding to the allegations in the complaint and raising any affirmative defenses that also includes (most, but not all) preliminary objections. The defendant has strategic reasons to file an answer that includes preliminary defenses, as we'll see, but the choice is largely its own to make (with, again, very limited exceptions). But, notice what happens if a defendant chooses the "one paper" route and files an answer that both addresses the merits and raises "wrong court" objections . . . but then does not promptly file a motion to have the court to dismiss the claim for lack of personal jurisdiction or venue. While subject matter jurisdiction cannot be waived, it is easy for a defendant to waive the two other "wrong court" objections. The defendant also has the option of doing nothing.

# Chapter 27

# The Defendant's Initial Set of Options

---

### Defendant's Initial Options Roadmap

This chapter explains the options available to a defendant.

---

The Rules give defendants principally three initial options, some or all of which may be available in a particular case: (1) filing a motion under Rule 12 (the filing of which will, at minimum, postpone the date on which an answer is due); (2) filing an answer (which can include most, but not all, of the issues that can be raised by a Rule 12 motion); or (3) doing nothing. FRCP 12(a)(4). In addition to—not instead of—filing an answer or a Rule 12 motion, the defendant may also be able to file a motion for summary judgment under Rule 56. *After* the defendant files an answer or Rule 12 motion, it may also have other options, such as moving to transfer venue from a proper venue to a more convenient one, options we'll explore later.

The facts and circumstances will dictate both which options are available as well as which option the defendant should choose as a matter of litigation strategy. Usually, doing nothing is not an option since it subjects the defendant to entry of a default judgment against it. Thus, the defendant will typically do something. This chapter explores its options.

## A. Filing a Motion Under Rule 12

Rule 12 authorizes several so-called "defenses," even though most of them aren't really defenses to the claim, but rather objections to procedures. The two that are not in Rule 12(b)—the motion to strike and the motion for more definite statement—*must* be made by pre-answer motion. All of the other defenses in Rule 12 may be included in the answer *or* can be raised in one pre-answer motion, but some of them *must* be included in whichever the defendant files first—a pre-answer motion or answer.

It is that last point that makes Rule 12 difficult: Rule 12 forces a defendant who files a Rule 12 motion to include in that one motion some, but not all, of any other Rule 12 defenses that it might then have available. If a defendant contends venue is improper, for example, and chooses to address the lack of venue with a Rule 12(b)(3) motion, it must include in that motion its objection (if it has one) to personal jurisdiction, or the objection to personal jurisdiction will be waived. On the other hand, the defendant doesn't have to include in a Rule 12(b)(3) motion its objection that the court lacks subject matter jurisdiction, or certain other objections in Rule 12. So, while filing a Rule 12 motion is one *option*, exercising that option may *require* the defendant to include other Rule 12 objections that it has available. We'll explore each Rule 12 motion in the coming chapters.

## B.  Filing an Answer

Another option of the defendant is to file an answer. With two narrow exceptions (the motion to strike and the motion for more definite statement under Rules 12(e) and (f)), a defendant can include in its answer every defense that it can include in a Rule 12 motion. Why, then, would a defendant choose just to file a Rule 12 motion?

A defendant who files an answer must respond to all of the plaintiff's allegations, must examine whether it has any counterclaims, must at least make a preliminary determination as to which parties it may or must join, and also include every "affirmative defense." It can cost money and take time to investigate the merits of a claim to determine whether the defendant has a claim against the plaintiff, or any non-party, and to determine what affirmative defenses might exist to the plaintiff's claims: filing a Rule 12 motion avoids those costs.

On the other hand, we'll see that filing an answer eliminates some procedural options that the plaintiff still has open to it if the defendant files only a Rule 12 motion. In other words, in some circumstances the defendant should only file its Rule 12 motion, while in others filing an answer that includes any Rule 12 defenses is the smarter move.

The important thing during law school is to master how to identify when each option is available, and how to exercise that option. Which option is best is a matter of circumstance, judgment and experience, not the Rules.

## C.  Doing Nothing

A defendant can choose to do nothing in response to being served with a complaint. If so, the plaintiff can seek entry of a default judgment. *See*

Chapter 44. Generally, if the defendant has assets, doing nothing is not a good option. For both practical and legal reasons, however, sometimes allowing a default judgment to be entered is the best choice.

As a practical matter, if the plaintiff has sued a defendant who has no assets and cannot afford to pay any judgment or an attorney to defend the suit, the only option the defendant may have is to do nothing and allow entry of a default judgment. The plaintiff will have a judgment, but will not be able to collect on it—a hollow victory—and the defendant will have avoided incurring attorneys' fees that it cannot afford to pay. The plaintiff at best becomes a judgment creditor and might recover some portion of the judgment someday. *See* Chapter 56.

Putting insolvent or nearly insolvent defendants to the side, there are also legal reasons why a defendant can choose to allow for entry of a default judgment despite having the ability to pay any judgment or defend the suit. Specifically, a defendant might choose not to respond to a complaint because it believes the court lacks power to enter the judgment against it, and so any resulting judgment would be void. *See* Chapter 59. This occurs most often when a defendant believes suit is filed in a court that lacks personal jurisdiction over the defendant, subject matter jurisdiction over the claim, or without having properly served the defendant. In those circumstances, a defendant can do nothing in response to the complaint, allow default judgment to be entered against it, but then "collaterally attack" the default judgment when the plaintiff seeks to execute it and collect its money. *See* Chapter 59.

This is a high-risk strategy for both practical and legal reasons. Obviously, it allows a plaintiff to obtain a default judgment against the defendant and to try to execute the judgment. Having a judgment against someone can create credit problems and practical difficulties. In addition, a defendant who believes that a court lacks personal or subject matter jurisdiction or that service was defective can raise those objections by Rule 12 motion. If the defendant does not raise the defense that way, then the burden of proof falls upon the defendant in the plaintiff's effort to enforce the judgment to establish under Rule 60(b)(4) that the defect should have prevented entry of the judgment. *See* Chapter 59.

## D. Limitations on the Defendant's Options

As we saw in Chapter 12, Rule 11 applies to all documents filed with a court. Thus, pertinent here, it limits the ability of a plaintiff to make claims, assert personal jurisdiction, allege the propriety of venue, or allege that subject matter jurisdiction exists. The same implied representations that apply to plaintiffs and their counsel apply to defendants and their counsel. As laid out in more detail in Chapter 12, the signature on a paper filed with a court implies these representations:

- Reasonable Inquiry under the Circumstances;
- No Improper Purpose;
- No Frivolous Legal Arguments, Defenses (or claims);
- No Unfounded Allegations; and
- No Unfounded Denials of Allegations.

Thus, in analyzing its options, a defendant is limited to asserting claims and defenses that have a reasonable basis in law and fact, and to denying an allegation against it only if the denial is supported by evidence.

# E. Moving to the Details

In the next several chapters, we'll explore the limitations on and availability of each option available to the defendant in detail. While we're learning about the options, remember that another option available to a defendant is to make claims against other parties who the plaintiff has joined as parties, and also to join parties that the plaintiff did not sue.

## Checkpoints

- Can you list the options available to a defendant?
- Do you understand why one might be a better choice than the others under particular facts?

# Chapter 28

# An Introduction to Motions

---

### Motions Roadmap

This chapter provides an overview of motions, including the Rules' technical requirements as well as the process that the parties and courts follow in deciding motions.

---

Recall that—perhaps with the exception of subject matter jurisdiction—federal judges do not sit in a courtroom, examining every pleading looking for mistakes or missteps, and raising up problems *sua sponte*. Instead, judges are very passive and typically only address issues raised by a party by motion. This chapter explains the mechanical aspects of motions and their common forms. After all, a motion under Rule 12 is one of the defendant's initial options.

## A. Technical Requirements for Motions

The required first step in filing most motions is a conference between counsel for the parties in which they try to resolve the issue without involving the court. Many Rules require counsel to certify in the motion that in good faith they attempted to resolve the issue before filing a motion. As a result, it is often required to hold a conference (it can be as simple as a telephone call), and then include a "certificate of conference" at the end of the motion.

If a conference is not required, or if it is held but counsel fail to resolve the issue, then the motion can be filed. The rest of this chapter addresses the components of motions and how they are resolved through, typically, three rounds of briefing—motion, response, reply—and then adjudication.

## 1. Writing, Caption, Grounds

Unless it is made during a hearing or trial, a motion must be in writing, state the relief sought, and state with particularity the grounds for seeking that relief. FRCP 7(b)(1). The motion must include a caption and be signed in accordance with Rule 11. FRCP 7(b)(2), (3). So, for example, the first page of a motion to dismiss for lack of subject matter jurisdiction in the suit between Mangia Pizza and Bob Smith, LP involving only a breach of contract claim might look like this:

---

IN THE UNITED STATES DISTRICT COURT FOR
THE WESTERN DISTRICT OF TEXAS

Mangia Pizza, Co.                                  Civ. A. No. 2007-01
   Plaintiff,

v.

Bob Smith, LP                                      Judge Rosenthal
   Defendant

DEFENDANT'S MOTION TO DISMISS FOR
LACK OF SUBJECT MATTER JURISDICTION
UNDER RULE 12(B)(1)

Defendant, Bob Smith, LP ("Smith") respectfully moves this Court to dismiss this case for lack of subject matter jurisdiction, since for purposes of subject matter jurisdiction, both Defendant and Plaintiff are citizens of Texas. In support of its motion, Smith would show the Court as follows ...

---

Defendant, Bob Smith, LP ("Smith") respectfully moves this Court to dismiss this case for lack of subject matter jurisdiction, since for purposes of subject matter jurisdiction, both Defendant and Plaintiff are citizens of Texas. In support of its motion, Smith would show the Court as follows ...

Depending on local rules of the court, sometimes the motion includes legal argument, or sometimes the argument must be included in a separate "brief in support" of the motion. It is there that the party's lawyer—you!—show why (in this hypothetical) the facts and law show that subject matter jurisdiction is lacking, and move the court as a result to dismiss.

## 2. Serving and Filing the Motion

A motion must also be "served," generally on the attorney for each party. FRCP 5(a), 5(b)(1). "Service" on attorneys for parties can be accomplished in several ways, and notice of a filing is done automatically by court electronic filing systems. The rules require that motions include a "certificate of service" stating that each party had been served. FRCP 5(d).

The party is also required to "file" the motion with the court. FRCP 5(e). Generally, this is accomplished either by using electronic filing or by delivering two copies of the motion to the court: one is filed, and the other is "time stamped" and returned to the lawyer for her files. E-filing is the norm in federal courts, however.

# B. Briefs, Affidavits, and Other Things Associated with Motions

Motions have different parts, and whether all parts, or only some, must be included in a particular motion depends on the circumstances, the local rules of the particular district court, and the type of motion. This section briefly describes some of the common components that will be pertinent to our later discussions.

Invariably, motions include legal argument to support the relief sought. As noted above, sometimes legal argument is physically included in the motion, while at other times local rules require that the legal briefing be kept separate from the motion in a separate "brief." In the argument, the party who files the motion will explain why it is entitled to have the motion granted. In the context of Rule 12 motions, for example, the defendant may explain that Section 1332 requires there be complete diversity but that because the defendant is a partnership it is deemed to be a citizen of the states of citizenship of each of its partners, and that, as a matter of fact, one partner has the same citizenship as the defendant. This argument might look something like this, to build off of what we learned earlier involving the one-count, diversity-based suit between Mangia Pizza and Bob Smith:

---

**ARGUMENT**

It is settled that 28 U.S.C. § 1332 requires complete diversity of citizenship between every plaintiff and every defendant. *Strawbridge v. Curtiss*, 7 U.S. (3 Cranch) 267 (1806). Thus, even if the amount in controversy exceeds $75,000, if defendant and plaintiff are citizens of the same State, subject matter jurisdiction is lacking.

Complete diversity is lacking here. Plaintiff is a citizen of Texas. Complaint, ¶ 1. While Plaintiff alleges that Defendant Bob Smith, LLP is a citizen of Illinois, the attached affidavit of Mr. Smith shows that Defendant is a limited liability partnership which has a general partner resident in Illinois but limited partners who are citizens of Texas. *See* Smith Affidavit ¶ 2 (attached as Exhibit A). A limited partnership has the citizenship of each of its limited partners. The citizenship of all partners, both general and limited, of a limited partnership count for diversity purposes. *Carden v. Arkoma Assocs.*, 494 U.S. 185 (1990). Therefore, this Court lacks subject matter jurisdiction, and should dismiss under Fed. R. Civ. P. 12(b)(1).

---

This hypothetical motion includes an "affidavit" of Bob Smith. An affidavit is a document that a lawyer prepares which consists of factual statements by the "affiant"—Bob Smith—that the affiant swears are true. Bob Smith's affidavit, for example, in part might look like this:

---

### IN THE UNITED STATES DISTRICT COURT
### FOR THE WESTERN DISTRICT OF TEXAS

Mangia Pizza, Co.
　　　　Plaintiff,　　　　Civ. A. No. 2007-01

v.

Bob Smith, LP　　　　　　Judge Rosenthal
　　　Defendant

#### AFFIDAVIT OF BOB SMITH

1.　　　My name is Bob Smith, I am over 21 years old and am competent to make this affidavit.

2.　　　Bob Smith, LP is a limited partnership with limited partners who have residences in each of the fifty states, including Texas.

Further, affiant sayeth not.

/s

Bob Smith

---

The affidavit must be signed and sworn to as true by Mr. Smith. Affidavits are common when, for example, a defendant makes "factual attack" on subject matter jurisdiction, personal jurisdiction, or venue. They're also very common in motions for summary judgment or motions to transfer venue. Affidavits are attached to motions and used to support factual assertions by the party made in the motion.

Often parties who include a "proposed order" whether filing the motion or responding to it. Although not required, it's good practice to include a proposed order since it may make it easier for the judge to properly and quickly decide the motion. A proposed order from the defendant filed with its motion to dismiss might look like this:

IN THE UNITED STATES DISTRICT COURT
FOR THE WESTERN DISTRICT OF TEXAS

| | | |
|---|---|---|
| Mangia Pizza, Co. | § | |
| Plaintiff, | § | Civ. A. No. 2007-01 |
| | § | |
| v. | § | |
| | § | |
| Bob Smith, LP | § | Judge Rosenthal |
| Defendant | § | |

ORDER GRANTING DEFENDANT BOB SMITH LP'S
MOTION TO DISMISS FOR LACK OF SUBJECT MATTER
JURISDICTION UNDER RULE 12(B)(1)

The Court having considered the arguments of the parties finds that this
Court lacks subject matter jurisdiction over this case because the parties
are citizens of the same State. Therefore, this Court dismisses this case.

_____
Hon. Lee Rosenthal
United States District Judge

# C. The Opposition to the Motion

When opposing counsel is served with a motion, as required by Rule 11 she
must first investigate the law and facts, and then prepare a written response
to the motion explaining why, legally, factually, or both, the motion should be
denied. Thus, in our example above, the plaintiff may have some factual basis
for contending that the defendant is not a citizen of Texas. What if, for example,
the plaintiff knew of facts showing that no limited partner was a citizen of Texas.
The plaintiff would likely include an affidavit that sought to establish that fact.

The next step is the filing with the court and service on opposing counsel the
response in opposition to it. Typically, local rules of court require that a response
or opposition to a motion be filed within 20 days of the filing of the motion
itself. Often there are strict page limits on motions, oppositions, and reply briefs.

# D. The Reply in Support of the Motion

The third, and typically final, brief comes from the party who filed the
motion and is usually referred to as a "reply" brief. A reply brief is generally

the movant's only chance to address points raised by the other party in its response. Generally, local rules strictly limit the length of reply briefs. Local rules typically prohibit parties from filing any more briefs, absent exceptional circumstances (*e.g.*, after the party files its last brief, a case is decided that is squarely on point). Reply briefs cannot raise new arguments not presented in the motion.

## E.  Court Dockets and Rules on the Motion

As each paper comes in — motion, response, reply — the clerk of the court (or the electronic filing system) enters them on the "docket" for the particular case. (Even though in federal court this is all done electronically, "docket sheet" persists as a means of describing the list of motions, briefs, and other papers received by a court for each case.) *See generally,* FRCP 79(a).

It may come to a surprise to you, and could be either a disappointment or a relief, but federal courts routinely resolve motions "on the papers" without oral argument. Oral arguments are becoming less common, meaning that persuasive, concise writing is a critical skill for lawyers. *See generally,* FRCP 78(b).

Either based upon the papers or after considering a brief oral argument, the district court will enter an "order" like the example above. *See generally,* FRCP 79(b). The clerk of the court will then mail a copy of the order on counsel for each party, or it will be sent electronically. The order can be quite brief (as in the proposed order above), or it can be a more lengthy writing in which the district court explains its rationale. Some of the opinions you read are, essentially, lengthy explanations of why a court issued an order.

As we'll see in Chapter 57, until there is an order that is a "final judgment on the merits," there will almost never be an appeal. In our hypothetical, if the court dismissed for lack of subject matter jurisdiction, an appeal could properly be taken by the plaintiff because there would be no further proceedings in the district court; but if the court denied the motion — if it kept jurisdiction over the claim because it concluded it had subject matter jurisdiction — then the case would proceed. The defendant could not immediately appeal because the order did not end litigation, and so is not a final judgment.

That last point bears emphasizing, because it may be counter-intuitive: there generally is no "second chance" to go on appeal immediately after a party loses a motion. Unless the order falls into one of a few narrow classes of orders that can be appealed on an "interlocutory" basis, no order of a district court can be appealed until after the entire case is finally resolved by entry of a "final judgment." Lawyers typically get only one chance.

## Checkpoints

- Can you identify the technical requirements for motions? For how motions are adjudicated?

- Do you understand the function of affidavits, briefs, and other parts of a motion? Do you understand what an "order" is and the distinction between it and a "final judgment"?

# Chapter 29

# When and Why Must a Defendant File an Answer or Rule 12 Motion?

---

### File an Answer or a Rule 12 Motion Roadmap

This chapter shows that, to avoid giving the plaintiff the power to seek entry of a default judgment, a defendant must timely file either an answer or, if it has grounds to do so, a Rule 12 pre-answer motion. Filing a Rule 12 motion delays the time for filing an answer, and an answer can be more expensive to prepare than a Rule 12 motion, since preparing an answer requires defense counsel to conduct a more vigorous legal and factual investigation into all allegations of the complaint, affirmative defenses, and joinder of claims and parties.

---

## A. When and Why Must a Rule 12 Motion or Answer Be Filed?

### 1. When Must a Rule 12 Motion or Answer Be Filed?

As we saw, when a plaintiff files a suit it must mail to the defendant a copy of the complaint along with a request for waiver of service of the summons. That form explains to the defendant that it can either waive service of process, in which case it has 60 days to respond to the complaint, or it can require service, in which case it will only have 21 days to answer the complaint after it is formally served. *See* Chapters 26 and 27; FRCP 12(a)(1).

### 2. Why Must a Rule 12 Motion or Answer Be Filed?

Rule 12(a) requires filing an answer but Rule 12(a)(4) extends the time to file an answer if the defendant files a Rule 12 motion. If a defendant does not either timely file its answer or a Rule 12 motion, then the plaintiff can move for entry of a default judgment. *See* Chapter 45. If default judgment is entered, then defendant is at risk of the plaintiff moving forward to execute the judgment, meaning having the government (typically a sheriff) force the defendant to sell property and pay money to the plaintiff, for example.

Filing a Rule 12 motion postpones the time that the defendant must file a responsive pleading, called an answer. If the court denies the Rule 12 motion, how much time the party gets to file its responsive pleading turns on which type of Rule 12 motion it filed and how the court ruled on it:

> (A) If the court denies the motion or postpones its disposition until trial, the responsive pleading must be served within 14 days after notice of the court's action; or
> (B) If the court grants a motion for more definite statement, the responsive pleading must be served within 14 days after the more definite statement is served.

Rule 12(A)(4). Obviously, if the motion is granted the case may be dismissed or transferred to a different district.

## B. What Must or Can be Raised in a Rule 12 Motion?

Two objections—as to scandalous or other improper material in the complaint and as to the indefiniteness of the complaint—*must* be made in a pre-answer motion. *See* FRCP 12(e) and 12(f). Seven others can be made *either* in an answer or, at the option of the defendant, in a—one—pre-answer motion, as Rule 12(b) tries to make clear:

> Every defense to a claim for relief in any pleading must be asserted in the responsive pleading if one is required. But a party may assert the following defenses by motion: (1) lack of subject matter jurisdiction; (2) lack of personal jurisdiction; (3) improper venue; (4) insufficient process; (5) insufficient service of process; (6) failure to state a claim upon which relief can be granted; and (7) failure to join an indispensable party.

This chart summarizes where, and so effectively when, Rule 12 defenses can be made.

| | 12(b)(1) | 12(b)(2) | 12(b)(3) | 12(b)(4) | 12(b)(5) | 12(b)(6) | 12(b)(7) | 12(e) | 12(f) |
|---|---|---|---|---|---|---|---|---|---|
| In the pre-answer motion? | √ | √ | √ | √ | √ | √ | √ | √ | √ |
| In answer (or amendment as of right?) | √ | √ | √ | √ | √ | √ | √ | | |
| Even without being included in the pre-answer motion or answer? | √ | | | | | √ | √ | | |

The next few chapters explore each Rule 12 objection, because defense counsel must promptly analyze whether any Rule 12 objection is available because many must be asserted no later than in the answer. Later, we'll explore the "consolidation requirement" and see that if the defendant files a Rule 12 pre-answer motion, *many of the Rule 12 objections* are waived if they are not "consolidated" and included in that Rule 12 pre-answer motion and, further, if one Rule 12 pre-answer motion is made, a second pre-answer Rule 12 motion is improper. *See* Chapter 36.

## Checkpoints

- Can you identify how long a defendant has to respond to receipt of a complaint?
- Can you explain why a defendant must file either a Rule 12 motion or an answer?
- Can you identify those Rule 12 objections that must be raised in a pre-answer motion? That may be?

# Chapter 30

# Rule 12(b)(1) Challenges to Subject Matter Jurisdiction

---

### Rule 12(b)(1) Roadmap

This chapter describes the two forms of Rule 12(b)(1) motions and how each is decided.

This chapter explains related doctrines, under which subject matter jurisdiction might literally exist, but other Constitutional or prudential concerns either require that the federal court dismiss the claim, or give it discretion to stay its hand pending resolution of related state court proceedings.

---

A party asserting lack of subject matter jurisdiction as to one or more claims can raise the objection at any time, including before filing an answer in a Rule 12 pre-answer motion and even while the case is on appeal after final judgment. Most often, a defendant will raise lack of subject matter jurisdiction early by pre-answer motion under Rule 12(b)(1), because a district court without subject matter jurisdiction over a claim must dismiss that claim.

## A. Two Forms of Attack

Motions to dismiss for lack of subject matter jurisdiction either are "facial attacks"—in which the defendant asserts that even if the allegations in the complaint are taken as true the complaint insufficiently invokes subject matter jurisdiction—or factual attacks (sometimes called "speaking motions"), where the defendant takes issue with and attempts to prove as false allegations in the complaint by, for example, submitting an affidavit attesting that certain facts alleged in the complaint (*e.g.*, the citizenship of the defendant) are inaccurate or untrue. *See Miller v. Mer*, 2006 WL 1735355 (S.D. Ohio 2006). Subject matter jurisdiction must be analyzed on a claim-by-claim basis.

## 1. Facial Attacks

If a party does not challenge the truth or accuracy of facts alleged in the complaint, the court must accept those allegations as true. *McCann v. Newman Irrevocable Trust*, 458 F.3d 281 (3rd Cir. 2006). The question for the court is, assuming the alleged facts are true, is there subject matter jurisdiction over the claim?

## 2. Factual Attacks

If a party in a Rule 12(b)(1) motion contests any of the allegations in the complaint by submitting evidence (through, for example, an affidavit), the plaintiff can include evidence in its response to the motion. The nonmoving party (*i.e.,* typically the party claiming jurisdiction exists) must introduce specific facts, not mere speculation. *Harleysville Mut. Ins. Co. v. Packer*, 60 F.3d 1116, 1119–20 (4th Cir.1995). These factual motions typically are litigated when diversity is the basis for subject matter jurisdiction, and the defendant contends the citizenship of one or more parties is not accurately alleged.

The court then decides the motion by weighing the evidence. The party asserting that subject matter jurisdiction exists has the burden to prove the facts by preponderant evidence. *McCann v. Newman Irrevocable Trust*, 458 F.3d 281 (3rd Cir. 2006). A live hearing may be needed in unusual circumstances.

# B. The Impact of Adjudication

If a court grants a motion to dismiss a claim for lack of subject matter jurisdiction, then the claim is dismissed but *without* prejudice. *See* FRCP 41(b). The claim can be refiled, but must be refiled in state court.

Whether dismissal of one claim of a multi-claim suit means the entire case is dismissed usually depends upon whether a claim over which the court has original jurisdiction remains pending. However, sometimes even if the only remaining claims are those over which the court lacks original subject matter jurisdiction, the court can still keep the case under 28 U.S.C. § 1367(c)(3). *See* Chapter 21.

# C. Additional Doctrines Related to Subject Matter Jurisdiction

In some instances even a federal court that has subject matter jurisdiction can, nonetheless, lack the power to adjudicate a claim or have discretion to refuse to do so. These objections may be available to a defendant at the time it is filing its answer or later.

In some circumstances, federal courts lack power to adjudicate claims because the Constitution limits judicial power to "cases or controversies." If a claim presents no "case or controversy," there is no constitutional authority for a federal court to act. As we will see, a "case or controversy" can be absent because the dispute is not yet ripe, the dispute has become moot, or the plaintiff lacks "standing"—it doesn't have a personal stake in the dispute distinct from any member of the public—to raise the claim.

These doctrines have different sources and different dimensions, but they all share the same basic principle of prohibiting or giving discretion to federal courts to choose not to adjudicate a claim. You may not reach these doctrines in your first year civil procedure course, but you might. They are covered in upper-year "federal courts" or "federal jurisdiction" classes, if not during the first year. They're covered here just briefly.

Even if there is an actual case or controversy presented by a claim, under some narrow circumstances the court, nonetheless, may—and sometimes, must—refuse to adjudicate the claim. Generally, we'll see that there are several differently named but closely related "abstention doctrines" under which federal courts refuse to decide a claim, usually because doing so will implicate a parallel or previous state suit on the same subject matter. We'll see that these doctrines are fairly straightforward—a party who lost in state court generally can't file a suit in federal district court to "overturn" the state court judgment for example— while others turn on somewhat complex balancing of competing and subtle policies.

The following chart summarizes the doctrines discussed in this chapter. Each is distinct and must be analyzed separately. It's possible that a claim could be ripe, but the plaintiff lack standing; or be subject to multiple bases for abstention, for example.

In addition to what it depicts, there are other limitations, such as the "political question doctrine" which deems non-justiciable questions that the Constitution assigns to other branches of government. *See, e.g., Nixon v. U.S.,* 506 U.S. 224 (1993) (no subject matter jurisdiction over challenge to trial procedure followed by the U.S. Senate); *Goldwater v. Carter,* 444 U.S. (1979) (same as to President's decision to unilaterally abrogate a treaty with a foreign country). This doctrine is sometimes studied in constitutional law, not civil procedure classes.

## 1. A Summary Chart

### CONSTITUTIONAL AND PRUDENTIAL
### LIMITATIONS ON FEDERAL SUBJECT MATTER JURISDICTION

| Doctrine | Source | Triggers | Impact |
|---|---|---|---|
| Constitutional Standing | Art. III | Plaintiff was not itself harmed by defendant's actions | Lacks subject matter jurisdiction; must dismiss claim. |
| Ripeness | Art. III | Plaintiff seeks relief for acts that have not yet occurred | Lacks subject matter jurisdiction; must dismiss claim. |
| Mootness | Art. III | Events have rendered the need for adjudication moot | Lacks subject matter jurisdiction; must dismiss claim. |
| Prudential Standing | Judicial self-governance | Domestic relations or Probate matters | Lacks subject matter jurisdiction; must dismiss claim. |
| *Rooker-Feldman* | 28 U.S.C. § 1257 | Party that lost suit in state court seeks to reverse it in federal district court | U.S. Supreme Court is the only federal court that has subject matter jurisdiction over appeals from state court judgments. |
| *Colorado River* | Principles of Comity | On-going state litigation over same subject | Court has subject matter jurisdiction, but may dismiss or stay resolution of the case pending resolution by the state court. |
| *Younger* | Principles of Comity | On-going state litigation over same subject | Similar to above, but abstain only. |
| *Pullman* | Avoiding Constitutional Questions | A federal constitutional question arises from an unsettled interpretation of state law | Court has subject matter jurisdiction, but has discretion to stay the case pending resolution of the underlying question of state law. |

## 2. Requirements Originating from Article III's Case or Controversy Clause

The first series of limitations all are anchored in the U.S. Constitution. Article III of the United States Constitution both grants and limits judicial power. In full, that Article provides:

Section 1. The judicial Power of the United States, shall be vested in one supreme Court, and in such inferior Courts as the Congress may from time to time ordain and establish. The Judges, both of the supreme and inferior Courts, shall hold their Offices during good Behaviour, and shall, at stated Times, receive for their Services, a Compensation, which shall not be diminished during their Continuance in Office.

Section 2. The judicial Power shall extend to all Cases, in Law and Equity, arising under this Constitution, the Laws of the United States, and Treaties made, or which shall be made, under their Authority;—to all Cases affecting Ambassadors, other public Ministers and Consuls;—to all Cases of admiralty and maritime Jurisdiction;—to Controversies to which the United States shall be a Party;—to Controversies between two or more States;—between a State and Citizens of another State;—between Citizens of different States;—between Citizens of the same State claiming Lands under Grants of different States, and between a State, or the Citizens thereof, and foreign States, Citizens or Subjects.

In all Cases affecting Ambassadors, other public Ministers and Consuls, and those in which a State shall be Party, the supreme Court shall have original Jurisdiction. In all the other Cases before mentioned, the supreme Court shall have appellate Jurisdiction, both as to Law and Fact, with such Exceptions, and under such Regulations as the Congress shall make.

The Trial of all Crimes, except in Cases of Impeachment, shall be by Jury; and such Trial shall be held in the State where the said Crimes shall have been committed; but when not committed within any State, the Trial shall be at such Place or Places as the Congress may by Law have directed.

Section 3. Treason against the United States, shall consist only in levying War against them, or in adhering to their Enemies, giving them Aid and Comfort. No Person shall be convicted of Treason unless on the Testimony of two Witnesses to the same overt Act, or on Confession in open Court.

The Congress shall have Power to declare the Punishment of Treason, but no Attainder of Treason shall work Corruption of Blood, or Forfeiture except during the Life of the Person attainted.

While obviously authorizing federal courts to decide disputes, this language includes important limitations: there must be a "case" or "controversy" to be adjudicated. The words "case" or "controversy" have a very specific, limited meaning, as we've already seen in other contexts. The grant of power in Article III is limited to the power to decide actual controversies between parties.

We've not focused on why the Framers chose to limit judicial power to cases or controversies. It wasn't by mistake. No "principle is more fundamental to the judiciary's proper role in our system of government that the constitutional limitation of federal-court jurisdiction to actual cases or controversies." *Raines v. Byrd*, 521 U.S. 811, 818 (1997). Why? Because if the courts had power to resolve just any question — one that didn't involve a concrete dispute between parties — then judicial power would extend to virtually "every subject proper for legislative discussion and decision. . . . The division of power [among the branches of government] could exist no longer, and the other departments would be swallowed up by the judiciary." 4 PAPERS OF JOHN MARSHALL 95 (C. Cullen ed. 1984). The "case or controversy" requirement keeps the courts from acting as executives or legislatures — issuing orders to govern solely future contemplated conduct, not to address existing or completed actions or to remedy their future impact. Thus, these limitations serve to check the unelected, unrepresentative judiciary in another-wise democratic government. *Allen v. Wright*, 468 U.S. 737, 760 (1984).

Most of the time, these doctrines are irrelevant to litigants. A party to a contract who sues because the other party has failed to deliver on time has a ripe, actual, case or controversy, and has standing to bring the claim. But the doctrines are important because they are invoked in civil lawsuits and, more importantly, they are fundamental to our system of divided government, and the principle of separation of powers.

Over time, Article III has been construed to create a number of prudential limitations on the exercise of federal judicial power. This chapter examines the more common limitations that arise out of Article III: standing, ripeness, and mootness (and its exception). If a claim is not ripe, or if it has become moot, or if the plaintiff lacks standing to bring the claim, then (absent an exception), the court lacks power to adjudicate the claim and must dismiss it. Parties cannot waive these requirements. This is true even if the Supreme Court is the first court to recognize that something is amiss. The requirements of standing, ripeness, and lack of mootness are constitutional jurisdictional requirements that cannot be waived by the parties. Accordingly, the courts have an independent obligation to examine whether a case or controversy is present. *DaimlerChrysler Corp. v. Cuno*, 126 S.Ct. 1854 (2006).

The doctrines examined in this section all originate in Article III's "case or controversy" requirement. *DaimlerChrysler Corp. v. Cuno*, 126 S.Ct. 1854 (2006). They are inter-related and in some cases an analysis of standing could be made under ripeness, and *vice versa. See Wilderness Soc'y v. Alcock*, 83 F.3d

386, 389–90 (11th Cir. 1996) (noting that courts confuse and conflate ripeness and standing analyses). Despite their relatedness and overlap, each must be analyzed separately.

### a. Constitutional Standing

"Standing" is a term that is used in various contexts. This section discusses the Constitutional aspect of "standing" that originates in Article III. The narrow "prudential" aspect of standing is discussed below in this chapter. The "case or controversy" requirement of Article III requires that the party asserting a claim have standing to do so. *DaimlerChrysler Corp. v. Cuno,* 126 S.Ct. 1854 (2006) (collecting cases). Constitutional standing is determined on a case-by-case basis. *Id.* Thus, it may be that a plaintiff has standing to bring one claim but not another. If the plaintiff lacks standing to bring a claim, then the court must dismiss the claim for lack of subject matter jurisdiction: federal jurisdiction is limited to cases or controversies, and a case or controversy requires that the party asserting the claim have standing to do so. *Id.* Neither the parties nor the courts can waive standing as it is a Constitutional requirement. *See id.*

The basic requirement of Constitutional standing is simple to state: (1) the plaintiff must have suffered an injury in fact; (2) there must be a causal connection between that injury and the conduct about which the plaintiff complains; and (3) it must be likely, and not just speculative, that the injury will be redressed by a favorable judicial decision. *Lujan v. Defenders of Wildlife,* 504 U.S. 555, 560–61 (1992). A court must conduct "careful . . . examination of a complaint's allegations to ascertain whether the particular plaintiff is entitled to an adjudication of the particular claims asserted." *Allen,* 468 U.S. at 752. Constitutional standing is measured at the time the complaint is filed. *Lujan,* 504 U.S. at 569 n. 4; *ACLU of Nev. v. Lomax,* 2006 WL 352579 (9th Cir. Dec. 8, 2006). Thus, events subsequent to the filing of the pleading containing the claim will not affect Constitutional standing, although the claim can become moot. *See* below.

### b. Ripeness

Article III's case or controversy limitation requires that a claim be "ripe" for decision. Because ripeness is a Constitutional requirement, the parties cannot waive it and the court should satisfy itself that a claim is ripe. *Nat'l Park Hospitality Ass'n. v. Dep't of Interior,* 538 U.S. 803, 808 (2003). Although Constitutional in origin, the ripeness requirement also has prudential aspects. *Id.* The Constitutional aspect arises from the limitation in Article III of federal judicial power to a "case or controversy"; the prudential aspects arise from the desire to prevent federal courts "from engaging in speculation or wasting their resources through the review of potential or abstract disputes." *Digital Props., Inc. v. City of Plantation,* 121 F.3d 586, 590 (11th Cir. 1997). At bottom, the ripeness doctrine prevents federal courts from deciding cases prematurely, before a judicial decision is actually necessary. A court must determine "whether the claim is sufficiently mature, and the issues sufficiently defined and concrete, to permit effective decision-making by the court." *Id.* at 589.

A claim is ripe only if the issues raised are concrete enough for judicial decision in light of the hardship to the parties of withholding judicial determination. *Abbott Labs. v. Gardner,* 387 U.S. 136, 149 (1967). In making the decision, the court must consider "(1) whether delayed review would cause hardship to the plaintiffs; (2) whether judicial intervention would inappropriately interfere with further administrative action; and (3) whether the courts would benefit from further factual development of the issues presented." *Ohio Forestry Ass'n, Inc. v. Sierra Club,* 523 U.S. 726, 733 (1998).

### c. Mootness

Mootness is a requirement for justiciability of a "case or controversy" under Article III. *Protestant Mem. Med. Center, Inc. v. Maram,* 2006 WL 3499943 (7th Cir. 2006). Similar to ripeness, the doctrine helps to avoid judicial pronouncements on legal questions that do not impact an existing controversy; with ripeness, the controversy has not yet become concrete enough, but with mootness, a judicial decision will not affect any existing right. Parties cannot waive mootness, and a court must ensure that a claim has not become moot.

"To qualify as a case fit for federal-court adjudication, an actual controversy must be extant at all stages of review, not merely at the time the complaint is filed." *Arizonans for Official English v. Arizona,* 520 U.S. 43, 67 (1997). "Federal courts have no power to hear moot cases, and because a case can become moot at any time — even after entry of a final judgment — the doctrine prevents a federal court of appeals from exercising its appellate jurisdiction in a moot case." *Brooks v. Vassar,* 462 F.3d 341, 348 (4th Cir. 2006). A once-ripe claim, therefore, can become moot.

### i. The Exception to the Mootness Limitation: Courts May Adjudicate Claims Capable of Repetition Yet Evading Review

A claim that has become moot may, nonetheless, be within the subject matter jurisdiction of the federal courts if it is "capable of repetition, yet evading review." There are two requirements to fall within this exception: (1) the challenged action must have been too short in its duration to be fully litigated prior to its cessation or expiration, and (2) there must be a reasonable expectation that the same plaintiff will again be subjected to the same conduct. *Lewis v. Cont'l Bank Corp.*, 494 U.S. 472, 481 (1990).

With respect to the first element, an action evades review if it is "almost certain to run its course before [an appellate court] can give the case full consideration." *ACLU of Nev. v. Lomax*, 2006 WL 3525179 (9th Cir. Dec. 2006). An example would be a challenge to an election procedure, since an election will likely end before a court could rule on the challenge to any election procedure or review on appeal any order issued by a district court concerning that procedure. *Id.* With respect to the second element, the party invoking the exception need only show that it is reasonable to expect that the defendant will engage in the same conduct again. *ACLU of Nev.*, 2006 WL 3525179 at *6. In one recent case, after a district court entered judgment for the plaintiff finding a statute unconstitutional in part, the legislature changed the statute to eliminate the infirmities identified by the district court, and so the question of mootness was raised on appeal. *Brooks v. Vassar*, 462 F.3d 341, 348 (4th Cir. 2006). The court of appeals explained that without it being reasonably likely that the legislature would re-enact the unconstitutional portions of the statute, the claims related to the unconstitutionality of that aspect were moot, and the second element could not be shown.

## 3. Prudential Standing Requirements

Prudential standing is distinct from Constitutional standing. *Elk Grove Unified School Dist. v. Newdow*, 542 US 1, 12 (2004). Although closely related to constitutional standing, prudential standing embodies "judicially self-imposed limits on the exercise of federal jurisdiction." *Id.* Prudential standing can preclude a federal court from adjudicating even a ripe, non-moot, actual case or controversy.

Prudential standing has not been "exhaustively defined." *Id.* It "encompasses 'the general prohibition on a litigant's raising another person's legal rights, the rule barring adjudication of generalized grievance more appropriately addressed in the representative branches, and the requirement that a plaintiff's complaint fall within the zone of interests protected by the law invoked.'" *Id.*(quoting *Allen v. Wright*, 468 U.S. 737, 751 (1984)). The Supreme Court has reasoned that without these self-imposed restraints, "courts would be called upon to decide abstract questions of wide public significance even though other governmental institutions may be more competent to address the questions and even though judicial intervention may be unnecessary to protect individual rights." *Id.* (quoting *Warth v. Sedlin*, 422 U.S. 490, 500 (1975)).

The principal subject matter to which the Court has held that prudential standing applies are domestic relations disputes, which is principally state law governing the legal relations between husband, wife, and children. *Id.* The Court has gone so far as to recognize a "domestic relations exception" that "divests federal courts of power to issue divorce, alimony, and child custody decrees." *Id.* at 12–13 (quoting *Ankenbrandt v. Richards,* 504 U.S. 689, 703 (1992)). Thus, even if two spouses seeking divorce resided in different states and are disputing an estate valued at more than $75,000, federal courts lack power to address the divorce case. *But cf. Palmore v. Sidoti,* 466 U.S. 429, 432–434 (1984) (court could answer a substantial federal question that existed apart from the state family law issues).

The *Elk Grove* decision arguably broadened this exception. In that case, a father filed a federal suit because state schools required teachers to lead recitation of the Pledge of Allegiance. However, the father was in a child-custody dispute in state court with the mother while this federal court action was proceeding. While at the time suit was filed he had the right to bring suit on her behalf, during pendency of the suit, that changed, and the mother was awarded that right. The Supreme Court held that prudential standing precluded jurisdiction over the case because the father's standing to prosecute the suit on his daughter's behalf was "founded on family law rights that are in dispute" and prosecution of the suit could "have an adverse effect on the person who is the source of the plaintiff's claimed standing." *Id.* at 18. Thus, in *Elk Grove* because the father's right to sue on his daughter's behalf had been taken away by a California state court while the *Elk Grove* decision was in litigation, the court held that "the prudent court is for the federal court to stay its hand rather than reach out to resolve a weighty question of federal constitutional law." *Id.* Several opinions were written in *Elk Grove,* one of which wondered why *Palmore* did not control, since the question of whether the Pledge could be required was a substantial federal question that existed apart from the question of custody. *Id.* at 21–22 (Rehnquist, J., concurring in the judgment). For now, *Elk Grove* probably represents an extreme illustration of prudential standing limitations.

Finally, federal courts similarly rely on prudential standing principles to decline to adjudicate probate matters. *Markham v. Allen,* 326 U.S. 490, 494 (1946). The parameters of this limitation on federal power and its exceptions are not as developed as the "domestic relations" exception.

## 4. Other Limitations on Federal Judicial Power

The foregoing limitations emanate directly from or at least are closely related to Article III's limitation of judicial power to "cases or controversies." The following doctrines also relate judicial power, but originate from more distant sources, policies, or concerns. With the exception of the *Rooker-Feldman* doctrine, they do not mean that the court lacks subject matter jurisdiction to address a dispute, but rather that it should "abstain" from adjudicating a claim even though it has power to do so. They are, as a result, known as the various "abstention doctrines." This section covers the principal abstention doctrines, each one known by the case in which it was first recognized.

### a. Rooker-Feldman: *Review of State Court Orders go to the Supreme Court, Not Federal District Courts*

A federal statute vests federal subject matter jurisdiction over appeals from state court judgments exclusively in the Supreme Court. *See* 28 U.S.C. § 1257. To enforce that statute, if a state court enters a judgment against a party in state court, but the loser files suit in federal district court that, in essence, seeks to reverse that state court judgment, then the federal district court lacks subject matter jurisdiction. *ExxonMobil Corp. v. Saudi Basic Indus. Corp.,* 544 U.S. 280 (2005). The plaintiff should have appealed, not filed another suit. Because the *Rooker-Feldman* doctrine is jurisdictional, the circuit courts hold that it may be raised at any time and cannot be waived by the parties. *Am. Reliable Ins. Co. v. Stillwell,* 336 F.3d 311, 316 (4th Cir. 2003) (collecting cases).

The *Rooker-Feldman* doctrine covers cases where a party who has lost a judgment in state court complains in federal court of injuries caused by that judgment. *Id.* To establish that jurisdiction is exclusive in the Supreme Court, the party invoking *Rooker-Feldman* must establish that: (1) there was a state court judgment entered before the federal suit was filed and (2) the federal suit is seeking to review and reject that judgment. *Id.*

With respect to the first element, the state court judgment must be prior to the filing of the federal suit. *Rooker-Feldman* does not apply where one party files a state court suit, and then while that suit is pending the other party files a mirror-image federal court lawsuit, and the state court case gets to judgment before the federal case. *Id.*(It may be that under such circumstances claim or issue preclusion might apply. *See* Chapter 60.) Thus, parallel state court litigation is no bar to federal court subject matter jurisdiction. *Id.* With respect to the second element, the doctrine *only* applies when a party is seeking to have the federal court review and reject the state court judgment. In both *Rooker* and *Feldman,* the federal court plaintiffs asked the federal court to overturn prior state court judgments. *Rooker v. Fidelity Trust Co.,* 263 U.S. 413 (1923) (state court judgment loser filed federal suit to have state judgment declared "null and void"). A "party losing in state court is barred from seeking what in substance would be appellate review of the state judgment in a United States district court." *Johnson v. De Grandy*, 512 U.S. 997, 1005–06 (1994). Thus, the doctrine applies only if the plaintiff is seeking to set aside a state court judgment; it does not apply if he is, in fact, presenting an independent claim. *Id.*

As a consequence, it is possible for a court to have subject matter jurisdiction over some, but not all, claims in a complaint. For example, in *Dist. of Columbia Court of Appeals v. Feldman*, 460 U.S. 462 (1983), two men who had lost a suit to have a state appellate court waive its rule imposing qualifications to practice law, filed federal court suit to overturn the court's decision to deny their request. The Court held that the district court lacked subject matter jurisdiction to overturn the court's decision that they personally could be admitted, but not over their claim that the challenged rule was itself unconstitutional. The rule could be challenged, but not its application in a particular case. *Id.* Thus, if a federal plaintiff pleads "some independent claim, albeit one that denies a legal conclusion that a state court has reached in a case to which he was a party . . . then there is jurisdiction and state law determines whether the defendant prevails under principles of [claim or issue] preclusion." *Exxon-Mobil*, 544 U.S. at 294.

Prior to *ExxonMobil*, appellate courts had given the *Rooker-Feldman* doctrine much greater breadth than the Court found appropriate in *ExxonMobil*. So, many cases decided prior to 2005 applying *Rooker-Feldman* may no longer be good law.

### b. Younger "Abstention"

Although it is not typical, it is also not rare for multiple suits to be filed arising out of the same dispute. If there are both an on-going state court proceeding and a federal suit arising out of the same dispute, there is no way for a federal court to "transfer venue" to the state court, and if subject matter jurisdiction exists, no way for the federal court to dismiss. What the federal court can do, however, is abstain from adjudicating the repetitious claims. That fact pattern — on-going state and federal court proceedings on the same subject — is the paradigm of *Younger* and *Colorado River* abstention doctrines.

*Younger* and *Colorado River* abstention doctrines are related to each other and, to a lesser extent, *Rooker-Feldman*. Under *Younger* and *Colorado River*, a federal court with subject matter jurisdiction over a claim can abstain from deciding the claim because there is parallel, on-going state court litigation involving the same issues. In such circumstances, the court should either stay or dismiss the federal suit pending resolution of the state court proceedings to avoid unnecessary intrusion into state matters and in recognition of the limited nature of federal government.

*Younger v. Harris*, 401 U.S. 37 (1971) established the strong federal policy against interfering in ongoing state court matters without "extraordinary circumstances" justifying doing so. This notion, called "comity," ensures "a proper respect for state functions, a recognition of the fact that the entire country is made up of a Union of separate state governments, and a continuance of the belief that that National Government will fare best if the States and their institutions are left to perform their separate ways." *Middlesex County Ethics Comm. v. Garden State B. Ass'n.*, 457 U.S. 423, 431 (1982). The federal court has subject matter jurisdiction, but refrains from acting. *Nivens v. Gilchrist*, 444 F.3d 237, 247–48 (4th Cir. 2006)

*Younger* abstention is proper when a parallel state court proceeding (1) is currently pending, (2) involves an important, substantial, or vital state interest, and (3) affords the plaintiff an adequate opportunity to raise constitutional claims. *See Nivens v. Gilchrist*, 444 F.3d 237 (4th Cir. 2006). Those circumstances permit the federal court to abstain, but there are exceptions which permit it to continue: (a) it's shown that the state officials responsible for the prosecution are acting in bad faith or to harass; (b) the law applied in the criminal proceeding flagrantly and patently violates express Constitutional provisions; or (c) "other extraordinary circumstances" exist. *Kugler v. Helfant*, 421 U.S. 117, 124 (1975). Despite exceptions, the "cost, anxiety, and inconvenience of having to defend against a criminal prosecution alone [does] not constitute irreparable injury. *Younger*, 401 U.S. at 46.

If, based on those factors the court finds a substantial risk of direct interference with on-going state proceedings, it can dismiss the federal claim or keep it but abstain from taking any further action pending resolution of the state court matter. *Nivens v. Gilchrist*, 444 F.3d 237 (4th Cir. 2006). A district court's decision to abstain or dismiss, or not, is reviewed for abuse of discretion. *Id.*

### c. Colorado River *Abstention*

Abstention under *Colorado River Water Conserv. Dist. v. U.S.*, 424 U.S. 800 (1976) is related to but distinct from *Younger* abstention. In *Colorado River*, the Court recognized that, as did *Younger*, the existence of an on-going state suit did not deprive the federal court of subject matter jurisdiction over a claim arising out of the same subject matter but considerations of federal-state comity and "wise judicial administration" can justify abstaining despite having jurisdiction.

There need not be identical claims or complete identity of parties to justify abstention under *Colorado River. Romine v. CompuServe Corp.*, 160 F.3d 337, 339 (6th Cir. 1998). Instead, various factors affect whether abstention under *Colorado River* is warranted: (1) whether the state court has assumed jurisdiction over any res or property; (2) whether the federal forum is less convenient to the parties; (3) avoidance of piecemeal litigation; (4) the order in which jurisdiction was obtained; (5) whether state or federal law provides the rule of decision; (6) the adequacy of the state court action to protect the federal plaintiff's rights; (7) the relative progress of the state and federal proceedings; and (8) the presence or absence of concurrent jurisdiction. *Id.* at 340–41.

### d. Pullman *Abstention*

The *Pullman* abstention doctrine arose from a case about Pullman railroad sleeping cars, where a federal court was asked to restrain an order of the Texas Railroad Commission requiring the use of attendants in railroad sleeping cars. *Tex. Railroad Comm'n. v. Pullman*, 312 U.S 643 (1941). The problem was that the federal issue was of constitutional import, but that issue had to be decided only if state law was interpreted a certain way, and the meaning of state law was very uncertain. So, if the state law was interpreted one way, there was no constitutional issue. The Fifth Circuit had gone ahead and interpreted state law and then affirmed an injunction against the order. However, the Court held that the federal courts, though having subject matter jurisdiction, should have abstained and let the state courts figure out the state law issue first, since that might have obviated the need to determine the federal constitutional issue. *Pullman* is thus about avoiding a constitutional question when reaching it turns on an interpretation of unsettled state law. The Court recognized that the Texas Supreme Court would have the final word on whether the Commission had acted within the scope of its authority under Texas law. *Id.* at 499–500. Nothing precluded that state court suit from being "brought with reasonable promptness, in the state court." *Id.* at 502. Thus, the Court held that the federal courts should retain jurisdiction over the action, but abstain while that state court process went forward. The court reached this result because the case touched a sensitive area of social policy, a state decision could obviate the need for federal constitutional adjudication, and any federal construction of the state law might be ignored or rejected by a state court, definitive decision.

Courts now characterize the purpose of *Pullman* as two-fold: (1) avoiding constitutional questions when their resolution is unnecessary and (2) allowing state courts to decide unsettled issues of state law. *Nivens v. Gilchrist*, 444 F.3d 237, 246 n. 6 (4th Cir. 2006). Over time, the *Pullman* analysis has become identified with these factors:

(1) The complaint touches a sensitive area of social policy upon which the federal courts ought not to enter unless no alternative to its adjudication is open.

(2) Such constitutional adjudication plainly can be avoided if a definitive ruling on the state issue would terminate the controversy; and

(3) The possibly determinative issue of state law is doubtful.

*Smelt v. County of Orange,* 447 F.3d 673 (9th Cir. 2006).

---

## Checkpoints

- Can you distinguish a facial attack from a factual attack?
- Can you explain whether a claim that is dismissed for lack of subject matter jurisdiction can be re-filed?
- Can you describe the various doctrines related to subject matter jurisdiction and their purposes?

# Chapter 31

# Rule 12(b)(2) Challenges to Personal Jurisdiction

---

### Rule 12(b)(2) Roadmap

This chapter describes the two different forms of motions to challenge personal jurisdiction and how they are decided.

This chapter also analyzes how an objection to personal jurisdiction can be waived, either by consent before the dispute even arose or after suit has been filed—by design or neglect.

---

A party that has a Rule 11 basis for asserting that a court lacks personal jurisdiction over one or more claims asserted against it has several options. Some options allow for immediate litigation of the objection, others waive the objection, and others delay litigation of the issue, at least for a while.

## A. Promptly and Timely Objecting to Lack of Personal Jurisdiction

The Rules give a party three places to raise an objection of lack of personal jurisdiction: in the pre-answer Rule 12(b)(2) motion; if there has not been a pre-answer motion, in the answer; or, an amendment to the answer that is allowed as a matter of right. FRCP 12(g), (h). *See* Chapter 41 (discussing amendments to pleadings).

## 1. Two Types of Challenges to Personal Jurisdiction

A party has the burden of establishing that the court has personal jurisdiction over each claim it asserts. *DiStefano v. Carozzi N. Am., Inc.*, 286 F.3d 81, 84 (2d Cir. 2001). How great that burden is depends on which of the two types of challenge the defendant makes. The type of challenge also affects the burden of proof and also the procedure that is used to adjudicate the motion.

### a. Facial Challenges

A facial challenge assumes the truth of the allegations in the pleading but nonetheless contends the court lacks personal jurisdiction. If a defendant makes a facial challenge, then the plaintiff must merely establish a *prima facie* showing of personal jurisdiction. The defendant basically says, "if everything the plaintiff pled is true, there still is no personal jurisdiction."

### b. Factual Challenges

In a factual attack on personal jurisdiction, the defendant disputes the jurisdictional facts pled in the pleading and submits evidence, such as affidavits, with its motion showing that, as a factual matter, the court lacks personal jurisdiction over one or more claims. In deciding how to adjudicate a factual attack, the district may use these procedures, or a combination, or all three:

(a) determine the motions based on affidavits alone;
(b) permit discovery which would help resolve the motion; or
(c) conduct an evidentiary hearing on the motion.

*See Intera Corp. v. Henderson,* 428 F.3d 605 (6th Cir. 2005). "When a non-resident defendant presents a motion to dismiss for lack of personal jurisdiction, the plaintiff bears the burden of establishing the district court's jurisdiction over the non-resident. The court may determine the jurisdictional issue by receiving affidavits, interrogatories, depositions, oral testimony, or any combination of the recognized methods of discovery." *Allred v. Moore & Peterson,* 117 F.3d 278, 281 (5th Cir. 1997).

Parties often choose to rely on affidavits alone. The defendant's lawyer will submit along with its motion to dismiss, a sworn statement from its client, third parties, or both, swearing as to facts which the lawyer will use to argue that requirements of the long-arm statute, minimum contacts, and "fair play" are not met. Plaintiff's counsel can do the opposite in the response to the motion to dismiss.

The district court may permit limited discovery into facts about personal jurisdiction, but if "a party needs jurisdictional discovery, that party has an obligation to request it in a timely manner." *Barrett v. Lombardi,* 239 F.3d 23, 28 (1st Cir. 2001). While a district court has discretion to deny jurisdictional discovery, "a diligent plaintiff who sues an out-of-state [defendant] and who makes out a colorable case for the existence of *in personam* jurisdiction may well be entitled to a modicum of jurisdictional discovery if the [defendant] interposes a jurisdictional defense." *Sunview Condo. Ass'n v. Flexel Int'l,* 116 F.3d 962, 964 (1st Cir. 1997).

## 2. Waiving Objection to Lack of Personal Jurisdiction

### a. Intentional Waiver

### i. Pre-Dispute Forum Selection Clauses

Parties can consent to personal jurisdiction through forum selection clauses in pre-dispute contracts. *See Nat'l Equip. Rental, Ltd. v. Szukhent,* 375 U.S. 311, 315–16 (1964). A party seeking to avoid enforcement of a forum selection clause must prove that it is unenforceable. To do so, it must prove one of three things.

First, that the clause was not reasonably communicated to the party. *See Effron v. Sun Line Cruises, Inc.,* 67 F.3d 7, 9 (2d Cir.1995). Second, that the forum selection clause "was obtained through fraud or overreaching." *Jones v. Weibrecht,* 901 F.2d 17, 18 (2d Cir. 1990) (*citing The Bremen v. Zapata Off-Shore Co.,* 407 U.S. 1, 15 (1972)). Finally, the party can show that enforcement of the clause clearly "would be unreasonable and unjust," *Jones,* 901 F.2d at 18. *See, e.g., Carnival Cruise Lines, Inc. v. Shute,* 499 U.S. 585 (1991) (enforcing forum selection clause printed in fine print on the back of a cruise line ticket because plaintiff did not carry a "heavy burden" of showing enforcement would inflict "unreasonable hardship" on her).

### ii. Post-Filing Deliberate Inaction

A party can intentionally or inadvertently waive an objection to personal jurisdiction in three ways. First, party who fails to properly raise an objection to personal jurisdiction as required by Rule 12 waives the objection, whether intentional or not. Second, sometimes counsel will realize that, although its client has an objection to personal jurisdiction, the suit is pending in a reasonably convenient forum and so, after consulting with the client, they decide not to object to personal jurisdiction. A party who appears in a suit without raising an objection to personal jurisdiction is often said to have filed a "general appearance," not a "special appearance." A general appearance waives objection to personal jurisdiction.

### iii. Filing of Suit

The third form of intentional waiver occurs by filing a suit: a plaintiff waives any personal jurisdiction objection to any *compulsory* counterclaim. *Competitive Tech. Inc. v. Fujitsu Ltd.,* 286 F. Supp. 2d 1118, 1141–42 (N.D. Cal. 2003) (collecting cases).

### b. Inadvertent Waiver: Pleading an Objection to Personal Jurisdiction in an Answer is not Enough

Pleading an objection to personal jurisdiction is not enough to preserve the objection. "[P]ersonal jurisdiction may also be waived, even if a defendant has nominally preserved the defense by reciting it in an answer, if that defendant participates in the litigation without actively pursuing its Rule 12(b)(2) defense." *Matthews v. Brookstone Stores, Inc.*, 431 F. Supp. 2d 1219, 1223 (S.D. Ala. 2006) (collecting cases). The party must in addition *promptly* file a Rule 12(b)(2) *motion* to dismiss. While there is no set time limit on how long is too long, or how much participation is too much, a defendant waives the defense if it engages in substantial litigation activities unrelated to the personal jurisdiction challenge. Cases provide some meaning to this rule.

For example, a defendant who litigates a case for two years by engaging in discovery and other motion practice unrelated to the personal jurisdiction defense probably waives the objection. *Hamilton v. Atlas Turner, Inc.*, 197 F.3d 58, 62 (2d Cir. 1999); *see Laborers' Welfare Fund v. Lowery*, 924 F.2d 731, 733 (7th Cir. 1991) (six years' participation waived defense). A defendant who then sued the plaintiff in a separate suit in the state allegedly lacking ties to the defendant or the dispute waives personal jurisdiction. *Gen'l Contracting & Trading Co., L.L.C. v. Interpole, Inc.*, 940 F.2d 20, 23 (1st Cir. 1991). Likewise, a defendant who files a motion for summary judgment before seeking adjudication of the personal jurisdiction defense waives the defense. *Bel-Ray Co. v. Chemrite Ltd.*, 181 F.3d 435, 444 (3d Cir. 1999).

On the other end of the spectrum, merely including a counterclaim in the answer that also included the personal jurisdiction objection does not waive the defense. *Rates Technology Inc. v. Nortel Networks Corp.*, 399 F.3d 1302 (Fed. Cir. 2005) (filing a permissive or compulsory counterclaim does not waive personal jurisdiction objection contained in that pleading).

On a related note, if a defendant fails to reasonably participate in discovery into personal jurisdiction, a court as a sanction may hold that the defendant waived even a properly preserved objection to personal jurisdiction. *Ins. Corp. of Ireland v. Compagnie des Bauxites de Guinee*, 456 U.S. 694 (1982).

# B. The Impact of Adjudication of the Motion

If a court concludes that it lacks personal jurisdiction, it may either dismiss the claim without prejudice, *see* Rule 41(b), or transfer the claim to a state where personal jurisdiction is proper. *See Goldlawr, Inc. v. Heiman*, 369 U.S. 463, 466 (1962) (if personal jurisdiction is lacking courts have authority to transfer a case to another district if the interests of justice so dictate). Often, a court will give the defendant the choice of dismissing — which means the decision can be appealed — or transferring the case and moving forward with the suit in another state, an order which is not appealable.

# C. Not Appearing and Later Collaterally Attacking the Judgment

A defendant can choose not to appear even if it has a proper objection to personal jurisdiction. By failing to appear, the plaintiff will be able to obtain a default judgment. *See* Chapter 44. A judgment is entitled generally to "full faith and credit" — meaning that it generally has to be honored by the courts of other states. To avoid enforcement of the out-of-state judgment in its home state, the defendant must "collaterally attack" the judgment and show the court which entered the judgment lacked jurisdiction to do so.

## Checkpoints

- Can you distinguish facial and factual attacks?
- Can you identify how objections to personal jurisdiction can be waived, either pre- or post-suit?
- If a claim is dismissed for lack of personal jurisdiction, does that mean the claim cannot be re-filed in a court that has personal jurisdiction?

# Chapter 32

# Rule 12(b)(3) Challenges to Improper Venue

---

### Rule 12(b)(3) Roadmap

This chapter describes the two ways that an objection to improper venue can be raised and the two types of objections, facial and factual.

This chapter also explains how an objection to venue can be waived, either intentionally prior to filing suit or after suit is filed through design or neglect.

---

## A. Objections to Improper Venue Must Be Made Promptly or Are Waived

### 1. Inadvertent Waiver

#### a. Failing to Timely File a Pre-answer Motion to Dismiss for Improper Venue

As with personal jurisdiction, a party who has a Rule 11 basis to contend that venue is improper—under Section 1391 or the rare federal claim-specific venue statute—must act properly and promptly or the objection is waived. Most likely because it affects the parties more than the federal court system, objection to venue is "a privilege personal to each defendant, which can be waived, and is waived . . . unless timely objection is interposed." *Concession Consultants, Inc. v. Mirisch*, 355 F.2d 369, 371 n. 1 (2d Cir. 1966).

As with personal jurisdiction there are three ways to raise an objection to venue. A party must object to improper venue either (a) in its Rule 12 pre-answer motion; (b) in a pleading (typically, the defendant's answer); or (c) an amendment to that pleading made as of right thereof. FRCP 12(g)(h). *See* Chapter 36.

A federal statute, 28 U.S.C. § 1406(a), authorizes district courts to dismiss or transfer cases that filed "in the wrong division or district." Courts view

Section 1406(a) as dependent on Rule 12(b)(3). That is, the Rule's approach to waiver controls. Consequently, once waived in terms of Rule 12(b)(3), venue is "proper"—no matter what—and so "the benefits of a § 1406(a) transfer for lack of venue are no longer available." *Orb Factory Ltd. v. Design Science Toys, Ltd.*, 6 F. Supp. 2d 203, 207 (S.D.N.Y. 1998).

### b. Including the Objection to Venue in a Pleading but Participating in Litigation Before Moving to Dismiss

A party who files a Rule 12(b)(3) motion has preserved its objection to improper venue. However, a party who chooses to include the objection, not in its pre-answer motion but in its answer must promptly follow-up by filing a motion to dismiss for improper venue. Even if an objection to venue is included in the answer, active participation in the suit can waive the venue objection. *See Sagent Technology, Inc. v. Micros Sys., Inc.*, 276 F. Supp. 2d 464, 471(D. Md. 2003) (finding no waiver where objecting party's post-answer conduct was minimal).

## 2. Intentional Waiver

### a. Post-Suit Deliberate Choice to Waive Objection

As with personal jurisdiction, counsel for a party may decide after consultation with its client to forego an objection to improper venue. The district may be as convenient as any district with proper venue, or countervailing considerations—the judge's prior rulings on the legal questions involved or her general reputation as being "pro-defendant," the likely jury pool compared to proper venues, and so on—may suggest that any objection be intentionally waived.

The fact that lawyers often fight over whether a case will be tried in Houston, or 45 miles away in Galveston, ought to indicate to you that variations in juries and judges can be critically important. *See, e.g., Smith v. Colonial Penn Ins. Co.*, 943 F. Supp. 782 (S.D. Tex. 1996) (denying motion for inter-divisional transfer from Galveston to Houston).

### b. Pre-Dispute Forum Selection Clauses

### i. Raising a Venue Objection Based on a Forum Selection Clause

It is increasingly common for parties in contracts to insist that disputes be litigated in certain locations. Sometimes these "forum selection" clauses specify merely the state where any suit arising out of the contract must be filed, while others specify the city, county (and, sometimes, specific court) where any suit must be filed. If a claim governed by a clause is not filed in the forum the clause specifies, then the other party may raise improper venue.

The fact that a claim is filed in a district contrary to a forum selection clause in an agreement between the parties does not mean venue is improper. Instead, as explained in Chapter 40, a motion to transfer venue to a more convenient district may be available.

The disagreement raises important issues for when an objection to venue must be raised. *See* Chapter 36. The issue is discussed more fully in that chapter and is often discussed in the casebooks.

### ii. Adjudicating Validity of Forum Selection Clauses

Pre-dispute forum selection clauses are presumptively valid. *M/S Bremen v. Zapata Off-Shore Co.*, 407 U.S. 1, 15 (1972). Even if a forum selection clause is properly raised as a basis to dismiss for improper venue, a court can refuse to enforce the forum selection clause when doing so would be clearly "unreasonable and unjust, or the clause is invalid for such reasons as fraud or overreaching." *Id.* Courts generally find that a clause is invalid only if the party seeking to avoid it establishes: (1) incorporation of the forum selection clause itself into the contract was the result of fraud, undue influence, or overwhelming bargaining power; (2) the forum selected is gravely difficult and so inconvenient that it will deprive the party seeking to avoid it of its day in court; or (3) public policy prohibits its enforcement. *Id.* at 12–18.

# B. Procedure for Adjudicating Objections to Improper Venue

## 1. Burdens of Proof

Generally the plaintiff bears the burden to establish proper venue. *Mohr v. Margolis, Ainsworth & Kinlaw Consulting, Inc.*, 434 F. Supp. 2d 1051, 1058 (D. Kan. 2006). Even so, some courts put the burden on the party challenging venue to establish its impropriety. *Barton v. Florida*, 2006 WL 2773238 (S.D. Ohio 2006).

A court may decide a venue issue on the pleadings alone, on affidavits submitted by either or both parties, or after allowing discovery into the facts relating to venue. *E.g., Controlotron Corp. v. Perry Printing Corp.*, 1990 WL 86085

(D. N.J. 1990) (granting limited discovery into venue facts). After all, venue often turns on where the defendant "resides" or where a substantial part of the events giving rise to the claim occurred, both of which can be fact-intensive issues. *Pierce v. Shorty Small's of Branson, Inc.*, 137 F.3d 1190, 1191 (10th Cir. 1998).

If the court decides venue on the pleadings alone, then the plaintiff must "present only a *prima facie* showing of venue." *Home Ins. Co. v. Thomas Indus., Inc.*, 896 F.2d 1352, 1355 (11th Cir. 1990). In all events, the court must draw all reasonable inferences in plaintiff's favor and resolve any factual disputes in plaintiff's favor. *Pinker v. Roche Holdings, Ltd.*, 292 F.3d 361, 368 (3rd Cir. 2002). Facts pled by the plaintiff are taken as true unless contradicted by the defendant. *Jyachosky v. Winter*, 2006 WL 1805607, *1 (D.D.C. 2006).

## 2. The Court Must Either Dismiss or Transfer If Venue Is Improper

28 U.S.C. § 1406(a) provides that if a case is filed in the wrong district *or* division, the court "shall dismiss, *or if it be in the interest of justice, transfer* such a case to any district or division in which it could have been brought." (Emph. added.) Section 1406(a) was adopted to give district courts an option other than dismissal, since venue can be improper simply because a plaintiff failed to fully appreciate where events occurred or the defendant resided. *See Wild v. Subscription Plus, Inc.*, 292 F.3d 256 (7th Cir. 2002) (discussing Section 1406(a)).

Don't confuse improper venue with convenient venue. A venue is proper if it's authorized by a statute, the general one being Section 1391; it may be that there's a better district for the claim to be tried, but that's not the same thing as concluding that venue is improper. If venue is improper, the court *must* either dismiss or transfer. It is within the sound discretion of the court to dismiss or, if it is in the interests of justice to do so, to transfer to a district where suit could have been brought. *First of Michigan Corp. v. Bramlet*, 141 F.3d 260, 262 (6th Cir. 1998). A court may transfer venue under Section 1406(a) even if it lacks personal jurisdiction over a defendant. *Goldlawr, Inc. v. Heiman*, 369 U.S. 463, 466 (1962). However, a court should dismiss a claim filed in an improper venue unless the party asserting it can show that "the interests of justice" require transfer. An involuntary dismissal for improper venue will be without prejudice. *See* FRCP 41(b).

A common reason for courts to transfer rather than dismiss is if the claim has become barred by the statute of limitations. *E.g., Smith v. Yale Univ.*, 2006 WL 1168446 (D. Conn. Apr. 28, 2006). Thus, a plaintiff can respond to a defendant's motion to dismiss for improper venue by pointing out that transfer is in the interest of justice because the claim has become time-barred. Often, a plaintiff faced with a defendant's persuasive motion to dismiss for improper venue will respond that the court should transfer rather than dismiss if the court finds venue is improper.

## 3. Where can the Court Transfer the Claim?

A claim filed in an improper venue can only be transferred to a district where the claim could have been properly filed. Thus, the proposed transferee court must (1) have personal jurisdiction over the defendants at the time the suit was filed (subject matter jurisdiction will be a given), and (2) venue must be proper in that district or division. Put the other way, a claim cannot be transferred to a district without personal jurisdiction or in which venue would have been improper, because that court is not one where the claim "might have been brought" in terms of Section 1406(a). This is true even if the defendant wants to waive its objection to personal jurisdiction or venue.

## 4. What if Venue Over Some Claims is Proper?

The question of whether the court should dismiss or transfer gets much more complex when venue is proper only some of the claims in the complaint. There are several different paths this could take.

In *Dobrick-Peirce*, the court had venue over one claim, but not over two related ones. We've seen above that some courts will invoke the doctrine of pendent venue and allow the entire case to proceed even though venue is improper as to some claims, so long as those claims are closely related to a claim over which venue is proper. Again, the doctrine often applies to state law claims which are related to a federal claim that has a statute giving different, or broader, venue.

Suppose pendent venue isn't recognized by the court, or doesn't apply because the claims aren't part of the same common nucleus of operative facts. What should a court do when it has venue over one claim, but another claim in the complaint ought to have been filed in another district or division?

One option is to dismiss the claim over which venue is improper, and keep the one with proper venue. This, however, could result in two suits proceeding between the same parties on somewhat similar facts. To avoid this, another option is to transfer the claims without venue to a proper forum and to use Section 1404(a), if available, to transfer the other claim to that same district. That is the option that the *Dobrick-Peirce* (yes, it's spelled "*Peirce*") court chose, doing so to avoid inefficiency. Other courts have done so, too but remember that venue must be proper in the transferee district over *each claim* to do this. *Munoz v. England,* 2006 WL 3361509, *7 (D.D.C. 2006).

Note also that to transfer the claim over which it lacks proper venue, the court must rely on Section 1406 and base its decision on a motion by a party brought pursuant to Rule 12(b)(3), but to transfer the claims *with* venue the court can rely on Section 1404, but must conclude that transfer is in the interest of justice. *See id.*

## 5. No Second-Guessing by Transferee Court

Absent "impelling and unusual circumstances," the transferee court cannot reexamine the transferor court's conclusion that venue is proper in the transferee court. *Brinderson-Newberg Joint Venture v. Pacific Erectors,* 690 F. Supp. 891, 893 (C.D. Cal. 1988).

---

### Checkpoints

• Can you list how objections to venue can be waived, either before or after suit is filed?

• Can you describe how courts determine whether venue is proper?

• Can you describe what a court can do if venue is improper?

# Chapter 33

# Rule 12(b)(4) and (5) Challenges to Process

---

### Rule 12(b)(4) Roadmap

This chapter explains how an objection to insufficient service must be raised.

This chapter also explains how an objection to insufficient service can be waived after suit is filed through design or neglect.

---

## A. The Scope of These Two Rules

Rules 12(b)(4) and 12(b)(5) are distinct but related means to challenge defects relating to service of process. Rule 12(b)(4) permits objections to "insufficient process" while Rule 12(b)(5) permits objections to "insufficient service of process." Both allow the defendant who has not waived service of process to challenge the content of, or the manner in which, process was served on it.

A Rule 12(b)(4) motion attacks the form of the process, not the manner or method of service. In contrast, a motion made under Rule 12(b)(5) challenges the mode of delivery, or lack of delivery, of process. *See Wasson v. Riverside County*, 237 F.R.D. 423, 424 (C.D. Cal. 2006). As that court explained:

> Although the distinction between the Rule 12(b)(4) and 12(b)(5) motions is easy to state, the line between them becomes blurred when the alleged defect is that the defendant either is misnamed in the summons or has ceased to exist. In these cases, the form of the process could be challenged under Rule 12(b)(4) on the theory that the summons does not properly contain the names of the parties, or a motion under Rule 12(b)(5) could be made on the ground that the wrong party—that is, a party not named in the summons—has been served.

As a result of the difficulty of distinguishing between objections under these two Rules, "several courts have . . . treated a combination of the two motions as proper procedure." *DakColl, Inc. v. Grand Central Graphics, Inc.,* 352 F. Supp. 2d 990, 1001 n.4 (D. N.D. 2005). "The distinction between the two insufficiencies is often blurred, and it is appropriate to present and analyze service under both rules." *Adams v. AlliedSignal General Aviation Avionics,* 74 F.3d 882, 884 n. 2 (8th Cir. 1996).

# B. Procedure to Make a Rule 12(b)(4) or 12(b)(5) Motion

A defendant who has a Rule 11 basis to object to service must include the objection in its Rule 12 pre-answer motion, in its answer, or in an amendment to its answer made as of right. As with personal jurisdiction and venue, failing to "consolidate" either a Rule 12(b)(4) or (5) objection waives it. Rule 12(g), (h).

# C. Waiver of Objection

A defendant who includes the objection in its answer must, as with the other Rule 12 objections, act promptly by filing a motion to dismiss for improper service, or the objection can be waived by time or substantial participation in the litigation. *Datskow v. Teledyne, Inc., Continental Products Div.,* 899 F.2d 1298, 1303 (2d Cir. 1990) (by attending a conference with the magistrate and participating in scheduling discovery and motion practice defendant waived defense of insufficiency of process even though it was asserted in its answer).

# D. The Impact of Adjudication

If a court grants a motion to dismiss for insufficient process or service of process, then the case is dismissed *without* prejudice. *See* FRCP 41(b). The claims that were pled in the pleading can be refiled and properly served. *See* FRCP 41(b) ("For failure of the plaintiff . . . to comply with [the FRCP] or any order of the court, a defendant may move for dismissal of an action. . . ."). Unless the statute of limitations has run on a claim, the plaintiff then simply re-serves process without the defect.

---

### Checkpoints

- Can you explain how an objection to service can be waived?
- Can you describe the impact of a court's grant of a Rule 12(b)(4) or (5) motion?

# Chapter 34

# Rule 12(b)(6) Challenges to Statement of a Claim by Plaintiff and under Rule 12(c) for Judgment on the Pleadings

---

### Rule 12(b)(6) Roadmap

This chapter describes how to raise an objection that a pleading fails to state a claim upon which relief can be granted.

This chapter also explains how even if the right to object in the pre-answer motion under Rule 12(b)(6) is waived, an objection that a pleading fails to state a claim can be raised by other rules besides Rule 12(b)(6).

This chapter also explains how Rule 12(b)(6) and those post-answer motions are adjudicated.

---

Of all the Rule 12 motions, only one under Rule 12(b)(6) addresses the merits of a claim. The other Rule 12 motions essentially raise the issue of whether the suit has been properly filed and postured. Rule 12(b)(6) allows a defendant to, essentially, say: "Even if every fact that the plaintiff alleges is true, the law won't allow the plaintiff to recover anything from me." If the defendant is successful, then the defendant can prevail without having to go through discovery, let alone a full trial. That is the core benefit of Rule 12(b)(6): it saves the parties and the judicial system time and resources.

Why have this? Think for a moment. If, at the very outset of a lawsuit, a defendant can show that even if after the parties go through discovery and hold a trial, it won't matter if the jury believes every factual allegation made by the plaintiff, because the law does not allow a remedy. If so, why make the defendant and the federal judicial system spend time on the claim? Why make the public coffers pay for it? (Put in terms you'll understand later, if after discovery and a trial the defendant would be entitled to judgment as a matter of law, why waste

313

time on discovery and conducting the trial?) Rule 12(b)(6) allows the parties and the courts to avoid wasting time.

Although powerful, there are limitations under Rule 12(b)(6) on what the court can consider and how it views what it can consider. Those points first.

# A. The Limitations in Rule 12(b)(6)

## 1. If the Court Does not Limit its Consideration to the Allegations of the Complaint, a Rule 12(b)(6) Motion Must be Treated as a Rule 56 Motion for Summary Judgment

The first limitation on Rule 12(b)(6) is what the court can consider. Under Rule 12(b)(6), the court can consider only the contents of plaintiff's complaint. If matters outside it are presented to the court by any party and not excluded by the court, the court must treat the motion as a motion for summary judgment filed under Rule 56. *See* Rule 12(d); Chapter 52. "Conversion" of a Rule 12(b) (6) motion into a Rule 56 motion is significant because Rule 56 requires that the non-moving party be afforded time to obtain discovery or affidavits to oppose the motion. Hence, if the moving party submits to the court anything beyond the pleading, the plaintiff should contend that the motion must be converted to one for summary judgment and establish its right under Rule 56 for time for discovery or obtaining affidavits. *See* Chapter 52.

Thus, the meaning of "the content of the complaint" can be critical. The battle over what can be considered without converting the motion is critical because it affects the value of the case, since conversion will delay dismissal and buy the plaintiff time. That is why there is so much litigation over the issue of what is "in" the complaint. The plaintiff typically will want a narrow view, since the plaintiff's allegations may be belied by documents not within the complaint; the defendant will want, generally, the broad view.

### a. What are the "Contents of the Complaint"?

Obviously, the "contents of the complaint" include the actual allegations in the complaint, but also documents attached by plaintiff's counsel to the complaint. *Marder v. Lopez*, 450 F.3d 445, 448 (9th Cir. 2005). "A copy of a written instrument that is an exhibit to a pleading is a part of the pleading for all purposes." FRCP 10(a); *see Durning v. First Boston Corp.*, 815 F.2d 1265, 1267 (9th Cir. 1987). So, if plaintiff attaches a copy of a contract to a complaint, the court may consider the contract without converting a Rule 12(b)(6) motion. *N. Ind. Gun & Outdoor Shows, Inc. v. South Bend,* 163 F.3d 449, 453–54 (7th Cir. 1998).

In some circumstances, a court may consider even documents not attached to the complaint without converting the motion. First, a court may consider documents incorporated by reference, *In re Silicon Graphics, Inc. Securities Litig.,* 183 F.3d 970 (9th Cir. 1999), or even merely referred to in the complaint without converting the motion to a motion for summary judgment. *See Branch,* 14 F.3d at 453. A complaint "refers" to a document if it is specifically mentioned in the complaint. *Id.* Second, "'when [a] plaintiff fails to introduce a pertinent document as part of his pleading, [a] defendant may introduce the exhibit as part of his motion attacking the pleading,'" so long as three conditions are met. *Branch v. Tunnell,* 14 F.3d 449, 453 (9th Cir. 1994). A court may consider such evidence without affording the protections of Rule 56 if: "(1) the complaint refers to the document; (2) the document is central to the plaintiff's claim; and (3) no party questions the authenticity of the copy attached to the 12(b)(6) motion." *Marder,* 450 F.3d at 448. Third, under some circumstances a court may consider filings made in earlier litigation between the parties without converting the motion. *Henson v. CSC Credit Servs.,* 29 F.3d 280, 284 (7th Cir. 1994).

### b. What if the Court Does not Exclude, but Does not Consider, Matters Outside the Complaint?

Even if the document is not deemed to be a part of the complaint, Rule 12(d) provides that if "matters outside the pleadings are presented to *and not excluded by the court,* the motion must be treated as one for summary judgment under Rule 56. All parties must be given reasonable opportunity to present all material that is pertinent to the motion." Accordingly, a district court has discretion to consider matters submitted with the motion, response, or reply, even if not "part of" the complaint, but only if it converts the motion to one for summary judgment. *See Cunningham v. Rothery,* 143 F.3d 546, 549 (9th Cir. 1998).

Either party may implicate conversion provision of Rule 12(d) by submitting materials which are not "part of" the complaint in the motion papers. Does the submission of such material, by itself, require that the court convert a Rule 12(b)(6) motion into one for summary judgment?

There is a split on the answer to that question. Some courts have held that the court may consider the materials without converting the motion unless the court actually relies on the materials in deciding the motion. *Alexander v. Okla.,* 382 F.3d 1206, 1213 (10th Cir. 2004). Other courts hold that consideration, alone, is sufficient to require conversion of a motion to dismiss into a motion for summary judgment. *N. Ind. Gun,* 163 F.3d at 453 n. 5. Still others hold that the mere acceptance of the material requires conversion. *Dempsey v. Atchison, Topeka & Santa Fe Ry. Co.,* 16 F.3d 832, 835–36 (7th Cir. 1994).

The plain language of Rule 12(d) would indicate that it is the failure to exclude the proffered materials — not reliance on or consideration of it — that requires conversion. *Max Arnold & Sons, LLC v. W.L. Hailey & Co.,* 452 F.3d 494, 503 (6th Cir. 2006). But with no clear answer yet, any time a party submits information that is not "part of" the complaint when litigating a Rule 12(b)(6) motion, the other party should analyze whether under controlling law the motion must be converted to one for summary judgment. If so, then the court must give both parties notice that it is converting the motion, and permit a "reasonable opportunity to present all the material that is pertinent to the motion." FRCP 12(d). It may be, for example, that a plaintiff can postpone consideration of the motion to conduct discovery. *See* FRCP 56.

## 2. The Plausible Facts in the Pleading are Taken as True: Rule 12(b)(6)'s Burden of Persuasion

The second limitation on Rule 12(b)(6) is the burden of persuasion. As we saw in our discussion of *Twombly* and *Iqbal,* the inquiry is whether, once the complaint is stripped of its legal conclusions and bare assertions, the remaining factual material, taken as true, plausibly states a claim upon which relief can be granted. This is the "so what" aspect of Rule 12(b)(6): even if the allegations are true, the law does not afford a remedy.

### *a. An Example Applied to a Claim*

In your torts class, you will probably learn there is no general duty to rescue. If I am walking down the street and see you drowning, I don't have to do a thing. If you're injured and sue me, you might allege something like this (in addition to all the bells and whistles):

---

Count I: Negligence

3. Defendant was a healthy male adult, capable of swimming.
4. Defendant saw plaintiff in distress in shallow water.
5. Defendant did nothing, causing plaintiff injuries.

---

Assume that those allegations are true, but also assume that under the law in the state where I left you stranded, there is no duty to rescue. I can avoid a trial by relying on Rule 12(b)(6) and saying, "so what": even if everything you allege is true, the law affords you no relief. You have "failed to state a claim upon which relief can be granted."

That's a simple example, but the rule is not limited to such clear cases: any time the law does not afford the plaintiff relief if its factual allegations are taken as true, Rule 12(b)(6) is a powerful weapon to reduce costs and exposure to a defendant.

### b. Rule 12(b)(6) and Affirmative Defenses

Can a Rule 12(b)(6) motion be used to dismiss a claim that is subject to an affirmative defense? Suppose, for example, that the pleading clearly states a claim, but it is subject to the defense of statute of limitations. Can the defendant move to dismiss under Rule 12(b)(6)? The answer is whether the complaint can be dismissed while taking its allegations as true:

> A complaint is subject to dismissal for failure to state a claim if the allegations, taken as true, show the plaintiff is not entitled to relief. If the allegations, for example, show that relief is barred by the applicable statute of limitations, the complaint is subject to dismissal for failure to state a claim; that does not make the statute of limitations any less an affirmative defense, *see* Fed. Rule Civ. Proc. 8(c). Whether a particular ground for opposing a claim may be the basis for dismissal for failure to state a claim depends on whether the allegations in the complaint suffice to establish that ground, not on the nature of the ground in the abstract. *See Leveto v. Lapina*, 258 F.3d 156, 161 (C.A.3 2001) ("[A] complaint may be subject to dismissal under Rule 12(b)(6) when an affirmative defense . . . appears on its face"). *See also Lopez-Gonzalez v. Municipality of Comerio*, 404 F.3d 548, 551 (C.A.1 2005) (dismissing a complaint barred by the statute of limitations under Rule 12(b)(6)).

*Jones v. Bock,* 127 S. Ct. 910, 920–21 (2007). *See also Eriline Co. S.A. v. Johnson,* 440 F.3d 648, 654 (4th Cir. 2006) (in rare circumstances courts may raise limitations defense *sua sponte*).

# B. Determining Whether the Pleading States a Claim for Relief

There are two steps for determining whether a pleading states a claim upon which relief can be granted: (A) determining the elements of the claim (by looking at the substantive law that creates the claim) and then (B) analyzing whether, stripped of legal conclusions and bare assertions, the complaint plausibly states facts which, if taken as true, satisfies each element of the claim. Plaintiffs must "set forth in their complaint factual allegations, either direct or inferential, regarding each material element necessary to sustain recovery under some actionable legal theory." *Dartmouth Review v. Dartmouth College*, 889 F.2d 13 (1st Cir. 1989).

So, for example, in a casebook case, *Langadinos v. Am. Airlines, Inc.*, 199 F.3d 68 (1st Cir. 2000), the district court granted a Rule 12(b)(6) motion to dismiss the plaintiff's complaint which pled a claim under a treaty, the Warsaw Convention, against an airline. The appellate court reversed. To determine the elements of the claim, it analyzed the language of the treaty, which stated that an airline was liable "for damage sustained . . . by a passenger . . . if the accident which caused the damage . . . took place on board the aircraft. . . ." The plaintiff had alleged that, while on an aircraft, the flight attendants had plied alcohol to an obviously intoxicated fellow passenger, who then assaulted the plaintiff. The court held that the element "accident" had been interpreted "flexibly" by the courts and included torts by other passengers so long as the airline had played a causal role in the commission of the tort. Thus, the plaintiff alleged each element of the tort: damage to a passenger caused by an accident that occurred on an airplane.

## C. Procedure for Making a Rule 12(b)(6) Motion

A defendant who believes that the plaintiff has failed to state a claim upon which relief can be granted can include the objection in its pre-answer motion, in its answer, or an amendment or right to its answer. Rule 12(g),(h). If the defendant includes the objection in the answer, it must promptly move to dismiss under Rule 12(b)(6): remember that the judge doesn't ferret out issues and do a party's job for it.

## D. Responding to a Rule 12(b)(6) Motion

As noted above, the party responding to a Rule 12(b)(6) motion should see if the movant submitted material beyond the complaint. If so, the party may in its response to the motion either move to exclude the material, move to have the motion converted to a Rule 56 motion and seek its protections, or both.

Another issue critical for the non-moving party to analyze whether it can fix any deficiency in the complaint by amending it. Suppose the plaintiff simply forgot to include an allegation that the defendant, in its motion to dismiss, argues is required, and the facts support making the allegation. The plaintiff should move to amend the complaint in response to the motion to dismiss (or amend as of right if that option is still available). While as a matter of course district courts often grant a party leave to amend a pleading subject to a Rule 12(b)(6) motion, they are not required to do so *sua sponte*. Consequently, a party responding to a Rule 12(b)(6) motion should seek leave to amend either during adjudication of the motion or promptly after the order dismissing the claim is entered, but before final judgment is entered. *See Fletcher-Harlee Corp. v. Pote Concrete Contractors, Inc.*, 482 F.3d 247 (3rd Cir. 2007) ("we hold that in ordinary civil litigation it is hardly error for a district court to enter final judgment after granting a Rule 12(b)(6) motion to dismiss when the plaintiff has not properly requested leave to amend its complaint").

## E. It's Hard to Waive the Objection of Failing to State a Claim

In a somewhat awkward way, the Rules permit a party to raise the issue of failure to state a claim at any time, up through trial, but not:

(a) *after* the defendant files a Rule 12 motion that does not include the defense but *before* it answers; *or*
(b) if adjudication of the defense will delay trial.

*See* Rule 12(c), (h)(2). But, the following shows that at any other time a defendant can move to dismiss a claim for failing to state a claim.

## 1. Rule 12(c)

### a. The Window of Rule 12(c)

Technically, a Rule 12(b)(6) defense that is not raised either in the pre-answer motion or answer (or amendment to the answer as of right) is waived. However, Rule 12(c) lets a party do exactly the same thing as Rule 12(b)(6), by permitting the defense of failure to state a claim to be raised so long as it does not delay trial, and so long as it is filed in or after the defendant has filed its answer. FRCP 12(c); *SEC v. Lucent*, 2006 WL 2168789 (D. N.J. 2006) (refusing to treat a waived Rule 12(b)(6) motion as a Rule 12(c) motion because defendant had not yet answered).

Thus, if it is filed within that window—after the answer is filed but before it will delay trial—courts tend to simply re-characterize "waived" Rule 12(b)(6) motions as motions for judgments on the pleadings under Rule 12(c). *See Trustees of the Univ. of Pennsylvania v. Mayflower Transit, Inc.*, U.S. Dist. Lexis

14577 (E.D. Pa. 1997) ("although 'a post-answer Rule 12(b) motion is untimely,' this timing requirement has customarily been treated as a mere technicality . . . a motion to dismiss under Rule 12(b)(6) made after an answer has been filed may be treated, in the court's discretion, as a Rule 12(c) motion for judgment on the pleadings."); *Prudential Prop. & Cas. Ins. Co. v. Stump*, 1994 U.S. Dist. Lexis 18072 (E.D. Pa. 1994) ("Technically, a 12(b)(6) motion filed after an answer is untimely and the court must deny it. However, under Rule 12(h)(2), 12(b)(6) motions are preserved from waiver . . . and . . . are then treated under Rule 12(c) as a motion for judgment on the pleadings. . . .").

Why? Think about it. If a defendant shows the plaintiff will not win even if everything alleged is true, why wait until trial because even if the jury finds the plaintiff proved everything it alleged, the defendant will prevail. So, even if the defendant raises the motion near trial, a court can grant it. It still saves time, just less time.

The first clause of Rule 12(c) makes it clear that a defendant cannot make a Rule 12(c) motion before it answers. We also know that if the defendant has already made its one Rule 12 motion, it cannot make a second Rule 12 motion until after it answers. If a defendant were able to make a Rule 12 motion, and then a Rule 12(c) motion before it answers, the defendant could engage in successive Rule 12 motion practice. *See SEC v. Lucent*, 2006 WL 2168789 (D. N.J. 2006). There is only *one* pre-answer motion permitted.

### b. The Same Standards Under Rule 12(b)(6) Apply Under Rule 12(c)

#### i. Burden of Proof

The standard for entry of judgment on the pleadings under Rule 12(c) is the same as that for failing to state a claim under Rule 12(b)(6). Thus, in ruling on a motion for judgment on the pleadings, a court must ignore the legal conclusions and bare allegations of the complaint and then ask whether the remaining material plausibly states facts which, if true, state a claim upon which relief can be granted.

#### ii. Conversion to a Rule 56 Motion for Summary Judgment

The same discussion above concerning conversion of Rule 12(b)(6) motions into motions for summary judgment when matters outside the pleadings are presented to and not excluded by the court applies to Rule 12(c) motions. FRCP 12(d).

## 2. At Trial

Under Rule 12(h)(2), the objection of failure to state a claim can also be raised in any pleading permitted or ordered or at trial on the merits. FRCP 12(h)(2). The impact of Rule 12(h)(2) in light of Rule 12(c) is to deny a defendant the right to raise the objection where it will delay trial, but to permit the objection to be raised at trial. This is the "window" noted above.

# F. The Impact of Adjudication of a Rule 12(c) Motion

Typically, a court will give a party one chance to amend a pleading that fails to state a claim upon which relief can be granted. So, for example, if plaintiff's counsel made a mistake in not including allegations necessary to state a claim, the court will permit the mistake to be remedied. If that cannot be done, and if instead the court grants a motion for failure to state a claim, then that claim is dismissed with prejudice. *See* FRCP 41(b). Absent reversal on appeal, the claim is subject to the defense of *res judicata* and so a party would likely violate Rule 11 by re-filing it. *See* Chapter 60.

---

### Checkpoints

- Can you explain when a motion under Rule 12(b)(6) must be converted into one under Rule 56, and why that as a practical matter may be significant?
- Do you see the relationship between Rule 12(b)(6)/Rule 12(c) and *Twombly* and *Iqbal?*
- Can you describe how a Rule 12(b)(6) objection is made and adjudicated?
- What impact does the grant of a Rule 12(b)(6) motion have? The denial of one?
- How can failure to state a claim be raised even if not included in a Rule 12 motion or in the answer?

# Chapter 35

# Rule 12(b)(7) and Indispensable Parties under Rule 19

A defendant should use Rule 12(b)(7) to raise the failure to join an indispensable party as required by Rule 19. Typically, a motion to dismiss for failure to join an indispensable party is filed either when the plaintiff has, for strategic reasons, failed to join a party—often in order to have diversity—*or* a party that was sued by the plaintiff gets dismissed from the case because, typically, the court lacks personal jurisdiction or subject matter jurisdiction over claims against that party. In the former case, the defendant will raise the objection; in the latter case, after a defendant is dismissed from the case, the remaining defendant will move to dismiss the case, contending that the dismissed party was indispensable. The same standards apply in either circumstance.

## A. Timing of Rule 12(b)(7) Objection

Rule 12(b)(7) objections can be raised either in the pre-answer motion or in the answer itself or in an amendment allowed as of right. Further, the objection that an indispensable party has not been joined can be raised in any pleading permitted or ordered, by Rule 12(c) motion, or at trial on the merits. FRCP 12(h)(2). Thus, as with Rule 12(b)(6), a Rule 12(b)(7) motion can be raised at any time, except:

(a) *after* the defendant files a Rule 12 motion that does not include the Rule 12(b)(7) defense but *before* it answers; *or*
(b) if adjudication of the defense will delay trial.

## B. Facial or Factual Attacks Permitted

When adjudicating a Rule 12(b)(7) motion, either party may submit evidence to the court, which is permitted to "go outside the pleadings and look to extrinsic evidence." *English v. Cowell,* 10 F.3d 434, 437 (7th Cir. 1993). The party making a Rule 12(b)(7) motion has the burden to produce "'evidence showing the nature of the interest possessed by an absent party and that the protection of that interest will be impaired by the absence,'" a burden that "'can be satisfied by providing "affidavits of persons having knowledge of these interests as well as other relevant extra-pleading evidence."'" *Sykes v. Hengel,* 220 F.R.D. 593 (S.D. Iowa 2004).

## C. The Impact of Adjudication

If the court grants a Rule 12(b)(7) motion, then the claim is dismissed but *without* prejudice. *See* FRCP 41(b). Absent reversal on appeal, the claim can be refiled, but must be refiled in another court where the indispensable parties may be joined.

# Chapter 36

# Rule 12's One-Motion-Consolidation Requirement

---

### Rule 12's One-Motion-Consolidation Requirement Roadmap

This chapter explains that a defendant may generally only make one pre-answer motion, and must include in that one motion certain objections under Rule 12, or it is waived.

---

The preceding chapters explored each Rule 12 objection. If a defendant intends to file a pre-answer motion to raise one objection, the defendant *must* include in that motion every other objection it then has under Rule 12(e), (f), or Rule 12(b)(2) to (5), or the objection is "waived" by Rule 12's "consolidation" requirement. The manner in which Rule 12 requires consolidation is not simple, but it can become intuitive.

## A. A Party Can Easily Waive Personal Protections

Rule 12 generally forces a party (typically the defendant) to raise in *its first response*—whether that response is a Rule 12(b) motion or an answer—those objections that it has that will not affect *whether* a claim will have to be adjudicated, but instead affect only *where* adjudication will occur or how easy it will be for the defendant to litigate the claim.

What the chart below shows is that objections that do impact the court are harder to waive, while those that largely protect a personal interest of the defendant—personal jurisdiction, venue, defects with service of process, and violations of the pleading rules by the plaintiff—are easier to waive. The chart also shows that the Rule requires those defenses that are personal to the defendant be raised early in the case, before the court spends much time proceeding on the case.

## Making Rule 12's Consolidation Requirement Intuitive

| | 12(b)(1) | 12(b)(2) | 12(b)(3) | 12(b)(4) | 12(b)(5) | 12(b)(6) | 12(b)(7) | 12(e) | 12(f) |
|---|---|---|---|---|---|---|---|---|---|
| Does waiver of the objection impact more than defendant's rights? | Yes (court lacks subject matter jurisdiction) | No (personal jurisdiction) | No (venue) | No (service of process) | No (service of process) | Yes (even if plaintiff proves allegation, defendant will win, so trial is waste of court's time) | Yes (not all parties are before the court who need to be) | No (pleading defects) | No (pleading defects) |
| Must this objection be pled in first response or be waived by the "consolidation" requirement? | No | Yes | Yes | Yes | Yes | No. See Rule 12(c) | No | Yes | Yes |

# B. The Requirement That Certain Rule 12 Objections Be Consolidated in the First Response or Be Deemed Waived, and the Three Exceptions to Waiver

The essence of the "consolidation" required of Rules 12(g) and 12(h) is that a party "who by motion invites the court to pass upon a threshold defense should bring forward all the specified defenses [personal jurisdiction, improper venue, insufficient process, or insufficient service] he then has and thus allow the court to do a reasonably complete job." FRCP advisory committee note, 1966 Amendment. Thus, if a defendant raises any Rule 12 objection in his first filing to the court, the defendant must raise all objections specified in Rule 12(h). Read Rule 12(g) and (h) closely to see why:

**(g) Joining Motions.**

    **(1) Right to Join.** A motion under this rule may be joined with any other motion allowed by this rule.

    **(2) Limitation on Further Motions.** Except as provided in Rule 12(h)(2) or (3), a party that makes a motion under this rule must not make another motion under this rule raising a defense or objection that was available to the party but omitted from its earlier motion.

**(h) Waiving and Preserving Certain Defenses.**

    **(1) When Some Are Waived.** A party waives any defense listed in Rule 12(b)(2)–(5) by:

        (A) omitting it from a motion in the circumstances described in Rule 12(g)(2); or

        (B) failing to either:

            (i) make it by motion under this rule; or

            (ii) include it in a responsive pleading or in an amendment allowed by Rule 15(a)(1) as a matter of course.

    **(2) When to Raise Others.** Failure to state a claim upon which relief can be granted, to join a person required by Rule 19(b), or to state a legal defense to a claim may be raised:

        (A) in any pleading allowed or ordered under Rule 7(a);

        (B) by a motion under Rule 12(c); or

        (C) at trial.

    **(3) Lack of Subject Matter Jurisdiction.** If the court determines at any time that it lacks subject matter jurisdiction, the court must dismiss the action.

**(i) Hearing Before Trial.** If a party so moves, any defense listed in Rule 12(b)(1)–(7) — whether made in a pleading or by motion — and a motion under Rule 12(c) must be heard and decided before trial unless the court orders a deferral until trial.

FRCP 12(g), (h).

If a defendant files a pre-answer motion, then each objection in the top row with a check mark must be included in its motion or that objection is waived; that objection cannot be put in an answer. If, instead of filing a pre-answer motion, the defendant files its answer, then each defense with a check mark in the bottom row must be pled in that answer or it is waived.

There are three exceptions. First, motions under Rules 12(e) and (f) cannot be pled in an answer. Second, motions under Rules 12(b)(6) and 12(b)(7) can effectively be made until and at trial. FRCP 12(h)(2). Finally, third, lack of subject matter jurisdiction may be raised at any time, by any party, or even by the court. FRCP 12(h)(3).

# C. Special Issues under Rule 12

## 1. One, and Only One, Pre-Answer Motion

As shown above, objections to lack of subject matter jurisdiction, failure to state a claim, and failure to join an indispensable party are not subject to the consolidation requirement. Even with respect to Rules 12(b)(1), 12(c) and Rule 12(b)(7), however, although the defendant can still raise these objections if it does not include them in a pre-answer motion, *it can raise them only an answer, not in a second Rule 12 motion.* As one court explained:

> At the outset, it is necessary to determine the nature of the motion brought by defendants. None of the movants have yet filed an answer. The motion submitted by the defendants is titled, "Motion to Dismiss For Failure To Join A Party Under Rule 19". The Motion argues that MMS is a necessary or indispensable party and requests dismissal of the complaint because of the failure of EP to join MMS. Although it is not mentioned in either defendants motion or their memorandum in support of the motion, defendants are apparently seeking dismissal pursuant to Rule 12(b)(7) . . . , which lists among the defenses that may be raised in a pre-answer motion to dismiss the failure to join a party under Rule 19.
>
> The Federal Rules clearly provide for a pre-answer motion to dismiss for failure to join a party under Rule 19. However, the Rules also govern how and when such a motion may be made. Rule 12(g) provides that
>
> > A party who makes a motion under this rule may join with it any other motions herein provided for and then available to the party. If a party makes a motion under this rule but omits therefrom any defense or objection then available to the party which this rule permits to be raised by motion, the party shall not thereafter make a motion based on the defense or objection so omitted, except a motion as provided in subdivision (h)(2) hereof on any of the grounds there stated.
>
> Therefore, if a party makes a Rule 12(b) motion, and does not include an additional defense or objection that could have been joined pursuant to Rule 12(g), that defense or objection is waived unless it is protected by Rule 12(h)(2). The same defendants who now move to dismiss

under Rule 12(b)(7) previously filed a motion to dismiss for lack of subject matter jurisdiction pursuant to Rule 12(b)(1). That Motion was filed March 8, 1993, and failed to raise any defense or objection of failure to join a party under Rule 19. Accordingly, that defense has been waived by the Defendants, unless the defense is discussed and preserved by Rule 12(h)(2). . . .

Rule 12(h)(2) preserves a defense based upon failure to join an indispensable party from waiver. However, it must be asserted in a manner consistent with that provision . . .

Defendant's second pre-answer motion to dismiss is clearly precluded by the Federal Rules of Civil Procedure. It is the role of the Court to apply the Rules to ensure the just, speedy, and efficient resolution of disputes. The filing of successive pre-answer motions to dismiss serves to frustrate these goals.

*EP Operating Ltd. Partnership v. Placid Oil Co.*, 1994 WL 507455 (E.D. La. 1994).

## 2. An Exception for Motions Under Rules 12(e) or (f)

Read literally, the consolidation requirement applies to any motion filed under Rule 12, including Rule 12(e) and (f). Consequently, if a party has any other Rule 12 defense available when it files a Rule 12(e) or (f) motion, the consolidation requirement applies. *Clark v. Associates Commercial Corp. v. Howard*, 149 F.R.D. 629, 632 (D. Kan. 1993)("the cases and commentators are overwhelmingly of the opinion that a party who makes a Rule 12(e) motion for a more definite statement may not thereafter assert by motion a Rule 12(b) defense that was available at the time of the initial motion."); *Martin v. Delaware Law School of Widener Univ.*, 625 F. Supp. 1288, 1296 (D. Del. 1985) (by not raising lack of personal jurisdiction, improper venue, and insufficient service of process in motion for more definite statement, defendant waived its right to assert those defenses in motion to dismiss). Though there is little case law on the subject, the consolidation requirement of Rule 12(g) also applies to motions filed under Rule 12(f): if the defendant files a Rule 12(f) motion and fails to include an objection that must be raised in the first response, the objection is waived. *Cima v. Wellpoint Healthcare Networks, Inc.*, 2007 WL 1068252 (S.D. Ill. 2007).

What if, however, the complaint is so indefinite that the defendant cannot ascertain whether, for example, personal jurisdiction, venue, or subject matter jurisdiction exists, and so it files a Rule 12(e) motion seeking a more definite statement? How can the defendant include in the Rule 12(e) motion its objection to personal jurisdiction when the basis for filing the Rule 12(e) motion is that it can't tell whether it has an objection to personal jurisdiction? In some circumstances, such as when a clearer pleading is necessary for a party to understand whether it has a basis to move under Rule 12(b), courts will not find waiver. *Nat'l Union Fire Ins. Co. of Pittsburgh, Pa. v. Aerowhawk Aviation, Inc.,* 259 F. Supp. 2d. 1096, 1100 (D. Idaho 2003).

### 3. Compelling a Party to Abide by a Pre-Dispute Arbitration Clause

Many commercial agreements include clauses that require any dispute arising out of the agreement be subject to binding arbitration, not litigation. If a party files suit in violation of such a clause, how does the other party enforce it? Specifically, must the party raise the issue under Rule 12(b)? If so, which part of Rule 12(b) applies?

The characterization can be critical: if a motion to raise an objection based upon an arbitration clause is, for example, one based upon improper venue, then the objection is easy to waive; but if it is one based on lack of subject matter jurisdiction, or failing to state a claim upon which relief can be granted, then it is much more difficult to waive. Further, the standards of review on appeal differ depending on which subsection of Rule 12(b) is implicated. *See Continental Cas. Co. v. Am. Nat'l Ins. Co.,* 417 F.3d 727 (7th Cir. 2005).

The policies cut both ways. On the one hand, allowing arbitration to be too easily waived would increase litigation, contrary to the parties' agreement and public interests. *See Palcko v. Airborne Express, Inc.,* 372 F.3d 588 (3rd Cir. 2004) (holding that, in part because of this policy, motions to dismiss based upon arbitration provisions fell within Rule 12(b)(6)). On the other hand, holding that a motion to compel arbitration can effectively never be waived would allow a party to participate in litigation, but then move to dismiss and compel arbitration if the litigation was not going its way.

Because arbitration agreements are increasingly common and arbitration is perceived by many to be pro-defendant, plaintiffs will often file suit rather than seek arbitration. Defense counsel must therefore be diligent to examine any agreement relating to a claim for an arbitration clause and to avoid waiving the client's right to compel arbitration.

## D. The Court Can Grant, Deny, or Carry a Rule 12 Motion With the Case

A court faced with a Rule 12 motion has three options: (1) grant it; (2) deny it; or (3) postpone its decision by carrying the motion along with the case until trial. Rule 12(i). A fourth option — converting a Rule 12(b)(6) or Rule 12(c) motion into one for summary judgment — arises where that motion refers to matters not part of the pleadings.

## 1. Impact of Granting a Rule 12 Motion

The impact of a court's grant of each of the Rule 12 motions is discussed in the chapter on that specific motion, above. This chart summarizes them:

| Motion | Impact of Grant of Motion |
| --- | --- |
| 12(b)(1) lack of subject matter jurisdiction | Dismissal without prejudice |
| 12(b)(2) lack of personal jurisdiction | Dismissal without prejudice |
| 12(b)(3) lack of proper venue | Dismissal without prejudice |
| 12(b)(4) insufficiency of process | Dismissal without prejudice |
| 12(b)(5) insufficiency of service of process | Dismissal without prejudice |
| 12(b)(6) failure to state claim | Dismissal with prejudice, if not curable through an amendment |
| 12(b)(7) failure to join indispensable party | Dismissal without prejudice |
| 12(c) judgment on the pleadings | Dismissal with prejudice, if not curable through an amendment |
| 12(e) motion for more definite statement | Party must re-plead |
| 12(f) motion to strike | Party must re-plead |

## 2. Impact of Denial of a Rule 12 Motion

The denial of the motion means the case moves on, and the defendant must next file an answer. Again, sequential motions under Rule 12 are not permitted. While a defendant may be able to include certain Rule 12 defenses in its *answer* that it did not include in its motion, it cannot file *another* Rule 12 motion — even one that was not required to be "consolidated" — but *must answer* and include in the answer any Rule 12 defenses that it has that were not waived.

## 3. Carrying the Motion with the Case

Courts will carry Rule 12 motions along until trial where, for example, the merits of the motion are intertwined with the merits of a claim and so the motion cannot be decided without adjudicating the claim itself. *Roberts v. Corrothers*, 812 F.2d 1173, 1177 (9th Cir. 1987). For example, if the court determines that a jurisdictional question and the merits of a claim are inextricably intertwined, it may not resolve genuinely disputed facts on a Rule 12(b)(1) motion but must wait until trial to resolve the jurisdictional issue, unless "the material jurisdictional facts are not in dispute and the moving party is entitled to prevail as a matter of law." *Id.*

# E. Should a Party with the Choice File an Answer or a Rule 12 Motion?

If a party has a Rule 12 defense that need not be pled only in a pre-answer motion, the defendant must determine whether to file a pre-answer motion or include its Rule 12(b) defenses in its answer. Which one to pick turns on several factors, including those summarized on this chart:

| Reasons to Only File Rule 12 Motion | Reasons to Answer and Include Rule 12 Defenses in the Answer |
| --- | --- |
| Filing a Rule 12 motion avoids the expense of having to conduct legal and factual research into an answer. As we have seen, an answer must admit or deny each allegation in a complaint, include affirmative defenses, and include counter- or crossclaims. Filing a Rule 12 motion at least delays those costs. | Filing a Rule 12 motion does not cut off the time for the plaintiff to amend its complaint as of right. |
| Filing a Rule 12 motion may result in dismissal of the lawsuit, or one or more claims in it. If dismissal can substantially narrow or eliminate the case, then the defendant can achieve that goal merely through filing the Rule 12 motion. | Filing a Rule 12 motion does not preclude the plaintiff from taking a voluntary non-suit under Rule 41. |

# F. Filing a Rule 56 Motion Should Not Postpone the Answer Date

It is unclear whether the filing of *only* a motion for summary judgment is an option. On the one hand, Rule 12(a)(4) literally requires *either* the filing of a Rule 12 motion *or* an answer. On the other hand, Rule 56 expressly permits the filing of a motion for summary judgment by a defending party at any time.

There is no clear answer to whether the filing of a motion for summary judgment postpones the filing of an answer. *Compare Ricke v. Armco, Inc.,* 158 F.R.D.

149 (D. Minn. 1994) (a motion for summary judgment that was not a Rule 12(b)(6) motion should not postpone the requirement of filing an answer) *with Rashidi v. Albright,* 818 F. Supp. 1354, 1356 (D. Nev. 1993) (reasoning that since a converted Rule 12(b)(6) motion postpones the need to file an answer, so too does the filing of a Rule 56 motion, but noting contrary authority). On a related note, it is clear that if a party files a Rule 12(b)(6) motion that the court "converts" into a Rule 56 motion for summary judgment, the motion is still treated as a Rule 12 motion for purposes of determining whether and if so when the party must file its answer.

## Checkpoints

- Can you identify those Rule 12 defenses that are "easy" to waive, and those that are more difficult to waive, and explain why they are treated differently?

- Can you list those Rule 12 defenses that may only be raised in a pre-answer motion? That must be raised in the first response? That may be raised in an answer even after a Rule 12 motion? That may, in substance at least, be raised even if not included in the answer?

# Chapter 37

# The Defendant's Answer

---

### Answer Roadmap

This chapter identifies the steps that defense counsel must follow to answer a complaint.

This chapter also describes when a "denial" of an allegation is insufficient to put a plaintiff on notice that the defendant intends to raise an "affirmative defense."

---

As we've seen, soon after service of a complaint the defendant must either file a Rule 12 motion or answer. Earlier chapters examined Rule 12 motions. Unless the Rule 12 motion is granted and results in dismissal of every claim, the defendant must next answer, even if it prevails on its Rule 12 pre-answer motion. This chapter examines the answer.

## A. Defense Counsel Must Investigate the Facts and Law

In its answer, the defendant must (a) admit or deny each allegation of a complaint; (b) plead every "affirmative defense" to plaintiff's claims; and (c) plead any counterclaim against the plaintiff. In addition, the defendant may need to implead or otherwise join non-parties. As a result, Rule 11 and competent lawyering require that defense counsel investigate both the facts and law before filing an answer. Satisfying that duty may require nothing more than speaking with the defendant and conducting, if any, only rudimentary legal research. In more complex cases, investigation may require a lot of time and money. The expense of an answer is, you will recall, one reason to file a Rule 12 motion if a grounds for doing so is available.

# B. Defense Counsel Must
# Address Each Allegation in the Complaint

The defendant is generally required to admit, deny, or state that it is without sufficient information to form a belief as to the truth of each allegation in a complaint. FRCP 8(b). A defendant may not deny an allegation, or state that it lacks sufficient information to admit or deny it, without making a reasonable investigation. *See* FRCP 11(b)(4). An allegation that is not denied is admitted, but if the defendant states that it lacks sufficient information to admit or deny a specific allegation, that allegation is deemed denied. FRCP 8(b)(5). So a defendant's answer might look in part like this:

---

4.  Admitted.
5.  Denied.
6.  Defendant is without sufficient information to form a belief as to the truth of this allegation.

---

The defendant is required both to "fairly respond to the substance of an allegation" and, if it intends to "deny only part of an allegation" it must "admit the part that is true and deny the rest." FRCP 8(b)(2) and (3). In *Zielinski v. Philadelphia Piers, Inc.,* 139 F. Supp. 408 (E.D. Pa. 1956), the plaintiff had alleged that the defendant "owned, operated and controlled" a forklift that had injured the plaintiff. In fact, the defendant owned the forklift, but had leased it to another party. The defendant in its answer denied the allegation. After limitations ran against the party that had been in control of the forklift that day, the defendant moved to dismiss the claim because it did not control or operate the forklift, and so could not be liable under a negligence theory. The court held that the defendant had not fairly met the substance of the allegation; the defendant should have admitted that it owned it, but denied that it controlled or operated the forklift on the day in question.

# C. The Answer Must Plead
# Every Affirmative Defense

Rule 8(c) provides in pertinent part:

> In responding to a pleading, *a party must affirmatively state any avoidance or affirmative defense, including*: accord and satisfaction, arbitration and award, assumption of risk, contributory negligence, discharge

in bankruptcy, duress, estoppel, failure of consideration, fraud, illegality, injury by fellow servant, laches, license, payment, release, res judicata, statute of frauds, statute of limitations, and waiver.

(Emph. added.) Each listed concept is an affirmative defense to some claims. Contributory negligence, for example, generally is an affirmative defense to a negligence claim. Fraud generally bars enforcement of a contract induced by fraudulent misrepresentation. Whether a listed defense can be used to defend against a specific claim turns whether under Rule 11 there is a good faith basis for asserting that it does so based upon substantive law that creates the claim.

There are three issues we'll next consider: First, what is an affirmative defense? Second, how much detail must be pled? Third, must a defendant be consistent in its positions?

## 1. What is an "Affirmative Defense"?

Obviously, if after reasonable investigation defense counsel concludes that the facts and law support asserting as a defense one or more of the nineteen defenses expressly listed in Rule 8(c), the answer must include them. It is the lead-in "catch-all" in Rule 8(c) that presents the difficulties: when is something that is *not* expressly listed in Rule 8(c) nonetheless "*an avoidance or affirmative defense*" that must be affirmatively pled? If something must be pled, but is not, then the defendant will not—under the new rules—even be allowed discovery into the matter, let alone be permitted to introduce evidence to support that affirmative defense. But, if it need not be pled, then pleading it will put the plaintiff on notice of facts that the defendant may not have had to disclose. Further, the defendant may by pleading something also undertake the burden to prove the facts underlying the "affirmative defense," even if it is not one.

Thus, while it is probably best to err on the side of pleading something as an affirmative defense, there are reasons not to. Sometimes the line should be clear: a contention that the defendant did not cause harm to the plaintiff is not an affirmative defense, since it simply denies an element of plaintiff's claim, and does not assume the claim is established but that is barred for a reason which is not an element of the claim. *See Ocean Atlantic Dev. Corp. v. Willow Treat Farm L.L.C.*, 2002 WL 485387 (N.D. Ill. 2002).

But the line between a denial and an affirmative defense is not always clear. As one court explained:

> the test applied is whether the defendant intends to rest his defense upon some fact not included in the allegations necessary to support

the plaintiff's case. A general denial places in issue all of the material allegations contained in plaintiff's petition necessary to support his claim and the defendant is entitled to prove any fact which tends to show plaintiff's cause of action never had any legal existence. On the other hand, if the defendant has a defense in the nature of a confession of the facts of the plaintiff's petition but avers that the plaintiff's theory of liability even though sustained by the evidence does not apply to it because of additional facts which place defendant in a position to avoid any legal responsibility for its action, then such defense must be set forth in his answer.

*Layman v. Southwestern Bell Tel. Co.,* 554 S.W.2d 477 (Mo. Ct. App. 1977). Put another way, whether a particular matter is an "affirmative defense" under the catchall in Rule 8(c) turns on whether denial of the allegation by itself will put the plaintiff on notice of the facts underlying the defendant's position. So, for example, in *Layman* the plaintiff brought a trespass claim against the telephone company for digging a trench on her land, and at trial the defendant sought to show that it had received an easement from a predecessor in interest to plaintiff's title. The court held that an easement was an affirmative defense, and should have been pled:

> the right of defendant to enter upon the land to which plaintiff has indisputable possessory right would have to be proven by some competent evidence which would give that right to defendant. This would not be in derogation of plaintiff's claim by way of showing that her claim was nonexistent but rather that despite her claim, the defendant had a positive right to enter and disturb the possessory rights of the plaintiff. Thus it is the obligation of a defendant in an action for trespass to affirmatively plead and prove matters in justification.

*Layman,* 554 S.W.2d at 480.

For these reasons, in response to a complaint, the defendant must plead not only each affirmative defenses in Rule 8(c) that it has a Rule 11 basis to plead, but also any which a court has or likely will conclude is covered by the catchall. For example, even though it is not listed, the plaintiff's failure to mitigate damages is nearly universally viewed as an affirmative defense that must be pled. *See Minn. Supply Co. v. Raymond Corp.,* 2003 WL 21303188 (D. MN. 2003) (collecting cases). *See also LaFont v. Decker-Angel,* 1999 U.S. App. LEXIS 8336 (10th Cir. 1999) (holding that the contention that a check the defendant had given to the plaintiff had been a "gift" was an affirmative defense to a claim that the defendant had committed fraud and conversion by using the check for the defendant's own purposes when it was in fact payment for the plaintiff's portion of land the two were to buy).

Finally, one important note: courts have observed that some of the "defenses" in Rule 12, such as Rule 12(b)(6), are not properly pled as affirmative defenses under Rule 8(c) because they do not raise matters outside the scope of the plaintiff's claim. *Ocean Atlantic Dev. Corp. v. Willow Treat Farm L.L.C.*, 2002 WL 485387 (N.D. Ill. 2002) (noting that simply asserting "this fails to state a claim" is insufficient under Rule 8). Even so, it is common for defendants to unnecessarily plead the "defense" of "failure to state a claim upon which relief can be granted."

## 2. How Much Detail About the Affirmative Defense Must be Pled in the Answer?

Courts split on the second issue — how much detail must be pled. Rule 8(c) requires that affirmative defenses be stated "affirmatively." Defendants typically do so by including a section after the admissions and denials of each paragraph of the answer that continues the sequential numbering of paragraphs and gives notice of any affirmative defenses. Typically, these affirmative defenses will state in a conclusory manner, for example, "Plaintiff's claim is barred by the statute of limitations."

But the courts are splitting on whether *Iqbal* and *Twombly* apply to affirmative defenses. Perhaps a majority of district courts hold that they do not, and so conclusory pleading of an affirmative defense is sufficient. But other courts disagree, and require that the *Iqbal/Twombly* approach applies to affirmative defenses, and so plausible facts must be pled. As a result, plaintiff's counsel should review the law and determine whether to move to strike an affirmative defense as insufficient.

## 3. May the Defendant Be Inconsistent in its Positions?

A party may plead inconsistent defenses. Rule 8(d)(2) provides:

> A party may set out 2 or more statements of a claim or defense alternatively or hypothetically, either in a single count or defense or in separate ones. If a party makes alternative statements, the pleading is sufficient if any one of them is sufficient.

In addition, a party "may state as on any separate claims or defenses as it has, regardless of consistency." FRCP 8(d)(3). A defendant may, for example, plead that there was no consideration for the contract; but if there was, it did not breach the contract; but if it did, the plaintiff's claim is barred by the statute of limitations; but if it's not . . .

## 4. An Example of Pleading Affirmative Defenses in Pre-*Iqbal/Twombly* Fashion

---

AFFIRMATIVE DEFENSES

9.     Because the bank declined payment on Plaintiff's check to Defendant, Plaintiff's claim for breach of contract is barred by failure of consideration.
10.    Because the alleged breach occurred more than four years before this suit was filed, Plaintiff's claim for breach of contract is barred by the statute of limitations

---

# D.  Defense Counsel Must Plead Any Rule 12(b) Objections

To the extent that the facts and law allow them and they have not been waived by failure to include them in the defendant's pre-answer motion, the defendant may plead every Rule 12(b) defense in its answer. Again, however, Rule 12(e) or (f) objections cannot be in answers but must be raised by motion and, again, only one pre-answer motion is permitted.

# E.  Defense Counsel Must Analyze Joinder of Claims and Parties

For defense counsel, the time to analyze joinder of claims and parties is early in the case, and principally at the time of filing the answer. There are several issues to consider. Of special concern is whether the defendant has a compulsory counterclaim that it must raise against the plaintiff. A defendant who has a counterclaim arising out of the transaction or occurrence that is the subject of the plaintiff's claim against it *must* assert that claim if it exists at the time the defendant serves its answer, unless it falls into the exceptions listed in Rule 13(a). FRCP 13(a). Likewise, the defendant *may* assert any other counterclaim it then has. FRCP 13(b). In addition, if the plaintiff has joined another defendant, the defendant may have a crossclaim to assert against a co-defendant. FRCP 13(g). In addition, with respect to both counter- and crossclaims, the defendant may need or want to join additional parties to the cross- or counterclaim. FRCP 13(h). Finally, a defendant may need to examine whether it can or must "implead" any third-party defendants under Rule 14(a). *See* Chapter 17.

# F. Defense Counsel Must Determine if a Jury Trial is Available and Desired

If the plaintiff has demanded a jury on any claim, the defendant can rely on that demand for that claim and need not make its own demand. FRCP 38(d), 39(a). If the plaintiff has not done so, the defendant must consider whether to demand a jury. *See* Chapter 54. In addition, if the defendant asserts a counterclaim, it may need to demand a jury trial on that counterclaim even if the plaintiff has demanded a jury on its claim. *See id.*

# G. Defense Counsel Must Timely File and Serve the Answer

A defendant must serve and file the answer within the time allowed by Rule 12(a)(2). In doing so, the defendant must include a "certificate of service" at the end of the answer indicating how defense counsel served the pleading on all other parties. FRCP 5(d), (e).

---

### Checkpoints

- Can you describe the steps that defense counsel must take in responding to receipt of a complaint?
- Can you describe the two circumstances when something is an "affirmative defense"?
- Can you describe when denial of an averment will be insufficient to allow a defendant to put in evidence of an "affirmative defense"?

# Chapter 38

# Rule 11's Reach and Special Procedures

---

### Rule 11's Reach Roadmap

This chapter explains how Rule 11 applies to pleadings and all other papers filed with the court except discovery.

This chapter also explains how a party, or the court on its own, can raise violations of Rule 11.

Finally, this chapter explains under what circumstances, and if so, what type of sanctions a court may impose for a violation of Rule 11, and who those sanctions may be imposed upon.

---

## A. Rule 11 Reaches all Papers, but not Discovery

Rule 11 applies to every "pleading, written motion, and other paper" filed with the district court, from the filing of the complaint until after the filing of the notice of appeal, except for discovery and motions related to discovery. FRCP 11(a); *see* FRCP 11(d). Thus, all pleadings and motions filed with the court, except those related to discovery, must comply with Rule 11. *See* Chapter 51. (Rule 11 even applies to Rule 11 motions themselves, resulting in the Kafka-esque filing of a Rule 11 motion for sanctions against a party for filing a Rule 11 motion for sanctions.) Though Rule 11 is broad and clearly applies to pleadings such as answer and to written motions under Rule 12 or Rule 56, Rule 11 has built-in limitations.

First, Rule 11 does not apply to oral statements as such, since it applies only to signed written documents filed with the court. However, Rule does apply to "later advocating" arguments included in written papers, and so Rule 11 does apply to some oral statements, but only those that flow directly from a document filed with the court. *See O'Brien v. Alexander,* 101 F.3d 1479, 1489 (2d Cir. 1996). Thus, arguing in open court that certain evidence is not admissible cannot violate Rule 11, unless the argument that the evidence was inadmissible was previously made in a document filed with the court. The "later advocating" prohibition is discussed more fully below. It is best thought of as an exception to the general rule that Rule 11 only applies to written documents filed with the court, and not to oral argument generally.

Second, Rule 11 does not apply to documents that are not actually filed with a district court. Thus, it does not apply to documents that had been filed in state court in a case removed to federal court. However, Rule 11 applies to papers filed in federal court to facilitate removal and applies to those filed after removal, and so it applies to the notice of removal itself, both because it is filed in federal court and the removal statute expressly says it is subject to Rule 11. 28 U.S.C. § 1446; *see* Chapter 10. However, if a party "later advocates" in federal court a statement or position that was taken in state court, then Rule 11 can be violated. *Brown v. Capitol Air, Inc.,* 797 F.2d 106, 108 (2d Cir. 1986).

Third, it does not apply to any aspect of discovery or initial disclosures. FRCP 11(d) ("This rule does not apply to disclosures and discovery requests, responses, objections, and motions under Rules 26 through 37."). Thus, even a motion to compel cannot violate Rule 11.

But Rule 11 covers all other papers filed with a district court. In addition, Rule 11 may cover letters to the court even though often they are not "filed." *See Legault v. Zambarano,* 105 F.3d. 24, 28 (1st Cir. 1997) (letter to the court is subject to Rule 11 only if letter is a "motion in disguise"). Finally, Rule 11 applies to a notice of appeal, since it is filed in the district court, but it does not apply to appellate filings; Federal Rule of Appellate Procedure 38 does. *See In re 60 East 80th St. Equities, Inc.,* 218 F.3d 109, 118–19 n. 3 (2d Cir. 2000); *Becker v. Montgomery,* 532 U.S. 757 (2001). *See* Chapter 58 for a discussion of appeals.

# B.  The Reach of Rule 11 Beyond "Filing" or "Submitting" a Paper to "Later Advocating"

A signature on a paper filed with a district court constitutes a representation by the signing lawyer that the paper complies with Rule 11. As noted in Chapter 12, Rule 11 applies a "snapshot" approach: if the paper *when filed* did not violate Rule 11, facts learned later cannot be used to "create" a violation in hindsight. Put the other way, if the paper when filed complied with Rule 11 there is no "duty to correct" the paper or to withdraw it based upon later-learned information.

Nonetheless, information learned after a lawyer files a paper covered by Rule 11 can limit the ability of the lawyer to later "advocate" what is in that paper if the lawyer learns that a position or argument in that paper, if submitted in light of the new knowledge, would now violate Rule 11. Although a 1993 Amendment to Rule 11 abrogated the duty to withdraw or amend a paper that the attorney or party later learns would violate Rule 11 if filed with later-gained knowledge, an attorney or party still cannot later advocate a position that it has learned has become frivolous under current Rule 11. This principle arises from Rule 11(b), which makes it a violation to "later advocat[e]" a statement in a paper that later is determined to have violated Rule 11. So for example, a defendant who includes an affirmative defense in its answer that, it later learns, is meritless would violate Rule 11 by later advocating that defense, even though the actual filing of the answer did not violate Rule 11.

# C. Two Ways to Raise Violations of Rule 11

## 1. Party's Motions for Sanctions

There is a three-step process for moving for sanctions under Rule 11:

(1) *Serve* the motion for sanctions on the party;

(2) *Wait 21 days* (the so-called "safe harbor") to give the party that filed the paper time to withdraw it; and then

(3) If the paper is not withdrawn, *file* the motion for sanctions with the court.

*See* FRCP 11(c)(2). (*See* Chapter 28 for a discussion of motion practice.) Rule 11 effectively gives a party 21 days to withdraw a paper that violates Rule 11.

Each step is important. Merely sending a letter to the other side pointing out the violation is insufficient; the party must serve the motion for sanctions, then wait the 21 days *See Roth v. Green,* 466 F.3d 1179 (10th Cir. 2006). Where a party moves for sanctions without giving the other side this 21-day "safe harbor" by serving the motion for sanctions before filing it, sanctions are improper, but the party against whom sanctions are sought *must object to the lack of receiving the 21 day safe harbor after receiving the motion, or the objection is waived. Rector v. Approved Fed. Sav. Bank,* 265 F.3d 248 (4th Cir. 2001).

## 2. Court's Own Motion for Sanctions

The procedure that a district court must follow when imposing sanctions *sua sponte* differs from that which applies to motions for sanction. *Compare* FRCP 11(c)(1)(A) *with* FRCP 11(c)(1)(B). A court may award sanctions on its own initiative by issuing what is called a "show cause" order: an order describing the specific conduct that appears to violate Rule 11. FRCP 11(c)(1)(B).

# D. The Proper Sanction Under Rule 11

## 1. A Violation Permits but Does not Require Imposition of any Sanction

Rule 11 permits, but does not require, a court to sanction conduct that violates the Rule. Specifically, Rule 11(c)(1) provides that if "after notice and a reasonable opportunity to respond, the court determines that Rule 11(b) has been violated, the court may, impose an appropriate sanction . . ." Thus, imposition of sanctions is permissive. *Perez v. Posse Comitatus*, 373 F.3d 321, 325 (2d Cir. 2004) ("Even if the district court concludes that the [paper] violates Rule 11 . . . the decision whether or not to impose sanctions is a matter for the court's discretion.")

Whether a court should impose sanctions turns on all the facts. The advisory committee notes to Rule 11 give examples of factors that help determine whether to impose sanctions:

> The rule does not attempt to enumerate the factors a court should consider in deciding whether to impose a sanction . . . ; but, for emphasis, it does specifically note that a sanction may be nonmonetary as well as monetary. Whether the improper conduct was willful, or negligent; whether it was part of a pattern of activity, or an isolated event; whether it infected the entire pleading, or only one particular count or defense; whether the person has engaged in similar conduct in other litigation; whether it was intended to injure; what effect it had on the litigation process in time or expense; whether the responsible person is trained in the law; what amount given the financial resources of the responsible person, is needed to deter that person from repetition in the same case; what amount is needed to deter similar activity by other litigants; all of these may in a particular case be proper considerations. The court has significant discretion in determining what sanctions, if any, should be imposed for a violation, subject to the principle that the sanctions should not be more severe than reasonably necessary to deter repetition of the conduct by the offending person or comparable conduct by similarly situated persons.

FRCP 11, Advisory Committee Note.

## 2. Who Can the Court Sanction?

Rule 11(c)(1) allows a court to "impose an appropriate sanction on any attorney, law firm, or party that violated the rule or is responsible for the violation."

Thus, the court may sanction only the person who violated Rule 11 or who is responsible for a violation. In that regard, Rule 11 allows the party itself to be sanctioned even though the party's lawyer, not the party, signed the paper that violated the Rule. *See Souran v. Travelers Ins. Co.*, 982 F.2d 1497, 1508 n. 14 (11th Cir. 1993) ("Even though it is the attorney whose signature violates the rule, it may be appropriate . . . to impose a sanction on the client.").

In contrast, sometimes only the lawyer, not the party, may be sanctioned. Specifically, only the lawyer may be sanctioned if the basis for the sanction is that the paper was legally frivolous. *See, e.g., Schrag v. Simpson*, 141 F.3d 1185 (10th Cir. 1998) (unpublished decision) (stating "such legal matters as the frivolousness of a claim . . . which are peculiarly [within] the province of lawyers, would not, without specific findings implicating knowing participation, support Rule 11 sanctions against a party"). Put the other way, Rule 11 requires sanctioning the attorney, not the party, when the conduct involves a representation regarding the legal sufficiency of a claim or position. *See* FRCP 11(c)(5)(A).

On the other hand, in some circumstances, sanctions only against the client are permissible. For example, sanctions can be levied against only a party if that party misrepresents facts, or when it is clear that the client is the "mastermind" behind a frivolous case. *See, e.g., Pelletier*, 921 F.2d 1465 (discussing client's scheme to institute frivolous litigation to extort settlement and noting that the client was skilled in the law). Likewise, if the client is responsible for a violation, the client may be sanctioned without also sanctioning its attorney. *Moore v. Western Surety Co.*, 140 F.R.D. 340, 345 (N.D. Miss. 1991), *aff'd*, 977 F.2d 578 (5th Cir. 1992).

Apart from those exceptions, "[w]ith any other violation, either the attorney or the client, or both, may be sanctioned; when the attorney reasonably relies upon the misrepresentations of a client, the client not the attorney should be sanctioned under Rule 11." *Horizon Unlimited, Inc. v. Richard Silva & SNA, Inc.*, 1999 WL 675469 (E.D. Pa. 1999).

## 3. Determining the "Appropriate" Sanction

If the court decides to impose sanctions, then it must exercise its discretion to determine which available sanction is "appropriate." FRCP 11(c)(1). Rule 11 limits the sanction to that which "suffices to deter repetition of the conduct or comparable conduct by others similarly situated." FRCP 11(c)(4). Thus, sanctions are limited to those necessary to deter similar conduct. In that regard, "The court has significant discretion in determining what sanctions, if any, should be imposed for a violation, subject to the principle that the sanctions should not be more severe than reasonably necessary to deter repetition of the conduct by the offending person or comparable conduct by similarly situated persons." Fed.R.Civ.P. 11, Advisory Committee Note.

In addition, Rule 11 has two other limitations. First, as noted above, monetary sanctions may not be imposed against a *party* (as compared to the lawyer for the party) for violating Rule 11(b)(2). FRCP 11(c)(5)(A). This makes sense, since Rule 11(b)(2) is prohibits a frivolous legal contention, and few clients are as equipped as their lawyer to abide by that prohibition. Second, sanctions which are imposed through the court's own initiative under Rule 11(c)(3) cannot be awarded unless the court issues a show cause order before the voluntary dismissal or settlement of the claims made by, or against, the party to be sanctioned. FRCP 11(c)(5)(B). Thus, if the plaintiff settles its claims against a defendant, and then the court issues a show cause order for sanctions, any sanctions would be improper. As we'll see in Chapter 44, filing the notice of voluntary dismissal terminates the power of the court to act, and allowing a court to sanction a party after settlement could obviously postpone or prevent settlement of litigation.

### a. Monetary Sanctions

As noted above, an objective test applies in determining whether Rule 11(b) has been violated: there is no "young lawyer's defense" or "pure heart, empty head" defense. However, courts *do* take into account the subjective facts when determining the amount or kind of sanction to impose. "Thus, the conduct of an experienced lawyer or of a lawyer who acted in bad faith is more apt to invite assessment of a substantial penalty than that of a less experienced or merely negligent one." *Lieb v. Topstone Indus., Inc.*, 788 F.3d 151, 158 (3rd Cir. 1986).

### b. Non-Monetary Sanctions, Including Dismissal

In some circumstances, a court can dismiss a complaint where the plaintiff has violated Rule 11, or strike the defendant's answer if it has done so. However, these are extreme sanctions and before imposing them the court must consider:

> (1) the degree of actual prejudice to the [moving party]; (2) the amount of interference with the judicial process; (3) the culpability of the litigant; (4) whether the court warned in advance that dismissal would be a likely sanction for noncompliance; and (5) the efficacy of lesser sanctions.

*Mobley v. McCormick*, 40 F.3d 337, 340 (10th Cir. 1994).

# E. Related Law: Sanctions Under 28 U.S.C. § 1927 and Inherent Power

## 1. Section 1927

28 U.S.C. § 1927 provides that any attorney "who so multiplies the proceedings in any case unreasonably and vexatiously may be required by the court to satisfy personally the excess costs, expenses, and attorneys' fees reasonably incurred because of such conduct." This statute "imposes an obligation on attorneys throughout the entire litigation to avoid dilatory tactics." *Bowler v. U.S. Immigration and Naturalization Serv.*, 901 F. Supp. 597, 604 (S.D.N.Y. 1995).

Rule 11 and Section 1927 are distinct sources of authority to sanction litigants. They aim at different kinds of misconduct, differ in scope, and are governed by different standards. *Byrne v. Nezhat*, 261 F.3d 1075, 1106 (11th Cir. 2001) (explaining that Rule 11 "is aimed primarily at pleadings" and covers both parties and attorneys while § 1927 covers "dilatory tactics throughout the entire litigation" and covers only attorney conduct); *Chambers v. NASCO, Inc.*, 501 U.S. 32, 47 (1991) (noting Rule 11 permits attorney's fees "for conduct which merely fails to meet a reasonableness standard," in contrast to a court's inherent powers, which require a higher showing).

Unlike Rule 11 sanctions, which take a snapshot and focus on a particular paper, sanctions under Section 1927 may involve any conduct that generates needless proceedings. As a result, "Section 1927 does not apply to initial pleadings, since it addresses only the multiplication of proceedings. It is only possible to multiply or prolong proceedings after the complaint is filed." *Matter of Yagman*, 796 F.2d 1165, 1187 (9th Cir.), *amended*, 803 F.2d 1085 (9th Cir. 1986). "The filing of a complaint may be sanctioned pursuant to Rule 11 or a court's inherent power, but it may not be sanctioned pursuant to § 1927." *In re Keegan Mgmt. Co., Sec. Litig.*, 78 F.3d 431, 435 (9th Cir. 1996).

## 2. Inherent Power to Sanction

Courts have a less well-defined "inherent power" to sanction even conduct that falls outside Rule 11 or Section 1927. *See Chambers v. NASCO, Inc.*, 501 U.S. 32, 50, (1991) (noting that "if in the informed discretion of the court, neither the statute nor the Rules are up to the task, the court may safely rely on its inherent power" in imposing appropriate sanctions).

A broad range of sanctions are authorized under inherent power, including striking of frivolous pleadings, claims or defenses, disciplining lawyers, punishing by contempt, and assessing attorney's fees. *E.g., Chambers*, 501 U.S. at

43–45; *Martin v. Automobili Lamborghini Exclusive, Inc.*, 307 F.3d 1332 (11th Cir. 2002) (dismissing complaint with prejudice); *Malautea v. Suzuki Motor Co., Ltd.*, 987 F.2d 1536 (11th Cir. 1993) (striking defendant's answer and entering default judgment); *State Exchange Bank v. Hartline*, 693 F.2d 1350, 1352 (11th Cir. 1982) (striking pleadings); *Telectron v. Overhead Door Corp.*, 116 F.R.D. 107 (S.D. Fla. 1987) (entering default judgment against defendant).

# F.  Sanctions Related to Discovery

This topic is covered in Chapter 51. Rule 11 does *not* apply to discovery.

---

## Checkpoints

- Can you describe how Rule 11 can be violated other than by filing a signed paper?
- Can you describe the steps that a party who believes a paper has been filed in violation of Rule 11 can raise it with the court?
- Can you describe when a court may sanction the lawyer? The client? Only one? Only the other?
- Can you describe how courts determine the proper sanction?

---

# Chapter 39

# Transfer from a Proper Venue to a More Convenient, Proper Venue

---

### Venue Transfer Roadmap

This chapter explains how and under what circumstances a case can be transferred from a district even though it is a proper venue.

---

Earlier we learned that there are improper venues and proper ones, and usually several districts could serve as a proper venue under the general federal venue statute. If there are several proper venues to choose from, the plaintiff gets to pick. If the venue is proper, then there's nothing in Section 1406 or Rule 12(b)(3) that permits a defendant change venues or to dismiss the case: Section 1406 only applies if the venue is *improper. See Kerobo v. Southwestern Clean Fuels, Corp.,* 285 F.3d 531 (6th Cir. 2002) ("venue in Michigan is not improper in this case, and the dismissal under Rule 12(b)(3) must be reversed. . . . [W]e are left with the § 1404(a) motion.").

However, another federal statute allows courts to transfer venue even from a proper venue to another district that is also proper *and* is more convenient for the parties, witnesses, and the judicial system. Specifically, 28 U.S.C. § 1404(a) provides: "For the convenience of parties and witnesses, in the interest of justice, a district court may transfer any civil action to any other district or division where it might have been brought." Unlike Section 1406(a) and Rule 12(b)(3), which concern dismissal or transfer from an improper venue to a district where suit could have been filed properly, Section 1404(a) is based on notions of convenience and allows transfer of a case even, and only, from a proper venue to a more convenient but still proper venue. The determination of whether to transfer is left to the "broad discretion of the district court and determined upon notions of convenience and fairness on a case-by-case basis." *Publicker Indus. Inc. v. U.S.,* 980 F.2d 110, 117 (2d Cir. 1992).

# A. How to Analyze a Section 1404(a) Motion to Transfer Venue

Any party may move to transfer a case to a more convenient forum. Whether transfer is proper requires analyzing three things: (1) Venue must be proper in the current district; (2) venue must be proper in the transferee district and that court must have personal jurisdiction over the defendant; and (3) the party moving to transfer bears the burden to clearly show that the transferee district is more convenient.

## 1. Venue Must be Proper in the Current District

A threshold requirement under Section 1404(a) is that the party seeking transfer must show that venue is proper in the current district. *VMS/PCA Ltd. Partnership v. PCA Partners Ltd. Partnership*, 727 F. Supp. 1167, 1173 (N.D. Ill. 1989). In part, this requirement is to ensure that a party seeking to transfer under Section 1404(a) is not attempting to transfer a case for improper venue in a case after it had waived an objection to improper venue. If venue is improper in the current forum, then Section 1404(a) is not the proper vehicle to use to seek transfer; Section 1406(a) and Rule 12(b)(3) are.

As noted in Chapters 8 and 9, a court that lacks personal jurisdiction over a defendant can rely on Section 1406(a) to transfer the case. May it also rely on Section 1404(a) in such circumstances? The courts split, with some courts holding that Section 1406(a) is the only vehicle, while others allow the motion to be made under Section 1404(a). In short, the courts try to transfer rather than dismiss if they can, so that the merits can be the focus.

Why might it matter whether a court without personal jurisdiction can rely on Section 1404(a) but not Section 1406(a)? For one thing, under Section 1406(a) the court should dismiss unless the *plaintiff* shows that the interests of justice warrant transferring the case, while under Section 1404(a) the court cannot dismiss but must transfer, but only if the *defendant* shows that it's clear that the balance of convenience is in the other forum. Depending on which section applies, the burden of proof and issues vary. Second, the appellate standard of review may differ, depending on precisely how the district court rules. *See Jumara v. State Farm Ins. Co.*, 55 F.3d 873 (3rd Cir. 1995).

Note that most of the time the moving party will argue that the court lacks power to transfer under Section 1404(a), since if the court lacks personal jurisdiction its only option otherwise is to dismiss unless the plaintiff shows under Section 1406(a) that the interests of justice necessitate transferring the case. The defendant is usually better served by dismissal rather than transfer since the plaintiff is more likely to lose interest in pursuing the case, and may fail to refile the claim in a timely fashion.

## 2. Venue in the Proposed Transferee District Must be Proper and the Defendant Must be Subject to Personal Jurisdiction in the Transferee Forum

A second requirement is that the transferee district — the place to which transfer is sought — must be a district where the claim "could have been brought." Although the decision on *whether* to transfer is left to the district court, the statute expressly limits the destination: the division and district must be one where the claim "might have been brought." In other words, the court in the proposed destination must have personal jurisdiction (subject matter will be a given), and venue must be proper in that district. *See Hoffman v. Blaski,* 363 U.S. 335 (1960) (transferee court must have had personal jurisdiction over defendant at time suit was commenced). Thus, a case cannot be transferred to a court where venue is improper or personal jurisdiction lacking. That court is not one where the claim "might have been brought."

## 3. The Party Seeking to Transfer the Case Bears the Burden to Establish the Transferee District is Clearly More Convenient

If the first two requirements are proven, then the question becomes whether transfer is warranted "for the convenience of parties and witnesses [and] in the interests of justice." 28 U.S.C. § 1404(a). Don't think that the court *must* transfer the case if the other district is more convenient. That's wrong for two reasons: first, the district court where the case is filed has wide discretion in deciding whether to transfer and, second, the general federal venue statutes only require that a suit be in a *proper* venue. Transfer to a convenient venue is purely for the convenience of the court, parties, and witnesses. *See D.H. Blair & Co. v. Gottdiener,* 462 F.3d 95, 106 (2d Cir. 2006). In that regard, remember that a Section 1404(a) motion effectively concedes that venue is proper in the pertinent district, but that it is more convenient somewhere else. Thus, a party seeking to transfer a case is trying to override a *proper* selection by the plaintiff. A party seeking transfer, as a result, bears the burden of making what some courts call a "clear-cut showing" that transfer is in the parties and witnesses' interests. *Smart v. Goord,* 21 F. Supp. 2d 309, 315 (S.D.N.Y. 1998) (collecting cases). *See Schultze v. DaimlerChrysler Corp.,* 2006 WL 3375373 (S.D.N.Y. Nov. 14, 2006) (explaining that defendant had burden to make a "clear and convincing showing" that the balance of convenience favors transfer); *PKWare v. Meade*, 79 F. Supp. 2d 1007, 1018 (E.D. Wis. 2000) (party seeking transfer must show transferee forum "is a clearly more convenient forum").

All pertinent factors come into play in determining whether the case should be transferred to that other district. Generally, courts consider the convenience of witnesses as the most important factor, but look to both the private and public concerns that could be affected by transfer. Among the private interests that courts consider are: (1) plaintiffs' privilege of choosing the forum; (2) defendant's preferred forum; (3) where the claim arose; (4) convenience of the parties and their witnesses; (5) convenience of witnesses, but only to the extent that witnesses may be unavailable for trial in one of the *fora*; (6) ease of access to sources of proof, such as documents and other tangible evidence; (7) applicability of each forum's law; (8) each party's ability to enforce a judgment; (9) comparative costs of each party to litigating in each forum; and (10) other pertinent facts. Among the public interest factors courts consider are: (1) the transferee court's familiarity with the law governing the claim; (2) the relative congestion between the transferor and potential transferee courts; and (3) whether there is a local interest in deciding local controversies near where they occurred.

Because of the fact-bound nature of Section 1404(a) motions, parties often will submit affidavits establishing, for example, who likely witnesses will be and where they reside; statistics showing that the case will be more quickly tried in one forum or the other; where the incident occurred; that the matter is one peculiar to one state's law or the other; where the bulk of the pertinent documentary evidence is stored; and so on. None of these factors "controls," and the lists above are not exclusive, but are the factors most often noted by the courts. Let's take a quick look at the key factors.

*Convenience of the Witnesses.* The convenience of the witnesses is often called a "primary" factor in the analysis of which district is more convenient. As you will see later, non-party witnesses can be compelled to testify at trial only to the extent they live within 100 miles of the courthouse where trial will occur. *See* FRCP 45(b)(2). Even if the witness is beyond subpoena range, it still may be more convenient for the case to be pending nearer to a large number of significant witnesses.

*Locus of Operative Events.* Another factor often labeled as "significant" is where the events that led to the suit occurred. "Courts routinely transfer cases to the district where the principal place events occurred, and where the principal witnesses are located in." *Schultze v. DaimlerChrysler Corp.*, 2006 WL 3375373 (S.D.N.Y. 2006)

*Plaintiff's Choice of Forum: The Oft-Ignored Choice.* Often both the district where the case was filed as well as the transferee district have some connection to the dispute. Courts often state that the "plaintiff's choice of forum is to be given considerable deference." *Eichenholtz v. Brennan,* 677 F. Supp. 198, 201 (S.D.N.Y. 1988). If so, courts will often give great weight to the fact that the plaintiff made a proper choice of forum, and deny transfer.

In close cases, this is correct, but courts are quite willing to give less weight to this factor when practical convenience or efficiencies point to transfer. So, for example, if all or the vast majority of the witnesses reside in the transferee forum and the events also occurred there, courts will not give much weight to the plaintiff's choice of some other forum with "no meaningful ties to the controversy and no particular interest in the parties or the subject matter." *Greater Yellowstone Coalition v. Bosworth,* 180 F. Supp. 2d 124, 128 (D. D.C. 2001). The courts say that "the defendant's burden in a motion to transfer decreases when the plaintiffs' choice of forum has no meaningful nexus to the controversy and the parties." *Id.*

Also, consider the weight that should be given to a plaintiff's choice of forum if it was chosen in violation of a forum selection clause. Courts typically state that enforceable forum selection clauses "negate" the weight usually accorded to a plaintiff's choice of forum. *E.g., Hodgson v. Gilmartin,* 2006 WL 2707397 (E.D. Pa. 2006).

Related to the question of giving the plaintiff some deference in its choice of venue is the problem of competing lawsuits: often, a defendant will respond to a lawsuit in the plaintiff's forum by filing a mirror image lawsuit in the defendant's home state. Courts generally give the first-filed suit some weight, but not if it was an improper "anticipatory" lawsuit. *See Ontel Prods., Inc. v. Project Strategies Corp.,* 899 F. Supp. 1144, 1150 (S.D.N.Y. 1995). For similar reasons, courts often permit a second-filed direct action to hold as the venue even though the party named as a defendant in that suit was the plaintiff in a previously filed mirror-image declaratory judgment action, if the first-filed declaratory judgment action had been filed in order to secure a venue more convenient to the defendant but without substantial connection to the dispute, or for other reasons. *See Hy Cite Corp. v. Advanced Marketing Int'l, Inc.,* 2006 WL 3377861 (W.D. Wis. 2006).

# B. Procedure to Move to Transfer Under Section 1404(a)

If venue is proper in the district where the suit is pending, but a party has a Rule 11 basis to assert that there is a more convenient district (or even division in the same district) to litigate the case, that party can move to transfer venue for convenience of the parties and witnesses under § 1404(a). *See Van Dusen v. Barrack,* 376 U.S. 612 (1964). The movant must file a written motion with the court where the case is filed that, typically, includes affidavits by the lawyers in the case as to where likely witnesses, documents, and related evidence is located and which includes statistics regarding the time-to-trial in the competing districts.

## 1. Is a Rule 12(b)(3) Motion Required to Move Under Section 1404(a)?

I believe the answer to that question is "no," but courts split on how motions to transfer from a proper venue to a more convenient one made pursuant to Section 1404(a) should be viewed for purposes of waiver and consolidation under Rule 12. As shown in Chapter 32, courts hold that a motion to dismiss or transfer for *improper* venue under Section 1406(a) is waived if the defense of improper venue under Rule 12(b)(3) is not properly raised either in any pre-answer motion or, if not, in the answer or an amendment thereto.

In contrast, a motion to transfer for the convenience of the parties under Section 1404(a) is *not* waived if it is not raised in the way required by Rule 12. Put the other way, a party who neither files a Rule 12(b)(3) motion nor objects to venue in the party's answer can still move to transfer the case to a more convenient forum. "A motion to transfer venue for the convenience of parties or witnesses or the interests of justice, brought pursuant to 28 U.S.C. § 1404(a), is not a motion under Rule 12(b)(3) of the Federal Rules . . . so the waiver provision of Rule 12(h) is inapplicable." *Red Wing Shoe Co. v. B-Jays USA, Inc.,* 2002 WL 1398538 (D. Minn. 2002) (collecting cases). *See Wilson v. U.S.,* 2006 WL 3431895 (E.D. Ark. 2006) (same).

## 2. Transfer, Not Dismissal, is the Only Option

If the transferor court concludes the transferee district is clearly more convenient, it has discretion to transfer — but it is not required to do so. Note that dismissal is *not* a proper result of a Section 1404(a) motion: transfer is. Decisions granting or denying motions to transfer under Section 1404(a) are reviewed for abuse of discretion. *Lony v. E.I. DuPont de Nemours & Co.,* 886 F.2d 628, 632 (3d Cir. 1989).

# C. Intra-District, Inter-Divisional Transfer Under Section 1404(a)

Some large districts are sub-divided further into two or more "divisions." The Southern District of Texas, for example, is quite large and extends from Houston to Galveston to parts of the Rio Grande Valley. Courts can transfer a case from one division to another division within a district. This is somewhat rare, and is known as interdivisional transfer. The same basic principles discussed above concerning section 1404(a) apply here. (Section 1406(a) does not apply to divisions. There is no such thing as an "improper division.")

For example, in *Smith v. Colonial Penn Ins. Co.*, 943 F. Supp. 782 (S.D. Tex. 1996), suit was filed in the Galveston Division of the Southern District of Texas, and the defendants sought to transfer it pursuant to Section 1404(a) to the Houston division, about 45 miles up I-45. The court denied the motion because the defendant failed to prove greater convenience to the parties and witnesses beyond the fact that Galveston did not have a commercial airport. Thus, when suit is filed in a geographically large or otherwise diverse district, intra-district, interdivisional transfer under Section 1404(a) should be considered.

---

## Checkpoints

- Can you describe when a court should grant a motion to transfer venue under Section 1404(a)?
- Can you explain why a motion to transfer venue under Section 1404(a) is best not viewed as a Rule 12(b)(3) motion?
- Can you list the showings that a party seeking to transfer a case must make?

# Chapter 40

# Special Venue Issues

---

### Special Venue Issues Roadmap

This chapter examines the impact of forum selection clauses on venue, and explores the doctrine of forum *non conveniens*.

---

This chapter addresses a number of special issues that can arise when addressing either whether venue is proper, or whether to transfer to a more convenient venue under Section 1404(a).

## A. The Impact of Forum Selection Clauses

### 1. Enforceability and Interpretation

It is common for commercial contracts to include forum selection clauses that specify where a suit over breach of the agreement must be filed. In *Bremen v. Zapata*, 407 U.S. 1, 15 (1972) the court reversed long-standing judicial hostility to such clauses and instead held that they should be enforced unless doing so "would be unreasonable or unjust" or that "the clause was invalid for such reasons as fraud or over-reaching." Even "boilerplate" clauses in consumer contracts have been upheld. This issue is explored in several casebooks.

Sometimes the clauses are unenforceable, however. For example, in *Jones v. GNC Franchising, Inc.*, 211 F.3d 495 (9th Cir. 2000), a franchisee sued the franchisor in California, where the franchise was located. The franchisor moved to dismiss or transfer under Section 1406(a) or to transfer under Section 1404(a), basing its argument in part upon a clause in the franchise agreement requiring suits be filed in Pennsylvania "and the parties waive all questions of personal jurisdiction or venue for the purpose of carrying out this provision." The district court denied the motion to dismiss, and also the motion to transfer, and stated that the clause was unenforceable under California's public policy against forum selection clauses. The Ninth Circuit affirmed because California had adopted a statute that stated that any provision in a franchise agreement precluding the filing of claims in California was void as against public policy. Because the policy was codified, the court held the clause was unenforceable.

But enforceability of the clause normally is not the issue: interpretation is. The contract may be enforceable but yet cover the claim in the suit. Just because I agree to litigate disputes over a cruise line with the company in Florida doesn't mean I have agreed to litigate a claim that arose when one of their employees happened to crash into my car while I was headed to the dock to board the ship. It is important for counsel to look closely at the language of the forum selection clause to determine if the clause requires the particular claim to be litigated in the designated forum. *See Hodgson v. Gilmartin,* 2006 WL 2707397 (E.D. Pa. 2006) (discussing various interpretive issues that accompany forum selection clauses).

## 2. Interplay Between Forum Selection Clauses and Rule 12(b)(3)

Suppose plaintiff files suit in a venue in violation of a forum selection clause. Must the defendant file a Rule 12(b)(3) motion or include an objection to improper venue in its answer or an amendment thereto, in order to have the court enforce the clause?

Until very recently, there was no clear answer to that question. However, in 2013 the Supreme Court held that whether venue is proper, or not, is determined by the venue statutes (primarily Section 1391). The Court held that "[w]hether the parties entered into a contract containing a forum-selection clause has no bearing on whether a case falls into one of the categories of cases listed in § 1391(b). As a result, a case filed in a district that falls within § 1391 may not be dismissed under § 1406(a) or Rule 12(b)(3)." *Atlantic Marine Const. Co., Inc. v. U.S. Dist. Court for Western Dist. of Texas,* 134 S.Ct. 568 (2014). Instead, a party enforces a forum selection clause through a motion to transfer venue under Section 1404. However, absent "extraordinary circumstances" the clause should be enforced. Further, the Court stated that the analysis under Section 1404 is changed in three fundamental ways:

- the plaintiff's choice of forum merits no weight, but because it is defying the forum-selection clause, it must establish "that transfer to the forum for which the parties bargained is unwarranted";
- the court should not consider the parties' private interests because when "parties agree to a forum-selection clause, they waive the right to challenge the preselected forum as inconvenient or less convenient for themselves or their witnesses, or for their pursuit of the litigation"; and

- the district court that decides the case—whether it is transferred or not—should apply the choice of law principles of the parties' selected state.

To sum up, a party who files suit in violation of a forum selection clause will have a hard time making his choice of forum stick. Finally, if suit is filed in federal court in violation of a clause that specifies that any dispute must be heard in state court, or in a foreign country, the Court in *Atlantic Marine* stated that a district court should address what to do in light of the doctrine of forum *non conveniens*, discussed next.

# B. Forum *Non Conveniens*

Forum *non conveniens* (often called just "forum *non*") is a narrow exception to the principle that if personal and subject matter jurisdiction and venue are proper and there is no more convenient forum, the district court where the suit is filed *must* hear the case.

## 1. International Application of Forum *Non*

The circumstances that can lead to application of forum *non* arise when the dispute has international elements. So, for example in *Piper Aircraft Co. v. Reyno,* 454 U.S. 235 (1981), a small airliner crashed in Scotland during a flight between foreign destinations. Suit was filed on behalf of several people killed on the flight, all Scottish citizens, in California against the aircraft manufacturer even though a related proceeding and various administrative investigations had occurred and were occurring in the United Kingdom. Some of those proceedings involved parties over whom a U.S. court could not get personal jurisdiction. Eventually the case was transferred to the Middle District of Pennsylvania under Section 1404(a).

At that point, the defendants moved to dismiss on the basis of forum *non conveniens*. The district court granted the motion; the appellate court reversed; the Supreme Court reversed the appellate court, holding that the district court had not abused its discretion in dismissing the case because it considered the various public and private factors that dismissal, compared to keeping the case, would create.

In more recent years, courts have created a process for addressing motions to dismiss for forum *non. E.g., Yavuz v. 61 MM, Ltd.,* 465 F.3d 418 (10th Cir. 2006). A federal court has discretion to dismiss a case when there is an alternative "adequate" forum to hear the case, trial in the current forum would be oppressive and vexatious out of all proportion to the convenience of the forum to the plaintiff or because the forum is inappropriate because of "considerations affecting the court's own administrative and legal problems." *Sinochem Int'l Co. Ltd. v. Malaysia Int'l Shipping Corp.*, 127 S.Ct. 1184, 1190 (2007).

An available forum is one that would have subject matter jurisdiction over the claim, and personal jurisdiction over the parties. *Alpine View Co. v. Atlas Copco AB*, 205 F.3d 208, 221 (5th Cir. 2000). A forum is "adequate" if it is one in which "differences in that forum's laws would not deprive the plaintiff of all remedies or result in unfair treatment." *Empresa Lineas Maritamas Argentinas, S.A. v. Schichau-Unterweser A.G.*, 955 F.2d 368, 372 (5th Cir. 1992). A forum is still "adequate" even if the plaintiff's claim would not be economically viable to bring because the foreign jurisdiction's law would provide less of a remedy. *Gonzalez v. Chrysler Corp.*, 301 F.3d 377, 383 (5th Cir. 2002).

If there is an adequate, available forum, then a variety of private and public factors influence the court's decision to determine whether to dismiss. The private factors include: (1) relative ease of access to sources of proof; (2) availability of compulsory process to compel attendance of witnesses at trial or deposition; (3) cost of obtaining attendance of non-willing non-party witnesses; (4) possibility of a view of the premises, if any and if appropriate; and (5) all other practical problems that make trial easier, more expeditious, or less expensive in one place or the other. *Baumgart v. Fairchild Aircraft Corp.*, 981 F.2d 824, 835 (5th Cir. 1993). If these private factors show that dismissal is proper, then the court should dismiss without proceeding further; however, if they do not support dismissal, then the court must consider whether the public interest factors weigh in favor of dismissal. *Id.* The public factors include: (1) administrative difficulties faced by courts with crowded dockets which can be exacerbated by cases not being filed where they arose; (2) the burden on jury duty of members of a community with no connection to the dispute or, perhaps, the parties; (3) the interest of the foreign venue of having local disputes decided at home; and (4) the fact that a foreign court will be more familiar with foreign law than will a court in the United States. *See Duha*, 448 F.3d at 872.

## 2. Narrow Domestic Application of Forum *Non*

Forum *non* generally does not apply in federal court where there is a district in the United States where venue is proper. "For the federal-court system, Congress has codified the doctrine and has provided for transfer, rather than dismissal, when sister federal court is the more convenient place for trial of the action." *Sinochem*, 127 S. Ct. at 1190 (citing 28 U.S.C. §§ 1404 and 1406). However, as noted above, the *Atlantic Marine* court held that if parties in a forum selection clause specify that any dispute must be filed either a state court in the United States or in a foreign tribunal, then a court may dismiss the action under the doctrine of forum *non.*

## 3. Appellate Review

A decision to dismiss under forum *non* is reviewed for abuse of discretion. *See Duha v. Agrium, Inc.,* 448 F.3d 867 (6th Cir. 2006). Finally, as with all aspects of venue, forum *non* is determined on a claim-by-claim basis, not on the basis of what the "dispute" is about. *Id.*

## 4. Waiver of Forum *Non*

A party must make a motion to dismiss based upon forum *non* "within a reasonable time after the facts or circumstances which serve as the basis for the motion have developed and become known or reasonably knowable" to it. *In re Air Crash Disaster Near New Orleans, La.,* 821 F.2d 1147, 1165 (5th Cir. 1987) (*en banc*), *vacated on other grounds sub nom., Pan Am. World Airways, Inc. v. Lopez,* 490 U.S. 1032 (1989).

# C. Venue in Removed Actions

Specific rules govern venue in removed actions, discussed in Chapter 10.

---

### Checkpoints

- Can you explain when forum selection clauses will be enforced?
- Can you explain how a party seeking to enforce a choice of venue specified in a forum selection clause can raise the issue?
- Can you describe the doctrine of forum *non conveniens*?

# Chapter 41

# Amending Pleadings

---

### Amending Pleadings Roadmap

This chapter explains when a party has a right to amend a pleading, and what standards govern a court's decision to grant an amendment once that right has expired.

This chapter also explains how to determine whether a claim added by an amended pleading "relates back" to an earlier time, and when relation back matters.

---

We'll see in the next chapter that in almost all federal litigation a scheduling order will control whether a party may amend a pleading. Nonetheless, there are two reasons to study the rules that apply only if there is no scheduling order: first, a few cases don't have scheduling orders that have deadlines for amending and, second, the standards that apply under a scheduling order are influenced by and in some circumstances are the same standards that apply without a scheduling order. In other words, you need to know both.

## A. The General Rule Regarding Amendment of Pleadings in Rule 15(a)

At the outset, note that the discussion here is limited to "pleadings." "Pleadings" is a term of art, limited to those papers identified as pleadings in Rule 7(a).

Why the need to amend? Suppose a party files a pleading but later realizes it forgot something: a plaintiff asserting a duty to rescue claim fails, for example, to allege facts showing that the claim falls into an exception to the general rule that there is no duty to rescue. Or, the plaintiff omits a claim that the facts also presented. Or, in the defendant's answer, the defendant fails to include an objection to personal jurisdiction, venue, or the sufficiency of service of process (and it did not make a pre-answer motion).

The Rules provide both a limited but unfettered right to amend a pleading and also, if the opposing party will not agree to allow an amendment, the right to move the court for leave to file an amended pleading.

## 1. The Right to Amend

Rule 15(a) creates two separate windows giving an unfettered right to amend one time: "A party may amend its pleading once as a matter of course: (A) 21 days after serving it, or (B) if the pleading is one to which a responsive pleading is required, 21 days after service of a responsive pleading or 21 days after service of a motion under Rule 12(b), (e), or (f)." Thus, a party has at least 21 days to serve and file an amended pleading—even if the other party files its responsive pleading or files a motion under Rule 12.

This is a recent amendment and a significant change from prior practice. As now structured, the rule gives a party 21 days to amend its pleading even after a Rule 12 motion is served, giving a plaintiff, for example, a significant incentive to review the sufficiency of its complaint if the defendant moves to dismiss under Rule 12. Note that Rule 15 applies to *all* pleadings, not just complaints.

## 2. Agreement From the Opposing Parties

As next shown, the law encourages courts to permit amendment. Consequently, often opposing parties will agree to an amendment even if the time to amend as of right has passed, particularly if the request to amend occurs before much discovery or other action has occurred.

## 3. Moving for Leave to Amend

### a. Rule 15(a)(2): The General Rule

The general rule governing amendments of pleadings is Rule 15(a)(2): Courts "should freely give leave when justice so requires." Courts have interpreted the Rule to be strongly biased toward allowing amendment, since denying the amendment means that the merits of the dispute will not be reached. The leading case emphasized:

> Rule 15(a) declares that leave to amend 'shall be freely given when justice so requires'; this mandate is to be heeded. If the underlying facts or circumstances relied upon by a plaintiff may be a proper subject of relief, he ought to be afforded an opportunity to test his claim on the merits. In the absence of any apparent or declared reason—such as

undue delay, bad faith or dilatory motive on the part of the movant, repeated failure to cure deficiencies by amendments previously allowed, undue prejudice to the opposing party by virtue of allowance of the amendment, futility of amendment, etc. — the leave sought should, as the rules require, be 'freely given.' Of course, the grant or denial of an opportunity to amend is within the discretion of the District Court, but outright refusal to grant the leave without any justifying reason appearing for the denial is not an exercise of discretion; it is merely abuse of that discretion and inconsistent with the spirit of the Federal Rules.

*Foman v. Davis*, 371 U.S. 178, 182 (1962). Delay, alone, is insufficient to deny amendment. *Id. See Laber v. Harvey*, 438 F.2d 404, 427 (4th Cir. 2006) (analyzing amendment offered after judgment had been entered).

What more, or besides, delay is sufficient to deny leave to amend a pleading?

**Futility.** An amendment is usually deemed to be futile because the claim the party seeks to add by the amendment is time-barred, *Bonerb v. Richard J. Caron Found.*, 159 F.R.D. 16, 18 (W.D.N.Y.1994), or the amendment does not cure the defect in the existing pleading, *Shell Oil Co. v. Aetna Casualty & Sur. Co.*, 158 F.R.D. 395, 403 (N.D. Ill.1994), or on its face the new claim in the proposed pleading fails to state a claim upon which relief can be granted, *see Clark v. Exxon Corp.*, 159 F.R.D. 26, 28 (M.D. La. 1994).

**Prejudice From Delay.** "A common example of a prejudicial amendment is one that raises a new legal theory that would require the gathering and analysis of facts not already considered by [the defendant, and] is offered shortly before or during trial." *Johnson v. Oroweat Foods Co.*, 785 F.2d 503, 509 (4th Cir. 1986). In contrast, if the amendment merely adds an additional legal theory to the facts already pled, or is offered before any discovery has occurred, prejudice is unlikely to arise. *Laber v. Harvey*, 438 F.2d 404, 427 (4th Cir. 2006).

**Prior Failures to Cure a Pleading Defect.** If a court grants leave for a party to cure a deficient pleading, but the party fails to properly amend the pleading, a subsequent request for leave to amend can be denied. *Glaser v. Enzo Biochem, Inc.*, 464 F.3d 474 (4th Cir. 2006) (affirming denial of motion for leave to amend where the plaintiff had been given four prior chances to correct its complaint).

**Evidentiary Prejudice.** Prejudice to the opposing party in the form of lost evidence or faded memories can be sufficient to deny amendment. A common example is evidentiary prejudice: "Undue prejudice is not mere harm to the non-movant but a denial of the opportunity to present facts or evidence which would have [been] offered had the amendments been timely." *Dove v. Wash. Area Metro. Transit Auth.*, 221 F.R.D. 246, 248 (D. D.C. 2004). Other examples of sufficient prejudice include where the proposed amendment will alter, late in litigation, the opposing party's strategy or choice of counsel. *See Atchinson v. Dist. of Columbia*, 73 F.3d 418, 427 (D.C. Cir. 1996) (indicating that "the district court's concerns regarding [the non-movant's] choice of counsel and litigation strategy seem well-founded").

**Other Forms of Prejudice.** Prejudice to both parties was at issue in *Beeck v. Aquaslide 'n' Dive Corp.*, 562 F.2d 537 (8th Cir. 1977), where the plaintiff had been injured in an accident on a pool slide. The plaintiff investigated and sued the company that apparently made the slide, Aquaslide. Based upon its own investigation, in its answer Aquaslide admitted that it had manufactured the slide. However, after a more complete investigation later, Aquaslide realized that it had not manufactured the slide, and so sought to amend its answer to change its admission to a denial. The plaintiff argued that it would be prejudiced because the statute of limitations had run against the proper defendant. The district court permitted the amendment. The appellate court found no abuse of discretion, agreeing with the district court that there had been no bad faith by the defendant to deny it the right to contest the question of whether it had, in fact, made the slide. The appellate court emphasized that the defendant would be prejudiced without the amendment — it would not be able to contest the issue of who made the slide — and the plaintiff had not established that it could not still sue the actual manufacturer of the slide.

# B. The Procedure to Amend a Pleading

A party with the right to amend simply files the amended pleading and serves it on the other parties. If the opposing parties agree to the amendment, then the party seeking to amend simply files an unopposed motion to amend the pleading (including a certification that the other parties have agreed to allow the amendment) along with a copy of the amended pleading, and serves those papers on the other parties.

If there is no agreement or right to amend, then the process is only slightly more involved. A party generally files a motion for leave to amend the pleading in which it argues why the amendment ought to be granted, attaching the proposed amended pleading as an exhibit to the motion. The party must include a certificate of conference in the motion explaining that the issue could not be resolved among counsel. If the motion is granted (after the other side gets its opportunity to respond to the motion, *see* Chapter 28), then the party must file and serve the amended pleading.

# C.  The Other Parties' Right to Respond if Amendment is Permitted

Suppose a plaintiff files an amended complaint after receiving leave of court. What then? The last sentence of Rule 15(a)(3) provides a partial answer: "Unless the court orders otherwise, any required response to an amended pleading must be made within the time remaining to respond to the original pleading or within 14 days after service of the amended pleading, whichever is later." Does this permit a defendant, for example, in response to an amended complaint, to raise counterclaims that it had omitted, or defenses that it had not raised in its original answer, or is a party limited in its to responding only to the new material introduced in the other party's amended pleading? There is no clear answer:

> Under the permissive view, a party is entitled to amend its answer once as of right upon the plaintiff's filing of an amended complaint. The philosophy underlying this approach appears to be that plaintiffs amend their complaint at their peril, opening themselves up to any and all counterclaims [the defendants] choose to assert. The permissive approach has been justified by reference to the "liberal standard for the amendment of pleadings" under Rule 15(a) . . .
>
> By contrast, courts that have adopted the narrow approach, generally hold that a party is only entitled to respond as of right to an amended complaint if its answer is strictly confined to the new issues raised by the amended complaint.
>
> To complete this exercise in triangulation, some courts have adopted the moderate view as a "third way" of approaching the Rule 15(a) dilemma. These courts agree with those taking the narrow view that Rule 15(a)'s "in response" language limits the ability of defendants to assert counterclaims. Moderate courts differ by concluding that this language only limits the breadth of the changes allowed in an amended response to the breadth of the changes made in the amended complaint. Thus, there is no requirement that a defendant specifically tailor its answer to the amended complaint; rather, moderate courts attempt to discern whether the defendant's answer affects the scope of the litigation in a manner commensurate with the amended complaint. . . . [T]he moderate approach is premised on a notion of equity that, if the plaintiff expands its case by adding new theories or claims, it cannot complain if the defendant seeks to do the same by averring new counterclaims.

*So. New England Tel. Co. v. Global NAPS, Inc.,* 2007 WL 521162 (D. Conn. 2007). This split in approach remains the law.

# D. Rule 15(c) Relation Back of an Otherwise Time-Barred Claim

The interplay between the statute of limitations and amended pleadings creates a somewhat complex problem which is addressed by Rule 15(c). Suppose a complaint is filed within the statute of limitations, but after the statute has run it is amended to add a new claim: should the new claim be treated as if it filing date of the original complaint, or only the later filing date of the amended complaint? If the former, it is timely; if the latter, it is barred by the statute of limitations. Be clear: This is an issue only where (a) the amended pleading adds a new claim and (b) that claim is time-barred by a statute of limitations if given the filing date of the amended pleading, but is not time-barred if given the benefit of the filing date of the pleading which is sought to be amended. Thus, the *only* fact pattern that implicates relation back is this:

TIME

Pleading Filed    Statute Runs    New Claim Added by Amendment

Typically, the issue of relation back is litigated when a plaintiff moves for leave to amend its complaint to add a new claim; in opposition to the motion to amend, the defendant contends the claim does not relate back, and so permitting the filing of the amended complaint is "futile" and so the motion to amend should be denied.

## 1. Rule 15(c)(1): The Rule Governing Relation Back

Rule 15(c)(1) creates three separate rules covering different circumstances by providing that an amendment "relates back to the date of the original pleading when:

(1) **When an Amendment Relates Back.** An amendment to a pleading relates back to the date of the original pleading when:

(A) the law that provides the applicable statute of limitations allows relation back;

(B) the amendment asserts a claim or defense that arose out of the conduct, transaction, or occurrence set out — or attempted to be set out — in the original pleading; or

(C) the amendment changes the party or the naming of the party against whom a claim is asserted, if Rule 15(c)(1)(B) is satisfied and if, within the period provided by Rule 4(m) for serving the summons and complaint, the party to be brought in by amendment:
   (i) received such notice of the action that it will not be prejudiced in defending on the merits; and
   (ii) knew or should have known that the action would have been brought against it, but for a mistake concerning the proper party's identity.

### a. Relation Back Under Rule 15(c)(1)(A)

If a statute specifically provides that the claim relates back, then it does. Such statutes are not common.

### b. Relation Back Under Rule 15(c)(1)(B)

Rule 15(c)(1)(B) is the most common basis for disputes over whether a claim relates back, since it involves only the addition of a new claim, not the addition of a new party. (Note that Rule 15(c)(1)(B) controls when a new claim is asserted against an existing party; Rule 15(c)(1)(C) applies when a new party is added or the name of an existing party is changed.) Under this Rule, a claim relates back if it "arose out of the conduct, transaction, or occurrence" in the pleading that is being amended.

The focus is on whether the factual circumstances alleged in the unamended pleading gave the opposing party notice of the facts underlying the newly-asserted claim. The "critical issue in Rule 15(c) determinations is whether the original complaint gave notice to the defendant of the claim now being asserted." *Moore v. Baker,* 929 F.2d 1129, 1131 (11th Cir. 1993). As stated in *Tri-Ex Enterprises, Inc. v. Morgan Guaranty Trust Co.,* 586 F. Supp. 930, 932 (S.D.N.Y. 1984):

> [T]he relation back doctrine is based upon the principle that one who has been given notice of litigation concerning a given transaction or occurrence has been provided with all the protection that statutes of limitation are designed to afford. Thus, if the litigant has been advised at the outset of the general facts from which the belatedly asserted claim arises, the amendment will relate back even though the statute of limitations may have run in the interim.

Thus, to determine whether a claim relates back, the allegations used to support to the newly asserted claim should be compared to the allegations used to support to the original claim: if they arise out of the same set of circumstances, the claim relates back.

So, for example, in *Bonerb v. Richard J. Caron Found.,* 159 F.R.D. 16 (W.D.N.Y. 1994), the original complaint alleged that plaintiff was injured when he slipped and fell on a wet, muddy basketball court "while participating in a mandatory exercise program . . ." at defendant's rehabilitation facility and the proposed amendment alleged that plaintiff "was caused to fall while playing in an outdoor basketball court . . . in an exercise program mandated as part of his treatment in the rehabilitation program . . ." and that "the rehabilitation and counseling care rendered . . . was negligently, carelessly and unskillfully performed." The court held that the claim related back even though the duties breached were distinct because both claims arose from "the injury suffered by plaintiff on November 29, 1991," which was the focus of the original pleading.

In contrast, however, if the claim arises out of a different set of circumstances, then it does not relate back. So, for example, in *Moore v. Baker,* the plaintiff's original complaint alleged that the defendant doctor had breached a statutory obligation to advise the patient of alternative therapy before conducting an operation that went awry. The complaint, therefore, focused on the events that occurred *before* the operation. After discovery and even after the defendant had moved for summary judgment, the plaintiff moved to amend the complaint to assert a claim that the operation had itself been conducted negligently. The district court held the amendment did not relate back, and the Eleventh Circuit affirmed:

> the allegations asserted in [the plaintiff's] original complaint contain nothing to put [the defendant] on notice that the new claims of negligence might be asserted. Even when given a liberal construction, there is nothing in [the plaintiff's] original complaint which makes reference to any acts of alleged negligence by [the defendant] either during or after surgery. The original complaint focuses on [the defendant's] actions before [the plaintiff] decided to undergo surgery, but the amended complaint focuses on [the defendant's] actions during and after the surgery. The alleged acts of negligence occurred at different times and involved separate and distinct conduct. In order to recover on the negligence claim contained in her amended complaint, [the plaintiff] would have to prove completely different facts than would otherwise have been required to recover on the informed consent claim in the original complaint.

*Moore,* 989 F.2d at 1132.

Likewise, in *Marsh v. Coleman Co.,* 774 F. Supp. 608 (D. Kan. 1991), the plaintiff initially filed breach of contract and age discrimination claims against his former employer arising out of his termination in 1988. Later, he sought to amend to add a fraud claimed arising out of statements made to him by his employer in 1985. The court held that the fraud claim did not relate back because the original complaint made no mention of any events in 1985, and so was "based on conduct substantially different in kind and time" from the 1988 termination.

A decision under Rule 15(c)(3) is reviewed *de novo*, with no deference to the district court's decision. *Slayton v. Am. Exp. Co.*, 460 F.3d 215, 227 (2d Cir. 2006). This is because an appellate court is in as good a position as the trial court to determine whether the new claim arose out of the same circumstances as those alleged in the original pleading.

### c. Relation Back Under Rule 15(c)(1)(C)

### i. Changing the Defendant or Defendant's Name

Rule 15(c)(1)(C) is the more problematic subsection of Rule 15(c), since it allows the party to change the identity of the party being sued. Rule 15(c)(1)(C) requires that:

(1) the claim arise out of the same transaction or occurrence as the original pleading;

(2) the party to be added had, within 120 days of the filing of the original pleading, received notice of the suit such that the party "will not be prejudiced in defending on the merits"; and

(3) the party to be added "knew or should have known that the action would have been brought against it, but for a mistake concerning the proper party's identity."

The analysis under the first step is the same as above.

In determining whether a defendant received notice such that it will not be prejudiced in defending the suit on the merits, the easy cases are those in which the right defendant is served, but its name is misspelled. This type of "mistake" relates back. *Edwards v. Occidental Chem. Corp.*, 892 F.2d 1442, 1446 (9th Cir. 1990). In those cases, the defendant likely had notice and was not prejudiced and should have known of the mistake if it was simply a typographical error.

More difficult are those cases in which the wrong party was named as a defendant. *See Braud v. Transp. Serv. Co. of Ill.*, 445 F.3d 801, 806 n. 12 (5th Cir. 2006) (explaining that if a different person or corporation is added, rather than merely fixing a typographical error, then the amending party must satisfy all elements of Rule 15(c)(1)(C)). In such cases, in addition to satisfying the first prong, the question of both "notice" and of whether the new defendant will have been prejudiced must be addressed. *Brink v. First Credit Resources*, 57 F. Supp. 2d 848 (D. Ariz. 1999).

In *Brink*, for example, the plaintiff initially sued a company for alleging violating the Fair Debt Collection Practices Act. After limitations had run on his claims, he sought to amend the complaint to (1) change the name of the corporate defendant and (2) add as defendant two individuals who were officers of that corporate defendant. The court explained that "notice" in terms of the second requirement can be either actual or constructive. *Id.* If the new defendant has an "identity of interest" with a named defendant, knowledge of the suit will be imputed from the named defendant to the new one. *Id.* Thus, for example, if a person owns all of the shares of a corporation, knowledge to the corporation is knowledge to that person for purposes of Rule 15(c)(1)(C). *Id.*

Other courts have likewise noted that constructive notice can arise in at least two ways:

(a) the "shared attorney" method, in which the plaintiff shows that "there was some communication or relationship" between the attorney for the named defendant and the proposed one before the 120 day period expired; *or*

(b) the "identity of interest" method, which requires the plaintiff demonstrate that the named defendant and the proposed one "are so closely related in business or other activities that it is fair to presume the added parties learned of the institution of the action shortly after it was commenced," such as when the unnamed defendant is a company that is closely related to, or is an officer or director of, the named defendant and has close connections to it.

*See Markhorst v. Rigid, Inc.,* 2007 WL 958604 (E.D. Pa. 2007). In addition, if the potential defendant misleads a plaintiff into thinking that the named party is the proper defendant, the unnamed defendant can be held to have had constructive notice or be estopped from denying that it had no notice. *See id.* If the newly named defendant was notified of the suit at the same time as the original defendant, then it is unlikely it will be able to show prejudice since it will have had the same amount of time to prepare its case as the original defendant. *Brink,* 57 F. Supp. 2d at 851.

Finally, the third prong "permits an amendment to relate back only where there has been an error made concerning the identity of the proper party and where that party is chargeable with knowledge of the mistake, but it does not permit relation back where ... there is a lack of knowledge of the proper party." *Wood v. Worachek,* 618 F.2d 1225, 1229 (7th Cir. 1980). A "mistake concerning the identity of the proper party" does not apply where the plaintiff simply lacks knowledge of the proper defendant. *Hall v. Norfolk So. Ry. Co.,* 469 F.3d 590, 595 (7th Cir. 2006).

## ii. Changing the Plaintiff

Read literally, Rule 15(c)(1)(C) permits amendment only changing the person against whom the claim is asserted, not the party asserting the claim. Nonetheless, under some circumstances an amendment can change the plaintiff and Rule 15(c)(3) will permit relation back of the claim. *See, e.g., Penn Millers Ins. Co. v. U.S.,* 472 F. Supp. 2d 705 (E.D. N.C. 2007). Although the law governing whether a new plaintiff's claim can be said to relate back is less developed than when the change is as to a defendant, *see Cliff v. Payco Gen'l Am. Credits, Inc.,* 363 F.3d 1113, 1131–32 (11th Cir. 2004), courts apply a different test to the question. One test is:

> Where a new plaintiff is added or substituted, the same conduct, trans-action, or occurrence originally alleged as a basis for the action must be relied upon by the substituted plaintiff. Moreover, (1) there must be a sufficient identity of interest between the new plaintiff, the old plaintiff, and their respective claims so that the defendant can be said to have received adequate notice of the latecomer's claim against the defendant so as to avoid prejudice; and (2) the defendant must have known or should have known that the new plaintiff would have brought the action against it but for a mistake concerning the identity of the proper party.

*Penn Millers,* 472 F. Supp. 2d at 715 (collecting cases). Note, however, that this "is not an open invitation to every plaintiff whose claim otherwise would be time-barred to salvage it by joining an earlier-filed action." *Young v. Lepone,* 305 F.3d 1, 14 (1st Cir. 2002).

The standard of review of decisions under Rule 15(c)(1)(C) is abuse of discretion because the district court is required "to exercise its discretion in deciding whether the circumstances of a given case are such that it would be unfair to permit the plaintiff to add a new defendant." *Percy v. San Francisco Gen. Hosp.,* 841 F.2d 975, 978 (9th Cir. 1988).

## 2. How the Question of Relation Back is Typically Litigated

It is settled that "an amendment which seeks to include time-barred claims is futile." *Aequitron Medical, Inc. v. CBS, Inc.,* 1994 WL 414361 at *2 (S.D.N.Y. Aug. 5, 1994). Thus, if a party moves for leave to amend to add a time-barred claim, the other party can oppose the amendment because permitting it would be "futile" under *Foman v. Davis. See id.* Accordingly, even though leave to amend normally must be freely given, if the claim does not relate back, then allowing the amendment would be futile, and so should be denied.

Finally, note that even if a claim relates back, the court must still consider whether allowing the amendment is proper under Rule 15(a). Simply because the claim relates back does not mean that the amendment must be allowed. It means only that the amendment is not futile—there could still be other reasons to deny leave to amend.

---

### Checkpoints

- Can you identify the three standards for amending a pleading that apply at different times?
- Can you describe when a court can properly deny leave to amend a pleading?
- Can you describe when relation back of a claim matters? How to determine whether a claim relates back, or not? The impact of that decision?

# Chapter 42

# Lawyer Responsibility for and Judicial Involvement in Case Management

In recent decades the Rules were amended to increase both the responsibility of counsel to cooperate and judicial involvement in managing litigation. Three Rules, in particular, are standouts: (1) Rule 26(f)'s requirement of an initial conference and the court's issuance of a scheduling order under Rule 16(b); (2) Rule 26(a)(2)'s requirement of the disclosure of expert reports and information; and (3) the requirement in Rule 26(a)(3) and Rule 16(e) of the preparation and submission of the final pretrial order.

First, lawyers are required to confer about the scope of discovery, timing of trial, and various other issues promptly after the defendant responds to the complaint and to prepare and file a report with the district court. After receiving the parties' report, the district court issues a scheduling order that establishes deadlines for amending pleadings, conducting discovery, submitting dispositive motions, and other actions. The passing of a deadline makes it more difficult for a party who misses one to amend a pleading or otherwise take action.

Second, the Rules require lawyers to disclose the identity of experts and to have certain experts prepare reports prior to being deposed. We'll see that a party who fails to timely disclose an expert and have a report prepared may have a difficult time overcoming their tardiness.

Finally, third, about a month before trial the parties are required to work together to prepare and submit the final pretrial order. And, again, we will see that a party who seeks to make a change to the pretrial order, while not completely precluded from doing so, nonetheless must jump over a higher hurdle.

The chart below brings these three requirements together in one place as a preview. Notice that a party who misses a deadline in a *scheduling* order has an easier time overcoming their tardiness than does a party who seeks to amend the *final pretrial* order. The hurdles are not impossible to clear, but the bar grows higher as the case progresses.

| Obligation | Source | Substance | To alter or amend after deadline has passed |
|---|---|---|---|
| Meet and Prepare Scheduling Order | 26(f) & 16(b) | Although it varies by local rule and practice, often the scheduling order establishes deadlines for amending pleadings, taking discovery, and filing dispositive motions, such as summary judgment motions. | Party seeking to amend must show "good cause" under Rule 16(b) and, to amend pleading, also meet Rule 15(a). |
| Make Expert Disclosures | 26(a)(2) | Identity of experts who may be used to testify, along with reports from certain experts, must be made 90 days before trial or as per scheduling order. | The party seeking to use information not properly disclosed must show that the nondisclosure was substantially justified. Rule 37(c)(1). |
| Comply with Final Pretrial Order | 26(a)(3) & 16(e) | Witnesses, exhibits, and deposition designations must be made 30 and 14 days before trial or as per scheduling order. | Party seeking to amend must show otherwise "manifest injustice" will result. |

# Chapter 43

# The First Steps After Pleadings Close: Conferences and Required Initial Disclosures

---

### After Pleadings Close Roadmap

This chapter explains how proceed once the pleadings are closed, including the scope of initial disclosures and the preparation of the scheduling order.

---

As we've seen, pleadings no longer play the primary role of identifying all facts that are likely to be relevant and dispositive of the claims or defenses. Instead, they provide only notice of the claims and defenses. The primary way that parties obtain access to information held by the opposing parties, or non-parties, now takes the form of discovery—a process where a party, and sometimes non-parties, must disclose information, but only to a limited extent and only upon proper request.

Although discovery is the principal way, it is not the only way that information beyond the pleadings is obtained from opposing parties. The Rules require each party to voluntarily disclose certain information that a party intends to use at trial, even without a request. This chart summarizes voluntary disclosures:

| What | When | Why | Where in This Book |
|---|---|---|---|
| Initial Disclosures | Near the start of the suit | FRCP 26(a)(1) | This chapter |
| Expert Testimony | About 90 days from trial or as per Rule 16 scheduling order | FRCP 26(a)(2) | Chapter 50 |
| Pretrial Disclosures | About a month from trial or as per Rule 16 scheduling order | FRCP 26(a)(3) | Chapter 53 |

These disclosures take place at separate and specific times during the suit, but Rule 26(a) lumps them together. We'll see each step as we move closer to trial. This chapter describes the first of these, initial disclosures.

## A. Required Initial Disclosures: Each Party Must Show its Best Hand

Discovery, as we will see, is the process by which one party uncovers information known to the other side by sending the other side written questions (called "interrogatories"), asking the other side to produce documents, and to submit to oral questioning at what are known as depositions, among other things. From the Rules' adoption in 1938 until the early 1990s discovery was the only means authorized by the Rules for a party to ascertain the facts known only to another party. There was, essentially, only one phase to the information exchange process of litigation, and that was discovery. It was an adversarial process in which a party had to provide information only if requested by another party.

Just in the last twenty-five years, the Rules added required "initial disclosures." Under the current Rules, parties are required, without request by another party, to produce significant information early in litigation. This chapter focuses principally on what occurs while the parties are waiting for discovery to begin, and how the process of initial disclosures required under Rule 26(a) (1) occurs.

The current approach to required initial disclosures was adopted in 2000, after 7 years of a different rule, under which parties had been required to disclose information that was relevant to any claim or defense, regardless of whether it helped or hurt that party's case. As you can imagine, lawyers construed "relevant" narrowly if the particular information was unfavorable, and broadly if that information was helpful. This led to changing the rule to require disclosure of, generally, all information that a party will use to support its positions.

This pre-discovery phase has a number of steps.

## B. The Parties Agree on a Plan for the Lawsuit at the Rule 26(f) Conference

Once a defendant appears in a case, either by filing a pleading, Rule 12 motion, or motion for summary judgment, the parties' attorneys are required to meet to confer to agree and identify any disagreements on a variety of subjects that will control the timing, scope, and order of the rest of the lawsuit.

## 1. When

The attorneys are required to confer so "as soon as practicable" but at least 21 days before the district court's date for the Rule 16(b) scheduling conference. FRCP 26(f)(1). The latest they can meet thus turns on when the district court sets the time for the scheduling conference under Rule 16(b), which, as amended in 2015, must be as soon as practicable, but no later than the earlier of (a) 90 days after any defendant has been served or (b) 60 days after any defendant has appeared. FRCP 16(b)(2). The 2015 amendments shortened the time in an effort to create earlier judicial involvement in a case and restricted the ability of the district court to delay entry of its Rule 16(b) order. Thus, now a district court has broad power to order the parties to meet more quickly, but it cannot extend the deadline for the Rule 16(b) conference absent good cause. FRCP 26(f)(1); FRCP 16(b)(2). (We'll come back to the Rule 16(b) conference and what results from it later in this chapter.) The attorneys for the parties are jointly required to set up this conference and to attempt in good faith to agree on a plan. FRCP 26(f)(2).

## 2. What

Rule 26(f)(2) requires the attorneys are required to confer (telephonically, in person, or otherwise) to in good faith attempt to agree on the following, and it must state the parties' views on these issues:

(a) The nature and basis of the parties' claims and defenses;

(b) The possibility of settlement or other resolution of the case;

(c) To arrange how to make the required initial disclosures;

(d) To develop a plan to manage discovery, including:

    (1) What if any changes should be made to the various required disclosures (both the initial disclosures and those that come later) and when they will take place;

    (2) The subjects on which discovery may be needed, when it must be completed, and whether it will be conducted in phases or limited to particular issues;

    (3) Any steps that need to be taken concerning preservation, disclosure, or discovery of electronically stored information;

    (4) Any agreement concerning what happens if privileged or work product information is inadvertently produced or disclosed;

    (5) Whether any of the limitations on discovery imposed by the Rules or a local rule of the district court need to be changed or whether other limitations need to be imposed; and

(6) Whether any protective orders under Rule 26(c) are needed, or whether any orders under Rule 16(b) or (c) are needed.

What does this list mean in practical terms? The first two items are designed to achieve broader goals than the others. In part, the goal of the conference is to ensure that the parties have a basic understanding of each other's claims or defenses and that settlement has been discussed. The requirement of paragraph (c) is mechanical: as we'll see, in making the required initial disclosures each party will have to get information and, in many cases, documents to the other party. Paragraph (c) requires that they agree on when and how to do so.

Rule 26(f)(2) and (f)(3) require lawyers to think through, at the outset of the suit, both timing and substantive issues. At the outset of the suit, the lawyer must have thought through, for example, whether she needs more than the 10 depositions allowed by the Rules, or more than the permitted 25 interrogatories. She'll need to know her likely work schedule in other cases (you'll be juggling a docket of cases for various clients; you don't handle one at a time) to know when trial can be set. She'll have to predict roughly how long it will take to conduct discovery, and how much time to prepare any motions for summary judgment. In addition, Rule 26(f)(3)(D) requires the lawyer to think about whether the case will require disclosure of information that may be proprietary or sensitive: if so, the lawyer may need to ask that the parties agree, or the court impose, a "protective order" under Rule 26(c) to limit disclosure of that sensitive information. *See* Chapter 51 for more on protective orders. Electronic discovery must be addressed, including the obligation to preserve it and how it will be produced.

There's a lot to think about and to report on. As a result, some district courts have adopted forms for these reports. Generally they ask a series of questions that force the lawyers to address all of the issues required by the Rule, and others. On the next page is a simplified version of one used in an Ohio district court, which is posted as a pdf file on the court's webpage, which you can find at http://www.ohsd.uscourts.gov/pdf/abreppar.pdf. It's set up so that the lawyers can fill in the blanks, and submit it to the court after signing it. A lot of it relates to dates and deadlines. As we will see, the court or parties use the report to generate a signed Rule 16 scheduling order, which we'll look at next.

It is common for attorneys to agree on most of the basic deadlines and other issues. To the extent they disagree, however, they include in the report a statement of each party's position on the disputed issue so that the district court can resolve the dispute when it enters the scheduling order, which is the major reason a conference is required.

## RULE 26(f) REPORT OF PARTIES

1. Pursuant to F.R.Civ.P. 26(f), a meeting was held on _____ and was attended by:

   _____, counsel for plaintiff _____

   _____, counsel for defendant _____

2. **Initial Disclosures.** The parties:

   ____ have exchanged the initial disclosures required by Rule 26(a)(1);

   ____ will exchange such disclosures by _____

   ____ are exempt from such disclosures under Rule 26(a)(1)(E).

   ____ have agreed not to make initial disclosures.

3. **Jurisdiction and Venue**

   a. Describe any contested issues relating to: (1) subject matter jurisdiction, (2) personal jurisdiction and/or (3) venue: _____

   b. Describe the discovery, if any, that will be necessary to the resolution of issues relating to jurisdiction and venue: _____

   c. Recommended date for filing motions addressing jurisdiction and/or venue: _____

4. **Amendments to Pleadings and/or Joinder of Parties.** Recommended date for filing motion/stipulation to amend the pleadings or to add additional parties:

   _____

5. **Recommended Discovery Plan**

   a. Describe the **subjects** on which discovery is to be sought and the nature and extent of discovery that each party will need: _____

   b. What **changes** should be made, if any, in the limitations on discovery imposed by the Federal Rules of Civil Procedure or the local rules of this Court? _____

   c. The parties recommend that discovery should proceed in **phases**, as follows: _____

   d. Describe the areas in which **expert testimony** is expected and indicate whether each expert will be specially retained within the meaning of F.R.Civ.P.26(a)(2): _____

      i. Recommended date for making **primary expert designations:** _____

      ii. Recommended date for making **rebuttal expert designations:** _____

   e. Recommended **discovery completion date:**

   _____

6. **Dispositive Motion(s).** Recommended date for filing dispositive motions:

   _____

7. **Settlement Discussions**

   a. Has a settlement demand been made? _____ A response? _____

   b. Date by which a settlement demand can be made: _____

   c. Date by which a response can be made: _____

**Signatures:**

Attorney(s) for Plaintiff(s):          Attorney(s) for Defendant(s):

_____          _____

## 3. Why

The parties are required to meet to confer because they must prepare and submit a report to the district court to help the court formulate a scheduling order that will state each major deadline for the lawsuit. If a party fails to participate in good faith "in the development and submission of a proposed discovery plan," the court may order the party or its attorney to "pay to any other party the reasonable expenses, including attorney's fees, caused by the failure." FRCP 37(f).

# B. The Rule 26(f) Conference's Impact on Discovery

Until the 2015 amendments, no discovery could be served prior to the Rule 26(f) conference. Then and now, the parties can exchange their required initial disclosures before the Rule 16(b) conference. Parties then and now must exchange their required initial disclosures within 14 days of the Rule 26(f) conference, unless they agree on another time or during the Rule 26(f) conference a party raises the objection that initial disclosures are not appropriate in the particular case. We'll come back to that.

The 2015 amendments permitted a party to serve requests for production, 21 days after a party has been served, to that party by any other party or by that party on any other plaintiff or party who has also been served. FRCP 26(d)(2). However, the requests are considered to be served only as of the date of the Rule 26(f) conference. *Id.*

As soon as the parties have completed the Rule 26(f) conference then, unless they've agreed otherwise, discovery can commence. FRCP 26(d)(1). Thus, these events — exchange of initial disclosures, holding of the Rule 16(b) conference, and commencement of formal discovery — can occur in different orders, depending on the facts, circumstances, and desires of the parties.

# C. The Rule 16(b) Conference and Order

The first thing a district court faced with a new lawsuit is required to do is receive the parties' Rule 26(f) report and issue a scheduling order under Rule 16(b). That Rule 16(b) scheduling order will set out the critical phases of the entire lawsuit, including when discovery can commence and end, when parties must be joined, and when trial will be held.

A formal conference is not required, and often the court will simply take the dates identified by the parties in their Rule 26(f) report and adopt them in its order. Because most suits, perhaps 95%, resolve without trial, and many without any judicial involvement whatsoever, typically the dates are of little practical importance to the court itself. But, the fact that the court enters an order setting deadlines is important for reasons we'll see in a moment. On the next page, is a real, fairly typical Rule 16(b) scheduling order from a case that a friend of mine litigated recently:

IN THE UNITED STATES DISTRICT COURT
FOR THE SOUTHERN DISTRICT OF TEXAS
HOUSTON DIVISION

| | | |
|---|---|---|
| CENTERPOINT ENERGY HOUSTON, | § | |
| | § | |
| VS. | § | CIVIL ACTION NO. H-04-2037 |
| | § | |
| AT&T WIRELESS SERVICE. | § | HONORABLE JOHN D. RAINEY |

### SCHEDULING ORDER

1. **TRIAL**
   a. Estimated days to try:                    3-4 Days
   b. Trial to be jury or bench:                Jury

2. **MOTION TO JOIN NEW PARTIES OR TO AMEND**
   **PLEADINGS** must be filed by:              Oct. 29, 2004
   Party requesting joinder will furnish a copy
   of this Scheduling Order to new parties.

3. **EXPERT WITNESSES** for **plaintiff** will be
   named and a report furnished by:             Nov. 12, 2004
   **EXPERT WITNESSES** for the **defendant** will be
   named and a report furnished within 30 days
   of the deposition of the plaintiff's last
   expert, but not later than:                  Dec. 31, 2004

4. **DISCOVERY** must be completed by:          Jan. 31, 2005
   Counsel may, by agreement, continue discovery beyond
   the deadline, but there will be no intervention by
   the court; no continuance will be granted because of
   information acquired in post-deadline discovery.

5. **DISPOSITIVE MOTIONS** filed by:            Dec. 31, 2004
   **ALL OTHER MOTIONS** filed by:              Feb. 18, 2005

6. **JOINT PRETRIAL ORDER** is due:             March 18, 2005
   The Plaintiff is responsible for filing the
   Pretrial Order on time. See local rules for
   requirement.

7. **DOCKET CALL** is set for:                  11:00 A.M.
                                                 March 25, 2005

   Case subject to call on short notice during
   the one month period of:                     April 2005

Signed at Houston, Texas this 16 day of September, 2004.

                                    NANCY K. JOHNSON
                                    UNITED STATES MAGISTRATE JUDGE

Attorney Conference must be held by December 31, 2004.

# D. Exchange of Required Initial Disclosures

As noted above, the parties may exchange initial disclosures before or after the Rule 16(b) conference. It simply turns on whether the conference is held before the parties have agreed to make the exchanges.

## 1. Exemptions

Rule 26(a)(1)(B) exempts only certain cases from initial disclosure requirements, and they are not common. It bears emphasizing that one thing does not constitute an exemption: Another party's failure to make initial disclosures does not excuse compliance. In other words, an opposing party's failure to properly make initial disclosures does not justify a tit-for-tat holding back. FRCP 26(a)(1)(E).

## 2. When

Unless the parties agree or the court orders otherwise, the parties must make their initial disclosures within 30 days of the Rule 26(f) conference. FRCP 26(a)(1)(D). If a party is joined to the suit after the Rule 26(f) conference occurred, that party must make its initial disclosures within 30 days after being served or joined, or as agreed, or as ordered by the court. *Id.*

## 3. What: The Good Stuff Reasonably Available to the Party

Four specific categories of information and documents are subject to the initial disclosure requirement. The first two are designed to force each party to disclose the information and documents that will support its claims or defenses—the good stuff, so far as that party is concerned. The second two categories are included to facilitate settlement. The four categories are:

(A) each witness likely to have discoverable information that the disclosing party may use to support its claims or defenses, unless solely for impeachment, identifying the subjects of the information;

(B) documents that the disclosing party may use to support its claims or defenses, unless solely for impeachment;

(C) a computation of damages or documents allowing for a computation to be done; and

(D) any insurance policy that may cover a claim.

FRCP 26(a)(1)(A). The list is fairly straightforward. A party who fails to make a proper initial disclosure can be barred from introducing the evidence at trial, as shown below.

## 4. Supplementation

If after making its initial disclosures, a party learns of information that is covered by Rule 26(a)(1), under some circumstances it must "supplement" its disclosures. FRCP 26(e)(1). Specifically, "in a timely manner," a party must supplement or correct their initial disclosures to include information acquired after the disclosure was made if "ordered to do so or if the party learns that in some material respect the disclosure or response is incomplete or incorrect, *and* if the additional or corrective information has not otherwise been made known to the other parties during the discovery process or in writing." FRCP 26(e)(1). Thus, the obligation to supplement does not arise if the parties have already received the information through discovery or some other written correspondence.

However, if the parties have not received the information and the party fails to supplement its disclosure, then the information that was not timely supplemented can be excluded from evidence, and the court can impose other sanctions under Rule 37(c)(1). Thus, when in doubt, supplement.

## 5. Sanctions and Exclusion From Evidence for Violating the Rule

The teeth of the initial disclosure requirement come from two rules.

First, an attorney or party must sign the required disclosures. FRCP 26(g)(1). The signature certifies that "to the best of the signer's knowledge, information, and belief, formed after a reasonable inquiry, any disclosure is complete and correct as of the time it is made." *Id.* A court may sanction a lawyer or party who, without substantial justification, signs a disclosure that violates that certification. FRCP 26(g)(3).

Second, if a party without substantial justification fails to disclose information covered by Rule 26(a)(1), then "unless the failure was substantially justified or is harmless" the party is prohibited from using that evidence at trial. FRCP 37(c)(1). In addition, other sanctions, including having the court tell the jury what happened, are available. *Id.*

Thus, it is important for a party to timely make required initial disclosures, particularly because initial disclosures largely cover the "good stuff." If a party fails to do so, then it won't be able to use the good stuff at trial unless the failure was substantially justified or the nondisclosure was harmless. As an extreme example of both behavior and sanction, the court in *Advance Financial Corp. v. Utsey*, 2001 WL 102484 (S.D. Ala. 2001), entered a default judgment as a sanction against a plaintiff whose lawyers had failed to make initial disclosures despite repeated orders to do so.

## E.  Amending a Deadline in a Rule 16 Scheduling Order: Good Cause Plus

If the parties have agreed on the dates in the scheduling order, why does it matter if the court enters an order? The answer to that question comes from Rule 16(b)(4): "A schedule may be modified only for good cause and with the judge's consent." That sentence is important for a number of reasons, many of which don't come through in typical civil procedure book.

First, if the scheduling order sets a deadline, that deadline is the one that applies, not the deadline that would apply under another rule. So, for example, under Rule 15(a) a party has the right to amend certain pleadings within a certain number of days. If the court enters a scheduling order, however, then the parties' right to amend ends when the scheduling order says so, not when stated by Rule 15(a).

Second, if a party needs to do something covered by a scheduling order after the deadline for doing so has passed, then the party must establish good cause to modify the order and seek the court's approval. So, for example, a party who wants to amend its pleading after the deadline in the scheduling order has passed must show the court in a motion that there is good cause to move the deadline. To establish good cause, at minimum movant must show that it could not have met the deadline with reasonable diligence. *Grochowski v. Phoenix Constr. Co.*, 318 F.3d 80, 86 (2d Cir. 2003). As a consequence, if the movant knew the facts necessitating the amendment before the deadline, good cause is usually not found. *Parker v. Colombia Pictures Indus.*, 204 F.3d 236, 241 (2d Cir. 2000); *Sosa v. Airprint Sys., Inc.*, 133 F.3d 1417, 1419 (11th Cir. 1998) (Rule 16(b) precludes modification "unless the schedule cannot be met despite the diligence of the party seeking the extension"). Some district courts consider several factors, including "1) the explanation for the failure to move timely for leave to amend; 2) the importance of the amendment; 3) the potential prejudice in allowing the amendment; and 4) the availability of a continuance to cure such prejudice." *Hawthorne Land Co. v. Occidental Chem. Corp.*, 431 F.3d 221, 227 (5th Cir. 2006); *U.S. v. First Nat'l Bank of Circle*, 652 F.2d 882 (9th Cir. 1981) (similar list of factors, and explaining that if denial of modification would result in injustice but allowing it would not substantially injury the other party nor inconvenience the court, the modification should be permitted).

Although general rules are difficult to come by, if the amendment to a pleading, for example, is sought while discovery is still open and does not create the need, for the sake of fairness and completeness, to re-take depositions, courts will generally allow the amendment. *E.g., Liberty Mut. Ins. Co. v. Midwest Cold Storage & Ice Corp.*, 1989 WL 21155 (D. Kan. 1989). This approach reflects the general principle in the Rules to resolve disputes on the merits unless prejudice will arise.

A district court has discretion to deny a motion to modify a scheduling order. *NAS Elecs., Inc. v. Transtech Elecs. Pte Ltd.*, 262 F. Supp. 2d 134, 150 (S.D.N.Y. 2003). Thus, the district court's decision is not likely to be overturned on appeal.

## 1. Amending Pleadings: Good Cause to Amend or Bias To Allow the Amendment?

Requiring a party seeking to amend a scheduling order show good cause is the opposite approach of Rule 15(a), which generally requires amendments to pleadings to be allowed unless the opposing party establishes that the party seeking the amendment acted in bad faith, had a dilatory motive, or there is another similar reason to deny amendment. *See* Chapter 41. So, the mere absence of prejudice, bad faith, futility, or similar factors by the party seeking the amendment is not sufficient to show good cause. *Carnite v. Granada Hosp. Group, Inc.*, 175 F.R.D. 439, 448 (W.D.N.Y. 1997). More is required by Rule 16(b) than Rule 15(a).

Suppose the party seeking amendment establishes good cause. Is that enough, given that Rule 15(a) has its own separate requirement? In other words, does Rule 16 supplant, or supplement, any requirement in Rule 15(a)? Courts hold that Rule 16 supplements showings required in other rules, but does not replace them. Thus, a party who establishes good cause to modify a scheduling order to change the deadline for amending a pleading must *also* establish that leave to amend should be granted under Rule 15(a). *S&W Enterp., L.L.C. v. Southtrust Bank of Alabama, NA*, 315 F.3d 533, 536 (5th Cir. 2003); *Sosa*, 133 F.3d at 1419 ("because Sosa's motion to amend was filed after the scheduling order's deadline, she must first demonstrate good cause under Rule 16(b) before we will consider whether the amendment is proper under Rule 15(a).")." The reason is that if a party could ignore a Rule 16(b) deadline by simply complying with the requirements of the other rule, then the scheduling order adds nothing. *Sosa*, 133 F.3d at 1419.

To sum up, if a party fails to comply with a deadline in a scheduling order, that party must show good cause to modify the scheduling order *and* meet the requirement imposed by any other rule. What this means is that the further into a suit one goes, the harder it is to make changes. We'll see, when we get to the final required disclosure that comes in the form of the Final Pretrial Order, that it becomes even more difficult to make changes because that disclosure occurs just before trial.

Think about the big picture: at the start, it is easy to amend pleadings, but over time it becomes more difficult. In large part this is because, until discovery is underway, there's been little reliance by one party on the other side's disclosures. The further into discovery, and the closer to trial, the greater that reliance has been, and thus the harder it is to change courses.

## Checkpoints

- Can you describe what each party must disclose as part of its "initial disclosures"?
- Can you list what the parties must consider during their Rule 26(f) conference?
- Can you explain the impact of the Rule 16 scheduling order on subsequent action in the case, and on amendment of pleadings?

# Chapter 44

# Adjudication or Resolution of Claims Before Discovery

---

### Adjudication Before Discovery Roadmap

This Chapter identifies the ways that a claim can be adjudicated without discovery, including through default judgment, voluntary dismissal (often because a case settled quickly after filing), involuntary dismissal, pursuant to Rules 12(b)(6), 12(c), or by way of summary judgment.

---

This Chapter shows the common ways claims are resolved without discovery and, often shortly after suit is filed. First, if a party fails to respond to the claims against it, the suit may be subject to entry of default judgment. Second, a party against whom a claim is asserted can contend that the pleading fails to state a claim upon which relief can be granted. (If the plaintiff asserted only one claim in its complaint, this can result in dismissal of the entire suit; if it contains more than one claim is asserted, then this can result in dismissal of a claim, but not the suit.) Third, many cases settle shortly after suit is filed and without much, if any, discovery. Finally, but only in extreme circumstances, a court can strike a party's pleading as a sanction.

## A.  Default Judgments

Rule 55 allows a party to move for entry of default judgment if it has asserted a claim against a party which "has failed to plead or otherwise defend, and that failure is shown by affidavit or otherwise . . ." FRCP 55(a). Rule 55 "tracks the ancient common law axiom that a default is an admission of all well-pleaded allegations against the defaulting party." *Vt. Teddy Bear Co. v. 1-800 Beargram Co.*, 373 F.3d 241, 246 (2d Cir. 2004).

392 · ADJUDICATION OR RESOLUTION OF CLAIMS

# 1. The Three Steps to Obtain a Default Judgment

There are three steps to determine whether entry of default judgment is proper. First, there must be an act of default: a party must have failed to "plead or otherwise defend" against a claim against it. Second, the party seeking default judgment must obtain entry of default. Third, the party seeking default must have default judgment entered. So, for example, if a defendant fails to respond to service of a complaint, the plaintiff may move for entry of default and then seek a default judgment.

It "is important to keep straight default language." *N.Y. Life Ins. Co. v. Brown*, 84 F.3d 137, 141 (5th Cir. 1996). "A *default* occurs when a defendant has failed to plead or otherwise respond to the complaint within the time required by the Federal Rules." *Id.* "An entry of default is what the clerk enters when the default is established by affidavit or otherwise." *Id.* "After defendant's default has been entered, plaintiff may apply for a judgment based on such default. This is a default judgment." *Id.* A party against whom default has been entered may move to set it aside; after default judgment is entered, the party must move to vacate the default judgment.

## a. An Act of Default: The Failure to "Plead or Otherwise Defend"

### i. Failure to Plead

Failing "to plead" means failing to file a pleading that is required to be filed in response to a pleading stating a claim. For example, if a defendant fails to file, that defendant has failed to "plead." Defaults are available against a party who was required to file a responsive pleading, but did not do so (and did not "otherwise defend," which we'll get to next).

While a defendant's failure to answer is the classic example, Rule 7(a) also requires these pleadings (or a Rule 12 motion) be filed in response to other pleadings:

> A plaintiff's reply to a defendant's counterclaim;
> A co-party's failure to file an answer to a crossclaim; and
> A third-party defendant's answer to a third-party complaint.

Thus, a plaintiff, a defendant, a third-party plaintiff, or a party that has asserted a counter- or cross-claim may move for default if the opposing party did not plead or otherwise defend the claim. *See* FRCP 55(a).

### ii. What Constitutes "Failure to Otherwise Defend"?

Default is not authorized if the party against whom it is sought, though failing to file a pleading, nonetheless has "otherwise defended" itself. Failure to "otherwise defend" means the party against whom entry of default is sought failed to take affirmative action sufficient enough to constitute "defending" itself. *Wickstrom v. Ebert*, 101 F.R.D. 26, 33 (E.D. Wis. 1984).

It includes defending the merits. For example, the phrase "otherwise defend" includes making any motion under Rule 12. *Id.* Likewise, it includes a party who moved for summary judgment, instead of answering or filing a pre-answer motion. *See Rashidi v. Albright*, 818 F. Supp. 1354, 1356 (D. Nev. 1993) ("If challenges less strenuous than those pleading to the merits can prevent the entry of default, clearly a summary judgment motion which speaks to the merits of the case and demonstrates a concerted effort and an undeniable desire to contest the action is sufficient to fall within the ambit of 'otherwise defend' for purposes of Fed.R.Civ.P. 55.").

Less merits-oriented conduct has also been held to constitute "otherwise defending." *See de Antonio v. Solomon*, 42 F.R.D. 320 (D.C. Mass. 1967) (denying motion for entry of default because defendant's obligation to plead or otherwise defend was satisfied by his assertion of privilege against self incrimination even though allegations of complaint were not addressed); *Pikofsky v. Jem Oil Co.*, 607 F. Supp. 727, 734 (E.D. Wis. 1985) (filing motion to transfer venue under Section 1404(a)); *N.Y. Life Ins. Co. v. Brown*, 84 F.3d 137, 141 (5th Cir. 1996) (participating in court conferences and simply engaging in conversation and exchanging letters with opposing counsel). Obviously, the less activity by the party against whom entry of default is sought, the more likely it is that the party will not have "otherwise defended" itself.

If a party has failed to plead or otherwise defend, then the party that asserted the claim may move for entry of default. Otherwise, it may not.

## b. Entry of Default and Setting Entry of Default Aside

### i. Entry of Default

If an opposing party has defaulted, the party seeking default judgment can request the clerk of the court to make an "entry of default" on the docket sheet (a list of activities in the case that the clerk keeps which, nowadays, is on-line). *Breuer Elec. Mfg. Co. v. Toronado Sys., Inc.*, 687 F.2d 182, 185 (7th Cir. 1982). Typically, the party asking for entry of default files a notice with the clerk along with an affidavit establishing that the opposing party was served with the pleading but failed to plead or otherwise defend itself. *See* FRCP 55(a). The clerk *must* enter default if the notice establishes that the other party has not plead or otherwise defended. Although the judge can also enter default, the clerk is authorized to do so and action by the judge is not required.

Entry of default cuts off the defendant's right to contest liability on the claims asserted against it. *Greyhound Exhibit Group, Inc. v. E.L.U.L. Realty Corp.*, 973 F.2d 155, 160 (2d Cir. 1992). The right to a jury also ends, unless a statute specifically preserves it. *In re Dierschke*, 975 F.2d 181, 185 (5th Cir. 1992) ("It is universally understood that a default operates as a deemed admission of liability. It is also clear that in a default case neither the plaintiff nor the defendant has a constitutional right to a jury trial on the issue of damages.").

### ii. Setting Aside Entry of Default

A party against whom default is entered may move the court to set it aside. The court may set it aside if the movant shows good cause. FRCP 55(c). The courts interpret "good cause" liberally, and the threshold to set aside entry of default is quite low. *Effjohn Int'l Cruise Holdings, Inc. v. A & L Sales, Inc.*, 346 F.3d 552, 563 (5th Cir. 2003). In deciding whether good cause exists, courts consider whether the moving party has a meritorious defense, whether it acted with reasonable promptness, the personal responsibility of the defaulting party (as opposed to its counsel), the prejudice to the party who obtained entry, whether there was a history of dilatory action, and the availability of sanctions less drastic than default. *Payne v. Brake*, 439 F.3d 198 (4th Cir. 2006). Although there is no express deadline to move to set aside entry of default, the motion must be made with reasonable promptness. *Id.*

### c. Entry of Default Judgment and Vacating Entry

### i. Can the Clerk or Must the Judge Enter Default Judgment?

A party who obtains entry of default then may move for entry of default judgment. A party against whom entry is made may not appeal it. *Ackra Direct Mktg. Corp. v. Fingerhut Corp.*, 86 F.3d 852, 855 (8th Cir. 1996). Unlike entry of default, which can be performed by the clerk, under some circumstances the court must enter default judgment.

The limits on the clerk's authority to enter default judgment are important because if the clerk cannot enter default judgment, then the party against whom default is sought must be given the protections of Rule 55(b)(2), which may require that notice and a hearing be afforded before default judgment is entered. *See Key Bank v. Tablecloth Textile Co.*, 74 F.3d 349, 352–53 (1st Cir. 1996). This table shows when the clerk may, or the judge must, enter default judgment:

| Clerk may enter default judgment if: | Judge must enter default judgment if: |
|---|---|
| the claim is for a "sum certain" *and* the defaulting party (a) did not "appear" or (b) file a responsive pleading | (1) the defaulting party "appeared" in the case; (2) the default occurred after the defaulting party filed its responsive pleading; (3) the defaulting party is a minor or incapacitated adult; *or* (4) the claim is for an unliquidated amount — if the claim is not for a "sum certain." |

Thus, the clerk can enter judgment only if the claim is for a "sum certain" *and* the defaulting party neither filed a responsive pleading *nor* "appeared." Whether the defaulting party has filed a responsive pleading is straightforward: if, for example, the defendant has filed an answer, the clerk cannot enter default judgment. The other two limitations on the ability of a clerk to enter default are less black and white.

### (a) What Is a "Sum Certain"?

If the damages sought are not for a "sum certain" or a "sum that can be made certain by computation" the clerk cannot enter default judgment. FRCP 55(b)(1), (2). Damages are "sum certain" when they are for a liquidated amount. Unliquidated damages may only be awarded without a hearing if the record accurately reflects the basis for award by detailed affidavits establishing the necessary facts. *Carter v. Macon Manor NRC, LLC,* 2007 WL 951419 (M.D. Ga. 2007). This table summarizes it:

| Clerk Can Enter If | Clerk Cannot Enter If |
|---|---|
| Liquidated damages or calculable sum; or Interest on a sum certain principal. | Attorney fees sought, unless a specific set amount was agreed to; Unliquidated amounts sought (*e.g.,* personal injury cases, most breach of contract cases); Punitive damages sought; or Prejudgment interest sought. |

### *(b) What is an "Appearance"?*

If the defaulting party has "appeared," the clerk may not enter default judgment. Courts tend to liberally construe what constitutes an "appearance." *Lutomski v. Panther Valley Coin Exchange*, 653 F.2d 270, 271 (6th Cir.1981) (defendants contacted plaintiffs and made clear that the damages sought were excessive); *H.F. Livermore Corp. v. Aktiengesellschaft Gebruder Loeppfe*, 432 F.2d 689, 691 (D.C. Cir. 1970) (exchanges between parties were normal effort to see if dispute could be settled and neither party doubted that suit would be contested if efforts failed); *Dalminter, Inc. v. Jessie Edwards, Inc.*, 27 F.R.D. 491, 493 (S.D.Tex.1961) (defendant contacted plaintiff's counsel by letter). However, the issue of what constitutes an "appearance" can be fact intensive. *Cf. Port-Wide Container Co. v. Interstate Maint. Corp.*, 440 F.2d 1195 (3rd Cir. 1971) (unlike *H.F. Livermore,* court held that oral and written communications between counsel for the parties in an effort to settle a dispute did not constitute an appearance).

### ii. Vacating a Default Judgment

As noted above, the issues of setting aside entry of default, as opposed to setting aside entry of default judgment, are distinct. While "good cause" is enough to set aside entry of default, after default judgment is entered the defaulting party must move to set it aside under Rule 60(b). FRCP 55(c). Rule 60(b) is discussed in Chapter 59.

# B. Voluntary Dismissal

Rule 41(a) provides:

> an action may be dismissed by the plaintiff without a court order by filing (i) a notice of dismissal before the opposing party serves either an answer or a motion for summary judgment, or (ii) a stipulation of dismissal signed by all parties who have appeared. Unless the notice or stipulation states otherwise, the dismissal is without prejudice. But if the plaintiff previously dismissed any federal or state court action based on or including the same claim, a notice of dismissal operates as an adjudication on the merits.

# 1. Voluntary Unilateral Dismissal of a Claim by a Party

### *a. Time for Filing Notice of Dismissal*

Under Rule 41(a)(1), until the defendant files a motion for summary judgment or an answer, the plaintiff has an unfettered right to voluntarily dismiss its complaint and do so without prejudice to refile it. No court approval is required: "Other than to determine, should the question arise, whether an answer or a motion for summary judgment has in fact been filed prior to the filing of a notice of dismissal, a court has no function under Rule 41(a)(1)(A)(i)." *D.C. Electronics, Inc. v. Nartron Corp.*, 511 F.2d 294, 298 (6th Cir. 1975).

Suppose a defendant files a Rule 12(b)(6) motion before the plaintiff moves to voluntarily dismiss. If the Rule 12(b)(6) motion includes materials beyond the pleadings that are not excluded by the court, does this unfettered right to dismiss extinguish? Although there is some minor disagreement, the more principled conclusion is that, so long as the notice of dismissal is filed before the district court notifies the parties that it will convert the Rule 12(b)(6) motion into one for summary judgment, it does not become a motion for summary judgment that terminates a plaintiff's right to voluntary dismissal under Rule 41(a)(1)(A)(i). *Marques v. Federal Reserve Bank of Chicago*, 286 F.3d 1014, 1017 (7th Cir. 2002) (plaintiffs had an absolute right to voluntary dismissal, even though defendant filed a motion to dismiss that was later converted to a motion for summary judgment on the same day the plaintiffs filed a notice of voluntary dismissal, where the trial court did not convert the motion to dismiss into a motion for summary judgment until after the plaintiffs' notice of voluntary dismissal was filed). *Cf. Swedberg v. Marotzke*, 339 F.3d 1139, 1142–45 (9th Cir. 2003) (a motion to dismiss for failure to state a claim upon which relief can be granted supported by extraneous materials cannot be regarded as a motion for summary judgment until a court converts the motion by indicating it will not those materials from consideration, and so such a motion will not, at the time it is served, preclude voluntary dismissal).

### b. Impact of Filing a Notice of Dismissal

The filing of a notice of voluntary dismissal divests a court of jurisdiction to proceed further:

> Rule 41(a)(1) is the shortest and surest route to abort a complaint when it is applicable. So long as plaintiff has not been served with his adversary's answer or motion for summary judgment he need do no more than file a notice of dismissal with the Clerk. That document itself closes the file. There is nothing the defendant can do to fan the ashes of that action into life and the court has no role to play. This is a matter of right running to the plaintiff and may not be extinguished or circumscribed by adversary or court. There is not even a perfunctory order of court closing the file. Its alpha and omega was the doing of the plaintiff alone. He suffers no impairment beyond his fee for filing.

*Am. Cyanamid Co. v. McGhee,* 317 F.2d 295, 297 (5th Cir.1963). The court cannot consider motions pending in the case when the notice is filed. *See Univ. of S. Ala. v. Am. Tobacco Co.,* 168 F.3d 405, 409 (11th Cir. 1999) ("Voluntary dismissal [under Rule 41(a)(1)(i)] normally may precede any analysis of subject matter jurisdiction because it is self-executing and moots all pending motions, obviating the need for the district court to exercise its jurisdiction.").

## 2. Only one Voluntary Dismissal *Without* Prejudice

Rule 41(a)(1)(B) provides that unless the notice or stipulation of dismissal states otherwise, voluntary dismissal is without prejudice—*unless* the plaintiff previously "dismissed any federal- or state-court action based on or including the same claim. . . ." So, a plaintiff gets one voluntary dismissal without prejudice; the second time, dismissal is *with prejudice.*

## 3. Dismissal by Stipulation of the Parties

The parties may voluntarily dismiss by filing a signed stipulation of dismissal by filing a stipulation of dismissal signed by all parties who have appeared. FRCP 41(a)(1)(A)(ii). This often happens after the parties settle a case, a process discussed later in this Chapter. While a properly stipulated dismissal under Rule 41(a)(1)(A)(ii) is self-executing and does not require judicial approval, *Aamot v. Kassel,* 1 F.3d 441, 445 (6th Cir. 1993), a court may, "exercising its inherent powers . . . look behind [a settlement] to determine whether there is collusion or other improper conduct giving rise to the dismissal." *U.S. v. Mercedes-Benz of North Am.,* 547 F. Supp. 399, 400 (N.D. Cal.1982).

### a. Dismissal After Answer or Summary Judgment or Without All Parties' Consent: Court Approval Required

If voluntary dismissal without court approval is unavailable, then Rule 41(a)(2) applies:

> Except as provided in Rule 41(a)(1), an action may be dismissed at the plaintiff's request only by court order, on terms that the court considers proper. If a defendant has pleaded a counterclaim before being served with the plaintiff's motion to dismiss, the action may be dismissed over the defendant's objection only if the counterclaim can remain pending for independent adjudication. Unless the order states otherwise, a dismissal under this paragraph (2) is without prejudice.

If the parties agree and file a stipulation of dismissal, then the court is divested of jurisdiction even if it does not approve the stipulation. *See Hester Indus., Inc. v. Tyson Foods, Inc.*, 160 F.3d 911, 916 (2d Cir.1998).

However, if all parties do not agree, then the court has discretion on whether to grant a motion for voluntary dismissal. "The basic purpose of Rule 41(a)(2) is to freely permit the plaintiff, with court approval, to voluntarily dismiss an action so long as no other party will be prejudiced." *Versa Prods., Inc. v. Home Depot, USA, Inc.*, 387 F.3d 1325 (11th Cir. 2004). Thus, the key inquiry is whether dismissal will result in prejudice in addition to the prospect of a second lawsuit. *See id.*

# C. Involuntary Dismissal with Prejudice for Violating Rules or Orders

Rule 41(b) provides:

> If the plaintiff fails to prosecute or to comply with these rules or a court order, a defendant may move to dismiss the action or any claim against it. Unless the dismissal order states otherwise, a dismissal under this subdivision (b) and any dismissal not under this rule—except one for lack of jurisdiction, improper venue, or failure to join a party under Rule 19—operates as an adjudication on the merits.

Rule 41(b) authorizes two very distinct forms of involuntary dismissal.

First, Rule 41(b) is the basis on which district courts dismiss claims for lack of subject matter or personal jurisdiction, improper venue, or for failure to join an indispensable party. Such dismissals are involuntary in that the plaintiff does not seek them. They are "without prejudice"—meaning the plaintiff can refile the claim because dismissal is not based on the merits of the claim.

Second, Rule 41(b) permits a court to dismiss claims or cases with prejudice—meaning the claim cannot be refiled—"for failure of the plaintiff to prosecute or to comply with these rules or a court order...." Although the Rules read as if involuntary dismissal can occur only upon the motion of the defendant, the a court may *sua sponte* involuntarily dismiss a claim. *See Link v. Wabash R.R.*, 370 U.S. 626, 630 (1962). A violation of Rule 11 can also permit a court to involuntarily dismiss with prejudice. *See* Chapter 44.

However, dismissal under Rule 41(b) is "a harsh remedy to be utilized only in extreme situations." *Theilmann v. Rutland Hospital, Inc.*, 455 F.2d 853, 855 (2d Cir. 1972). Typically courts consider all circumstances including: "(1) whether the party's failure is due to willfulness, bad faith, or fault; (2) whether the adversary was prejudiced by the dismissed party's conduct; (3) whether the dismissed party was warned that failure to cooperate could lead to dismissal; and (4) whether less drastic sanctions were imposed or considered before dismissal was ordered." *U.S. v. Reyes*, 307 F.3d 451, 458 (6th Cir. 2002). "Although no one factor is dispositive, dismissal is proper if the record demonstrates delay or contumacious conduct." *Id.*

In addition, a court has discretion to dismiss a complaint where the plaintiff failed to diligently prosecute the case. A court contemplating dismissing under Rule 41(b) for failure to prosecute must consider: "[1] the duration of the plaintiff's failures, [2] whether plaintiff had received notice that further delays would result in dismissal, [3] whether the defendant is likely to be prejudiced by further delay, [4] whether the district judge has take[n] care to strik[e] the balance between alleviating court calendar congestion and protecting a party's right to due process and a fair chance to be heard . . . and [5] whether the judge has adequately assessed the efficacy of lesser sanctions." *Alvarez v. Simmons Mkt. Research Bureau, Inc.*, 839 F.2d 930, 932 (2d Cir. 1988).

# D. Dismissal of a Claim Based Upon a Motion Under Rules 12(b)(6) or 12(c)

As we explored in Chapter 34, a claim can be dismissed involuntarily without any discovery to the extent it fails to state a claim upon which relief can be granted. However, a grant of a dismissal under Rule 12(b)(6) or 12(c) is *not* viewed as a Rule 41(b) involuntary dismissal, which is reviewed for abuse of discretion, but is instead reviewed *de novo. Ajifu v. Int'l Ass'n. of Machinists & Aerospace Workers*, 205 Fed. Appx. 488 (9th Cir. 2006).

# E. Settling the Case

It is common for parties to settle disputes promptly after a plaintiff files suit. If so, defendants typically require the plaintiff dismiss the claims *with prejudice* (*i.e.,* so that *res judicata* precludes refiling the claim) and require the plaintiff to "release" the claims (and more). A release provides additional protection to a defendant. As we will see in Chapter 60, the law of *res judicata* is often unsettled in some areas, or provides less protection to a defendant than it may want. As a result, parties often include in their settlement agreements "releases" whereby the parties agree not to raise claims not just arising out of or related to the dispute, but to claims that are unknown and even vaguely connected to the dispute. Releases are governed by state law, and it often requires specific words be used to release certain types of claims.

## Checkpoints

- Can you identify the steps to obtain a default judgment, and when the court, as opposed to the clerk, must be involved?
- Can you describe when a plaintiff may take voluntary dismissal without impact on their claim? When voluntary dismissal will bar their claim?
- Can you describe when involuntary dismissal is proper?

# Chapter 45

# The Foundations of Choice
of Law in Federal Court

---

### Foundations of Choice of Law Roadmap

This Chapter explains that one consequence of our Republican form of government is that each State has autonomy to enact laws as it sees fit, and the federal government has the power, to the extent authorized by the States in the Constitution to do so, to do the same.

---

## A. Federal Power is Limited

Federal power is limited. Remember that unless the States delegated power to the federal government to enact laws about a subject, power over that subject is "reserved" to the States under the Tenth Amendment. As a consequence, a federal statute, called the Rules of Decision Act, 28 U.S.C. § 1652, provides that State law controls unless federal law requires otherwise:

The laws of the several States, except where the Constitution or treaties of the United States or Acts of Congress otherwise require or provide, shall be regarded as rules of decision in civil actions in the courts of the United States, in cases where they apply.

We saw that the States gave Congress power to set up courts to decide disputes between citizens of different States; they did not give Congress the power to displace state law governing those disputes. A court has only subject matter jurisdiction — power — to decide the state claim.

The question of whether state or federal law applies turns on whether the claim arises under an area that is reserved to the States under the Constitution? If so, then state law must apply, since the States have not delegated to the federal government the power to regulate that area. So, a federal court deciding a state claim should apply state law "except where the Constitution or treaties of the United States or Acts of Congress otherwise require or provide . . ."

# B. States Authorized Congress to Create Federal District Courts

Think for a moment about the grant in Article III by the States to Congress to create courts. The States empowered Congress to create lower federal courts. Does that mean the States also delegated to Congress power to enact rules of procedure to govern proceedings in federal court? When deciding a state law claim, does the federal court apply federal procedural law, or state procedural law? If so, what's "procedure" and what's not?

# C. Limits on State Power

Not only is Congress's power limited by the Constitution to enact laws covering certain subject matter, each state's power is also limited, but more so by geography than subject matter. Because each State is equal and sovereign, its laws end at its borders. Consider also that it is quite common for the laws of one state on a subject to vary, often dramatically, from those of another state on exactly that same subject. Thus, it may be that a certain set of facts, if proven, would constitute a claim upon which relief can be granted under the laws of one state, but not under the laws of another. As one court:

> For example, the meaning of the concept of negligence and subsidiary concepts such as duty of care, foreseeability, and proximate cause varies amongst the states. Furthermore, as Defendant catalogued in its appendices, many states vary the limitations period under which a cause of action for negligence or products liability may be brought. The same can be said for the limitations periods governing breach of warranty claims.

*Drooger v. Carlisle Tire & Wheel Co.*, 2006 WL 1008719 (W.D. Mich. 2006).

As a result, "choice of law" principles have arisen that dictate which state's law will apply to a particular claim, if the claim is governed by state law. Just because a suit is filed in Delaware state court doesn't mean Delaware law will apply to the state law claims. Instead, as we'll see, the Delaware state court must conduct a "choice of law" analysis to identify which state's laws apply to each claim before it. Each state not only has different substantive law, often they use different "choice of law" rules to determine which state's law applies to a particular claim.

Now envision a federal court in Delaware that happens to have subject matter jurisdiction over a state law claim because of diversity jurisdiction. That federal court must also apply the "choice of law" principles of the forum state—the state in which the federal court sits, here, Delaware—to decide which law applies, so that the same law is applied to a state law dispute whether it's filed in state, or federal, court in Delaware.

# D. The Complexities of Choice of Law

Those principles—that federal law only applies to areas in which the States granted the federal government power to act; that when the matter is one of state law, each state's law often varies; and that it may be awkward for a federal court to have to follow state procedural law—create several issues, which are interrelated at some levels. Viewed broadly, there are at least three issues to keep in mind, though each presents a number of sub-issues.

First, what law should a federal court apply when deciding state law claims? We'll see that when deciding state law claims, a federal court must apply state law, generally the law of the state in which it sits. So, a New Hampshire federal district court deciding a claim for breach of a New Hampshire contract will look to the substantive law developed by New Hampshire state courts in deciding that claim.

Second, what if a case is filed in a federal court in a state with no real connection to the dispute? Suppose, for example, that a plaintiff files a suit in the defendant's home state because the plaintiff could not obtain personal jurisdiction over the defendant in the plaintiff's home state. If all of the activities that led to the suit occurred in the plaintiff's home state, doesn't that indicate that the plaintiff's state's law, not the defendant's state's law, ought to apply? How does a federal court determine which state's law to apply to a particular dispute? We'll see that a federal district court must apply the same choice of law principles as does a state court in that State—with some narrow exceptions involving cases where venue has been transferred.

Third, although state substantive law will control in deciding state claims, federal courts will apply their own rules of procedure (e.g., the FRCP). Only when an issue is one of substance—not procedure—must a federal court follow state law. Usually that distinction is clear; sometimes it is not.

## Checkpoints

- Can you explain the reasons why state substantive law will generally apply unless a federal statute creates the claim?

- Do you understand why it is necessary to identify which state's law applies to a particular claim, and that there are constitutional limitations on the ability of a state to have its law apply to a claim?

# Chapter 46

# Vertical and Horizontal Choice of Law

---

### Choice of Law Roadmap

This chapter explains "vertical" choice of law: how to determine which law — state or federal — applies to civil lawsuits filed federal court, and the resulting need to distinguish between substantive and procedural law.

This chapter also explains "horizontal" choice of law: how federal courts determine, if state law applies to an issue, *which* state's law applies, including resulting need to understand how the transfer of a case from one federal district court to one in a different state affects that analysis.

Finally, this chapter explains how federal courts determine the content of state law, including when they have to do so by "guessing."

---

## A. Federal Law and Federal Procedure Apply to Claims Arising Under Federal Law

Like almost everything in civil procedure, it is important to analyze issues on a claim-by-claim basis. It may be that federal law will apply to one claim, and state to another.

If a federal court is adjudicating a claim created by federal law, the analysis is straightforward: the court applies federal substantive law since federal law created the claim, and it also applies federal procedural rules. Why?

The fact that federal substantive law applies to claims created by federal law — or "arising under" federal law — should be pretty straightforward. In the Constitution, States granted to Congress the power to enact laws concerning certain subjects. If Congress has done so by creating a claim, the States have allowed federal law to control. So, if Congress has created a federal claim, federal law applies.

With respect to procedure, the analysis is a little murkier. The States in the Constitution gave Congress power to create federal courts. Implicit in the power to create courts is the power to regulate what happens in them. Put another way, creating federal procedure is implicit in the power to create federal courts in the first place. Congress recognized this. Not only are there statutes that create federal district courts, and the appellate courts, but Congress enacted the Rules Enabling Act, 28 U.S.C. § 2072, to "enable" the Supreme Court to adopt (and amend) what we now call the Federal Rules of Civil Procedure. Section 2072 provides in pertinent part: "The Supreme Court shall have the power to prescribe, by general rules, the forms of process, writs, pleadings, and motions, and the practice and procedure of the district courts and courts of appeals of the United States in civil actions. . . ."

Thus, federal courts have power—indeed, the mandate—to apply federal substantive law and federal procedure when adjudicating a claim that arises under federal law. When federal law creates the claim, the analysis is pretty simple.

# B. State Substantive Law, but Federal Procedural Law, Applies to Claims Arising Under State Law

Remember that federal courts have diversity subject matter jurisdiction. That means they can decide claims created by state law. Claims adjudicated in federal court but created by state law require more analysis, including the need to distinguish between "substantive" law and "procedural" law. There are three things to keep in mind in this analysis.

First, remember that the States in the Constitution gave Congress only limited power to legislate, and only Congress, not the courts, can enact statutes: federal courts have no power to legislative, only to decide disputes between parties. So there is only a limited body of federal substantive law and it is almost created by federal statutes, not "federal common law." In fact, courts often say there is no "general federal common law." So, if a claim is created by state law, state law is going to control.

Second, federal courts have limited power to adjudicate state law claims. (As we saw, original subject matter jurisdiction exists generally only if a claim is between citizens of different states and the amount in controversy exceeds $75,000, but there can be supplemental jurisdiction over closely related claims or a state law claim that is closely related to a federal claim.) Logically, the law that applies to a claim should not be different simply because a state law claim happens to fall within one of these categories and so is being heard in federal court. The outcome should be the same, whether the claim is in state or federal court.

Third, and this is where it gets messy, as explained above, implicit in the power to create federal courts is the power to create rules governing the proceedings in those courts. This is where the difficult issues exist: if a state law is arguably substantive and it conflicts with federal procedural law, what happens? How do courts distinguish between state *procedural* law—which will *not* apply in federal court—and state *substantive* law, which will if the claim arises under state law?

## 1. The *Erie* Decision: State Substantive Law Applies to State Law Claims Being Adjudicated in Federal Court

It may sound axiomatic: if state law creates a claim, the fact that a federal court happens to have jurisdiction to decide the claim should not change the substance of that state law. The law has evolved, slowly, to that point. Most casebooks spend some time explaining how we got here. We will be brief.

The story begins with the Rules of Decision Act, 28 U.S.C. § 1652, which provides: "The law of the several states, except where the Constitution or Acts of Congress otherwise require or provide, shall be regarded as rules of decision in civil actions in the courts of the United States, in cases where they apply." This statute seems to say that state law applies unless a federal statute or the U.S. Constitution says otherwise.

A long time ago, however, the Court held that the Rules of Decision Act did not require federal courts to follow state *common law* decisions, meaning opinions by state judges. *Swift v. Tyson*, 41 U.S. 1 (1841). Instead, the *Swift* Court held that federal judges could ignore state judicial opinions—state common law—when deciding what state law required, and they only had to follow state *statutes* (and certain other narrow "types" of "law") because only statutes and those other narrow types were the "law."

As a result, of *Swift*, for nearly 100 years, federal judges applied "federal common law" when there was no state statute on a particular issue, and in doing so held that this federal law could differ from, and even contradict, state law. Thus, and for a long time, if a claim created by state common law claim was being adjudicated in federal court, a judge could apply different "federal law" to it than would a state court judge deciding the same claim in state court.

Think about that for a second. Whether a plaintiff could win or lose a claim would depend upon whether the defendant was from a different state and the amount in controversy exceeded the statutory minimum!

Things had gotten that weird when the issue finally returned to the Court in *Erie v. Tomkins*. It took nearly 100 years, but the *Erie* Court overruled *Swift*. In *Erie*, the plaintiff, Tompkins, had been walking along a railroad track in Pennsylvania when a train operated by Erie Railroad injured him. Tompkins brought a state law claim. To prevail on that claim under Pennsylvania state law, he was required to allege and prove that the railroad had acted willfully or wantonly. To avoid this, Tompkins sued in federal district court, basing subject matter jurisdiction on diversity. Because under *Swift* the federal judge was not required to follow state common law, the district court relied on opinions from federal courts applying "federal common law" to railroad accidents. Federal common law only required Tompkins plead and prove lack of due care by the railroad, an easier standard for the plaintiff than willful or wanton misconduct. Tompkins obtained a jury verdict and judgment in his favor based on that lower federal standard.

On appeal, the Supreme Court overruled *Swift* and replaced it with what seemed to be a simple rule: a federal court deciding a state claim must apply state law, whether created by a court (in a judicial opinion announcing the common law) or a legislature (in a statute). In justifying its overruling of *Swift*, the Court noted the "mischief" that *Swift* had created, including the fact that out-of-state citizens like Tompkins were able to invoke federal law, which could be more favorable than the law applicable to an in-state plaintiff. The Court also recognized that the States had not delegated to *Congress* the power to create general law on anything—just to enact statutes on limited subjects—and yet under *Swift* the federal *courts* were creating their own common law on topics far beyond the limited power of Congress. The *Erie* court concluded that *Swift* constituted an "unconstitutional assumption of powers by courts of the United States which no lapse of time or respectable array of opinion could make us hesitate to correct."

*Erie* thus enforces the limited power that the States gave to the federal government to make law. *Erie* ensures that the Tenth Amendment is followed. Another core policy *Erie* furthers is that which forum decides the claim—state or federal court—should not be outcome determinative. *Guaranty Trust Co. v. York*, 326 U.S. 99, 108–10 (1945). Thus, the *York* Court held that a state statute of limitations that would bar a claim if the claim were brought in state court also bar it if the claim were adjudicated in federal court. *Id.*

To sum up, if state law creates the claim, state substantive law will apply to that claim in federal court. The happenstance that the federal judiciary has subject matter jurisdiction over the claim for one of the three reasons above will not change the substance of the law.

## 2. The Federal Power to Regulate Federal Procedure and its Limitations

Again, as part of the Constitutional power given Congress to create "inferior" courts, it is "necessary and proper" (in terms of the Constitution) for Congress to adopt rules to regulate proceedings in those courts. Thus, "*Erie* and its offspring cast no doubt on the long-recognized power of Congress to prescribe housekeeping rules for federal courts." *Hanna v. Plumer,* 380 U.S. 460 (1965).

This Constitutional power to create procedure governing in federal court is codified in the Rules Enabling Act. To ensure that only procedure, not substance, is regulated, Section 2072(b) of the Rules Enabling Act provides: "Such rules shall not abridge, enlarge or modify any substantive right." Thus, so long as a federal procedural rule does not affect "substantive rights" created by state or federal law, it should apply in federal court.

This creates a dichotomy between procedural rules and substantive law. Federal procedural law applies so long as it does not affect a substantive right. This can be an issue where a claim is created either by federal or state law, but it is a much more common problem where state law creates a claim because state substantive law applies, but federal procedural law applies. How do we distinguish between state "substantive" and "procedural" law, since only state "substantive" law applies? And, what if there is a conflict between state substantive law and federal procedural law, since federal procedural law should apply in federal court?

Often, of course, there is no doubt whether some state law is procedural or substantive. State common law defines the elements of a state common law tort. The level of misconduct required by state law in *Erie,* as a result, was substantive: under state law willful and wanton misconduct was required, and that is substantive. Likewise, state law that provides the requirements to form a valid contract necessary to support a breach of contract claim is substantive.

But there is grey at the dividing line between "substance" and "procedure." That uncertainty must be resolved if federal procedural law would affect a "substantive" right. The approach taken by the Court in trying to distinguish substance from procedure has varied over the years. Accordingly, the development of the law is important to grasp the current state of the law and to see the remaining ambiguities.

For a time after *Erie,* the Court seemed to encourage courts to defer to state law in doubtful circumstances. For example, in *Guaranty Trust Co. v. York,* 326 U.S. 99 (1945), the plaintiff's state law claim was barred by New York's statute of limitation; the plaintiff, however, filed in federal court and argued that *Erie* created a distinction between substance and procedure, and that the statute of limitation was procedural, not substantive, and so federal law applied, and under federal law, the claim was not time-barred. The *Guaranty Trust* Court held that it was "immaterial" under *Erie* whether the statute was characterized as substantive or procedural. It characterized *Erie* as expressing "a policy that touches vitally the proper distribution of judicial power between State and federal courts." In essence, *Guaranty Trust* sought to make it so that the result of a state law claim filed in federal court should be substantially the same as if it had been filed in state court. The distinction between substance and procedure was recast as to whether the state law "concerns merely the manner and the means by which a right to recover, as recognized by the State, is enforced, or whether such statutory limitation is a matter of substance in an aspect that alone is relevant to our problem, namely, does it significantly affect the result of a litigation for a federal court to disregard a law of a State that would be controlling in an action upon the same claim by the same parties in a State court?" *Id.* The Court held that the state statute of limitation controlled adjudication of the state claim in federal court.

Whether, or not, the distinction between "manner and mode" and "substance" is exactly the same line drawn in *Erie*, the *Guaranty Trust* Court suggested that even what arguably was state procedural law could control in federal court if failing to do so would change the result. So, a state statute that simply said precluded corporations that hadn't paid state taxes from suing applied in federal courts. It is hard to characterize that sort of statute as "substantive." *E.g., Woods v. Interstate Realty Co,* 337 U.S. 535 (1949).

The story becomes more complicated because of a related, but distinct, line of cases involving the validity of the Federal Rules of Civil Procedure. Specifically, later in *Hanna,* the Court considered a state statute that required that process be served "in hand," a stricter approach than required by the federal rules in Rule 4. In *Hanna,* the plaintiff served the defendant in a way that was proper under Rule 4, but was not proper under the state law. Which controlled? The Court stated that under the Rules Enabling Act, the Rules applied in federal court unless a Rule violated either the terms of the Rules Enabling Act (because it was substantive, not procedural) or Constitutional limitations. It then held:

> To hold that a [Rule] must case to function whenever it alters the mode
> of enforcing state-created rights would be to disembowel either the
> Constitution's grant of power over federal procedure or Congress'
> attempt to exercise that power in the Enabling Act.

Applying this principle, the *Hanna* Court held that Rule 4 was a valid exercise of the Rules Enabling Act, not unconstitutional, and so controlled despite being contrary to state law.

This means that a federal rule of civil procedure will apply unless it is not "procedural" but instead "substantive" (or otherwise unconstitutional). What is "procedure" and so authorized by the Rules Enabling Act? Luckily it is quite broad: Enactments that are "'rationally capable of classification' as procedural rules are necessary and proper for carrying into execution the power to establish federal courts vested in Congress by Article III, § 1." *Budinich v. Becton Dickinson & Co.*, 486 U.S. 196, 199 (1988). As one court recently explained:

> As recognized by the Supreme Court, however, "[c]lassification of a law as 'substantive' or 'procedural' for *Erie* purposes is sometimes a challenging endeavor." *Gasperini v. Center for Humanities, Inc.*, 518 U.S. 415, 416 (1996). To aid courts in this "challenging endeavor" the Supreme Court developed a two-part test in *Hanna v. Plumer*, 380 U.S. 460 (1965). Under the *Hanna* test, "when the federal law sought to be applied is a congressional statute or Federal Rule of Civil Procedure, the district court must first decide whether the statute is 'sufficiently broad to control the issue before the court.'" *Alexander Proudfoot Co. World Headquarters L.P. v. Thayer*, 877 F.2d 912, 917 (11th Cir. 1989). If the federal procedural rule is "sufficiently broad to control the issue" and conflicts with the state law, the federal procedural rule applies instead of the state law. *See Cohen v. Office Depot, Inc.*, 184 F.3d 1292, 1296 (11th Cir.1999) (explaining that "if the state law conflicts with a federal procedural rule, then the state law is procedural for Erie / Hanna purposes regardless of how it may be characterized for other purposes"). If the federal rule does not directly conflict with the state law, then the second prong of the Hanna test requires the district court to evaluate "whether failure to apply the state law would lead to different outcomes in state and federal court and result in inequitable administration of the laws or forum shopping." *Cohen*, 184 F.3d at 1297 (citing *Hanna*, 380 U.S. at 468)

*Burke v. Smith*, 252 F.3d 1260 (11th Cir. 2001). The following have been held to be procedural issues, and so are governed by federal law:

- An issue addressed by the Federal Rules of Civil Procedure. *Com/Tech Commn. Tech., Inc. v. Wireless Data Sys., Inc.*, 163 F.3d 149, 150–51 (2d Cir.1998) ("it is settled that the [FRCP] applies regardless of contrary state law.").
- What constitutes a "final decisions of the district courts" in terms of the final judgment rule in 28 U.S.C. § 1291. *Budinich v. Becton Dickinson & Co.*, 486 U.S. 196, 199 (1988).

- An issue addressed by the Federal Rules of Evidence. *Legg v. Chopra*, 286 F.3d 286, 289 (6th Cir. 2002).
- Questions of appealability of district court orders. *Cohen v. Beneficial Industrial Loan Corp.*, 337 U.S. 541 (1949).

Thus, unless a Rule is not "procedural," it will control. But, what if a federal procedural rule is contrary to state law so that the rule, if applied, would alter substantive rights?

## 3. Where We Are Today

### a. A Validly Enacted Rule Will Control Absent State Substantive Law to the Contrary

As just shown, over time *Hanna* and *Erie* have come to stand for the proposition that federal courts when deciding a state law claim must "apply state substantive law and federal procedural law." *Gasperini v. Ctr. for Humanities, Inc.*, 518 U.S. 415, 427 (1996). Likewise, a rule adopted under the Rules Enabling Act will control, unless there is state *substantive* law to the contrary. What has happened is that over time courts have concluded that *Erie* helps maintain the limited delegation of authority in the Constitution to the federal government to create substantive law, while *Hanna* helps to ensure that the federal government's power to create federal courts included the necessary ability to enact rules of *procedure*, but not more than that.

Taken together, they both reflect the straightforward principle that there is no reason why a claim "which concededly would be barred in the state courts . . . should proceed through litigation to judgment in federal court solely because of the fortuity that there is diversity of citizenship. . . ." *Walker v. Armco Steel Corp.*, 446 U.S. 740, 752 (1980). Although rare, these issues continue to arise today. *See, e.g., Moreland v. Barrette*, 2006 WL 3147651 (D. Ariz. 2006) (holding that state statute that required that a doctor provide an affidavit before a medical malpractice claim could be filed did not conflict with the Rules and controlled in federal court because affidavit's absence would preclude a state court from trying the claim); *Caiola v. Berkshire Med. Ctr., Inc.*, 2004 WL 2607805 (N.D.N.Y. 2004) (state law requiring medical malpractice plaintiff to first submit its claim to a medical "tribunal" controlled under *Erie* and did not conflict with the Rules).

The key is to focus on what law creates the claim. At that point, the substantive law that creates the claim will control in either state or federal court, and federal procedural law will apply in all circumstances. If a federal court's failure to apply state law would change the outcome, then careful application of *Hanna* and *Erie* is required.

# B. Determining Which State's Law Applies and Then Identifying the Content of that State's Law

## 1. Which State's Law Applies?

The building block for understanding horizontal choice of law is something that you are picking up on in your other classes: state courts come to different conclusions about what the law is or ought to be. You've probably seen that states draw the line for proximate cause in tort law in different places. It may be, consequently, that conduct is actionable as a tort in one state, but not in another. Also, some states recognize certain torts — negligent infliction of emotional distress is a good example — which other states simply do not. So, what might be a tort under one state's laws is not under another.

Those differences are outcome determinative!

It is also important you recognize that it is common for suits to be filed in one state, but for another state's law to control the claim. For example, a defendant who engaged in wrongdoing in New Mexico might have to be sued in his state of domicile, say Arizona, because personal jurisdiction is lacking in New Mexico. As noted at the outset of this chapter, even on common issues, common law (and statutes, for that matter) varies enormously between states. It is very possible that a set of facts will state a claim for a plaintiff under one state's law but not under another's. Long ago, courts held that simply because a suit was filed in a particular state did not mean that the law of that state where the suit was filed controlled. Georgia law won't apply to a car wreck that happened in New York simply because the plaintiff files the suit in Georgia.

### a. Choice of Law in Federal Courts: The General Rule

How do federal courts figure out which state's law applies to a state law claim? A federal court must apply the same substantive law as would a state court where the federal court sits. Thus, the first question is to ask which state's law would the forum's state courts apply to the claim.

Instead of simply applying the law of the forum state, courts apply what are called "choice of law" principles. Although they vary, most states apply the law of the State with the most "significant contacts" to the claim. So, a state court would ask: what state has the most significant contacts with this claim? That state's law applies, no matter where the suit was filed. So, in our car wreck hypo above, a car wreck that occurred in New York will be governed by New York law — whether the suit is filed in state court in Georgia, New York, or any other state's court.

With an exception that applies when a case is transferred by a federal court out of the state in which it sits — cases that we'll get to in a moment — a federal court must apply the same approach to legal rules governing choice of law as do the state courts in the forum where the federal court sits. *Klaxon Co. v. Stentor Elec. Mfg. Co.,* 313 U.S. 487 (1941). So, a federal district court in Georgia must apply Georgia's choice of law rules to determine whether the laws of New York, New Mexico, or some other state apply to a claim. In theory, therefore, the fact that a claim is filed in federal court will make no difference.

### b. Choice of Law After Transfer of Venue to a Different State

What happens when a federal court transfers a case to a district in another state? Does the transferee court apply the choice of law rules — the rules that determine which law applies to an interstate dispute — of the transferor's state, or its own state?

You ask: why would it matter that different states have different law about choice of law? After all, the tort occurred "somewhere" and that place's law ought to apply. Most of the time, that is true: there's not going to be much disagreement about what law applies in a car wreck case. But what law applies where, for example, a defendant in Missouri mails fraudulent statements to a plaintiff in Texas about land in Iowa? The "most significant contacts" analysis might lead to different answers; and, the law of one state might be highly more favorable than another.

Just as they disagree about tort law itself, courts in different states sometimes use different choice of law rules to determine which law applies to an interstate dispute, and sometimes they just take slightly different approaches — even though using the exact same approach. As a consequence, sometimes, a good plaintiff's lawyer might be able to pick a forum that has the "right" choice of law rules, so that the law of a state that is favorable to the plaintiff will be chosen over less favorable law. Thus, it can matter greatly how a court determines the applicable law after transfer.

### i. Choice of Law After a Section 1404(a) Transfer to a More Convenient Forum

If a court transfers a case under Section 1404(a), what happens? Does the transferee court pretend like it's in the transferor's state for the purpose of determining which state's law applies?

Yes. In *Van Dusen v. Barrack,* 376 U.S. 612 (1964), the Court held that the transferor's state's law, including the transferor's state's choice of law rules, applied in the transferee court. The court reasoned that because the transferor forum was proper, the fact that the case was transferred for the convenience of parties and witnesses should not change which law applied to the dispute. Note that this does not mean, necessarily, that the laws of the transferor's state will apply: it means that the transferee court will look to the laws of the transferor state to determine which laws apply. That's true whether the plaintiff or defendant seeks transfer.

In some states the statute of limitation is "procedural" and not "substantive" and so a plaintiff could file suit in that state, and have the court apply that state's longer statue of limitations to a claim that is otherwise governed by another state's law. Once the plaintiff gets the favorable law selected, can it then transfer the case to the state where it's most convenient, under section 1404(a), and still get the benefit of the longer statute of limitations?

The answer is "yes" and it happens more often than you might think. For example, in *Ferens et ux. v. John Deere Co.*, 494 U.S. 516 (1990), the plaintiff's hand was injured by a John Deere combine. In an attempt to avoid a statute of limitations defense, the plaintiff filed two suits. In his home state of Pennsylvania, he filed a complaint with two claims that were not barred by limitations. But, he had other claims that were, under Pennsylvania's law, time-barred. So, he filed a second suit in Mississippi, because he knew that the Mississippi federal court would follow Mississippi's choice of law rules, under which it would apply Mississippi's longer statute of limitations because it was procedural. As a result, the claim would not be barred, even though Pennsylvania law provided all the substantive law to the claim.

Then, to finish this remarkable lawyering feat, plaintiff's counsel sought under Section 1404(a) to transfer the Mississippi case to Pennsylvania so that it could be consolidated with the case with the two other claims. Plaintiff's counsel believed that under *Van Dusen* the Pennsylvania court would apply the same choice of law rules as the Mississippi court, and end up holding that the claim filed in Mississippi was not barred because Mississippi's procedural statute of limitation would control.

The defendant did not oppose the transfer (why would it?). After transfer, the Pennsylvania district court rejected the plaintiff's attempt and held that Pennsylvania's shorter statute applied, and refused to apply Mississippi law. The Court, however, ultimately reversed, reasoning that *Erie* required that federal courts apply to a transferred case the same law that would have been applied by a state court in the transferor forum. So, the Court held that the Pennsylvania federal court had to apply Mississippi's statute of limitation to the claim, and so the claim was not time-barred.

Thus, no matter which party invokes transfer under Section 1404(a), the transferee court must apply the same law and choice of law principles that the state courts in the transferor forum would have applied. The transferee court, in other words, has to pretend like it is in the transferor's forum for this purpose. If the transferor court would apply Mississippi's statute of limitations, so must the transferee. Remember that under Section 1404(a) the plaintiff's choice of venue was proper; the law shouldn't change simply because there was also a more convenient, proper venue.

### ii. Choice of Law After a Section 1406(a) Transfer for Improper Venue (or Lack of Personal Jurisdiction)

The rule of *Van Dusen* does not apply to transfers made under Section 1406(a), from an improper venue to a proper one, or from a court lacking personal jurisdiction to one with personal jurisdiction. Instead, "following a transfer under § 1406(a), the transferee district court should apply its own state law rather than the state law of the transferor district court." *Jackson v. West Telemarketing Corp. Outbound*, 245 F.3d 518 (5th Cir. 2001).

So for example, if a plaintiff files suit in a California district where venue is improper, or personal jurisdiction lacking, and the case is transferred under Section 1406(a) to a Texas federal court, the Texas court would apply Texas's choice of law rules to determine what law governed the dispute, not California's. *Id.* The result would be the opposite if the transfer had been for convenience under Section 1404(a).

## 2. How Does a Federal Court Determine What State Law is — the "Content" of State Law?

Once a court identifies which state's law applies to a claim, it must determine what state law provides. How does it do so?

First, a court should look to decisions of the supreme court of the state which law applies to the dispute. If that state supreme court has decided the issue, its decision must be followed. If it has not, then the court must follow decisions of the state's intermediate appellate courts absent a strong showing that the state supreme court would have ruled differently. *Lawler v. Fireman's Fund Ins. Co.*, 322 F.3d 900, 903 (6th Cir. 2003).

If there is no definitive answer, the federal district court must guess — what is called the the "*Erie* guess." The court should do its best to predict what the state's supreme court would find the law to be if it were faced with the issue. Under some circumstances, a federal court can "ask" the state supreme court for its answer!

## 3. Constitutional Limitations on Imposition of Substantive State Law

The question of whether a state can assert personal jurisdiction over a defendant turns on the defendant's contacts with the state. *See* Chapter 6; *see also* Chapter 7 (discussing *in rem* jurisdiction). Does the fact that a state court has personal jurisdiction mean that it can apply its law to the dispute, regardless of the connection between the dispute and the state?

There are Constitutional limitations arising from the Due Process Clause and the Full Faith and Credit Clause on the power of a court to apply its state's substantive law to a dispute even if it has personal jurisdiction over the defendant. The Court in *Allstate Ins. v. Hague*, 449 U.S. 301 (1982), held that if "a State has only an insignificant contact with the parties and the occurrence or transaction, application of its law is unconstitutional." *See also Phillips Petroleum Co. v. Shutts*, 472 U.S. 797 (1985) (holding court could not apply Kansas law to leases that had no connection to Kansas even in a nationwide class action). On the other hand, states may constitutionally apply their *procedural* law to disputes in the forum. *Sun Oil Co. v. Wortman*, 486 U.S. 717 (1988).

# D. Appellate Review

An appellate court reviews a district court's determination of which law applies *de novo*. *Olympic Sports Prods., Inc. v. Universal Athletic Sales Co.*, 760 F.2d 910 (9th Cir. 1985). Likewise, the *Erie* "guess" is reviewed *de novo*, *Salve Regina College v. Russell*, 499 U.S. 225 (1991), as is a district court's determination that an issue is "procedural" or "substantive." *Am. Reliable Ins. Co. v. Navratil*, 445 F.3d 402 (5th Cir. 2006).

---

### Checkpoints

• Can you describe when *Erie* requires application of state law?

• Can you describe what *Hanna* held concerning the Rules?

• Can you identify when law will be classified as "procedural" as opposed to "substantive"? What impact does that classification have?

• Can you describe how a federal court identifies which state's law applies, either in a case that has, or has not, been transferred?

# Chapter 47

# Discovery

---

## Discovery Roadmap

This chapter explains the purpose of discovery and the ways by which the Rules require lawyers to cooperate and plan the scope and timing of discovery.

This chapter describes the scope of discovery, both in general and as to each method of discovery.

---

Before adoption of the Rules, very little information was exchanged between the parties before trial. Because pleadings were often done in multiple rounds, some information was disclosed through the process of pleading, but trial was the principal way that one side learned the full details of the facts possessed by the other side. Generally, one party did not learn facts known only to the other party until the witnesses were on the stand. "Trial by ambush" was not uncommon.

Under the Rules, however, the importance of pleadings has diminished, since they need only provide notice of the claims and defenses. Remember that the under *Iqbal* and *Twombly*, the Rules require that a plaintiff put very little information in a complaint: the plaintiff must plead factual material that, if true, plausibly states a claim upon which relief can be granted. But recall that, although a plaintiff must have a Rule 11 basis to plead its allegations, simply because the plaintiff can do so does not mean that there is no evidence that undermines the allegations; it also does not mean that a plaintiff cannot violate Rule 11 by pleading an allegation without evidence to support it. The same is true, of course, for a defendant's answer.

Instead of multiple rounds of pleadings, the Rules now provide multiple mechanisms—forms of discovery—for each side to learn information known by the other side, and by third parties. Although parties are free—within the bounds of ethics—to simply use informal means to gather information, discovery is the Rules' way to force parties to give up even damaging information.

Thus, rather than learning the bulk of information at trial or through informal investigation, parties now learn information from other parties and non-parties through "discovery." Because of the discovery rules, trial by ambush is the exception, not the rule. The thought is that it is better to try cases on the merits, rather than by last minute evidentiary surprises.

The net effect of discovery is to shift forward from trial the time when each party should be fully informed of all relevant information bearing on the parties' claims or defenses. In theory, therefore, discovery should reduce the time needed to resolve disputes. However, in fact discovery has proven quite expensive and, although trials are less frequent than they were without discovery, costs have generally increased, not decreased. The focus of dispute resolution, however, has shifted from courtroom to discovery process.

As a consequence, litigators must be very familiar with all aspects of discovery. Discovery is the process by which facts are gathered. Summary judgment and trial are the means by which those facts are used in creative but legitimate ways to tell a story and persuade the judge or jury that liability should, or should not, be imposed.

# A.  Purpose of Discovery

As we saw above, as part of the required initial disclosures, shortly after suit is filed the Rules require parties to disclose information that they will likely want to use at trial to support their claims or defenses (and other information, such as damages and insurance) and to do so without a request. Boiled down, under initial required disclosures, each party must disclose to the other its "good stuff"—what it will use to support its case or defense. In discovery, each party is required to produce all relevant evidence—even evidence that undermines or contradicts allegations needed to prove their claim or defense—*if sought by an opposing party through a proper discovery request.*

Although the Rules create means to discover information from opposing parties and non-parties, the Rules also limit what can be discovered. All discovery, for example, is—for the first time—limited to discovering information that is relevant to a claim or defense. But, even some relevant information can be protected from disclosure where the costs exceed the likely benefit of producing the information, or the information is subject to a privilege, including the attorney-client privilege. Finally, each specific method of discovery has its own limitations: some forms of discovery can only be used against parties, for example, not non-parties; other forms of discovery are limited in number.

Despite eliminating trial by ambush (and so saving costs) and eliminating multiple rounds of pleadings, discovery is expensive, intrusive, and time-consuming.

*See In re Brand Name Prescription Drugs Antitrust Litig.*, 123 F.3d 599, 614 (7th Cir. 1997) ("Pretrial discovery included the taking of a thousand depositions and the production of fifty million pages of documents."). Think that's an extreme case? It is, but it's not unique. *See Mitzel v. Westinghouse Elec. Corp.*, 72 F.3d 414 (3rd Cir. 1995) (in a simple injury case, 5100 attorney hours were spent conducting 19 depositions and producing 22 linear feet of documents).

Before learning about discovery and related to how much its costs, it is important to emphasize that litigants do not always have to get information through formal discovery. Instead, they are generally free to engage in informal information gathering. For example, a lawyer can discuss an accident with a non-party witness without having to take that witness's deposition, and, indeed, a lawyer probably should interview a non-party witness before noticing that witness's deposition. Instead of taking a witness's deposition, for example, a lawyer can interview the witness and obtain a sworn affidavit as to who ran the red light.

While ethical rules limit a lawyer's ability to talk to opposing parties who are represented by counsel (including, to some extent, current and former employees of an entity-opponent), generally lawyers are free to learn information from non-parties. Likewise, lawyers are generally free to use undercover investigators, to search public databases and the Internet for factual information that may help to bring or defend a lawsuit. Formal discovery is an important part of the information gathering process that lawyers must do, but only a part of it.

# B. Party Responsibility for Setting the Boundaries for Discovery and Making Initial Disclosures

Disputes between lawyers over the scope of discovery have existed since discovery became the norm. A lot of judges spent enormous amounts of time and energy resolving arguments about whether one side was asking for too much, or the other side giving up too little. As a result, beginning in the 1980s, the Rules were amended to require parties to negotiate their disagreements more fully before going to a judge. Most disagreements are resolved by negotiation between lawyers without involving the court through motion practice. But disputes continued. As a result, the Rules in 2015 were again amended to encourage early judicial management of discovery and require greater party management of its scope.

# C. Greater Judicial Involvement in and Lawyer Management of Discovery

The parties' obligations to manage discovery are clear, and recent amendments require greater, earlier judicial involvement.

## 1. Each Lawyer Must Participate in the Rule 26(f) Conference

At the start of a lawsuit, at a Rule 26(f) conference the parties' lawyers must meet to discuss and agree upon the scope of discovery. *See* Chapter 42. If have disagreements, they must articulate and submit them promptly to the court for decision. *See id.*

## 2. New Amendment Requires Early, More Judicial Involvement

The Rules require judges be more proactive in managing discovery than ever before. The changes are subtle. The rule used to state the court would enter the scheduling order "after consulting with the parties, attorneys and any unrepresented parties at a scheduling conference by telephone, mail, or other means"; but it was changed to delete "telephone, mail, or other means." A committee note states that the rule still allows a scheduling order to be based on the parties Rule 26(f) report without holding an in-person conference, but emphasizes the court should use "direct simultaneous communication" to the text of the rule is intended to encourage judges to participate in direct exchanges with the parties early on in the litigation process.

Another change was to shorten the time period for issuing the scheduling order, from 120 days to 90 days (generally after the first defendant was served), unless the judge finds good cause for a longer deadline. FRCP 16(b)(2).

A third change was, as pointed out in Chapter 42, to expand what must be in the Rule 42 report in the first place.

Taken together, the rules as amended are intended to get even more information to the judge, even earlier in the case, and to get judges more involved earlier in managing discovery.

## 3. Each Party Must Make Initial Disclosures

Each party must make its "initial disclosures." *See* Chapter 42.

## 4. A Discovery Request Is Certified as Reasonable

The Rules require parties to take into account the burden that their discovery requests will impose on the opposing party, and to certify that each discovery request is reasonable in light of the stakes in the case. Specifically, Rule 26(g)(1) requires every request for discovery be signed by a party's lawyer, and the signature certifies that: (A) the request is consistent with the rules, or at least is not frivolous under them; (B) is not made for "any improper purpose" including causing harassment, unnecessary delay, or "needless" increase in litigation costs; and (C) is "not unreasonable nor unduly burdensome or expensive, considering the needs of the case, prior discovery in the case, the amount in controversy, and the importance of the issues at stake in the action." FRCP 26(g)(1).

These Rules require attorneys to determine before sending a request that it is reasonable in light of the circumstances in the case. This is intended to rein in discovery by requiring lawyers to self-police and to not seek discovery that is unduly difficult to gather given the circumstances of the case.

## 5. Lawyers Must Meet and Confer Before Raising Disputes with the Court, and Must Request a Conference with the Court Before Filing a Discovery Motion

If a discovery dispute arises, the Rules require that the lawyers first attempt in good faith to resolve their dispute, and — in a new amendment — to first ask for a conference with the court before filing any discovery motion. FRCP 37(B).

The Rules are designed to require the lawyers to be reasonable in discovery, to work without judicial intervention in both in setting the boundaries and timing of discovery, and to resolve disputes over discovery.

### Checkpoints

- Can you describe how the Rules require lawyers to cooperate in discovery, and judicial involvement in managing it?

# Chapter 48

# Scope of Discovery: Relevancy and Other Boundaries

---

## Scope of Discovery Roadmap

This chapter explains the basic tools of discovery: requests for production of documents; interrogatories; requests for admission; and depositions.

This chapter describes how the Rules limit discovery to, at most, "relevant" information.

This chapter also explains how sometimes even relevant information may not be discovered, either because the usefulness of the evidence is outweighed by the cost to obtain it, or because the information is protected from discovery because of competing policies including those embodied in the attorney-client privilege, the work-product doctrine, or principles of privacy.

---

Significant amendments were made in December 2015 to those rules governing discovery. As always, the Rules have express limitations on discovery—but as amended they are different and seemingly more restrictive. Those boundaries must be enforced by a party: if the other side seeks, for example, undiscoverable information, the party from whom that information is sought must object, or the objection will be waived if the party tries to assert it later. The same is true even for efforts to discover information that, while relevant, is not discoverable because it is protected from discovery by the attorney-client privilege or other doctrines. It is very easy to waive an objection that the other party is seeking "too much" information.

The proper way to object to a discovery request that exceeds the scope authorized by the Rules varies depending on what type of discovery is being sought (*i.e.*, whether what is sought is documents, or deposition testimony, for example.). The proper way to object, therefore, is discussed in connection with how a party must respond to each type of discovery is being requested. *See* Chapter 49.

# A. Relevancy to a Claim and Proportionality as a Key Limit on Discovery

Since their inception, the Rules have limited discovery to "relevant" information. "Relevant *to what*" has undergone recent changes and sometimes even relevant information is not discoverable.

Until 2000, information was discoverable without court approval if it was at least "reasonably calculated to lead to discovery of" information that was "relevant to the subject matter" of the suit.

But in 2000, the rule was narrowed to allow discovery only to information that was reasonably calculated to lead to discovery of information that "relevant to a claim or defense" in the suit, and so narrower than the "subject matter" of the suit. But the rule still permitted discovery of information that was merely "relevant to the subject matter"—but only if the party seeking that information showed "good cause" to allow it. *See Sanyo Laser Prods., Inc. v. Arista Records, Inc.,* 214 F.R.D. 496 (S.D. Ind. 2003) (discussing the 2000 amendment).

Then in December, 2015, the scope of discovery was narrowed in two ways, and a third change was made that is intended to heighten awareness of the need for discovery to be "proportional" to a case, and likely will narrow discovery even if that was not its intent.

First, the amended rule eliminates the 2015 provision which had allowed a court for good cause to permit discovery of information that, while not relevant to a claim or defense, was relevant to the subject matter of the suit.

Second, the rule after 2015 no longer states that information is discoverable if it is "reasonably calculated" to lead to evidence relevant to the claim or suit.

Third, the 2015 amendment made a change by moving, and re-ordering, language that had been "buried" in Rule 26(b)(2)(C) to a more prominent spot. Now the rule more specifically states that a discovery request seeking information relevant to a claim or defense is not proper unless the request is also was "proportional to the needs of the case, considering the importance of the issues at stake in the action, the amount in controversy, the parties' relative access to relevant information, the parties' resources, the importance of the discovery in resolving the issues, and whether the burden or expense of the proposed discovery outweigh its likely benefit." Fed. R. Civ. P. 26(b)(1).

This language had existed in earlier rules, but in explaining when discovery was "unduly burdensome."

Thus, since 2000 the rules have substantially narrowed the scope of discovery:

| Prior to 2000 | 2000–15 | 2015– |
|---|---|---|
| Request was proper if it sought information reasonably calculated to lead to discovery of information relevant to the subject matter of a suit, even if the information was not admissible at trial. | Request was proper if it sought information reasonably calculated to lead to discovery of information relevant to a claim or defense, and, with good cause, to the subject matter of a suit; in both instances, the information need not have been admissible at trial. | Request was proper if it sought information relevant to a claim or defense, and meets the proportionality test, even if the information is itself not admissible at trial. |

This chapter now takes a closer look at the requirements of the new rule.

First, the information must be "relevant" to a claim or defense. The Rules do not and have never defined "relevance," stating instead only that relevant evidence is discoverable even if it is not admissible at trial. The Federal Rules of Evidence define "relevant evidence" as "evidence having any tendency to make the existence of any fact that is of consequence to the determination of the action more probable or less probable than it would be without the evidence." Taken together, then, information is discoverable—again, even if it will not be admissible at trial—so long as the information is reasonably likely to lead to evidence that is admissible at trial that makes the existence of a fact of consequence at trial more or less probable.

A lot of this is beyond your first year civil procedure course, but not all of it. What facts will matter at trial turns on what claims or defenses are in the pleadings. A deposition question in a car wreck case asking the defendant "did you run the red light" obviously goes to a fact that has consequence at trial, and the defendant's testimony about what he did, or didn't do, is admissible because the defendant has personal knowledge of his own action.

When would a question seek information that, while itself is not admissible, is reasonably calculated to lead to discovery of admissible evidence? You can't learn the rules of evidence in civil procedure, but you probably have some idea that "hearsay" is inadmissible. So, for example, a lawyer could object at trial if a witness were asked, "did someone tell you whether she saw the defendant run the red light?" However, during a deposition in discovery, that question would be proper, since it is reasonably calculated to lead to discovery of the identity of the person who made that statement, and that person's testimony as to whether she saw the defendant run the red light would be admissible. So, information is discoverable even if it is not admissible. The two are related, but separate, concepts. *See Bank of the Orient v. Superior Court,* 136 Cal. Rptr. 741 (Cal. App. 1977) (court held information that would be inadmissible at trial because it was a "subsequent remedial measure" in terms of the Rules of Evidence was discoverable).

The casebooks typically use a few cases to illustrate the meaning of "relevance." In *Davis v. Precoat Metals,* 2002 WL 1759828 (N.D. Ill. 2002), for example, the plaintiffs' claim was that the defendant engaged in unlawful racial and sex discrimination at a particular plant. The court held that the plaintiffs were entitled to discovery of information that could show that other employees — besides the plaintiffs — had been discriminated against. Why was that relevant to the plaintiffs' claim? Because it might show that any explanation offered by the defendant for its actions was pretextual: if the defendant had legitimate reasons for its hiring decisions concerning plaintiffs, why were there so many other instances of discrimination? The court held the plaintiff was entitled to discover evidence that would be probative of that point. *Cf. Steffan v. Cheney,* 920 F.2d 74 (D.C. Cir. 1990) (because judicial review of an administrative action was limited to the ground upon which it was based, discovery into conduct that might also have supported administrative action was irrelevant).

Similarly, in *Pacitti v. Macy's,* 193 F.3d 766 (3rd Cir. 1999), Macy's department store worked with producers of the musical "Annie" to locate the "next Annie" by conducting a star search. The advertisements stated that the winner would be the star on Broadway in the upcoming production of Annie. The eventual winner of the search performed in the off-Broadway road show, but was fired just before the show began its Broadway run. The girl's parents then sued Macy's, contending that Macy's had intended all along not to actually let the winner perform on Broadway, asserting several claims including fraudulent inducement: the plaintiffs contended that Macy's had a secret deal with the producers by which the winner in fact would not appear on Broadway. Plaintiffs alleged they relied on the fraudulent misrepresentation to the contrary. Even so, the district court denied discovery into communications between Macy's and the producers. The district court reversed, finding that the information was relevant because the information that "Macy's possessed when [the girl] relied on its representations and participated in the Search forms the very basis of plaintiff's fraudulent misrepresentation claims."

As noted above, the Rules recently were amended to narrow the scope of relevance by requiring the information be relevant to a claim or defense, and not allowing discovery into information relevant to the subject matter, even with "good cause" for the court to do so. Again, before 2000, discovery was allowed — without court approval — if the information sought was relevant to the "subject matter" of the suit, and not only if it was relevant to a claim or defense. "Relevant to the subject matter" had been construed "broadly to encompass any matter that bears on, *or that reasonably could lead to other matter* that could bear on, any issue that is or *may be* in the case." *Oppenheimer Fund, Inc. v. Sanders,* 473 U.S. 340 (1978) (emph. added).

What difference does it make that information is discoverable now only if it is relevant to the claim or defense, as compared to relevant to the subject matter? It is clear that the amendment was "designed to involve the court more actively in regulating the breadth of sweeping or contentious discovery." *In re Sealed Case,* 381 F.3d 1205, 1215 (D.C. Cir. 2004). Beyond that, the courts are disagreeing on the degree of the limitation.

On the one hand, one could read the requirement that the information be relevant to a claim or defense to mean that discovery cannot be used to uncover facts that relate to potential claims or defenses, but ones that have not already been pled. *Toms v. Links Sports Mgmt. Group, L.P.,* 2006 WL 3255865 (W.D. La. 2006) ("Absent an order expanding the scope of discovery for good cause shown, discovery generally should not be allowed for the purpose of developing new claims or defenses not already pleaded."). On the other hand, courts have rejected that reading. *Thompson v. Dep't of Housing & Urban Dev.,* 199 F.R.D. 168, 172 (D. Md. 2001) (stating that it was a mistake to conclude that the 2000 amendment means that "no fact may be discovered unless it directly correlates with a factual allegation in the complaint or answer" but recognizing that the amendment was intended to narrow the scope of discovery "in some meaningful way"). Other courts have indicated the change is not so great as either end of that spectrum suggest. *See Anderson v. Hale,* 2001 U.S. Dist. Lexis 7538 (N.D. Ill. 2001) ("None of the decisions suggest that amended Rule 26(b)(1) will bring about a dramatic effect on the scope of discovery).

The third limitation is the "new" proportionality requirement. Thus far, courts are holding that the movement of the language — from when it described when discovery was "unduly burdensome" into the rule defining the scope of discovery — and the slight changes made to the language when moved, do not change the scope of discovery. One court stated flatly that the burdens to show "unduly burdensome" under the old rule, or "lack of proportionality" under the new, "have not fundamentally changed" *Carr v. State Farm Mut. Auto. Ins. Co.,* 312 F.R.D. 459 (N.D. Tex. 2015) (party objecting to discovery as not proportional must make a specific objection and come forward with specific information to address, insofar as that information is available to it, importance of issues at stake in action, amount in controversy, parties' relative access to relevant information, parties' resources, importance of discovery in resolving issues, and whether burden or expense of the proposed discovery outweighs its likely benefit).

# B. Sometimes Even a Request for Information that is Relevant to a Claim or Defense and which is Proportional to the Case is Objectionable

Sometimes even a request for information that is relevant to a claim or defense and which is proportional to the case is objectionable. "All discovery is subject to the limitations imposed by Rule 26(b)(2)(C)." FRCP 26(b)(1). Those limitations include:

- Court orders may limit the number of depositions or interrogatories, or the length of depositions;
- Court orders or local rules may limit the number of requests for admission;
- Electronically stored information that is not "reasonably accessible because of undue burden or cost" may not need to be produced absent a showing of good cause by the party seeking it;
- The party opposing the discovery shows that the discovery sought is unreasonably cumulative or duplicative, or is obtainable from some other source that is more convenient, less burdensome, or less expensive;
- The party opposing the discovery shows that the party seeking the discovery has had ample opportunity by discovery in the action to obtain the information sought; or
- The party opposing the discovery shows that the burden or expense of the proposed discovery outweighs its likely benefit, taking into account the needs of the case, the amount in controversy, the parties' resources, the importance of the issues at stake in the litigation, and the importance of the proposed discovery in resolving the issues.

So, for example, even if a party seeks information that is discoverable, if it is available in another form or duplicates information already known to the party, discovery can be denied, even though the information is relevant to a claim or defense.

# C. Privilege and Work Product as Boundaries to Discovery

The attorney-client privilege and work product doctrines both limit discovery, but one is largely absolute (at least under the Rules) while the other may be overcome. This section briefly describes both the attorney-client privilege and the work product doctrine and explains how each serves as boundaries under the Rules.

# 1. Privileged Information Is Protected from Disclosure

Rule 26(b)(1) limits discovery to "any non-privileged matter" that is relevant to a claim or defense. While this sounds like a party has an obligation not to ask for privileged information, instead the Rules work exactly in the opposite fashion: a party must object to disclosing privileged information, or the objection is waived.

A privilege means the right not to reveal certain information. The term "privileged" in the Rule has the same meaning in discovery as at trial, and so is defined by the Federal Rules of Evidence. *U.S. v. Reynolds*, 345 U.S. 1 (1953). Under the Federal Rules of Evidence, a privilege can arise from various sources, including the Constitution (*e.g.*, the privilege against self-incrimination), substantive law, rules of evidence, and "principles of the common law as they may be interpreted by courts of the United States in light of reason and experience." Federal Rule of Evidence 501; *see Jaffe v. Redmond*, 518 U.S. 1 (1996) (adopting a federal privilege protecting psychotherapist-patient communications). State privilege law provides the scope of any privilege where state law provides an element of the claim or defense. *Id.* The attorney-client privilege is a common privilege, and our sole focus here.

Although there are entire books on the scope of the attorney-client privilege, only a basic understanding is necessary here. Information is generally subject to a claim that it is protected by the attorney-client privilege only if:

> (1) the asserted holder of the privilege is or sought to become a client; (2) the person to whom the communication was made (a) is a member of the bar of a court or his subordinate and (b) in connection with this communication is acting as a lawyer; (3) the communication relates to a fact of which the attorney was informed (a) by his client (b) without the presence of strangers (c) for the purpose of securing primarily either (i) an opinion on law or (ii) legal services or (iii) assistance in some legal proceeding, and not (d) for the purpose of committing a crime or tort; and (4) the privilege has been (a) claimed and (b) not waived by the client.

*In re Sealed Case*, 737 F.2d 94, 98–99 (D.C. Cir.1984) (*quoting U. S. v. United Shoe Machinery Corp.*, 89 F. Supp. 357, 358–59 (D. Mass. 1950)).

The privilege creates special issues when the client is not a person, but a business entity such as a corporation: is everyone employed by a corporate party a "client" for purposes of the privilege? If not everyone, who? The answer to the question is important because if a communication is not from or to a "client," there can be no privilege. *Upjohn Co. v. U.S.*, 449 U.S. 383 (1981) is the oft-cited case analyzing privilege in the context of entities. The Court reasoned that federal law would recognize a privilege over communications between an attorney and an employee of a business entity would be privileged if the employee is someone who is a member of the "control group" of the company—who can cause the company to act on the advice—or who gave the information in the course of enabling the lawyer to give sound advice. Thus, the content of communications (though not the facts in the communications) from either type of employee may be privileged if all the elements are satisfied.

A person or party who believes that a party is seeking discovery of privileged information must object, either by interposing an objection to an interrogatory or deposition question and not disclosing the privileged information, or, in the case of requests for production, by producing a "privilege log" of documents that are withheld from production. These procedures will be explored more fully in the next chapter. The key thing is to realize that privileged information is not discoverable *but that the party withholding it has an obligation to object and preserve the privilege.*

Privilege may be waived in other ways as well, for example by intentionally disclosing part of a privileged communication or using it "offensively" against a party. *See Santelli v. Electro-Motive,* 188 F.R.D. 306 (N.D. Ill. 1999) (party avoided waiver of psychotherapist-patient privilege by eliminating any claim for emotional distress damages in sexual discrimination case). Again, however, the key issue is to recognize how to claim the privilege, a process that will be discussed in connection with each form of discovery.

## 2. Work Product or "Trial Preparation" Materials Receive Qualified Protection

Suppose litigation is anticipated and defense counsel interviews witnesses and memorializes their statements in several memoranda, putting them in his file. Later, in fact, a suit is filed. The information is not privileged, since it was not communicated between client and attorney. Is there any protection for it? What if one of the memos reveals the lawyer's litigation strategies, and includes his impressions on how good each witness might do at trial?

Before a specific Rule governing this type of litigation materials was adopted, in *Hickman v. Taylor,* 329 U.S. 495 (1947), the Court held that communications could be protected from disclosure even if they were not privileged because attorneys needed to have a "certain degree of privacy, free from unnecessary intrusion by opposing parties and their counsel" to properly prepare a client's case. However, the Court also recognized that this protection had to give way sometimes, at least as to factual information: "Where relevant and non-privileged facts remain hidden in an attorneys' file and where production of those facts is essential to the preparation of [the other party's] case, discovery may properly be had." With that phrase, the court made a narrow limit on protection of work product: *factual* information could be had, but only if they were essential to the other side's case.

Today a rule controls but *Hickman* influenced the rule. Rule 26(b)(3) protects work product or trial preparation information from discovery—even when it is relevant to a claim or defense—but unlike the protection afforded to privileged communications, the protection granted to some forms of work product can be overcome under some circumstances:

### (3) Trial Preparation: Materials.

(A) *Documents and Tangible Things.* Ordinarily, a party may not discover documents and tangible things that are prepared in anticipation of litigation or for trial by or for another party or its representative (including the other party's attorney, consultant, surety, indemnitor, insurer, or agent). But, subject to Rule 26(b)(4), those materials may be discovered if:

(i)   they are otherwise discoverable under Rule 26(b)(1); and

(ii)  the party shows that it has substantial need for the materials to prepare its case and cannot, without undue hardship, obtain their substantial equivalent by other means.

(B) *Protection Against Disclosure.* If the court orders discovery of those materials, it must protect against disclosure of the mental impressions, conclusions, opinions, or legal theories of a party's attorney or other representative concerning the litigation.

(C) *Previous Statement.* Any party or other person may, on request and without the required showing, obtain the person's own previous statement about the action or its subject matter. If the request is refused, the person may move for a court order, and Rule 37(a)(5) applies to the award of expenses. A previous statement is either:

(i)   a written statement that the person has signed or otherwise adopted or approved; or

(ii)  a contemporaneous stenographic, mechanical, electrical, or other recording—or a transcription of it—that recites substantially verbatim the person's oral statement.

FRCP 26(b)(3). Thus, something can be work product if:

(1) it is a document or a tangible thing;
(2) it was prepared in anticipation of litigation; and
(3) had been prepared by or for a party, or by his representative.

Note that only tangible things are protected, not information memorialized in them. Simply because a witness tells a lawyer a fact which the lawyer writes down doesn't make that fact "protected"; the document itself is. Because facts themselves are not protected simply because they are memorialized in a document by a lawyer in anticipation of litigation, work product is often misunderstood. In a recent case the district court tried to clarify the limitations on what is, and is not, work product:

> Interrogatories which seek to discover facts regarding an attorney's mental thought process seek improper work product information. "Although the work product doctrine is most commonly applied to documents and things, unjustified disclosure of the opinions or mental processes of counsel may occur when questions are posed which seek information at depositions or in interrogatories." *United States v. Dist. Council of New York City and Vicinity of the United Brotherhood of Carpenters and Joiners of Am.*, 1992 WL 208284 (S.D.N.Y. 1992). In *United Brotherhood*, the court found,
>
> > How a party, its counsel and agents choose to prepare their case, the efforts they undertake, and the people they interview is not factual information to which an adversary is entitled. Disclosure of this information would inevitably teach defendants which individuals the [plaintiff] considered more or less valuable witnesses and how it was preparing for trial.
>
> Similarly, in *Commonwealth of Massachusetts v. First National Supermarkets, Inc.*, 112 F.R.D. 149 (D. Mass. 1986), the court distinguished between interrogatories seeking discoverable facts and those seeking attorney work product, finding a "distinction between asking the identity of persons with knowledge, which is clearly permissible, and asking the identity of persons contacted and/or interviewed during an investigation, which is not." *First National*, 112 F.R.D. at 152. Likewise, in *Morgan v. City of New York*, 2002 WL 1808233 (S.D.N.Y. 2002), the court directed plaintiff to answer an interrogatory requesting the identity of "every person whom Plaintiff believes has knowledge of any facts concerning Plaintiff's claims in this litigation[,]" but not an interrogatory requiring plaintiff to "[i]dentify every person whom Plaintiff or her agents have contacted, interviewed or communicated with concerning

Plaintiff's allegations in this case." *See also Seven Hanover Assocs., LLC v. Jones Lang LaSalle Americas, Inc.,* 2005 WL 3358597 (S.D.N.Y. 2005) ("Defendant is free to ask for the names of persons with knowledge of the facts, but it is not entitled, through plaintiffs, to the identification of who among such knowledgeable individuals may have been interviewed by plaintiffs' attorney."); *Donson Stores, Inc. v. American Bakeries Co.,* 1973 WL 791 (S.D.N.Y. 1973) (striking the clause "including your counsel" from the interrogatory requesting, "State whether you, including your counsel, made any investigation regarding any possible violations of any company policy. . . .").

*Weiss v. Nat'l Westminster Bank, PLC,* 2007 WL 1460933 (E.D. N.Y. 2007). *See also ECDC Envtl., L.C. v. New York Marine and Gen. Ins. Co.,* 1998 WL 614478 (S.D.N.Y. 1998) ("because the work product privilege does not protect facts in that document (the privilege protects documents, not facts), the party seeking those facts may obtain them through [means other than document requests], such as through depositions and interrogatories.").

Thus, work product does not make facts secret. In addition, some of what is protected by work product can be discovered. Consistent with *Hickman,* Rule 26(b)(3)(B) creates a three-tiered system—(1) factual or "ordinary" work product, (2) "opinion" work product, and (3) a party or person's own statement. Only factual work product, not opinion work product, can be discovered, and it only if the party seeking its discovery makes the showing required by Rule 26(b)(3)(A).

> Thus, Rule 26(b)(3) provides that, even if the party seeking discovery of information otherwise protected by the work product doctrine has made the requisite showing of need and undue hardship, courts must still protect against the disclosure of mental impressions, conclusions, opinions, or legal theories of an attorney and his agents. Stated differently, Rule 26(b)(3) establishes two tiers of protection: first, work prepared in anticipation of litigation by an attorney or his agent is discoverable only upon a showing of need and hardship; second, "core" or "opinion" work product that encompasses the "mental impressions, conclusions, opinion or legal theories of an attorney or other representative of a party concerning the litigation" is "generally afforded near absolute protection from discovery." Thus, core or opinion work product receives greater protection than ordinary work product and is discoverable only upon a showing of rare and exceptional circumstances.

*In re Cendant Corp. Sec. Litig.,* 343 F.3d 658, 663 (3d Cir. 2003).

It is rare for opinion work product to be discoverable. For example, in *Holmgren v. State Farm Mut. Ins. Co.*, 976 F.2d 573 (9th Cir. 1992), the court held that opinion work product was discoverable when "mental impressions are the pivotal issue in the current litigation and the need for the material is compelling." At issue were notes written by State Farm's adjuster evaluating a claim against its insured, and the suit was a claim by the insured against State Farm for not settling that claim in good faith. Thus, the notes reflected an opinion made during litigation, but that opinion—the amount of liability the insured faced—was critical in the bad faith suit.

## D. Other Boundaries

As noted in Chapter 50, courts generally do not permit a party to discover facts known to or opinions held by an opposing party's consulting expert.

Finally, Rule 33(d) permits a party responding to an interrogatory request to provide the raw business information that can lead to the answer to the interrogatory if "the burden of deriving or ascertaining the answer [to the interrogatory] is substantially the same for either party. . . ." FRCP 33(d).

## E. Enforcing the Boundaries

A party who believes that another party is seeking either irrelevant information or information that is otherwise undiscoverable must object and may move for a protective order. *See* Chapter 51. Conversely, a party who believes that it is entitled to overcome a boundary—by seeking information that is relevant only to the subject matter, or which is protected by the work product doctrine, for example—must file a motion to compel that information if the opposing party objects.

---

### Checkpoints

- Can you explain when information will be relevant to a claim or defense?
- Can you identify those circumstances when even relevant information will not be discoverable, and how a party goes about precluding discovery into relevant information?
- What information is protected from discovery by the attorney-client privilege? The attorney-work product doctrine? When can either protection be overcome, if ever?

# Chapter 49

# Forms of Discovery

---

### Forms of Discovery Roadmap

This chapter describes the forms of discovery, their limitations, and how lawyers typically use each.

---

There are five major forms of discovery: document requests; requests for admission; interrogatories; requests for physical exams; and oral depositions. (In addition, the rules allow "depositions on written questions," which have a limited but useful purpose.) This chapter explores each form of discovery.

In a typical case, lawyers use discovery in a fairly predictable order: each side requests documents from the other side, which once received are put in chronological order and examined by the recipients' lawyers. Then, interrogatories, requests for admission, and depositions on written questions are used for specific purposes (for reasons we'll see below). Finally, lawyers depose fact witnesses and, then, finally, expert witnesses. We won't analyze discovery in the order the Rules are in, because examining the discovery tools in the order they're usually used in will give you a better intuition about them. Casebooks, however, generally follow the order of the Rules.

## A. Requests for Production of Documents and Things

Typically, but especially in commercial litigation, lawyers first send "document requests" or "requests for production" to other parties to the lawsuit in order to require them to produce existing documents, documents that were created at the time of the events that led to the lawsuit. Generally, once those documents are produced, then the lawyer who requested the documents will place them in chronological order. The lawyer can then read the documents in the order they were created, and thus learn much of the story of what went on, who was involved, and what issues might arise in the lawsuit. Particularly in large law firms, young lawyers spend significant time reviewing documents that have been produced by the other parties to the suit. At times, document review produces "smoking guns" which greatly affect the value of a case.

As you can imagine, it can be quite expensive and disruptive to force a business to rummage through files—including e-mails and other electronic files (called Electronically Stored Information, or ESI)—to locate documents that respond to a document request. Lawyers receiving a document request must examine carefully whether a request is not proportional, since it can cost a lot to gather and produce documents. This section next describes how parties send requests and respond to them.

## 1. Obligations of the Requesting Party

A party wishing to obtain documents from another party to a suit does so by serving written requests for production. *See* FRCP 34. The requests must be signed by an attorney and must include the attorney's name and address, and the signature of the lawyer constitutes a certification that the request is proper, as discussed in Chapter 47. As noted in Chapter 47, a request must seek information relevant to a claim or defense and be proportional. The amended rules emphasize that a lawyer sending a request must consider the proportionality requirement in drafting a request. However, a party seeking information may have no idea how expensive or otherwise burdensome it will be for the other party to respond. While the parties should discuss these issues at their Rule 26(f) conference, they may not have done so sufficiently because they could not then appreciate the issues in the case or difficulties that would develop during discovery, particularly of electronically stored information, or ESI.

In practice, what attorneys do in creating requests for production is to put together a list of descriptions of documents that they believe the other party might have, and which would either contain or lead to the discovery of admissible evidence. See the examples below. Obviously, the claims and defenses and the particular facts determine which kinds of documents might exist and might be relevant. The rules simply require that the party serving the requests to set forth the categories of documents "with reasonable particularity." FRCP 34(b)(1)(A). If a party wants electronically stored documents to be produced in a certain way, for example in pdf format, then it must state the form in the request.

## 2. Obligations of the Recipient

The Rules give the recipient 30 days or as otherwise agreed to respond to requests for production. FRCP 34(b)(2); *see* FRCP 29. During that time, the party may have a lot of work to do.

The first step is for the lawyer responding to the request to analyze the document requests to determine if any are not proportional, or otherwise seek irrelevant or otherwise undiscoverable information. Objections are subject to Rule 26(g), and must be made only after investigation. *See St. Paul Reinsurance Co. v. Commercial Fin. Corp.,* 198 F.R.D. 508 (N.D. Iowa 2000) (requiring lawyer to publish an article on why boilerplate objections are improper).

If the lawyer has a reasonable basis for this belief, then he can object and must object to preserve the objection. FRCP 34(b)(2)(B). The 2015 amendments made a significant change to objections. For the first time, if a party objects it must state whether it is withholding documents on the basis of that objection. FRCP 34(a)(2)(C). Notice that if the attorney only objects in part to a request, he must produce documents that are not objectionable. FRCP 34(b)(2)(C) ("An objection to part of a request must specify the part and permit inspection of the rest.") The new rule also requires that, if a party specifies in a request the format of how it wants ESI produced (*e.g.,* pdf, TIFF, *etc.*), the responding party must make its objection; if the requesting party does not specify the format, then the responding party must identify what format it will use. FRCP 34(d).

As a practical matter, to respond to requests, a lawyer will have a secretary re-type the requests, and beneath them the lawyer will state her objections. So, for example, a response to one of the requests above might look like this:

---

REQUEST: Produce all documents that refer to failures of the widget.
RESPONSE: Defendant objects to this response to the extent it seeks information covered by the attorney-client privilege or the work product doctrine. In addition, Defendant objects to producing documents which refer to any failure of the widget, since the failure in this case relates to metal fatigue. Accordingly, documents that refer to other failures are irrelevant, and also not proportional to the needs of the case. Subject to and without waiving such objections, Defendant will produce documents responsive to this request, and is withholding documents on the basis of this objection. Defendant will produce ESI in pdf format.

---

A party must state objections in the response or they are waived. *See Drexel Heritage Furnishings, Inc. v. Furniture USA Inc.,* 200 F.R.D. 255 (M.D. N.C. 2001) (recognizing that waiver is implicit Rule 34's requirement that objections be specifically stated). Thus, for example, a party that fails to include an objection to producing privileged documents waives the right to withhold such documents from copying and inspection, unless the court excuses the waiver for good cause shown. *Starlight Int'l Inc. v. Herlihy,* 181 F.R.D. 494 (D. Kan. 1998) (attorney's negligence is not good cause). As a result, responses to request for production invariably include objections to producing privileged or work product information, information that is not reasonably calculated to lead to discovery of admissible evidence, or information held by experts which is not otherwise discoverable. Typical objections to discovery requests include:

*The request is non-proportional, over broad, unduly burdensome, or harassing.* This objection is typically proper where a request is not limited to the claims or defenses in suit by time or subject matter. So, for example, a document request in the products liability case would be objectionable where it sought documents concerning widgets that were unrelated to the widget in suit. A similar objection is that the request seeks information that is "not reasonably calculated to lead to the discovery of admissible evidence."

*The request seeks information subject to the attorney-client privilege or attorney work product doctrine.* As a general rule, attorney-client privileged communications are not discoverable, and attorney-work product can be discovered only upon special showings. *See* Chapter 48. As a result, a party should object to requests for production that seek protected documents. (In addition, a party withholding documents on the basis of privilege or work product must prepare a privilege log, as discussed below.)

*The request seeks information held by experts but protected from disclosure by Rule 26(b)(4).* As shown below, expert witnesses are subject to special rules and procedures. A request for production that exceeds those boundaries is objectionable.

In addition to preparing objections and the written responses, the attorney must work with the client to use reasonable efforts locate all responsive documents or electronically stored information. The phrase "documents or electronically stored information" is broad and includes "writings, drawings, graphs, charts, photographs, sound recordings, images, and other data or data compilations—stored in any medium from which information can be obtained either directly or, if necessary, after translation by the responding party into a reasonably usable form." FRCP 34(a)(1)(A). Thus, it is not just paper documents, but x-rays, e-mail, electronic files such as Microsoft Word files, pdf files, voicemail recordings, and the like.

This can be quite time consuming, particularly where large corporations are responding to a request. The recipient of a document request has an obligation to produce non-objectionable, responsive documents that it has in its "possession, custody, or control." FRCP 34(a). Attorneys, therefore, have an obligation to ensure that their clients search out responsive "documents" that the client possesses, has custody of, or controls.

What does "possession, custody, or control" mean? The word "control" is probably the broadest, and it includes all documents that the responding party has a legal right to access. *Searock v. Stripling*, 736 F.2d 650, 654 (11th Cir. 1984). Thus, a party must produce not just documents in its actual possession or custody, but also those that it has the right to control. Therefore, a document in possession of the agent of a party—including its attorneys or employees—is within that party's control. For example, a common issue that arises when a corporation is a party is whether it must produce documents that are possessed, not by the corporate entity that is named as a party to the suit, but by a related corporation, such as a parent, subsidiary, or affiliate. Courts tend to hold that if the corporate party has the right to access the documents, then they are under its control and must be produced. *E.g., Gerling Int'l Ins. Co. v. Comm'r of Internal Rev.*, 839 F.2d 131, 140 (3rd Cir. 1988). Absent control, then a *subpoena duces tecum* must be served on the affiliated corporation, since a non-party controls the document. *See* below.

How much of an effort must the client take to find "documents" that it possesses, controls, or has custody of? The short answer is a "reasonable" one. *See Chambers v. Capital Cities/ABC*, 154 F.R.D. 63 (S.D.N.Y. 1994). What is "reasonable" obviously turns on the facts of the case. However, the 2015 amendments state that a "party need not provide discovery of electronically stored information from sources that the party identifies as not reasonably accessible because of undue burden or cost." FRCP 26(b)(2)(B).

As a practical matter, how do lawyers respond to requests for production? Clients often do not understand that they have an obligation to disclose documents that contain information that could harm their case. They do have that obligation and the withholding of responsive information can not only subject the lawyer and client to sanctions, it can result in the judge or jury concluding that the party is hiding the truth—that is never a good thing.

As a result, what generally happens is that a lawyer will first send a letter to a client who has been served with a set of document requests listing which categories of "documents" need to be located, and then meet with the client to discuss where responsive documents might be located. In the electronic environment, this may include talking to IT personnel to learn where e-documents are stored or backed-up electronically. Voicemail, e-mail, and all documents of the usual kind need to be gathered.

Once documents are gathered, the next typical step is to stamp (software and scanners do it now) each page of each document with its own unique number, called a "Bates Stamp." Bates stamping is important because it gives each page its own unique identifier. Typically, the plaintiff will use numbers starting with "P" or some other letter indicating the source of the document, and the defendant will use "D" or some other letter, followed by a unique number for each document.

After that, lawyers representing the producing party will examine each page to determine whether, though responsive, the document can be withheld because it discloses privileged or work product information. (An objection can be made to production of the whole document, or to a part of it by "redacting" information that is not discoverable by blacking it out with a marker or some form of electronic obliteration.) Often when literally read, document requests will call for production of documents protected by the attorney-client privilege, work product doctrine, or both. If the producing party has withheld any responsive documents on the basis of privilege or work product, the party must not only explicitly state the objection in the response, but must also prepare what is called a "privilege log." A privilege log identifies every document being withheld from production on the basis that, though responsive to a request for production, it is protected from disclosure by privilege (or work product). *See* FRCP 26(b)(5).

A responding party withholding documents on the basis of privilege must prepare a list of withheld documents—which provides enough information so that the party seeking the document can fairly assess whether privilege was properly claimed—and serve that list either along with the response to the request for production of documents, or later if agreed by the parties. *See Burlington Northern & Santa Fe Ry. Co. v. U.S. Dist. Ct.*, 408 F.3d 1142, 1147 (9th Cir. 2005). A portion of a typical privilege log might look like this:

| From | To | Subject | Privilege Claimed | Bates Nos. |
|------|-----|---------|-------------------|------------|
| Bob Smith, esq. | Ernie Engineer | Advice re widget compliance with environmental laws | Attorney client privileged communication | P001-008 |
| Ann Jones, esq. | Susie Developer | Memo regarding related lawsuit | Attorney Work Product | P1005-06 |

A privilege log includes a statement from counsel identifying Ann Jones and Bob Smith as attorneys and Susie and Ernie as employees party. These logs can take many hours to prepare. Young lawyers are often tasked to do "privilege reviews" of potentially responsive documents so that documents that can be claimed as privileged can be withheld from production and identified on a privilege log, as set out above.

The final step for the producing party is to organize the documents for production: how this must be done turns on whether the documents are paper or electronically stored. With paper documents, the producing party can either produce them as they were kept in the usual course of the party's business *or* labeled to respond to the requests for production. Rule 34(b)(2)(E)(i). With respect to electronically stored information, if the requesting party asked for it to be produced in a certain form, the party must produce it in that form (unless it objected to doing so); if the request did not specify the format, then it can be produced either in which it is ordinarily maintained or in "a reasonably usable form or forms." Rule 34(b)(2)(E)(ii). A party need not produce the same ESI in more than one form. Rule 34(b)(2)(E)(iii).

Why must a party go through all this trouble? Why not just ignore the document request and keep back the "bad" information (after all, the "good" information will have been disclosed during as part of the initial disclosures). First, a party who fails to respond to a request under Rule 34 may be sanctioned, such as precluding the use of evidence at trial, and also award attorneys' fees to the party that served the unanswered requests. FRCP 37(a)(3)(B)(iii). Second, the party who served the requests may move to compel, and if the failure to respond (or an incomplete or evasive response) was not substantially justified, the party who failed to answer may also be sanctioned. FRCP 37(a)(5)(A); *see* below, discussing motions to compel. If a party believes that a request for production is objectionable, it must confer with the party that served it and if that does not resolve the matter, it may file a motion for protection or wait to see if the party moves to compel production. *See* FRCP 26(c).

In this regard, a real world note bears emphasizing. Lawyers face pressure to interpret document requests narrowly or awkwardly to avoid producing the "smoking gun" or bad documents. In *Washington State Physicians Ins. Exchange & Ass'n. v. Fisons Corp.*, 858 P.2d 1054 (Wash. 1993), for example, the plaintiff had sued the defendant for injuries sustained by ingesting a defective medicine. The defendant held back a document that showed that it knew the medicine was defective by making evasive objections and doing its best to simply avoid producing the document even though it was responsive to a request for production. When it eventually came out, the plaintiff moved for sanctions. The Washington Supreme Court published an opinion detailing the misconduct. Although you will be tempted to play these games, don't do so. It's much more fun to win when you play fair than when you cheat.

The next step is for the producing party to sign and serve its response to the request for production on each party. FRCP 34(b). The producing party is not obligated to actually copy and serve the documents. Instead, the obligation is to make the documents available for copying under reasonable circumstances.

FRCP 34(b). Despite the fact that no such obligation is owed, in practice if only a few documents are responsive, the producing party will simply copy and produce them to all parties. However, if a voluminous number of pages are responsive, then the responding party will let the other parties come to inspect and designate which, if any, of those documents they want copied and produced. The producing party may be required, if the document is in electronic format, to convert it into a perceivable, reasonably useable form. FRCP 34(b)(2)(E). However, Rule 34 cannot be used to force a party to *create* a document. *Rockwell Int'l Corp. v. H. Wolfe Iron & Metal Co.*, 576 F. Supp. 511, 513 (W.D. Pa. 1983).

After receiving responsive documents or copying those that it wants from all that the party makes available for inspection, the party that served the requests for production then, as noted above, typically makes a copy of the documents (in case they get marked up or damaged) and then "chrons" the copy set, putting the documents into chronological order in order to study them and determine what happened and who from the other side were involved in the matter that led to the lawsuit. In that regard, review of the documents may lead the attorneys to realize that their client has additional claims or defenses. Further, the documents may reveal which of the other side's employees are likely to be key witnesses at trial, and so be subject to a pre-trial deposition. *See* below. Finally, reviewing the documents will suggest areas for further inquiry by interrogatory, requests for admission, or further requests for production.

If during document production a privileged or work product document is inadvertently produced, then under a recent amendment to Rule 26(b)(5)(B):

> If information produced in discovery is subject to a claim of privilege or of protection as trial-preparation material, the party making the claim may notify any party that received the information of the claim and the basis for it. After being notified, a party must promptly return, sequester, or destroy the specified information and any copies it has; must use or disclose the information until the claim is resolved; must take reasonable steps to retrieve the information if the party disclosed it before being notified; and may promptly present the information to the court under seal for a determination of the claim. The producing party must preserve the information until the claim is resolved.

This new "claw back" provision ostensibly will result in less privilege waiver through inadvertent production of privileged documents.

If the party that served the requests believes that one or more documents on the privilege log were not privileged, they can, after conferring with the party claiming privilege, move to compel production of privileged documents. The process by which district courts determine whether a document is in fact privileged often involves the district judge examining the challenged documents *in camera* (*i.e.*, without the party seeking their production present, or the party claiming privilege), so that the judge can review the document to determine whether it is, in fact, privileged. *See Banks v. Office of Senate Sergeant-at-Arms*, 2007 WL 949738 (D. D.C. 2007) (describing role of privilege logs and process of *in camera* examination of documents by the court).

## 3. Obtaining Documents from Non-Parties by Rule 45 Subpoena *Duces Tecum*

A party to a lawsuit can compel non-parties to produce documents only by serving the non-party with a "subpoena *duces tecum*." *See* Rules 34(c) & 45(d)(1). The non-party has the same obligations to search for documents, and the same options in how it will produce them, as a party does. Those are discussed above.

A non-party can choose to comply with a subpoena. A non-party who wants to comply with a subpoena subject to some objections must serve a written response to the subpoena on the party who served it. FRCP 45(c). For example, a party may be willing to produce documents, but the subpoena may call for production of privileged documents. The subpoenaed party may, therefore, serve a written response objecting to the requests for production to the extent they call for privileged documents, but otherwise agreeing to produce responsive documents. FRCP 45(d)(2).

If the non-party chooses to comply, either subject to objections or not, then the non-party must make the documents available for inspection and copying at a reasonable time and place, or simply produce them. FRCP 45(d)(1). If the lawyers cannot agree, the non-party may move the court to order that inspection be held at a convenient location, particularly if the volume of documents or other circumstances makes production at other locations unduly burdensome. *Caruso v. Coleman Co.*, 157 F.R.D. 344, 349 (E.D. Pa. 1994).

If the party serving the subpoena believes that the non-party is withholding responsive, discoverable documents or otherwise refusing to comply with the subpoena, it may move to compel compliance. *In re Sealed Case*, 121 F.3d 729, 741 (D.C. Cir. 1997).

# B. Requests for Inspection of Land and Other Locations to Parties or Non-Parties

Rule 34 is also the means by which one party may gain access to land, property or other physical locations in the possession, custody, or control of a party or, through subpoena, a third party. FRCP 34(a)(2). A party may seek access for any purpose reasonably likely to lead to discovery of admissible evidence, including to inspect, measure, survey, photograph or sample property. *Id.* Because entry onto land obviously can be intrusive, the party seeking the request should state what it intends to do on the property and why it is reasonably necessary for the claim or defense. *Belcher v. Basset Furn. Indus.*, 588 F.2d 904, 908 (4th Cir. 1978) (applying a balancing test to determine propriety of request for inspection). In addition, requests for inspection are not proper means to interview or depose persons who are on the land. *Id.*

A party who wants to inspect land or property owned by a non-party may do so through a subpoena. *See* Rules 34(c) & 45.

## C. Interrogatories to Parties

Interrogatories are written questions that a party may serve on another party. They provide an efficient but inherently limited means to uncover useful information. For example, interrogatories are often used to ask for the identity of *all* persons with knowledge of relevant facts (rather than those who know information the opposing party will use to support its claims or defenses, as required by initial disclosures). Another useful and common interrogatory is the "contention interrogatory." A contention interrogatory asks what the opposing party will contend is the basis, in law or fact, of a claim, position, or defense in the lawsuit. For example, a plaintiff can ask a defendant why it contends that a claim is barred by the affirmative defense of statute of limitations.

### 1. Serving Party's Obligations

Parties may serve interrogatories on parties to uncover any information that is relevant to a claim or defense of the suit. FRCP 26(b)(1). A party may serve interrogatories only on another party. FRCP 33(a). They may not be served, even when accompanied by a subpoena, on a non-party. *Univ. of Tex. v. Vratil*, 96 F.3d 1337, 1340 (10th Cir. 1996).

Absent court order or agreement of counsel, a party may serve no more than 25 interrogatories, including discrete subparts. FRCP 33(a). In practice, what exactly is a "subpart" that counts as an interrogatory is a source of controversy. What if, for example, a party serves an interrogatory which reads: "Please state the name, address, and telephone number of all witnesses to the accident." Is that one interrogatory, or three? *See Williams v. Bd. Of City Comm'rs.*, 192 F.R.D. 698, 701 (D. Kan. 2000) (holding that it was one, not three). When forced to decide such issues, the courts apply a functional test, asking whether the subparts are related to the primary question, or logically instead would be separate questions and so should each "count" toward the limit of 25. *Kendall v. GES Exposition Servs., Inc.,* 174 F.R.D. 684 (D. Nev. 1997). If a party believes more than 25 are necessary and cannot secure agreement from opposing counsel to let it ask more, then it can seek a court order increasing the number available. FRCP 26(b)(2); 33(a).

Before including an interrogatory in its requests, a party must determine it is a proper request, both in that it seeks relevant information and is proportional. FRCP 26(g)(1)(B). A proper interrogatory is a "contention" interrogatory. The first item in the example below is a proper contention interrogatory:

---

1.  Identify the facts supporting your contention that defendant breached the agreement.
2.  Identify every person with knowledge of relevant facts.

---

## 2. Recipient's Obligations

A party served with interrogatories must first conduct a reasonable inquiry into the subject of each interrogatory. FRCP 26(g)(1). Then it must, within 30 days of service of the interrogatories, serve its objections and answers to each interrogatory. FRCP 33(b)(2).

Objectionable interrogatories would include those that inquire into irrelevant matters, are not proportional, or which seek disclosure of privileged or work product information. Objections must be specifically stated. FRCP 33(b)(4). Before interposing an objection, however, the party must determine that the objection is consistent with the Rules, not interposed for an improper purpose, and is not unreasonable given the scope of the case. FRCP 26(g)(1)(B).

Why must a party go through all this trouble? Why not just ignore the interrogatory and keep back the "bad" information (after all, the "good" information will have been disclosed during as part of the initial disclosures)? For the same reasons we saw above: a party who fails to answer an interrogatory may be sanctioned, such as precluding the use of evidence at trial, and the court may also award attorneys' fees to the party that served the unanswered requests. FRCP 37(a)(3)(B)(ii). Second, the party who served the interrogatories may move to compel, and if the failure to answer (or an incomplete or evasive answer) was not "substantially justified," the party who failed to answer may also be sanctioned. FRCP 37(a)(5); *see* below, discussing motions to compel. If a party believes that an interrogatory is objectionable, it must confer with the party that served it and if that does not resolve the matter, file a motion for protection. FRCP 26(c).

# D. Requests for Admission

## 1. Serving Party's Obligations

Rule 36(a) allows a party to serve "requests for admission" on another party. "A party may serve upon any other party a written request to admit, for purposes of the pending action only, the truth of any matters within the scope of Rule 26(b)(1) relating to: (A) facts, the application of law to fact or opinions about either; and (B) the genuineness of any described documents." Thus, typical requests for admission may ask:

> 1.    Admit that the document attached as Exhibit A and bates stamped P001-005 is genuine.
> 2.    Admit that the defendant is incorporated in Texas and has its principal place of business in Illinois.
> 3.    Admit that the defendant was negligent.

## 2. Recipient's Obligations

The party must respond to a request for admission within 30 days of service or each request is "deemed" admitted. FRCP 36(a)(3). The lawyer must reasonably investigate before answering requests for admission. She then has these options: object, admit, deny, admit in part and deny in part, or state that it has investigated and cannot admit or deny. A district court summarized the obligations of a party responding to requests for admission:

> A party may not avoid responding based on technicalities. For example, a party who is unable to agree with the exact wording of the request for admission should agree to an alternate wording or stipulation. When the purpose and significance of a request are reasonably clear, courts do not permit denials based on an overly-technical reading of the request.
>
> Instead of admitting or denying the request for admission, a party may respond by claiming inability (lack of sufficient information) to admit or deny the matter stated in the request. But a party responding in this manner must also state that he or she has made "reasonable inquiry and that the information known or readily obtainable by the party is

insufficient to enable the party to admit or deny." The responding party is required to undertake a "good faith" investigation of sources reasonably available to him or her in formulating answers to request for admissions (similar to the duty owed in responding to interrogatories).

"Reasonable inquiry" is limited to persons and documents within the responding party's control (*e.g.*, its employees, partners, corporate affiliates, etc.). It does not require the responding party to interview or subpoena records from independent third parties in order to admit or deny a Request for admission. Likewise, a party cannot be forced to admit or deny facts testified to by a third party witness as to which the responding party has no personal knowledge. Because request for admissions can have dire consequences, the responding party's duty to obtain information is no broader than that owed in responding to interrogatories; i.e., generally limited to obtaining information from persons and entities over which it has actual control.

The responding party's simple statement that he or she has made a "reasonable" inquiry and is unable to admit or deny the request because insufficient information is available may not suffice as an answer to the request for admission. Moreover, the fact that the party has not done so may be asserted as a basis for challenging the response. Alternatively, costs may be awarded against a party for failure to inform himself or herself before answering, as provided by Rule 37(c).

Finally, it is not ground for objection that the request is "ambiguous" unless so ambiguous that the responding party cannot, in good faith, frame an intelligent reply. Parties should admit to the fullest extent possible, and explain in detail why other portions of a request may not be admitted. Failure to do so may result in sanctions.

*U.S. ex rel. Englund v. Los Angeles County*, 235 F.R.D. 674 (E.D. Cal. 2006).

A party who believes that a request for admission exceeds the boundaries of discovery or inquires into protected information such as privileged or work product materials should object on that basis. However, it is not a proper basis to object to a request for admission that it asks an ultimate question, such as whether the party was negligent in the underlying matter or breached a contract at issue in the case.

Why not deny everything and make the other side prove it at trial? If a party fails to properly admit a request for admission and forces the other side to do so, the party who served the request may move for sanctions, including attorneys' fees. The court *must* impose sanctions unless (a) the request was held to be objectionable; (b) the admission was "of no substantial importance"; (c) the party failing to admit had "reasonable ground to believe" it might prevail on the issue; or (d) "there was other good reason for the failure to admit." FRCP 37(c)(2).

## 3. Scope of Admission and Withdrawal of an Admission

Under Rule 36(b) if a party either fails to timely respond to a request, or admits a request, that matter is "conclusively established" unless that party succeeds in withdrawing the admission. A party may withdraw (and, so, amend) an answer only if it persuades the court doing so would promote "presentation of the merits of the action" will be subserved thereby and the party who obtained the admission wouldn't be prejudiced "in maintaining or defending the action on the merits." FRCP 36(b).

An admission is only for the purposes of the civil action in which the admission is made. It cannot be used as an admission in any other lawsuit. *Id.*

# E. Depositions on Written Questions

Depositions on written questions can be served on parties or, if accompanied by a subpoena, on non-parties. FRCP 31(a). Depositions on written questions have limited utility, but can effectively be used to obtain testimony from a third party custodian of records that certain documents are authentic, or constitute "business records" in terms of an exception to the hearsay Rule of Evidence.

## 1. Sender's Obligations

A party who wants to depose another party on written questions may do so by agreement or without court order unless (A) the proposed deposition would result in more than 10 being taken in the case; (B) the proposed deponent has already been deposed once; or (C) the deposition is sought before the Rule 26(f) conference has occurred. FRCP 31(a)(2).

The sender simply includes in the notice a series of questions that the recipient must answer, under oath, and in writing. FRCP 31(a)(3). The other parties then serve crossquestions which they want the person to answer. FRCP 31(a)(5). The party noticing the deposition on written questions can serve redirect questions, and then the other parties may serve re-crossquestions. *Id.* Ultimately, a person authorized to take the deposition takes the testimony of the person or the person simply provides the answers in writing. FRCP 31(b).

## 2. Recipient's Obligations

The recipient must answer the questions and its lawyer must interpose any objections that the questions exceed a boundary on discovery, such as by inquiring into irrelevant matters or seeking privileged or work product information. A party who fails to respond to a written deposition request may be sanctioned. *See* FRCP 37.

# F. Oral Depositions

## 1. Overview

Oral depositions are the most expensive but typically the most fruitful form of discovery. The attorney for each party will be allowed to ask questions of the witness (called a deponent) while sitting across the table from him and so obtain spontaneous answers to those questions, without coaching or other input from the attorney (at least during the deposition). The deposition is recorded, either only by a stenographer or by both a stenographer and by videotape. Typically, depositions are taken only after documents are exchanged and interrogatories and requests for admission answered, so that the attorney can ask questions after having already reviewed the story told through the contemporaneous documents produced by the other side.

## 2. Procedure for Taking the Deposition of Parties or Non-Parties

Depositions may be taken of a party, an employee of a party (under Rule 30(b)(6)), and of non-parties (through a subpoena). The following sections explore the differences between these depositions, but they share a lot in common, and we'll discuss that first.

A party who wants to depose another party or person may do so by agreement and without agreement or court order unless (A) the proposed deposition would result in more than 10 being taken in the case; (B) the proposed deponent has already been deposed once; or (C) the deposition is sought before the Rule 26(f) conference has occurred. FRCP 30(a)(2); *see also* FRCP 27 (allowing a deposition to be taken under some narrow circumstances before suit is filed).

The party seeking the deposition must give written notice stating the time and place for the deposition and indicating who will be deposed and how the deposition will be recorded (by videotape or only stenographically, typically).

If another party wants the deposition to be recorded in another way, it may designate that method, at its expense. FRCP 30(b)(3).

On the day designated for the deposition, the parties appear before a person authorized by Rule 28 (often called a "court reporter"), who swears the witness to tell the truth, and then the lawyers take the deposition. The court reporter types every word said by a lawyer, the deponent, or any one else present at the deposition so that the transcript may be used at trial.

The party who noticed the deposition asks its questions first, and then the other parties' lawyers may ask questions as well. Before the witness answers each question, lawyers for the other parties may interpose an objection, which must be stated "concisely in an nonargumentative and nonsuggestive manner." FRCP 30(c)(2). The witness may be instructed not to answer a question only to preserve a privilege, enforce a limitation ordered by the court previously, or to present a motion to the court to terminate the deposition. *Id.* The deposition may last no more than one day of seven hours, absent court order. FRCP 30(d)(1).

Once the deposition is complete, a copy with exhibits is sent by the court reporter to the witness, who has 30 days to make corrections and sign the deposition as being accurate. FRCP 30(e). The court reporter then sends the deposition transcript along with any documents that were used as exhibits at the deposition to the lawyer who noticed the deposition, who must store and protect that material. FRCP 30(f)(1). If other parties want a copy of the transcript and exhibits, they must pay the court reporter for their copy. FRCP 30(f)(2).

Here, for example, might be a deposition transcript:

---

Hricik:   I am handing you what has been marked as plaintiff's exhibit 1, which is bates stamped D005-008. Have you seen that before?
Smith:   Yes.
Hricik:   Can you tell me what that is?
Smith:   This is the contract I executed with your client, the defendant.
Hricik:   Was that executed on or about the date shown, April 5, 2007?
Smith:   Yes.
Hricik:   Turning your attention to the third page of that document, bates stamped D008, do you see the handwriting in the margin on the left side?
Opposing lawyer: Hold on, there's handwriting at the top and the bottom.
Hricik:   I'm calling your attention to the handwriting at the top. Do you see that?
Smith:   Yes, I do.
Hricik:   Do you recognize that as your handwriting . . .

---

Why go through all this trouble? Why not just ignore the deposition notice and keep back the "bad" information (after all, the "good" information will have been disclosed during as part of the initial disclosures). First, a party who fails to attend its own deposition (or who fails to show up for a Rule 30(b)(6) deposition) may be sanctioned, such as precluding the use of evidence at trial, and also award attorneys' fees to the party that served the unanswered requests. FRCP 37(d). Second, the party who noticed the deposition may move to compel, and if the failure to attend was not substantially justified, the party who failed to answer may also be sanctioned. FRCP 37(d); *see* below, discussing motions to compel.

## 3. Deposing a Natural Person Who Is Already a Party to the Suit

The procedures above are all that are required to depose a natural person who is a party to the suit.

## 4. Deposing Corporations and Other Entities: Rule 30(b)(6)

What does a party do if it wants to take deposition testimony from an entity? There is no "person" named "Ford Motor Company," after all. How does a party take the deposition of a large corporation about its accounting practices if the party has no idea who at the company would know about those practices? (If the party does know the name of the individual it wishes to depose, then it can proceed under the normal rules, and does not need to rely on Rule 30(b)(6). *See* FRCP 30(b)(6), last sentence.) Although one could imagine forcing the party seeking the information to hope to guess the name of the right employee, the Rules take a different approach.

### a. The Procedure for Obtaining a Rule 30(b)(6) Deposition

Rule 30(b)(6) provides a straightforward mechanism to obtain deposition testimony from entities. The first step is for the party seeking the deposition to serve a deposition notice, or subpoena if a non-party, that specifies the subject matter on which testimony is desired. Thus, the first sentence of Rule 30(b)(6) provides: "In its notice or subpoena a party may name as the deponent a public or private corporation, a partnership, an association, a governmental agency, or other entity and must describe with reasonable particularity the matters for examination."

The recipient has several obligations. First, the second sentence of Rule 30(b) (6) requires the recipient "designate one or more" officer, director, "managing agent" or "persons who consent to testify on its behalf" and list for each designee the subject "matters on which the person will testify." This limitation is important because by implication it precludes using a 30(b)(6) notice to take the deposition of an ordinary employee. *Williams v. Lehigh Valley R.R. Co.*, 19 F.R.D. 285, 286 (S.D. N.Y. 1956). *See also* FRCP 37(d) (court may sanction only party, officer, director, or managing agent who does not appear for a deposition). "Once served with a Rule 30(b)(6) notice, the corporation is compelled to comply, and it may be ordered to designate [an officer, director, or managing agent as] witnesses if it fails to do so." *United States v. J.M. Taylor*, 166 F.R.D. 356, 360 (M.D.N.C. 1996).

In addition, the designee is required to testify as to "matters known or reasonably available to the organization." Thus, the party that receives the notice must present a witness who can testify on its behalf, after engaging in a reasonable investigation as to the subject matters designated in the Rule 30(b)(6) notice. "Corporations must act responsively; they are not entitled to declare themselves mere document-gatherers. They must produce live witnesses who know or who can reasonably find out what happened in given circumstances." *Wilson v. Lakner*, 228 F.R.D. 524, 530 (D. Md. 2005).

### b. Issues Concerning the Designee's Testimony

Rule 30(b)(6) testimony creates several issues concerning the scope of the deposition and the use of the testimony. Foremost, to what extent is the testimony of the 30(b)(6) witness binding on the designating entity? Suppose, for example, the witness makes a statement that is an admission that, if "made by the company" would constitute a judicial admission under the Rules of Evidence. Suppose, for instance, the witness said, "I admit we were negligent in marketing the product that hurt the plaintiff." Would that bind the company? Does the fact that the company designated the individual to testify under Rule 30(b)(6) make the testimony binding? Put the other way, if a 30(b)(6) witness testifies X is true, does that preclude the corporation from adducing evidence showing that X is not true?

Courts are split on this question. Some courts hold that 30(b)(6) testimony is the equivalent of a judicial admission. "By commissioning the designee as the voice of the corporation, the Rule obligates a corporate party 'to prepare its designee to be able to give binding answers' in its behalf." *Rainey v. Am. Forest & Paper Ass'n., Inc.*, 26 F. Supp. 2d 82 (D.D.C. 1998) (quoting *Ierardi v. Lorillard, Inc.*, 1991 WL 158911 (E.D. Pa. 1991). Other courts, however, reject that approach. *See Industrial Hard Chrome, Ltd. v. Hetran, Inc.*, 92 F. Supp. 2d 786, 791 (N.D. Ill. 2000) (Rule 30(b)(6) "testimony is not a judicial admission that ultimately decides an issue. The testimony given at a Rule 30(b)(6) deposition is evidence which, like any other deposition testimony, can be contradicted and used for impeachment purposes.").

Second, may the interrogating party question beyond the scope of the subjects listed in the 30(b)(6) notice? "Courts are divided on whether a party noticing a Rule 30(b)(6) deposition is limited to the topics set forth in the notice." *U.S. ex rel. Tiesinga v. Dianon Systems, Inc.*, 2006 WL 3332883 (D. Conn. 2006).

One the one hand, a majority of courts hold that a Rule 30(b)(6) witness may be examined as to any relevant subject. *See King v. Pratt & Whitney,* 161 F.R.D. 475 (S.D. Fla. 1995). Courts following this approach reason that questions outside the scope of the notice are objectionable only as with a normal deponent. *See Bracco Diagnostics, Inc. v. Amersham Health Inc.,* 2005 U.S. Dist. LEXIS 26854 (D.N.J. 2005) (noting string of district courts have followed the *King* court's reasoning). Thus, the subject matters listed in the 30(b)(6) notice "cannot be used to limit what is asked of a designated witness at deposition." *Detoy v. San Francisco,* 196 F.R.D. 362, 367 (N.D. Cal. 2000). Instead, "the scope of the deposition is determined solely by relevance under Rule 26, that is, that the evidence sought may lead to the discovery of admissible evidence." *Id.*

On the other hand, some courts hold that the deposition is limited to "matters included in the notice." *Paparelli v. Prudential Ins. Co.,* 108 F.R.D. 727, 730 (D. Mass. 1985); *see Hoechst Celanese Corp. v. Nat'l Fire Union Fire Ins. Co. of Pittsburgh,* 623 A.2d 1099, 1113 (Del. Supr. 1991). These courts reason that implicit in the approach of Rule 30(b)(6) is a limitation that the deposition be limited to the subjects designated, reasoning that if "a party were free to ask any questions, even if 'relevant' to the lawsuit, which were completely outside the scope of the 'matters on which examination is requested,' the requirement that matters be listed 'with reasonable particularity' would make no sense." *Paparelli,* 108 F.R.D. at 730.

A third issue implicated by Rule 30(b)(6) depositions is whether any testimony beyond the scope of the notice is binding on the corporation. If a 30(b)(6) notice seeks testimony as to topic A, testimony as to topic B ought not bind the corporation even if the question was not objectionable as outside the scope of the notice. *See U.S. E.E.O.C. v. Caesars Entertainment, Inc.,* 237 F.R.D. 428, 433 (D. Nev. 2006).

A fourth issue, related to the third, is whether counsel presenting the 30(b)(6) witness for the deposition must object to questions outside the scope at the deposition. District courts have suggested that lawyers make objections at the deposition and ask the judge to exclude the testimony as not intended to be the answers of the designating party. *Id.*

Finally, the question of where the deposition takes place sometimes is a litigated issue. There is a presumption that the deposition should take place at the corporation's principal place of business. *Cadent Ltd v. 3M Unitek Corp.*, 232 F.R.D. 625 (C.D. Cal. 2005). However, either party can move for a protective order under Rule 26(c) and show that justice requires that the deposition be held elsewhere. *Id.* In fact, "corporate defendants are frequently deposed in places other than the location of the principal place of business, especially in the forum [where the action is pending], for the convenience of the parties and in the general interests of judicial economy." *Id.*

Like all discovery disputes, fights over where a deposition should take place are to be avoided, as judges find the inability of counsel to agree on such matters troubling. As one court recently wrote in deciding a motion brought to determine where a 30(b)(6) deposition should take place wrote:

> This matter comes before the Court on Plaintiff's Motion to designate location of a Rule 30(b)(6) deposition. Upon consideration of the Motion — the latest in a series of Gordian knots that the parties have been unable to untangle without enlisting the assistance of the federal courts — it is ORDERED that said Motion is DENIED. Instead, the Court will fashion a new form of alternative dispute resolution, to wit: at 4:00 P.M. on Friday, June 30, 2006, counsel shall convene at a neutral site agreeable to both parties. If counsel cannot agree on a neutral site, they shall meet on the front steps of the Sam M. Gibbons U.S. Courthouse.... Each lawyer shall be entitled to be accompanied by one paralegal who shall act as an attendant and witness. At that time and location, counsel shall engage in one (1) game of "rock, paper, scissors." The winner of this engagement shall be entitled to select the location for the 30(b)(6) deposition to be held somewhere in Hillsborough County during the period July 11–12, 2006. If either party disputes the outcome of this engagement, an appeal may be filed and a hearing will be held at 8:30 A.M. on Friday, July 7, 2006 before the undersigned ...

*Avista Mgmt., Inc. v. Wausau Underwriters Ins. Co.*, Civ. A. No. 6:05-cv-1430-Orl-31JGG (M.D. Fla. 2006).

## 5. Taking Oral Deposition of a Non-Party by Service of a Subpoena

The general rules regarding *when* discovery may be served applies to subpoenas, even though Rule 45 does not itself contain any time limits. *See Alper v. U.S.*, 190 F.R.D. 281, 283 (D. Mass. 2000).

Rule 45(a) requires certain formalities in subpoenas, all of which can be satisfied by using a common form subpoena available online. An attorney for a party is authorized to complete the subpoena to compel a non-party to give an oral deposition, to produce documents, or both, an attorney is authorized where the deposition will be held or documents produced issue a subpoena requiring the non-party to testify, produce the documents, or both. FRCP 45(a). (Subpoenas may also be used to compel trial testimony. *See id.*)

A party requesting a subpoena, like all discovery, has an affirmative obligation to avoid imposing undue burden or expense. FRCP 45(c)(1). Improper use of subpoenas may result in sanctions. *Id.*

The subpoena must be served, along with a check to cover attendance and mileage of the witness, by a non-party who is at least 18 years old. FRCP 45(b). Court reporters typically provide this service for a fee. There are geographic limitations on a court's subpoena power. Generally, a subpoena is ineffective if either the person is served outside of the district which issues the subpoena or more than 100 miles from the place where the activity demanded by the subpoena will occur. FRCP 45(b)(2).

A non-party served with a subpoena can seek to challenge it by moving to quash it, or comply with it without or subject to objections. FRCP 45(c). A non-party who wants to object to complying with the subpoena must object or move to quash it. FRCP 45(c). A non-party who wants to comply with a subpoena *duces tecum* but subject to objections must serve a written response on the party who served it. For example, a party subpoenaed to produce documents, but the document requests may call for production of privileged documents. The subpoenaed party may, therefore, serve a written response objecting to the requests for production to the extent they call for privileged documents, but otherwise agreeing to produce responsive documents.

# G. Physical and Mental Examinations

Under Rule 35, a party may request a physical or mental examination under some circumstances. These are often called "IMEs" or "independent medical examinations."

## 1. Obtaining an Order for an Examination

What is required to obtain an examination? Examinations are available by court order, either as the result of an agreement by the parties or after an opposed request for an exam. (Often the parties simply agree to a physical exam and avoid the order entirely.) If the request for an exam is opposed, however, the party seeking the exam must move the court for an order and in it show that (A) the person is a party, under the control of the party, or in the custody of the party; (B) that the condition of the party is "in controversy"; and (C) that there is "good cause" for the examination(s) sought. FRCP 35(a).

### a. Who May Be Examined?

Only a party or a person "who is in the custody or under its legal control" can be ordered to undergo an exam. Thus, it allows for an examination of any party, whether plaintiff, defendant, or otherwise. FRCP 35(a)(1). *See Schlagenhauf v. Holder,* 379 U.S. 104 (1964). The phrase "custody or legal control" includes, for example, a minor or incapacitated adult, but it does *not* include an employee of a party. *Lewis v. Herrman's Excavating, Inc.,* 200 F.R.D. 657 (D. Kan. 2001).

### b. When Is a Condition "in Controversy"?

To establish that the person's condition is "in controversy" the movant must show that "each condition as to which the examination is sought is really and genuinely in controversy" and normally cannot rely on pleadings alone. Nonetheless, often little is required. The classic example of "in controversy," for example, occurs when a plaintiff pleads in a personal injury action that the defendant caused it specific harm. A plaintiff who claims that the defendant's negligence broke the plaintiff's finger, for example, puts the condition of the plaintiff's finger "in controversy." *See Schlagenhauf.*

At other times this element requires a greater showing. For example, in *Schlagenhauf,* the plaintiff was injured when the bus in which he was riding plowed into the back of a tractor-trailer that was parked along the side of a freeway. The plaintiff sued the bus driver as well as the bus company. The plaintiff sought several medical exams of the defendant bus driver. To establish that there was good cause for several medical exams, the plaintiff argued in its motion seeking an exam that the driver had admitted that he had seen the red lights of the tractor-trailer for 15 seconds before the collision, but had done nothing, and that he had been involved in a similar prior accident. The Court held that this was insufficient to establish that his mental or physical condition was "in controversy." The Court further held that it was insufficient to order only an eye exam.

### c. What Constitutes "Good Cause"?

Generally "good cause" exists where the exam sought will "determine the existence and extent of" the condition. *Schlagenhauf.* Thus, for example, the facts of *Schlagenhauf* might constitute good cause for an eye exam, but not heart exam. But "good cause" also takes into account whether the information might be obtainable through means other than the desired examination. *Benham v. Rice,* 238 F.R.D. 15 (D.D.C. 2006). Thus, even if a condition is in controversy, there may be "good cause" only for one type of exam and not another.

# H. Special Issues

## 1. E-Discovery

In December 2006 substantial revisions to the Rules came into effect designed largely to address problems and concerns arising from the fact that today many "documents" are in electronic format, and sometimes difficult and expensive to access or locate. The critical, broad issue that E-discovery creates is the need for lawyers to become familiar with their client's document management systems, so that a lawyer can accurately certify that responsive documents have been produced. Electronic discovery can be massively expensive, and courts are only just beginning to struggle with how to allocate costs and address the difficult amounts of material that must be reviewed in response to a request for production that includes electronic materials. *See, e.g., Zubalake v. UBS Warburg LLC,* 217 F.R. D. 309 (S.D.N.Y. 2003).

# I. Practical but Crucial Big Picture View of Discovery

In order to recover at trial, a plaintiff must produce sufficient evidence of each element of every claim that it pleads. Some of the information that the plaintiff has it does not need to acquire through discovery: for example, a plaintiff who has pled a breach of contract against a pizza box manufacturer for delivering defective boxes does not need to use formal discovery to prove that its restaurants actually received the boxes, since its own records and witnesses can establish that fact (if receipt of the boxes is even disputed by the defendant). But a plaintiff in such a case would have to prove that the boxes were defective or otherwise failed to meet the specifications set forth in the parties' contract. It may be able to do that through its own testing, or it may need access to the defendant's plant and documents in the defendant's possession in order to show that the boxes were in fact below standard.

In this sense, discovery is about gap filling: any element of a claim that the plaintiff lacks evidence for, it must find, either through informal investigation or formal discovery. The same is true for defendants: a defendant who pleads that the statute of limitations has expired can rely on the date of filing suit for when limitations ceased to run, but will likely have to conduct discovery to find out, for example, when plaintiff discovered the alleged breach of duty to it. Discovery allows parties to fill gaps in their own cases.

At the same time, it allows parties to gather evidence that undermines the other side's claims or defenses. A plaintiff could, for example, take discovery of employees of the defendant to show that, even though limitations might have appeared to have expired, defendant engaged in active concealment of the facts, and so limitations should be "tolled."

Ultimately, each side's lawyer will have to determine whether it has sufficient, credible evidence on each element of each claim or defense. That assessment typically comes near the end of discovery, since it is only at that time that the parties have fully exchanged information and can accurately assess the strengths and weaknesses of each side's positions. At that time, settlement is very common, as is the filing of summary judgment by one or both parties.

## Checkpoints

- Can you describe each discovery tool, and when it likely will be best to use?
- Can you explain how to avoid production of privileged or work product information when responding to each type of discovery request?
- Can you explain the process for obtaining a Rule 30(b)(6) deposition, and when using Rule 30(b)(6) may be useful or necessary?
- Can you explain when a court will likely order a mental or physical exam of a party and who is "controlled" by a party for purposes of that rule?

# Chapter 50

# Expert Witnesses: Disclosure, Discovery, and Protection

---

### Expert Witnesses Roadmap

This chapter explains how to identify the three different types of "experts" created by the Rules, and the obligations that a party has with respect to each different type.

This chapter also explains how the rules prohibit discovery of information known to certain experts, and identifies the exceptions to those prohibitions.

---

As explained earlier, the Rules require parties to disclose information without having been served a discovery request to do so. One circumstance that may require disclosure concerns expert witnesses. (We saw required initial disclosures in Chapter 43, and you'll see that additional disclosures are required in connection with the final pretrial order in Chapter 53.)

The Rules state that "a party must disclose to the other parties the identify of any witness it may use at trial to present evidence" under the Rules of Evidence relating to expert testimony. FRCP 26(a)(2)(A). Thus, whether someone is an "expert" turns on the rules of evidence, not the rules of civil procedure.

"Experts" are more common than you may think, and so the rules requiring disclosure of information about certain experts are triggered more often than you might intuit. Specifically, the rules of evidence say that someone is an expert if she has "scientific, technical, or other specialized knowledge that will help the trier of fact to understand the evidence or to determine a fact in issue." FRE 702. A carpenter testifying about the proper way to make a chair is just as much of an expert as is a chemist describing a new patented formula.

If someone is going to offer an expert opinion at trial, then the party intending to do so has certain required disclosures they must make. Conversely, sometimes a party may retain an expert and plan *not* to use the testimony at trial; in those cases, it may be that the opposing parties cannot discover information about that witness. The rules treat the three categories of experts very differently from each other:

| Type | Example |
|---|---|
| A fact witness who also has expertise ("hybrid-expert witnesses") | A doctor who will testify at trial because he treated the plaintiff in the emergency room after an accident |
| Testifying Expert | A marketing expert hired by defense counsel to testify at trial to rebut plaintiff's damage claim |
| Consulting Expert | An accounting expert hired by defense counsel to assist on the case, but who will not testify at trial |

# A. Required Disclosures from Parties Intending to Use Testifying Experts and Hybrid Experts at Trial

## 1. An Overview of the Two Rounds of Disclosures

Rule 26(a)(2)(D) requires that at least 90 days before trial, or as required by the scheduling order or the parties' agreement, the parties must begin a process of disclosing certain information about experts and expert witnesses. Unless modified by the scheduling order or agreement, the Rules require two rounds of disclosures.

First, each party must to disclose (a) the identity of each hybrid expert and a summary of the subject matter on which the expert will give expert testimony along with a summary of the facts and opinions about which she is expected to testify (FRCP 26(a)(2)(C)); and (b) the identify of each testifying expert along with a report prepared and signed by the expert that includes:

(i) a complete statement of all opinions the witness will express and the basis and reasons for them;

(ii) the facts or data considered by the witness in forming them;

(iii) any exhibits that will be used to summarize or support them;

(iv) the witness's qualifications, including a list of all publications authored in the previous 10 years;

(v) a list of all other cases in which, during the previous 4 years, the witness testified as an expert at trial or by deposition; and

(vi) a statement of the compensation to be paid for the study and testimony in the case.

FRCP 26(a)(2)(B). So, imagine a car wreck case. The plaintiff saw a doctor in the emergency room and both plaintiff and defendant have hired accident reconstruction experts. In that case, 90 days before trial, the plaintiff must identify the doctor from the emergency room if he is going to give opinions ("the plaintiff had a broken bone") and a summary of those opinions, and the plaintiff would have to identify the accident reconstruction expert and provide his written report. Likewise, the defendant at that time would have to disclose the identity of her accident reconstruction expert and provide his written report. Note that, often, a hybrid expert will have been identified much earlier as a person that the party intends to call at trial as a fact witness, but a hybrid expert must still be listed as an expert in these disclosures.

The second round comes, if not modified by the scheduling order, 30 days later (*i.e.*, 60 days before trial). At that point, if a party has expert evidence that is intended solely to contradict or rebut evidence on the same subject matter by an expert of another party, then it must disclose the (a) identity of the expert and (b) with respect to testifying experts but not hybrid experts, provide reports. So, for example, if a defendant intends to offer an expert's testimony solely to rebut the testimony offered by an expert identified by the plaintiff in the first round of disclosures, the defendant need only identify this expert 60 days prior to trial, and if a testifying expert, provide the report. If, on the other hand, the defendant had an expert to testify concerning an affirmative defense, the defendant must identify that expert 90 days out, and if the plaintiff has an expert to rebut the defendant's expert, the plaintiff must identify that expert 60 days from trial.

### a. Disclosure of the Identity of Each Testifying Expert and Hybrid Expert

Rule 26(a)(2)(a) requires a party to disclose *the identity* of "any witness it may use at trial to present evidence under Federal Rule of Evidence 702, 703, or 705." The Rules of Evidence generally do not permit witnesses to give opinions, only to state facts the witnesses observed. However, the rules of evidence allow "experts" to give opinions. Again, what is "expert testimony" in terms of the Rules of Evidence includes a lot. Studies show that there are "experts" in about 90% of cases, and the average case has over three experts involved.

Any witness who is expected to offer "expert opinion" at trial—even if that witness is *also* a fact witness—must be identified 90 days prior to trial, unless the testimony is rebuttal. If the testimony is not purely factual, the witness should be identified and, again, should be identified as a person who will offer expert testimony even if the witness was previously identified as a fact witness.

*In re Illusions Holdings, Inc.*, 189 F.R.D. 316 (S.D.N.Y. 1999), the plaintiff was injured while scuba diving in the Virgin Islands. The plaintiff sought to exclude two of the defendant's witnesses from testifying at trial because they were not identified as experts, only as fact witnesses. The two men were professional scuba divers had been deposed by plaintiffs' counsel and had testified not just about their familiarity with the area where the accident occurred and what they heard and saw, but also as to scuba diving training methods, proper procedures for diving, their opinions about currents, and other information. The court therefore excluded the two witness's testimony from trial and imposed other sanctions.

Thus, the identity of two of the three kinds of experts—hybrid experts and testifying experts—must be disclosed. Although there is a split, many courts hold that the identity of a consulting expert may be obtained only upon a showing of "exceptional circumstances." *Ager v. Jane C. Stormont Hosp. & Training School for Nurses*, 622 F.2d 496, 502 (10th Cir. 1980) (requiring exceptional circumstances).

### b. Disclosure of Reports of Testifying Experts and Summaries from Hybrid Experts

Parties are required to disclose far more than just the identity of testifying experts, and somewhat more with respect to hybrid experts. This section describes the two types of testifying experts and what must be disclosed about each, before describing the summaries that must be provided along with hybrid experts.

### i. Who is a "Testifying Expert" and so Must Prepare a Report?

Two categories of testifying experts must prepare written, signed reports: (1) any witness who was retained or specially employed to provide expert testimony in the case; or (2) any witness whose duties as an employee of a party regularly involve giving expert testimony. FRCP 26(a)(2)(B).

Who is covered by the first category? The typical expert witness is a person who has expert knowledge in a field who is hired by a party to testify for a specific case. If a witness does not have personal knowledge of the facts of the case, but was retained to testify about his opinions based on the testimony of those who do have that knowledge, that person is an expert witness.

Who is covered by the second category? It is not as broad category as the first. If a party's employee's job regularly entails testifying as an expert and the employee will be offering opinions, then she is a testifying expert and must prepare a report. Where an employee regularly testifies, complicated issues concerning the scope of discovery can arise. *E.g., People ex rel. Wheeler v. So. Pac. Transp. Co.,* 1993 WL 816066 (E.D. Cal. 1993) (examining scope of discovery over employee who regularly testified but also used discoverable information and other information in conducting his job).

Who would not be covered by either category? The doctor who treated the plaintiff before the accident, or the doctor who treated him afterward, would not—absent more—be required to prepare a report. Likewise, a mechanic employed by a party who will testify about proper maintenance procedures when maintaining the employer's vehicle fleet will not—without more—be covered by this Rule. In the former case, the doctors would have to be retained as experts in the case; in the latter case, the employee's duties would have to regularly involve giving testimony. Again, those witnesses would likely be hybrid experts: they don't have to prepare a report, but the lawyer who intends to use their opinion testimony must provide a written summary, discussed at the end of this section.

### ii. What Must Be in the Report of a Testifying Expert?

Rule 26(a)(2)(B) requires that the report include:

- a complete statement of all opinions the witness will express and the basis and reasons for them;
- the facts or data considered by the witness in forming the opinions;
- any exhibits to be used as a summary of or support for the opinions;
- the qualifications of the witness, including a list of all publications authored by the witness during the last ten years;
- the compensation to be paid for the study and testimony; and
- a listing of any other cases in which the witness has testified as an expert at trial or by deposition within the preceding four years.

FRCP 26(a)(2)(B). Expert reports can be voluminous. The Federal Rules of Evidence impose requirements concerning minimum qualifications to be an expert as well as limitations on what expert testimony may address. Substantive law, as well, must be consulted because it may limit the extent to which an expert may testify, or impose other requirements. Two issues are worth emphasizing here.

First, the term "data or other information considered" by the expert means what it says. The term "considered" includes more than just "relied upon," referring instead to any information furnished to a testifying expert that such an expert generates, reviews, reflects upon, reads, and/or uses in connection with the formulation of his opinions, even if the expert ultimately rejected relying on the information. *Compare Amway Corp. v. Procter & Gamble Co.,* 2001 WL 1877268 (W.D. Mich. 2001) (holding that documents supplied to testifying expert, but which he did not read, review, or consider in forming opinions, were not discoverable under Rule 26(a)(2)(B)) *with Vitalo v. Cabot Corp.,* 212 F.R.D. 472, 474 (E.D. Pa. 2002) (defining "consider" as reflecting on, reviewing, or using, even if ultimately rejected by expert).

Second, and related to that point, until recently, privileged or work product information was generally not exempted from "data or information considered" by the expert. Until recently, if a lawyer provided a testifying expert with a document that revealed the lawyer's litigation strategy and key opinions, the majority of courts held that there is complete waiver, even as to opinion work product. *In re Pioneer Hi-Bred Int'l, Inc.,* 238 F.3d 1370 (Fed. Cir. 2001). Other courts did not permit discovery of "core" or "opinion" work product, but find protection as to all other types of protected information has been waived. *E.g., Krisa v. Equitable Life Assurance Soc'y,* 196 F.R.D. 254, 259 (M.D.Pa. 2000) (finding that disclosure of core work product to a testifying expert does not abrogate the privilege that attaches to such materials).

As amended in 2010, however, the rule expressly states that certain information is not discoverable: (1) draft reports or disclosures of testifying experts; (2) communications between testifying experts and the party's attorneys; and (3) facts known or opinions held by consulting (non-testifying) experts. FRCP 26(b)(4)(B)-(D). However, if an expert "considers" information from someone other than a party's attorney, tbose communications are discoverable. *Whole Women's Health v. Lakey,* 301 F.R.D. 266 (W.D. Tex. 2014) (collecting cases).

### iii. What Must the Summary of a Hybrid Expert Contain?

Hybrid experts need not prepare reports, but the lawyer intending to call a hybrid expert as a witness must prepare a summary of the facts and opinions regarding the witnesses testimony. Obviously, the detail in a testifying expert's report is not required. Courts have held that simply stating that a treating physician will rely upon medical records is not sufficient since that is not a "summary." *E.g., Smothers v. Solvay Chem., Inc.,* 2014 WL 3051210 (D. Wyo. July 3, 2014) (collecting cases).

## 2. Each Party Must Supplement Expert Disclosures

Rule 26(a)(2)(E) requires that every report be supplemented, and, in addition, that information disclosed by the expert during his deposition also be supplemented. So, for example, if the expert conducts additional experiments or reaches additional conclusions not disclosed in the expert report or which were queried about at his deposition, the information must be supplemented. The latest time for supplementation is at the time the Rule 26(a)(3) disclosures are due, which is either when stated in the scheduling order or 30 days prior to trial.

## 3. Incomplete or Late Reports, Summaries of Hybrid Experts, or Deposition Testimony

Suppose at trial or in connection with summary judgment motions a party seeks to introduce evidence that was not properly *and* timely disclosed by the expert in his report or summary, or at deposition, or afterward by supplementation. The other parties can seek to exclude the evidence under Rule 37(c)(1), which provides that if "a party fails to provide information or identify a witness as required by Rule 26(a) or 26(e), the party is not allowed ot use that information or witness to supply evidence on a motion, at a hearing, or at trial unless the failure was substantially justified or was harmless." In addition, the court, on motion and after hearing can impose other, or additional, sanctions. *Id.*

Thus, unless the nondisclosure was either "substantially justified" *or* "harmless," a district court must exclude the undisclosed witness or evidence from being used. *Salgado v. Gen'l Motors Corp.,* 150 F.3d 735, 742 and n.6 (7th Cir. 1998). The sanction of "exclusion is automatic and mandatory unless the sanctioned party can show that its violation of Rule 26(a) was either justified or harmless." *Id.* Importantly, the filing of a *late but complete* report also must be "substantially justified" or "harmless." *J&J Celcom v. AT&T Wireless Serv., Inc.,* 2006 WL 3825343 (9th Cir. 2006).

"Substantial justification" turns on all the facts, including prejudice to the other party. But it is a high hurdle. Courts have held that a party who fails to identify a plaintiff's treating physician as an expert is not substantially justified in doing so, because the case law is fairly clear that disclosure is required. *E.g., Musser v. Gentiva Health Serv.,* 356 F.3d 751 (7th Cir. 2004). In *Musser,* the plaintiffs brought a medical malpractice claim against a home nursing service, alleging that its negligent monitoring led to their baby's death. As part of initial required disclosures, the plaintiffs identified various treating physicians and nurses as fact witnesses. Depositions were taken of various witnesses, including those doctors and nurses.

When the time came for expert witness disclosures, however, plaintiffs' counsel did not identify any of these witnesses as persons who would give expert opinion testimony. The defendant then moved for summary judgment, arguing that plaintiffs could not produce any evidence of causation, since proof of causation requires expert testimony and plaintiffs had not identified any expert witnesses. When the plaintiffs' lawyer realized the problem, she argued that she had misunderstood the law, and didn't realize that, even though these witnesses had been disclosed as part of required initial disclosures as fact witnesses, they also had to be identified as expert witnesses.

The district court excluded the witnesses and the Seventh Circuit affirmed. It noted that, though the exclusion of the evidence meant dismissal of the case, under the facts presented it was not an abuse of discretion for the district court to find that the omission was not substantially justified. 356 F.3d at 759–60.

A "harmless" omission requires both an honest mistake by the nondisclosing party *and* sufficient knowledge on behalf of the other party of the withheld information. *Vance v. U.S.*, 1999 WL 455435 (6th Cir. 1999). So, for example, if the nondisclosure occurred at such a time as to prejudice a party in preparing a motion for summary judgment, or responses to one, the nondisclosure is not harmless. *Hermeling v. Montgomery Ward & Co.*, 851 F. Supp. 1369, 1376 (D. Minn. 1994).

A trial court's decision that nondisclosure was not substantially justified or was not harmless is reviewed for abuse of discretion. *Southern States Rack & Fixture, Inc. v. Sherwin-Williams Co.*, 318 F.3d 592, 597 (4th Cir. 2003). However, if the court does *not* find substantial justification or harmlessness, then it *must* exclude the evidence or witness. *Id.*

# B. Non-Testifying (*aka* Consulting) Experts

## 1. The Rule: No Discovery of Consulting Experts

When a party intends to have an expert testify at trial, the disclosure obligations above are triggered. Suppose, and this happens a lot, a lawyer retains an expert who provides his opinion to the lawyer . . . and it's not good. The expert basically thinks that the other side's right. Or, suppose the expert's opinion is favorable to the lawyer's client, but the expert just makes an awful witness. In either case, what, if anything, is the party required to disclose?

"Nothing" is the short answer: the required disclosure obligations concerning experts do not apply unless the party intends for the expert to testify at trial. There's a longer answer, though: although the *required disclosure obligations in Rule 26(a)* do not apply to non-testifying experts, in some circumstances *discovery* can be had of these experts.

Stop and consider the extreme rules that could apply to this issue. The rule could provide that nothing known to a consulting expert is discoverable; or, it could permit discovery of everything known to a consulting expert. We instead have a rule that provides broad protection to facts known or opinions held by a non-testifying expert, but which has an exception. Here is the Rule, which both authorizes access to such information while conditioning it:

> Ordinarily, a party may not, by interrogatories or deposition, discover facts known or opinions held by an expert who has been retained or specially employed by another party in anticipation of litigation or to prepare for trial and who is not expected to be called as a witness at trial. But a party may do so only:
>
> (i)   as provided in Rule 35(b); or
>
> (ii)  *on showing exceptional circumstances under which it is impracticable for the party to obtain facts or opinions on the same subject by other means.*

FRCP 26(b)(4)(D) (emph. added).

Thus, apart from medical examinations under Rule 35, facts known to or opinions held by a non-testifying expert can be discovered through deposition or interrogatories, but only if "exceptional circumstances" as defined in the emphasized language exist. Make sure you get the rule and exception: the rule "forbids the judge to order disclosure in pretrial discovery of the facts found or opinions formulated by an opponent's non-testifying experts except ... 'upon a showing of exceptional circumstances under which it is impracticable for the party seeking discovery to obtain facts or opinions on the same subject by other means.'" *Braun v. Lorillard Inc.,* 84 F.3d 230, 236 (7th Cir. 1996).

Why not one extreme or the other, and why the narrow exception? The Rules generally prevent disclosure concerning non-testifying experts so that each party can hire experts and get the case fairly evaluated without fear that an adverse opinion will become "grist for the adversary's mill." *Long Term Capital Holdings v. U.S.,* 2003 U.S. Dist. LEXIS 14579 (D. Conn. 2003). Think about it for a moment: if you knew that any unfavorable opinion you obtained from an expert that *you paid* could be used by the other side, you'd not hire truly neutral experts, but instead a partisan you knew you could count on for a favorable, not neutral, opinion. So, don't lose sight of the broad prohibition into discovery of consulting experts, even though the rest of this section focuses on the exception, not the general rule.

## 2. The "Exceptional Circumstances" Exception

A party seeking discovery from a non-testifying expert carries a "heavy burden" of proving "exceptional circumstances." *Spearman Indus., Inc. v. St. Paul Fire & Marine Ins. Co.,* 128 F. Supp. 2d 1148, 1151 (N.D. Ill. 2001). The party seeking the discovery must show it is unable to obtain equivalent information from other sources. The requisite "exceptional circumstances" are typically found under three fact patterns:

(A) the consulting expert observed an event, object, or condition that no longer is observable but the event relates to a material issue at trial, and the party seeking discovery could not reasonably have been expected to observe it;

(B) the cost to replicate the event, object, or condition is prohibitively expensive; *or*

(C) there are no other available experts in the field.

*See Braun v. Lorillard Inc.*, 84 F.3d 230, 236 (7th Cir. 1996). These are fairly rare circumstances: if the plaintiff claims it was injured by a defective product, for example, each side can usually have its own expert examine the product *See Grindell v. Am. Motors Corp.*, 108 F.R.D. 94, 95 (W.D.N.Y. 1985) (quashing subpoena for non-testifying expert that had been retained by the defendant because plaintiffs could hire their own expert to examine the car and so there were no exceptional circumstances); *Hermsdorfer v. Am. Motors Corp.*, 96 F.R.D. 13, 14 (W.D.N.Y. 1982) (plaintiffs had access to the car model in question to same extent as defendant, and so no exceptional circumstances existed).

### a. The Condition Is No Longer Observable and Could Not Have Been Observed by the Party Seeking Discovery from the Consulting Expert

Casebooks use a few cases to illustrate when courts will allow access because a condition that is relevant to the suit is no longer observable and could not have been observed by the party seeking the discovery. In *Thompson v. Haskell Co.*, 65 F. Empl. Prac. Cas. (BNA) 1088 (M.D. Fla. 1994), the court found "exceptional circumstances" where the plaintiff, who was claiming mental anguish from sexual harassment and who had alleged that she had been severely depressed by the harassment, had seen a psychologist immediately after she had been fired from her job, but suit was not filed until many months later. Her mental condition immediately after she had been fired obviously was essential to her case, and could not be recreated by the defendant. *See Braun v. Lorillard Inc.*, 84 F.3d 230, 236 (7th Cir. 1996) (Because the tissue samples had been destroyed, the "only way defense could find out whether there were . . . asbestos fibers in the tissues that the plaintiff's experts had tested was to get the test results.")

On the other hand, in *Chiquita Int'l Ltd. v. M/V Bolero Reefer*, 1994 U.S. Dist. Lexis 5820 (S.D.N.Y. 1994), the court found no exceptional circumstances where, in a dispute over a spoiled commercial shipment by boat of bananas, both parties could have investigated the conditions on the dock that resulted in the bananas being left to rot, but only one party did so, even though the dock was at the critical time equally accessible to both of them.

### b. The Event or Condition Can be Recreated Only at Great Expense

This exception is not designed to permit a party from building its case by using the other side's financial resources, diligence, or better preparation. Consequently, it is not enough to satisfy this prong to show that testing or examination take time and money. *In re Shell Oil Refinery,* 132 F.R.D. 437 (E.D. La. 1990) (cost of $300,000 insufficient to constitute "exceptional circumstances"). In other words, this exception is narrow but courts will grant discovery in extreme circumstances, but will not let one party "free ride" on the work of the other.

### c. There's No Other Expert in the Field Available

This is an extremely rare occurrence.

# C. Special Issues

## 1. Deposing a Testifying Expert's Non-Testifying Assistants

Generally, as we've seen, a non-testifying expert is treated quite differently from a testifying expert: full discovery is allowed of a testifying expert, but rarely is discovery concerning a non-testifying expert even allowed. Suppose, though, that a testifying expert has been substantially assisted in the preparation of his report by an assistant, who is not going to testify. Is that assistant a non-testifying expert, or does involvement in the report allow for discovery of the person as a testifying expert?

The answer generally seems to turn on whether the assistant was a collaborator in the sense that the testifying expert did not independently verify the work. To that extent, while the assistant may not need to testify at trial, the other parties may be able to take discovery of the assistant. *Dura Automotive Sys., of Indiana, Inc. v. CTS Corp.,* 285 F.3d 609, 612–14 (7th Cir. 2002) (an assistant or collaborator may be deposed to "make sure they performed their tasks competently."); *Herman v. Marine Midland Bank,* 207 F.R.D. 26, 31 (W.D.N.Y. 2002) (allowing discovery of assistant's work because the report was "the result of substantial collaborative work"). If a testifying expert is simply using a report prepared by a non-testifying expert, courts sometimes find "exceptional circumstances" and permit discovery of the non-testifying expert. *See Heitmann v. Concrete Pip Machinery*, 98 F.R.D. 740 (E.D. Mo. 1983).

## 2. Waiver of Protection of Non-Testifying Expert's Opinions

If the opinions of a non-testifying expert are provided to a testifying expert, has the party waived protection of opinions known to the consulting expert? What if an opinion of a consulting expert is provided to a third party, such as a government agency? Is protection lost, not just for that document, but for all related communications? "The rule itself does not mention waiver, and the courts are divided." *In re Polymedica Corp. Sec. Litig.*, 235 F.R.D. 28, 35 (D. Mass. 2006) (collecting the few cases on this point).

## 3. De-Designating a Testifying Expert

Suppose a lawyer designates a person as a testifying expert, but then changes her mind. Can she "de-designate" the expert and thus make it so that, rather than having unfettered discovery of the person, the expert must be treated as a consulting expert and so discovery can be had only if "exceptional circumstances" are established? The issue puts various policies in play and has split the courts and resulted in fact-intensive decisions. *E.g., Commerce & Indus. Ins. Co. v. Grinnell Corp.*, 1999 WL 731410 (E.D. La. 1999).

---

### Checkpoints

- Can you describe the two forms of disclosures that apply to testifying experts?
- Can you define when a fact witness is also an expert?
- Can you explain what must be in an expert report, and who must submit one?
- Can you identify when facts known to or opinions held by a consulting expert?

# Chapter 51

# Adjudication of Discovery Disputes

---

### Adjudication of Discovery Disputes Roadmap

This chapter explains how lawyers must first attempt to resolve discovery disputes by conferring, and only if that fails can either the party seeking discovery move to compel disclosure or the party opposing a discovery request move for protection from complying with it.

This chapter also explains how a party who violates a prior order — either compelling disclosure or protecting against it — can face additional sanctions.

---

## A. Penalties for Noncompliance with Discovery Requests and Disclosure Obligations

In prior chapters, we discussed the rules that create obligations on both the party serving and the party responding to discovery requests. If one party believes the other side has violated the rules, then it must first confer to resolve the dispute. If that fails, a party may move for an order preventing the discovery or compelling it. (A non-party from whom discovery is sought may also file a motion to prevent discovery sought against it.) A party or non-party may use a motion for a protective order to prevent discovery; and its mirror image, the motion to compel, is used by a party to force another party (or non-party) to comply with a discovery request. Sanctions can be imposed on a party, non-party or its counsel for violating the rules.

### 1. The Process for Adjudicating Disputes About Discovery

The rules have been repeatedly amended over the last twenty years to increase judicial management of cases, particularly with respect to discovery. Early and increased judicial involvement was seen as a way to reduce the scope and frequency of disagreements between counsel concerning the scope of discovery. In addition, the fact that the Rules now require counsel to consider proportionality before serving a discovery request also has reduced disputes because it imposes some self-restraint. But, disputes still occur.

Where parties do disagree, the Rules first require that the parties meet and confer over their disagreement. FRCP 37(a)(2)(1) (conference required before a party can move to compel discovery or compliance with initial disclosure obligation); FRCP 26(c)(1) (conference required before a person or party may move for a protective order). These "conferences" need not be formal face-to-face meetings, but they must be meaningful attempts to resolve the disagreement. In my experience, often after receiving a set of discovery requests, or after sending back objections and responses, the parties will negotiate and come to an agreement on the scope of the requests. *See, e.g., Davis v. Precoat Metals,* 2002 WL 1759828 (N.D. Ill. 2002) (court noted that plaintiffs limited their requests in scope from those which were actually served prior to bringing a motion to compel). Most discovery disputes are resolved in this way, and the requirement of conference was designed for that to happen more. They are required, and a motion to compel or for protective order must include a certificate of conference. *Shuffle Master Inc. v. Progressive Games, Inc.,* 170 F.R.D. 166 (D. Nev. 1996) (denying motion for sanctions where motion was unaccompanied by certificate of conference).

Courts take the obligation to confer seriously. Courts insist that parties negotiate over the scope of requests in light of the needs of the case, and to limit or comply with the requests when the case warrants. *See Thompson v. Dept. of Housing & Urban Dev.,* 199 F.R.D. 168 (D. Md. 2001) (admonishing lawyers for not taking into account the stakes in the case and the volume of information sought in attempting to "set aside their differences as adversaries and make a good faith effort to reach common ground on the disputes"). Typically, the certificate of conference is included at the end of the motion to compel or for protection, and may state simply: "Counsel has conferred in a good faith effort to secure the information without court action, but counsel could not resolve the matter and require the court's involvement." Lawyers often sign these certificates separately from the motion itself. If a certificate of conference is omitted, the clerk or court will reject a motion.

If the conference fails to resolve the dispute, or to resolve it completely, then a party who believes it is entitled to discovery that the other party, or non-party, refuses to provide may file a "motion to compel" under Rule 37. A party or non-party who believes that a party is seeking discovery to which it is not entitled may file a "motion for a protective order" under Rule 26(c). This section addresses the more common bases for each motion and describes their adjudication. They are mirror images of each other.

## 2. Adjudicating a Party's Motion to Compel

### a. The Process for Moving to Compel

Where a party believes that another party is refusing to disclose discoverable information, it may move for a motion to compel production of the information. FRCP 37(a)(3)(B). Likewise, if a party believes that another party failed to make its required disclosures under Rule 26(a), it may move to compel production. FRCP 37(a)(3)(A). A motion to compel may be used when a party has entirely failed to disclose or made an incomplete or evasive disclosure. FRCP 37(a)(4).

Common bases for motions to compel include disagreements over what is, or is not, "relevant" to a claim or defense. Likewise, often parties will argue that, although the information sought is relevant, it is too expensive for the case, duplicative of other discovery which has already been answered, or otherwise harassing. Another common basis for motions to compel is the scope of the attorney-client privilege or work product doctrine: a party will claim privilege over certain communications, and the party that sought the information (say through a document request) will move to compel because the parties disagree over whether the information is protected from discovery, or whether protection has been waived. There are numerous reasons that lead to discovery disputes.

If a party files a motion to compel, the other parties or persons against whom it is filed have the opportunity to respond as the chapter on motion practice points out. *See* Chapter 28. What happens next depends on whether the court grants, grants in part, or denies the motion entirely:

| If court grants a motion to compel in its entirety: | If court grants a motion to compel in part, but denies it in part: | If court denies a motion to compel in its entirety: |
|---|---|---|
| The court *must*, in addition to ordering the disclosure, award attorneys' fees to the party who filed the motion unless (a) the party failed to confer in good faith prior to filing the motion; (b) the non-disclosure, response, or objection that necessitated the motion "was substantially justified"; *or* (c) "other circumstances make an award of expenses unjust." FRCP 37(a)(5)(A). | The court must order disclosure be made to the extent the motion was granted *and* may enter a protective order to the extent the motion was denied, and *may* apportion reasonable expenses incurred. FRCP37(a)(5)(C). | The court may enter a protective order and *must* require the party that filed the motion, its attorney, or both, to pay the attorneys' fees the motion caused the other party to incur unless (a) the filing of the motion was "substantially justified" *or* (b) "other circumstances make an award of expenses unjust." FRCP 37(a)(5)(B). |

So for example, in *Poole v. Textron, Inc.,* 192 F.R.D. 494 (D. Md. 2000), the plaintiff moved to compel answers and objections to a set of requests for admissions that it had served. The court granted the motion to compel in its entirety. It held the defendant had not been substantially justified in making excessive qualifications to its answers to 92% of the requests for admission and so awarded the plaintiff 92% of the attorneys' fees it incurred in bringing the motion.

### b. Violation of an Order Compelling Discovery

Suppose after a motion to compel is adjudicated, a party or non-party violates an order by not responding to the discovery as the court ordered? Under Rule 37(b), the court may impose various sanctions, including striking pleadings, precluding evidence, and other sanctions. *See* FRCP 37(b)(1), (2). Thus, if a party or non-party loses a motion to compel filed against it, it faces the prospect of paying attorney fees incurred by the movant in making the motion; if it violates the order the court issues when it grants that motion, the party faces losing the ability to introduce evidence or, even dismissal of its case or entry of default judgment against it. FRCP 37(b)(2).

An example of this latter circumstance is *Chrysler Corp. v. Carey,* 186 F.3d 1016 (8th Cir. 1999). The district court granted a plaintiff's motion to compel, but the defendants nonetheless did not comply with the order and, in addition, engaged in a systematic pattern to avoid complying with the district court's orders and the Rules. The district court sanctioned the defendants by striking their answer. The appellate court affirmed, in part because the district court found that defense counsel had repeatedly lied during discovery, including denying that responsive documents existed and making unfounded objections to discovery. Although emphasizing that dismissal was a rare sanction, dismissal was proper if there has been a "blatant disregard of the Court's orders and the discovery rules" accompanied by actual deceit.

*Poole v. Textron, Inc.*, 192 F.R.D. 494 (D. Md. 2000) also involved violation of an order granting a motion to compel. There, the defendant did not act reasonably in responding to the district court's order granting the plaintiff's motion to compel the defendant to produce certain documents. The court found that the defendant, a large company, had attempted to stonewall the plaintiff, and as a result imposed sanctions of about $40,000 for violating its order granting the motion to compel.

## 3. Adjudication of a Party's or Non-Party's Motion for Protective Order

Rule 26(c) permits a party or a non-party who believes a discovery request is improper to ask the court to protect it from the request. The party or person is first required to confer with the party seeking the discovery to resolve the disagreement. If that fails, the party or person may move the court for an order protecting it from discovery which exceeds the scope of discovery and, further, from "annoyance, embarrassment, oppression, or undue burden or expense." The rule allows a court deny discovery or "to regulate the terms, conditions, time or place of discovery." *Pro Billiards Tour Ass'n. v. R.J. Reynolds Tobacco Co.*, 187 F.R.D. 229, 230 (M.D.N.C. 1999).

The first step is for the recipient of a discovery request who believes the request is improper is to confer with the party seeking the discovery. If that fails to resolve the entire disagreement, then the recipient of the request may move for a protective order. (And, again, conversely the party seeking the discovery may move to compel, as discussed above.)

The party or person seeking a protective order must file a motion that establishes "good cause" to preclude or limit the discovery and show that "good cause requires [granting the protective order] to protect a party or person from annoyance, embarrassment, oppression, or undue burden or expense." FRCP 26(c). "For good cause to exist, the party seeking protection bears the burden of showing specific prejudice or harm will result if no protective order is granted." *Phillips v. General Motors Corp.*, 307 F.3d 1206, 1211 (9th Cir. 2002).

An interesting example of the issuance of protective orders arose in *Stalnaker v. Kmart Corp.*, 71 Fair Empl. Prac. Cas. (BNA) 705 (D. Kan. 1996). There, a female employee brought a claim that her supervisor had sexually harassed her and created a hostile work environment. To support her claim, she sought to depose other women who worked in her department, but who were not parties. She did not argue that they had witnessed the defendant's harassment of her, or made any claim against them. Instead, she wanted to depose them to find out if he had sexually harassed them. The defendant sought a protective order, arguing that such questions would invade the non-parties' right to privacy. The court recognized that inquiry into voluntary romantic or sexual relationships invaded a matter of privacy between the defendant and the non-party women, but nonetheless held that the plaintiff could inquire about even voluntary relationships to the extent they showed "conduct on his part to encourage, solicit, or influence any employee . . . to engage or continue in such activity." The court further limited use of the discovery to the pending suit. The court thus balanced the privacy rights with the need to discover relevant information.

If the court determines that a protective order is proper, then it may take any action it deems "just" to protect the moving party from the annoyance, oppression, undue expense, or embarrassment. That can include ordering that the discovery be conducted another way (*e.g.,* interrogatories rather than depositions), that certain matters not be inquired into (as in *Stalnaker*), and various other steps or limitations be observed. FRCP 26(c).

If the motion is denied in whole or in part, then the court may enter an order to the extent that it is granted ordering the party that filed the motion to produce the information. FRCP 26(c)(2).

| If the court grants the motion for protection in its entirety: | If the court grants the motion for protection in part, but denies it in part: | If a court denies the motion for protection in its entirety: |
|---|---|---|
| The court *must* issue the protective order, and, in addition, it must award attorneys' fees to the party who filed the motion unless (a) the party failed to confer in good faith prior to filing the motion; (b) the nondisclosure, response, or objection that necessitated the motion "was substantially justified"; *or* (c) "other circumstances make an award of expenses unjust." FRCP 37(a)(5)(A). | The court must order disclosure be made to the extent the motion was denied *and* may enter a protective order to the extent the discovery was denied, and *may* apportion reasonable expenses incurred in the motion among the parties "in a just manner." FRCP 37(a)(5)(C). | The court may enter an order compelling disclosure and *must* require the party that filed the motion, its attorney, or both, to pay the attorneys' fees the motion caused the other party to incur unless (a) the filing of the motion was "substantially justified" *or* (b) "other circumstances make an award of expenses unjust." FRCP 37(a)(5)(B). |

## Checkpoints

- Can you describe the process for adjudicating motions to compel? Motions for protective orders?

- Can you explain the sanctions available when a court grants, denies, or grants in part each motion?

# Chapter 52

# Summary Judgment: Adjudication of Claims Before Trial but Usually After Discovery Closes

---

### Summary Judgment Roadmap

This chapter explains how summary judgment motions are used to resolve claims or defenses for which the party with the burden of proof at trial has been unable, despite having the opportunity during discovery to do so, to produce sufficient evidence to reach a jury on a claim or defense.

This chapter also explains how courts determine whether there is a "genuine issue" of "material fact" and the process for adjudicating motions for summary judgment.

---

A lawyer for a defendant who realizes that even if the factual allegations in the complaint do not plausibly show a basis for relief should quickly file a motion under Rule 12(b)(6) or 12(c) to dismiss the claim. There is no need to wait and the motion will eliminate the expense of discovery and of litigation generally. If the complaint does state a claim, then the case will move into discovery.

The filing of a motion for summary judgment is typically the next time the defendant can test the merits of the plaintiff's case. The most common use of a motion for summary judgment is for the defendant to show that the plaintiff, although making a certain allegation, cannot produce evidence to support that allegation. While Rule 56(b) allows a motion for summary judgment to be filed even before an answer is filed, or at any time up until 30 days after discovery closes (or as the scheduling order provides) if a defendant files the motion before the plaintiff has had opportunity for discovery, the plaintiff can show that it needs time to take discovery. FRCP 56(d). For that reason, usually defendants file motions for summary judgment are filed shortly after discovery closes. (Timing is discussed more fully below.)

Summary judgment motions will be filed after discovery and used to show there is no evidence of something that a party (usually the plaintiff) bears the burden of persuasion on at trial (*e.g.*, the plaintiff's claim). What this means is that during discovery, the plaintiff must gather some evidence of every element of each claim; the defendant should gather evidence to undermine that evidence. Conversely, the defendant should gather evidence to support each element of any affirmative defense it has pled, and the plaintiff should gather evidence to undermine that evidence.

Here is a simple example. Suppose the plaintiff alleges in the complaint that while she was swimming, the defendant saw her drowning and yet failed to rescue her. Further, because the law provides that there is no duty to rescue unless there is a "special relationship" between the plaintiff and defendant, suppose the plaintiff alleges in the complaint that the plaintiff and defendant had an attorney-client relationship between them. Suppose, finally, that under applicable state law, an attorney-client relationship is sufficient under state law to create a "special relationship" sufficient to create a duty to rescue.

Thus, the allegations state a claim upon which relief can be granted because the factual allegations taken as true plausibly show the plaintiff is entitled to relief. Suppose, however the defendant tells his lawyer that, in fact, he never had an attorney-client relationship with the plaintiff but instead had told her to get a different lawyer, and soon after that he saw her drowning. If that is true and there is no dispute about it, then no reasonable jury could find there had been an attorney-client relationship. The rules could make the defendant wait to show that there is no evidence of an attorney client relationship, despite the allegation in the complaint.

This is where Rule 56 comes in: it moves forward—from trial—the court's determination that no reasonable jury could find for the plaintiff on its claim. Why wait until trial if the evidence will be undisputed that the party with the burden of proof (a plaintiff on each element of a claim, for example) though given the opportunity during discovery, did not produce sufficient evidence to support a jury verdict in its favor.

If the party with the burden of proof on an claim lacks any evidence on just one element on that claim, then a jury cannot find for it. To show a duty to rescue, the plaintiff must show duty, breach, causation, and damages: if there is no duty, then the plaintiff loses. If there were no damages, the plaintiff loses; and so on. No reasonable jury can find for a party with the burden of proof on a claim or defense if there is no evidence on one or more of its elements. Thus, summary judgment can be used to point out that the other party won't have enough evidence (we'll see how much is enough below) for a reasonable jury to find for it even though it's had an opportunity to conduct discovery. Summary judgment exists because there is no reason to wait after discovery but until trial to decide that there is no evidence.

Notice that in the example above the defendant moved for summary judgment on an issue that the plaintiff has the burden of proof on: an element of the plaintiff's claim. Now think about the defendant and an affirmative defense. Suppose the defendant in this same duty to rescue case has pled an affirmative defense of statute of limitations, alleging that the plaintiff had failed to file suit within two years from the date of the incident, as required by the applicable state statute of limitations. Suppose the defendant believes no reasonable jury could reject that defense—the evidence is so overwhelming that no reasonable jury could find that the plaintiff's claim was not barred by limitations.

In that circumstance, the defendant would be moving for summary judgment on an issue that it has the burden of proof on at trial: its affirmative defense. It's not enough for the defendant to show there's no evidence on an element (indeed, it loses if that happens; be sure you understand why). Instead, the defendant has to show the opposite: that there is so much evidence that no reasonable jury could not find that it had not proven its affirmative defense. That, obviously, is a lot harder to accomplish: it's easier to show there's no evidence of one element of the other side's issue that to show there's so much evidence of every element of your issue that a reasonable jury couldn't come out any other way than for you.

We'll come back to this more below, but that example should make you realize that it is critical to identify whether the party moving for summary judgment is the party who bears the burden of proof on the claim or defense that is the subject of the motion, or not. Now for the details.

# A. Timing: When Motions for Summary Judgment Can Be and Typically Are Filed

Either party may move for summary judgment at any time, up until 30 days after discovery closes or the scheduling order provides. FRCP 56(b). Nonetheless motions for summary judgment are typically not filed until or near the conclusion of discovery. There are several reasons why that is so. First, Rule 56(d) allows a party opposing a motion for summary judgment to file an affidavit with the court explaining why it needs time to conduct discovery to oppose the motion. Thus, as a practical matter a party who files a motion for summary judgment will not have the motion promptly decided by the court: instead, filing the motion will simply give the opposing party an early peak at the party's theory as to why a trial will be unnecessary. Other reasons are more practical, and relate to the fact that often a party will not be able to get evidence to support a summary judgment motion without taking the deposition of the other party's witnesses or of third parties. Thus, although a party can file a motion for summary judgment early in the case, as general practice they are filed once discovery ends.

## B. What a Court May Consider in Adjudicating a Motion for Summary Judgment

Unlike motions under Rule 12(b)(6) or Rule 12(c), which are limited to the pleadings, in deciding a summary judgment motion the court may consider admissible evidence submitted to the court by either party in the motion, the response, or the reply. The rule allows the parties to submit, and the court to consider, discovery responses, deposition testimony, admissible documents, answers to interrogatories, answers to requests for admissions, and also "affidavits." FRCP 57(c).

"Affidavits" are signed, written, sworn statements that lawyers obtain from their own clients or non-parties. (Ethical rules will generally prevent a lawyer from obtaining an affidavit from an opposing party who is represented by counsel in a matter.) So, for example, a lawyer representing a defendant accused of failing to rescue the plaintiff who wants to show that there was no attorney-client relationship between the plaintiff and defendant might obtain an affidavit from the defendant in which the defendant swears that he never had an attorney-client relationship with the plaintiff. Or, defense counsel might obtain an affidavit from his client's secretary in which the secretary testifies that he has examined the books and records of the defendant's law firm and no document showed that the law firm had ever represented the plaintiff. Or, defense counsel could do both.

Notice that if a party relies on an affidavit in a summary judgment proceeding, Rule 56(d) allows the opposing party the opportunity to file a motion that includes an affidavit that explains why it needs time to obtain discovery or other affidavits. Finally, note that if an affidavit is made in bad faith, the court may impose sanctions. FRCP 56(h).

# C. The Burden of Persuasion is on the Party Moving for Summary Judgment Movant

## 1. The Burden of Persuasion

Why does a party gather together discovery responses and affidavits to file a motion for summary judgment? It does so because it believes the court should decide, before trial, that there is nothing for the jury to decide at trial. Again, what a motion for summary judgment does is move forward in time from the middle of trial to the end of discovery the question of whether there is enough evidence so there is something for the jury to decide. The party moving for summary judgment must persuade the court there is no evidence. Specifically, the movant must show that "there is no genuine issue as to any material fact *and* that the movant is entitled to a judgment as a matter of law." FRCP 56(a). Let's break that down further.

### a. No Genuine Issue of Material Fact

The moving party must show that there is no real dispute—that's what "genuine issue" means—over an important ("material") fact. The moving party has the burden of demonstrating the absence of any disputed material facts. In deciding whether the movant has carried that burden the court must resolve all ambiguities and draw all inferences in favor of the party against whom summary judgment is sought. *Matsushita Elec. Indus. Co. v. Zenith Radio Corp.*, 475 U.S. 574, 587 (1986).

#### i. When Is a Fact "Material"?

"Material" means "important." If it doesn't matter to the success or failure of the claim or defense that is the subject of the motion, then it's immaterial and a dispute over the fact doesn't matter. Suppose, for example, that the plaintiff in our duty to rescue hypothetical had alleged that the defendant lawyer had represented the plaintiff in a breach of contract suit. It would be immaterial if the defendant came forward and showed that, in fact, the defendant had represented the plaintiff, but only in a car wreck case: what matters to the element of whether a special relationship existed is whether there was an attorney-client representation, not what any representation was about.

Thus, to know whether a fact is material to the outcome of a dispute, the court must be guided by the substantive law. The key question is whether the fact important to an element of the claim or defense that is the subject of the motion.

## ii. When Is There a "Genuine Issue"?

A factual dispute is "genuine" only when there is "sufficient evidence favoring the non-moving party for a jury to return a verdict for that party." *Anderson v. Liberty Lobby, Inc.*, 477 U.S. 242, 249 (1986). An example of the need to show a genuine issue of material fact that sheds light on the meaning of the phrase occurred in *Bias v. Advantage Int'l., Inc.*, 905 F.2d 1558 (D.C. Cir. 1990). There, Len Bias, a Maryland basketball star died of a cocaine overdose shortly after being drafted in the first round of the NBA draft. His parents sued Advantage, which had been Len's agent, contending that it had agreed to but had failed to buy life insurance on Len's life. The insurance company moved for summary judgment, contending that the plaintiff could not prove that its breach of contract caused any harm.

The defendant in moving for summary judgment relied on deposition and affidavits from two groups of people. First, it filed evidence with the court showing eyewitnesses had seen Len use cocaine at various times. Second, it filed evidence showing that every insurance company inquired about drug use, and would deny coverage to anyone who admitted drug use. (Obviously, the parents could not contend that Len would have lied and so avoided the obligation.) Thus, the defendant asserted that there was no causation: even if it had breached the contract by not applying for insurance for Len, he would not have been issued a policy because (a) he used cocaine and (b) every insurer asked about drug use before issuing a policy and no insurer would issue a policy to a cocaine user.

To try to establish there was a "genuine issue" on both points (showing there was a dispute as to *one* would have been sufficient), the parents introduced (a) affidavits from people who said they had never seen Len use cocaine and (b) affidavits from insurance companies that said they did not inquire at certain stages of the application process about drug use. The district court granted the defendant's motion for summary judgment, holding that the plaintiffs had failed to establish there was a genuine dispute over causation.

The appellate court affirmed. The fact that some people had not seen Len use cocaine on other days did not create a dispute with those who swore they had seen him use cocaine on certain other days. Further, the fact that some insurers did not inquire about drug use at certain stages of the application process did not create a dispute with plaintiff's showing that all of them did before issuing a policy and none would issue a policy to a cocaine user.

Thus, the moving party carries the burden to show that there is no "genuine issue"—no "disputed issue"—and in *Bias* the defendant insurer did so. We'll come back to this point below when we talk about the procedure of deciding summary judgment motions, but to avoid having summary judgment rendered against it, the non-movant can show that there *is* a dispute about the issue targeted by the movant. So, for example, in *Bias* Len's parents could (only hypothetically, it seems) have obtained affidavits from other people who had been at the parties and places where Len supposedly used cocaine in which they swore, for example, they were with Len the whole time and he never did cocaine at the parties where defendants' witnesses said they saw him do so. That would create a dispute of material fact on the first issue: who is telling the truth about whether he used cocaine at those parties? Or, Bias's lawyers could have obtained evidence that some insurance companies insured admitted cocaine users: thus, there would be some evidence for a jury to find the defendant could have obtained an insurance policy.

### b. When Is a Movant "Entitled to Judgment as a Matter of Law"?

As noted above, it's easier for a party to obtain summary judgment when the motion is directed to an issue that the party moving for summary judgment does not have the burden of proof on at trial. From the defendant's perspective, for example, it's easier to show there's no evidence on *one* element of plaintiff's claim than it is to show that there's so much evidence on *every element* of an affirmative defense that no jury could decide against the defendant. Although we haven't talked about in using the terminology yet, that fact is a reflection of the phrase "the moving party is entitled to a judgment as a matter of law."

Before we get into the details, when will this be an issue? If there is a disputed issue of material fact, then summary judgment is improper. If there is no disputed issue of material fact, why shouldn't the court have to either grant summary judgment for one side or the other?

Simply because there's no dispute about material facts doesn't mean that the moving party is entitled to judgment—it doesn't mean no jury could come out for the other side. Indeed, often the opposite is true. Suppose, for example, in the *Bias* case one person testifies that he was with Bias at every one of the parties and didn't see him use cocaine. That means there is a disputed issue of fact on whether he used cocaine at those parties, or not. Does that mean a jury *must* believe that witness, when ten others say they saw Bias use cocaine at those parties? No, it simply means that there is some evidence that *could support* a jury's verdict, not that a jury *must* rule for it. Now to look at the second step.

## 2. The Burden of Production, Not Persuasion, Is Usually What Matters

Your understanding what "entitled to judgment as a matter of law" means starts with understanding this: How much evidence does a party who has the burden of proof on an issue (a plaintiff on its claim; a defendant on an affirmative defense, for instance) have to *produce* during trial for there to be something for the jury to decide? The answer to that question is measured, not just on a claim-by-claim basis, but on an element-by-element basis. (Likewise, affirmative defenses also have elements, and the same analysis applies to the amount of evidence the defendant must produce on an element-by-element basis.)

It may be helpful to think of a claim or defense as a series of boxes. Each element is represented by one box, and the party with the burden of proof must produce "enough" evidence in *each* box for a reasonable jury to find for the party. Again, that doesn't mean the jury *must* find for that party, just that it *can*. So, for example, you might think of a negligence claim in this fashion:

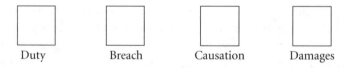

Duty        Breach        Causation        Damages

In terms of Rule 50(a)(1) (the rule that governs "judgments as a matter of law," and to which Rule 56(a) refers) puts the burden of production in these terms: by the time a party with the burden of proof on an issue finishes putting on its evidence (so, by the time the plaintiff rests), it must during trial have put into evidence a "legally sufficient evidentiary basis for a reasonable jury to find for that party on that issue." If not, then if the defendant moves for "judgment as a matter of law," then the plaintiff should lose. To break this down further, in terms of the example above, by the time the plaintiff rests at trial, there must be "legally sufficient" evidence in *each box*.

Summary judgment moves this question of is there sufficient evidence earlier, from the middle of trial to the end of the discovery period. When a party is moving for summary judgment against the party that has the burden of proof—for example, if the defendant is moving for summary judgment on a plaintiff's claim—the defendant has the burden to show that the plaintiff has not come forward—has not gathered enough evidence durig discovery—with "enough" evidence in every box. If discovery shows that there is *no evidence* of an element of a claim—no evidence in one or more boxes—then because a jury could not find for the plaintiff at trial, the defendant is entitled to sum- mary judgment: the plaintiff had the chance in discovery but found no evidence.

So, if one box—say duty—is completely empty (there is, for example, no evi- dence of any special relationship between the plaintiff and defendant), then the plaintiff has not met its *burden of production* on an element on which it bears the burden of proof. It doesn't matter if the defendant's failure to rescue caused the plaintiff damages, because there was no duty. This element-by-element analysis is critical in legal reasoning and in understanding summary judgment.

### a. How Much Evidence Is Sufficient?

Clearly, producing no evidence is legally insufficient evidence. On the other end of the spectrum, if there's undisputed and overwhelming evidence of an element, then obviously that is enough for a reasonable jury to find for the party. Suppose, for example, everyone concedes that the plaintiff and defen- dant had a "special relationship" and it is in fact admitted at trial. Or the evi- dence is that every insurance company agreed to insure cocaine users. Clearly, that would be "legally sufficient."

The difficult conceptual issue is the middle ground: when is some evidence still not enough? The courts state that if there is more than a "scintilla" of evi- dence on an element, then judgment as a matter of law is improper. If there is at least a scintilla of evidence in the box, in other words, then there is some- thing for the jury to decide.

Note that the question is not whether there is "more" evidence against that "scintilla." If there is a "scintilla" of evidence, then there is something the jury must decide even if there is a lot of evidence to the contrary. All that shows is that there's a disputed issue of fact, not that the party with the burden of proof didn't meet its burden to produce more than a scintilla of evidence.

Return to our duty to rescue case. Suppose the defendant moves for sum- mary judgment and to support it produces affidavits from the attorney- defendant, deposition testimony of her secretary, and the deposition of another witness all of which states that the attorney had never represented the plaintiff. If the plaintiff in opposition to the defendant's motion produces (sub- mits to the court) his deposition testimony where he testified that he had met with the defendant as a lawyer for an hour. If believed, that deposition testi- mony is some evidence the plaintiff had an attorney-client relationship with the defendant, and so some evidence of the "special relationship" element of the plaintiff's duty to rescue claim. That would be sufficient evidence for the jury to find for the plaintiff because plaintiff has produced more than a scin- tilla of evidence on the element.

In other words, don't confuse avoiding summary judgment with winning at trial. Juries will weigh the plaintiff's weak evidence with the defendant's strong evidence. But credibility is for the jury: judges in summary judgment motions cannot weigh the movant's evidence against the non-movants "scintilla" to decide whether or not there's a scintilla. If there's more than a scintilla, then summary judgment is improper, regardless of the credibility of the evidence and weight to the contrary. Who to believe is for the jury to decide (in most cases!).

## D. The Summary Judgment Process: Shifting Burdens of Production

While the burden of *persuasion* is always on the summary judgment movant to show there is no genuine issue of material fact and that it is entitled to judgment as a matter of law, summary judgment itself is litigated with shifting burdens of *production*.

Think about those boxes, above, and the fact that summary judgment is available to both plaintiffs and defendants and as to both claims and defenses. A party who is seeking to obtain summary judgment on an issue on which the other party bears the burden of proof at trial has an easier burden: if there is not at least a scintilla of evidence for each element of a claim—in every box— the party with the burden of proof loses. Why? Because there is no dispute about a material fact because there is no evidence—not even a scintilla—to support that fact. But, as shown above, if a party moving for summary judgment has the burden of proof at trial, it must show that there is "so much" evidence and no dispute about it that no reasonable jury could find for the other side. Thus, a key step in determining what "the party is entitled to a judgment as a matter of law" means is determining whether, or not, the party moving for summary judgment has the burden of proof at trial on the subject of the motion.

In the vast majority of cases, the party moving for summary judgment will not have the burden of proof at trial. In those circumstances (*e.g.*, the defendant is moving for summary judgment on the plaintiff's claim), the movant (defendant) must persuade the court there is no dispute about a material fact. FRCP 56. How does it do so? It must support its assertion that there is no dispute about a fact by citing to "particular parts of materials in the record, incldugin depositions, documents, electronically stored information, affidavits or declarations, stipulations (including those made for purposes of the motion only), admissions, interrogatory answers, or other materials" or, instead, "showing that the materials cited do not establish the absence or presence of a genuine dispute, or that an adverse party cannot produce admissible evidence to support the fact" FRCP 56(c)(1). What does that mean? We turn there next.

# 1. The Movant's Initial Burden of Production and the Shift to the Responding Party

If a party moves for summary judgment, the burden of production it faces depends on whether it bears the burden of proof at trial on the claim or defense for which it is moving for summary judgment. Only if the movant meets its burden of production does the responding party have *any* obligation. This section summarizes the movant's burden of production and the responding party's burden.

### a. The Burden of Production If the Party Moving for Summary Judgment Does Not Have the Burden of Proof at Trial

The most common use of summary judgment is defensively: the party against whom a claim is asserted (typically a defendant) will move for summary judgment with respect to the claim by contending that the plaintiff cannot produce evidence on each element of the claim. The Supreme Court in *Celotex v. Catrett*, 477 U.S. 317 (1986) addressed this fact pattern. The plaintiff brought a product liability claim against several asbestos manufacturers, one of whom moved for summary judgment, contending that the plaintiff could not produce evidence that its product (as opposed to something else) had caused the plaintiff's cancer.

What exactly must a defendant in that circumstance do? Must it affirmatively negate the plaintiff's claim — *i.e.,* show that it could not have been its product that caused the harm? Or, is it sufficient to show that the plaintiff can't prove that it *was* the defendant's product that caused the harm? If the latter, how does the defendant prove the plaintiff can't prove it?

How does a party show there *isn't* "more than a scintilla" of evidence in one or more boxes supporting the other side's position? It must, in its motion, show the materials in the record — the depositions, interrogatory answers, and other items in Rule 56(c) — show there is no genuine disputed issue of material fact. *Celotex Corp. v. Catrett*, 477 U.S. 317, 323 (1986). In other words, a movant for summary judgment *cannot* simply file a motion that says, "there's no evidence of" an element: it must show that the discovery in the case shows there is no evidence of an element of the plaintiff's claim.

Again, the defendant cannot simply say "the plaintiff has no evidence of" an element. If the party moving for summary judgment does that, it fails to discharge that burden of production, then the court *should* deny the motion for summary judgment without even addressing the type of showing needed by the non-movant. *Clark v. Coats & Clark, Inc.,* 929 F.2d 604, 608 (11th Cir. 1991). In other words, if a defendant moves for summary judgment but fails to show that the record fails to show there's no genuine dispute of material fact, the plaintiff technically doesn't even have to respond to the motion (of course, it will, and in its response it will point this defect out) and it would be *improper* to grant the defendant's motion.

The moving party instead of saying "there is no evidence" must instead support its assertion that there is no genuine issue of material fact by citing to the discovery materials and (optionally) affidavits and explaining why they show there is no evidence. The moving party has a "burden of production" to cite to the record which shows there is no evidence on an issue. The *Celotex* Court thus held that the movant must demonstrate in its motion that the non-movant has, through discovery, been unable (or by affidavit shows that it will be unable) to produce any evidence at trial supporting an essential element of an issue on which the non-movant bears the burden of proof.

But, if the movant does not meet its burden of production—if it does not cite support for its assertion that there is no disputed issue of material fact— that does not shift the burden onto the non-movant to come forward with evidence to show there is some evidence to support the challenged element. Only if the motion cites the record and shows why that establishes the lack of evidence must the non-movant produce to the court in its opposition to the motion evidence sufficient to demonstrate an issue for trial. *Celotex,* 477 U.S. at 323

### b. The Burden of Production If the Party Moving for Summary Judgment Also Has the Burden of Proof at Trial

It is much less frequent for a party to believe it has a Rule 11 basis to move for summary judgment on an issue on which it bears the burden of proof at trial, but it does happen. The party must show that there is no genuine issue of disputed fact and that it is entitled to judgment as a matter of law. Thus, the movant must show that (1) there is no genuine issue of material fact and (2) as a matter of law the evidence is so compelling or conclusive that it is entitled to judgment; no reasonable jury could *not* find for it. *Calderone v. U.S.,* 799 F.2d 254, 259 (6th Cir. 1986). For that reason, it is much rarer for a party to move for, let alone for a court to grant, summary judgment offensively—on an issue the party has the burden of persuasion on at trial. *See, e.g., Arbegast v. Bd. of Ed. Of S. New Berlin Central H.S.,* 480 N.E.2d 365 (N.Y. 1985) (defendant was properly granted JMOL on affirmative defense of assumption of the risk to negligence claim by plaintiff who had ridden a donkey in a game of "Donkey Ball" after being told that donkeys buck and that she could play "only at her own risk").

Recall that a motion can be directed to just an element of a claim or a defense. If a plaintiff (or defendant) believes it is entitled to partial summary judgment, it may not be worth the cost. For example, if a plaintiff believes that it is clear that the defendant owed it a duty to rescue—no jury would find there was *not* a special relationship—filing that motion likely would not save much time or money, and there will still be a trial on breach, causation, and damages. So, these "offensive" motions are rarer but they do happen.

## 2. The Burden of Production Shifts Only if the Summary Judgment Movant Meets Its Burden of Production

If the moving party does not satisfy its burden of production, it is not proper to grant summary judgment. Why? Because Rule 56 authorizes entry of summary judgment only when the party seeking it has shown that there is no genuine issue of disputed fact and the movant is entitled to judgment as a matter of law. So, if a defendant simply says, without citing to the record, "plaintiff has no evidence to support a special relationship," the court should deny the motion.

Significantly, however, the non-movant *must raise the failure of the movant to meet its burden of production, or this argument is waived. Logan v. Commercial Union Ins. Co.*, 96 F.3d 971, 978 (7th Cir. 1996) (citing *Celotex*). Thus, a non-movant should always examine whether the movant has satisfied its burden of production. Only if the party moving for summary judgment makes the required showing (depending on whether it has the burden of persuasion at trial on the issue, or not), has it carried its burden of production on the motion.

In response to a motion for summary judgment that *does* meet the burden of production, the non-movant cannot rest on its pleadings, but instead must use evidence from depositions, answers to interrogatories, requests for admission, as well as affidavits in its response in opposition to the motion to show that a genuine issue of material fact remains, requiring trial. *See Celotex* at 324. In determining whether the non-movant has identified a "material" issue of fact for trial, courts look to the applicable substantive law, and "[o]nly disputes that could affect the outcome of the suit under governing law will properly preclude the entry of summary judgment." *McGinn v. Burlington Northern R.R. Co.*, 102

F.3d 295, 298 (7th Cir.1996). As noted above, a factual dispute is "genuine" only when there is "sufficient evidence favoring the non-moving party for a jury to return a verdict for that party." *Anderson*, 477 U.S. at 249 (1986). Hence, a "metaphysical doubt" regarding the existence of a genuine fact issue is not enough to stave off summary judgment, and "the non-movant fails to demonstrate a genuine issue for trial 'where the record taken as a whole could not lead a rational trier of fact to find for the non—moving party. . . .'" *Logan*, 96 F.3d at 978 (quoting *Matsushita*, 475 U.S. at 587 (1986)).

# E. Examples with Explanations and a Flow Chart

## 1. Examples with Explanations

Several oft-cited cases all adjudicated motions filed by the party that did not have the burden of proof at trial.

In *Celotex Corp. v. Catrett*, 477 U.S. 317 (1986) for example, the plaintiff brought a products liability claim against several asbestos manufacturers, alleging that her husband had died as a result of exposure to their products. One element of that claim is that the defendant made the product that injured the person. The defendant moved for summary judgment on the plaintiff's claim. In its motion it met its burden of production by showing that during discovery the plaintiff had not identified in response to an interrogatory any person who knew that the plaintiff's husband had been exposed to defendant's products. In that way, the defendant showed there was less than a scintilla of evidence to support an element of the plaintiff's claim. (In response to the defendant's motion, the plaintiff had sought to show that it had more than a scintilla of evidence supporting this element by submitting with its opposition to the motion three items: the deposition of the husband and two letters, each of which tended to suggest that the husband had been exposed to defendant's products.) The Court held that the defendant had met its burden of production, and remanded for consideration of whether the plaintiff had met its burden to show that there was more than a scintilla of evidence to support the element of its claim.

In *Anderson v. Liberty Lobby, Inc.*, 477 U.S. 242 (1986), the plaintiff brought a defamation claim against a publisher. Under the circumstances of the case, the First Amendment required that the plaintiff prove each element of its case, not just by the usual "preponderance of the evidence" standard, but by clear and convincing evidence. In addition, one element of a defamation claim under the circumstances was "actual malice" by the defendant in publishing the article.

The defendant moved for summary judgment, arguing that there had to be more than a scintilla of clear and convincing evidence for each element of the defamation claim, and it was lacking. The defendant met its burden of production by including with its motion for summary judgment an affidavit of the author of the allegedly defamatory article explaining that he had spent a lot of time substantiating the facts in the article and still believed them to be true. Defendant contended plaintiff could not produce more than a scintilla of clear and convincing evidence to support its claim.

The Court held, first, that the higher standard of proof did matter on summary judgment: "in ruling on summary judgment the judge must view the evidence presented through the prism of the substantive evidentiary burden." Thus, the question of whether there was more than a scintilla had to be viewed in light of the fact that it had to be clear and convincing evidence. The appellate court had not applied this standard, and so the Court reversed and remanded the case.

Finally, in *Matsushita Elec. Indus. Co., Ltd. v. Zenith Radio Corp.*, 475 U.S. 574 (1986), the Court addressed summary judgment in the context of a complex antitrust suit. Plaintiff claimed that defendants had conspired to price television sets below cost to drive the plaintiff from the market. One element of that claim was intent: the plaintiff had to show that they priced low to hurt it, not just to compete by gaining sales. The defendants moved for summary judgment, contending plaintiff could not adduce any evidence of that intent. They met their burden of production by showing there was no "smoking gun" direct evidence of intent, and that it was as plausible that they had lowered prices in order to gain market share, rather than to drive the plaintiff out of business.

The Court held that the defendants had met their burden of production, and the plaintiff as a result should have been required to come forward with "sufficiently unambiguous" evidence to support this element of its claim, and remanded for it to do so. The Court emphasized that it was not enough to create metaphysical doubt over the defendants' plausible inference that their intent had been to compete, not monopolize: because the evidence gave rise to the reasonable inference that defendants had acted legally, on remand the plaintiff "must come forward with more persuasive evidence to support their claim than would otherwise be necessary."

## 2. A Flow Chart

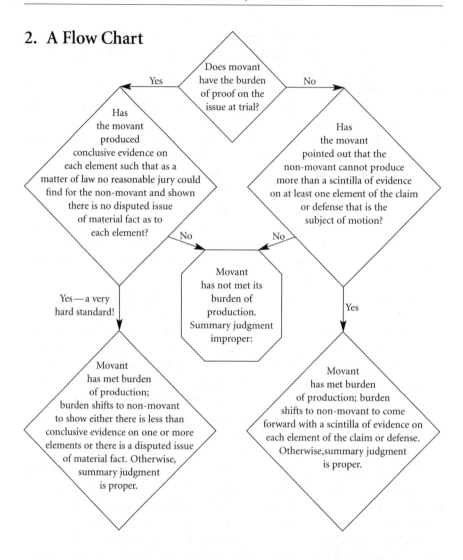

## Checkpoints

- Can you explain why it is more difficult for the party with the burden of proof on an issue at trial to obtain summary judgment than otherwise?

- Can you explain when a fact is "material" and what impact it has on the propriety of summary judgment when there is a dispute over a material fact?

- Can you explain how a party must "point out" that the other side lacks evidence on an element of its claim or defense?

# Chapter 53

# The Final Set of Required Disclosures: The Pretrial Order

---

### Pretrial Order Roadmap

This chapter explains the requirements for preparation of the final pretrial order.

---

In Chapter 43 we saw that each party is required to unilaterally initially disclose the "good stuff" to the other parties. In Chapter 50, we saw that each party is also required to disclose expected expert testimony to the other parties, sometimes in the form of reports. The third and final form of required disclosures comes in the form of the pretrial order, which the parties are jointly required to prepare and submit to the court. This document will effectively override the pleadings and becomes the roadmap for trial for both the court and the parties.

The process described by Rules 26(a)(3) and 16 and is frequently modified by local rule or custom, under which the parties are required to jointly prepare and file a pretrial order. Nonetheless, we'll start out with explaining what that Rule requires before briefly turning to the more common form of jointly prepared pretrial orders required by the courts today.

## A. Pretrial Disclosures Required by Rule 26(a)(3) 30 Days Before Trial

The two-step set of filings set out in Rule 26(a)(3) is usually not followed; instead, the one-step set of filings discussed in the next section is usually required by a court's local rules. But the rules gives the basics for understanding what typically happens.

As envisioned by Rule 26(a)(3), thirty days before trial (or as per the Rule 16(b) scheduling order), each party must file with the court and provide to each other party the following information, unless it is to be used solely for impeachment:

    (i)   the name and, if not previously provided, the address and telephone number of each witness—separately identifying those the party expects to present and those it may call if the need arises;

    (ii)  the designation of those witnesses whose testimony the party expects to present by deposition and, if not taken stenographically, a transcript of the pertinent parts of the deposition; and

    (iii) an identification of each document or other exhibit, including summaries of other evidence—separately identifying those items the party expects to offer and those it may offer if the need arises.

Paragraph (i) requires preparing a witness list, categorizing the witnesses by whether the party expects that it "may call" or "will call" that person to testify at trial. This is commonly referred to as a "witness list."

Paragraph (ii) requires preparing a "deposition designations" or "depo degs" as they're commonly referred to. To prepare this, lawyers must go through the depositions they have taken and decide which testimony they expect to offer, and provide a written list designating it page by page and line by line.

Paragraph (iii) requires preparing an "exhibit list." Each party must identify the documents and other physical evidence that it expects to, or may, offer at trial. Typically, a party will examine the documents that it used as exhibits at depositions and prepare a list identifying those exhibits so that the parties can tell that the document is the same as the one used at the deposition.

Thus, the first step for each party to file and provide this information to each other party. Then, fourteen days (or by any deadline in a Rule 16 scheduling order) after each party files this information, each party then does the second step: object to the other party's submissions. FRCP 26(a)(3) requires two objections be made or they will be waived. First, each party state its objections to the extent that the deposition designations are not permitted by Rule 32. Second, with respect to both the deposition designations and the exhibits listed, each party must state any evidentiary objection it may have, except for those arising under Federal Rule of Evidence 402 or 403. Thus, for example, if a document listed on a party's witness list contains hearsay, the opposing party must object to that portion of the document or it waives the objection. (Rule 402 and 403 relate to lack of relevant and unfair prejudice; those objections need not be made.) The objections made in this second step, under the rule, must be filed and provided to other parties within 14 days of the filing of each party's original filing of its witness list, deposition designations, and exhibit list.

Once these two-steps of filings are complete, then the trial court then has this material in advance of the trial so that it can rule on any objections, or at least be prepared to do so.

## B. The More Common, Jointly Prepared Pretrial Order and Commonly Required Additional Materials

It is much more common for parties to be required by local rule or as part of the Rule 16 scheduling order to prepare, jointly, a pretrial order that includes materials required by Rule 26(a)(3) in a format that is a bit more helpful to the district court, and to also include additional information to get the court up to speed on the legal and factual issues likely to be presented at trial.

Specifically, whether by local rule or standing order, most federal courts require the parties do the two steps, but file only a joint pretrial order. Thus, each side will first provide to the other the materials required in the first step, above, but they do not file it with the court. Then, they make objections to each other's witnesses and documents, and combine those materials into one filing with the court, not four filings, as the rule would suggest occurs.

In addition to the materials required by Rule 26(a)(3), many courts require the parties to provide a summary of the claims and defenses and a "trial brief" from each side laying out its position of the law and facts. This approach permits the trial court to get an advanced, organized look at the legal and factual issues for trial. In addition, courts often require the parties to lay out which claims and which defenses pled in their pleadings they were going to actually take to trial. (It's common for a party to plead several claims or defenses, but to not actually try each claim or defense. When a lawyer is drafting a complaint or answer, she doesn't know how the evidence will turn out and so often pleads multiple claims or defenses just in case.)

## C. Impact of the Pretrial Order on Subsequent Events

Suppose after the parties submit the pretrial order, or their submissions as required by Rule 26(a)(3), a party realizes it omitted a critical document from the exhibit list, or deposition testimony from the designations, or witness from the witness list? Can a party freely amend the pretrial order?

Rule 16(e) ends with this sentence: "The court may modify the order issued after a final pretrial conference only to prevent manifest injustice." This is a difficult standard to reach, but courts consider "the need for doing justice on the merits between the parties (in spite of the errors and oversights of their attorneys) against the need for maintaining efficient procedural arrangements." *Laguna v. Am. Export Isbrandtsen Lines,* 439 F.2d 97 (2d Cir. 1971). As another court put it, although the rule "does impose some restraint on the trial court's normal broad discretion in decisions to amend pleadings and pretrial orders, Rule 16(e) does not supplant the court's discretion." *Schmitt v. Beverly Health & Rehab. Serv., Inc.,* 993 F. Supp. 1354, 1365 (D. Kan. 1998).

The countervailing circumstance is the fact that a pretrial order is due only after the parties have gone through discovery and will be on the eve of trial. So, it "manifest injustice" can arise because of the sunk cost of litigation and the burden on the courts and parties. So, in *U.S. v. First Nat'l Bank of Circle,* 652 F.2d 882 (9th Cir. 1981), the federal government sued a bank. The government claimed that the bank had failed to withhold certain taxes on loans that it made to a builder, an obligation imposed by a federal statute on banks that made certain loans. The bank in the final pretrial order had agreed with a statement that it had made loans covered by the statute. On the first day of trial, however, the bank put on evidence that in fact it had not made any loan covered by the statute. The trial court granted judgment to the bank. On appeal, the court held that the district court had erred in modifying the final pretrial order to permit introduction of this evidence since doing so caused substantial prejudice to the government. The court emphasized that in determining whether to permit an amendment to a pretrial order to allow evidence not included in it, the district court should measure the prejudice to the party seeking the amendment, the prejudice to the party opposing it, the impact of such a late modification on the proceedings at such a late stage, and the degree of willfulness, bad faith or inexcusable neglect by the party seeking modification. *See McKey v. Fairbairn,* 345 F.2d 739 (D.C. Cir. 1965) (holding district court did not abuse its discretion in denying plaintiff leave, at trial, to amend final pretrial order to change theory of liability).

Thus, if an exhibit, witness, or deposition designation is omitted, or if the court requires that claims or defenses also be included in the party's pleading, and one is omitted from the final pretrial order, it may be waived or abandoned unless the party can establish "manifest injustice" would result. As one court explained:

While pretrial orders entered earlier in the life of a case often deal with interstitial questions like discovery staging and motions practice and are relatively easy to amend as a result, a final pretrial order focused on formulating a plan for an impending trial may be amended "only to prevent manifest injustice." Fed. R. Civ.P. 16(e). Even that standard isn't meant to preclude any flexibility—trials are high human dramas; surprises always emerge; and no judge worth his salt can forget or fail to sympathize with the challenges the trial lawyer confronts. For all our extensive pretrial procedures, even the most meticulous trial plan today probably remains no more reliable a guide than the script in a high school play—provisional at best and with surprising deviations guaranteed. *See, e.g., Sill Corp. v. United States*, 343 F.2d 411, 420 (10th Cir. 1965) (pretrial orders should not be treated as "hoops of steel"). At the same time, the standard for modifying a final pretrial order is as high as it is to ensure everyone involved has sufficient incentive to fulfill the order's dual purposes of encouraging self-editing and providing reasonably fair disclosure to the court and opposing parties alike of their real trial intentions. *See, e.g., Case v. Abrams*, 352 F.2d 193, 195 (10th Cir. 1965) ("A policy of too-easy modification not only encourages carelessness in the preparation and approval of the initial order, but unduly discounts it as the governing pattern of the trial." (quoting A. Sherman Christenson, The Pre–Trial Order, 29 F.R.D. 362, 371 (1961))).

*Monfore v. Phillips*, 778 F.3d 849 (10th Cir. 2015).

If a party has included a claim in a pleading, but not in the pretrial order, then amending the pretrial order will cure the problem. What if the plaintiff had never pled the claim which it seeks to add to the final pretrial order? The final pretrial order supplants the pleadings and controls from its entry forward. FRCP 16(d). Thus, if the final pretrial order is amended, there is no reason to seek amendment of the pleadings. Consequently, unlike a party who is seeking to amend a scheduling order in order to amend a pleading, a party seeking to amend a final pretrial order need only meet the requirements of Rule 16(e), not both it and Rule 15(a).

---

## Checkpoints

- Can you describe what each party must include in the final pretrial order?
- Can you explain how to analyze a motion to amend the pretrial order?

# Chapter 54

# Adjudication of Claims by Trial

---

### Adjudication of Claims by Trial Roadmap

This chapter identifies the procedures that take place prior to taking testimony that relate to the Rules, including the filing of motions in limine, the question of whether a jury will decide a claim, and the process of jury selection.

This chapter also explains briefly the turn-taking nature of civil trials, and how the Rules allow, but limit, the use of discovery at trial.

This chapter also explains how Rule 50(a) allows a judge to grant "judgment as a matter of law" against a party if it fails to produce sufficient evidence on an issue on which it bears the burden of proof.

---

Your evidence and trial practice classes will focus more upon trial procedure than will your civil procedure class. This chapter provides brief but important context for much of pre- and post-trial practice, describes the extent to which discovery responses may used at trial, the basics of how to object at trial, and summarizes the trial process.

## A. Pretrial Motions *in Limine*

Usually the local rules require that the final pretrial order include any pretrial motion that a party wants resolved. Many of the motions authorized by the Rules can be raised at trial, such as motions for separate trial, consolidation, and the like.

One motion that is not mentioned in the Rules but which is extremely common is the motion *in limine*. This motion essentially permits a party to obtain a pre-trial ruling on admissibility of certain evidence prior to trial. Suppose, for example, that defense counsel believes that plaintiff's counsel will attempt at trial to get before the jury some damaging fact about the defendant that defense counsel believes is irrelevant to the case. Defense counsel can prepare a motion *in limine* to advise the trial court of the expected dispute to seek an order requiring plaintiffs' counsel to approach the bench before mentioning or seeking testimony about that subject in front of the jury.

# B. Juries

## 1. Will a Jury Hear the Claim?

### a. Is There a Right to Trial by Jury?

The Seventh Amendment to the U.S. Constitution provides that in "suits at common law, where the value in controversy shall exceed twenty dollars, the right of trial by jury shall be preserved...." *See* FRCP 38(a). The Amendment has been interpreted literally: if a jury right existed in a suit "at common law" in the year the Seventh Amendment was adopted, 1791, then it is "preserved" today. *See Chauffers, Teamsters Helpers Local No. 391 v. Terry*, 494 U.S. 558 (1990). This part of the Bill of Rights does not create any right: it simply preserves one.

In practice, determining whether a jury trial right is available for most claims is a matter of simple legal research. A claim for conversion, negligence, damages for trespass, and other common claims carry a right to trial by jury, for example. Similarly, many statutes create rights and specify a jury trial right. (The Seventh Amendment does not prevent Congress from expanding the jury trial right, just from failing to preserve it.)

Complexities arise when a post-1791 statute creates a claim but does not expressly grant a jury trial right. Rather than holding that such claims are not subject to the Seventh Amendment, the Court has held that the question is whether the claim resolves rights that would have been subject to trial by jury in 1791. *Chauffers, supra.* Although recognizing that invariably the form of relief will dictate whether the claim is "legal"—meaning subject to jury trial—or "equitable"—meaning subject to decision by the judge alone—the Court in *Chauffers* held that a court must analyze two factors. First, the court must identify the claim that could have been brought in England prior to 1791 that is most "analogous" to the statutory claim. If that claim carried a right to trial by jury, that fact indicates that the statutory claim has a jury trial right, too. Second, the court must look to the relief that is sought: if the relief is money damages, rather than equitable relief, then it is more likely that a jury trial is available. *See, e.g., Tull v. U.S.*, 481 U.S. 412 (1987) (holding that there was a jury trial right for a claim by the government for a civil penalty for violating the Clean Water Act, but not for determining the amount of the penalty since historically governments could determine the amount of a penalty).

## b. Was the Right Waived or, if Made, Can It be Revoked?

Rule 38(b) authorizes two ways for a party to demand a trial by jury: (1) it may include the demand in a pleading (*e.g.*, putting "plaintiff demands a jury trial" in a complaint); or (2) it may serve a jury demand on the parties within 10 days after service of the last pleading directed to the issue (*e.g.*, 10 days after a defendant serves its answer, it could serve a jury demand on all the parties, as could the plaintiff). If a party fails to demand a jury trial in either way, then the right is waived. FRCP 38(d).

The demand for a jury trial can be partial or full. FRCP 38(c). For example, a plaintiff can demand a jury trial on one of its two claims; a defendant can demand it only on its affirmative defense. If one party demands only a partial jury trial, the other party can demand one on other issues by serving a demand for a jury trial on the other issues within 10 days.

The Rules specifically allow one party to rely on the jury demand made by another. "A proper demand may be withdrawn only if the parties consent." FRCP 38(d). Thus, if a plaintiff demands a trial by jury in the complaint, the defendant does not need to demand one on the claims against it. Indeed, the jury demand must be honored unless the parties file a written stipulation with the court that a jury trial is waived, or do so orally in open court. FRCP 39(a).

The issue of whether a demand is necessary becomes more complicated when counterclaims are involved. Suppose plaintiff does not demand a jury, but defendant makes a counterclaim and demands a jury trial on its counterclaim, but not on plaintiff's claim. If the defendant's counterclaim does not arise out of the same transaction or occurrence as the plaintiff's claim, then the plaintiff must ask for a jury trial on its claim. *Cf. Cal. Scents v. Surco Prods., Inc.*, 406 F.3d 1102, 1109 (9th Cir. 2005) (plaintiff could rely on demand in defendant's counterclaim where plaintiff's claim arose out of same "matrix of facts" as counterclaim).

## c. Power of the Court to use a Jury on Non-Jury Questions, or Despite the Parties' Waiver of the Right to One

Even if a party fails to properly demand a jury trial, the court has discretion to order a jury trial. FRCP 39(b). *See Lewis v. Time Inc.*, 710 F.2d 549 (9th Cir. 1983) (court may, but need not, grant a tardy effort to obtain a jury trial when waiver occurred through oversight or inadvertence). In addition, even where there is no right to jury trial, a court may use an "advisory jury"—one whose verdict will not control the court, but simply advise it—if either a party moves for one or the court decides on its own to use an advisory jury. FRCP 39(c). In addition, the court may with the consent of the parties try the case to a binding jury verdict even where no right to jury is recognized, unless the United States government is a party to the case. FRCP 39(c).

## 2. Jury Selection

### a. Jury Pools

Each district is required to have a system to randomly select jurors and to do so in a way that results in a fair cross section of the community. 28 U.S.C. §§ 1861 to 1865. There are specific procedures for lawyers to challenge these systems. 28 U.S.C. § 1867. While challenges were once common, they are of diminishing importance as the law has grown clearer and courts have become familiar with how to properly summon a potential jury.

Although the precise methods vary among the courts, generally potential jurors are summoned to the courthouse and gather in a large room, waiting to be called to a specific courtroom. Many citizens are called to jury duty and never leave that large room, where dozens if not hundreds of others are gathered to wait. Others wait for hours before being summoned to a courtroom to be considered as a juror for a particular case.

### b. Jury Strikes

A judge will typically summon far more potential jurors to a courtroom than she needs to try the case because some jurors will be "struck" for cause, and others peremptorily. It is not uncommon for 25 to 40 people to be seated as potential jurors for a civil case, even if the jury will consist only of eleven jurors.

Typically, before potential jurors arrive the clerk of the court will give each lawyer a very brief form that each potential juror had completed that lists, typically, the person's address, workplace, spouse's employer, and certain other factual information. Then the judge will conduct and may permit lawyers to participate in *voir dire*. This is a process where the judge alone, sometimes with input from the parties, or the judge and then each lawyer will have the opportunity to ask questions of the panel in order to identify bias, interest, or prejudice and to simply learn more about the potential jurors. *See Fietzer v. Ford Motor Co.*, 622 F.2d 281 (7th Cir. 1980) (holding that although a district judge has wide discretion to choose the scope and means of *voir dire*, the process chosen must create a reasonable assurance that bias or prejudice would be discovered if it was present).

### i. Striking for Cause

Each party is allowed an unlimited number of "challenges for cause or favor." 28 U.S.C. § 1870. These may be used where, for example, a potential juror is related to a party or employed by one. A lawyer who believes that a person should be struck "for cause" typically approaches the bench with opposing counsel and explains the reasons for his belief. If the court agrees, it grants the motion to strike, typically only advising the lawyers, privately, of that determination.

Arguments among lawyers about striking for cause can become quite heated. *See, e.g., Thompson v. Altheimer & Gray,* 248 F.3d 621 (7th Cir. 2003). Suppose, for example, that a potential juror states in response to a question that she believes that medical malpractice claims are what cause insurance rates to go up, and many malpractice plaintiffs exaggerate their injuries. That person would make a great juror for the defense, and so defense counsel will do their level best to have the person "rehabilitated" by stating that she can be fair and impartial despite those beliefs. The plaintiff's counsel, on the other hand, wants the person struck "for cause" because otherwise the person will be seated, unless plaintiff's counsel uses a "peremptory strike."

## ii. Striking Peremptorily

Each party in a civil case gets three peremptory strikes. 28 U.S.C. § 1870. Where multiple parties are involved, the court has discretion to allow for additional strikes, or to require them to be exercised jointly, and to otherwise equalize the number of strikes. *Id.*

A peremptory strike can be made for any reason, unless the reason violates the constitutional rights of the potential juror or a litigant. So, for example, if that potential juror who believed malpractice claims were causing insurance problems and malpractice plaintiffs often exaggerated their injuries was not struck for cause, plaintiff's counsel could use one of the three "peremptory strikes" to prevent him from being seated as a juror.

There are limits to the proper use of peremptory strikes. In a series of cases, the Court has held that it violates the constitutional rights of a potential juror if she is stricken on the basis of race, gender, ethnicity or other protected traits. *See* William C. Slusser, David Hricik & Matthew P. Eastus, *Batson, J.E.B., and Purkett: A Step-By-Step-By-Step Guide to Making and Challenging Peremptory Challenges in Federal Court,* 37 S. Tex. L. Rev. 127 (1996). *See, e.g., Hidalgo v. Fagen,* 206 F.3d 1013 (10th Cir. 2000) (rejecting plaintiff's motion for new trial based upon defense counsel's alleged *Batson* violation); *Edmonson v. Leesville Concrete Co.,* 500 U.S. 614 (1991) (holding trial court should have required race-neutral explanations for counsel's striking of two African American jurors in case brought by African American plaintiff). The American Bar Association continues to state that, while a lawyer may not discriminate on the basis of race and other protected classes during jury selection, a *Batson* violation by itself does not violate that rule. *See* Am. B. Ass'n. Model R. Prof. Conduct 8.4(g) (2016).

### c. Jury Seated

Generally, what happens during jury trial is that after *voir dire* and strikes for cause are decided, the parties look at the first 15 or so potential jurors who were not struck for cause and consider what they know about them. Each lawyer then makes a judgment and advises the clerk by written note which, if any, potential jurors she wants to strike peremptorily. The clerk then seats the first 11 (or whatever number of jurors the court has decided to seat) who were neither struck for cause by the court or peremptorily by either party. Those people are seated in the jury box. Trial then begins.

# C. Trial

## 1. Turns and Burdens

Trials are conducted largely in turns, and each turn is itself divided into smaller turns. In the typical one-plaintiff-one-defendant case, the plaintiff goes first: it decides which witnesses to call, and in what order, with the minimum goal being to establish, by the time it rests its case, that there is sufficient evidence of each element of each claim to require resolution by the jury. Thus, after each side makes opening statements, plaintiff's counsel begins.

## 2. Plaintiff's Case in Chief

A plaintiff's counsel must determine what evidence it needs to introduce during its case in chief—before it rests and defendant gets its turn—and determine who can "sponsor" that evidence—we've seen already that to avoid entry of judgment as a matter of law against it, the plaintiff must produce more than a scintilla of evidence on each element of each claim. Unfortunately, putting on a case cannot follow the order of elements of a claim.

The Rules of Evidence generally permit a witness to testifying only as to the witness's personal knowledge. The rules of trial conduct generally permit a party to call a witness only once. Taken together, that results in an awkward, non-linear, non-chronological trial where each witness can testify only as to his personal knowledge, and only one time. So, for example, a witness who was involved in early negotiations of a contract, but then who had no involvement until the contract was breached, will testify once, and will address the early negotiations and then the breach, but will say nothing about the actual execution of the agreement, since the witness has no personal knowledge about it. The next witness might know only of the execution of the agreement, but not its breach. And so on. Also because of the requirement of personal knowledge, a witness can also only testify as to documents that they can "lay a foundation for." If the witness doesn't have personal knowledge of a document, the lawyer can't use that witness to "get the exhibit into evidence." This, again, leads to disjointed presentation of evidence.

And there is one more turn within a turn: after a plaintiff conducts direct examination of a witness, the defendant then gets the opportunity to cross-examine that witness. The plaintiff then gets the opportunity to re-direct. Then the plaintiff calls its next witness, and the process continues, witness-by-witness, turn-by-turn, in an unfamiliar and strange format.

Plaintiff's counsel must be sure to get admitted evidence to support each element of each claim. This may require calling the defendant's employees during the plaintiff's case in chief, or admitting excerpts from depositions taken during discovery. The need to have this evidence available at trial is why lawyers will depose witnesses who are under the control of the opposing party—such as employees. Rule 32 governs the use of depositions at trial or hearings. Absent agreement or court order, the Rule permits unfettered use of deposition testimony if the witness is "unavailable." A deponent is "unavailable" only if the court finds that the party seeking to use the deposition testimony has proven:

(A) that the witness is dead;

(B) that the witness is more than 100 miles from the place of trial or hearing, or is the United States, unless it appears that the witness's absence was procured by the party offering the deposition;

(C) that the witness is unable to attend or testify because of age, illness, infirmity, or imprisonment;

(D) that the party offering the deposition could not procure the witness's attendance by subpoena; or

(E) on motion and notice, that exceptional circumstances make it desirable, in the interest of justice and with due regard to the importance of live testimony orally in open court, to permit the deposition to be used.

FRCP 32(a)(4). This Rule allows depositions—which are normally inadmissible under the Rules of Evidence because they are hearsay—to be used at trial. *Angelo v. Armstrong World Indus., Inc.*, 11 F.3d 957, 962–63 (10th Cir.

1993) (holding that Rule 32(a)(4) created an exception to the rule against admissibility of hearsay). Even so, Rule 32(a)(4) also reflects the bias toward live testimony, and so the party seeking to use deposition testimony has the burden to prove the testimony fits within an exception in this rule. *Young & Assocs. Public Relations, LLC v. Delta Air Lines, Inc.,* 216 F.R.D. 521, 522 (D. Utah 2003).

If a party offers part of a deposition in evidence, an adverse party may invoke the rule of "optional completeness," which requires "the offeror to introduce any other part which ought in fairness to be considered with the part introduced" and, in addition, once part of a deposition is introduced, "any party may introduce any other parts." While objections are made to the deposition testimony as if "the witness were then present and testifying," objections are typically interposed during the designation of deposition excerpts during preparation of the pretrial order.

## 3. Defendant's Turn

### a. JMOL under Rule 50(a): aka "Motions for Directed Verdict"

The first thing a defendant should do when the plaintiff's lawyer rests is examine whether that is the best time to move under Rule 50(a) for judgment as a matter of law. The purpose of a Rule 50(a) motion is to allow the judge to take away a claim or issue from the jury when no reasonably jury could decide for the non-movant.

### i. Timing of Rule 50(a) Motion

The earliest time during trial that a party against whom a claim is asserted can move for judgment as a matter of law on that claim is at the time the party asserting the claim rests its case in chief, since at that time the party asserting the claim has been "fully heard" on that claim. FRCP 50(a)(1). Thus, for example, when the plaintiff rests, the defendant can move for JMOL under Rule 50(a)(1).

A defendant is not required to raise JMOL at the close of plaintiff's case-in-chief; instead, it may wait until the close of all evidence (*i.e.,* after the plaintiff and defendant have both rested their cases and any rebuttal is over). FRCP 50(a)(2). However, a party waives important rights if it does not move under Rule 50(a) prior to submission of the case to the jury. As shown later, if a party fails to move for JMOL before jury submission, the most it can hope for a is a new trial, not an order turning it from the verdict-loser into the judgment-winner. *See* Chapter 54.

## ii. Two Motions

A Rule 50(a) motion may be in writing but need not be. FRCP 7(b)(1). The lawyer must explain how the law and specific facts show the movant is entitled to judgment. FRCP 50(a)(2).

The reason the motion must be made prior to submission to the jury is two-fold. First, the opposing party must be given an opportunity to cure any defect in its proof. The motion thus effectively alerts "the opponent to deficiencies that he may still have time to repair—by asking to reopen his case in chief, or by reshaping his cross-examination of the defendant's witnesses, or by putting in evidence in rebuttal to the defendant's case." *McKinnon v. City of Berwyn*, 750 F.2d 1383, 1388 (7th Cir. 1984). Remember that the Rules favor resolving cases on the merits and so if a lawyer has mistakenly failed to put in evidence that was available, the Rules want that cured. Second, it is unconstitutional to "reexamine" a jury's finding. U.S. Const. Am. VII. We'll come back to that point later.

## iii. Movant's Burden of Proof

A movant under Rule 50(a) must show that "a reasonable jury would not have a legally sufficient evidentiary basis to find for that party on that issue . . ." FRCP 50(a)(1). If so, then the court may resolve that issue against the party and, if under the controlling law the claim or defense can be maintained or defeated only with a favorable finding by the non-movant on that issue, enter judgment as a matter of law in favor of the movant. FRCP 50(a)(1). The process for determining whether JMOL can be granted consists of two steps: (1) identifying each element of the claim (or defense) on which JMOL is sought; and (2) analyzing whether there is "legally sufficient" evidence on each element.

The first step turns on substantive, or "controlling" law. Before the case is submitted to the jury, a party asserting a claim must introduce evidence of each element of its claim, or it has failed to prove its entitlement to relief. A party who proves, for example, the existence of a contract and its breach, but fails to produce any evidence of causation of damages has failed to prove breach of contract. Likewise, a party asserting an affirmative defense must introduce at trial legally sufficient evidence on each element of that affirmative defense.

The second step is to determine whether there is "legally sufficient evidence" for each element. How much is "enough" turns on what law created the claim. When a Rule 50(a) motion is directed against a federal question claim, the burden of proof is often stated as follows:

On motions for directed verdict [*i.e.,* under Rule 50(a)] and for judgment notwithstanding the verdict [*i.e.,* under Rule 50(b)] the Court should consider all of the evidence—not just that evidence which supports the nonmover's case—but in the light and with all reasonable inferences most favorable to the party opposed to the motion. If the facts and inferences point so strongly and overwhelmingly in favor of one party that the Court believes that reasonable men could not arrive at a contrary verdict, granting of the motions is proper. On the other hand, if there is substantial evidence opposed to the motions, that is, evidence of such quality and weight that reasonable and fair-minded men in the exercise of impartial judgment might reach different conclusions, the motions should be denied, and the case submitted to the jury.

*Boeing Co. v. Shipman,* 411 F.2d 365 (5th Cir.1969). Put in terms of the movant's burden, the movant must show that there is not enough evidence on at least one element such that fair minded men could reach different conclusions, with all reasonable inferences taken in favor of the non-movant. If there is *no evidence* on an element then obviously JMOL is proper; it is also proper if there is less than a scintilla; it is improper if there is more than a scintilla.

The district court may not resolve any conflicts in the testimony nor weigh the evidence, except to the extent of determining whether substantial evidence could support a jury verdict: "a mere scintilla of evidence will not suffice." *Von Zuckerstein v. Argonne Nat'l Lab.,* 984 F.2d 1467, 1471 (7th Cir.1993) There must be more than a scintilla of evidence to support a verdict. Generally, "to create a jury question, there must be a dispute in the substantial evidence, that is, evidence which is of such quality and weight that reasonable and fair-minded men in the exercise of impartial judgment might reach different conclusions," such that "a mere scintilla of evidence is insufficient to present a question for the jury" but that "[e]ven if the evidence is more than a scintilla . . . some evidence may exist to support a position which is yet so overwhelmed by contrary proof as to yield to a directed verdict." *Sobley v. So. Natural Gas Co,* 302 F.3d 325, 336 (5th Cir. 2002). Thus, there may be a small amount of evidence to support a verdict, but an overwhelming amount of evidence is to the contrary.

In contrast, the circuits are split on whether state or federal standards control the amount of evidence the non-movant must have introduced to avoid entry of JMOL against it on a state law claim. *See Dick v. N.Y. Life Ins. Co.,* 359 U.S. 437, 444 (1959) (noting that the Court had not resolved the issue). In some circuits, when a Rule 50 motion for judgment as a matter of law is based on a challenge to the sufficiency of the evidence, the court applies the burden used by the courts of the state whose substantive law governs the claim or defense to determine how much evidence is "sufficient." *Kusens v. Pascal Co., Inc.,* 448 F.3d 349 (6th Cir. 2006). Some other circuits, however, deem this question to be procedural, not substantive, and so apply the same standard applied to federal claims. *Magnum Foods, Inc. v. Continental Cas. Co.,* 36 F.3d 1491, 1504 (10th Cir. 1994).

### iv. Grant or Denial of Motion

A district court has discretion to grant or deny a motion for JMOL under Rule 50(a). Many district judges will deny the motion, even if she believes there is legally insufficient evidence to support a verdict. They do so because it is easier to uphold a jury verdict than it is to uphold the grant of a motion for JMOL: to uphold a jury verdict, there merely must be substantial evidence to support the verdict; to uphold the grant of a JMOL motion, there must be virtually no evidence to support one or more elements of a claim. Thus, if the judge's instincts are correct about the lack of evidence on one side, the jury will likely reach the same result, and the party that "should have" been granted JMOL will win the jury's verdict and be in a better position than had the judge granted the Rule 50(a) motion. Further, if the jury gets it "wrong" the judge can still grant the party's renewed motion under Rule 50(b). Thus, for various reasons, Rule 50(a) motions are not as frequently granted as the circumstances might actually warrant.

JMOL motions are made on a claim-by-claim, defense-by-defense, and element-by-element basis. Thus, even if a court decides to grant a motion, it may only be on one claim of several raised.

## 4. Plaintiff's Rebuttal Case and Plaintiff's JMOL Against Defendant's Counterclaims or Affirmative Defenses

After the defendant rests and makes any Rule 50(a) motions, the plaintiff may have an opportunity to present rebuttal testimony. The plaintiff also has its first opportunity to make Rule 50(a) motions with respect to any issues on which the defendant had the burden of proof. Thus, if the defendant had a counterclaim, or if it raised an affirmative defense, the plaintiff can at the close of the defendant's case move for JMOL under Rule 50(a) because, at that time, the defendant has been "fully heard" on those issues.

## 5. JMOL on Issues on Which the Movant Has the Burden of Proof

The Rule 50(a) motions discussed so far were brought by the party that did *not* have the burden of proof on the issue at trial: a defendant moving for JMOL on a plaintiff's claim, or a plaintiff moving for JMOL on a defendant's counterclaim or affirmative defense. A party may also move for JMOL on issues on which it carries the burden of proof at trial. Thus, a plaintiff may move for JMOL on its claim, or a defendant may move for JMOL on its affirmative defense. These motions can be brought no earlier than the close of the defendant's case-in-chief.

These motions are rarely granted because of the burden of proof the movant carries: grant of JMOL in favor of a party bearing the burden of proof may be granted only where (1) the movant "has established [its] case by evidence that the jury would not be at liberty to disbelieve" and (2) "the only reasonable conclusion is in [the movant's] favor." *Hurd v. American Hoist & Derrick Co.*, 734 F.2d 495, 499 (10th Cir. 1984).

## 6. JMOL Examples with Explanations

Several cases are commonly cited that address JMOL. Note that some of these are pre-submission JMOL decisions (*aka* directed verdicts) while others are post-judgment JMOL motions (*aka judgment nonobstante verdicto,* or JNOV). The standard that applies to both motions is the same, although as we'll see the post-judgment motion is limited to those issues that were raised in the pre-submission motion. But, for purposes of understanding how JMOL works, the cases are equally applicable.

In *Lavender v. Kurn,* 327 U.S. 645 (1946), a man was killed while working on a railroad. His estate brought a claim under a federal statute that required as an element of the claim that the railroad's negligence had caused his death. However, there was no eyewitness to the accident. The plaintiff relied on circumstantial evidence, pointing out that the location of the body and the injuries to it led to the inference that he had been hit by a mail hook hanging from a train. The defendant argued that the evidence showed that he had been murdered, relying on the fact that there were tramps in the area and the decedent's pistol was found beneath him, and he was found without any money. The jury returned a verdict for the plaintiff, but the defendant obtained (what was then) judgment notwithstanding the verdict, or JNOV. The Court held that there was sufficient evidence for a jury to reasonably infer that the mail hook had killed him. It emphasized that although there was evidence showing it might have been impossible for the hook to hit him, and which might have shown he was murdered, the jury had made a reasonable inference of which had been the cause of death. "Whenever the facts are in dispute or the evidence is such that fair-minded men may draw different inferences, a measure of speculation and conjecture is required on the part of those whose duty it is to settle the dispute by choosing what seems to them to be the most reasonable inference." JMOL would have been proper, though, if there had been "a complete absence of probative facts to support" the verdict.

In contrast, in *Reid v. San Pedro, Los Angeles & Salt Lake R.R.*, 118 P. 1009 (Utah 1911), a cow was found near railroad tracks after having been killed by a train. An element of plaintiff's claim was proof that the cow had wandered onto the tracks through a breach of duty by the railroad. The railroad had a duty to maintain a fence around the tracks. So, plaintiff had to show that the cow came through a hole in the fence. But, there was also a gate nearby, and the railroad was not responsible if the cow had wandered through the gate. The court held that under these circumstances, the evidence was in equipoise and so the party with the burden of proof lost: JMOL was proper because a reasonable jury could only speculate as to how the cow wandered onto the tracks.

In *Pennsylvania Railroad v. Chamberlain*, 288 U.S. 333 (1933), a man was also killed while working on a railroad, and again without actual eyewitnesses. However, many people had been near the scene of the accident. The court granted a directed verdict to the defendant. The Supreme Court affirmed, even though the plaintiff had presented the testimony of an eyewitness who said he had heard a crash emanating from a railroad car on which the plaintiff had been standing just before being found dead. The Court emphasized, however, that several other witnesses who had actually seen the car did not see any collision. The Court believed that because the plaintiff had shown only an inference that a collision had occurred, which contradicted direct evidence from witnesses who actually saw the car, that the plaintiff had failed to produce evidence on an issue of causation: "here there really is no conflict in the testimony as to the *facts*. The witnesses for [defendant] flatly testified that there was no collision" and the plaintiff's witness merely testified that he heard a crash and *inferred* that there had been a collision. Given that the railroad yard had many crashes, the inference was not reasonable that it was the decedent's car that had been involved in a collision, especially when that inference contradicted the direct testimony.

In *Honaker v. Smith*, 256 F.3d 477 (7th Cir. 2001), the plaintiff's house burned down. He filed several claims. One was a claim under 28 U.S.C. § 1983, which allows a claim against a defendant only for acts undertaken "under the color of" law. The plaintiff contended at trial that the mayor of the city had set fire to the plaintiff's house, but produced no evidence to show that even if the mayor had done so, there was no evidence to show that he had acted as mayor while doing so. Thus, the appellate court properly held the district court had properly granted a post-judgment Rule 50 motion. The plaintiff had also claimed that the fire department had negligently worked to stop the fire. The district court had granted a pre-verdict JMOL motion on that claim because no one had testified that the fire department had not acted properly; the only evidence to support the claim was plaintiff's opinion that the fire took too long to put out. Third, the district court also granted a pre-submission JMOL motion as to plaintiff's claim for intentional infliction of emotional distress. On this claim, the appellate court held that the plaintiff had produced more than a scintilla of evidence to show that the mayor had been involved in setting the fire, the act of setting a house on fire would be reasonably foreseeable to cause severe emotional distress, and that the plaintiff had in fact experienced severe emotional distress in seeing his house burn down. Thus, the appellate court remanded for a new trial on that claim, but affirmed the entry of JMOL on the other two claims.

Finally, in *Howard v. Wal-Mart Stores, Inc.,* 160 F.3d 358 (1998), a plaintiff sued Wal-Mart over a slip and fall claim, alleging she had fallen on a puddle of liquid soap. As an element of her claim and under the circumstances of the case, the plaintiff had to prove that a Wal-Mart employee, not a customer, had spilled the soap. The jury found for the plaintiff and the judge denied both Wal-Mart's pre-submission and post-judgment Rule 50 motions. On appeal, the court held there was sufficient evidence — more than a scintilla — to support the verdict because the accident had occurred in the morning, which the evidence shows was a time when Wal-Mart employees stocked the shelves and that the container was never found, which the court concluded created the reasonable inference that an employee had spilled it, since a customer would not buy a bottle of soap with half its contents spilled out.

# D. Conferring on the Charge and Verdict Form

Most local rules require the parties to work together to submit a joint jury charge for the court to read to the jury. The jury must be instructed as to what the elements of each claim and defense involved in the case require. They are often instructed on what the burden of proof requires, how to determine credulity, and the weight to give testimony.

Often bar associations publish "model jury charges" that provide the bulk of a jury charge and the parties agree to and follow these model charges. *See*

*Mitchell v. Gonzales,* 819 P.2d 872 (Cal. 1991). To the extent that the parties disagree on how the jury should be charged, the court will hold a "charge conference" to hear the arguments and examine the competing charges. Rule 51 requires that any objection to instructions state "distinctly the matter objected to and the grounds of the objection."

In addition to agreeing upon the instructions and hearing disagreements, the parties are typically ordered to work together to create a verdict form for the jury. A verdict form can be "general" in that it simply asks which party won, and how much money, if any, to award, or it can be quite specific, accompanied by "special interrogatories" as to whether the party with the burden of proof established each element of its clam or defense by a preponderance of the evidence.

Under Rule 49, the decision to use a general verdict form, a special verdict form, or a general verdict form with special interrogatories is within the sound discretion of the trial court. *Workman v. Frito-Lay, Inc.,* 165 F.3d 460, 465 (6th Cir. 1999). As a general principle, plaintiffs' counsel favor general verdicts, while defense counsel favor special verdicts, since if the jury finds "no" to just one element on a claim listed on special verdict, the plaintiff's claim fails. In addition, because of its complexity, a special verdict is more likely to create an inconsistent verdict which may result in a new trial. *See generally, McClaughlin v. Fellows Gear Shaper Co.,* 786 F.2d 592 (3rd Cir. 1986) (addressing complications created by an inconsistent verdict, but upholding denial of new trial under the facts).

# E.  Closing Arguments

In closing argument, each attorney summarizes the evidence and explains how it satisfies the burden that the party has, or fails to satisfy the burden that the other party faces. Thus, plaintiff's counsel in a breach of contract action will contend that it has established that there was a contract; that it was breached; and that the breach caused damage to plaintiff; defense counsel will argue the opposite. If the defendant has raised an affirmative defense, defense counsel will contend that the evidence shows defendant has met its burden of proof; plaintiff will argue the opposite.

As with all aspects of civil procedure, there are limits but those limits must be enforced by an objection. *Brokopp v. Ford Motor Co.,* 139 Cal. Rptr. 888 (Cal. App. 1977) (defense counsel failed to object to various improper arguments made by plaintiff's counsel in closing).

# F. Charging the Jury

Once the parties have completed closing argument, the judge will read aloud the jury charge. Sometimes the jurors are also given a copy of the charge.

After the charge is read to the jury, a party who has an objection likely must again assert it. *See Meagher v. Long Island R.R. Co.,* 261 N.E.2d 384 (N.Y. 1970) (analyzing whether objection was properly preserved). Some circuits hold even if the "initial request is made in detail, the party who seeks but did not get the instruction must object again after the instructions are given but before the jury retires for deliberations." *Gray v. Genlyte Group, Inc.,* 289 F.3d 128, 134 (1st Cir. 2002)

# G. Jury Deliberation

Juries deliberate in secret. Federal Rule of Evidence 606(b) reinforces that:

> Upon an inquiry into the validity of a verdict or indictment, a juror may not testify as to any matter or statement occurring during the course of the jury's deliberations or to the effect of anything upon that or any other juror's mind or emotions as influencing the juror to assent to or dissent from the verdict or indictment or concerning the juror's mental processes in connection therewith. But a juror may testify about (1) whether extraneous prejudicial information was improperly brought to the jury's attention, (2) whether any outside influence was improperly brought to bear upon any juror, or (3) whether there was a mistake in entering the verdict onto the verdict form. A juror's affidavit or evidence of any statement by the juror may not be received on a matter about which the juror would be precluded from testifying.

*See Warger v. Shauers,* 135 S.Ct. 521 (2014) (holding that a party cannot seek a new trial based upon a juror's testimony that another jury lied during voir dire). It is improper under Rule 606(b) to receive testimony from the jury that it misunderstood the jury instructions. *Peterson v. Wilson,* 141 F.3d 573 (5th Cir. 1998). In *Peterson,* after a jury had found for the plaintiff, the district court met with jurors after the verdict and outside the presence of counsel. The district court granted a motion for new trial based upon the jurors' comments. The Fifth Circuit reversed the grant of new trial because it relied on information obtained during the post-verdict conversation, and not because the requirements for the grant of a new trial in terms of Rule 59 were present.

# H. Return of Verdict

Unless a mistrial occurs, the jury will return its verdict after deliberating. (In my experience with complex federal cases, it takes about three days. Those are long, anxious days!)

After the jury returns its verdict, there typically will be a party that "wins" and one that "loses," although split or mixed verdicts are also possible. What happens after verdict is addressed in the next chapter, even though some of the actions must take place while the jury is still in the box.

## Checkpoints

- Can you define when a right to jury trial will subsist for a claim that existed prior to 1791? To one created afterward?

- Can you describe how to demand a right to trial by jury, and how a court can even absent the right to, or a request for, a jury, have a jury provide binding or advisory verdicts?

- Can you define when a challenge for cause is proper? A peremptory strike?

- Do you understand the limited rights to use discovery at trial?

- Do you understand the operation of Rule 50(a)?

- Do you understand why people refer to juries as "black boxes"?

Chapter 55

# After Verdict: In the District Court

---

### After Verdict Roadmap

This chapter identifies the procedure that a party must undertake immediately after verdict and shortly after judgment is issued in a case.

This chapter thus analyzes when a post-judgment motion under either to turn the loser into the winner under Rule 50(b) or to grant a new trial under Rule 59 may be granted.

---

After the jury has returned its verdict, several steps follow quickly, a few of which must take place before the jury is discharged. After the jury is discharged, the district court will enter judgment, triggering a 28-day deadline for parties—usually only one party, the loser, but sometimes both sides can "lose" at trial—to file post-trial motions. For example, if a plaintiff has one claim and the jury finds for the defendant, the plaintiff will be the only loser. If the plaintiff has two claims and prevailed on one, but lost on one that would have resulted in greater damages, then the plaintiff and the defendant both "lost." A defendant who wins on the claim against it, but lost on a counterclaim, likewise has "lost" something. This chapter discusses post-verdict practice. It also explains how the rules require trial courts to structure their post-verdict rulings to allow for efficient review and resolution of the case.

## A. Options for the Verdict Loser That Must Be Taken before Jury Discharge

The verdict loser has a few options that are not taken very often and are not often successful, but which must be taken immediately after the verdict is announced if they are to be taken at all.

One possible issue is the inconsistent verdict. What if when the jury returns its verdict, there is an inconsistency on the verdict form? For example, suppose that in answer to a specific interrogatory on whether there was a contract, the jury found "no," but yet it found for the plaintiff and awarded it damages for breach of that, ostensibly nonexistent, contract? If there is inconsistency, a party must object before the jury is dismissed. *Corpus v. Bennett,* 430 F.3d 912 (8th Cir. 2005); *Correia v. Fitzgerald,* 354 F.3d 47, 57 (1st Cir. 2003) (failure to object to an alleged inconsistency while the jury is still in the box waives a party's objection); *Wennik v. Polygram Group Distrib., Inc.,* 304 F.3d 123, 130 (1st Cir. 2002) (a party waives verdict inconsistency claims by failing to object before the jury is dismissed as "iron-clad"); *Skillin v. Kimball,* 643 F.2d 19, 19–20 (1st Cir. 1981) (the "only efficient time to cure . . . possible problems of [verdict] inconsistency would be after the jury announced the results of its deliberations and before it was excused").

Another possible, but rarely fruitful, option is to "poll the jury." The verdict-loser may ask the trial judge for permission to ask each juror whether the verdict was, in fact, its intended verdict. This request must be made before the jury is dismissed. *Audette v. Isaksen Fishing Corp.,* 789 F.2d 956 (1st Cir. 1986). This is an unusual request, and the inquiry is generally limited to asking each juror if he or she agrees with the verdict. Only if a juror actually disagrees with the verdict—believe it or not, sometimes a juror or even the jury may think that he's or it's doing precisely the opposite of what the verdict actually does—is there basis for a new trial. *Grossheim v. Freightliner Corp.,* 974 F.2d 745, 750 (6th Cir. 1992).

Another uncommon event is a request by the verdict-loser to interview jurors before they are dismissed. The problem is that there is very little that jurors are allowed to discuss. As noted above, Federal Rule of Evidence 606(b) prohibits jurors from testifying "as to any matter or statement occurring during the course of the jury's deliberations or to the effect of anything upon that or any other juror's mind or emotions as influencing the juror to assent to or dissent from the verdict . . . or concerning the juror's mental processes in connection therewith." There are two narrow exceptions: a juror can testify as to whether there was extraneous prejudicial information improperly brought to the jury's attention or whether there was a mistake in entering the verdict on the form. *Id. See Warger v. Shauers,* 135 S.Ct. 521 (2014) (holding that a party cannot seek a new trial based upon a juror's testimony that another jury lied during voir dire).

That's it for what can happen to challenge the verdict before discharge. The jury process by design is a black box, one that lawyers and parties are not readily able to impeach by taking apart what the jury did. More likely the jury verdict will be overcome, if at all, by showing not that the jury process was somehow misguided, but that there were procedural mistakes made at trial by the judge that caused the jury to err, or that the evidence does not support the verdict. Those issues can be raised, however, not only after the jury has discharged, but only after judgment has been entered on the verdict.

# B. After the Jury Discharge: Verdict Winner Moves for Entry of Judgment

## 1. Process for Entry of Judgment

As noted above, the verdict winner will generally ask the trial court to enter judgment in its favor. Typically, the prevailing party submits a draft judgment along with a motion for the court to enter the judgment. In some circumstances, the clerk may enter judgment, while in others the court must do so.

| Clerk May Prepare and Enter | Court Must Approve Before Clerk Enters |
|---|---|
| General verdict returned; Verdict awarded only costs; Verdict awarded a sum certain; or Verdict denied all relief. | Special Verdict or one accompanied by interrogatories; or Court grants relief not listed in Rule 58(a)(2). |

In either circumstance, it is often wise for the verdict winner to file a motion with the court to have it enter the judgment, as entry of the judgment begins the time for accrual of post-judgment interest and also the time-tables for the verdict-loser to file its post-judgment motions. Entry of judgment triggers a 28-day window for the verdict loser to file its post trial motions. There are two common post-trial motions: Post-judgment motions for judgment as a matter of law under Rule 50(b) (formerly known as motions for judgment *non obstante verdicto,* or "JNOV") and motions for new trial under Rule 59. We now turn to those two motions. Then, we examine the final means by which a verdict loser can challenge a judgment in the trial court, which is by filing a motion under Rule 60(b) for relief from the judgment.

## 2. Form of Judgment

A judgment must be contained in a separate document and be in writing. FRCP 58. A judgment is not an opinion: it simply identifies which party won, and what relief was awarded, but without identifying the reasons therefore. *See Clough v. Rush,* 959 F.2d 182, 185 (10th Cir. 1992) (15 page opinion is not a "judgment").

# C. Within 28 Days of Entry of Judgment, the Verdict Loser Must File Any Motions for New Trial and Rule 50(b) Renewed Motions for JMOL

The Rules require that two post-trial motions be made, if at all, within 28 days of entry of the judgment. FRCP 50(b). This period cannot be extended.

## 1. Post-Judgment Rule 50(b) JMOL Motions (aka JNOV)

### a. Predicate: Pre-Submission Rule 50(a) JMOL Motion

A party who failed to timely move under Rule 50(a) for JMOL before the case is submitted to the jury waives the right to move for post-judgment JMOL. The filing of *both* a pre-submission and post-judgment motion under Rule 50 is required for a judgment-loser to be made the judgment winner. *Unitherm Food Sys., Inc. v. Swift-Eckrich*, 126 S.Ct. 980, 985 (2006). If a party fails to file a post-judgment JMOL then it cannot properly assert that it should be made the judgment-winner, either after judgment or on appeal: it can at most assert that it should be entitled to a new trial. *Id.*; *Fuesting v. Zimmer, Inc.*, 448 F.3d 936 (7th Cir. 2006) (verdict loser may still be awarded a new trial even without complying with Rule 50).

However, the failure to object to a post-judgment Rule 50(b) motion on the basis that the moving party failed to make a pre-verdict JMOL motion waives the objection. So, if a verdict loser makes a post-judgment Rule 50(b) motion without having made a Rule 50(a) motion before submission of the case to the jury, the verdict winner must object to the motion.

### b. Scope of Post-Judgment Rule 50(b) Motion Limited to Pre-Verdict Rule 50(a) Motion

A post-judgment JMOL motion cannot raise issues that were not raised in the pre-submission JMOL motion. *Phillips v. Bowen*, 115 F. Supp. 2d 303, 305 (N.D.N.Y. 2000), *aff'd*, 278 F.3d 103 (2d Cir. 2002). As noted in the prior chapter, this is a limitation for two reasons: to allow the non-movant during trial at the time the Rule 50(a) motion is made to cure the evidentiary defect, and for Constitutional reasons, to avoid "reexamination" of facts found by a jury. *Fruend v. Nycomed Amersham*, 347 F.3d 752, 761 (9th Cir. 2003) (reversing district court's order granting defendant's Rule 50(b) motion because it was based on an argument that defendant failed to raise in its Rule 50(a) motion); *Lifshitz v.*

*Walter Drake & Sons, Inc.*, 806 F.2d 1426, 1429 (9th Cir. 1986) (in affirming district court's rejection of argument made for the first time in its Rule 50(b) motion, court held that a party may secure a Rule 50(b) judgment only based on the specific grounds raised in the Rule 50(a) motion because otherwise "the directed verdict motion would not serve its purpose of providing clear notice of claimed evidentiary insufficiencies and of preserving the issue of the sufficiency of the evidence on a particular matter as a question of law").

However, the objection that a post-judgment JMOL motion raises issues that were not raised in the movant's pre-verdict Rule 50(a) motion itself can be waived. "[W]here a party did not object to a movant's Rule 50(b) motion specifically on the grounds that the issue was waived by an inadequate Rule 50(a) motion, the party's right to object on that basis is itself waived." *Williams v. Runyon*, 130 F.3d 568, 572 (3d Cir. 1997). Put another way, if a party raises an issue in a Rule 50(b) motion that it did not raise in its pre-submission Rule 50(a) motion, the party opposing that motion must in its response point out that fact. Otherwise, that objection is itself waived. *Canny v. Dr. Pepper/Seven-Up Bottling Group, Inc.*, 439 F. 3d 894 (8th Cir. 2006).

### c. Burden of Proof

Any issue that would permit the trial court to hold that judgment on one or more claims or defenses should be rendered in favor of the verdict-loser can serve as the basis of a motion for JMOL. The issue can be a pure question of law: suppose, for example, that the parties disputed which statute of limitations applied to a claim — the defendant arguing that a statute that imposed a two-year period applied, the plaintiff, that a statute imposing a four-year period applied — and under one party's position it was undisputed that the plaintiff's claim was barred, but under the other's, that the plaintiff's claim was timely.

Another common issue in JMOL motions is the legal insufficiency of the evidence — a "no evidence" argument. Suppose, for example, that the jury verdict was for the plaintiff, but the defendant believes that there was no evidence of one or more elements of the claim. Let's say that the plaintiff brought a claim that the defendant failed to rescue the plaintiff from drowning; that applicable state law imposes such a duty only if there is a blood or marriage relationship between plaintiff and defendant; but that the plaintiff introduced no evidence of any such relationship between plaintiff and defendant. Nonetheless, the jury found for the plaintiff. The same standard — there must be more than a scintilla of evidence supporting the verdict with all reasonable inferences viewed in a light most favorable to the verdict winner — applies to Rule 50(b) post-judgment JMOL motions. *See* the examples in Chapter 54.

### d. Impact of Rulings

If a court finds that JMOL is proper as to one or more claims, then it vacates its prior judgment and enters judgment accordingly. In one-claim cases, the verdict winner becomes the judgment loser. The result of trial where a new trial is not granted (discussed next) is a final judgment that can be appealed. The party on appeal — the verdict-winner — will now be the judgment-loser.

## 2. Motions for New Trial under Rule 59

As with post-judgment JMOL motions, a motion for new trial must be filed within 28 days of entry of the judgment. FRCP 59(b). In addition, within that same period, the district court on its own initiative may order a new trial. FRCP 59(d).

### a. The Two Common Bases for New Trial Motions

Rule 59 grants discretion to district courts to permit a new trial whether either the court made procedural errors or the evidence in favor of the verdict, though sufficient to uphold the verdict, is against the "great weight of the evidence."

With respect to errors by the district court, error is not enough to grant a new trial. Erroneous rulings do not justify a grant of a new trial unless they affected the "substantial rights" of the parties. FRCP 61. Thus, the fact that a judge gave an erroneous jury instruction can warrant a new trial only where the objecting party can show that it was prejudiced by the erroneous instruction. *Fink v. Foley-Belsaw Co.*, 983 F.2d 111, 113–14 (8th Cir. 1993) (improper jury instructions or failure to comply with Rule 51 may be ground for a new trial, but only if movant shows material prejudice).

The district court has broad discretion to grant a new trial if the basis for doing so is a ruling on a matter that initially rested within the discretion of the court (such as evidentiary rulings), *see Bhaya v. Westinghouse Elec. Corp.*, 922 F.2d 184, 187 (3d Cir. 1990) or prejudicial statements made during trial by counsel, *see Lind v. Schenley Indus., Inc.*, 278 F.2d 79, 90 (3d Cir. 1960). To establish a right to new trial based upon a procedural error, the movant must show (1) that an error was in fact made, (2) that the party seeking a new trial objected to the erroneous ruling at the time; and (3) that the error was so prejudicial that a refusal to grant a new trial would affect a party's "substantial rights." FRCP 61.

So for example, in *Tesser v. Bd. of Ed.*, 190 F. Supp. 2d 430 (E.D.N.Y. 2002), the plaintiff brought an employment discrimination claim. The jury found for the defendants, and the plaintiff moved for a new trial, making three arguments. First, she argued that the court had committed harmful error by refusing to allow her to testify after she had put two defendants on the stand during her case in chief. The court held that she had failed to object and that, in any event, the ordering and presentation of evidence had been a proper exercise of its discretion. Second, she argued that the trial court had committed prejudicial error by allowing the defense to admit into evidence unredacted versions of her tax returns, which showed she was wealthy, which was irrelevant. The trial court held it had not erred because one of plaintiff's experts had considered them in formulating his report, thus rendering it admissible and the court had, further, cured any substantial prejudice by instructing the jury not to consider the amount of her income other than in connection with the expert's report. Finally, third, she argued that defense counsel in closing argument had improperly suggested that plaintiff had destroyed evidence. The court held that these statements were insufficient to sway the jury and that any prejudice had been cured by instructions to the jury that arguments of counsel are not evidence.

Motions based on the verdict "being against the great weight of the evidence" are seldom granted, especially if the subject matter of the suit was not particularly complex and instead dealt with issues which are familiar to a lay jury. *Lind v. Schenley Indus., Inc.*, 278 F.2d 79, 90–91 (3d Cir. 1960). The party challenging the verdict must bear the heavy burden of showing that the verdict is against the weight of the evidence and that a miscarriage of justice would result if the verdict were to stand. *Williamson v. Consol. Rail Corp.*, 926 F.2d 1344, 1353 (3d Cir. 1991).

For example, in *Lind* the district court granted a new trial to the verdict loser based upon the verdict being against the great weight of the evidence. Though noting that the question was only whether the district court had "abused its discretion," the Third Circuit emphasized that where there is evidence to support the verdict but the judge nonetheless grants a new trial to the verdict loser, the judge "has, to some extent at least, substituted his judgment of the facts and the credibility of the witnesses for that of the jury." As a result, appellate courts were to examine the order with "a closer degree of scrutiny" than otherwise applies to the grant of a motion for new trial based on procedural errors. *Id.* Thus, although the district court may in analyzing a motion for new trial consider the credibility of witnesses and even weigh the evidence, it must "exercise restraint to avoid usurping the jury's primary function." *Blakey v. Continental Airlines, Inc.*, 992 F. Supp. 731, 734 (D.N.J. 1998).

Similarly, in *Latino v. Kazer*, 58 F.3d 310 (7th Cir. 1995) the plaintiffs brought false arrest and Section 1983 claims against two police officers. In an earlier trial, the jury had found for the defendants. However, the district judge had granted a new trial because he concluded that the police officer's version of the incident had been perjurious and so entitled to no weight, and thus he granted a new trial. At the second trial, the jury found for the plaintiffs. After final judgment was entered against them, the defendants appealed the order that granted the new trial after the first trial. In reversing, the appellate court emphasized that the Seventh Amendment limits the ability to reexamine the jury's verdict as being against the great weight, and that a "more exacting standard of review" applies when such a motion is granted. Because the court believed that the judge had "act[ed] as a 13th juror" rather than merely giving no weight to evidence that no reasonable juror could believe. As a result, it vacated the order granting new trial in the first case, and reinstated the jury verdict in that case for the defendants. *See Dadurian v. Underwriters at Lloyd's of London*, 787 F.2d 756 (1st Cir. 1986); *U.S. v. An Article of Drug*, 725 F.2d 976 (5th Cir. 1984).

### b. New Trial Awarded Based Only on the Amount of Damages

Suppose a district judge believes that the jury's verdict on liability is supported by the evidence, but that the jury either awarded far too much or far too little in damages. Only if the jury awards too much does a federal court judge have the ability to order a new trial.

### i. Remittitur

What if the damages awarded by the jury in its verdict seem far too high, and seemingly resulted not from the proof of damage to the plaintiff, but of passion or prejudice from a highly emotional case? In extreme — extreme — cases a trial court can order *remittitur*. It's available only if the "verdict exceeds any rational appraisal or estimate of the damages that could be based on the evidence before the jury." *Rivera Castillo v. Autokirey, Inc.*, 379 F.3d 4, 13 (1st Cir. 2004). In considering whether the award is too high, courts compare the amounts awarded in similar cases. *See, e.g., Sylvester v. City of N.Y.*, 2006 WL 3230152 (S.D.N.Y. 2006) (comparing award of $30,000 in false arrest case to similar awards and denying remittitur).

If the trial court determines *remittitur* is appropriate, it cannot simply award the amount it thinks justified by the evidence; instead, it issues an order that grants the defendant's motion for new trial unless the plaintiff agrees to take the lesser amount set by the court. *See, e.g., Brown v. McBro Planning & Dev. Co.*, 660 F. Supp. 1333, 1337 (D.V.I.1987) ("The court has the power to grant a new trial on the issue of damages, conditioned on plaintiff's refusal to file a remittitur (that is, a reduction in the amount of the award), if the size of the verdict is so grossly excessive that it is not rationally related to any evidence adduced at trial."). If the plaintiff accepts, then judgment is entered for that amount, and the defendant can appeal. If it rejects, then there will be a new trial. (We'll see below that the plaintiff won't be able to appeal the grant of a new trial until after judgment is entered after the next trial.)

### ii. *Additur:* Unconstitutional in Federal Court

If the damages awarded by the jury verdict seems too low, a federal court may not grant a new trial to the plaintiff unless the defendant agrees to pay more. Under *Dimick v. Schiedt*, 293 U.S. 474, 486–87 (1935), federal courts may not use additur because it violates the Seventh Amendment's right to a jury trial. *Id.* The only thing the court can do is grant a motion for new trial conditioned on the defendant's agreement to pay more.

## D. Motions to Amend the Judgment under Rule 59(e)

Rule 59(e) permits a motion to alter or amend the judgment to be filed within 28 days of entry of judgment. These motions are uncommon and generally cannot be used to turn the verdict-loser into the verdict winner, or to obtain a new trial. Instead, generally district courts may alter or amend judgment "to correct a clear error of law or prevent manifest injustice." *Collision v. Int'l Chem. Workers Union, Local 217*, 34 F.3d 233, 236 (4th Cir. 1994). For example, parties have moved to amend a judgment that failed to award the relief that the court had previously found was warranted, or which failed to award interest on the judgment. *See, e.g., Continental Cas. Co. v. Howard*, 775 F.2d 876 (10th Cir. 2000). A district court's denial of a party's motion to alter or amend judgment under Rule 59(e) is reviewed for an abuse of discretion. *Devlin v. Transp. Communications Int'l Union*, 175 F.3d 121, 132 (2d Cir. 1999).

## E. What Does the Verdict and Judgment Winner Have to Do?

The verdict winner must look at two issues.

### 1. Did the Verdict Deprive It of Any Relief?

The verdict winner should analyze whether the verdict in fact awarded it all that it was entitled to. If, for example, a plaintiff won one of two claims and the claim on which it lost had a greater damage remedy, the "winner" may not have won all it was entitled to. It may need to file a post-judgment JMOL motion, or motion for new trial, in the same way the losing defendant would.

## 2. Respond to the Loser's Motions

The only other task for the judgment winner is to respond to the other party's motions.

# F. Impact of Entry of Judgment on Execution and Appeals

The principal reason most plaintiffs file suit is to obtain monetary damages. Once 14 days have passed after a judgment is entered, a prevailing plaintiff may "execute the judgment" and take actions authorized by state law to collect up to the amount awarded by the court. FRCP 69(a); 62(a). *See* Chapter 56. (Remember *Pennoyer v. Neff*?)

In addition, entry of judgment starts the time period for appeal. *See* Chapter 58. Normally, a notice of appeal must be filed within 30 days of entry of the judgment. Fed R. App. P. 4(A)(1)(a). *Id.* The filing of a post-judgment JMOL motion or a motion for new trial delays the running of the appellate timetable. When one or more such motions have been timely filed, "the time to file an appeal runs for all parties from the entry of the order disposing of the last such remaining motion." Fed. R.App. P. 4(a)(4)(A). *See* Chapter 58.

However, the filing of such motions does not prohibit the prevailing party from starting to execute on the judgment. Instead, the Rules specifically authorize motions to stay execution pending the district court ruling on a motion for JMOL or new trial, or a few other less common motions. FRCP 62(b). Consequently, the losing party often, along with its post-judgment motions, files a motion to stay execution of the judgment. FRCP 62.

# G. Possible Actions by the Trial Court and the Impact on Appeal

What makes post-trial practice somewhat confusing is that a verdict-loser can combine a motion for JMOL with a motion for new trial, and argue that it's entitled to judgment despite the verdict, but that if not judgment, it's at least entitled to a new trial. The system wants one appeal, and if on appeal the appellate court decides that the verdict loser should remain so, it should also address whether, in the alterative, the verdict loser was entitled to a new trial. A trial judge, therefore, can grant or deny the relief sought in the alternative, or conditionally. As a result, the trial when presented with appropriate post-trial motions for JMOL or, in the alternative, for a new trial, can:

| Deny both motions | Grant JMOL and conditionally grant the verdict-loser's motion for new trial | Deny the JMOL motion, but grant the new trial motion | Deny the motion for new trial, but grant the JMOL motion |
|---|---|---|---|
| This is probably the most common outcome. The trial court will uphold the verdict, and deny the motion for new trial. The party that lost the jury verdict can appeal both the denial of its JMOL motion and the denial of the motion for new trial. | This would mean both that the verdict-loser should be made the verdict-winner (by granting its post-judgment JMOL motion) and that if the judge's decision granting that motion is re-versed on appeal, that then a new trial should be ordered. In that case, the judge will grant the motion JMOL and conditionally grant the motion for new trial: if the appellate court holds that the verdict should not have been set aside, then on appeal the verdict-loser can still argue that the trial judge properly granted the motion for new trial. The verdict-loser can appeal. | In this circumstance, the court likely has concluded that, although sufficient evidence supports the verdict, either flaws in the process made the verdict suspect, or that, although supported by enough evidence, the evidence in support of the verdict was out-weighed by the evidence to the contrary. There is no appeal under these circumstances until after the new trial, at which time the party that won the first verdict may argue that the grant of new trial was an abuse of discretion. | Under this circum-stance, the court rejects the position that a new trial is warranted due to procedural defects, but holds that insufficient evidence supports the verdict. The verdict-loser becomes the judgment-winner. The party that won the jury trial, but lost the JMOL motion, can appeal the grant of the verdict-loser's JMOL motion. |

This chart depicts all of this graphically:

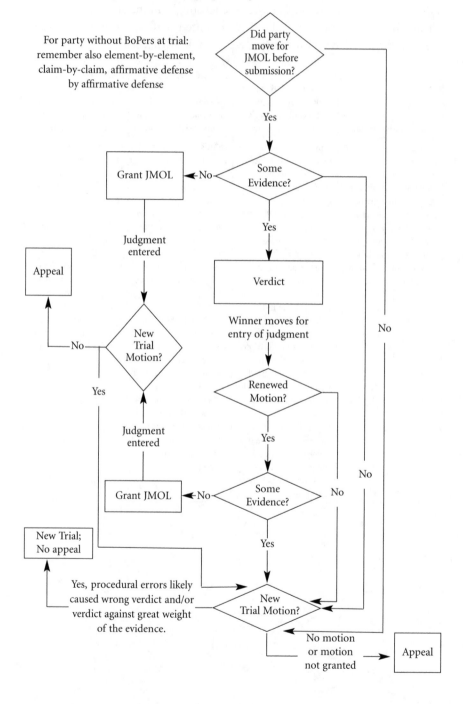

## Checkpoints

- Can you describe the steps that a verdict loser must take before the jury is discharged? After judgment is entered to obtain judgment in its favor? To obtain a new trial?

- Do you understand the process for entry of judgment?

- Do you understand how the rules require the trial court to rule so that, no matter the decision on appeal, the questions of who "won" and whether there should be a new trial can both be decided?

# Chapter 56

# Obtaining Relief after Prevailing on a Claim

---

### Obtaining Relief Roadmap

This chapter explains that a party who obtains a judgment granting relief against another party generally can "execute" that judgment. "Executing a judgment" permits the prevailing party as a judgment creditor to utilize state methods for collecting the judgment, such as attachment of real or personal property (so it can be sold) and garnishment of wages.

---

## A. Execution of Judgment and Discovery in Aid of Execution

Rule 69(a) controls execution of a judgment, and has two main provisions. The first explains the execution process, and the second allows the holder of a judgment to obtain discovery in aid of execution. It provides:

(1) **Money Judgment; Applicable Procedure.** A money judgment is enforced by a writ of execution, unless the court directs otherwise. The procedure on execution—and in proceedings supplementary to and in aid of judgment or execution—must accord with the procedure of the state where the court is located, but a federal statute governs to the extent it applies.

(2) **Obtaining Discovery.** In aid of the judgment or execution, the judgment creditor or a successor in interest whose interest appears of record may obtain discovery from any person—including the judgment debtor—as provided in these rules or by the procedure of the state where the court is located.

Execution is how a judgment creditor turns the judgment—a piece of paper—into money. A judgment creditor must rely on the execution procedures of the state in which the district court sits. FRCP 69(a); *Fuddruckers, Inc.*

*v. KCOB I, LLC,* 31 F. Supp. 2d 1274, 1279 (D. Kan. 1998) ("a judgment creditor is confined to the methods authorized by state law with respect to execution procedures, including the method for conducting a formal hearing in aid of execution"). Most states have various procedures that can be used, including garnishment of wages, writs of attachment (to force sale of real or personal property), and other mechanisms.

If the creditor needs to obtain discovery to identify assets or otherwise execute the judgment, it can rely upon *either* state or federal discovery procedures. *See In re Clerici,* 2007 WL 840327 (11th Cir. 2007); *see also F.D.I.C. v. LeGrand,* 43 F.3d 163, 171 (5th Cir. 1995) (rejecting judgment debtor's argument that "state procedural rules apply to the determination of the post-judgment discovery issue"). The scope of post-judgment discovery is broad so a judgment creditor can discover assets upon which to execute. *LeGrand,* 43 F.3d at 172.

# B. The Judgment Loser Can Move in Federal Court to Stay Execution of the Judgment Pending Appeal

Federal Rule of Civil Procedure 62(a) provides that a prevailing party may not execute a judgment until fourteen days after the entry of judgment. There are three ways to stay a judgment pending appeal. Unless the federal court stays execution, the judgment holder is free to seek execution of the judgment, pursuant to Rule 69. First, the judgment-creditor can agree to stay execution. Although not unheard of, agreeing to a stay will greatly reduce the leverage that the judgment creates.

Second, the rules provide two grounds to stay execution of money judgments under Rule 62(d) or 62(f).

First, under Rule 62(d), execution of a money judgment is automatically stayed pending appeal if the judgment-debtor posts a *supersedeas* bond of a type and in an amount left to the discretion of the trial court. *Acevedo-Garcia v. Vera-Monroig,* 296 F.3d 13, 17 (1st Cir. 2002). The requirement of a bond can be excused if: (1) the defendant's ability to pay is so plain that the posting of a bond would be a waste of money; or (2) the bond would put the defendant's other creditors in undue jeopardy. *Olympia Equipment Leasing Co. v. Western Union Tel. Co.,* 786 F.2d 794, 796 (7th Cir. 1986).

Second, Rule 62(f) provides that if "a judgment is a lien upon the judgment debtor's property . . . , a judgment debtor is entitled to the same stay of execution the state court would give." The district court must grant a stay without a bond if the requirements of Rule 62(f) are met. *Id* .To obtain a stay pending appeal, a movant must establish a strong likelihood of success on the merits or, failing that, nonetheless demonstrate a substantial case on the merits provided that the harm factors militate in its favor. *Hilton v. Braunskill*, 481 U.S. 770, 778 (1987). In deciding whether to grant a stay pending appeal, a court "assesses the movant's chances of success on the merits and weighs the equities as they affect the parties and the public." *E.I. du Pont de Nemours & Co. v. Phillips Petroleum Co.*, 835 F.2d 277, 278 (Fed. Cir. 1987).

---

## Checkpoints

- Can you explain the process that a judgment-winner uses to obtain money awarded by a court?
- Can you explain why federal courts have a limited role in that process, and describe it?

# Chapter 57

# Limited Availability of Appeals: The Final Judgment Rule and Its Exceptions

---

### Final Judgment Rule Roadmap

This chapter explains the final judgment rule, which provides that ordinarily there can be no appeal until final judgment, which means essentially when the case is "over."

This chapter also identifies the few, narrow exceptions to the final judgment rule.

---

Most of law school is spent reading decisions of the state or federal supreme or appellate courts. As a result, you may believe that appeals are both common and easily obtained. That's not the case. One of the more counter-intuitive aspects of civil procedure is that appeals are the exception, not the rule. Although we could have a system in which the decisions of district court judges are readily reviewed on appeal, and in which any error can be corrected, we do not. Instead, as a general rule an appeal cannot take place until the district court has completely resolved the parties' dispute and entered a final judgment.

Other doctrines also limit the ability of a litigant to obtain relief on appeal. For example, many decisions by district court judges are reviewed for an "abuse of discretion," and so an appellate court will not reverse even if it were, on its own, to have decided the issue the other way. It gives deference to the trial court. Similarly, appellate courts give deference to factual findings of district court judges: by reversing them generally only if a fact finding is "clearly erroneous." Finally, even if a district court judge has erred, an appellate court will not reverse unless the error caused a certain amount of harm: there is such a thing as "harmless error."

These various procedures and doctrines make appeals the exception, not the rule, and make it difficult to reverse a judge on appeal. It is important to grasp the breadth of the final judgment rule and the narrowness of exceptions to that rule, along with doctrines that limit the ability of litigants to obtain reversal of district court decisions, because together they give tremendous power to district court judges and that should make you understand that getting it right is important, because chances are there will only be one opportunity to do so and any mistake will not be easily overturned.

# A. Who Can Appeal?

As a general rule, a party can appeal only when it has both suffered an adverse impact — when it has been "aggrieved" — by a trial court's judgment or order and it has preserved its objection to the error. To be clear, a party who failed to preserve its objection can still appeal, but the hurdle that it must clear to reverse the district court — called "plain error" — is incredibly high.

Whether a party suffered an adverse impact is often clear: the plaintiff suffers an adverse impact where a jury returns a verdict for the defendant against the only claim brought by the plaintiff, for example. Conversely, if the jury were to have found for the defendant, it would suffer an adverse impact. A plaintiff who wins only one claim out of more than one filed may also suffer an adverse impact. For example, a plaintiff who pleads both fraud and breach of contract but who prevails only on the breach of contract claim likely suffers an adverse impact because fraud allows for punitive damages and for a somewhat greater measure of damages than contract claims.

But a party who obtains a judgment that awarded it all that it had sought is not aggrieved and cannot appeal. *Armotek Indus., Inc. v. Employers Ins.*, 952 F.2d 756, 759 n. 3 (3rd Cir. 1991) (defendant's appeal dismissed because it was not aggrieved by a judgment in its favor); *Watson v. City of Newark*, 746 F.2d 1008, 1010 (3d Cir. 1984) ("Generally, a party who receives all of the relief which he sought is not aggrieved by the judgment affording the relief and cannot appeal from it."); *In re Arthur Treacher's Franchisee Litig.*, 689 F.2d 1137, 1149, n. 16 (3d Cir. 1982) (party who is successful in district court has "no right of appeal from a judgment in its favor for the purpose 'of obtaining a review of findings he deems erroneous which are not necessary to support the decree'"). A party who is not aggrieved includes a plaintiff who voluntarily dismisses its complaint. *See, e.g., Bell v. City of Kellogg*, 922 F.2d 1418 (9th Cir. 1991). Consequently, a party may have been subject to court errors of even constitutional proportions, but if the final decision, order, or judgment gives it all the relief it sought, those errors are beyond appellate review.

Even if the party was aggrieved, it can realistically appeal issues only to the extent its lawyer preserved the error in the district court. Preservation of error is a complex subject. *E.g., Rush v. Smith*, 56 F.3d 918, 922 (8th Cir.1995) (party failed to lodge a timely objection to the trial judge's comments); *Dupre v. Fru-Con Eng'g, Inc.*, 112 F.3d 329, 336 (8th Cir. 1997) ("[o]ne of the most fundamental principles in the law of evidence is that in order to challenge a trial court's exclusion of evidence, an attorney must preserve the issue for appeal by making an offer of proof," and where the offer is unrecorded, review of the exclusion of evidence is for "plain error"); *Yannacopoulos v. Gen'l Dynamics Corp.*, 75 F.3d 1298, 1304 (8th Cir. 1996) ("When a party waits until the end of a case to complain of juror misconduct . . . the objection is waived . . . and we will reverse the District Court only if it has committed plain error"); *McKeel v. City of Pine Bluff*, 73 F.3d 207, 211 (8th Cir. 1996) (to preserve the error of exclusion of evidence, the party objecting must lodge an objection at trial, and failure to object limits the appellate court to "plain error" review).

As a general rule, though, counsel's failure to make a timely and specific objection at trial "results in a waiver of the objection advanced on appeal, and the jury verdict can be reversed only for plain error." *Preferred RX, Inc. v. Am. Prescription Plan, Inc.*, 46 F.3d 535, 547 (6th Cir. 1995). Plain error exists "where the error was obvious and prejudicial and require[s] action by the reviewing court in the interests of justice." *Ivey v. Wilson*, 832 F.2d 950, 955 (6th Cir. 1987).

# B. When is the Earliest an Appeal Can Be Taken? The Final Judgment Rule and Its Few Exceptions

The final judgment rule is embodied in 28 U.S.C. § 1291, which creates and limits appellate authority. That statute provides that appeals lie "from all final decisions of the district courts." The negative implication is that appeals lie *only* from final judgments of district courts. An attempt to appeal made prior to a final judgment is, therefore, premature unless it falls within one of the several exceptions to the final judgment rule. This section addresses what constitutes a "final judgment." The next section addresses exceptions to the rule.

The importance of knowing when a "final judgment" has been entered comes from the need for timely filing of an appeal after a "final judgment" has been entered, and from recognizing when an order is not a final judgment, and so cannot be appealed from. The issue is jurisdictional, and so an appellate court on its own must address the issue, even if the parties do not. *See also* FRCP 12(h)(3) (district courts may address subject matter jurisdiction *sua sponte*).

The rules require that a final judgment must "be set forth on a separate document" unless it an order disposing of a motion: (1) for judgment under Rule

50(b); (2) to amend or make additional findings under Rule 52(b); (3) for attorney's fees under Rule 54; (4) for a new trial, or to alter or amend the judgment, under Rule 59; or (5) for relief under Rule 60. *See* FRCP 58.

The separate document rule is "designed to reduce uncertainty on the part of an aggrieved party as to when the time to file a notice of appeal begins to run." *RR Vill. Ass'n Inc. v. Denver Sewer Corp.*, 826 F.2d 1197, 1201 (2d Cir. 1987). Rule 58(a) "must be mechanically applied . . . to avoid new uncertainties as to the date on which a judgment is entered." *U.S. v. Indrelunas*, 411 U.S. 216, 221– 22 (1973) (per curiam). "[A] one-sentence order denying a motion satisfies the separate document rule." *RR Vill.*, 826 F.2d at 1201. "[A]n order that is part of an opinion or memorandum, however, does not." *Id.*

So, a document that is a separate document that is a "final judgment" must be appealed from within 30 days. But what is a final judgment?

The definition of a final judgment is straightforward: it "is one which ends the litigation on the merits and leaves nothing for the court to do but execute the judgment." *Catlin v. U.S.*, 324 U.S. 229, 233 (1945). Applying the final judgment rule is also straightforward in many common circumstances. Certain things are clearly "final judgments" and so are appealable as of right. For example, a paper labeled "final judgment" issued after a jury verdict resolving all the claims in a suit is a "final judgment." On the other end of the spectrum, certain things are clearly *not* "final judgments" and so do not create a right of appeal unless they fall within an exception. For example, orders granting or denying discovery are not final decisions and cannot be reviewed until final judgment. *See U.S. v. Diabetes Treatment Centers of Am., Inc.*, 444 F.3d 462, 471 (6th Cir. 2006).

In between those two extremes lie ambiguity, and what the comments to the Federal Rules of Appellate Procedure themselves call "a trap for an unsuspecting litigant." Timing is the culprit: appeal too soon, and unless there's an exception to the final judgment rule, the appeal will be dismissed as "premature." Appeal too late, and the right of appeal is waived. Thus, identifying exactly when a "final judgment" exists is crucial.

Labels do not count. Thus, a district court captioning an otherwise interlocutory order as a "final judgment" does not make it so. *E.g., Liberty Mut. Ins. Co. v. Wetzel*, 424 U.S. 737 (1976) (dismissing appeal from district court order which "directed that final judgment be entered . . ."). Instead, it is the substantive impact of whether the paper ends litigation on the merits.

But "ends the litigation on the merits" is not the same as "completely ends activities in the trial court." Thus, even if there are questions "remaining to be decided after an order ending litigation" that does not prevent a paper from being a final judgment, so long as the answers to those questions will not "moot or revise decisions embodied in the order." *Budnich v. Becton Dickinson & Co.,* 486 U.S. 196, 199 (1988). So, for example, the fact that the district court must still decide a request for attorneys' fees does not render the judgment issued by the court non-final. *Id.* (collecting cases). Similarly, an order imposing sanctions on an attorney is not appealable as a final order even where the attorney no longer represents a party to the case. *Cunningham v. Hamilton County,* 527 U.S. 198 (1999).

## 1. Exceptions to the Final Judgment Rule

Federal appellate jurisdiction is statutorily circumscribed. Appeals of anything but a "final decision" are, therefore, available only in very narrow circumstances. As a result, an interlocutory order may not be appealed unless: (1) the district court has directed entry of a partial final judgment under Rule 54(b); (2) the district court certified a controlling issue of law under § 1292(b); (2) the order includes the grant or denial of an injunction, § 1292(a)(1); (4) the order is appealable under the judge-made collateral order doctrine; or (5) mandamus relief is available. *See Great Rivers Co-op. of S.E. Ia. v. Farmland Indus., Inc.,* 198 F.3d 685, 688–89 (8th Cir. 1999). The following table summarizes the exceptions.

EXCEPTIONS TO THE FINAL JUDGMENT RULE

| Exception | Source |
|---|---|
| Express Determination in Cases with multiple claims | FRCP 54(b) |
| Collateral Order | Judge-made |
| Grant or Denial of Injunctive Relief | 28 U.S.C. § 1291(a) |
| Certification for Appeal | 28 U.S.C. § 1292(b) |
| Mandamus | 28 U.S.C. § 1651 |

### a. Rule 54(b)

The final judgment rule does not permit appeals unless the *case* is "over." What if, however, the case involves multiple parties, and claims by, or against, one of them are entirely dismissed? Under the final judgment rule, no appeal will lie because there is still more for the court to do beyond executing the judgment: it has to resolve the remaining claims of the parties.

Rule 54(b) applies only when a suit "presents more than one claim for relief—whether as a claim, counterclaim, crossclaim, or third-party claim—or when multiple parties are involved." In that circumstance, the rule makes it clear that an order—no matter what it is labelled by the court—"that adjudicates fewer than all the claims or the rights and liabilities of fewer than all the parties does not end the action as to any of the claims or parties . . ." FRCP 54(b). Consequently, for example, a defendant in a multi-defendant suit, against whom even all claims have been dismissed, still must monitor the lawsuit and is still a "party" to the suit. There is no final judgment even as to that defendant. The judge can reconsider his decision at any time and there is no appeal because there is no final judgment. That's the general rule.

But there is an exception in Rule 54(b). It creates a procedure for a party to have the district court enter a *partial* final judgment, permitting an immediate appeal from a judgment even when some of the case remains pending. That exception comes from the first sentence of Rule 54(b):

> When an action presents more than one claim for relief . . . or when multiple parties are involved, the court may direct entry of a final judgment as to one or more, but fewer than all, claims or parties only if the court expressly determines that there is no just reason for delay.

FRCP 54(b).

Taken as a whole, if a case involves more than one claim or party and if the court has not resolved it all, then the any order disposing of part of the case can be modified at any time by the district court, and so is not appealable, *unless* (1) the order adjudicates at least one claim in a multiple claim suit and (2) the district court (a) "expressly determines" that there is no just reason to delay and (b) expressly directs entry of a final judgment on the claim, or claims, adjudicated. So, the general rule is that the adjudication of some, but not all, claims does not constitute an appealable order. We turn to the exception in Rule 54(b) now.

### i. Adjudication of at Least One of Multiple Claims

Rule 54(b) only gives a district court power to direct entry of a partial final judgment if it has adjudicated at least one claim in a suit involving more than one claim, or if it involves multiple parties.

Multiple claims generally do not exist where the claims are related to each other. Instead, they exist where one claim is factually independent or could be enforced separately from another, or where there is more than one type of relief requested or potential recovery. *See Advanced Magnetics v. Bayfront Partners,* 106 F.3d 11, 16, n. 21 (2d Cir. 1997); *Ginett v. Computer Task Group,* 962 F.2d 1085, 1096 (2d Cir.1992) ("Only those claims 'inherently inseparable' from or 'inextricably interrelated' to each other are inappropriate for rule 54(b) certification.").

When is a claim adjudicated? A judgment can be certified for appeal under Rule 54(b) only when it reflects "an ultimate disposition of an individual claim entered in the course of a multiple claims action." *Sears, Roebuck & Co. v. Mackey*, 351 U.S. 427, 436 (1956). The requirement of a final disposition of a claim is mandatory and is not a matter of discretion. *Houston Indus. Inc. v. U.S.*, 78 F.3d 564 (Fed. Cir. 1996). Thus, an order which states that a plaintiff has established one element of a claim, or which otherwise decides an issue but which does not adjudicate a claim, cannot properly be the subject of a Rule 54(b) motion. The resolution of individual issues within a claim does not satisfy the requirement in Rule 54(b) that a claim be adjudicated. *Compare Liberty Mut. Ins. Co. v. Wetzel*, 424 U.S. 737, 742–43 (1976) (entry of judgment under Rule 54(b) was not proper where district court determined issue of liability in employment discrimination claim but requests for relief, including damages, remained).

## ii. Express Determination There Is No Just Reason for Delay

Often a district court will state in its certification order the words required in Rule 54(b): there is no just reason for delay. That language is required in some circuits, but even when it is required, it may not control. When it is required, its absence precludes appeal. In some circuits, "when district courts fail to make express determinations, we do not consider the parties' arguments about finality and no just reason for delay." *New Mexico v. Trujillo*, 813 F.3d 1308 (10th Cir. 2016). Even when it is present, a court will review the determination for an abuse of discretion. If a circuit does nto require the language, it will look at the order together with the record in the district court to determine if the district court had an unmistakable intent to render the issue appealable under Rule 54(b). *Ford v. Elsbury*, 32 F.3d 931, 934–35 (5th Cir. 1994).

The reason certification is required is because Rule 54(b) balances two policies: avoiding the "danger of hardship or injustice through delay which would be alleviated by immediate appeal" and "avoid[ing] piecemeal appeals." *PYCA Indus. v. Harrison County Waste Water Management Dist.*, 81 F.3d 1412, 1421 (5th Cir.1996). The purpose of Rule 54(b) is to provide the opportunity to appeal adjudication affecting some, but not all, of the parties or some but not all of the claims against a single party.

The first policy, the "historic federal policy against piecemeal appeals," cuts against certifying cases for appeal under Rule 54(b). *Reiter v. Cooper*, 507 U.S.

258 (1993). Respect for that policy requires that the court's power to enter a final judgment before the entire case is concluded, in order to permit an aggrieved party to take an immediate appeal, be exercised sparingly. The Supreme Court has emphasized that "[n]ot all" dismissals of "individual claims should be immediately appealable, even if they are in some sense separable from the remaining unresolved claims." *Curtiss-Wright Corp. v. General Electric Co.*, 446 U.S. 18 (1980). Likewise, Rule 54(b) "should be used only in the infrequent harsh case," *Cullen v. Margiotta*, 618 F.2d 226, 228 (6th Cir. 1980), such as when "there exists 'some danger of hardship or injustice through delay which would be alleviated by immediate appeal,'" *id.* (quoting *Brunswick Corp. v. Sheridan*, 582 F.2d 175, 183 (2d Cir.1978)).

Piecemeal appeals result in additional work for courts and the parties. For example, if a plaintiff's claims against one of two defendants are adjudicated and an appeal is permitted, the plaintiff will be proceeding in the district court against one defendant while having to appeal the judgment in favor of the other defendant.

The second policy, danger of hardship, is a reason to certify, but it is personal to a party and finding it too readily will create the risk of unnecessary appeals and violations of the final judgment rule. As a result, great hardship is required. Courts emphasize that certification under Rule 54(b) should be "exercised sparingly," and "only if there are interests of sound judicial administration and efficiency to be served, or in the infrequent harsh case where there exists some danger of hardship or injustice through delay which would be alleviated by immediate appeal." *Harriscom Svenska AB v. Harris Corp.*, 947 F.2d 627, 629 (2d Cir. 1991). This means that "[n]ot all" dismissals of "individual claims should be immediately appealable, even if they are in some sense separable from the remaining unresolved claims." *Curtiss-Wright Corp.*, 446 U.S. at 8. "The power which this Rule confers upon the trial judge should be used only in the infrequent harsh case," *Cullen v. Margiotta*, 618 F.2d 226, 228 (2d Cir. 1980), such as "if there exists 'some danger of hardship or injustice through delay which would be alleviated by immediate appeal.'" *Id.* That means, for example, that if the district court dismisses some but not all claims in an action, but the remaining claims will require "the same or closely related issues . . . to be litigated," the court generally should not certify its judgment as appealable under Rule 54(b), *Nat'l Bank of Washington v. Dolgov*, 853 F.2d 57, 58 (2d Cir.1988), unless it concludes "that adherence to the normal and federally preferred practice of postponing appeal until after a final judgment has been entered . . . will cause unusual hardship or work an injustice." *Hogan v. Consolidated Rail Corp.*, 961 F.2d 1021, 1026 (2d Cir. 1992).

For these reasons, the need to avoid a second trial in cases where the dismissed claims are closely related to the still-surviving claims is generally not a proper ground to certify a case for appeal. *See Hogan*, 961 F.2d at 1026 ("Though we sympathize with the district court's desire to avoid a retrial of the entire case . . . the interrelationship of the dismissed and surviving claims is generally a reason for not granting a Rule 54(b) certification. . . . To deem sufficient under Rule 54(b) a finding simply that an immediate appeal might avoid the need for a retrial . . . could only contravene the federal policy against piecemeal appeals." *Harriscom*, 947 F.2d at 631 ("[T]he federal scheme does not provide for an immediate appeal solely on the ground that such an appeal may advance the proceedings in the district court."); *see also Brunswick Corp. v. Sheridan*, 582 F.2d 175, 185 (2d Cir.1978) (disapproving district court's Rule 54(b) certification and cautioning that "[t]he policy against piecemeal appeals of intertwined claims should not be subverted by the specters of additional trials summoned up by . . . able district judge[s]").

### iii. Express Entry of Final Judgment

Again, normally a district court that certifies a case for appeal under Rule 54(b) simply captions the order as a "final judgment" and includes a statement that the judgment is intended to be appealable. However, the words are not required and are not enough, by themselves, to indicate the intent to permit an interlocutory appeal under Rule 54(b).

### iv. Waiver of the Right to Seek Rule 54(b) Certification

Although Rule 54(b) does not have a time limit on seeking certification, delay can waive the right to use the procedure. The court in *Schaefer v. First Nat'l Bank of Lincolnwood*, 465 F.2d 234, 236 (7th Cir.1972), held that absent exceptional circumstances it would be an abuse of discretion for a district court to enter judgment under Rule 54(b) when the motion for certification had been filed more than 30 days after the entry of the order. Otherwise, a party would have more time to appeal during a lawsuit than it would after final judgment.

### v. Appellate Review

A party on appeal of a Rule 54(b) order can argue that certification was improper, and so the appeal should be dismissed. Appellate courts review a district court's Rule 54(b) certification for abuse of discretion. *Curtiss-Wright Corp.*, 446 U.S. 1, 8–10. However, because Rule 54(b) severance is consistent with the final judgment rule, certification is rarely reversed on appeal. *See, e.g., In re First T.D. & Inv., Inc.*, 253 F.3d 520, 531–33 (9th Cir. 2001).

## b. Collateral Orders

A "collateral order" may be appealed before final judgment. The collateral order doctrine is a common law exception that grew out of *Cohen v. Beneficial Indus. Loan Corp.*, 337 U.S. 541(1949). The Supreme Court has repeatedly characterized the collateral order doctrine as "narrow," and described conditions for its application as "stringent," explaining that it "should stay that way and never be allowed to swallow the general rule." *Digital Equip. Corp. v. Desktop Direct Inc.*, 511 U.S. 863, 868 (1994). In addition, strict construction of the collateral order doctrine is consistent with the statutory policy against piecemeal appeals that underlies the final judgment rule. Thus, courts apply the test "without regard to the chance that the litigation at hand might be speeded, or a particular injustice averted, by a prompt appellate court decision." *Digital Equip.*, 511 U.S. at 868. The reason for the strict construction is the concern that the collateral order doctrine "will overpower the substantial finality interests § 1291 is meant to further: judicial efficiency, for example, and the 'sensible policy "of avoid[ing] the obstruction to just claims that would come from permitting the harassment and cost of a succession of separate appeals from the various rulings to which a litigation may give rise."'" *Will v. Hallock*, 546 U.S. 345 (2006).

In narrow circumstances, *Cohen* and the collateral order exception permit appeal, before final judgment, of a district court order but only one that (i) "conclusively determine[s]" the disputed question; (ii) "resolve[s] an important issue completely separate" from the merits of the action; and (iii) is "effectively unreviewable" on appeal from a final judgment. *Coopers & Lybrand v. Livesay*, 437 U.S. 463, 468–69 (1978). If the order does not satisfy each requirement, appellate review must await final judgment. *See Gulfstream Aerospace Corp. v. Mayacamas Corp.*, 485 U.S. 271, 276 (1988). Many orders will meet the first two requirements, but not the third.

### i. Conclusive Determination

It is usually clear whether or not the district court's decision conclusively determines an issue, and when it does not. *See, e.g., Blake v. Gov't of V.I. Dept. of Housing*, 198 Fed. Appx. 216 (3rd Cir. 2006) (order staying discovery on affirmative defense did not conclusively resolve whether affirmative defense was proper); *Reyes v. Freebery*, 192 Fed. Appx. 120 (3rd Cir. 2006) (order which trial court entered "without prejudice" to party to re-urge its motion did not conclusively determine the issue).

### ii. An Important Issue Separate From the Merits

The right at issue must be jurisprudentially "important." Generally courts weigh the importance of the issue to the parties to the litigation against "the policies militating against interlocutory appeals." *Lauro Lines S.R.L. v. Chasser*, 490 U.S. 495, 502 (1989) (Scalia, J., concurring). The issue must be important in light of the fact that it will result in piecemeal appeals. *Id.*

### iii. Effectively Unreviewable After Appeal

This is the hardest element to satisfy. "It is not mere avoidance of trial, but avoidance of a trial that would imperil a substantial public interest, that counts when asking whether an order is 'effectively' unreviewable if review is to be left until later." *Sinochem*, 126 S.Ct. at 959. The decision in *Lauro Lines* illustrates this point. In that case, a man was killed by terrorists who had hijacked a cruise liner. The man's estate filed a wrongful death action against the owner of the cruise line, which moved to dismiss based upon a forum selection clause which ostensibly obligated all suits to be brought in Naples, Italy. The district court denied the motion to dismiss, and the defendant sought to appeal.

The Supreme Court held that the order was not within the collateral order exception because it was reviewable after appeal, even though that meant that the cruise ship owner would have to go through the entire trial and then, after final judgment, appeal and get the case dismissed, then have the suit brought again, if at all, in Italy. The Court emphasized that an order was "effectively unreviewable" only if the right would be *destroyed* if not vindicated prior to trial. The right to have the case heard in Italy would not be destroyed by trial in the U.S.: "If it is eventually decided that the District Court erred in allowing trial in this case to take place in New York, petitioner will have been put to unnecessary trouble and expense, and the value of its contractual right to an Italian forum will have been diminished," but that was not enough to "essentially destroy" the right. *Lauro Lines*, 490 U.S. at 502. *See Digital Equip. Corp. v. Desktop Direct, Inc.*, 511 U.S. 863 (1994) (district court's order vacating its prior order dismissing a case pursuant to parties' settlement was not a final judgment).

Few orders meet this hurdle, but some do — usually those that involve the right not to be sued, at all. *Puerto Rico Aqueduct and Sewer Auth. v. Metcalf & Eddy, Inc.*, 506 U.S. 139, 144 (1993) (state sovereign immunity immediately appealable); *Mitchell v. Forsyth*, 472 U.S. 511, 526 (1985) (qualified executive immunity immediately appealable); *Larsen v. Senate of Commonwealth of Penn.*, 152 F.3d 240, 245 (3d Cir.1998) (legislative immunity immediately appealable). Finally, the fact that courts split on whether even an order that will result in disclosure of privileged information meets the test gives some idea of its narrow nature. *See U.S. v. Diabetes Treatment Centers of Am., Inc.*, 444 F.3d 462, 471 (6th Cir. 2006) (explaining that some circuits permit collateral order review of discovery orders involving claims of privilege).

### c. *Orders Granting or Denying Injunctive Relief:*
### *28 U.S.C. § 1292(a)(1)*

There are generally three types of injunctions: permanent, preliminary, and temporary. Permanent injunctions are issued with final adjudication and so are appealable as part of a final injunction. Permanent injunctions are issued before then, but last (at the longest) only until final adjudication. While that may only "a few" months, even that amount of time can be disruptive of a business, and litigation can take years. Temporary injunctions, or "TROs" last only 30 days and are typically available only, in a civil case, to maintain the status quo for a short time until the court can more fully adjudicate the claims.

The availability of an appeal prior to final judgment thus matters only if the court has entered a preliminary or temporary injunction since permanent injunctions by definition only exist after final judgment. Permanent injunctions are appealable as of right under Section 1292(a)(1) and by its express terms. *See also Continental Training Services, Inc. v. Cavazos,* 893 F.2d 877, 880 (7th Cir.1990) (where a permanent injunction has been granted that supersedes the original preliminary injunction, appeal from an interlocutory preliminary order is properly dismissed); *New York State Nat. Organization for Women v. Terry,* 886 F.2d 1339, 1350 (2d Cir.1989) ("the appealability of the district court's grant of a preliminary injunction is moot . . . because the district court subsequently granted a permanent injunction").

28 U.S.C. § 1292(a)(1) creates appellate jurisdiction over "[i]nterlocutory orders of the district courts . . . granting, continuing, modifying, refusing or dissolving injunctions, or refusing to dissolve or modify injunctions, except where a direct review may be had in the Supreme Court." This statute "was intended to carve out only a limited exception to the final-judgment rule." *Carson v. Am. Brands, Inc.,* 450 U.S. 79, 84 (1981).

This statute presents several issues that are common to all forms of injunctions. For example, although an order denying or granting a preliminary injunction would be immediately appealable, orders that would seem to have the same substantive impact are not appealable, such as denying a motion for summary judgment where the plaintiff contended it was entitled to a preliminary injunction. Second, orders that are not labeled "injunctions" but which have the same effect as an injunction may be appealable if they otherwise meet the requirements of the statute. We turn briefly to those issues before turning to issues that turn on which type of injunction is entered, preliminary or temporary.

Suppose a court denies a motion for summary judgment in a case where the only relief the plaintiff seeks is an injunction. Sounds like the district court denied a preliminary injunction? It did not. Conversely, suppose the court grants a summary judgment motion of the plaintiff in that same case, or even one where it sought permanent injunctive relief upon entry of summary judgment. Neither results in an order granting or denying injunctive relief. Instead, "the denial of summary judgment is not a final, appealable decision. Moreover, even when a district court denies a summary judgment motion seeking a permanent injunction, § 1292(a)(1) does not provide a basis for appellate jurisdiction. In *Switzerland Cheese Ass'n, Inc. v. E. Horne's Market, Inc.*, 385 U.S. 23, 25 (1966), the Supreme Court characterized the denial of such a summary judgment motion because of disputed issues of fact as relating only to "pretrial procedures" and therefore not "'interlocutory' within the meaning of § 1292(a)(1)." *United Keetoowah Band of Cherokee Indians in Oklahoma v. U.S. ex rel. Norton*, 2007 WL 2562352 (10th Cir. Sept. 6, 2007).

On the other hand, sometimes a court can grant summary judgment and order a defendant (or other party) to do something. An order that someone do, or not do, something is injunctive relief. Under those circumstances the grant of summary judgment along with the order requiring action (or not acting) is appealable, even if the case remains pending below (for adjudication of other claims, damages, and so on). *See Gon v. First State Ins. Co.*, 871 F.2d 863, 866 (9th Cir. 1989) ("The order [directing the insurer to pay defense expenses] met the general definition of an injunction in that it was directed to [the insurer], was enforceable by contempt, and provided most of the substantive relief the insureds sought.").

We turn to the aspects of Section 1291(a)(1) which depend on the type of injunction issued: preliminary or temporary.

### i. Orders Granting or Denying Preliminary Injunctions: Appealable as of Right

A district court's order granting or denying a preliminary injunction is generally immediately appealable under 28 U.S.C. § 1292(a)(1). But even if the injunction runs through trial, to be appealable, the order must "either grant or deny the relief sought by a claimant in more than a temporary fashion." *Cohen v. Bd. of Trustees of the Univ. of Med. & Dentistry of N.J.*, 867 F.2d 1455 (3rd Cir. 1989).

### ii. Temporary Restraining Orders: Generally Not Appealable

As a general rule, a temporary restraining order that does nothing but preserve the status quo is not appealable under Section 1292(a)(1). *See Office of Pers. Mgmt. v. Am. Fed'n of Gov't Employees, AFL-CIO*, 473 U.S. 1301, 1303–04 (1985). The reasons are largely practical: TROs last less than a month and usually terminate with a prompt ruling on a preliminary injunction, from which the losing party has the right to immediately appeal. *See Vuitton v. White*, 945

F.2d 569, 573 (3d Cir.1991). "Therefore, an appeal of the TRO is not necessary to protect the rights of the parties, and practical reasons favor waiting for an appeal of the preliminary injunction." *Northeast Ohio Coalition for Homeless and Serv. Employees Int'l. v. Blackwell*, 467 F.3d 999 (6th Cir. 2006).

However, appeal of a narrow type of order is permitted, even if the district court captions the order as a "TRO" or "temporary restraining order." "The label attached to an order by the trial court is not decisive, and the court looks to the nature of the order and the substance of the proceeding below to determine whether the rationale for denying appeal applies." *Id.* "An order may be appealed under section 1292(a)(1) if it has the practical effect of an injunction and 'further[s] the statutory purpose of "permit[ting] litigants to effectually challenge interlocutory orders of serious, perhaps irreparable, consequence."'" *Id.* (quoting *Carson v. Am. Brands, Inc.*, 450 U.S. 79, 84 (1981)). Thus, an "order granting a TRO may be appealable as an order granting a preliminary injunction when three conditions are satisfied: (1) the duration of the relief sought or granted exceeds that allowed by a TRO (ten days), (2) the notice and hearing sought or afforded suggest that the relief sought was a preliminary injunction, and (3) the requested relief seeks to change the status quo." *AT&T Broadband v. Tech Communications, Inc.*, 381 F.3d 1309 (11th Cir. 1004).

Under this exception, interlocutory appeals of TROs have been allowed if the TRO threatened to inflict irretrievable harm before it expired. *See Ross v. Rell*, 398 F.3d 203 (2d Cir. 2005). In addition, courts have allowed interlocutory appeal of TROs that do not preserve the status quo but rather act as a mandatory injunction requiring affirmative action. *See Belknap v. Leary*, 427 F.2d 496, 498 (2d Cir. 1970). When a TRO does not "merely preserve the status quo pending further proceedings," but rather "directs action so potent with consequences so irretrievable, we provide an immediate appeal to protect the rights of the parties." *Adams*, 570 F.2d at 953; *see Am. Fed'n of Gov't Employees*, 473 U.S. at 1304–05 (noting that "[o]nly if the District Court granted the temporary restraining order would it have disturbed the status quo" by preventing the implementation of new regulations, and implying that interlocutory appeal would be available).

### d. Appeals under 28 U.S.C. § 1292(b)

Under 28 U.S.C. § 1292(b), a district court may certify an otherwise non-final order for interlocutory appellate review if the order "involves a controlling question of law as to which there is substantial ground for difference of opinion and . . . an immediate appeal from the order may materially advance the ultimate termination of the litigation." A court of appeals may then, in its discretion, determine whether the order warrants prompt review. *Id.*

## i. Requirements

The first sentence of Section 1292(b) provides: "When a district judge, in making in a civil action an order not otherwise appealable under this section, shall be of the opinion that such order involves a controlling question of law as to which there is substantial ground for difference of opinion and that an immediate appeal from the order may materially advance the ultimate termination of the litigation, he shall so state in writing in such order." Section 1292(b) thus clearly requires that the order (1) involve a controlling question of law; (2) as to which there is substantial ground for difference of opinion and (3) an immediate appeal may materially advance termination of the litigation. *See Garner v. Wolfinbarger*, 433 F.2d 117 (5th Cir. 1970) (holding that an order granting or denying a motion to transfer venue under Section 1404(a) was not reviewable under Section 1292(b)).

### (a) Controlling Question of Law

Questions are "controlling" when they "materially affect issues remaining to be decided in the trial court." *Marriott Int'l Resorts, L.P. v. U.S.*, 63 Fed. Cl. 144, 145 (Fed. Ct. Cl. 2005). Controlling is not the same as "important." Otherwise, interlocutory appeals would neither be exceptional nor rare. *See Singh v. George Washington University*, 383 F. Supp. 2d 99, 105 (D.D.C.2005).

The phrase "question of law" is used "much the same way a lay person might, as referring to a pure question of law rather than merely to an issue that might be free from a factual contest. The idea was that if a case turned on a pure question of law, something the court of appeals could decide quickly and cleanly without having to study the record, the court should be enabled to do so without having to wait till the end of the case." *Ahrenholz v. Bd. of Trustees of Univ. of Ill.*, 219 F.3d 674, 677 (7th Cir. 2000).

### (b) Substantial Ground for Difference of Opinion

There are at least four ways that a party seeking certification can show that there is "substantial ground" for difference of opinion.

First, there may be two different but plausible interpretations of a line of cases addressing the legal question. *See Vereda, Ltda. v. United States*, 271 F.3d 1367, 1374 (Fed. Cir. 2001) (agreeing with district court that "substantial ground for difference of opinion" was present regarding interaction between two controlling circuit court cases). Second it can be shown by splits among the circuit courts. *See Marriott Int'l Resorts*, 63 Fed. Cl. at 146. Third, the party can show that there is an intra-circuit conflict or a conflict between an earlier circuit precedent and a later Supreme Court case. *See Ins. Co. of the West v. United*

*States*, 1999 WL 33604131 at *4 (Fed.Cl.1999). Finally, at minimum, the party can argue that there is a substantial difference of opinion among the district courts. *See Hermes Consol., Inc. v. United States*, 58 Fed. Cl. 409, 419–20 (2003), *rev'd on other grounds*, 405 F.3d 1339 (Fed. Cir. 2005).

It is not enough that the case present a question of first impression. "Unsettled" is not the same as a substantial ground for difference of opinion. *In re Flor*, 79 F.3d 281, 284 (2d Cir.1996) ("the mere presence of a disputed issue that is a question of first impression, standing alone, is insufficient to demonstrate a substantial ground for difference of opinion.").

### (c)  *Interlocutory Appeal May Materially Advance Litigation*

This is a pragmatic inquiry. "Whether interlocutory review of this question would materially advance the resolution of this case depends in large part on considerations of judicial economy and the need to avoid 'unnecessary delay and expense' and piecemeal litigation." *Coast Fed. Bank, FSB v. United States*, 49 Fed. Cl. 11, 14 (Fed. Cl. 2001).

### ii.  Process in the District Court

The first sentence of Section 1292(b) requires a district court to state in writing in an order that the order "involves a controlling question of law as to which there is substantial ground for difference of opinion and that an immediate appeal from the order may materially advance the ultimate termination of the litigation." Typically, a party will by motion ask the district court, either after it entered its order or in connection with briefing the motions underlying the order, to certify the order under Section 1292(b). Even if the elements for certification are present, the trial court can still deny certification, as it is a matter of discretion.

### iii.  Process in the Appellate Court

The second sentence of Section 1292(b) provides: "The Court of Appeals which would have jurisdiction of an appeal of such action may thereupon, in its discretion, permit an appeal to be taken from such order, if application is made to it within ten days after the entry of the order . . ." Thus, even if the district court certifies the order for appeal, the party seeking to appeal must also apply to the appellate court for it to certify the order as appealable. Even if the district court believes the requirements of Section 1292(b) are satisfied, the appellate court can still deny review, and it gives no deference to the district court's decision to grant certification:

Even when all of those factors are present, the court of appeals has discretion to turn down a § 1292(b) appeal. And we will sometimes do so. The proper division of labor between the district courts and the court of appeals and the efficiency of judicial resolution of cases are protected by the final judgment rule, and are threatened by too expansive use of the § 1292(b) exception to it. Because permitting piecemeal appeals is bad policy, permitting liberal use of § 1292(b) interlocutory appeals is bad policy.

*McFarlin v. Conseco Serv., LLC,* 381 F.3d 1251 (11th Cir. 2004). The Seventh Circuit in 2000 noted that it had denied certifications in roughly two-thirds of appeals under Section 1292(b). *See Ahrenholz,* 219 F.3d at 675.

### iv. Waiver

Under the statute, an appellant who fails to move appellate court within 10 days of entry of the district court's order waives the right to appeal. In addition, a party who does not promptly ask the district court to certify the order for appeal can waive the right to seek certification, since the language of that statue requires that an "immediate appeal" from the order will materially advance the litigation. As such, the statute clearly contemplates an expedited procedure for seeking certification to appeal. *See Martens v. Smith Barney, Inc.,* 238 F. Supp. 2d 596, 600 (S.D.N.Y.2002) (denying motion certification where movant had waited almost 5 months and had no reasonable explanation for that delay).

### e. Mandamus

Mandamus is the least well defined but, nonetheless, narrowest of the various exceptions to the final judgment rule. "The remedy of mandamus is a drastic one, to be involved only in extraordinary situations." *Kerr v. United States Dist. Court,* 426 U.S. 394, 402 (1976). The writ of mandamus "has traditionally been used in the federal courts only 'to confine an inferior court to a lawful exercise of its prescribed jurisdiction or to compel it to exercise its authority when it is its duty to do so.'" *Id. (quoting Will v. United States,* 389 U.S. 90, 95 (1967)) *(quoting Roche v. Evaporated Milk Ass'n,* 319 U.S. 21, 26 (1943)). Courts have developed multi-factor tests for evaluating its propriety, such as this:

(1) The party seeking the writ has no other adequate means, such as a direct appeal, to attain the relief he or she desires.
(2) The petitioner will be damaged or prejudiced in a way not correctable on appeal.

(3) The district court's order is clearly erroneous as a matter of law.

(4) The district court's order is an oft-repeated error, or manifests a persistent disregard of the federal rules.

(5) The district court's order raises new and important problems, or issues of law of first impression.

*Silver Sage Partners, Ltd. v. U.S. Dist. Court,* 1998 WL 246526 (9th Cir. 1998). *See also In re Chimenti,* 79 F.3d 534 (6th Cir. 1996) (applying similar five factor test).

No doubt to prevent it from swallowing the final judgment rule and the other narrow exceptions, mandamus has been held unavailable to obtain appellate review of various rulings including awards of new trials, *Silver Sage, supra,* but it has been found proper to review orders compelling disclosure of privileged information. *See U.S. v. Diabetes Treatment Centers of Am., Inc.,* 444 F.3d 462, 471 (6th Cir. 2006) (discussing availability of mandamus and in some circuits collateral orders for review).

## C. The Big Picture

Appeals are rare. Appeals prior to final judgment are exceedingly rare. Those facts highlight important realities about lawyering. First, what the district court decides will very likely be the final decision. Second, all error — from the day of filing the complaint 'til the day of final judgment — must be appealed in *one* appeal, in a brief that typically is limited to about 50 pages. Third, many issues that a district judge gets wrong will not be corrected. What does all of that mean? You will get one shot at getting a judge to rule your way.

---

### Checkpoints

- Can you describe how the requirement that a party have been aggrieved by a district court limits who can appeal?
- Can you identify a final judgment?
- Can you articulate the exceptions to the final judgment rule and each of their requirements?

# Chapter 58

# A Brief Word on Appeals

---

### Appeals Roadmap

This chapter summarizes the appellate process, including the constraints on appellate review.

---

## A. Timing of Filing of Notice of Appeal

The entry of final judgment triggers the 30 day deadline to file a notice of appeal. Fed. R. App. P. 4(a). That deadline can be extended for good cause under some circumstances. *Id.*

Importantly, however, six post-trial motions suspend the time for filing the notice of appeal. In other words, even though a final judgment has been entered, if one of the following motions has been filed, the 30 day period does not begin to run if one or more of these motions are filed: (1) a post-judgment JMOL motion under Rule 50(b); (2) a motion for new trial under Rule 59(b); (3) a motion to alter or amend the judgment under Rule 59(e); (4) a motion to reopen the judgment under Rule 60(b) *if* that motion is filed within 10 days of entry of judgment; (5) a motion to amend or make additional findings of fact under Rule 62(b); and (6) a motion for attorneys' fees under Rule 54 *if* the district court extends the time to appeal under Rule 58.

If one of those motions is filed, then the 30-day period begins to run for all parties once the district court enters "the order disposing of the last such remaining motion." Fed. R. App. P. 4(a)(4)(A). However, an appellant does not have to wait: if a party files a notice of appeal after judgment has been entered but before the court has ruled on of motion listed above, the notice of appeal simply does not "become[] effective" before an order disposing of that motion has been entered. Fed. R. App. P. 4(a)(4)(B)(i).

# B. The Appellate Process

Very briefly, an appellant must file a single brief with the appellate court for the circuit in which the district court sits. In that one brief, which generally can run no more than about 50 pages (federal circuits now limit the length of brief by the number of words, and require certification of the number of words in a brief), the appellant must explain the facts of the case, its procedural posture, why the district court erred, and how the appellant was aggrieved by the judgment below. The appellee gets one brief of roughly the same length to demonstrate that the district court's judgment should be affirmed. The appellant then can file a short reply brief.

## 1. Reversible Error and Harm Must Be Established

Parties are not guaranteed perfect trials, but instead can obtain a relief on appeal only if there was error *and* the error was harmful. Whether a district court committed error turns on what "standard of review" is applied. Whether the error was harmful turns on whether the appellant can show that the error harmed its substantial rights, and may require more depending on whether the appellant properly preserved its objection.

### a. Standards of Review

Appellate courts are courts of review, not places where a second trial occurs. They receive only written trial transcripts and exhibits used at trial, or otherwise properly in the appellate record. They do not receive testimony from witnesses, and except in extraordinary circumstances the record of what transpired in the district court cannot be enlarged on appeal. If a document or testimony was not introduced at trial, for example, it cannot be relied upon on appeal.

As a result, appellate courts are generally deferential to trial courts, particularly where the error involves an act that by law is discretionary with a trial judge, or when the appellate court is reviewing fact findings made by a district court (or jury). In contrast, appellate courts review errors of law closely, since a three judge panel of an appellate court is more likely to get the law right and has no real reason to defer to a district judge where the question is a purely legal one. But, again, error is not enough: the error must have caused harm.

There are entire law review articles addressed to which is the proper standard of review for a particular issue on appeal. The following chart only summarizes the broad categories, but it applies only if the error was properly preserved below—if the lawyer objected. Otherwise, the appellate court may apply a much more deferential standard, finding error only under if the error was "plain." *Katzenmeier v. Black Powder Prods., Inc.*, 628 F.3d 948 (8th Cir. 2010) ("When a party seeks to exclude evidence in a motion in limine, but fails to interpose an objection to the evidence during trial, we review under the plain error standard because the party failed to preserve the alleged error.").

|  | De novo | Clearly Erroneous | Abuse of Discretion | Substantial Evidence |
|---|---|---|---|---|
| *Applies to:* | Questions of Law | Question of fact | Discretionary action | Jury finding |
| *Made by:* | District Judge | District Judge | District Judge | Jury |
| *Amount of deference:* | None | Reject finding of fact only if appellate court is "left with a definite and firm conviction that a mistake has been committed." | Reverse only if the district court clearly made an error of judgment. | Reverse only if it is not supported by substantial evidence, even if there is strong evidence to the contrary. |

Many errors reviewed by appellate courts involve mixed questions of law and fact, or are legal determinations based on subsidiary fact findings. The standard of review is critical on appeal, since the less discretion afforded to the decision below, the more likely it is that the appellate court will reverse. Hence, appellants do their best to characterize all errors as legal questions, and appellees portray all issues as being discretionary or factual, or at best, a mixture of law and fact.

## b. Harmful Error Is Required to Reverse

A district court's mistake does not require reversal or remand. Instead, the party asserting error must demonstrate that the error was harmful by showing that the error affected that party's substantial rights *See* FRCP 61; *Federico v. Order of St. Benedict in R.I.*, 64 F.3d 1, 3 (1st Cir. 1995) (burden of showing harmful error in a civil case is on party asserting error). "In determining whether an error affected a party's substantial right[s], the central question is whether this court can say with fair assurance . . . that the judgment was not substantially swayed by the error." *Ahern v. Scholz*, 85 F.3d 774, 786 (1st Cir. 1996).

Whether harmful error occurred depends on context. Suppose, for example, that the alleged error was in admitting evidence over an objection. Under those circumstances, courts rely on various factors to determine the likelihood that the jury verdict was substantially swayed by the error include the centrality of the evidence and the prejudicial effect of its admission or exclusion. *See Ahern*, 85 F.3d at 786.

On the other hand, if the error concerns assigning the burden of proof to the wrong party, then whether the error was harmful turns on how close the case was. Therefore, the only conceivable prejudice from the district court's error is the possibility that its misallocation of the ultimate burden of proof affected the outcome of the case. For this to occur, the evidence presented would have to be in sufficient balance so that the outcome would depend on who had the burden. *See, e.g., U.S. ex rel. Bilyew v. Franzen*, 686 F.2d 1238, 1248 (7th Cir. 1982) ("If the evidence is closely balanced, then common sense indicates there is a reasonable possibility that who bears the burden of proof will determine the outcome."); *New York Life Ins. Co. v. Taylor*, 147 F.2d 297, 301 (D.C. Cir. 1945) (harmful error found where burden of proof was placed on wrong party because "the evidence was such that the result might well have depended on where the ultimate burden of proof lay").

## 2. Affirm, Reverse, Render or Remand

A three judge panel typically decides each appeal, often without receiving oral argument. Generally, an appellate panel can, with respect to each claim or defense raised on appeal, either affirm the district court, reverse it, render (turning the judgment loser below into the judgment winner on appeal), or remand for further proceedings.

## 3. Panel Reconsideration and Rehearing En Banc

A party that loses the appeal can file for the panel for reconsideration or seek rehearing of the panel's decision by all of the active members of the court, called "rehearing en banc." Both motions are rarely granted.

# C. Petition for Certiorari to the United States Supreme Court

The last possible phase in the typical civil suit is the filing by the party that suffered an adverse result in the appellate court a petition for writ of certiorari with the United States Supreme Court. In large measure, the Court has absolute discretion as to what cases it will review, and only a tiny percentage of cases for which "cert" is sought are ultimately reviewed by the Court.

## Checkpoints

- Can you explain why error, alone, is insufficient for an appellate court to reverse a trial court's ruling or action?

- Can you explain when the different standards of review apply and articulate which presents a greater challenge to an appellant?

# Chapter 59

# Attacking a Judgment in District Court under Rule 60(b)

---

### Rule 60(b) Roadmap

This chapter explains how a party can attack a judgment by way of a "collateral" attack under Rule 60(b), rather than "directly" by an appeal after the judgment, and the severe limitations that such a party faces.

---

## A. Motions to Reopen the Judgment under Rule 60(b)

Ordinarily, a party who wants to challenge a judgment must do so within 28 days of its entry by moving for a new trial or JMOL, and then by appealing. *Parke-Chapley Constr. Co. v. Cherrington*, 865 F.2d 907, 915 (7th Cir. 1989) ("an appeal or motion for new trial, rather than a FRCP 60(b) motion, is the proper avenue to redress mistakes of law committed by the trial judge, as distinguished from clerical mistakes caused by inadvertence . . . parties should not be allowed to escape the consequences of their failure to file a timely appeal by addressing questions of law to the trial court for reconsideration. That is the function of appellate courts").

Rule 60(b) presents a narrow exception to that general rule. The key point is that Rule 60(b) gives district courts much less power to vacate a judgment than its plain meaning would suggest to you. The reason for that? Finality, foremost, and also to encourage parties to vigorously litigate cases: if a party could easily reopen a case it had lost, there would be no finality and less incentive to litigate aggressively, since the result could always be undone later. To avoid that, Rule 60(b) is construed narrowly.

## B. The Six Narrow Bases of Rule 60(b) and the Short Time Limits

Rule 60(b) sets out five specific, and one general, bases for granting relief from a final judgment:

> On motion and just terms, the court may relieve a party or its legal representative from a final judgment, order, or proceeding for the following reasons:
> (1) mistake, inadvertence, surprise, or excusable neglect;
> (2) newly discovered evidence that, with reasonable diligence, could not have been discovered in time to move for a new trial under Rule 59(b);
> (3) fraud (whether previously called intrinsic or extrinsic), misrepresentation, or misconduct by an opposing party;
> (4) the judgment is void;
> (5) the judgment has been satisfied, released, or discharged; it is based on an earlier judgment that has been reversed or vacated; or applying it prospectively is no longer equitable; or
> (6) any other reason that justifies relief.

A Rule 60(b) motion must be made within one year after entry of judgment under subsections (1), (2), and (3), and otherwise, within a reasonable time. FRCP 60(c).

## C. Adjudication of Rule 60(b) Motions

### 1. Rule 60(b)(1): Mistake, Inadvertence, Surprise, or Excusable Neglect

Excusable neglect is the most common basis urged to set aside a default judgment. The factors to be considered in deciding a motion to set aside a default judgment are identical to those under Rule 60(b)(1): "(1) whether the default was willful; (2) whether the plaintiff will be prejudiced if the default is set aside; and (3) whether the defendant has any meritorious defenses to the complaint." *Gucci America, Inc., v. Gold Ctr. Jewelry,* 158 F.3d 631, 634 (2d Cir. 1998). Although the criteria is "identical to those used to determine whether to vacate a default judgment under the Rule 60(b)(1) standard of 'mistake, inadvertence, surprise, or excusable neglect,' although the 'good cause' standard is less rigorous because the concepts of finality ... are more deeply implicated in cases of default judgment under Rule 60." *Richardson v. Nassau County,* 184 F.R.D. 497, 501 (E.D.N.Y. 1999).

Whether to set aside a default judgment is a discretionary decision, but one that must be viewed in light of the "oft-stated preference for resolving disputes on the merits." *Enron Oil Corp. v. Diakuhara,* 10 F.3d 90, 96 (2d Cir. 1993). Default judgments are "not favored, particularly when the case presents issues of fact, and doubts are to be resolved in favor of a trial on the merits." *Meehan,* 652 F.2d at 277. Setting aside defaults when business entities are parties is, as a practical matter, more difficult than with less sophisticated laymen. *See EMI April Music, Inc. v. 1064 Old River Rd., Inc.,* 214 Fed. Appx. 589 (6th Cir. 2007) (fact that corporation's president's brother died did not excuse failure of corporation to file an answer).

## 2. Rule 60(b)(2): Newly Discovered Evidence

If a party discovers new evidence after trial—that it could not with reasonable diligence have otherwise had—that may satisfy the first requirement of this subsection. Obviously, if after final judgment a party first learns of the existence of evidence, that evidence is "newly discovered."

Courts do afford some flexibility beyond that, recognizing for example, that a party may have thought during trial that a document that once existed had been destroyed, and later finding it. In one case, the court found evidence "newly discovered" under those circumstances, when the pivotal document, thought to have been destroyed, was later discovered unexpectedly to have been have survived a disaster because it had been moved to an unanticipated place. *See Serio v. Badger Mut. Ins. Co.,* 266 F.2d 418 (5th Cir. 1959). However, "[w]hile awareness of evidence, standing alone, does not categorically preclude considering the evidence to be 'newly discovered' under Rule 60(b)(2), a party's unannounced awareness of evidence can affect the assessment of whether it exercised the 'reasonable diligence' contemplated by the Rule. Fed.R.Civ.P. 60(b)(2)." *Bain v. MJJ Prods., Inc.,* 751 F.3d 642 (10th Cir. 2014).

While newly discovered evidence that could not have been found without reasonable diligence is required, it is not enough. The movant must also must show that the evidence likely would have caused a different result. *Rozier v. Ford Motor Co.,* 573 F.2d 1332 (5th Cir. 1978).

## 3. Rule 60(b)(3): Fraud

In *Rozier v. Ford Motor Co.,* 573 F.2d 1332 (5th Cir. 1978), the plaintiff sued Ford after his wife was killed in a car fire after an accident. During discovery, the plaintiff had requested any documents analyzing whether the fuel tank could have been put in a safer place, but Ford responded hat no such documents existed. The jury after trial found for Ford. Less than a year later, plaintiff's counsel happened upon a document concerning a similar model of Ford that did analyze the fuel tank's placement, and sought to reopen the judgment on the basis of fraud under Rule 60(b)(3).

The court held that a party seeking to reopen a judgment under Rule 60(b)(3) had to show by clear and convincing evidence that the adverse party obtained a verdict through fraud *and* that the information prevented the party that had lost from fully and fairly presenting its case. In adjudicating that motion, Ford's counsel admitted that he had known of the document prior to the first trial, but chose not to disclose it. The court held this satisfied the first element. As to the second the court found that the document would have made a difference in the way the case was presented, and that was sufficient—it was not necessary to show the document itself would have changed the outcome. That is not required under Rule 60(b)(3), which requires fraud, but it is under Rule 60(b)(2), which does not.

## 4. Rule 60(b)(4): Judgment is Void

"A void judgment is a legal nullity . . . . [I]t suffices to say that a void judgment is one so affected by a fundamental infirmity that the infirmity may be raised even after the judgment becomes final. The list of such infirmities is exceedingly short; otherwise, Rule 60(b)(4)'s exception to finality would swallow the rule." *United Student Aid Funds, Inc. v. Espinosa,* 130 S. Ct. 1367 (2010). The narrow "infirmities" that have been found to render a judgment "void" in terms of Rule 60(b)(4) are limited to "the rare instance where a judgment is premised either on a certain type of jurisdictional error or on a violation of due process that deprives a party of notice or the opportunity to be heard." *Id.* Thus, a judgment issued by a court that lacks subject matter jurisdiction to do so is void only in "the exceptional case in which the court that rendered judgment lacked even an 'arguable basis' for jurisdiction." *Id.*

## 5. Rule 60(b)(5): Judgment has been Satisfied, Released, Discharged, Reversed, or Become Inequitable

Rule 60(b)(5) allows a court to reopen a judgment that was satisfied, released, discharged, or if it has been vacated or reversed on appeal, or if it has prospective application that has become inequitable. The last phrase principally covers only judgments that awarded injunctive relief, not orders granting or denying monetary damages. *DeWeerth v. Baldinger,* 38 F.3d 1266 (2d Cir. 1994).

## 6. Rule 60(b)(6): The Narrow Catch-all

The final "catch-all" provision, Rule 60(b)(6), provides that a court may relieve a party from a final judgment for "any other reason that justifies relief." This "any other reason" clause is a "grand reservoir of equitable power" to do justice in a case, but only if *both* relief is and was *not* warranted by the five other enumerated grounds, and "extraordinary circumstances" are present. *Batts v. Tow-Motor Forklift Co.*, 66 F.3d 743, 747 (5th Cir. 1995).

Perhaps the most famous Rule 60(b)(6) case is *DeWeerth v. Baldinger*, 38 F.3d 1266 (2d Cir. 1994). The plaintiff, several years before filing this suit, had in 1982 filed suit to obtain possession of a Monet painting that American soldiers had taken from her home during World War II, and that the defendant had acquired from a Swiss art dealer. The district court in 1987 held a trial and awarded the painting to the plaintiff. However, on appeal in late 1987, the Second Circuit held that the plaintiff's claim was barred by the New York statute of limitations because, the Second Circuit held, it required proof that the plaintiff had acted reasonable diligence in locating stolen property, and plaintiff had not done so. Three years later, however, New York's highest court in an unrelated case issued an opinion holding that the statute of limitations did not require reasonable diligence by the plaintiff.

The plaintiff then moved the court under Rule 60(b)(6) (and, as well, (b)(5)) to re-open the prior judgment. The district court granted the motion, but the Second Circuit reversed. It reasoned that "*Erie* simply does not stand for the proposition that a plaintiff is entitled to reopen a federal court case that has been closed for several years in order to gain the benefit of a newly announced decision of a state court." It further held that, although the court had been wrong in its *Erie* guess, that was a risk the plaintiff had brought on herself by filing a diversity action in the first place.

---

### Checkpoints

- Can you explain why it is more difficult to challenge a judgment under Rule 60(b) than through direct appeal?
- Can you articulate what each subsection of Rule 60(b) requires in order to set aside a judgment?

# Chapter 60

# After Appeals: Claim and Issue Preclusion

---

### Claim and Issue Preclusion Roadmap

This chapter explains the doctrines of claim and issue preclusion.

This chapter also explains how claim and issue preclusion are litigated.

---

Claim preclusion and issue preclusion are related but distinct doctrines that are often confused with each other. In part, the confusion stems from their similar names, and in part because courts often use the phrase "*res judicata*" to describe both claim and issue preclusion, while others limit "*res judicata*" to refer only to claim preclusion, and use "collateral estoppel" to refer to issue preclusion. So, normally if you see "collateral estoppel" you know it's issue preclusion, but if a court uses the phrase "*res judicata*," you need to read it closely to determine which doctrine the court was using. Let's turn to each.

Claim preclusion helps ensure finality over "disputes." Broadly stated, after a lawsuit, a party to that lawsuit—and sometimes others—cannot later asserts a claim in a different lawsuit if it was the "same" or closely related to one in the first suit—whether the party later asserting the claim won, or lost, the first suit. To understand this, back up and think for a moment about the fact that we want lawsuits to be efficient and final. To meet those goals, once a party files a lawsuit, the law of claim preclusion generally requires that party to assert all related claims it then has. Likewise, if a defendant is sued, to force efficiency and finality, claim preclusion generally forces the defendant to raise related claims it then has against the plaintiff. So, for example, a plaintiff who sues for medical malpractice from a botched back operation cannot later sue for the same surgery. Claim preclusion prevents later asserting the "same claim" and more than just the identical claim. For example, a plaintiff who brings a negligence claim for a botched back operation could not later in a different suit bring a battery claim for the same the operation. Claim preclusion precludes later asserting not just the "same claim" from the first suit, but also every claim that, for policy reasons, is similar enough to a claim brought in the first suit that it "should have been" pled in the first suit. And it applies even if the plaintiff won in the first suit, and even if the later-asserted claim wasn't filed in the first suit.

Issue preclusion is different. It does not address whether a claim is barred. Instead, issue preclusion generally prevents a party who has *actually* litigated an issue—a question of fact or law—from litigating that issue again. So, for example, if a court holds in the medical malpractice case against the doctor that his license had been obtained through forgery, the doctor would not be able to relitigate whether his license had been forged—and hope to persuade another jury or court to find that his license had been properly granted. Notice that with issue preclusion, the issue has to have been actually decided; with claim preclusion, a claim that was not brought, but "should" have been, is barred.

## A. Choice of Law

When issue or claim preclusion is adjudicated in federal court, the question of whether the federal court applies federal or state law arises. If the judgment was entered by a federal court which had federal question subject matter jurisdiction, then federal law applies to determine its preclusive effect; if subject matter jurisdiction was based on diversity, then state law would apply. *See Taylor v. Sturgell*, 553 U.S. 880 (2008) (claim preclusion). If the prior judgment was entered by a state court, then state law would apply. *See Semtek Int'l Inc. v. Lockheed Martin Corp.*, 531 U.S. 497 (2001).

What if a prior judgment adjudiated both state and federal claims but is in federal court? Ordinarily, of course, a suit that contains both state and federal claims, will be related to each other, and chances are choice of law won't matter. Courts reason that federal law likely will control the preclusive effect of a federal judgment with both state and federal claims. 18B Charles Alan Wright et al., Federal Practice and Procedure § 4472 (2d ed. 2011) ("[I]f state questions are decided as an incident of federal-question litigation, the clear right of federal courts to insist on their own preclusion rules as to the federal questions may carry over to include all questions in a uniform body of doctrine.").

One interesting wrinkle is if the first suit was a federal suit dismissed under Rule 41 If a federal court dismisses a case under Rule 41, whether that dismissal is "on the merits" turns on state law, not Rule 41. For example in *Semtek*, the federal court dismissed under Rule 41, but the plaintiff refiled in state court. The court held that beause the dismissal would not have been "on the merits" under state law, the dismissal was not on the merits under federal law if the suit were filed in a state court or different federal court. However, the Court stated that if "state law is incompatible with federal interests," then federal law might preclude later assertion of the claim in federal court. *Id.* The gave as an example state law that "did not accord claim-preclusive effect to dismissal for willful violation of discovery orders . . . ." *Id.*

# B. Claim Preclusion

## 1. Purpose of Claim Preclusion

Claim preclusion is to make lawsuits efficient and final. "To preclude parties from contesting matters that they have had a full and fair opportunity to litigate protects their adversaries from the expense and vexation attending multiple lawsuits, conserves judicial resources, and fosters reliance on judicial action by minimizing the possibility of inconsistent decisions." *Montana v. U.S.,* 440 U.S. 147, 153–54 (1979). In essence, claim preclusion bars later assertion of a claim that was asserted—or one that efficiency dictates should and could have been asserted—in an earlier suit. As a consequence, if a party had an opportunity to assert a claim, it can be precluded from litigating that claim and related claims later—even if it inadvertently failed to raise a related claim in the earlier suit. Thus, while courts often portray claim preclusion as preventing asserting the same claim twice, it does far more than that, since a later claim can be barred even if it was never asserted in a suit—if it was related to one that was raised.

The rules don't require plaintiffs assert related claims. Rule 20 *authorizes* a plaintiff to bring every claim that it has against a defendant that arises out of the same transaction or occurrence as another claim, but does not *require* the plaintiff do so. The law of claim preclusion is what requires plaintiffs to assert certain claims. Unlike Rule 20, claim preclusion forces a party who has filed a claim or been sued to include in that suit all of the claims that it has that are "close enough" to the dispute that it would be convenient and efficient to litigate it in that suit. On the other hand, claim preclusion doesn't *force* a party to file *un*related claims that it might have, since that would expand the suit beyond one general dispute, and might increase litigation by forcing parties to assert even unrelated claims that they otherwise might not even want to bring.

What about counterclaims? Rule 13(a) does require defendants to file "compulsory counterclaims," which are speaking generally those claims which are related to the plaintiff's claims against the defendant. So, not does Rule 13 require defendants to bring such counterclaims, the law of claim preclusion reinforces the Rule's requirements and, we will see, fills a couple of gaps in Rule 13.

## 2. The Elements of Claim Preclusion

The elements of claim preclusion generally are:

A. Could the later-asserted claim have been brought in the first suit?
B. Is the later-asserted claim:
   1. the "same" claim as a claim in the first suit (*i.e.*, is it identical or to on that was asserted, or related "enough?");
   2. a compulsory counterclaim to a claim in the first suit; or
   3. a defense to a claim in the first suit that, if allowed to be raised, could nullify rights established in the first suit?
C. Was the party who is bringing the later-asserted claim a party to the first suit or in privity with someone who was a party to the first suit?
D. Did the first suit end with a final judgment "on the merits."

Notice that there is no requirement that the later-asserted claim *actually* have been asserted in the first suit. This is because claim preclusion forces parties to assert claims that, for the sake of efficiency, should be brought. Also, there is no requirement that the party later asserting the claim have lost the earlier suit: claim preclusion applies whether the party later asserting the claim won, or lost, the first suit. This section now explores each element.

### *a. Could the Later-Asserted Claim Have Been Brought in the First Suit?*

Claim preclusion bars a later-asserted claim only applies if it could have been asserted in the first suit. As a simple example, a claim that arose after the complaint had been filed in the first suit is not barred. So, if a plaintiff sues a doctor for malpractice, and later the doctor punches the plaintiff, the claim for battery arising out of the punch is not barred.

Another example of when a later-asserted claim could not have been brought is when the first court was a state court, and the later-asserted claim is one over which the federal courts have exclusive subject matter jurisdiction. For example, in *Gargallo v. Merrill Lunch, Pierce, Fenner & Smith*, 918 F.2d 658 (6th Cir. 1990), the first suit included a state law fraud claim that ended in a final judgment. The same plaintiff later sued the same defendant, but asserted a securities fraud claim over which federal courts had exclusive subject matter jurisdiction. Because the law of the state of the court that issued the judgment did not preclude the filing of claims that the first court would have lacked subject matter jurisdiction to hear, the *Gargallo* court held that claim preclusion did not apply since the state court would have lacked subject matter jurisdiction over the later-asserted federal securities law claim.

Casebooks often discuss *Sopha v. Owens-Corning Fiberglas Corp.*, 601 N.W.2d 627 (Wis. 1999). In that case, in the first suit the plaintiff alleged his lungs had been injured by long-term exposure to asbestos. While the defendants motion for summary judgment based upon the statute of limitations was pending, the plaintiff voluntarily dismissed the case but *with* prejudice. Later, he died of more serious complications, and his surviving spouse filed suit, claiming his death had also caused by asbestos exposure. The defendants raised claim preclusion, asserting the later-asserted claim was simply for other injuries caused by the same exposure raised earlier. The court held for the plaintiff, reasoning that those who tried to bring an action when the non-malignant injuries appeared would not be able to recover for being "afraid" of getting the more malignant injuries, as they would be speculative. Thus, the court held that because the claim for damages from the malignant injury could not have been brought, claim preclusion did not bar the later-asserted claim.

### b. Should the Later-Asserted Claim Have Been Asserted in the First Suit: is it the "Same Claim" as one in the Earlier Suit?

Claim preclusion has the goal of forcing parties to bring all the claims that they have that arise out of the "same" claim as one being litigated. If a later-asserted claim was related "enough" to one in an earlier suit, then for efficiency's sake it should have been asserted. There are three things to watch for: is the later-asserted claim so identical or at least related "enough" that it should have been asserted in the first suit? Was the later-asserted claim a compulsory counterclaim in the first suit? Or, rarely, is the later-asserted claim something that was a defense to the first suit, and if it is allowed to proceed as a claim later, it could nullify rights that were established in the earlier suit?

### i. Is the Later-Asserted Claim so Identical to or Closely Related to one in the Earlier Suit that "Should Have Been" Brought Earlier?

Sometimes it's clear whether a later-asserted claim is, or is not, close "enough" to one in the first suit that it should have been raised then. If Bob sues Susie over a car wreck, and later sues her over a bar fight, the claim arising out of the bar fight isn't the "same claim" as the car wreck. On the other end of the spectrum, if Bob had in the first suit sued Susie for damages only to his car, but then filed a second suit seeking damages for a broken pinky he had suffered in that wreck, that would be the same claim: negligence from a car wreck, with just a different item of damage sought.

The trouble of course lies in the middle and is compounded by the fact that courts, including federal courts, apply different definitions of what constitutes close "enough," ranging from very broad tests to very narrow. The broader the definition of what's "close enough," more claims that must be brought in a suit, and so each suit will be more complicated; the narrower the definition, fewer claims, must be brought, but that, of course, means there may be more suits.

At the broadest end of the spectrum, probably a majority of courts hold a later-asserted claim is must be asserted if it arose out of the same transaction or series of transactions out of which the earlier claim arose. *E.g.,* Restatement (Second) of Judgments § 24. This test focuses on pragmatic issues and generally operates to require that a claim be brought if it would be convenient to try it in the same suit as another claim. *Apotex, Inc. v. Food & Drug Admin.,* 393 F.3d 210 (D.C. Cir. 2004); *Porn v. Nat'l Grange Mut. Ins. Co.,* 93 F.3d 31 (1st Cir. 1996); *O'Brien v. City of Syracuse,* 429 N.E.2d 1158 (N.Y. 1981).

A smaller number of courts apply a narrower approach. Some courts apply a "same cause of action" or "same evidence" test which focuses on whether "the evidence necessary to sustain a second verdict would sustain the first." *See, e.g., Redfern v. Sullivan,* 444 N.E.2d 205, 208 (Ill. App. 1983); *Snell v. Mayor and City Council of Havre de Grace,* 837 F.2d 173 (4th Cir. 1988); *Smith v. Kirkpatrick,* 111 N.E.2d 209 (N.Y. 1953).

There are variations. Sometimes, courts saying that they are using the narrower test in fact apply it as broadly as the "convenient trial unit" approach of the majority. *See Snell,* 847 F.2d at 176–77 (explaining that Maryland courts use the narrow-sounding test but apply it in a pragmatic fashion). Beyond the two primary tests, other courts apply distinct ones, such as California's "primary rights" definition of a "claim." *See Los Angeles Branch NAACP v. Los Angeles Unified School Dist.,* 750 F.2d 731 (9th Cir. 1984) (en banc).

Most of the time, the answer to the question of whether a later-asserted claim will be barred will the same under either test. Obviously, asserting what is literally a claim twice is covered. Also, simply changing the legal theory—asserting negligent misrepresentation in the sale of a car in the first, and then fraud for selling the car in the second suit—does not make a claim "different" under either test. Similarly, if the later-asserted claim merely seeks different damages for the same wrong as the earlier claim, it is barred under either suit. So, for example, a claim for damages to a car would be the same as a later claim for personal injuries, if both arose out of the same car wreck. it is easy to tell if a claim is close enough, and to do so under either test. (The trick is to remember that even if the plaintiff won the first suit, the later claim will be barred! That's why the importance of this step may not be intuitive!)

But the result can depend on which test is applied. For example, in *Frier v. City of Vandalia*, 770 F.2d 699 (7th Cir. 1985), the plaintiff in its first suit brought replevin claims against the city government for allegedly wrongfully towing his cars. Later, he filed suit claiming that the city had violated his Due Process rights by not giving him a hearing before towing the cars. The majority held that the claim for violation of Due Process was the "same claim" as the claim to replevin his cars under the narrower "same cause of action" test applied by Illinois courts; the dissent argued that the claim for due process "requires an entirely different factual showing" and so was not barred, and contended that the majority had improperly applied the broader Restatement test to a claim covered by the narrower test.

### ii. Was the Later-Asserted Claim a Compulsory Counterclaim in the First Suit?

As noted above, Rule 13(a) requires parties to plead compulsory counterclaims, and claim preclusion rests upon and reinforces that rule. *See, e.g., Publicis Communication v. True North Communications Inc.*, 132 F.3d 363, 365 (7th Cir. 1997) ("The definition of a compulsory counterclaim mirrors the condition that triggers a defense of claim preclusion (res judicata) if a claim was left out of a prior suit."). If a later-asserted claim "should have been" a compulsory counterclaim in prior litigation, then it is barred.

First off, you have to look at what court system the first suit was in. If the prior judgment was issued by a state court, then whether the later-asserted claim was a compulsory counterclaim turns on state, not federal, law. *See Stone v. Dept. of Aviation*, 453 F.3d 1271, 1280–81 (10th Cir. 2006) (applying Colorado's rule on compulsory counterclaim because prior judgment had been issued by a Colorado state court).

If the prior judgment was issued by a federal court, then the Federal Rules of Civil Procedure would determine whether a later-asserted claim was a compulsory counterclaim to the first suit. Remember two things about Rule 13(a). First under Rule 13(a), certain counterclaims are not compulsory even if they arise out of the same transaction or occurrence as the plaintiff's claim:

> those that it did not have at the time it served the pleading responding to the claim;
> those that were already pending in another suit at the time the suit was commenced;
> those that require joinder of parties over whom the court cannot obtain jurisdiction; or
> those where jurisdiction was based on *in rem*.

*See* Chapter 16. Second, if a defendant did not file an answer, then Rule 13(a) does not apply: no counterclaim was required to be pled because there was no pleading. *Martino v. McDonald's Sys., Inc.*, 598 F.2d 1079 (7th Cir. 1979).

But, if a later-asserted claim was a compulsory counterclaim — under state or federal law governing the underlying judgment — then its later assertion is barred by claim preclusion. In addition, claim preclusion law may go a bit further than state or federal law about compulsory counterclaims. This is where claim preclusion fills some gaps.

### iii. Could the Later-asserted Claim Have Been a Defense to the First Suit That, if Successful, Would Nullify Rights Established in the First Suit?

What if a defendant does not file an answer, and so the compulsory counterclaim rule is not triggered? What if the facts form both a defense, and a counterclaim?

The general rule is that if the defendant does not file an answer, or if facts form the basis of both a defense and a counterclaim, that defendant is not precluded from "relying on those facts in an action subsequently brought by him against the plaintiff." *Martino v. McDonald's Sys., Inc.*, 598 F.2d 1079, 1084 (7th Cir. 1979). However, courts have used claim preclusion law to create a narrow exception to that rule, barring a later-asserted claim if allowing it would nullify rights established in an earlier lawsuit.

For example, in *Martino,* McDonald's sued a franchisee, alleging that the franchisee had violated a restrictive covenant in the franchise agreement. The parties entered into a consent judgment pursuant to which the franchisee sold his franchise back to the franchisor. Later, the franchisee sued McDonald's alleging that the enforcement of the restrictive covenant in the franchise agreement violated antitrust laws. *Id.* at 1081. The district court granted summary judgment in favor of McDonald's. The Seventh Circuit affirmed and held that the antitrust claim was barred:

> Both precedent and policy require that res judicata bar a counterclaim when its prosecution would nullify rights established by the prior action. Judicial economy is not the only basis for the doctrine of res judicata. Res judicata also preserves the integrity of judgments and protects those who rely on them.

*Id.* at 1085. If the antitrust counterclaim had merit, then the franchise agreement was illegal, and so it would have nullified the rights established by the prior consent judgment in favor of McDonald's. Therefore, the court held the later-asserted claim was barred even though it was not within the scope of Rule 13(a). *See Mendota Ins. Co. v. Hurst,* 965 F. Supp. 1290 (W.D. Mo. 1997) (following *Martino*); *A.B.C.G. Enterp., Inc. v. First Bank Southeast, N.A.,* 515 N.W.2d 904 (Wis. 1994) (explaining *Martino* and other cases).

### c. If the Party Bringing the Later-Asserted Claim was not a Party to the First Suit, is it Nonetheless Bound by the Prior Judgment Because it is in "Privity" with a Party to the First Suit?

Typically, claim preclusion is raised when someone who was a party in the first suit tries to avoid the judgment. A plaintiff lost, but then tries to sue a different defendant. As a general rule, claim preclusion only applies where the second suit is against someone who was a party to the first suit. The general rule is subject to exceptions, but these exceptions cut against the principle that Due Process requires that a person be given a full and fair opportunity to litigate a claim (or defense to one).

Courts often state that if a person falls into one of the exceptions, then it is "in privity" with a party to the earlier suit, and so bound by the judgment in that case. The word "privity" has a somewhat unintuitive meaning in this context, however. "Privity may exist for the purpose of determining one legal question but not another depending on the circumstances and legal doctrines at issue." *Chase Manhattan Bank v. Celotex Corp.,* 56 F.3d 343, 346 (2d Cir.1995). "Whether there is privity between a party against whom claim preclusion is asserted and a party to prior litigation is a functional inquiry in which the formalities of legal relationships provide clues but not the solutions." *Id.*

The Supreme Court recently summarized the narrow exceptions — when "privity" exists — that exist to the rule that only a party is bound by a judgment entered by a federal court when it has federal question subject matter jurisdiction, and so federal law applies:

- A person who agrees to be bound by the judgment entered in a suit between others is bound by that agreement.
- A person is bound by a prior judgment if there was a pre-existing "substantive legal relationship" between the person asserting the later claim and a party to the judgment in the first case. Those relationships include: preceding and succeeding owners of property, bailee and bailor, and assignee and assignor.
- In "limited certain limited circumstances," a party asserting a claim is bound by an earlier judgment because she was "adequately

represented" by someone who was a party to the first suit. But this is generally limited to when the prior suit was a class action, or a suit brought by a trustee, guardian, or other fiduciary, and the later suit is by a member of the class or someone whose interests the fiduciary was obligated to protect.

- A party asserting a claim is bound by an earlier judgment if she "assumed control" over the first case, and so effectively "already "had his day in court" even though not a formal party.

- A party is bound by a judgment may not avoid it by bringing a second suit through a proxy that it controls, so for example a person who was not a party to the first suit who brings the second suit as an agent for someone who was a party to the first suit would be bound.

- Finally, statutes may expressly bar successive litigation, but these include things like bankruptcy and somewhat unusual claims.

*Taylor v. Sturgell*, 553 U.S. 880 (2008).

Some exceptions—some examples of "privity"—are easy to spot. If Bob agrees to be bound by what a court decies in a suit between Juanita and Julia, he's going to be bound by it. Likewise, for example, if property is sold, the exception should be easy to spot. For example, suppose in the first suit Bob obtained a judgment about the property lines between his property and that of his neighbor, Susie. If Susie later sold her land to Jill, Jill would be in privity with Susie. Whatever happened in the first suit would bind Jill. Likewise, if Bob sold his land after the suit, that buyer would be bound as well.

When a person has actual control of how a party to the first suit litigated it, again it may be relatively easy to spot. But there must be actual control: the Supreme Court has rejected holding a person bound by an earlier judgment if the person had been "virtually represented" in the first suit. *Taylor, supra.* The Court rejected analyzing whether the person's interests were "close enough" to those of a party to the first suit, and to balance competing equitable concerns, instead favoring the general rule that a person is not bound by a prior judgment unless within the narrow categories above.

### d. Did the First Suit End with a Final Judgment "On the Merits"?

Normally, whether the first suit ended with a final judgment on the merits is fairly straightforward: if the court granted summary judgment or entered judgment based upon a jury verdict, the judgment is "on the merits." Once the district court enters its judgment, it's final even if there may be appeals or motions for costs and other items to be decided. *See Coover v. Saucon Valley Sch. Dist.*, 955 F. Supp. 392, 410 (E.D. Pa. 1997). But there are some complexities.

First, in a case discussed in casebooks, *Fed. Dept. Stores, Inc. v. Moitie*, 452 U.S. 394 (1981), the court faced unusual facts which illuminate the basic contours of claim preclusion. Seven lawsuits alleging antitrust violations were filed against a department store. The suits were filed in, or removed to, federal court. The district courts held that the plaintiffs did not and could not allege a required element of the claim, and so dismissed all seven suits with prejudice. Five plaintiffs appealed their cases, but two re-filed their suits, which eventually were again dismissed by federal courts, though this time on claim preclusion grounds. Those two plaintiffs appealed the dismissals. While those two appeals were pending, the Supreme Court issued a decision that changed the substantive law governing the claims, and in light of the change each plaintiff could now allege a claim. As a result, the appellate court reversed the judgment against the five plaintiffs who had appealed, since the judgment had been based on an incorrect understanding of antitrust law. It also reversed the judgments against the two plaintiffs, even though they were based on claim preclusion. The Supreme Court reversed. It held that a suit by the same plaintiff against the same defendant over the same conduct was barred, and a "judgment merely voidable because based upon an erroneous view of the law is not open to collateral attack, but can be corrected only by [a direct appeal] . . . and not by bringing another action upon the same" claim. *Id.*

Second, recall that a federal court judgment entered in a diversity case is given the preclusive effect of state law. If a federal court dismisses a claim under Rule 41(b), the *Semtek* Court has held that state law governs the preclusive effect, unless federal interests override. When federal law applies, dismissals are generally "on the merits" even though it was entered as a sanction. *Goel v. Heller*, 667 F. Supp. 144 (D. N.J. 1987); *see* FRCP 41(b). State law generally is similar. *See, e.g., Jaffe v. Accredited Surety & Cas. Co., Inc.*, 294 F.3d 584 (4th Cir. 2002) (analyzing impact of involuntary dismissals under Florida law).

Third, if a court dismisses a claim for failing to state a claim upon which relief can be granted, the dismissal is "with prejudice" and "on the merits" for the purpose of claim preclusion. *Federated Dep't Stores v. Moitie*, 452 U.S. 394, 399 n. 3 (1981).

# C. Issue Preclusion

## 1. Purpose of Issue Preclusion

Issue preclusion, or "collateral estoppel," is related but distinct from claim preclusion. The doctrine "applies to prevent issues of ultimate fact from being relitigated between the same parties in another lawsuit if that issue has once been determined by a valid and final judgment. *Vines v. Univ. of La. at Monroe*, 398 F.3d 700, 705 (5th Cir. 2005). Once a court decides an issue, it is, for that party and those in privity with it, decided once and for all—with narrow exceptions.

Suppose, for example, Susie sues Bob for breach of contract and a judgment issues that could only have issued if there was a finding that there had been no contract between them. If Susie again sued Bob—even on an *un*related claim— Bob could use the prior judgment to preclude Susie from attempting to prove that there was a contract between them. Bob could estop Susie from contradicting the finding implicit in the first judgment.

The doctrine of issue preclusion exists for two principal reasons. First, it serves efficiency for both court and parties: it "has the dual purpose of protecting litigants from the burden of re-litigating an identical issue with the same party or his privy and of promoting judicial economy by preventing needless litigation." *Parklane Hosiery Co. v. Shore*, 439 U.S. 322, 326 (1979). Second, issue preclusion protects "the integrity of the prior judgment by precluding the possibility of opposite results by two different juries on the same set of facts . . ." *Ill. Central R. Co. v. Parks*, 390 N.E.2d 1078 (Ind. App. 1979). In other words, courts recognize that a jury in a subsequent suit on precisely the same issue could reach the opposite conclusion from a first jury. To protect the first jury verdict's integrity, a second trial can be precluded when the elements of issue preclusion are met. Think about that for a second. Issue preclusion prevents us from seeing that juries do not find the truth; they just decide who won.

## 2. Elements of Issue Preclusion

The elements of issue preclusion have only been broadly stated by the Supreme Court, which relies upon the Restatement, which "explains that subject to certain well-known exceptions, the general rule is that 'when an issue of fact or law is actually litigated and determined by a valid and final judgment, and the determination is essential to the judgment, the determination is conclusive in a subsequent action between the parties, whether on the same or a different claim." *B & B Hardware, Inc. v. Hargis Indus., Inc.*, 135 S. Ct. 1293 (2015) (quoting Restatement (Second) of Judgments § 27, p. 250 (1980)). Although the circuits vary slightly in how they cast them, this requires that five questions must be analyzed to know whether issue preclusion applies:

A.  Was the same issue litigated and actually determined in the first suit?
B.  Was the issue essential to the judgment in the first case, such that the judgment could not have issued without that issue having been decided?

C. Was there a valid, final judgment on the merits in the first suit?

D. Can issue preclusion be applied against the party in the second suit?

E. Can the party in the second suit assert issue preclusion?

*See Robinette v. Jones,* 476 F.3d 585 (8th Cir. 2007); *NAACP, Detroit Branch v. Detroit Police Officers Assoc.,* 821 F .2d 328, 330 (6th Cir.1987).

## a. Was the Same Issue Litigated and Actually Determined in the First Suit?

Normally, this issue is fairly straightforward: if a party in the first suit claims the plaintiff was negligent, and in the second suit claims that same party was negligent, the issue is the same; if in the first case, the issue was breach of contract and in the second it is fraud, the issue is not the same.

The conceptual problem with this issue concerns changes in the burden of proof: for purposes of issue preclusion, the "issue decided" has to be cast in terms of the burden of proof. The simple example involves a civil suit followed by a criminal suit: suppose in a civil suit, a jury finds that a defendant had caused the wrongful death of his ex-girlfriend. Because the burden of proof in that case would have been preponderance of the evidence, that jury's finding that the defendant had killed the ex-girlfriend would not constitute the "same issue" in a subsequent criminal case for murder against the man. Because of the difference of degree of proof necessary, an issue of fact already adjudicated in a civil case is never "the same issue" in a criminal case. *See, e.g., U.S. v. Konovsky,* 202 F.2d 721, 726–27 (7th Cir.1953). For purposes of claim preclusion, what was proven in the first case was not that the man had killed the woman: it was that the plaintiff had proven by a preponderance of the evidence that the man had killed the woman. That is *not* the same issue as proof beyond a reasonable doubt that the man had killed the woman. *See also Ferrell v. Pierce,* 785 F.2d 1372 (7th Cir. 1986) (prior judgment in civil action did not constitute proof of "same issue" in later contempt proceeding, as it had a higher burden of proof of clear and convincing evidence). So, for example, acquittal in a prior criminal action does not bar a subsequent civil suit for wrongful death on the basis that the "issue" of whether the man killed the woman had been decided, as O.J. Simpson found out.

Notice, though, that if the burden of proof was *higher* in the case that led to judgment, the "same issue" would be present. *See Studio Art Theatre of Evansville, Inc. v. City of Evansville, Ind.,* 76 F.3d 128 (7th Cir. 1996) (applying Indiana law to prior state court judgment and holding prior criminal conviction supported "same issue" element of issue preclusion).

Also, the Court has held that findings by an administrative agency in an adjudicatory proceeding can be given preclusive effect: "courts may take it as given that Congress has legislated with the expectation that the principle [of issue preclusion] will apply except when a statutory purpose to the contrary is evident." *B & B Hardware, Inc. v. Hargis Indus., Inc.,* 135 S. Ct. 1293 (2015).

### b. Was the Issue Essential to the Judgment in the First Case, Such That the Judgment Could Not Have Issued Without That Issue Having Been Decided?

In stark contrast to claim preclusion, which applies whether or not the later-asserted claim was decided in the prior suit, issue preclusion only arises if the issue was actually litigated in the prior suit. "As a general rule, an issue is 'actually litigated' only when it is properly raised by the pleadings, submitted for a determination, and actually determined." *Matter of Gober,* 100 F.3d 1195, 1203 (5th Cir. 1996); *see Ill. Central R. Co. v. Parks,* 390 N.E.2d 1078 (Ind. App. 1979) (analyzing impact of prior jury verdict closely to determine what issues were clearly "actually litigated). Normally this is fairly straightforward: did the fact have to be decided for the first judgment to be entered?

But it can be difficult to apply. For example, *Rios v. Davis,* 373 S.W.2d 386 (Tex. Civ. App.—Eastland 1963, writ ref'd), involved two suits arising out of a single car wreck. Rios had been driving a truck owned by his employer when it was involved in an accident with Davis. The employer sued Davis to recover damages to the truck. Davis impleaded Rios, contending that Rios had been contributorily negligent, and seeking money damages for the damages to Davis' car. The jury in the first case found that all three parties had been negligent but that Davis had proximately caused the accident. The court entered judgment that Davis and the employer take nothing. Then in the second suit, Rios sued Davis for personal injuries. The appellate court reversed entry of judgment based upon issue preclusion, holding that a finding that Davis had been negligent was not essential to the judgment, since a judgment against Davis could have been entered based upon Davis' own negligence in the accident, without having found that Rios had been negligent. Therefore, the finding against Davis was not essential to the judgment, particularly because Rios could not have appealed that finding since no adverse judgment had been entered against him.

Similarly, in *Illinois Central Gulf Railroad v. Parks,* 390 N.E.2d 1078 (Ind. App. 1979), a car carrying a husband and wife collided with a train. In the first suit, both of them sued the railroad company, but she sought damages for her injuries, while he only sought loss of consortium damages (*i.e.,* compensation for injuries caused to their marriage because of her injuries, not compensation for his own personal injuries). The railroad raised the issue of contributory negligence. The jury awarded her $30,000, but awarded him nothing without specifying why. Later, he brought suit for his injuries. The railroad argued that the award by the jury in the first case of nothing to him meant that the jury had found him contributorily negligent. The court disagreed, recognizing that the verdict could mean *either* that they found him contributorily negligent *or* that there had been no loss of consortium damages incurred. As a result, it could not be said that a finding of contributory negligence was essential to the first judgment. Often, this requires examining the claims and defenses in the first suit as well as the jury instructions that were given. *Herrera v. Reicher,* 608 S.W.2d 539 (Mo. App. 1980) (analyzing jury instructions to determine if issue had been actually decided in prior case). *See also, Cunningham v. Outten,* 2001 WL 428687 (Del. Supr. 2001) (prior criminal judgment that party had violated an "inattentive driving" statute did not preclude litigation of "liability which consists of more than guilt or innocence").

However, there are exceptions to the "actual litigation" requirement, where a judgment will be given preclusive effect even though clearly the issues were not actually litigated. First, as noted above, an order dismissing a case "with prejudice" is "on the merits" for purposes of claim preclusion, even if it was entered as a sanction, and so obviously was not in any meaningful sense "on the merits." When a state court strikes a pleading and enters a judgment, whether a federal court will give that judgment preclusive effect turns on state law. *See Matter of Gober,* 100 F.3d at 1204–05 (analyzing how Texas courts treat various forms of default including those entered after striking a pleading). Federal courts appear to hold that under federal law the entry of a default judgment is *not* sufficient to satisfy the "actually litigated" requirement unless the party substantially participated prior to entry of the default. *See In re Daily,* 47 F.3d 365 (9th Cir. 1995).

The problem can arise, however, where two separate independent findings support the entry of judgment in the first case. Suppose, for example, that a court dismisses both because it lacks personal and subject matter jurisdiction. Are both preclusive, or neither? The federal courts split. *See Jean Alexander Cosmetics, Inc. v. L'Oreal USA, Inc.,* 458 F.3d 244 (3rd Cir. 2006) (collecting cases and discussing split). In some circuits, both issues will be deemed necessary to the outcome, while in others, neither will. *See also Aldrich v. New York,* 494 N.Y.S. 2d 662 (N.Y. App. Div. 1985) (holding that one of two alternative grounds sufficed because record showed the alternative was, in fact, fully litigated).

### c. Was There a Valid, Final Judgment on the Merits in the First Suit?

Whether the prior judgment ended on the merits is usually fairly straight-forward: a judgment after a jury trial, or after summary judgment has been granted, clearly is on the merits, for example. Any decision based upon lack of personal jurisdiction, subject matter jurisdiction, venue, improper service of process, or failure to join an indispensable party, on the other hand, obviously are not.

Normally, of course, voluntary dismissal will be without prejudice. But not always. In *Robinette v. Jones*, 476 F.3d 585 (8th Cir. 2007) the court observed that in the context of claim preclusion "final" may require less finality than claim preclusion. "Finality in the context of issue preclusion may mean little more than the litigation of a particular issue has reached such a stage that a court sees no really good reason for permitting it to be litigated gain." *Id.* at 590. In that case, the court held that a final judgment had arisen even though the plaintiffs had voluntarily dismissed their complaint in the prior action because they had done so after the defendant had answered and while its motion for summary judgment was pending.

"On the merits" means different things when the prior judgment issued from state court, however. For example, a dismissal of a claim as barred by the statute of limitations is not uniformly viewed as "on the merits." Thus, the plaintiff in *Semtek* filed suit in California state court, and the defendants removed the case to California federal district court based on diversity subject matter jurisdiction. The court later dismissed the suit as barred by California's two-year statute of limitations. 531 U.S. at 499. After that dismissal, the plaintiff filed suit in Maryland state court, asserting the same claims but arguing that Maryland law applied, and Maryland had a three-year statute of limitations. The state court granted the defendant's motion for summary judgment based upon claim preclusion. The appellate courts affirmed the dismissal. The United States Supreme Court granted certiorari, and concluded that "federal common law governs the claim-preclusive effect of a dismissal by a federal court sitting in diversity." *Id.* at 508. In addition, the Court concluded that the federal court should adopt "the law that would be applied by state courts in the State in which the federal diversity court sits." *Id.* Consequently, the Supreme Court concluded that the Maryland appellate courts erred in holding that the dismissal in California necessarily precluded the subsequent action in Maryland: under California law a dismissal of an action on statute-of-limitations grounds by a California state court would not be claim preclusive. *Id.* at 509.

### d. Can Issue Preclusion be Applied Against the Party in the Second Suit?

Issue preclusion can be applied against a person who was a party in the first suit or who is in privity with a party who was. The same principles above concerning claim preclusion apply.

### e. Can the Party in the Second Suit Assert Issue Preclusion?

Issue preclusion can be used offensively or defensively. "[O]ffensive use . . . occurs when the plaintiff seeks to foreclose the defendant from litigating an issue the defendant has previously litigated unsuccessfully in an action with another party." *Parklane Hosiery Co. v. Shore*, 439 U.S. 322, 326 n. 4 (1979). However, they are not available on equal terms.

Until fairly recently, they were, because issue preclusion required "mutuality." If the plaintiff could not use issue preclusion against the defendant, the defendant could not use it against the plaintiff. Why it was that a party who had had a full opportunity to litigate an issue, but lost, could not be precluded from re-litigating it simply because the party asserting issue preclusion was not bound by that determination because it had not been a party was never quite clear. *See Berhard v. Bank of Am.*, 122 P.2d 892 (Cal. 1942) ("No satisfactory rationalization has been advanced for the requirement of mutuality.").

Now, federal courts permit non-mutual issue preclusion, but if the party asserting issue preclusion is using it offensively — against a party that lost a case — the federal courts have discretion to deny its use. On the other hand, defensive use — if a party loses an issue but then sues another defendant — is permitted as of right if the elements are otherwise satisfied.

The reason for unfettered non-mutual defensive use of issue preclusion was made clear in *Blonder-Tongue Labs., Inc. v. Univ. of Ill.*, 402 U.S. 313 (1971). In that case, a patent owner sued a defendant, but the patent was found to be invalid. The plaintiff then sued a second defendant for infringing that same patent. The second defendant argued that the issue of invalidity of the patent had been decided in the first case, and the plaintiff should as a result be estopped from contending that its patent was valid. The Supreme Court agreed even though, had the plaintiff won the first suit, it obviously could not have used the finding that the patent was valid against the second defendant. (Due process requires that, unless a person was a party to or in privity with a party to a suit, that it get at least one chance to litigate an issue.) The court recognized that any time a defendant "is forced to present a complete defense on the merits to a claim which the plaintiff has fully litigated and lost in a prior action, there is an arguable misallocation of resources."

The reason for limiting offensive non-mutual use of issue preclusion was stated in *Parklane Hosiery Co. v. Shore*, 439 U.S. 322 (1979). In that case, a plaintiff filed a private securities fraud action against the defendant. While that suit was pending, the SEC brought a serious securities action in federal district court against a company for misstatements in those same corporate filings. The SEC proceeding resulted in judgment against the company. The plaintiffs in the private suit then moved for partial summary judgment, arguing that the judgment against the company in the SEC action precluded the company from re-litigating issues found against it. Thus, the private plaintiffs were using the SEC judgment offensively—against the party that had lost the prior case—and it was non-mutual because, again, obviously they could not be bound by a judgment in a case that they were neither parties to, nor in privity with a party to.

The Court held that district courts would have discretion to permit offensive use of issue preclusion. It held that it should not be available as a matter of right, unlike defensive issue preclusion, for several reasons. First, offensive use could increase the amount of litigation: a party who was aware of a lawsuit on the same issue could avoid joining that suit, and if the plaintiff in that case won, it could then file suit and use offensive issue preclusion, but if the plaintiff lost, there would be no impact on it—it could freely litigate the issue. Thus, allowing unfettered offensive issue preclusion would result in more, not less, social cost. Second, it could cause over-litigation in the first suit: suppose a defendant is sued for a small amount of money. If offensive issue preclusion is always available, it would have to "over litigate" the case to avoid having a judgment entered that someone else, in a more serious case, might be able to use against it. Likewise, if the first suit was in a forum where full discovery was not permitted, or other limitations on presenting evidence existed, it would be unfair. As a result, the court held that discretion, not right, guided the availability of non-mutual offensive issue preclusion.

Inconsistent prior judgments are a rare basis for denying non-mutual offensive use, but one mentioned by *Parklane* and involved in other suits. For example, in *State Farm Fire & Cas. Co. v. Century Home Components*, 550 P.2d 1185 (Or. 1976), a series of lawsuits were filed by plaintiffs whose property was damaged during a fire. Sometimes the plaintiff won, but sometimes it did not. The court adopted the "rule" from the few cases that dealt with actual inconsistent verdicts and held that "where outstanding determinations are actually inconsistent on the matter sought to be precluded, it would be patently unfair to estop a party by the judgment it lost." *Id.*

# D. Procedure for Litigating Claim Preclusion

## 1. Claim Preclusion is *"Res Judicata"* and So Must be Pled as an Affirmative

*"Res judicata"* — which includes both claim and issue preclusion — is an affirmative defense under Rule 8(c). Under that Rule, in "a pleading to a preceding pleading," a party must affirmatively plead certain defenses, including claim and issue preclusion. Thus, a party who fails to plead the defense waives it. *Scherer v. Equitable Life Assurance Soc'y*, 347 F.3d 394, 398 (2d Cir. 2003) ("The preclusion doctrines . . . are waiveable affirmative defenses").

A federal court may on its own motion raise claim (or issue) preclusion. *Plaut v. Spendthrift Farm, Inc.*, 514 U.S. 211 (1995). So, for example, "if a court is on notice that it has previously decided the issue presented, the court may dismiss the action *sua sponte*, even though the defense has not been raised. This result is fully consistent with the policies underlying *res judicata*: it is not based solely on the defendant's interest in avoiding the burdens of twice defending a suit, but is also based on the avoidance of unnecessary judicial waste." *U.S. v. Sioux Nation*, 448 U.S. 371, 432 (1980) (Rehnquist, J., dissenting) (citations omitted). *See, e.g., Transclean Corp. v. Jiffy Lube Int'l., Inc.*, 474 F.3d 1298 (Fed. Cir. 2007) (affirming district court's dismissal raising issue preclusion *sua sponte*).

## 2. Ordinarily Claim Preclusion can be Resolved by Moving for Summary Judgment

Typically, a party who believes that a claim against it is barred by claim preclusion raises the issue through summary judgment, providing a copy of the prior judgment and any other papers necessary to prove the elements of the affirmative defense to the court.

# E. Procedure for Litigating Issue Preclusion

## 1. Pleading Requirements

### a. Because Issue Preclusion is *"Res Judicata"* it must be Pled as an Affirmative Defense Under Rule 8(c)

As noted above, *"res judicata"* is an affirmative defense. Generally, failure to plead issue preclusion waives it, unless the court raises it *sua sponte* in rare instances.

### b. Offensive Use: Must Plaintiff Plead Issue Preclusion?

Offensive use of issue preclusion by a plaintiff creates a problem: does the *plaintiff* have to plead offensive use? The defendant would have to, since it is an affirmative defense, but is the plaintiff required to be plead it? So far the courts have generally held that the Rules do not require that issue preclusion be pled in the complaint. *Harvey by Blankenbaker v. United Transp. Union*, 878 F.2d 1235 (10th Cir. 1989).

## 2. Litigating Issue Preclusion by Moving for Summary Judgment

Because proof of the prior adjudication is an element of issue preclusion, as with claim preclusion, the party relying on it must prove the prior adjudication occurred. Where facts are not disputed, it is typically done through a summary judgment.

# F. Special Issues

## 1. Co-Pending Suits with Same Claims

Where two suits with the same claims are pending at the same time, a defendant must also act. Even though a motion for summary judgment based upon claim or issue preclusion cannot be filed until the first suit goes to judgment, a motion to dismiss based on improper claim-splitting—filing the "same claim" in two separate suits—"need not-indeed, often cannot-wait until the first suit reaches final judgment." *Hartsel Springs Ranch of Co., Inc. v. Bluegreen Corp.*, 296 F.3d 982 (10th Cir. 2002) (recognizing that, if two suits based on the same claim are pending, but the defendant waits to file a motion to dismiss until "after judgment enters on one of the two," then "the motion should be denied"); *Bockweg v. Anderson*, 428 S.E.2d 157, 164 n. 2 (N.C. 1993) ("While it is clear that defendants could not raise their *res judicata* defense until and unless the [prior] court action resulted in a final judgment, defendants could have moved to dismiss on the grounds of a prior action pending involving the same claim."); *Lake v. Jones*, 598 A.2d 858, 861–62 (Md. 1991) ("[Defendant] may not lie in wait silently until one of the two actions is brought to judgment to ambush the plaintiff and defeat the other action.").

Thus, even if there is no judgment, the defendant faced with claim-splitting can move the court in the second suit to hold that it is precluded pursuant to claim preclusion. *E.g., Klipsch, Inc. v. WWR Tech., Inc.*, 127 F.3d 729, 734–35

(8th Cir.1997) (district court erred in granting summary judgment in favor of defendant on *res judicata* defense because defendant had acquiesced in the splitting of plaintiff's claims); *Clements v. Airport Auth. of Washoe County,* 69 F.3d 321, 328 (9th Cir.1995) (defendant waived res judicata defense by acquiescing in the splitting of plaintiff's claims); *Calderon Rosado v. General Elec. Circuit Breakers, Inc.,* 805 F.2d 1085, 1087 (1st Cir.1986) (refusing to apply claim preclusion because defendant acquiesced to splitting of claim when he failed to object or complain while the two actions were pending).

## Checkpoints

- Can you explain the purposes of claim and issue preclusion?
- Can you articulate each element of claim preclusion? Issue preclusion?
- Can you explain the impact of concluding that a claim or issue is precluded?
- Do you understand the difference between offensive and defensive issue preclusion?
- Can you explain the procedure for raising claim or issue preclusion?

# Part C

# Special Procedures for Resolving Similar Claims among Many Parties

# Chapter 61

# A Brief Introduction to Mass and Class Actions

Especially in the last few decades, courts have been forced to resolve claims of enormous numbers of plaintiffs that arise out of a single set of facts. For example, the rise of mass manufacturing techniques and distribution channels have enabled a single model of a product to be sold to thousands, if not millions, of consumers, each of whom may then have a claim if the product causes injuries or is otherwise defective. Recent class actions suits involving allegedly defective drugs have gained national headlines, and other class action suits have been litigated for years in the federal courts.

The Rules generally permit each plaintiff to file its own suit. A defendant facing multiple suits over the same basic set of facts will rarely be able to force joinder of one of those plaintiffs into a suit by another because Rule 19 requires joinder only rarely, and t would never require joinder of two plaintiffs who assert, for example, personal injuries caused to each when each bought a defective product. While having two separate lawsuits over the same product may not be socially intolerable, where there are hundreds or thousands of plaintiffs, the courts, the parties (or at least the defendant), and society may want more efficient resolution of the claims.

Two procedures exist to help resolve multiple parties' claims more efficiently than individual suits might: (1) class action lawsuits and (2) use of multi-district litigation, or "MDL."

Boiled down, a class action allows for enormous numbers of plaintiffs (and in some cases, defendants) to be joined in one lawsuit where efficiency would be served by doing so. In recent years, class actions have become regulated by statute, and in some ways restricted and reduced in utility and scope.

If a series of disputes does not qualify as a class action, it may nonetheless be subject to special management procedures as "multi-district litigation." Suppose, for example, there are a dozen or two suits filed around the United States over the same issue, against the same defendants, but each with its own plaintiff, but the cases cannot be brought as a class action. It may make sense to combine the cases for some purposes, particularly discovery, so that different judges do not have to repeatedly address and resolve the same issues among the various parties. The tools to manage multi-district litigation can be used when the dispute is "more" than a typical lawsuit, but "less" than is required to create a class action suit.

In recent years, class actions have become subject to federal statutes, and particularly the Class Action Fairness Act ("CAFA"), and their prominence is probably waning. Some firms specialize in bringing or defending class suits, but most lawyers will have no involvement in class action, or mass action, suits during their careers. This chapter, as a result, simply provides the basics.

# A. Class Actions

## 1. Overview of Class Actions

The rules impose two broad requirements on whether a class is proper. First, Rule 23 creates four requirements class actions only if: (1) the class is so numerous that joinder of all members is impracticable, (2) there are questions of law or fact common to the class, (3) the claims or defenses of the representative parties are typical of the claims or defenses of the class, and (4) the representative parties will fairly and adequately protect the interests of the class. FRCP 23(a).

Second, Rule 23(b) requires that *one* of the following three be present:

> (1) the prosecution of separate actions by or against individual members of the class would create a risk of
> (A) inconsistent or varying adjudications with respect to individual class members which would establish incompatible standards of conduct for the party opposing the class, or
> (B) adjudications with respect to individual class members which would, as a practical matter, be dispositive of the interests of the other members not parties to the individual adjudications or substantially impair or impede their ability to protect their interests; or
> (2) the party opposing the class has acted or refused to act on grounds that apply generally to the class, so that final injunctive relief or corresponding declaratory relief respecting the class as a whole; or
> (3) the court finds that the questions of law or fact common to the class members predominate over any questions affecting only individual members, and that a class action is superior to other available methods for the fairly and efficiently adjudicating of the controversy.

The matters pertinent to the findings include: (A) the class members' interests in individually controlling the prosecution or defense of separate actions; (B) the extent and nature of any litigation concerning the controversy already begun by or against members of the class; (C) the desirability or undesirability of concentrating the litigation of the claims in the particular forum; (D) the likely difficulties in managing a class action.

FRCP 23(b).

If a plaintiff files a suit seeking to represent a class, then it must "at an early practicable time" have the court decide whether to certify the action as a class action. FRCP 23(c)(1)(A). In addition to examining whether the two conditions for certification noted above are present the court must also certify counsel to represent the class. FRCP 23(g). The class action plaintiff's lawyer will be responsible for adjudicating the rights of large numbers of plaintiffs with whom she will likely not have the normal direct form of attorney-client relations. As a result, certification of counsel is a means by which courts protect the class.

If the court issues a certification order, it must identify the class, appoint class counsel, and provide various notices to class members. FRCP 23(c). During litigation, the court has power to make various rulings to streamline proceedings. FRCP 23(d). Cases may not be dismissed or settled except by approval of the court and notice to class members. FRCP 23(e).

## 2. Impact of CAFA

In 2005, CAFA and amendments to Rule 23 almost completely replaced the law governing class actions. Together, they have radically increased the ability of federal courts to hear class actions involving state claims. CAFA adopted the constitutional "minimal diversity" for interstate class actions. Congress amended the diversity jurisdiction statute (28 U.S.C. § 1332) by allowing diversity jurisdiction if any one class member is diverse from any one defendant. Although CAFA still has an "amount in controversy" requirement of $5 million, the amount of each class member's claim may be aggregated for purposes of satisfying that amount in controversy requirement. *Id.* The statute made numerous changes to existing class action law and will likely be the subject of an advanced litigation course, not your basic civil procedure class. *See, e.g., Blockbuster, Inc. v. Galeno,* 2006 WL 3775326 (2d Cir. 2006) (discussing CAFA's impact on removability of class actions); *Miedema v. Maytag Corp.,* 450 F.3d 1322 (11th Cir. 2006) (same).

# B. Multi-District Consolidation: 28 U.S.C. § 1407

Suppose there are a significant number of suits filed all across the country, each by a separate plaintiff but against a common defendant and arising out of the same basic facts. Suppose, for example, a drug maker sells an allegedly defective drug that harms thousands of consumers across the country, resulting in dozens, hundreds, or even thousands of lawsuits. *See, e.g., In re Zyprexa Prods. Liability Litig.*, 2006 WL 3495667 (E.D.N.Y. Dec. 5, 2006).

If there is no class formed or it is for some reason a class is unavailable, federal courts have the power to consolidate these suits through 28 U.S.C. § 1407. That statute allows civil actions that involve at least one common question of law in fact that are pending in different district to be "transferred to any district for coordinated or consolidated pretrial proceedings." A special "MDL panel" then handles the cases through pre-trial procedures "for the convenience of parties and witnesses" and to "promote the just and efficient conduct of such actions." *Id.* Once pretrial proceedings are finished — in other words, when the cases are ready to be tried, each action is transferred back to the district where it came from for trial. *Id.*

# Mastering Civil Procedure Master Checklist

For cases originally filed in federal court, is there an anchor claim—which is a claim over which the court has personal jurisdiction, venue, and subject matter jurisdiction because of diversity or federal question jurisdiction? If not, then the defendant should move to dismiss the case.

- ❏ Subject matter jurisdiction over the anchor claim:

    - ◼ Does the claim "arise under" federal law?

        - • Is there a "substantial federal question" raised by a state law claim that does not satisfy diversity requirements?

    - ◼ Is there complete diversity between the parties and does the amount in controversy, exclusive of costs and interest, exceed $75,000? If there is more than one claim, can the amounts be aggregated to reach $75,000?

- ❏ Personal jurisdiction over the anchor claim:

    - ◼ Did the defendant consent, either contractually or by operation of law such as through incorporation, registration, or operation of a motor vehicle?

    - ◼ Has the party voluntarily appeared, waived, or consented to personal jurisdiction either pre- or post-suit?

- ❏ Is jurisdiction *in rem* sufficient?

- ❏ If a federal long-arm statute applies to the claim, or if a state long-arm statute applies to the claim, are its requirements met?

- ❏ If only a state long-arm statute applies, if the requirements of the state long-arm statute is met, does assertion of personal jurisdiction over the claim comport with Due Process requirements?

- ▪ Is there general jurisdiction over the defendant because (a) the defendant is a natural person and is domiciled in the state or (b) the defendant is a corporation and it is incorporated in the state, the state is its principal place of business, or there are "exceptional circumstances"?

- ▪ Is there specific jurisdiction over the claim because the defendant has minimum contacts with the forum and assertion of personal jurisdiction would not offend traditional notions of fair play and substantial justice?

❏ Venue over the anchor claim:

- ▪ Is venue over the claim proper under a specific statute?

- ▪ Is venue over the claim proper under the general federal venue statute, in that either it is filed (a) in a judicial district where any defendant resides and all the defendants reside in that state; (b) it is filed in a district in which a substantial part of the events or omissions occurred; or (c) it is in a district where any defendant can be found if venue is not proper elsewhere?

**If defendant is seeking to remove to federal court a case pending in state court:**

❏ Did the removing parties file to remove within 30 days of receipt of the pleading or other paper showing the case was removable?

❏ For diversity-type removal, in addition ask:

- ▪ Is there complete diversity over one claim? If not, is the non-diverse defendant fraudulently joined?

- ▪ Is there a forum defendant? If so, has it been fraudulently joined?

- ▪ Is the amount in controversy established?

- ▪ Did the defendants comply with the one-year deadline? If not, is there an equitable exception to the one-year deadline?

❏ Has the right to seek removal been waived by conduct?

❏ Did all properly joined defendants join in the removal? If not, were they fraudulently joined?

❏ Is the case subject to remand by the plaintiff?

- ▪ Is any state law claim "separate and independent" and so subject to remand?

**For each additional claim:**

❏ Is there authority in Rules 13, 14, 18, 19, 20, 21, 22, 23, or 24 to join the claim? Does a federal statute, such as those governing intervention or interpleader authorize joinder?

❏ Is there personal jurisdiction or pendent personal jurisdiction over the claim, or has an objection to personal jurisdiction been waived or provided by consent?

❏ Is there original subject matter jurisdiction or supplemental jurisdiction over the claim?

❏ Is there venue, pendent venue, or is venue over the claim unnecessary because of consent or other reasons?

**Complaints**

❏ Does the complaint allege facts showing subject matter and personal jurisdiction?

❏ Does the complaint allege factual material that, if true, states a claim upon which relief can be granted?

❏ Are allegations of fraud or mistake pled with particularity as required by Rule 9(b)?

❏ Are damages prayed for, and special damages specifically pled?

❏ Is it signed in accordance with Rule 11?

**Defendant's Choices Upon Receipt of a Complaint:**

❏ Make a pre-answer motion.

  ▪ Is a pre-answer motion required because the complaint contains scandalous material or is indefinite?

  ▪ Is a pre-answer motion permitted because subject matter jurisdiction, personal jurisdiction, or venue are lacking, or the complaint fails to state a claim upon which relief can be granted, was improperly served, or fails to join an indispensable party?

  ▪ If a pre-answer motion is permitted or required, all available defenses except lack of subject matter jurisdiction, failure to join an indispensable party, and failure to state a claim must be consolidated or they are waived.

❑ File and serve an Answer.

    ▮ Which averments must the defendant deny? Admit? Plead insufficient information?

    ▮ Which affirmative defenses must be pled?

    ▮ Which "compulsory counterclaims" must be pled?

❑ Do nothing.

    ▮ This generally allows the plaintiff to obtain a default judgment.

❑ Defendant must file and serve any answer or motion in the time allowed, and sign in accordance with Rule 11.

## Even if Venue is Proper, is There a More Convenient Venue, or or is Forum Non Available?

❑ Even if a claim is properly filed a court, if the convenience of parties and witnesses indicates another forum is clearly more convenient, is there basis for any party to move to transfer venue under 28 U.S.C. 1404(a)?

❑ Is there a forum selection clause which supports transfer of venue?

❑ Does forum *non conveniens* necessitate dismissal?

## Amendments to Pleadings.

❑ If the amendment adds a claim (or a party), and if limitations has run on that claim, then the amendment would be futile if the claim does not "relate back" under Rule 15(c).

❑ If no scheduling order is in effect:

    ▮ A party may amend its pleading as a matter of right for 21 days after serving it even if the opposing party serves a responsive pleading or a motion under Rule 12(b),(e), or (f).

    ▮ A party may amend its pleading with consent of the opposing parties;

    ▮ A party may even without the right or consent of the opposing party amend its pleading upon motion, which shall be freely given.

❑ If a scheduling order is in effect and the deadline has passed, then the party must show good cause to modify the scheduling order and also move to amend the pleading.

❑ If a final pretrial order is in effect and the deadline has passed, then the party must show "manifest injustice" will result.

## Rule 26(f) Conference, Initial Disclosures, Scheduling Conference, and Discovery

❑ Each party must confer more than 21 days before the scheduling conference date set by the judge and, within 14 days after conferring, disclose to each other party certain information under Rule 26(a)(1) that it may use to support a claim or defense.

❑ The court must issue a Rule 16 scheduling order, which sets deadlines that will control the case.

❑ The parties may serve requests for production before the conference, but if so they are deemed served on the date of the conference, and other discovery can begin only after the discovery conference under Rule 26(f) has occurred:

- Up to 25 interrogatories may be served, but only on parties.

- Requests for admissions may be served only on parties, and may be limited in number by local rule.

- Document requests may be served on parties and, by way of subpoena, on non-parties.

- Up to 10 depositions per side may be taken of parties and, by way of subpoena, of non-parties.

- Other forms of discovery such as physical examination and deposition on written questions are available.

- All discovery is limited, absent court order, to that which is relevant to a claim or defense in the lawsuit and which is proportional to the case.

- Expert witnesses must be identified and, for testifying experts, reports must be prepared before the expert may be deposed, and for hybrid experts, a summary must be prepared.

- Facts known and opinions held by consulting experts are generally not discoverable.

## Which Law Applies to the Merits?

❏ Federal Claims: Federal substantive and procedural law applies.

❏ State Claims: Federal procedural law, but state substantive law, applies.

▪ Which state's law applies turns on which state has the most significant contacts with the facts giving rise to the claim.

▪ Whether state law is characterized as "substantive"—and so controls over a contrary federal procedural rule—turns on the *Erie* doctrine.

## Adjudication Prior to Trial

❏ Default judgment can be taken if the defending party fails to answer or otherwise appear.

❏ A party asserting the claim can voluntarily dismiss under Rule 41.

❏ A party defending a claim can move to dismiss for failure to state a claim upon which relief can be granted or for judgment on the pleadings under Rule 12.

❏ A party may seek summary judgment on a claim or defense asserted by or against it.

▪ If the party moving for summary judgment does not have the burden of proof on the issue at trial, then it need only show that there is no genuine issue of disputed fact and the summary judgment evidence shows there is insufficient evidence for a reasonable jury to find for the non-movant on one or more elements of the claim or defense.

▪ If the party moving for summary judgment has the burden of proof on the issue at trial, then it must show there is no genuine issue of disputed fact and the summary judgment evidence is so compelling that no reasonable jury could find for the non-movant.

## Adjudication by Trial

❏ The parties must submit the final pretrial order including exhibits, witnesses, and other information required by Rule 26(a)(3).

❏ Whether the court, or jury, will decide a claim turns on whether there is a right to trial by jury and whether a party properly invoked that right under Rule 38.

❏ Once the party with the burden of proof on an issue has had an opportunity to be fully heard, then the opposing party may move for judgment as a matter of law under Rule 50.

## Post-trial

❏ After verdict, an aggrieved party must promptly poll the jury or argue that the jury's verdict is inconsistent.

❏ After verdict, the clerk or court must enter judgment on a separate document.

❏ Post-trial motions for new trial and for judgment as a matter of law must be made within 28 days of entry of the judgment.

■ A post-judgment Rule 50(b) motion can be granted only to the extent the issues it raises were raised prior to submission of the case to the jury.

■ New trial motions under Rule 59 may be based upon either errors at trial or the fact that the verdict was against the great weight of the evidence.

❏ The judgment winner can "execute" on the judgment unless execution is stayed pending appeal.

❏ Absent an exception to the final judgment rule, only after judgment is entered can anyone appeal.

■ The exceptions to the final judgment rule are narrow and include the collateral order doctrine, orders affecting certain types of injunctive relief, certified appeals, and appeals under Rule 54(b).

❏ Collateral attacks by way of Rule 60(b) are extremely limited in order to avoid the final judgment rule.

# Index